EFFICIENT READING

EFFICIENT READING
REVISED FORM B

JAMES I. BROWN
University of Minnesota

Houghton-Mifflin

D. C. HEATH AND COMPANY
Lexington, Massachusetts Toronto

TO THE STUDENT

Your academic success depends very largely on how well you can read. That's why this book is so important.

To get down to particulars, suppose you decide to spend two hours of preparation for every hour spent in class. In carrying a normal load you will read an average of thirty hours a week. We'll say also that you read textbooks at about 200 words a minute with average comprehension.

Now what does increasing your reading efficiency mean? Well, an improvement in rate of only 100 words a minute without any loss in comprehension means you can do one hour's reading in forty minutes. That saves you ten hours a week, 100 hours a quarter, and 300 hours a year. In four years of college that adds up to a grand total of 1200 hours saved, or the equivalent of 150 eight-hour days. And that's only a beginning, for there's the much bigger problem of keeping up professionally for the rest of your life. In short, by taking the time somewhere along the way to develop greater reading efficiency, you literally *make* the time you need for additional reading as well as for a variety of other activities — social, professional, and otherwise. Yes, getting full value from the printed page with a minimum of time and effort does indeed deserve top priority.

That brings us to another point you will want to remember. No matter how poorly or how well you now read, the chances are you are reading below your maximum potential. For example, that hypothetical 50 percent increase just mentioned should be relatively easy to attain. At least reports from various reading programs around the country mention student gains of well over 100 percent. You may want to work toward matching the record made by one group of incoming freshmen. In one quarter they were able to improve their comprehension from 66 to 79 percent and their rate from 220 to 438 words a minute.

Furthermore the average and above-average readers seem to have as much room for improvement as the others, if not more. A group of bankers, after ten sessions, improved from 71 to 72 percent in comprehension and from 250 to 425 words a minute in rate, a 70 percent increase in efficiency. This group, made up largely of executives, indicated that they ordinarily spent about three hours a day in reading. For them even a 50 percent increase would have been well worth the time invested for the training.

It is evidence of this kind that suggests that no matter how well you now read, you still have room for improvement.

But your progress in reading, if it is to be rapid and lasting, needs to be based on the solid foundation of the language or communication arts, of which it is a part. Reading, writing, speaking, and listening are actually so closely interrelated that improvement in any one facilitates improvement in all the others, provided you have learned to think in terms of these interrelationships instead of in terms of isolated skills. Since, according to research findings, 70 percent of your waking time is spent in reading, writing, speaking, or listening, the value of a broadly based approach seems obvious.

This book is organized to emphasize these interrelationships and to help you take advantage of them as effective aids in learning to read.

The first section contains background information necessary for understanding the complex nature of the whole communication process. In it you will have a fresh look at language, at grammar, and at our use of signs and symbols in communicating. You will see how to cope with propaganda; to understand the key factors of attitude, interest and habit; and to recognize the role of observation as an important preliminary to effective expression. In addition you will be introduced to the new area of nonverbal communication. Articles on word study, human potential, and the learning process itself will round out the picture. Such background information will provide a firm foundation for the rapid growth of reading efficiency.

The next five sections point up the important role of reading in learning to communicate more effectively. Section II offers specific help with many of your reading problems. Sections III and IV, while treating problems of written and spoken expression, are reminders that what you learn about words, sentences, and paragraphs from writing and speaking will help you read and listen more effectively. Section V contributes insights about listening. Often the personal factor in a lecture or speech awakens the interest needed for increasing concentration and comprehension as you read. Listening can also contribute much to your awareness of denotative and connotative word values, to your building of general and specialized backgrounds, and to your acquaintance with methods of developing and organizing ideas. And if you find that you listen better than you read, you have added reason for expecting to make rapid progress in reading improvement. Section VI emphasizes your dependence on words in all the language arts.

The last section shifts the emphasis from *how* to communicate to *what* to communicate, a reminder that communication is a means toward an end, not an end in itself. As Earl J. McGrath puts it: "In a very real sense the destiny of our society and of each of us individually will be determined by our ability to communicate with one another and with citizens of other nations about contemporary problems."

Your first step in using this book will be to get better acquainted with your strengths and weaknesses as a reader, writer, speaker, and listener.

Do you write better than you read, for instance? One student, a poor reader, scored consistently low on objective tests where rapid, accurate reading was required. In one course where both objective and subjective tests were given, his grades on the objective type ranged from C down to F. On the subjective tests in the same course he never scored below a B. He told of spending twenty hours preparing for a botany quiz, which, because it was objective, brought him only a C. Yet, whenever he was asked to demonstrate his grasp of a subject in writing, he communicated well. If he had learned to carry over into his reading common elements mastered in writing, that inequality would probably not have existed.

Your first move, then, will be to use this book to find out how fast you read and how much you comprehend. See at what difficulty levels you read with adequate understanding. Find out whether you read better than you listen, or listen better than you read. Check up on yourself, also, as a writer and speaker, noticing such things as your grasp of sentence and paragraph structure and your ability to organize material effectively. Find out if your vocabulary is adequate for your communication needs.

This book is designed to help you with those explorations. For example, the ten questions about each selection give you a check on comprehension. The first five measure how well you read for details. The last five measure how well you interpret, evaluate, draw inferences, or get central ideas — skills coming under the general heading of critical or reflective reading. These comprehension check questions are equally useful in exploring your listening ability. Get someone to read one of the selections aloud to you; then answer the questions to check your listening comprehension. The

five vocabulary questions provide an opportunity for checking the size and accuracy of your vocabulary as well as the effectiveness with which you use contextual clues in arriving at word meanings.

Whenever you disagree with the answers in the key, go back over the selection carefully to find concrete evidence both for your answer and for the given answer. Discuss questionable items with someone else in an attempt to uncover all relevant data. Such analyses and discussions will do much to bring increased awareness of how you can secure emphasis, clarify organization, develop ideas, and avoid ambiguities in your writing and speaking.

Word counts and timing aids are for your convenience in exploring the relationship between word-per-minute rate and comprehension. Read one selection at your normal rate, checking both rate and comprehension. Then read another selection for full comprehension to see if you can score a 90 or 100. Finally, read still another selection as fast as you can, again checking both rate and comprehension. The difference between your slowest and fastest rate is a kind of "index of flexibility," indicating the range of rates at your command. Your comprehension on each of these trials is an indication of the skill that accompanies those variations in rate.

Although all selections are arranged for self-timing, you will want to consider what specific purposes or what kinds of material lend themselves most appropriately to rapid rates. When you are reading strictly for information, what rate is appropriate? Does slow reading tend to overaccent details and obscure the main ideas? And how rapidly should you read for enjoyment? Would seeing a full-length movie in slow motion tend to increase or to lessen your enjoyment? Keep these questions in mind as you make your preliminary explorations.

The *Exercises* based on each selection provide additional help with a diversity of problems related to reading and the other areas of communication.

After you have a clear picture of yourself as a communicator from these initial explorations, you are ready for the next step — intelligently planned practice. Actually the first step insures the success of the second. Only when you know exactly what your problems are can you direct your attention properly for immediate results.

If your difficulty is comprehension, the reason may be lack of concentration. Increasing your reading rate may help bring needed concentration. Or the cause may be inadequate vocabulary or lack of experience with material at a certain difficulty level. Knowing that you tend to miss details or main ideas will help you direct attention more intelligently. As you work on the problem from several angles, you will soon begin to see improvement.

If you find that you are a "one-speed" reader, again

you will know where to direct your energies. Stepping up your rate beyond the point of comfort may bring a drop in comprehension, but don't worry. You can hardly expect to read with real efficiency at an entirely new rate the first time you try. And without trying you can never get the experience needed for effective performance. If your goal is to read comfortably at, say, 500 words a minute, practice for a time at a faster rate. Then when you drop back to the slower 500 rate, you will feel much more comfortable and confident. Similarly, well-directed practice should be attempted in other areas as your needs suggest.

Finally, as you go ahead to attain the reading ability so necessary for college adjustment, as well as for success after graduation, you have the satisfaction of knowing that you are getting skills basic to he highest educational endeavor. As Carlyle said: "If we but think of it, all that a University or final highest school can do for us is still but what the first school began doing — teach us to *read*."

TO THE INSTRUCTOR

The first edition of *Efficient Reading* was published in 1952, followed in 1962 by a revised edition. This revision — the third, *Efficient Reading, Revised Form B,* provides further opportunity to incorporate changes and improvements suggested by those teachers and students who used the earlier editions.

This latest revision contains thirty-six selections from the earlier edition and thirty-nine entirely new selections, a total of seventy-five, seven more than before. The number of one-page reading-type exercises was also increased from two to eight, most of the added exercises with a strong how-to emphasis. These increases provide wider choice and improved coverage.

This text is designed for use in college and adult efficient reading programs and in reading laboratories and clinics. It is also useful in freshman English courses that emphasize reading. As Lambuth says in his *Golden Book on Writing,* the vocabulary, usage, and idiom "so essential to good writing can be acquired only by wide and intelligent reading. And in no other way whatsoever." Furthermore the focus on communication touches a broad, significant area of concern. After all, communication permeates every process of life, making the study of communication in a sense the study of society. The broad communication setting also provides the best possible foundation for maximum improvement in reading, through increased facility and growth in the companion skills areas of writing, speaking, and listening.

To make this revision even more useful, it was decided to apply item-analysis procedures, which are essential in preparing a standardized test, to additional comprehension check questions. In the previous edition twenty-six of the sixty-eight selections were so treated, all items of low or negative discrimination replaced by new or revised items. In this revision thirty-four of the seventy-five selections have comprehension tests of known validity — .47 on the average — assurance that the tests do discriminate well. Those comprehension tests, analyzed and improved where necessary, are marked with an asterisk in the Index According to Order of Difficulty on page 327. This use of item-analysis techniques in a text of this kind is unique, as far as is known.

To add further usefulness, a new type of pacing sheet has been added. Students feel that pacing is the single most helpful device for improving reading efficiency. The newly designed pacing sheets make it possible to pace students at any of six speeds, thus taking the place of costly individual reading accelerators. (For a more detailed treatment of the pacing approach, read James I. Brown, "A Pacing Technique for Classroom Teaching of Reading," *College English,* December 1956, pp. 164–65.)

With two editions — *Revised Form A* and *Revised Form B* — closely parallel in plan, treatment, and format, yet with different selections, instructors will be able to select the one best suited to the specific needs and interest of their students. They will also be able to alternate the two editions from year to year, for sake of variety and interest. Some teachers use one form for classroom work only, with the other as the required text for the class, an arrangement permitting more extensive coverage of any desired area and greater opportunity for accelerating and individualizing instruction.

The book lends itself both to classroom and individual use. The questions and exercises are easily self-scored and the word-per-minute rates easily figured by use of the conversion table and word counts for each selection. Listening ability can also be checked by having someone read a selection aloud, then comparing the comprehension with that usually obtained by reading.

Some instructors have asked for more detailed suggestions for structuring a college or adult reading course. Here are three suggested plans that have been used with good results in classes at the University of Minnesota. Each plan provides a practical framework of developmental steps or stages into which a variety of selections can be fitted.

(1) *Guide to Effective Reading* (Heath). This text, when used with *Efficient Reading,* provides a ready-made course organization, which still permits wide choice of selections from this text. In the *Guide* the thirty-two 500-word readings fall into nine sequential steps to move the student toward more efficient reading. The *Guide* was written initially as a how-to manual to accompany *Efficient Reading.* For that reason it was kept short — less than 100 pages — and inexpensive.

The Preface to the *Guide* indicates the steps, the first being *proper orientation and diagnosis of reading strengths and weaknesses.* Selections 1, 4, 5, and 32 in the *Guide* cover that step. *Efficient Reading,* then, supplies all the selections needed for additional exploration, practice, and coverage.

The remaining eight steps are covered similarly, as indicated in the Preface. For example, the third step — *proper management of the learning process* — is considered of prime importance and is covered by seven selections (2, 8, 9, 10, 11, 12, and 13). This step fits neatly into a two-week period. At a 500 word-per-minute rate these selections take only a minute to read, plus additional time for the comprehension test. This leaves plenty of time for additional practice in longer selections. Both texts may be required or the teacher may utilize the *Guide* as a helpful companion text for in-class use only.

(2) *Reading Power* (Heath). This provides still another possible structuring, somewhat more gradual and beginning at a somewhat easier level. This text is built around five major steps — the Check-Up, the Build-Up, the Speed-Up, the Shape-Up, and the Ease-Up. Fourteen instructional readings cover specific points under each step, taking the students step by step toward improved reading efficiency. Students are led from "Reading for Meaning" on to the reading of words, paragraphs, and entire selections, then to "Getting Better Grades," "Generating New and Wider Interests," and finally to "Reading for Life."

(3) *Success Through Efficient Reading* (a series of videotaped aids for the teaching of reading).* This se-

---

*Available through Telstar, 366 North Prior Avenue, St. Paul, Minnesota 55104.

ries has been under experimental development since 1960. For schools or learning centers with videotape playbacks, these tapes provide a variety of instructional units and exercises for use with *Efficient Reading* to accelerate student progress.

A listing of twelve key programs will suggest the structure. (1) Exploring Your Potential, (2) Spotlight on You — the Reader, (3) Putting Word Power to Work, (4) Step Up Your Learning Speed, (5) Traveling the Pacing Road, (6) Purposeful Skimming and Scanning, (7) Improving Word Grouping Habits, (8) Applying the SD4 Formula, (9) Paragraph Reading Skills, (10) Getting the Writer's Plan, (11) Getting the Main Ideas, (12) The Dynamic Role of Reading.

ACKNOWLEDGMENTS

Acknowledgment should be made of my obligation to those authors and publishers granting permission for the use of their material and to my colleagues teaching reading here at Minnesota — Eugene S. Wright, Richard O. Horberg, Starling W. Price, Thomas E. Pearsall, Warren Y. Gore, James R. Holloway, and William M. Marchand. They provided teacher and student reactions of particular help in deciding which selections to retain for this revised edition.

Dr. Horberg, head of the Freshman Communication program, deserves special mention for his help with many of the writing exercises. And for much of the section on listening, particular thanks must go to Dr. Ralph G. Nichols, whose book *Are You Listening?* provided useful insights. Finally, Dr. Wright's doctoral research, which pointed up the significant relationship between academic success and training in reading, continued to serve as added incentive in the preparing of this new revision. The experimental group in his study used the first edition as a basic text.

CONTENTS

PART ONE: READING SELECTIONS

Section IV: On Speaking

Section V: On Listening

Section VI: On Vocabulary

Section VII: Current Problems

PART TWO: COMPREHENSION AND VOCABULARY CHECK QUESTIONS AND EXERCISES

Appendix

Part One

READING SELECTIONS

Section I: Background

Language as a Tool

J. Samuel Bois

Everywhere around us you will find tools. But is there such a thing as a tool to increase brain power? Indeed there is. This entire text is designed to help you sharpen that very tool. For an explanation, read on.

There are many things you can do with a hammer: you may drive nails and pull them, split a board, break stones, bang someone on the head, and so forth. But there are things that you cannot do with a hammer: you cannot saw a piece of wood, drive a screw, or bore a hole.

A tool has a function, a range of uses. The limits of that range are not always very sharp; a skillful worker may achieve wonders with the most primitive tools. But there is a point where he has to stop because the tool is totally inadequate to do what has to be done. With a stethoscope and a thermometer a good physician can diagnose many ailments, but he will need a microscope to examine a sample of tissue that he suspects of being cancerous.

The tool is not independent of the tool-user, and the tool-user is not independent of his tool. Taken together, they form an operating unit that works as a whole. Tools can be considered as extensions of man's sense organs, and of his arms, hands, and legs. The automobile gives us the seven-league boots of fairy tales, the airplane gives us wings, the hydraulic press gives us the muscular strength of a Titan.

What of our brain? Have we any tools that have increased its power, its speed, and efficiency? Yes, we have. A child in the elementary grades of school can now perform long multiplications and divisions that were considered as the exclusive achievements of experts in the Middle Ages. The tool that he is using is the positional notation of numbers, or the device of giving a number ten times its original value when we write it in the first column to the left, one hundred times its value when we write it in the second column, and so forth. This was a great invention which came from India through Arab scholars. History shows that it was resisted very strongly for generations, just as the first labor-saving devices were not welcomed by manual laborers in the early days of machinery. To appreciate the difference between this mathematical tool and those that were used before, divide CVIII by IX, using exclusively the Roman numeral notation, and see how long it will take you to get the answer.

Like physical tools, the brain tools have their limitations. They are very useful within a certain range of operation, but they cannot cope with problems outside that range. For instance, the metric system, based on the decimal notation, passes much more easily from volume to weight than does the cumbersome English system of feet and pounds. But if you try to express *exactly* in decimals the one-third of a meter, you cannot. To profit by the advantages of the metric system, you must forego the measurements that are inconsistent with it. No tool can do everything; no system is an all-purpose system. If your brain adopts a tool, it increases its capacity and limits it at the same time. We choose our tools according to what we have to do; we have to become better acquainted with our brain tools and change them freely when we have to.

We are coming now to a most important notion. Unless we agree about it, we are bound to misunderstand each other in the following pages. So, please take time to ponder over the statement emphasized a few lines further down. You may find it obvious, baffling, mysterious, exaggerated, or what not — I don't know. To me, it is a key statement. If you don't accept it, please do not go beyond it, — or proceed at your own risk. Here it is:

OUR EVERYDAY LANGUAGE CAN BE VIEWED AS A BRAIN TOOL

Language as a tool. What does this mean in the light of what has been said before? It means this:

1. Language is the tool we use to do most of our thinking. In other words, thinking could be described as *talking to ourselves.*

2. The better the tool, the better the job. A rich and flexible language makes thinking rich and flexible.

3. The language and the thinker (the tool and the tool-user) form a working unit, in which each element helps and limits the activities of the other.

4. Language is organized into a system by virtue of its rules of syntax, and it throws out of our thinking unit — that is, out of our functioning brain — all statements that are inconsistent with its system, just as the

metric system forces us to ignore the exact third of a meter.

5. If we become aware of the limitations of our language, we may recognize what limitations it imposes upon our brain.

6. By pushing outward the limitations of our language (by improving the tool range and the functioning of the tool) we may increase the capacity of the human brain, as the mathematicians did when they removed the shackles of the Roman numerals and introduced the positional notation.

Are we going to compare languages, say French and English, Russian and German, Nootka and Cree, and decide which is the "best" thinking tool? No. I am not a linguist, and I don't think anyone has both the competence and the authority to promote such a change.

Are we going to insist on those "increase-your-vocabulary" exercises and tests that appear in the *Reader's Digest* and similar publications? No. A larger and more precise vocabulary is surely a good thing, but while it increases the *elements* of our language, it does not affect its *structure;* it does not bring it to a higher dimension.

Are we to advocate a new language, either simplified from a current one, like Basic English, or derived from a whole family of related idioms, like Esperanto, Volapük, or Interlingua? Not at all.

Are we going to become purists, people who dabble in etymology, Greek roots, and word history, for the purpose of restoring the *pure, original* meaning of words? Nothing is further from our purpose.

These questions, and similar ones, are all going in directions where countless pathways have been trodden down by pioneers and their eager followers. If you expect a new version of any of these schemes, or a combination of some or all of them, you will be disappointed.

Our explorations will take us in other directions and into other dimensions. Our starting point is that language can be viewed as a tool that combines with our brain to form one thinking unit. You have noticed it when you attempted to learn French, Spanish, or any other language. For a while you kept *thinking in English* while clothing your thoughts with the terms of the new language. Eventually, the new thinking tool became "homogenized" with your brain, and you discovered that you could think either in English or in the new language. Translation meant "rethinking" the experience or the stream of thoughts in a different language.

The tool and the tool-user form a complex unit. We may separate them "mentally," but in practice they work as a whole.

Number of Words 1180
See page 171 for Questions

Reading Time in Seconds _____
See page 323 for Conversion Table

SELECTION 2

I'll Remember It in a Minute

Corey Ford

Do you have trouble remembering things? Don't let that worry you. By the time you finish reading this article, you will feel distinctly superior — just by contrast with the forgetful author. Go ahead. Enjoy his difficulties.

Let's see, what was I going to say? It was right on the tip of my tongue. Oh, yes, about my memory.

Frankly, I've got a mind like a steel sieve. Things go in one ear, but that's as far as they get. Right now if you asked me, for instance, I couldn't tell you where I'm meeting my wife for lunch. I can't recall the license of my car, I have to look up my own phone number in the book, and I haven't the slightest idea what this string around my finger is for. People are always coming up to me and saying, "I bet you don't know who I am," and, what's more, they're always right. I never remember names.

Maybe I don't concentrate properly when I'm introduced. I'm so busy trying to look the other person smack in the eye — some book I read, I forget the title, said the first impression is very important — that I don't catch his name when he gives it. I thrust out my jaw — that's what the book said — seize his hand in a vice-like grip, yank it toward me and downward at the same time and pronounce my own name in a forceful tone: "Ford." As a result, the name "Ford" is fixed firmly in my mind, and I can remember it the rest of the evening, but when I meet the other person again I call him "Hi-ya boy," or "Hi," for short. Most of the people I know are named "Hi-ya boy."

On the other hand, I always forget a face. That is, I recognize the face, but I can't place the person it belongs to. When I join a cocktail party I'll snub the host completely, stare coldly at an important business client with whom I had dinner last night, and make a bee-line across the room to pump the hand of an old college classmate whom I've been trying to avoid for years and who takes advantage of my enthusiastic greeting to borrow ten dollars.

The safest solution, I've found, is to nod to everyone I meet, creating the impression that I'm running for public office. If I see anybody waving in a crowd, I smile and wave in return. Usually it turns out that he is trying to attract the attention of someone standing behind me, which means that I must arrest my gesture in midair and pretend that I was just reaching up to scratch my ear, or that I was waving at someone behind him. The trouble is that the person behind him is apt to wave back.

It's even worse when I spot a familiar-looking face on the street. I halt and stare intently into a store window, occasionally glancing over my shoulder to see if the owner of the face is still there. Unfortunately, he spots me at the same time and halts before another store window casting furtive looks in my direction. Sooner or later our glances meet, and we greet each other with well-feigned surprise, exclaiming, "Well, what do you know!" and clapping each other on the back to cover the fact that we're both a little guilty about having failed to keep in touch all these years.

We start walking down the street together, assuring each other that we haven't changed a bit and asking how everything is and what's new lately, while I thumb frantically through the pages of memory's album in search of some revealing clue. *Met him at Cape Cod last summer? Member of the club? Cousin Ettie's husband?* "How's the wife?" I try, just a feeler.

"Oh, Myrtle's fine thanks," he replies, dashing that hope.

I turn the corner, he turns it too. *Can't I ever get rid of him?* "Sure I'm not taking you out of your way?" I ask pointedly.

"Not a bit," he insists. "It's right in my direction."

By this time our conversation has dwindled to a few sporadic remarks like, "Hot enough for you?" or "How do you like the Giants?" and I wonder what I'll do if I meet somebody and have to introduce him. *Played golf together once? Sells insurance? Friend of Bill's?* "Ever hear from Bill?" I attempt.

"Bill who?" he counters, and we lapse into silence again.

I start down my own block, but he clings stubbornly to the last. I halt before my house in relief, and we shake hands. "Well, it's been great seeing you," I nod, starting up my path.

"We'll have to do it more often," he nods, and starts up the path of the house next door.

It's hard enough for me to remember a story I've heard, but it's even harder to remember where I heard it. Just as I'm halfway through a good one that somebody told me lately, I detect a certain glassy expression on my listener's face, which can be compared roughly to the sympathetic look you might give a doddering uncle who is well-meaning but not quite bright. The further I get with the story, the more patient his smile becomes. Along about the time I reach the point, the horrid realization dawns that I told the same story to him yesterday. Not only that, but he's the one who told it to me the day before.

I have the same trouble when I try to buy a shirt. Somehow the figure "36" sticks in my mind, but I'm not sure whether it's my neck size or the waistband of my trousers. Probably the number is printed on the bottom of the shirt I'm wearing, but I'd look pretty silly pulling out my shirttail in front of a storeful of people. I point vaguely to the pile on the counter and tell the clerk, "That one seems about right," which accounts for the way my sleeves hang down around my wrists — and is why my collar looks like that of a Rangeley guide who has driven into Bangor for the weekend.

I'm no good at all on birthdays or wedding anniversaries or dental appointments, but for some reason my wife never forgets a date. This isn't because women have better memories than men, I'm convinced, but because they forget different things. For instance, a woman can't recall where she put something, whereas a man knows right where he put it, but he can't think what it was he put there.

My wife has an uncanny faculty for remembering something I said six years ago, which she brings up triumphantly at the appropriate moment during an argument. She has never forgotten that I admitted once I had a weakness for redheads, and she hasn't let me forget it either. She's able to tell exactly when Elsie's baby is due, she'll report the entire menu they served at the bridge-club luncheon, and she can quote verbatim what that idiotic salesgirl said to her and what she told the salesgirl. On the other hand, when we start out of the house together she can never remember whether she left her cigarette burning.

It isn't that I don't retain. My mind is a veritable storehouse of assorted facts, like the names of all the living ex-Presidents, the declension of the Latin noun *tuba* (tuba, tubae, tubae or not *tubae*), the weight of the world's-record brook trout, or the first six verses of The Ancient Mariner. In short, I can remember anything, provided it is useless. I can count up to ten in Navajo, border the state of Tennessee and order a fried egg in Malay (*mata sapi*, in case you think I'm kidding); but when I try to give a taxi driver the address of my insurance company in the city, I draw a total blank. I'd go back to my hotel room and look it up, but I've forgotten the address of the hotel.

I suppose the answer is to train your memory. This book I was reading — I wish I could tell you its name — claims that the best way to remember a name is to associate it with the name of something else. It seems to me this means you'd have two things to remember instead of one, but probably the author knows what he's talking about. All right. Let's say, for instance, that I meet a Mr. Garden, and I want to establish his name in my mind. A garden needs fertilizer, and fertilizer suggests a barn, and a barn usually has cows in it, and cows produce butter, and butter reminds me of that grease spot on my necktie. So, the next time I meet Mr. Garden, I glance at my necktie — I assume I'm still wearing the same necktie — run through the list backward, extend my hand, smile pleasantly and say, "How do you do, Mr. Fertilizer." It's as easy as that.

It's just as easy to remember telephone numbers.

Suppose I want to think of Ocean 9-2561. The 9 is a baseball team, of course, and 2 and 5 are the respective ages of my wife's sister's two children, and 6 plus 1 makes 7, which is my hat size. So I can think of my wife's sister's two children playing baseball with my hat in the ocean, or else I can look up the number in the directory and save myself all the trouble. The main thing to realize is that the mind is a muscle which can be developed with proper exercise, according to this book on memory. It's funny I can't think of the title. I know it as well as I know my own name —

My name? That's easy. It's right here at the top of this article, if I could remember where I put the magazine.

Number of Words 1620
See page 173 for Questions

Reading Time in Seconds _____
See page 323 for Conversion Table

SELECTION 3

The Art of Discovery

J. Frank Dobie

How to stay alive as long as you live! That's one of life's major problems. And the art of discovery is apparently at the heart of that problem, so J. Frank Dobie feels. Take a mind open to discovery; add a book open to be read and you have an ideal combination.

Happily for the human race, it does not always take a great deal of intelligence to enjoy discovery. The intelligence comes from observing.

Of course, awareness and desire to see are requisite for any discovery. If I were running a school of so-called creative writing, I'd have one requisite for enrolling and two courses for the people enrolled. The requisite would be intelligence or alertness, which amount pretty much to the same thing. The main course would be in observing; a secondary course would be in writing sentences. Every day and Sunday too I'll choose a writer who is strong in observing powers, though lacking in style, over one who is syntactically perfect but dull-eyed.

Luck is being ready for the chance; so is discovery. When I went to New York to attend Columbia University, my first free afternoon was spent in the Metropolitan Museum of Art. Among the many paintings I scanned, one made a stronger impression on me than any other. It was of a snow scene, and some of the snow was rose-coloured, a kind of purple. Coming from the lower end of Texas, I had seen little snow. I had always

understood that snow was snow-white. There was plenty of snow in New York that winter. Not long after seeing the picture of rose-coloured snow, I went across the Hudson River on a Sunday afternoon to ramble over the New Jersey countryside. I was not looking for anything in particular. I wanted fresh air and natural ground. The sun was shining. Under some bushes, partly in shadow, I saw rose-coloured snow. Probably I should not have noticed it had the painting not called my attention to such a phenomenon. I discovered two things: snow tinted by light and a verification of Oscar Wilde's assertion that nature follows art. The artist had followed nature, but nature through my eyes was following art. This discovery gave me an idea on the function of art, including literature, that has grown.

Many years ago a ranchman named Richard Merrill told me about a one-man horse he had owned and ridden. The horse would allow nobody but his owner to mount him. He was strong, intelligent, enduring. One evening Merrill brought a new pair of leggin's (called chaps in some parts of the West) home from town. The next morning he saddled his horse for the purpose of riding out in a pasture. The horse was docile as usual. Before mounting him, Merrill pulled on his new leggin's. Upon being approached by the fresh, smelly leather, the horse became frantic, uncontrollable. The only way to mount him, Merrill said, was either to tie him up like a freshly caught mustang and blindfold him or take off the leggin's. He took them off.

One coldish morning a year or so later, Richard Merrill, his wife, and her visiting sister proposed riding horseback to a mountain several miles away from the ranch. The sister-in-law had put on Merrill's old jacket. By accident she came near the one-man horse and the horse sniffed her familiarly. "He's easier in the saddle than the horse I was going to let you ride," Merrill said. "He seems to like you. Maybe he'll let you ride him." He did.

The three took their lunch. By the time they had eaten it on the mountain, the afternoon was warm. The visiting lady had cast aside Merrill's old jacket. Now the horse would not allow her to approach him. Merrill had to ride him home.

This account was told to illustrate the power of smell in horse behaviour. The subject was not entirely new to me, but for the first time I seemed to have discovered something on it. I began noticing for myself, not only in what I saw but in what others told or wrote. I came to realize what the Spanish-Indian *vaqueros* of California knew a hundred years and more ago: that after capturing wild horses the first step in controlling them was to accustom them to the smell of man. I remembered how when I was a boy on our ranch in southern Texas a Mexican *vaquero* (cowboy) would blow his breath into the nostrils of a colt or wild cow that was roped for taming — the cow to become a milk cow.

I took to observing deer from the point of view of smell. For instance, one afternoon I saw three in brush at the instant they saw me. The wind was from them to me. At the moment of our mutual glimpses I became immobile against a low tree. They knew something foreign was there, but they didn't know exactly what, and deer are very inquisitive. After they had watched me for a while without seeing another movement, I watching them at the same time, they got out of sight in the growth. I knew they were still inquiring and I kept still. About thirty minutes after their discovery I heard one of them snort behind me and turned just in time to catch a glimpse of disappearing white tails. The deer had "taken roundance" in order to get my smell. Like many other animals, they were relying more on nostrils than on eyes. They were demonstrating that the road to comprehension of wildlife is through the sense of smell.

Furthermore, someday I may write an essay on Love at First Smell. Manufacturers of French perfumes would do well to circulate it.

"The thing that hath been, it is that which shall be; and that which is done is that which shall be done; and there is no new thing under the sun," wrote the Solomonic author of *Ecclesiastes*. He had seen all of life that — for him — there was to see. He had grown shut-eyed in the manner of the man who said that when he was *out* there was no place left to go but *in* and when he was *in,* no place to go but *out*. In short, he was through; he had come to the finality of being old, which is considerably more than being aged. He was the antipodes of those Athenians who "spent their time in nothing else" but telling, hearing or seeing "some new thing."

An ancient folk anecdote tells of a philosopher who had resigned from life because, he declared, he wasn't seeing or learning anything new. While in this comatose state, he asked a servant to light his (the philosopher's) pipe at the hearth fire. He watched the servant rake out a coal with a swift stroke, pick it up and shift it rapidly from one hand to the other while transporting it to the pipe bowl, on top of the tobacco. "Why, you've taught me something," the philosopher exclaimed, though it seems not plausible to me that after being around fire all his life he should not have known how to carry a live coal. Anyhow, he took to discovering again — and lived happily ever afterwards.

For the learner, the liver, the new thing is new to him, however old it be to another. I have no idea who first magnetized iron, but I doubt if the accomplishment gave him more of a thrill than a magnet gave me and my brothers and sisters one Christmas while we were children. Homer had written his epics maybe two thousand and seven hundred years back and the *Odyssey* and the *Iliad* had been translated many times before John Keats picked up and read a two-hundred-years-old translation by an Elizabethan dramatist, poet, lover, and scholar named George Chapman. The discovery — discovery for himself — so excited him that he wrote a sonnet "On First Looking into Chapman's Homer" —

Then felt I like some watcher of the skies
When a new planet swims into his ken.

No southward sailing sailor can now report a new land mass or a new constellation. All the land masses of earth and all the constellations visible to the naked eye were long ago charted, but looking at the Southern Cross for the first time can be as wondrous to an individual of the twenty-first century as it was to the first mariner of antiquity who beheld it. There is a book, perhaps there are several books, on the kiss — though there is only one Rodin masterpiece of sculpture on it. Until the day of doom every lover will discover for himself with the freshness of creation's first dawn the meaning of a kiss.

The commonest phenomena of life, "What Every Woman Knows," are the phenomena most often written about and talked about. They are the most vital. Yet they do not really exist for a person until he has discovered them for himself. They are perennially new because every human being among the hundreds of millions on earth is in a new pattern. Having mind and senses open to discovery is more important to him than any discovery he makes is likely to be. Whoever wants to see, observe, discover, will. The stuff for discovery is everywhere. "I have travelled a good deal in Concord," Henry David Thoreau said and "to be awake is to be alive."

Number of words 1520
See page 175 for Questions

Reading Time in Seconds _____
See page 323 for Conversion Table

SELECTION 4

The Importance of Being Interested

H. Addington Bruce

Emerson once said: "Beware of what you want — for you will get it." Was this true with Franklin, Darwin, and Mozart? Perhaps it's want-to, not I.Q., *that is most important. If so, how strong is your interest in improving your reading and communicating abilities?*

Many years ago there lived in the city of Boston a small boy whose days were spent in a singularly wearisome way. At the age of ten, when most boys are dividing their time between school and play, he was busy all day boiling soap, cutting wicks for tallow candles, filling candle molds, and otherwise drudging as assistant to his father in the soap and candle business. It was a business in which the father took an honest pride, and in thus apprenticing his youngest son to it, he did so with the expectation of giving him full charge and ownership in later years.

As it happened, the son's mind was filled with thoughts of other things than soap and candles. He worked faithfully enough at the kettles and wicks and molds; but he worked with such scant enthusiasm and such little skill that his father soon perceived that he would never become an expert candle-maker. Bitterly disappointed, he nevertheless appreciated the folly of compelling his son to persist in an occupation manifestly uncongenial to him. To another and much older son he one day said:

"Will you take Ben into your printing shop? He will never be a successful chandler, but he may make a fair printer. At any rate, I wish you would give him a chance."

Into the printing shop, accordingly, young Ben went, somewhat against his will, for the handling of inky type seemed to him only a trifle less unpleasant than dealing with greasy molds. But he presently made the important discovery that through typesetting he was in a position both to gain knowledge for himself and to make knowledge available for other people by putting it into print. Forthwith he became interested in printing as he had never been in candle-making; also, he became fired with a desire to learn all he could about as many subjects as possible, and he developed, besides, an ambition to turn author and see his own thoughts take form on the printed page.

Behold him, then, sometimes sitting up the whole night long over Plutarch's *Lives, The Spectator,* Locke's *Essays,* and kindred works of information and literary power. Behold him in the fervor of his zeal turning vegetarian at the age of sixteen, because the greater cheapness of his meals would allow him more money for books. Behold him scribbling and rescribbling in the effort to give clear expression to the ideas forming in his mind as a result of his wide reading and hard thinking. Finally, behold him timidly slipping under the door of his brother's newspaper office an unsigned essay written in a disguised hand — an essay so good that, on publication, its authorship was variously ascribed to leading writers of the day.

Thereafter he toiled more industriously than ever — printing, reading, thinking, writing. Ere he was thirty he was widely known, and long before his death he was acclaimed on two continents as one of the wisest of men. We of to-day, looking back from the vantage-point of more than a century later, feel that the praise of his contemporaries was not misplaced. For the whilom candle-maker who thus rose to eminence was none other than Benjamin Franklin, philosopher, scientist, diplomat, and apostle of America's freedom.

Take, similarly, the history of an English lad born some twenty years after Franklin died. More happily circumstanced, being the son of a successful physician, this boy was given all the advantages of good schooling. But he did not seem to draw much profit from his lessons. In fact, as he himself has told us, both his father and his teachers were inclined to regard him as "rather below the common standard in intellect." To make matters worse from the father's point of view, he showed a marked distaste for the tasks of the school-

From the *Outlook,* July 18, 1914.

room, and an equally marked fondness for vagabondage.

Gun in hand, he would roam for hours through verdant lanes or across the open country. "You care for nothing but shooting, dogs, and rat-catching, and you will be a disgrace to yourself and all your family," his father once predicted, mournfully. As the boy grew older, his propensity for idling seemed only to increase. In spite of this, hoping against hope that he would settle down to serious things, his father entered him at the University of Glasgow, with the idea of fitting him for the practice of medicine. "It is no use," the boy frankly avowed after a few months at Glasgow. "I hate the work here, and I cannot possibly be a physician." So earnest were his protests that he was transferred to Cambridge University, on the understanding that he would study to be a clergyman.

At Cambridge, as good fortune would have it, he entered the natural history class of an eminent and enlightened scholar, Professor Henslow, who sent him into the woods and fields to make collections of plants and insects. Free again to roam under the clear blue skies, but this time with a lofty purpose set before his mind, a passion for achievement took possession of him. The boy whom other teachers had found dull and lazy proved himself, under Professor Henslow's inspiring guidance, a marvel of industry and mental vigor. There was no longer any thought of the "last resort" plan of putting him into the ministry. He would, he assured his now delighted father, devote his whole life to the study of nature's laws.

Thus it came about that, when his college days were over, he eagerly accepted an opportunity to accompany a Government exploring expedition. During that long voyage in southern seas he accumulated a remarkable collection of specimens. What was far more important, he brought back with him to England, after a five years' absence filled with hardships, a mass of new ideas regarding fundamental principles in natural science — ideas which, being masterfully scrutinized and sifted, were afterwards to make him world-famous as Charles Darwin, originator of the doctrine of evolution.

Again, there was born in the German city of Salzburg, about the middle of the eighteenth century, a bright-eyed boy, the son of a Court musician. As was inevitable by reason of his father's vocation, this child, from the hour he first opened his eyes and ears to the world about him, daily heard melody from violin, clavier, and harpsichord. Before he was three years old it was noticed that he not only seemed to take great delight in listening to music, but also that he often attempted with his little fingers to strike harmonious intervals on the clavier. His father, amused but impressed, offered to give him lessons; joyfully the child accepted, and at once a start was made.

Thenceforth music dominated his waking thoughts. The toys of childhood were cast aside, and in their stead he played with the keyed and stringed instruments to which his father gave him ready access. From the first he astonished all around him by his wonderful skill. By the time he was four he could play several minuets on the harp and he was busily composing themes, and in his sixth year he was able to play the violin so well that he once assisted his father and a celebrated violinist in rehearsing trios which the latter had recently composed. Modest, unassuming, bending his every effort to progress in the art which had so fascinated him, the youngster passed in quick succession from one notable feat to another. On all sides the prediction was heard: "If this boy keeps on as he has begun, he will be one of the world-masters of music." Those who are familiar with Mozart's marvelous compositions for church, opera-house, and concert-room know well that the prediction was amply fulfilled.

Now, I have recalled these beginnings of the careers of Franklin, Darwin and Mozart because they strikingly illustrate a profound psychological truth the significance of which can scarcely be overestimated. It is a truth, to be sure, that has long been partially recognized. But its full meaning has not been — and could not be — appreciated until quite recently. Only within the past few years has scientific research effected sundry discoveries which make its complete recognition possible and of supreme importance — of such importance that practical application of the principles involved would make for an immediate and stupendous increase in human happiness, efficiency, and welfare.

Stated briefly, the truth in question is that success in life, meaning thereby the accomplishment of results of real value to the individual and to society, depends chiefly on sustained endeavor springing out of a deep and ardent interest in the tasks of one's chosen occupation. It is not enough merely to be a "hard worker." The world is full of people who slave faithfully at their respective duties, perhaps earn a handsome living, but know in their hearts that they have failed to achieve their possibilities. Yet the trouble with them simply is that they are not really interested in what they are doing. They are "misfits," as Franklin was in his father's candle-shop and Darwin at the University of Glasgow. Unlike Franklin and Darwin, they have not been so fortunate as to stumble eventually upon a vocation capable of inciting in them a passionate enthusiasm; unlike Mozart, they have not had a father wise enough to perceive their natural inclinations and brave enough to safeguard the development of these by an early education. Had they been thus circumstanced, who knows but that they might have attained results fairly comparable with the results attained by Franklin and Darwin and Mozart — all through the dynamic power of interest.

Indeed, evidence is accumulating that it is in this, rather than in any exceptional structure of the brain, that we have the true explanation of the wonderful achievements of so-called "men of genius." Looked at superficially, the mental processes of the man of genius undoubtedly seem to differ greatly from those of the ordinary man. In the case of the former, great ideal, marvelous "inspirations," often spring into consciousness seemingly of their own accord. Napoleon used to say that his battles frequently were won by tactics devised by him on the spur of the moment. "The decisive moment approached, the spark burst forth, and one was victorious." Goethe has testified that not a few of his themes, and sometimes whole poems, came to him from he knew not where. On Schiller's own testimony, when he was consciously at work, creating and constructing, his imagination did not serve him "with the same freedom as it had done when nobody was looking over its shoulder." Likewise we have Mozart's statement that his compositions "came involuntarily, like dreams."

All this, I say, seems very different from the workings of the mind of the ordinary man. Yet, after all, exactly the same sort of thing occurs to the latter. He, too, has his "happy thoughts," his occasional "flashings" of wise decisions, correct solutions of baffling problems, etc. Noticeably, however, his happy thoughts and flashings are always connected with matters to which he has devoted much conscious attention, matters which have been of great interest to him. It is as though, by thinking of them earnestly, he has set in motion some hidden mechanism that has enabled him, smoothly and easily, and all unknown to himself, to arrive at definite conclusions *beneath the threshold of consciousness.*

Precisely thus with the man of genius. A Napoleon's inspirations are not concerned with nature's laws; those of a Darwin have nothing to do with military conquest; those of a Mozart relate neither to problems of science nor problems of war. No, the inspirations of every man of genius are concerned solely with the subject in which, perhaps from earliest childhood, he has taken the greatest interest, and to which he has devoted the greatest thought. Napoleon, it is known, was so absorbed in military matters that, even at the opera, his mind would be incessantly occupied with some such problem as: "I have ten thousand men at Strasbourg, fifteen thousand at Magdeburg, twenty thousand at Würzburg. By what stages must they march so as to reach Ratisbon on three successive days?" The flowering of Darwin's great discovery was not the work of a moment, but was preceded by years of patient, arduous observation.

Mozart, beginning the study of music at the age of three, remained a zealous student all his days.

"Nobody," runs his own account, "takes as much pains in the study of composition as I. You could not easily name a famous master in music whom I have not industriously studied, often going through his works several times." Walking, or at the theater, or even while engaged in social amusements, he lived in a self-created atmosphere of music. "In Prague," Otto Jahn has recorded, "it once happened that Mozart, while he was playing billiards, was humming a motif, and from time to time would look into a book he had with him. Afterward he confessed he had been at work upon the first quintette of the 'Zauberflöte'!" And we have his wife's testimony: "In truth, his head was working all the time, his mind was ever moving, he composed almost unceasingly." As with Napoleon, Darwin, and Mozart, so with all men of genius of whose lives we have any detailed record.

It may, then, be stated as a well-established fact that intense interest plus persistent effort is the prime essential to the highest success in any sphere of human activity. . . .

Number of words 2250
See page 177 for Questions

Reading Time in Seconds _____
See page 323 for Conversion Table

SELECTION 5

The Fifty-First Dragon

Heywood Broun

"Believe that life is worth living, and your belief will help create the fact," said William James. Was belief the essential difference between the fiftieth and the fifty-first dragon in the story that follows? By comparison, how well do you tap the power of positive thinking?

Of all the pupils at the knight school Gawaine le Cœur-Hardy was among the least promising. He was tall and

sturdy, but his instructors soon discovered that he lacked spirit. He would hide in the woods when the jousting class was called, although his companions and members of the faculty sought to appeal to his better nature by shouting to him to come out and break his neck like a man. Even when they told him that the lances were padded, the horses no more than ponies and the field unusually soft for late autumn, Gawaine refused to grow enthusiastic. The Headmaster and the Assistant Professor of Pleasaunce were discussing the case one spring afternoon and the Assistant Professor could see no remedy but expulsion.

"No," said the Headmaster, as he looked out at the purple hills which ringed the school, "I think I'll train him to slay dragons."

"He might be killed," objected the Assistant Professor.

"So he might," replied the Headmaster brightly, but he added, more soberly, "we must consider the greater good. We are responsible for the formation of this lad's character."

"Are the dragons particularly bad this year?" interrupted the Assistant Professor. This was characteristic. He always seemed restive when the head of the school began to talk ethics and the ideals of the institution.

"I've never known them worse," replied the Headmaster. "Up in the hills to the south last week they killed a number of peasants, two cows and a prize pig. And if this dry spell holds there's no telling when they may start a forest fire simply by breathing around indiscriminately."

"Would any refund on the tuition fee be necessary in case of an accident to young Cœur-Hardy?"

"No," the principal answered, judicially, "that's all covered in the contract. But as a matter of fact he won't be killed. Before I send him up in the hills I'm going to give him a magic word."

"That's a good idea," said the Professor. "Sometimes they work wonders."

From that day on Gawaine specialized in dragons. His course included both theory and practice. In the morning there were long lectures on the history, anatomy, manners and customs of dragons. Gawaine did not distinguish himself in these studies. He had a marvelously versatile gift for forgetting things. In the afternoon he showed to better advantage, for then he would go down to the South Meadow and practice with a battle-ax. In this exercise he was truly impressive, for he had enormous strength as well as speed and grace. He even developed a deceptive display of ferocity. Old alumni say that it was a thrilling sight to see Gawaine charging across the field toward the dummy paper dragon which had been set up for his practice. As he ran he would brandish his ax and shout "A murrain on thee!" or some other vivid bit of campus slang. It never took him more than one stroke to behead the dummy dragon.

Gradually his task was made more difficult. Paper gave way to papier-mâché and finally to wood, but even the toughest of these dummy dragons had no terrors for Gawaine. One sweep of the ax always did the business. There were those who said that when the practice was protracted until dusk and the dragons threw long,

fantastic shadows across the meadow Gawaine did not charge so impetuously nor shout so loudly. It is possible there was malice in this charge. At any rate, the Headmaster decided by the end of June that it was time for the test. Only the night before a dragon had come close to the school grounds and had eaten some of the lettuce from the garden. The faculty decided that Gawaine was ready. They gave him a diploma and a new battle-ax and the Headmaster summoned him to a private conference.

"Sit down," said the Headmaster. "Have a cigarette."

Gawaine hesitated.

"Oh, I know it's against the rules," said the Headmaster. "But after all, you have received your preliminary degree. You are no longer a boy. You are a man. To-morrow you will go out into the world, the great world of achievement."

Gawaine took a cigarette. The Headmaster offered him a match, but he produced one of his own and began to puff away with a dexterity which quite amazed the principal.

"Here you have learned the theories of life," continued the Headmaster, resuming the thread of his discourse, "but after all, life is not a matter of theories. Life is a matter of facts. It calls on the young and the old alike to face these facts, even though they are hard and sometimes unpleasant. Your problem, for example, is to slay dragons."

"They say that those dragons down in the south wood are five hundred feet long," ventured Gawaine, timorously.

"Stuff and nonsense!" said the Headmaster. "The curate saw one last week from the top of Arthur's Hill. The dragon was sunning himself down in the valley. The curate didn't have an opportunity to look at him very long because he felt it was his duty to hurry back to make a report to me. He said the monster, or shall I say, the big lizard? — wasn't an inch over two hundred feet. But the size has nothing at all to do with it. You'll find the big ones even easier than the little ones. They're far slower on their feet and less aggressive, I'm told. Besides, before you go I'm going to equip you in such fashion that you need have no fear of all the dragons in the world."

"I'd like an enchanted cap," said Gawaine.

"What's that?" answered the Headmaster, testily.

"A cap to make me disappear," explained Gawaine.

The Headmaster laughed indulgently. "You mustn't believe all those old wives' stories," he said. "There isn't any such thing. A cap to make you disappear, indeed! What would you do with it? You haven't even appeared yet. Why, my boy, you could walk from here to London, and nobody would so much as look at you. You're nobody. You couldn't be more invisible than that."

Gawaine seemed dangerously close to a relapse into his old habit of whimpering. The Headmaster reassured him: "Don't worry; I'll give you something much better than an enchanted cap. I'm going to give you a magic word. All you have to do is to repeat this magic charm once and no dragon can possibly harm a hair of your head. You can cut off his head at your leisure."

He took a heavy book from the shelf behind his desk and began to run through it. "Sometimes," he said, "the charm is a whole phrase or even a sentence. I might, for instance, give you 'To make the' — No, that might not do. I think a single word would be best for dragons."

"A short word," suggested Gawaine.

"It can't be too short or it wouldn't be potent. There isn't so much hurry as all that. Here's a splendid magic word: 'Rumplesnitz.' Do you think you can learn that?"

Gawaine tried and in an hour or so he seemed to have the word well in hand. Again and again he interrupted the lesson to inquire, "And if I say 'Rumplesnitz' the dragon can't possibly hurt me?" And always the Headmaster replied, "If you only say 'Rumplesnitz,' you are perfectly safe."

Toward morning Gawaine seemed resigned to his career. At daybreak the Headmaster saw him to the edge of the forest and pointed him to the direction in which he should proceed. About a mile away to the southwest a cloud of steam hovered over an open meadow in the woods and the Headmaster assured Gawaine that under the steam he would find a dragon. Gawaine went forward slowly. He wondered whether it would be best to approach the dragon on the run as he did in his practice in the South Meadow or to walk slowly toward him, shouting "Rumplesnitz" all the way.

The problem was decided for him. No sooner had he come to the fringe of the meadow than the dragon spied him and began to charge. It was a large dragon and yet it seemed decidedly aggressive in spite of the Headmaster's statement to the contrary. As the dragon charged it released huge clouds of hissing steam through its nostrils. It was almost as if a gigantic teapot had gone mad. The dragon came forward so fast and Gawaine was so frightened that he had time to say "Rumplesnitz" only once. As he said it, he swung his battle-ax and off popped the head of the dragon. Gawaine had to admit that it was even easier to kill a real dragon than a wooden one if only you said "Rumplesnitz."

Gawaine brought the ears home and a small section of the tail. His school mates and the faculty made much of him, but the Headmaster wisely kept him from being spoiled by insisting that he go on with his work. Every clear day Gawaine rose at dawn and went out to kill dragons. The Headmaster kept him at home when it rained, because he said the woods were damp and unhealthy at such times and that he didn't want the boy to run needless risks. Few good days passed in which Gawaine failed to get a dragon. On one particularly fortunate day he killed three, a husband and wife and a visiting relative. Gradually he developed a technique.

Pupils who sometimes watched him from the hill-tops a long way off said that he often allowed the dragon to come within a few feet before he said "Rumplesnitz." He came to say it with a mocking sneer. Occasionally he did stunts. Once when an excursion party from London was watching him he went into action with his right hand tied behind his back. The dragon's head came off just as easily.

As Gawaine's record of killings mounted higher the Headmaster found it impossible to keep him completely in hand. He fell into the habit of stealing out at night and engaging in long drinking bouts at the village tavern. It was after such a debauch that he rose a little before dawn one fine August morning and started out after his fiftieth dragon. His head was heavy and his mind sluggish. He was heavy in other respects as well, for he had adopted the somewhat vulgar practice of wearing his medals, ribbons and all, when he went out dragon hunting. The decorations began on his chest and ran all the way down to his abdomen. They must have weighed at least eight pounds.

Gawaine found a dragon in the same meadow where he had killed the first one. It was a fair-sized dragon, but evidently an old one. Its face was wrinkled and Gawaine thought he had never seen so hideous a countenance. Much to the lad's disgust, the monster refused to charge and Gawaine was obliged to walk toward him. He whistled as he went. The dragon regarded him hopelessly, but craftily. Of course it had heard of Gawaine. Even when the lad raised his battle-ax the dragon made no move. It knew that there was no salvation in the quickest thrust of the head, for it had been informed that this hunter was protected by an enchantment. It merely waited, hoping something would turn up. Gawaine raised the battle-ax and suddenly lowered it again. He had grown very pale and he trembled violently. The dragon suspected a trick. "What's the matter?" it asked, with false solicitude.

"I've forgotten the magic word," stammered Gawaine.

"What a pity," said the dragon. "So that was the secret. It doesn't seem quite sporting to me, all this magic stuff, you know. Not cricket, as we used to say when I was a little dragon; but after all, that's a matter of opinion."

Gawaine was so helpless with terror that the dragon's confidence rose immeasurably and it could not resist the temptation to show off a bit.

"Could I possibly be of any assistance?" it asked. "What's the first letter of the magic word?"

"It begins with an 'r,' " said Gawaine weakly.

"Let's see," mused the dragon, "that doesn't tell us much, does it? What sort of a word is this? Is it an epithet, do you think?"

Gawaine could do no more than nod.

"Why, of course," exclaimed the dragon, "reactionary Republican."

Gawaine shook his head.

"Well, then," said the dragon, "we'd better get down to business. Will you surrender?"

With the suggestion of a compromise Gawaine mustered up enough courage to speak.

"What will you do if I surrender?" he asked.

"Why, I'll eat you," said the dragon.

"And if I don't surrender?"

"I'll eat you just the same."

"Then it doesn't make any difference, does it?" moaned Gawaine.

"It does to me," said the dragon with a smile. "I'd rather you didn't surrender. You'd taste much better if you didn't."

The dragon waited for a long time for Gawaine to ask "Why?" but the boy was too frightened to speak. At last the dragon had to give the explanation without his cue line. "You see," he said, "if you don't surrender you'll taste better because you'll die game."

This was an old and ancient trick of the dragon's. By means of some such quip he was accustomed to paralyze his victims with laughter and then to destroy them. Gawaine was sufficiently paralyzed as it was, but laughter had no part in his helplessness. With the last word of the joke the dragon drew back his head and struck. In that second there flashed into the mind of Gawaine the magic word "Rumplesnitz," but there was no time to say it. There was time only to strike and, without a word, Gawaine met the onrush of the dragon with a full swing. He put all his back and shoulders into it. The impact was terrific and the head of the dragon flew away almost a hundred yards and landed in a thicket.

Gawaine did not remain frightened very long after the death of the dragon. His mood was one of wonder. He was enormously puzzled. He cut off the ears of the monster almost in a trance. Again and again he thought to himself, "I didn't say 'Rumplesnitz'!" He was sure of that and yet there was no question but that he had killed the dragon. In fact, he had never killed one so utterly. Never before had he driven a head for anything like the same distance. Twenty-five yards was perhaps his best previous record. All the way back to the knight school he kept rumbling about in his mind seeking an explanation for what had occurred. He went to the Headmaster immediately and after closing the door told him what had happened. "I didn't say 'Rumplesnitz,' " he explained with great earnestness.

The Headmaster laughed. "I'm glad you've found out," he said. "It makes you ever so much more of a hero. Don't you see that? Now you know that it was you who killed all these dragons and not that foolish little word 'Rumplesnitz.' "

Gawaine frowned. "Then it wasn't a magic word after all?" he asked.

"Of course not," said the Headmaster, "you ought to be too old for such foolishness. There isn't any such thing as a magic word."

"But you told me it was magic," protested Gawaine. "You said it was magic and now you say it isn't."

"It wasn't magic in a literal sense," answered the Headmaster, "but it was much more wonderful than that. The word gave you confidence. It took away your fears. If I hadn't told you that you might have been killed the very first time. It was your battle-ax did the trick."

Gawaine surprised the Headmaster by his attitude. He was obviously distressed by the explanation. He interrupted a long philosophic and ethical discourse by the Headmaster with, "If I hadn't of hit 'em all mighty hard and fast any one of 'em might have crushed me like a, like a — " He fumbled for a word.

"Egg shell," suggested the Headmaster.

"Like a egg shell," assented Gawaine, and he said it many times. All through the evening meal people who sat near him heard him muttering, "Like a egg shell, like a egg shell."

The next day was clear, but Gawaine did not get up at dawn. Indeed, it was almost noon when the Headmaster found him cowering in bed, with the clothes pulled over his head. The principal called the Assistant Professor of Pleasaunce, and together they dragged the boy toward the forest.

"He'll be all right as soon as he gets a couple more dragons under his belt," explained the Headmaster.

The Assistant Professor of Pleasaunce agreed. "It would be a shame to stop such a fine run," he said. "Why, counting that one yesterday, he's killed fifty dragons."

They pushed the boy into a thicket above which hung a meager cloud of steam. It was obviously quite a small dragon. But Gawaine did not come back that night or the next. In fact, he never came back. Some weeks afterward brave spirits from the school explored the thicket, but they could find nothing to remind them of Gawaine except the metal parts of his medals. Even the ribbons had been devoured.

The Headmaster and the Assistant Professor of Pleasaunce agreed that it would be just as well not to tell the school how Gawaine had achieved his record and still less how he came to die. They held that it might have a bad effect on school spirit. Accordingly, Gawaine has lived in the memory of the school as its greatest hero. No visitor succeeds in leaving the building to-day without seeing a great shield which hangs on the wall of the dining hall. Fifty pairs of dragons' ears are mounted upon the shield and underneath in gilt letters is "Gawaine le Cœur-Hardy," followed by the simple inscription, "He killed fifty dragons." The record has never been equaled.

Number of words 3000
See page 179 for Questions

Reading Time in Seconds _____
See page 323 for Conversion Table

The Lord of Creation

Susanne K. Langer

As a reader you must of necessity deal with symbols. What importance do you attach to that fact? Do you find yourself agreeing or disagreeing with the author as she identifies what she feels is the "highest and most amazing achievement of the human mind"?

A symbol is not the same thing as a sign; that is a fact that psychologists and philosophers often overlook. All intelligent animals use signs; so do we. To them as well as to us sounds and smells and motions are signs of food, danger, the presence of other beings, or of rain or storm. Furthermore, some animals not only attend to signs but produce them for the benefit of others. Dogs bark at the door to be let in; rabbits thump to call each other; the cooing of doves and the growl of a wolf defending his kill are unequivocal signs of feelings and intentions to be reckoned with by other creatures.

We use signs as animals do, though with considerably more elaboration. We stop at red lights and go on green; we answer calls and bells, watch the sky for coming storms, read trouble or promise or anger in each other's eyes. That is animal intelligence raised to the human level. Those of us who are dog lovers can probably all tell wonderful stories of how high our dogs have sometimes risen in the scale of clever sign interpretation and sign using.

A sign is anything that announces the existence or the imminence of some event, the presence of a thing or a person, or a change in a state of affairs. There are signs of the weather, signs of danger, signs of future good or evil, signs of what the past has been. In every case a sign is closely bound up with something to be noted or expected in experience. It is always a part of the situation to which it refers, though the reference may be remote in space and time. In so far as we are led to note or expect the signified event we are making correct use of a sign. This is the essence of rational behavior, which animals show in varying degrees. It is entirely realistic, being closely bound up with the actual objective course of history — learned by experience, and cashed in or voided by further experience.

If man had kept to the straight and narrow path of sign using, he would be like the other animals, though perhaps a little brighter. He would not talk, but grunt and gesticulate and point. He would make his wishes known, give warnings, perhaps develop a social system like that of bees and ants, with such a wonderful efficiency of communal enterprise that all men would have plenty to eat, warm apartments — all exactly alike and perfectly convenient — to live in, and everybody could and would sit in the sun or by the fire, as the climate demanded, not talking, but just basking, with every want satisfied, most of his life. The young would romp and make love, the old would sleep, the middle-aged would do the routine work almost unconsciously and eat a great deal. But that would be the life of a social, superintelligent, purely sign-using animal.

To us who are human, it does not sound very glorious. We want to go places and do things, own all sorts of gadgets that we do not absolutely need, and when we sit down to take it easy we want to talk. Rights and property, social position, special talents and virtues, and above all our ideas, are what we live for. We have gone off on a tangent that takes us far away from the mere biological cycle that animal generations accomplish; and that is because we can use not only signs but symbols.

A symbol differs from a sign in that it does not announce the presence of the object, the being, condition, or whatnot, which is its meaning, but merely *brings this thing to mind.* It is not a mere "substitute sign" to which we react as though it were the object itself. The fact is that our reaction to hearing a person's name is quite different from our reaction to the person himself. There are certain rare cases where a symbol stands directly for its meaning: in religious experience, for instance, the Host is not only a symbol but a Presence. But symbols in the ordinary sense are not mystic. They are the same sort of thing that ordinary signs are; only they do not call our attention to something necessarily present or to be physically dealt with — they call up merely a conception of the thing they "mean."

The difference between a sign and a symbol is, in brief, that a sign causes us to think or act *in face of* the thing signified, whereas a symbol causes us to think *about* the thing symbolized. Therein lies the great importance of symbolism for human life, its power to make this life so different from any other animal biography that generations of men have found it incredible to suppose that they were of purely zoological origin. A sign is always embedded in reality, in a present that emerges from the actual past and stretches to the future; but a symbol may be divorced from reality altogether. It may refer to what is *not* the case, to a mere idea, a figment, a dream. It serves, therefore, to liberate thought from the immediate stimuli of a physically present world; and that liberation marks the essential difference between human and nonhuman mentality. Animals think, but they think *of* and *at* things; men think primarily *about* things. Words, pictures, and memory images are symbols that may be combined and varied in a thousand ways. The result is a symbolic structure whose meaning is a complex of all their respective meanings, and this kaleidoscope of *ideas* is the typical product of the human brain that we call the "stream of thought."

The process of transforming all direct experience into imagery or into that supreme mode of symbolic expression, language, has so completely taken possession of the human mind that it is not only a special talent but a dominant, organic need. All our sense impressions leave their traces in our memory not only as signs disposing our practical reactions in the future but also as symbols, images representing our *ideas* of things; and the tendency to manipulate ideas, to combine and abstract, mix and extend them by playing with symbols, is man's outstanding characteristic. It seems to be what his brain most naturally and spontaneously does. Therefore his primitive mental function is not judging reality, but *dreaming his desires.*

Dreaming is apparently a basic function of human brains, for it is free and unexhausting like our metabolism, heartbeat, and breath. It is easier to dream than not to dream, as it is easier to breathe than to refrain from breathing. The symbolic character of dreams is fairly well established. Symbol mongering, on this ineffectual, uncritical level, seems to be instinctive, the fulfillment of an elementary need rather than the purposeful exercise of a high and difficult talent.

The special power of man's mind rests on the evolution of this special activity, not on any transcendently high development of animal intelligence. We are not immeasurably higher than other animals; we are different. We have a biological need and with it a biological gift that they do not share.

Because man has not only the ability but the constant need of *conceiving* what has happened to him, what surrounds him, what is demanded of him — in short, of symbolizing nature, himself, and his hopes and fears — he has a constant and crying need of *expression.* What he cannot express, he cannot conceive: what he cannot conceive is chaos, and fills him with terror.

If we bear in mind this all-important craving for expression we get a new picture of man's behavior, for from this trait spring his powers and his weaknesses. The process of symbolic transformation that all our experiences undergo is nothing more nor less than the process of *conception,* which underlies the human faculties of abstraction and imagination.

When we are faced with a strange or difficult situation, we cannot react directly, as other creatures do, with flight, aggression, or any such simple instinctive pattern. Our whole reaction depends on how we manage to conceive the situation — whether we cast it in a definite dramatic form, whether we see it as a disaster, a challenge, a fulfillment of doom, or a fiat of the Divine Will. In words or dreamlike images, in artistic or religious or even in cynical form, we must *construe* the events of life. There is great virtue in the figure of speech, "I can *make* nothing of it," to express a failure to understand something. Thought and memory are processes of *making* the thought content and the memory image; the pattern of our ideas is given by the symbols through which we express them. And in the course of manipulating those symbols we inevitably distort the original experience, as we abstract certain features of it, embroider and reinforce those features with other ideas, until the conception we project on the screen of memory is quite different from anything in our real history.

Conception is a necessary and elementary process; what we do with our conceptions is another story. That is the entire history of human culture — of intelligence and morality, folly and superstition, ritual, language, and the arts — all the phenomena that set man apart from, and above, the rest of the animal kingdom. As the religious mind has to make all human history a drama of sin and salvation in order to define its own moral attitudes, so a scientist wrestles with the mere presentation of "the facts" before he can reason about them. The process of *envisaging* facts, values, hopes, and fears underlies our whole behavior pattern; and this process is reflected in the evolution of an extraordinary phenomenon found always, and only, in human societies — the phenomenon of language.

Language is the highest and most amazing achievement of the symbolistic human mind. The power it bestows is almost inestimable, for without it anything properly called "thought" is impossible. The birth of language is the dawn of humanity. The line between man and beast — between the highest ape and the lowest savage — is the language line. Whether the primitive Neanderthal man was anthropoid or human depends less on his cranial capacity, his upright posture, or even his use of tools and fire, than on one issue we shall probably never be able to settle — whether or not he spoke.

Number of words 1740
See page 181 for Questions

Reading Time in Seconds _____
See page 323 for Conversion Table

15

The Future of Grammar

Paul Roberts

Being bad grammar, you shouldn't use no dangling participles. Furthermore, subject and verb has to always agree. Ain't it about time to look into this here grammar business to see what linguistic scientists are saying about grammar and communication. Do "ain't" and "isn't" communicate equally well?

The last few decades have witnessed an amiable but spirited battle between linguistic scientists and defenders of traditional ways of teaching English. Linguists have been in revolt against two assumptions that underlie the tradition: (1) that there are absolute criteria — logical, analogical, etymological, or whatever — by which correctness can be measured; and (2) that there are universal, nonlinguistic concepts through which the linguistic categories of any language can be identified and defined. Ultimately this revolt will succeed; there need be no doubt of that. Provided only that our society retains the orientation it has had for the past several centuries, nothing can prevent the establishment in the school system of the views of linguistic science. Wherever, in our civilization, science and non-science conflict, it is non-science that gives way, as astrology gave way to astronomy and alchemy to chemistry. In the same way, linguistic science and structural analysis will triumph over traditional language teaching, although it may take a similarly long time. It is true that astrology does not now play the role that it did in 1350, but astrologers are still around.

Our purpose here is not to discuss when or whether the transition will take place but rather to suggest what its effects on English teaching are likely to be.

Some effects there have been already, and not all of them are good. Linguists have long argued that correctness is altogether relative, having nothing to do with logic or the order of the universe, but depending on such variables as time, place, circumstance, age, sex. The language forms used, correctly, in addressing an umpire, may be incorrect in addressing a bishop. And vice versa. The sentence "We heard the sweetest little bird singing the dearest little song" is correct if you're a twelve-year-old girl but incorrect if you're a fifty-year-old bartender. In some circles, "Ain't you comin' back?" will get you blackballed; in others, "Shall you not return?" will get you tossed out on your ear.

Logic has nothing to do with it. When they ask, "Is it correct?" linguists don't mean, "Is it logical?" They mean, "Would it be well received — at this time, in this place, in this social situation — from a person of this age and sex?" It doesn't matter whether or not, in

algebra, two negatives make a positive. What matters is whether, in the language area being considered, it is customary to say, "We don't want no trouble," and, if so, whether it would be generally understood that the speaker wants trouble or doesn't.

All this is old stuff. It is a principle now fully accepted by dictionaries, which don't tell us what to say but rather what we and our countrymen *do* say. It has also been accepted, to some degree, by most handbooks and by many teachers of English. But the implications for classroom procedure are still to be understood and faced.

One thing that the idea of relativity of correctness does *not* mean is that it doesn't matter how we talk or write. Recently some educators have been disposed to tell us: "It isn't important *how* you say a thing; what is important is what you say." This is a pious thought, and it may be true in the sight of God, but it isn't true as the world goes and never will be. Possibly this notion is the linguists' responsibility, but it isn't the linguists' notion.

Certainly it matters how you say a thing. Saying the right thing in the wrong way can get you fired, divorced, arrested, or expelled from the P.T.A. It's nice to be intelligible, but sometimes it is infinitely better to be unintelligible than incorrect. It makes a tremendous difference how you say a thing; it just doesn't always make the same difference. In fact, it probably never makes the same difference twice.

This is what the growing heaps of linguistic information, like the Linguistic Atlas and the dialect dictionaries, are showing ever more clearly. We may suppose that any bit of speech, any word or phrase or sentence, will, when uttered, be either correct or incorrect. But we cannot predict which without knowing all about the nonlinguistic environment in which the utterance occurs. The criteria of correctness are real enough, but they are staggeringly complex and constantly in motion, shifting subtly about us as we go from work to play, from night to morning, from anteroom to inner office, from Broadway to Cypress Street, from Peter to Paul. There is probably no American expression of which we can say, "This will always be correct." And none of which we can say, "This will always be wrong."

So far we have tried to meet this difficulty with the concept of "levels of usage," dividing usage into several strata, usually three — standard, colloquial, vulgate. Now this concept has its uses where the intent is purely descriptive, as for example in a dictionary or a descriptive grammar. But as a device for instructing students in how to behave linguistically, it is using nets to catch the wind. The "levels of usage" concept has not led us, as some would say, to teach descriptively rather than prescriptively. It has simply led us to be prescriptive in a much more complicated way — and yet in a way not nearly complicated enough for the linguistic reality which our students face. If we must be prescriptive, it is more reasonable to select some single, more or less graspable area of usage — say the usage of *The Atlantic Monthly* — and make the student learn that and only that and bat his ears down when he departs from it.

The alternative is to abandon the prescriptive idea altogether, to give up the notion of bringing the student to a fore-determined pattern of usage, and to seek other results entirely. We might aim not at conformity but at range, flexibility, adaptability. We might teach the student to observe his own language and the language of others and to describe them accurately. We might develop sensitivity for the nuances of speech and prose, an ear and an eye for the eternal subtle changes going on in them. We might train the student to use dictionaries as their makers intend them to be used — not as oracles but as collections of linguistic fact to be consulted in areas into which the user's experience does not reach and to be believed whenever they do not conflict with the user's own accurate observation.

Experiments in this direction are already underway in many schools throughout the country. But it may be generations before the thing is done in the school system generally. Our teaching materials will need to be thoroughly revised, the curriculum in teacher-training institutions drastically modified. Most important, beliefs and attitudes as deep-seated as the belief of the Middle Ages in astrology will have to give way. But there is no reason to believe that the change will not take place — in someone's lifetime — and that the change will not be generally for the better, resulting in a major improvement in the morale of English classes and in a general rise in the ability to speak and write fluently, intelligibly, gracefully, accurately, and even — in the best sense of the word — correctly.

Along with this must go a quiet revolution in our techniques for describing language. We are still tied to a superstition of "universal grammar," which rests in fact on the grammar of Latin. We can make it work in English only by the most rigorous exclusion of the realities of English, and what we study when we study "English grammar" is an artificial language, a concoction of made-up sentences with which no one could possibly communicate for any length of time on any subject of importance. Any student of English can prove this for himself simply by taking a page — any page — of actual English writing and trying to analyze it with the tools of what passes for English grammar.

But probably the most discouraging thing about traditional grammar is the set of tautologies in which it wanders: "a noun is a name," "a verb is an action," "an interrogative sentence is a sentence which asks a question." These statements are more or less true, but they don't tell us anything we don't already know, any more than would definitions like "a man is a man," "a rose is a rose." Let us grant that a noun is the name of something. What we want to discover is how we know, in any particular sentence, which words name things and are therefore nouns. We do not grasp this by any metaphysical intuition, but by our understanding of a complicated set of structural signals which mark off nouns from other word classes. These signals are indeed complex (and of course entirely different from language to language), but they are tangible, real and rather interesting. It is sometimes urged for grammar that it is valuable as an intellectual discipline, and it may be, provided it is real description of actual language. But when it is a half-baked hodge-podge of improbable abstractions, there is no intellectual discipline in it but only disillusion and despair.

Somebody will have to do something about this, and many people are already trying — seeking to look at the language and see what's there and find ways of describing it. Specialists disagree about whether to scrap everything and begin again or to try to save as much as possible from the tradition — terminology, for instance — and simply to change and add whatever is necessary. Whichever choice is made, the task will be long and difficult, but it will be done, and the grammar that emerges will make English studies more pleasant than they are now. People are disposed to believe that traditional grammar is dull and difficult, but useful. As generally taught, grammar is difficult and dull, but it isn't useful. The new grammar may not be useful either, and will be difficult, but won't be dull.

Number of words 1660
See page 183 for Questions

Reading Time in Seconds _____
See page 323 for Conversion Table

The Educated Man

James Ansara

At what point in life can it be said that a person is truly educated? Lin Yutang once said, "The wise man reads both books and life itself." Does the following dramatic story say much the same thing? How differently can ideas be communicated!

My father was a man steeped in the aphorisms and parables of his race, with which he spiced even his everyday conversation. Best of all I liked the stories he often resorted to to illustrate truisms. I remember the first time he told the one about the education of Sheikh Yusif's son. I had finished college, and my problem was whether to continue my intellectual pursuits or to launch myself into the practical activities of the world. One evening I sought to discuss the matter with him, but instead of giving me his advice he offered to tell me a story that his father had once told him. It was after dinner and we were having black coffee flavored with the essence of roses. Between long, satisfying sips, this was the story he told: —

Once there was a sheikh, Yusif al-Hamadi, who was determined that some day his only son, Ali, should become a learned man.

When Ali completed his elementary studies under his tutors, the Sheikh called together his advisers and asked them where his son could acquire the best possible education. With one voice, they answered, "The University of El-Azhar, in Cairo."

So at El-Azhar, then the most renowned university in the whole world, the son of Sheikh Yusif studied with great energy and soon proved himself a true scholar. After eight years of study, the Ulama of the university pronounced Ali an educated man, and the son wrote that he was returning home.

As a scholar, Ali scorned the vanities of life and departed from Cairo riding a jackass and wearing the coarse raiment of an ascetic. Jogging along with his books behind him and his diploma fastened to his side, Ali lost himself in meditating upon the writings of the poets and philosophers.

When he was only a day's journey from his home, the young scholar entered a village mosque to rest for a while. It was Friday and the place was full of worshipers. A Khatib was preaching on the miraculous deeds of the Prophet.

Now Ali, as a result of his profound study of the teachings of the Prophet, had become an uncompromising puritan of the Faith. Therefore, when the Khatib told his credulous congregation that Mohammed caused

springs to flow in the desert, moved mountains, and flew on his horse to heaven, Ali was outraged.

"Stop!" cried Ali. "Believe not this false man. All that he has told you are lies, not the true faith. Our teacher, Mohammed, was not a supernatural being, but a man who saw the light, the truth —"

The Khatib interrupted to ask the young man upon what authority he contradicted him. Ali proudly informed him that he was a scholar, a graduate of the great University of El-Azhar. The preacher, with a sneer on his face, turned toward his congregation.

"This man, who calls himself a scholar, is a heretic, an atheist who dares come among you, the Faithful, and throw doubt upon the greatness of our Prophet Mohammed, blessed be his name. Cast him out of the mosque; he contaminates its sanctity."

The people seized Ali and dragged him to the street, beating and kicking him and tearing his clothes. Outside, his books and diploma were destroyed, and the unconscious Ali was tied to his jackass backward and stoned out of the village.

When word came of the approach of Ali, Sheikh Yusif and the neighboring sheikhs, whom the proud father had invited to join him to receive and honor his scholarly son, rode forth to meet the learned graduate of El-Azhar. But lo, the scholar was dangling from the back of a jackass, his learned head bouncing against its haunches. Bruised, half naked, he was muttering like an idiot.

Not for several days was Ali well enough to tell his father what had befallen him. When he finished, Sheikh Yusif sighed deeply and said, "Ali, you have come back to me only half educated. You must return to Cairo." The young man protested that there was nothing more the university could teach him, and Sheikh Yusif agreed. The rest of his education was to be outside of El-Azhar.

Back in Cairo, Ali was to discover a new world. According to his father's instructions, he spent the first six months in the shop of a merchant, bartering and wrangling in the busiest bazaar of Cairo. Following that, the chief of police took him in hand and introduced him to the life of the city in all its varied aspects. For a time he was a beggar outside one of the great mosques, a disciple of a magician, a waiter in a low café. Ali also came to know the life of a sailor, a wandering trader, and a laborer.

At the end of the fifth year, Ali informed his father

Reprinted by permission from *The Atlantic Monthly*, November 1937.

that his education was completed and he was again returning home.

This time, the son of Sheikh Yusif left Cairo riding a spirited Arabian, dressed in silks and satins, and attended by a train of servants. His stops during the journey were brief, until he reached the village of the Khatib. It was again Friday and the same Khatib was declaiming the same miracles to the credulous peasants. Ali joined the congregation and listened to the words of the preacher with a rapture equal to that of his neighbors. His "Ah" and "Great is our Prophet" were even more fervent than those about him.

When the Khatib concluded his sermon, Ali humbly begged to be heard.

"In spite of my youth," said Ali, "I have studied much and traveled wide, seeking the truth and wisdom of our great Prophet, blessed be his name. But never have I heard or read a sermon equal in truth and piety to that of your reverend Khatib. Not only is he a learned man, but a holy one, for his knowledge of the life of the Prophet comes only from the deepest source of faith and piety, a knowledge denied to ordinary men. Fortunate are you in having such a saint. Fortunate am I too, for here ends my search for the holiest man of our age.

"O holy Khatib, fit companion of Caliphs, I beg of you a boon!"

The bewildered Khatib could only ask the nature of that boon.

"It is written in the Holy Koran that a relic from a saint brings endless blessings to the Faithful. A hair from they beard, O Saintly One!"

Still perplexed, the Khatib could not, before his whole congregation, deny such a pious request. The young man with bowed head slowly mounted the *mumbar* and, in sight of all the people, with two extended fingers pulled a hair from the outthrust, flowing beard. Ali kissed it with deep reverence, folded it meticulously in a white silk kerchief, and placed it inside his shirt next to his heart.

A murmur arose from the congregation — their Khatib was a holy man! Even before Ali left the *mumbar,* the stampede toward the preacher had begun. By the time the son of Sheikh Yusif had forced his way through the mad crowd to the street, not a hair was left on the Khatib's face or head, not a shred of clothing on his body, and he lay behind the *mumbar* writhing and gasping like a plucked rooster.

That evening, Ali arrived home and there was great rejoicing in his father's house. His wit and dignity, his profound store of knowledge, his tact and manners, charmed all the guests and swelled the heart of his father with pride.

When at last the guests departed and Ali was alone with his father, he recounted to him his second visit to the village of the Khatib. The old Sheikh nodded his head approvingly and said: —

"Now, my son, I can die in peace. You have tempered book learning with worldly wisdom and returned a truly educated man."

Number of words 1320
See page 185 for Questions

Reading Time in Seconds _____
See page 323 for Conversion Table

SELECTION 9

Detecting Propaganda

Ralph G. Nichols

How to cope effectively with propaganda is an important aspect of your overall communication effort. As you read, listen, and observe, what specific propaganda devices should you be most aware of if you are to avoid being manipulated to disadvantage? Read all about them.

Most techniques of propaganda have been well defined by the Institute for Propaganda Analysis. The institute calls them "propaganda techniques," perhaps somewhat inaccurately according to the dictionary definition of the word "propaganda." However, the techniques are used by persuasive talkers, both in the trained-speaker cate-

gory and in the conversational, person-to-person category. The institute has identified seven techniques and given them titles:

1. Name calling. As we know, people tend to summarize whole areas of their experience under labels. The labels, when heard, flood the listener with emotion, his mind stops working on a logical basis, and he may, without giving his decision careful thought, take the action desired of him by the persuasive talker. With this technique the labels are usually selected by the talker to produce a negative reaction in the listener against some thing, cause or person.

For example, the term "Communist" has been an emotion-laden label in America and has sometimes been devastatingly applied to people who have not been Communists.

2. Glittering generalities. This technique works in a fashion similar to the first one, but here the labels are likely to illuminate the talker's cause, or anything or anybody supporting it, in a favorable light. Examples of such labels are: freedom-loving, democratic, American, Christian, efficient, patriotic and friend. Such words often cause good feelings to fill the listener on an emotional level, and again he may make a decision to accept the speaker's proposition without reasoning it out.

A political candidate may be introduced as "that great, democratic, freedom-loving, patriotic American." In the face of these "glittering generalities" it's sometimes hard for a listener to believe otherwise.

3. Transfer. With this device the speaker frequently refers to sources of authority, prestige or reverence that his listener respects. He will not explicitly say that the sources support his cause, but he gives the impression that they do. Such sources might include a church, a highly respected civic organization, the flag, the will of the people or public education.

As the political candidate speaks he tells about attending church, belonging to civic groups, attending local schools and having respect for the will of the people. Many listeners are likely to make a "transfer," assuming that these things mentioned by the candidate all rally behind the man, even though he really does not say so.

4. Testimonial. In support of his cause the speaker employing this technique cites testimony from respected, well-known people, or he may call on them to give the testimony personally.

On the television screen a famous movie star appears, testifying to all the favorable mechanical features of a new-model car that is being advertised. Because the star is well known the noncritical listener fails to question how qualified the actor is to talk about technical factors in a car, and the actor's words persuade the listener to buy the vehicle without question.

5. Plain folks. As listeners we will often readily accept the word of a person who seems to be very much like us, while, on the other hand, we become suspicious of people who are different from us. The persuasive

talker may take advantage of this inconsistency to sway his listeners by doing things to make himself appear to be one of them.

A well-dressed salesman visiting the foreman of a machine shop will remove his coat and necktie before entering the shop. Inside, he practically forces handshakes out of the grease-smeared workmen to show that he, like them, doesn't mind dirty hands, and he uses bad grammar mixed with considerable cursing because he figures that that is how the average shophand talks. If his outward change of character is accepted by the foreman, the salesman has a better chance to gain acceptance of what he says in his sales talk.

6. Card stacking. When a persuasive talker "stacks his cards" he edits his oral material in his own favor. Any evidence that supports his proposition will be spoken, but adverse evidence will be shrouded in silence.

"This vacuum cleaner," says the salesman, "has nine wonderful features." And he enumerates them, but he makes no reference to the disadvantages, of course. The noncritical listener accepts what he hears, failing to look beyond the spoken words for the full evidence.

7. Band wagon. This device appeals to follow-the-herd instincts that are strong in most of us. The persuasive speaker points out that many people are accepting his proposition, often leaving the listener with a feeling that he too should join the crowd.

The television announcer appears on the screen holding a package of cigarettes. "Two billion of these were sold last year," he states. "Everyone is buying them. This year we expect to sell three billion or more." The announcer may give no solid evidence regarding the cigarettes' quality, but the listener, not exercising critical abilities, may buy the cigarettes simply because he understands that everyone else is buying them.

In addition to these seven devices there are, of course, other techniques used in oral persuasion. In their book, *General Speech,* A. Craig Baird and Franklin H. Knower point out a number of other things that persuasive talkers use or play upon to their advantage: "flattery; appeals to fear, hate, anger, frustration or discontent growing out of lack of opportunity or misfortune; the creation of devils on which to place blame; repetition and more repetition; wishful thinking, rationalization, rumor, distrust; identification with the great, the beautiful and the good; prophecies and positive suggestion."

Number of words 910
See page 187 for Questions

Reading Time in Seconds _____
See page 323 for Conversion Table

Why Word Study Is Necessary

Denver Ewing

Sometimes one thing only exerts a strong spreading circle of influence, as a stone dropped into a quiet pool. Every new word has that effect on your ability to communicate. Every new word helps you read, write, speak, listen, and even think more effectively. Word study is, therefore, perhaps your best shortcut to effective communication, as you will soon see.

Though the reasons for success in life are too complicated to be traceable to any one source, a close correlation does exist between big achievement and big vocabulary. Despite Thomas Gray's contradictory tribute to "Some mute inglorious Milton" in "Elegy in a Country Churchyard," the fact remains that poets sing because they must, and their evocative powers are commensurate with their vocabularies. "Don't just stand there — say something" is the eternal challenge that only man with his ready wit can answer. "Speak that I may know thee" somehow epitomizes the fact that language is a great revealer of character and training. Words are not only fossil poetry but pegs on which to hang ideas. Thus looking up a word in the dictionary may be almost synonymous with the beginning of wisdom. Yet the reluctance with which the average student uses his lexicon undoubtedly has some connection with the failure of mass education. To overcome that reluctance is more than any teacher or any book can do. All that can be done here is to point out that word study is necessary (1) because in college almost every assignment requires reading, writing, speaking, listening, and thinking that involve vocabulary extension and (2) because in the business, social-service, and learned professions for which students are trained a vocabulary that even Shakespeare could not have evoked is now, far more than ever before, not only necessary but indispensable.

VOCABULARY AND READING

Probably the most rewarding of all activities for vocabulary extension is the reading done not only in the field of one's choice but also in other fields, not only in the native tongue but also in other tongues. Since only about fifteen percent of a college freshman's time is spent in reading, even the most elementary courses in social, political, physical, and natural sciences, history, and humanities can tax beyond his powers of comprehension the student who has not come to terms with his dictionary. A college student with the vocabulary of only an eighth grader is hardly likely to succeed in a course where the basic terms are beyond his grasp. On the other hand simplification of subject matter can go too far. It can eviscerate a subject. Just how much, for example, can the authors of biology texts concede to the average student with no Latin background without irreparable damage to the course? Granted that the average student in such a course does have to absorb more strange, unpronounceable words than are required in any first-year foreign-language course, the omission of terms means the omission of ideas and ideas are the quintessence of not only biology but all other subjects. As Ruskin has the books say, "If you will not rise to us, we cannot stoop to you." In short, in order to come into coincident thinking with an author, the student must work "as an Australian miner would," Ruskin further says, for "the metal you are in search of" is "the author's mind or meaning," and "his words are as the rock which you have to crush and smelt in order to get at it."

If the present is an age of marvelous opportunity for the printed word, it is also an age of marvelous opportunity for other and more facile means of communication. Radio and television — the attractive alternative to the printed word — could prove the undoing of the more jaded civilizations. The newer and more virile civilizations that are attempting to do in one generation what it took the older ones some four hundred years to do are dubious of radio, television, and movies because they are passive devices. Since they want to exercise their minds they read books. They are determined to become literate, and they know that viewing and listening are alternatives but not substitutes for the more powerful and lasting medium of print. In connection with shortcuts it is said that a people who know only one language know no language. Most Americans are often surprised at how many languages exchange students from the more backward countries can speak. Certainly in international affairs failure to understand other peoples in their own languages is an almost insuperable barrier to sound diplomacy, commerce, trade, and understanding. If Saul, son of Kish, could go out to find his father's asses and find a city, the student of words might go out and stagger into a whole new kingdom — the kingdom of words.

By permission. From the February issue of *World Study* © 1963 by G. & C. Merriam Co., Publishers of the Merriam-Webster Dictionaries.

VOCABULARY AND WRITING

Though Bacon grants that reading "maketh a full man," he also contends that writing makes an exact man. So in order to be an exact man the college freshman spends about three percent more time in writing than in reading. Lamb was a voracious reader, but he also enjoyed setting down the outcroppings of his own mind. Artistically, much of the writing that men do is worthless, but the writing which endures is, as Milton says, "the precious life-blood of a master-spirit, embalmed and treasured up on purpose to a life beyond life." The act of putting the proper words in their proper places in sentences is of the essence of style. A mature style is not something that just happens. It is a deliberate act and requires more effort than either reading, speaking, listening, or thinking. Without a large store of words, however, the writer may search long before he finds the one word which is a perfect fit. Yet he should know that the most difficult and most rewarding aspect of exact wording is not in the writing itself but in the rewriting. As soon as he realizes that the first fine careless rapture of yesterday's creativity is today's disappointment, drastic revision sets in. The unruly word goes out and a more tractable one takes its place. Sometimes a whole reference library is brought under contribution, but all the proper words have found all their proper places and no longer sound "jangled, out of tune and harsh." For it must be borne in mind that in reading and in listening the context of a particular word is provided and that in writing the context must be created. Moreover, writing is the only literary activity that requires syllabication a part of the time and proper spelling all the time. Bacon therefore might almost have said that writing makes a meticulous man.

VOCABULARY AND SPEAKING

Concerning the power and command of the spoken word, Marjorie Kinnan Rawlings has Quincey Dover say of the Widow Tippett in "Cocks Must Crow": "She licked her lips. I could see her drawing back her tongue like I'd done mine. And when she let it loose, seemed to me like I'd been casting mine full of backlashes, and not coming within ten yards of putting it where I aimed to. For she takened her tongue and she laid it down so accurate I had to stand and admire a expert." Apparently Quincey herself was no slouch in the art of slinging words, for it takes an expert to admire an expert. Until, however, the phonograph was invented, posterity could no more ascertain the speaking power of those gone before than one can be sure of the song the Sirens sang. More specifically, no one knows how the great orators of other days spoke their speeches, nor does he know how the great conversationalists like Dr. Johnson, Coleridge, and Lamb conversed. As a matter of fact most who write like angels do not speak with the tongues of angels. Donne's longing "to talk with some old lover's ghost" might, if granted, have proved disap-

pointing. Though Oliver Goldsmith was a most charming writer of informal essays, Garrick says that the writer talked like poor Poll. Certainly anyone's speech is more deceptive and harder to judge than is his writing. The gleam of the eye, the modulation of the voice, and the gestures of the hands and movements of the body can sometimes cast a spell over the hearer even when the words of the speaker are as chaff in the wind. On the one hand, stripped of bodily aids, the writer must remember that he has to depend on bare script or print. On the other, deprived of time to meditate, the speaker must remember what Lear told Cordelia: "Mend your speech a little,/Lest it may mar your fortunes." Moreover, the eye, the voice, and the bodily movements are not all. The misuse and mispronunciation (particularly a misplaced accent) of a word can betray a person's background as nothing else can do. Ruskin therefore warns that if words "are not watched closely, they will do deadly work" and "that a false accent of a mistaken syllable is enough in the parliament of any civilized nation to assign to a man a certain degree of inferior standing forever." Though Wordsworth was no doubt surprised that the old leech gatherer replied "With something of a lofty utterance . . ./Choice word and measured phrase, above the reach/Of ordinary men: a stately speech," the opposite effect is far more frequent. Silence is golden, but Solomon says that "A word fitly spoken is like apples of gold in pictures of silver." Thus, since a college freshman spends about twenty-five percent of his time talking and speaks thousands of words to every word he writes, he can hardly overemphasize the importance of the spoken word in human associations.

VOCABULARY AND LISTENING

Of all the aspects of communication, listening, as has already been implied, is the most passive. Without a pencil and notebook the hearer is liable to forget all the unusual pronunciations, words, and ideas or anecdotes that at the time he is listening seem too important ever to forget. For example, a speaker may be talking of automation and mention *cybernetics,* a relatively new word and only recently recorded in the dictionaries. The listener may never have heard it before and may not know whether it begins with an *s* or a *c.* Finally, after a futile search, he may give up and forget it. Since, on the other hand, so many more people are deficient in hearing than in any other of the five senses, the listener may have received so garbled a sensation as to have been unable himself to pronounce or visualize the word at all. Moreover the art of effective listening is being recognized, especially in college classrooms, as a very important discipline. Like most other disciplines, effective listening, alas, is "more honored in the breach than the observance." The sobering truth is that few people can emerge from a listening experience with anything much better than a garbled account of what has been said. Granted that the speaker is impeccable — a big concession — either the vocabulary is beyond their comprehension, the correct pronunciation is alien to their ears, or the distractions are too fascinating. Always the onus is on the uneducated person. He cannot allow for the nuances and subtleties of the highly cultivated speaker, and what happens is the reverse of the observation that "the hand of little employment hath the daintier sense." He says *rigamorole, twelth, maintainance, modren,* and a hundred or more other crude expressions without ever knowing the difference between his pronunciations and what he has heard. The pity is that he is revealing his lack of education every time he opens his mouth. He does not know that listening to sloppy speakers day in and day out can often make for one's also being a sloppy speaker. The careful speaker can usually understand the careless one, but the reverse is not so likely. Yet, since about forty percent of a student's time is spent in listening, his passing or failing in college may easily depend upon his ability or inability to improve his listening power.

VOCABULARY AND THINKING

Before, during, and after all reading, writing, speaking, and listening comes thinking — the handmaiden of all communications. Even though the power to think effectively is, like Paul's definition of faith, "the substance of things hoped for, the evidence of things not seen," it is nevertheless indispensable. Its logicalities and illogicalities reveal themselves most clearly, however, in writing and speaking, which should be planned, executed, and criticized in the light of the communicative power of the end product. Since the writer or speaker cannot be entirely sure that he knows what he means until he has put it into written or spoken words and realizes how it looks or sounds, both writing and speaking involve a risk that is not involved in reading and listening. Except in a general way the student does not plan his reading and listening experiences as he does his writing and speaking experiences because the materials of the former two are not of his making. To think of the unique verbal relationships that make an interesting theme or

speech is the despair of the mediocre student and the pride of the brilliant one. To attempt to perform mental feats without an ever-expanding vocabulary is like trying to win athletic contests without a powerhouse of reserve energy acquired through much training. The student without vocabulary has nothing to think with. Words make words, and it might be said that to him who hath shall be given and to him who hath not shall be taken away even that which he has.

VOCABULARY AND A VOCATION

Finally, when the student has been graduated from college and goes into business, social service, or a learned profession, he will no doubt already know many of the terms that are peculiar to his field of specialization, but he can hardly know them all, and, anyway, terminology sometimes changes, especially when new procedural methods are adopted. To the businessman such words as *competition, underselling, credit, liability, corporation, mortgage, inventory, bankruptcy, stocks, bonds, negotiability consignment, demurrage,* and *fluctuation* are the staple of conversation. To the social-service worker the dictionary is largely a matter of words having to do with *status seekers, suburbanites, hovels, delinquents, squalor, prostitution, alcoholism, mendicancy,* and *perversion.* And, finally, to the professional man (lawyer, doctor, professor, or artist) the verbal resources are almost limitless: *intestate, legacy, quit-claim deed, absolve, accomplice,* and *indictment; hemorrhage, emetic, anesthetic, diagnosis, malignancy, acute, contusion,* and *therapeutic;* and *gaucherie, parody, limpidness, naturalism, virtuosity, chiaroscuro, plagiarism,* and *dissonance.*

It is therefore clear that the student in college must come to terms with words, for "In the beginning was the word, and the word was with God, and the word was God." In the end too will be the word, and the student will have to fill in between the words, words, words from his reading, writing, speaking, listening, and thinking and finally with words from whatever vocation he happens to follow in later life.

Number of words 2440
See page 189 for Questions

Reading Time in Seconds _____
See page 323 for Conversion Table

Habit! Make It Your Friend, Not Your Enemy

William James

In this world, what is strongest? Ovid, born back in 43 B.C., *thought he knew. He put it this way — "Nothing is stronger than habit." How do you put habit formation directly behind all your efforts to improve reading and communication skills? Get help from this selection.*

"Habit a second nature! Habit is ten times nature," the Duke of Wellington is said to have exclaimed; and the degree to which this is true no one probably can appreciate as well as one who is a veteran soldier himself. The daily drill and the years of discipline end by fashioning a man completely over again, as to most of the possibilities of his conduct.

"There is a story," says Professor Huxley, "which is credible enough, though it may not be true, of a practical joker who, seeing a discharged veteran carrying home his dinner, suddenly called out, 'Attention!' whereupon the man instantly brought his hands down, and lost his mutton and potatoes in the gutter. The drill had been thorough, and its effects had become embodied in the man's nervous structure."

Riderless cavalry-horses, at many a battle, have been seen to come together and go through their customary evolutions at the sound of the bugle-call. Most domestic beasts seem machines almost pure and simple, undoubtingly, unhesitatingly doing from minute to minute the duties they have been taught, and giving no sign that the possibility of an alternative ever suggests itself to their mind. Men grown old in prison have asked to be readmitted after being once set free. In a railroad accident a menagerie-tiger, whose cage had broken open, is said to have emerged, but presently crept back again, as if too much bewildered by his new responsibilities, so that he was without difficulty secured.

Habit is thus the enormous fly-wheel of society, its most precious conservative agent. It alone is what keeps us all within the bounds of ordinance, and saves the children of fortune from the envious uprisings of the poor. It alone prevents the hardest and most repulsive walks of life from being deserted by those brought up to tread therein. It keeps the fisherman and the deckhand at sea through the winter; it holds the miner in his darkness, and nails the countryman to his log-cabin and his lonely farm through all the months of snow; it protects us from invasion by the natives of the desert and the frozen zone. It dooms us all to fight out the battle of life upon the lines of our nurture or our early choice, and to make the best of a pursuit that disagrees, because there is no other for which we are fitted, and it is too late to begin again. It keeps different social strata from mixing. Already at the age of twenty-five you see the professional mannerism settling down on the young commercial traveller, on the young doctor, on the young minister, on the young counsellor-at-law. You see the little lines of cleavage running through the character, the tricks of thought, the prejudices, the ways of the "shop," in a word, from which the man can by-and-by no more escape than his coat-sleeve can suddenly fall into a new set of folds. On the whole, it is best he should not escape. It is well for the world that in most of us, by the age of thirty, the character has set like plaster, and will never soften again.

If the period between twenty and thirty is the critical one in the formation of intellectual and professional habits, the period below twenty is more important still for the fixing of *personal* habits, properly so called, such as vocalization and pronunciation, gesture, motion, and address. Hardly ever is a language learned after twenty spoken without a foreign accent; hardly ever can a youth transferred to the society of his betters unlearn the nasality and other vices of speech bred in him by the associations of his growing years. Hardly ever, indeed, no matter how much money there be in his pocket, can he even learn to *dress* like a gentleman-born. The merchants offer their wares as eagerly to him as to the veriest "swell," but he simply *cannot* buy the right things. An invisible law, as strong as gravitation, keeps him within his orbit, arrayed this year as he was the last; and how his better-clad acquaintances contrive to get the things they wear will be for him a mystery till his dying day.

The great thing, then, in all education, is to *make our nervous system our ally instead of our enemy.* It is to fund and capitalize our acquisitions, and live at ease upon the interest of the fund. *For this we must make automatic and habitual, as early as possible, as many useful actions as we can,* and guard against the growing into ways that are likely to be disadvantageous to us, as we should guard against the plague. The more of the details of our daily life we can hand over to the effortless custody of automatism, the more our higher powers of mind will be set free for their own proper work. There is no more miserable human being than one in whom nothing is habitual but indecision, and for whom the lighting of every cigar, the drinking of every

From *Psychology: Briefer Course,* Henry Holt and Company, 1892.

cup, the time of rising and going to bed every day, and the beginning of every bit of work, are subjects of express volitional deliberation. Full half the time of such a man goes to the deciding, or regretting, of matters which ought to be so ingrained in him as practically not to exist for his consciousness at all. If there be such daily duties not yet ingrained in any one of my readers, let him begin this very hour to set the matter right.

In Professor Bain's chapter on "The Moral Habits" there are some admirable practical remarks laid down. Two great maxims emerge from his treatment. The first is that in the acquisition of a new habit, or the leaving off of an old one, we must take care to *launch ourselves with as strong and decided an initiative as possible.* Accumulate all the possible circumstances which shall re-enforce the right motives; put yourself assiduously in conditions that encourage the new way; make engagements incompatible with the old; take a public pledge, if the case allows; in short, envelop your resolution with every aid you know. This will give your new beginning such a momentum that the temptation to break down will not occur as soon as it otherwise might; and every day during which a breakdown is postponed adds to the chances of its not occurring at all.

The second maxim is: *Never suffer an exception to occur till the new habit is securely rooted in your life.* Each lapse is like the letting fall of a ball of string which one is carefully winding up; a single slip undoes more than a great many turns will wind again. *Continuity* of training is the great means of making the nervous system act infallibly right. As Professor Bain says:

"The peculiarity of the moral habits, contradistinguishing them from the intellectual acquisitions, is the presence of two hostile powers, one to be gradually raised into the ascendant over the other. It is necessary, above all things, in such a situation, never to lose a battle. Every gain on the wrong side undoes the effect of many conquests on the right. The essential precaution, therefore, is so to regulate the two opposing powers that the one may have a series of uninterrupted successes, until repetition has fortified it to such a degree as to enable it to cope with the opposition, under any circumstances. This is the theoretically best career of mental progress."

The need of securing success at the *outset* is imperative. Failure at first is apt to damp the energy of all future attempts, whereas past experiences of success nerve one to future vigor. Goethe says to a man who consulted him about an enterprise but mistrusted his own powers: "Ach! you need only blow on your hands!" And the remark illustrates the effect on Goethe's spirits of his own habitually successful career.

The question of "tapering off," in abandoning such habits as drink and opium-indulgence comes in here, and is a question about which experts differ within certain limits, and in regard to what may be best for an individual case. In the main, however, all expert opinion would agree that abrupt acquisition of the new habit is the best way, *if there be a real possibility of carrying it out.* We must be careful not to give the will so stiff a task as to insure its defeat at the very outset; but, *provided one can stand it,* a sharp period of suffering, and then a free time, is the best thing to aim at, whether in giving up a habit like that of opium, or in simply changing one's hours of rising or of work. It is surprising how soon a desire will die of inanition if it be *never* fed.

"One must first learn, unmoved, looking neither to the right nor left, to walk firmly on the strait and narrow path, before one can begin 'to make one's self over again.' He who every day makes a fresh resolve is like one who, arriving at the edge of the ditch he is to leap, forever stops and returns for a fresh run. Without *unbroken* advance there is no such thing as *accumulation* of the ethical forces possible, and to make this possible, and to exercise us and habituate us in it, is the sovereign blessing of regular work."

A third maxim may be added to the preceding pair: *Seize the very first possible opportunity to act on every resolution you make, and on every emotional prompting you may experience in the direction of the habits you aspire to gain.* It is not in the moment of their forming, but in the moment of their producing *motor effects,* that resolves and aspirations communicate the new "set" to the brain. As the author last quoted remarks: "The actual presence of the practical opportunity alone furnishes the fulcrum upon which the lever can rest, by means of which the moral will may multiply its strength, and raise itself aloft. He who has no solid ground to press against will never get beyond the stage of empty gesture-making. . . ."

As a final practical maxim, relative to these habits of the will, we may, then, offer something like this: *Keep the faculty of effort alive in you by a little gratuitous exercise every day.* That is, be systematically ascetic or heroic in little unnecessary points, do every day or two something for no other reason than that you would rather not do it, so that when the hour of dire need draws nigh, it may find you not unnerved and untrained to stand the test. Asceticism of this sort is like the insurance which a man pays on his house and goods. The tax does him no good at the time, and possibly may never bring him a return. But if the fire *does* come, his having paid it will be his salvation from ruin. So with the man who has daily inured himself to habits of concentrated attention, energetic volition, and self-denial in unnecessary things. He will stand like a tower when everything rocks around him, and when his softer fellow-mortals are winnowed like chaff in the blast.

The physiological study of mental conditions is thus the most powerful ally of hortatory ethics. The hell to be endured hereafter, of which theology tells, is no worse than the hell we make for ourselves in this world by habitually fashioning our characters in the wrong way. Could the young but realize how soon they will become mere walking bundles of habits, they would give more heed to their conduct while in the plastic state. We are spinning our own fates, good or evil, and never to be undone. Every smallest stroke of virtue or of vice leaves its never so little scar. The drunken Rip Van Winkle, in Jefferson's play, excuses himself for every fresh dereliction by saying, "I won't count this time!" Well! he may not count it, and a kind Heaven may not count it; but it is being counted none the less. Down among his nerve-cells and fibers the molecules are counting it, registering and storing it up to be used against him when the next temptation comes. Nothing we ever do is, in strict scientific literalness, wiped out. Of course this has its good side as well as its bad one. As we become permanent drunkards by so many sepa-

rate drinks, so we become saints in the moral, and authorities and experts in the practical and scientific spheres, by so many separate acts and hours of work. Let no youth have any anxiety about the upshot of his education, whatever the line of it may be. If he keep faithfully busy each hour of the working day, he may safely leave the final result to itself. He can with perfect certainty count on waking up some fine morning, to find himself one of the competent ones of his generation, in whatever pursuit he may have singled out. Silently, between all the details of his business, the *power of judging* in all that class of matter will have built itself up within him as a possession that will never pass away. Young people should know this truth in advance. The ignorance of it has probably engendered more discouragement and faint-heartedness in youths embarking on arduous careers than all other causes put together.

Number of words 2245
See page 191 for Questions

Reading Time in Seconds _____
See page 323 for Conversion Table

New Light on the Human Potential

Herbert A. Otto

Your creative potential and your reading potential may well be amazingly high, but there's still a problem. How can you tap a major portion of that potential when "negative conditioning" is at work to limit confidence? New light is indeed needed.

William James once estimated that the healthy human being is functioning at less than 10 percent of his capacity. It took more than half a century before this idea found acceptance among a small proportion of behavioral scientists. In 1954, the highly respected and widely known psychologist Gardner Murphy published his pioneering volume *Human Potentialities*. The early Sixties saw the beginnings of the human potentialities research project at the University of Utah and the organization of Esalen Institute in California, the first of a series of "Growth Centers" that were later to be referred to as the Human Potentialities Movement.

Today, many well-known scientists such as Abraham Maslow, Margaret Mead, Gardner Murphy, O. Spurgeon English, and Carl Rogers subscribe to the hypothesis that man is using a very small fraction of his capacities. Margaret Mead quotes a 6 percent figure, and my own estimate is 5 percent or less. Commitment to the hypothesis is not restricted to the United States. Scientists in the U.S.S.R. and other countries are also at

work. Surprisingly, the so-called human potentialities hypothesis is still largely unknown.

What are the dimensions of the human potential? The knowledge we do have about man is minimal and has not as yet been brought together with the human potentialities hypothesis as an organizing force and synthesizing element. Of course, we know more about man today than we did fifty years ago, but this is like the very small part of the iceberg we see above the water. Man essentially remains a mystery. From the depths of this mystery there are numerous indicators of the human potential.

Certain indicators of man's potential are revealed to us in childhood. They become "lost" or submerged as we succumb to the imprinting of the cultural mold in the "growing up" process. Do you remember when you were a child and it rained after a dry spell and there was a very particular, intensive earthy smell in the air? Do you remember how people smelled when they hugged you? Do you recall the brilliant colors of leaves, flowers, grass, and even brick surfaces and lighted signs that you experienced as a child? Furthermore, do you recall that when father and mother stepped into the room you

Abridged from *Saturday Review*, December 20, 1969. Reprinted by permission of Saturday Review/World.

knew how they felt about themselves, about life, and about you — at that moment.

Today we know that man's sense of smell, one of the most powerful and primitive senses, is highly developed. In the average man this capacity has been suppressed except for very occasional use. Some scientists claim that man's sense of smell is almost as keen as a hunting dog's. Some connoisseurs of wines, for example, can tell by the bouquet not only the type of grape and locality where they were grown but even the vintage year and vineyard. Perfume mixers can often detect fantastically minute amounts in mixed essences; finally there are considerable data on odor discrimination from the laboratory. It is also clear that, since the air has become an overcrowded garbage dump for industrial wastes and the internal combustion engine, it is easier to turn off our sense of smell than to keep it functioning. The capacity to experience the environment more fully through our olfactory organs remains a potential.

It is possible to regain these capacities through training. In a similar manner, sensory and other capacities, including visual, kinesthetic, and tactile abilities, have become stunted and dulled. We perceive less clearly, and as a result we feel less — we use our dulled senses to close ourselves off from both our physical and interpersonal environments. Today we also dull our perceptions of how other people feel and we consistently shut off awareness of our own feelings. For many who put their senses to sleep it is a sleep that lasts unto death. Again, through sensory and other training the doors of perception can be cleansed (to use Blake's words) and our capacities reawakened. Anthropological research abounds with reports of primitive tribes that have developed exceptional sensory and perceptive abilities as a result of training. Utilization of these capacities by modern man for life-enrichment purposes awaits the future.

Neurological research has shed new light on man's potential. Work at the UCLA Brain Research Institute points to enormous abilities latent in everyone by suggesting an incredible hypothesis: The ultimate creative capacity of the human brain may be, for all practical purposes, infinite. To use the computer analogy, man is a vast storehouse of data, but we have not learned how to program ourselves to utilize these data for problem-solving purposes. Recall of experiential data is extremely spotty and selective for most adults. My own research has convinced me that the recall of experiences can be vastly improved by use of certain simple training techniques, provided sufficient motivation is present.

Under emergency conditions, man is capable of prodigious feats of physical strength. For example, a middle-aged California woman with various ailments lifted a car just enough to let her son roll out from under it after it had collapsed on him. According to newspaper reports the car weighed in excess of 2,000 pounds. There are numerous similar accounts indicating that every person has vast physical reserve capacities that can be tapped. Similarly, the extraordinary feats of athletes and acrobats — involving the conscious and specialized development of certain parts of the human organism as a result of consistent application and a high degree of motivation — point to the fantastic plasticity and capabilities of the human being.

Until World War II, the field of hypnosis was not regarded as respectable by many scientists and was associated with stage performances and charlatanism. Since that time hypnosis has attained a measure of scientific respectability. Medical and therapeutic applications of hypnosis include the use of this technique in surgery and anesthesiology (hypnoanesthesia for major and minor surgery), gynecology (infertility, frigidity, menopausal conditions), pediatrics (enuresis, tics, asthma in children, etc.), and in dentistry. Scores of texts on medical and dental hypnosis are available. Dr. William S. Kroger, one of the specialists in the field and author of the well-known text *Clinical and Experimental Hypnosis,* writes that hypnotherapy is "directed to the patient's needs and is a methodology to tap the 'forgotten assets' of the *hidden potentials* of behavior and response that so often lead to new learnings and understanding." (My italics.) As far as we know now, the possibilities opened by hypnosis for the potential functioning of the human organism are not brought about by the hypnotist. Changes are induced by the subject, utilizing his belief-structure, with the hypnotist operating as an "enabler," making it possible for the subject to tap some of his unrealized potential.

The whole area of parapsychology that deals with extrasensory perception (ESP), "mental telepathy," and other paranormal phenomena, and that owes much of its development to the work of Dr. J. B. Rhine and others is still regarded by much of the scientific establishment with the same measure of suspicion accorded hypnosis in the pre-World War II days. It is of interest that a number of laboratories in the U.S.S.R. are devoted to the study of telepathy as a physical phenomenon, with research conducted under the heading "cerebral radiocommunication" and "bioelectronics." The work is supported by the Soviet government. The reluctance to accept findings from this field of research is perhaps best summarized by an observation of Carl C. Jung's in 1958.

(Some) people deny the findings of parapsychology outright, either for philosophical reasons or from intellectual laziness. This can hardly be considered a scientifically responsible attitude, even though it is a popular way out of quite extraordinary intellectual difficulty.

Although the intensive study of creativity had its beginnings in fairly recent times, much of value has been discovered about man's creative potential. There is evidence that every person has creative abilities that can be developed. A considerable number of studies indicate that much in our educational system — including conformity pressures exerted by teachers, emphasis on memory development, and rote learning, plus the overcrowding of classrooms — militates against the development of creative capacities. Research has established that children between the ages of two and three can learn to read, tape record a story, and type it as it is played back. Hundreds of children between the ages of four and six have been taught by the Japanese pedagogue Suzuki to play violin concertos. Japanese research with infants and small children also suggests the value of early "maximum input" (music, color, verbal, tactile stimuli) in the personality development of infants. My own observations tend to confirm this. We have consistently underestimated the child's capacity to learn and his ability to realize his potential while *enjoying* both the play elements and the discipline involved in this process.

In contrast to the Japanese work, much recent Russian research appears to be concentrated in the area of mentation, with special emphasis on extending and enlarging man's mental processes and his capacity for learning. As early as 1964 the following appeared in *Soviet Life Today,* a U.S.S.R. English language magazine:

> The latest findings in anthropology, psychology, logic, and physiology show that the potential of the human mind is very great indeed. "As soon as modern science gave us some understanding of the structure and work of the human brain, we were struck with its enormous reserve capacity," writes Yefremov (Ivan Yefremov, eminent Soviet scholar and writer). "Man under average conditions of work and life, uses only a small part of his thinking equipment. . . . If we were able to force our brain to work at only half its capacity, we could, without any difficulty whatever, learn forty languages, memorize the large Soviet Encyclopedia from cover to cover, and complete the required courses of dozens of colleges."
>
> The statement is hardly an exaggeration. It is the generally accepted theoretical view of man's mental potentialities.
>
> How can we tap this gigantic potential? It is a big and very complex problem with many ramifications.

Another signpost of man's potential is what I have come to call the "Grandma Moses effect." This artist's experience indicates that artistic talents can be discovered and brought to full flowering in the latter part of the life cycle. In every retirement community there can be found similar examples of residents who did not use latent artistic abilities or other talents until after retirement. In many instances the presence of a talent is suspected or known but allowed to remain fallow for the best part of a lifetime.

Reasons why well-functioning mature adults do not use specific abilities are complex. Studies conducted at the University of Utah as a part of the Human Potentialities Research Project revealed that unconscious

blocks are often present. In a number of instances a person with definite evidence that he has a specific talent (let's say he won a state-wide contest in sculpture while in high school) may not wish to realize this talent at a later time because he fears this would introduce a change in life-style. Sometimes fear of the passion of creation is another roadblock in self-actualization. On the basis of work at Utah it became clear that persons who live close to their capacity who continue to activate their potential, have a pronounced sense of well-being and considerable energy and see themselves as leading purposeful and creative lives.

Most people are unaware of their strengths and potentialities. If a person with some college background is handed a form and asked to write out his personality strengths, he will list, on an average, five or six strengths. Asked to do the same thing for his weaknesses, the list will be two to three times as long. There are a number of reasons for this low self-assessment. Many participants in my classes and marathon group weekends have pointed out that "listing your strengths feels like bragging about yourself. It's something that just isn't done." Paradoxically, in a group, people feel more comfortable about sharing problem areas and hang-ups than they do about personality resources and latent abilities. This is traceable to the fact that we are members of a pathology-oriented culture. Psychological and psychiatric jargon dealing with emotional dysfunction and mental illness has become the parlance of the man in the street. In addition, from early childhood in our educational system we learn largely by our mistakes — by having them pointed out to us repeatedly. All this results in early "negative conditioning" and influences our attitude and perception of ourselves and other people. An attitudinal climate has become established which is continually fed and reinforced.

As a part of this negative conditioning there is the heavy emphasis by communications media on violence in television programs and motion pictures. The current American news format of radio, television, and newspapers — the widely prevalent idea of what constitutes news — results from a narrow, brutalizing concept thirty or forty years behind the times and is inimical to the development of human potential.

The news media give much time and prominent space to violence and consistently underplay "good" news. This gives the consumer the impression that important things that happen are various types of destructive activities. Consistent and repeated emphasis on bad news not only creates anxiety and tension but instills the belief that there is little except violence, disasters, accidents, and mayhem abroad in the world. As a consequence, the consumer of such news gradually experiences a shift in his outlook about the world leading to the formation of feelings of alienation and separation. The world is increasingly perceived as a threat, as the viewer becomes anxious that violence and mayhem may be perpetrated on him from somewhere out of the strange and unpredictable environment in which he lives. There slowly grows a conviction that it is safer to withdraw from such a world, to isolate himself from its struggles, and to let others make the decisions and become involved.

As a result of the steady diet of violence in the media, an even more fundamental and insidious erosion in man's self-system takes place. The erosion affects what I call the "trust factor." If we have been given a certain amount of affection, love, and understanding in our formative years, we are able to place a certain amount of trust in our fellow man. Trust is one of the most important elements in today's society although we tend to minimize its importance. *We basically trust people.* For example, we place an enormous amount of trust in our fellow man when driving on a freeway or in an express lane. We trust those with whom we are associated to fulfill their obligations and responsibilities. The element of trust is the basic rule in human relations. When we distrust people, they usually sense our attitude and reciprocate in kind.

The consistent emphasis in the news on criminal violence, burglarizing, and assault makes slow but pervasive inroads into our reservoir of trust. As we hear and read much about the acts of violence and injury men perpetrate upon one another, year after year, with so little emphasis placed on the loving, caring, and humanitarian acts of man, we begin to trust our fellow man less, and we thereby diminish ourselves. It is my conclusion the media's excessive emphasis on violence, like the drop of water on the stone, erodes and wears away the trust factor in man. By undermining the trust factor in man, media contribute to man's estrangement from man and prevent the full flourishing and deeper development of a sense of community and communion with all men.

. . . .

Human potentialities is rapidly emerging as a discrete field of scientific inquiry. Exploring the human potential can become the meeting ground for a wide range of disciplines, offering a dynamic synthesis for seemingly divergent areas of research. It is possible that the field of human potentialities offers an answer to the long search for a synthesizing and organizing principle which will unify the sciences. The explosive growth of the Human Potentialities Movement is indicative of a growing public interest. Although there exist a considerable number of methods — all designed to tap human potential — work on assessment or evaluation of these methods has in most instances not progressed beyond field testing and informal feedback of results. The need for research in the area of human potentialities has never been more pressing. The National Center for the Exploration of Human Potential in La Jolla, California, has recently been organized for this purpose. A nonprofit organization, the center will act as a clearing house of information for current and past approaches that have been successful in fostering personal growth. One of the main purposes of the center will be to conduct and coordinate basic and applied research concerning the expansion of human potential.

Among the many fascinating questions posed by researchers are some of the following: What is the relationship of body-rhythms, biorhythms, and the expansion of sensory awareness to the uncovering of human potential? What are the applications of methods and approaches from other cultures such as yoga techniques, Sufi methods, types of meditation, etc.? What is the role of ecstasy and play vis-à-vis the realizing of human possibilities? The exploration of these and similar questions can help us create a society truly devoted to the full development of human capacities — particularly the capacities for love, joy, creativity, spiritual experiencing. This is the challenge and promise of our lifetime.

Number of words 2885
See page 193 for Questions

Reading Time in Seconds _____
See page 323 for Conversion Table

In Other Words

Peter Farb

If you want to say something, you have to use language and words. Or do you? Recently we have been made aware of silent or wordless language, part of which is sometimes called "body" language. Take a quick look now into this paradoxical area of wordless words.

Early in this century, a horse named Hans amazed the people of Berlin by his extraordinary ability to perform rapid calculations in mathematics. After a problem was written on a blackboard placed in front of him, he promptly counted out the answer by tapping the low numbers with his right forefoot and multiples of ten with his left. Trickery was ruled out because Hans's owner, unlike owners of other performing animals, did not profit financially — and Hans even performed his feats whether or not the owner was present. The psychologist O. Pfungst witnessed one of these performances and became convinced that there had to be a more logical explanation than the uncanny intelligence of a horse.

Because Hans performed only in the presence of an audience that could see the blackboard and therefore knew the correct answer, Pfungst reasoned that the secret lay in observation of the audience rather than of the horse. He finally discovered that as soon as the problem was written on the blackboard, the audience bent forward very slightly in anticipation to watch Hans's forefeet. As slight as that movement was, Hans perceived it and took it as his signal to begin tapping. As his taps approached the correct number, the audience became tense with excitement and made almost imperceptible movements of the head — which signaled Hans to stop counting. The audience, simply by expecting Hans to stop when the correct number was reached, had actually told the animal when to stop. Pfungst clearly demonstrated that Hans's intelligence was nothing but a mechanical response to his audience, which unwittingly communicated the answer by its body language.

The "Clever Hans Phenomenon," as it has come to be known, raises an interesting question. If a mere horse can detect unintentional and extraordinarily subtle body signals, might they not also be detected by human beings? Professional gamblers and con men have long been known for their skill in observing the body-language cues of their victims, but only recently has it been shown scientifically that all speakers constantly detect and interpret such cues also, even though they do not realize it.

An examination of television word games several years ago revealed that contestants inadvertently gave their partners body-language signals that led to correct answers. In one such game, contestants had to elicit certain words from their partners, but they were permitted to give only brief verbal clues as to what the words might be. It turned out that sometimes the contestants also gave body signals that were much more informative than the verbal clues. In one case, a contestant was supposed to answer *sad* in response to his partner's verbal clue of *happy* — that is, the correct answer was a word opposite to the verbal clue. The partner giving the *happy* clue unconsciously used his body to indicate to his fellow contestant that an opposite word was needed. He did that by shifting his body and head very slightly to one side as he said *happy,* then to the other side in expectation of an opposite word.

Contestants on a television program are usually unsophisticated about psychology and linguistics, but trained psychological experimenters also unintentionally flash body signals which are sometimes detected by the test subjects — and which may distort the results of experiments. Hidden cameras have revealed that the sex of the experimenter, for example, can influence the responses of subjects. Even though the films showed that both male and female experimenters carried out the experiments in the same way and asked the same questions, the experimenters were very much aware of their own sex in relation to the sex of the subjects. Male experimenters spent 16 percent more time carrying out experiments with female subjects than they did with male subjects; similarly, female experimenters took 13 percent longer to go through experiments with male subjects than they did with female subjects. The cameras also revealed that chivalry is not dead in the psychological experiment; male experimenters smiled about six times as often with female subjects as they did with male subjects.

The important question, of course, is whether or not such nonverbal communication influences the results of experiments; the answer is that it often does. Psychologists who have watched films made without the knowledge of either the experimenters or the subjects could predict almost immediately which experimenters would obtain results from their subjects that were in the direction of the experimenters' own biases. Those experimenters who seemed more dominant, personal, and relaxed during the first moments of conversation with their subjects usually obtained the results that they secretly hoped the experiments would yield. And they somehow communicated their secret hopes in a completely visual way, regardless of what they said or their paralanguage when they spoke. That was made clear when these films were shown to two groups, one of which saw the films without hearing the sound track while the other heard only the sound track without seeing the films. The group that heard only the voices could not accurately predict the experimenters' biases — but those who saw the films without hearing the words immediately sensed whether or not the experimenters were communicating their biases.

A person who signals his expectations about a certain kind of behavior is not aware that he is doing so — and usually he is indignant when told that his experiment was biased — but the subjects themselves confirm his bias by their performances. Such bias in experiments has been shown to represent self-fulfilling prophecies. In other words, the experimenters' expectations about the results of the experiment actually result in those expectations coming true. That was demonstrated when each of twelve experimenters was given five rats bred from an identical strain of laboratory animals. Half of the experimenters were told that their rats could be expected to perform brilliantly because they had been bred especially for high intelligence and quickness in running through a maze. The others were told that their rats could be expected to perform very poorly because they had been bred for low intelligence. All the experimenters were then asked to teach their rats to run a maze.

Almost as soon as the rats were put into the maze it became clear that those for which the experimenters had high expectations would prove to be the better performers. And the rats which were expected to perform badly did in fact perform very badly, even though they were bred from the identical strain as the excellent performers. Some of these poor performers did not even budge from their starting positions in the maze. The misleading prophecy about the behavior of the two groups of rats was fulfilled — simply because the two groups of experimenters unconsciously communicated their expectations to the animals. Those experimenters who anticipated high performance were friendlier to their animals than those who expected low performance; they handled their animals more, and they did so more gently. Clearly, the predictions of the experimenters were communicated to the rats in subtle and unintended ways — and the rats behaved accordingly.

Since animals such as laboratory rats and Clever Hans can detect body-language cues, it is not surprising that human beings are just as perceptive in detecting visual signals about expectations for performance. It is a psychological truth that we are likely to speak to a person whom we expect to be unpleasant in such a way

that we force him to act unpleasantly. But it has only recently become apparent that poor children — often black or Spanish-speaking — perform badly in school because that is what their teachers expect of them, and because the teachers manage to convey that expectation by both verbal and nonverbal channels. True to the teacher's prediction, the black and brown children probably will do poorly — not necessarily because children from minority groups are capable only of poor performance, but because poor performance has been expected of them. The first grade may be the place where teachers anticipate poor performances by children of certain racial, economic, and cultural backgrounds — and where the teachers actually teach these children how to fail.

Evidence of the way the "Clever Hans Phenomenon" works in many schools comes from a careful series of experiments by psychologist Robert Rosenthal and his co-workers at Harvard University. They received permission from a school south of San Francisco to give a series of tests to the children in the lower grades. The teachers were blatantly lied to. They were told that the test was a newly developed tool that could predict which children would be "spurters" and achieve high performance in the coming year. Actually, the experimenters administered a new kind of IQ test that the teachers were unlikely to have seen previously. After IQ scores were obtained, the experimenters selected the names of 20 percent of the children completely at random. Some of the selected children scored very high on the IQ test and others scored low, some were from middle-class families and others from lower-class. Then the teachers were lied to again. The experimenters said that the tests singled out this 20 percent as the children who could be expected to make unusual intellectual gains in the coming year. The teachers were also cautioned not to discuss the test results with the pupils or their parents. Since the names of these children had been selected completely at random, any difference between them and the 80 percent not designated as "spurters" was completely in the minds of the teachers.

All the children were given IQ tests again during that school year and once more the following year. The 20 percent who had been called to the attention of their teachers did indeed turn in the high performances expected of them — in some cases dramatic increases of 25 points in IQ. The teachers' comments about these children also were revealing. The teachers considered them more happy, curious, and interesting than the other 80 percent — and they predicted that they would be successes in life, a prophecy they had already started to fulfill. The experimenters plainly showed that children who are expected to gain intellectually do gain and that their behavior improves as well.

The results of the experiment are clear — but the explanation for the results is not. It might be imagined that the teachers simply devoted more time to the children singled out for high expectations, but the study showed that was not so. Instead, the influence of the teachers upon these children apparently was much more subtle. What the teachers said to them, how and when it was said, the facial expressions, gestures, posture, perhaps even touch that accompanied their speech — some or all of these things must have communicated that the teachers expected improved performance from them. And when these children responded correctly, the teachers were quicker to praise them and also more lavish in their praise. Whatever the exact mechanism was, the effect upon the children who had been singled out was dramatic. They changed their ideas about themselves, their behavior, their motivation, and their learning capacities.

The lesson of the California experiment is that pupil performance does not depend so much upon a school's audio-visual equipment or new textbooks or enriching trips to museums as it does upon teachers whose body language communicates high expectations for the pupils — even if the teacher thinks she "knows" that a black, a Puerto Rican, a Mexican-American, or any other disadvantaged child is fated to do poorly in school. Apparently, remedial instruction in our schools is misdirected. It is needed more by the middle-class teachers than by the disadvantaged children.

Number of words 1930
See page 195 for Questions

Reading Time in Seconds _____
See page 323 for Conversion Table

Of Happiness and of Despair We Have No Measure

Ernest van den Haag

What do the radio, television, movies, and newspapers do for us — or to us? Are they substitute gratifications — packaged dreams that encourage us to continue sleeping — or do they have the opposite effect, encouraging us to glimpse reality more clearly through an uncovering of essentials? See how convincing you find this selection.

All mass media in the end alienate people from personal experience and, though appearing to offset it, intensify their moral isolation from each other, from reality and from themselves. One may turn to the mass media when lonely or bored. But mass media, once they become a habit, impair the capacity for meaningful experience. Though more diffuse and not as gripping, the habit feeds on itself, establishing a vicious circle as addictions do.

The mass media do not physically replace individual activities and contacts — excursions, travel, parties, etc. But they impinge on all. The portable radio is taken everywhere — from seashore to mountaintop — and everywhere it isolates the bearer from his surroundings, from other people, and from himself. Most people escape being by themselves at any time by voluntarily tuning in on something or somebody. Anyway, it is nearly beyond the power of individuals to escape broadcasts. Music and public announcements are piped into restaurants, bars, shops, cafes, and lobbies, into public means of transportation, and even taxis. You can turn off your radio but not your neighbor's, nor can you silence his portable or the set at the restaurant. Fortunately, most persons do not seem to miss privacy, the cost of which is even more beyond the average income than the cost of individuality.

People are never quite in one place or group without at the same time, singly or collectively, gravitating somewhere else, abstracted, if not transported by the mass media. The incessant announcements, arpeggios, croonings, sobs, bellows, brayings and jingles draw to some faraway world at large and by weakening community with immediate surroundings make people lonely even when in a crowd and crowded even when alone.

We have already stressed that mass media must offer homogenized fare to meet an average of tastes. Further, whatever the quality of the offerings, the very fact that one after the other is absorbed continuously, indiscriminately and casually, trivializes all. Even the most profound of experiences, articulated too often on the same level, is reduced to a cliché. The impact of each of the offerings of mass media is thus weakened by the next one. But the impact of the stream of all mass-media offerings is cumulative and strong. It lessens people's capacity to experience life itself.

Sometimes it is argued that the audience confuses actuality with mass-media fiction and reacts to the characters and situations that appear in soap operas or comic strips as though they were real. For instance, wedding presents are sent to fictional couples. It seems more likely, however, that the audience prefers to invest

Excerpted from *The Fabric of Society* by Ernest van den Haag and Ralph Ross, Harcourt, Brace & World, Inc., 1957.

fiction with reality — as a person might prefer to dream — without actually confusing it with reality. After all, even the kids know that Hopalong Cassidy is an actor and the adults know that "I Love Lucy" is fiction. Both, however, may attempt to live the fiction because they prefer it to their own lives. The significant effect is not the (quite limited) investment of fiction with reality, but the de-realization of life lived in largely fictitious terms. Art can deepen the perception of reality. But popular culture veils it, diverts from it, and becomes an obstacle to experiencing it. It is not so much an escape from life but an invasion of life first, and ultimately evasion altogether.

Parents, well knowing that mass media can absorb energy, often lighten the strain that the attempts of their children to reach for activity and direct experience would impose; they allow some energy to be absorbed by the vicarious experience of the television screen. Before television, the cradle was rocked, or poppy juice given, to inhibit the initiative and motility of small children. Television, unlike these physical sedatives, tranquilizes by means of substitute gratifications. Manufactured activities and plots are offered to still the child's hunger for experiencing life. They effectively neutralize initiative and channel imagination. But the early introduction of de-individualized characters and situations and early homogenization of taste on a diet of meaningless activity hardly foster development. Perhaps poppy juice, offering no models in which to cast the imagination, was better.

The homogenizing effect of comic books or television, the fact that they neither express nor appeal to individuality, seems far more injurious to the child's mind and character than the violence they feature, though it is the latter that is often blamed for juvenile delinquency. The blame is misplaced. Violence is not new to life or fiction. It waxed large in ancient fables, fairy tales, and in tragedies from Sophocles to Shakespeare.

Mom always knew that "her boy could not have thought of it," that the other boys must have seduced him. The belief that viewing or reading about violence persuades children to engage in it is Mom's ancient conviction disguised as psychiatry. Children are quite spontaneously bloodthirsty and need both direct and fantasy outlets for violence. What is wrong with the violence of the mass media is not that it is violence, but that it is not art — that it is meaningless violence which thrills but does not gratify. The violence of the desire for life and meaning is displaced and appears as a desire for meaningless violence. But the violence which is ceaselessly supplied cannot ultimately gratify it because it does not meet the repressed desire. . . .

A little more than a hundred years ago, Henry David Thoreau wrote in *Walden*: "The mass of men lead lives of quiet desperation. . . . A stereotyped but unconscious despair is concealed even under what are called the games and amusements of mankind." Despair, we find, is no longer quiet. Popular culture tries to exorcise it with much clanging and banging. Perhaps it takes more noise to drone it out. Perhaps we are less willing to face it. But whether wrapped in popular culture, we are less happy than our quieter ancestors, or the natives of Bali, must remain an open question despite all romanticizing. (Nor do we have a feasible alternative to popular culture. Besides, a proposal for "the mass of men" would be unlikely to affect the substance of popular culture. And counsel to individuals must be individual.)

There have been periods happier and others more desperate than ours. But we don't know which. And even an assertion as reasonable as this is a conjecture like any comparison of today's bliss with yesterday's. The happiness felt in disparate groups, in disparate periods and places cannot be measured and compared. Our contention is simply that by distracting from the human predicament and blocking individuation and experience, popular culture impoverishes life without leading to contentment. But whether "the mass of men" felt better or worse without the mass-production techniques of which popular culture is an ineluctable part, we shall never know. Of happiness and of despair, we have no measure.

Number of words 1124
See page 197 for Questions

Reading Time in Seconds _____
See page 323 for Conversion Table

SELECTION 15

How to Read a River

Mark Twain

The dictionary reminds us that we read many things besides words. You may read a person's character in his face. You may read someone's mind — particularly if it's like an open book. You may read the skies to determine the weather. And here is Mark Twain to help you read a river.

Now I had often seen pilots gazing at the water and pretending to read it as if it were a book; but it was a book that told me nothing. A time came at last, however, when Mr. Bixby seemed to think me far enough advanced to bear a lesson on water-reading. So he began:

"Do you see that long, slanting line on the face of the water? Now, that's a reef. Moreover, it's a bluff reef. There is a solid sand-bar under it that is nearly as straight up and down as the side of a house. There is plenty of water close up to it, but mighty little on top of it. If you were to hit it you would knock the boat's brains out. Do you see where the line fringes out at the upper end and begins to fade away?"

"Yes, sir."

"Well, that is a low place; that is the head of the reef. You can climb over there, and not hurt anything. Cross over, now, and follow along close under the reef — easy water there — not much current."

I followed the reef along till I approached the fringed end. Then Mr. Bixby said:

"Now get ready. Wait till I give the word. She won't want to mount the reef; a boat hates shoal water. Stand by — wait — *wait* — keep her well in hand. *Now* cramp her down! Snatch her! snatch her!"

He seized the other side of the wheel and helped to spin it around until it was hard down, and then we held it so. The boat resisted, and refused to answer for a while, and next she came surging to starboard, mounted the reef, and sent a long, angry ridge of water foaming away from her bows.

"Now watch her; watch her like a cat, or she'll get away from you. When she fights strong and the tiller slips a little, in a jerky, greasy sort of way, let up on her a trifle; it is the way she tells you at night that the water is too shoal; but keep edging her up, little by little, toward the point. You are well up on the bar now; there is a bar under every point, because the water that comes down around it forms an eddy and allows the sediment to sink. Do you see those fine lines on the face of the water that branch out like the ribs of a fan? Well, those are little reefs; you want to just miss the ends of them, but run them pretty close. Now look out — look out! Don't you crowd that slick, greasy-looking place; there ain't nine feet there; she won't stand it. She begins to smell it; look sharp, I tell you! Oh, blazes, there you go! Stop the starboard wheel! Quick! Ship up to back! Set her back!"

The engine bells jingled and the engines answered promptly, shooting white columns of steam far aloft out of the 'scape-pipes, but it was too late. The boat had "smelt" the bar in good earnest; the foamy ridges that radiated from her bows suddenly disappeared, a great dead swell came rolling forward, and swept ahead of her, she careened far over to larboard, and went tearing away toward the shore as if she were about scared to death. We were a good mile from where we ought to have been when we finally got the upper hand of her again.

During the afternoon watch the next day, Mr. Bixby asked me if I knew how to run the next few miles. I said:

"Go inside the first snag above the point, outside the next one, start out from the lower end of Higgins's woodyard, make a square crossing, and — "

"That's all right. I'll be back before you close up on the next point."

But he wasn't. He was still below when I rounded it and entered upon a piece of the river which I had some misgivings about. I did not know that he was hiding behind a chimney to see how I would perform. I went gaily along, getting prouder and prouder, for he had never left the boat in my sole charge such a length of time before. I even got to "setting" her and letting the wheel go entirely, while I vaingloriously turned my back and inspected the stern marks and hummed a tune, a sort of easy indifference which I had prodigiously admired in Bixby and the other great pilots. Once I inspected rather long, and when I faced to the front again my heart flew into my mouth so suddenly that if I hadn't clapped my teeth together I should have lost it. One of those frightful bluff reefs was stretching its deadly length right across our bows! My head was gone

---

From *Life on the Mississippi*, 1883.

in a moment; I did not know which end I stood on; I gasped and could not get my breath; I spun the wheel down with such rapidity that it wove itself together like a spider's web; the boat answered and turned square away from the reef, but the reef followed her! I fled, but still it followed, still it kept — right across my bows! I never looked to see where I was going, I only fled. The awful crash was imminent. Why didn't that villain come? If I committed the crime of ringing a bell I might get thrown overboard. But better that than kill the boat. So in blind desperation, I started such a rattling "shivaree" down below as never had astounded an engineer in this world before, I fancy. Amidst the frenzy of the bells the engines began to back and fill in a curious way, and my reason forsook its throne — we were about to crash into the woods on the other side of the river. Just then Mr. Bixby stepped calmly into view on the hurricane-deck. My soul went out to him in gratitude. My distress vanished; I would have felt safe on the brink of Niagara with Mr. Bixby on the hurricane-deck. He blandly and sweetly took his toothpick out of his mouth between his fingers, as if it were a cigar — we were just in the act of climbing an overhanging big tree, and the passengers were scudding astern like rats — and lifted up these commands to me ever so gently:

"Stop the starboard! Stop the larboard! Set her back on both!"

The boat hesitated, halted, pressed her nose among the boughs a critical instant, then reluctantly began to back away.

"Stop the larboard! Come ahead on it! Stop the starboard! Come ahead on it! Point her for the bar!"

I sailed away as serenely as a summer's morning. Mr. Bixby came in and said, with mock simplicity:

"When you have a hail, my boy, you ought to tap the big bell three times before you land, so that the engineers can get ready."

I blushed under the sarcasm, and said I hadn't had any hail.

"Ah! Then it was for wood, I suppose. The officer of the watch will tell you when he wants to wood up."

I went on consuming, and said I wasn't after wood.

"Indeed? Why, what could you want over here in the bend, then? Did you ever know of a boat following a bend up-stream at this stage of the river?"

"No, sir — and I wasn't trying to follow it. I was getting away from a bluff reef."

"No, it wasn't a bluff reef; there isn't one within three miles of where you were."

"But I saw it. It was as bluff as that one yonder."

"Just about. Run over it!"

"Do you give it as an order?"

"Yes. Run over it!"

"If I don't, I wish I may die."

"All right; I am taking the responsibility."

I as just as anxious to kill the boat, now, as I had been to save it before. I impressed my orders upon my memory, to be used at the inquest, and made a straight break for the reef. As it disappeared under our bows I held my breath; but we slid over it like oil.

"Now, don't you see the difference? It wasn't anything but a *wind* reef. The wind does that."

"So I see. But it is exactly like a bluff reef. How am I ever going to tell them apart?"

"I can't tell you. It is an instinct. By and by you will just naturally *know* one from the other, but you never will be able to explain why or how you know them apart."

It turned out to be true. The face of the water, in time, became a wonderful book — a book that was a dead language to the uneducated passenger, but which told its mind to me without reserve, delivering its most cherished secrets as clearly as if it uttered them with a voice. And it was not a book to be read once and thrown aside, for it had a new story to tell every day. Throughout the long twelve hundred miles there was never a page that was void of interest, never one that you could leave unread without loss, never one that you would want to skip, thinking you could find higher enjoyment in some other thing. There never was so wonderful a book written by man; never one whose interest was so absorbing, so unflagging, so sparklingly renewed with every reperusal. The passenger who could not read it was charmed with a peculiar sort of faint dimple on its surface (on the rare occasions when he did not overlook it altogether); but to the pilot that was an *italicized* passage; indeed, it was more than that, it was a legend of the largest capitals, with a string of shouting exclamation-points at the end of it, for it meant that a wreck or a rock was buried there that could tear the life out of the strongest vessel that ever floated. It is the faintest and simplest expression the water ever makes, and the most hideous to a pilot's eye. In truth, the passenger who could not read this book saw nothing but all manner of pretty pictures in it, painted by the sun and shaded by the clouds, whereas to the trained eye these were not pictures at all, but the grimmest and most dead-earnest of reading-matter.

Number of words 1734
See page 199 for Questions

Reading Time in Seconds _____
See page 323 for Conversion Table

Feeding the Mind

Lewis Carroll

It has been said, "Tell me what you eat, and I will tell you what you are."
In the following selection Lewis Carroll seems to say that that is not so. It's not
so much what you eat but what you read that makes you what you are. Do you
find his case convincing?

Breakfast, dinner, tea; in extreme cases, breakfast, luncheon, dinner, tea, supper, and a glass of something hot at bedtime. What care we take about feeding the lucky body! Which of us does as much for his mind? And what causes the difference? Is the body so much the more important of the two?

By no means; but life depends on the body being fed, whereas we can continue to exist as animals (scarcely as men) though the mind be utterly starved and neglected. Therefore Nature provides that, in case of serious neglect of the body, such terrible consequences of discomfort and pain shall ensue as will soon bring us back to a sense of our duty; and some of the functions necessary to life she does for us altogether, leaving us no choice in the matter. It would fare but ill with many of us if we were left to superintend our own digestion and circulation. "Bless me!" one would cry, "I forgot to wind up my heart this morning! To think that it has been standing still for the last three hours!" "I can't walk with you this afternoon," a friend would say, "as I have no less than eleven dinners to digest. I had to let them stand over from last week, being so busy — and my doctor says he will not answer for the consequences if I wait any longer!"

Well it is, I say, for us, that the consequences of neglecting the body can be clearly seen and felt; and it might be well for some if the mind were equally visible and tangible — if we could take it, say, to the doctor and have its pulse felt.

"Why, what have you been doing with this mind lately? How have you fed it? It looks pale, and the pulse is very slow."

"Well, doctor, it has not had much regular food lately. I gave it a lot of sugar-plums yesterday."

"Sugar-plums! What kind?"

"Well, they were a parcel of conundrums, sir."

"Ah! I thought so. Now just mind this: if you go on playing tricks like that, you'll spoil all its teeth, and get laid up with mental indigestion. You must have nothing but the plainest reading for the next few days. Take care now! No novels on any account!"

Considering the amount of painful experience many of us have had in feeding and dosing the body, it would,

I think, be quite worth our while to try and translate some of the rules into corresponding ones for the mind.

First, then, we should set ourselves to provide for our mind its *proper kind* of food; we very soon learn what will, and what will not, agree with the body, and find little difficulty in refusing a piece of the tempting pudding or pie which is associated in our memory with that terrible attack of indigestion, and whose very name irresistibly recalls rhubarb and magnesia; but it takes a great many lessons to convince us how indigestible some of our favorite lines of reading are, and again and again we make a meal of the unwholesome novel, sure to be followed by its usual train of low spirits, unwillingness to work, weariness of existence — in fact by mental nightmare.

Then we should be careful to provide this wholesome food in *proper amount*. Mental gluttony, or overreading, is a dangerous propensity, tending to weakness of digestive power, and in some cases to loss of appetite; we know that bread is a good and wholesome food, but who would like to try the experiment of eating two or three loaves at a sitting?

I have heard of a physician telling his patient — whose complaint was merely gluttony and want of exercise — that "the earliest symptom of hypernutrition is a deposition of adipose tissue," and no doubt the fine long words greatly consoled the poor man under his increasing load of fat.

I wonder if there is such a thing in nature as a *fat* mind? I really think I have met with one or two minds which could not keep up with the slowest trot in conversation, could not jump over a logical fence to save their lives, always got stuck fast in a narrow argument, and, in short, were fit for nothing but to waddle helplessly through the world.

Then, again, though the food be wholesome and in proper amount, we know that we must not consume *too many kinds at once*. Take the thirsty haymaker a quart of beer, or a quart of cider, or even a quart of cold tea, and he will probably thank you (though not so heartily in the last case!). But what think you his feelings would be if you offered him a tray containing a little mug of beer, a little mug of cider, another of cold tea, one of hot tea, one of coffee, one of cocoa, and corresponding vessels of milk, water, brandy-and-water,

From *Feeding the Mind, London:* Chatto and Windus, 1907.

and buttermilk? The sum total might be a quart, but would it be the same thing to the haymaker?

Having settled the proper kind, amount, and variety of our mental food, it remains that we should be careful to allow *proper intervals* between meal and meal, and not swallow the food hastily without mastication, so that it may be thoroughly digested; both which rules for the body are also applicable at once to the mind.

First as to the intervals: these are as really necessary as they are for the body, with this difference only, that while the body requires three or four hours' rest before it is ready for another meal, the mind will in many cases do with three or four minutes. I believe that the interval required is much shorter than is generally supposed, and from personal experience I would recommend any one who has to devote several hours together to one subject of thought to try the effect of such a break, say once an hour — leaving off for five minutes only, each time, but taking care to throw the mind absolutely "out of gear" for those five minutes, and to turn it entirely to other subjects. It is astonishing what an amount of impetus and elasticity the mind recovers during those short periods of rest.

And then as to the mastication of the food: the mental process answering to this is simply *thinking over* what we read. This is a very much greater exertion of mind than the mere passive taking in of the contents of our author — so much greater an exertion is it, that, as Coleridge says, the mind often "angrily refuses" to put itself to such trouble — so much greater, that we are far too apt to neglect it altogether, and go on pouring in fresh food on the top of the undigested masses already lying there, till the unfortunate mind is fairly swamped under the flood. But the greater the exertion, the more valuable, we may be sure, is the effect; one hour of steady thinking over a subject (a solitary walk is as good an opportunity for the process as any other) is worth two or three of reading only.

And just consider another effect of this thorough digestion of the books we read; I mean the arranging and "ticketing," so to speak, of the subjects in our minds, so that we can readily refer to them when we want them. Sam Slick tells us that he has learned several languages in his life, but somehow "couldn't keep the parcels sorted" in his mind; and many a mind that hurries through book after book, without waiting to digest or arrange anything, gets into that sort of condition, and the unfortunate owner finds himself far from fit really to support the character all his friends give him.

"A thoroughly well-read man. Just you try him in any subject, now. You can't puzzle him!"

You turn to the thoroughly well-read man: you ask him a question, say, in English history (he is understood to have just finished reading Macaulay); he smiles good-naturedly, tries to look as if he knew all about it, and proceeds to dive into his mind for the answer. Up comes a handful of very promising facts, but on examination they turn out to belong to the wrong century, and are pitched in again; a second haul brings up a fact much more like the real thing, but unfortunately along with it comes a tangle of other things — a fact in political economy, a rule in arithmetic, the ages of his brother's children, and a stanza of Gray's *Elegy;* and among all these the fact he wants has got hopelessly twisted up and entangled. Meanwhile every one is waiting for his reply, and as the silence is getting more and more awkward, our well-read friend has to stammer out some half-answer at last, not nearly so clear or so satisfactory as an ordinary schoolboy would have given. And all this for want of making up his knowledge into proper bundles and ticketing them!

Do you know the unfortunate victim of ill-judged mental feeding when you see him? Can you doubt him? Look at him drearily wandering round a reading-room, tasting dish after dish — we beg his pardon, book after book — keeping to none. First a mouthful of novel — but no, faugh! he has had nothing but that to eat for the last week, and is quite tired of the taste; then a slice of science, but you know at once what the result of that will be — ah, of course, much too tough for *his* teeth. And so on through the old weary round, which he tried (and failed in) yesterday, and will probably try, and fail in, tomorrow.

Mr. Oliver Wendell Holmes, in his very amusing book *The Professor at the Breakfast-table,* gives the following rule for knowing whether a human being is young or old. "The crucial experiment is this. Offer a bulky bun to the suspected individual just ten minutes before dinner. If this is easily accepted and devoured, the fact of youth is established." He tells us that a human being, "if young, will eat anything at any hour of the day or night."

To ascertain the healthiness of the *mental* appetite of a human animal, place in its hands a short, well-written, but not exciting treatise on some popular subject — a mental *bun,* in fact. If it is read with eager interest and perfect attention, *and if the reader can answer questions on the subject afterwards,* the mind is in first-rate working order; if it be politely laid down again, or perhaps lounged over for a few minutes, and then, "I can't read this stupid book! Would you hand me the second volume of *The Mysterious Murder?*" you may be equally sure that there is something wrong in the mental digestion.

If this paper has given you any useful hints on the important subject of reading, and made you see that it is one's duty no less than one's interest to "read, mark, learn, and inwardly digest" the good books that fall in your way, its purpose will be fulfilled.

Number of words 1866
See page 201 for Questions

Reading Time in Seconds _____
See page 323 for Conversion Table

Open Every Door

T. E. Murphy

If life is a corridor with many doors, as the author suggests, what are books? Could they be the all-important doorknobs? Reading the following selection could push open all kinds of doors down the long corridor ahead.

If nature continues faithful to her trust we shall have, in the future, saucer eyes, ears like loving cups and double-spread bottoms — the better to see, hear and sit. Our arms and legs will shrink to sausagelike appendages; the head will atrophy to a tiny thread connecting the used senses of eyes and ears. For we are fast becoming a nation of watchers and listeners; we have too much to see and hear, not enough to do.

A process that began four decades ago is now reaching its logical conclusion with the advent of television. We watch other men fight, make love, play baseball or football, even attend religious services. (Catholics have had to be warned that hearing Mass by television does not fulfill the requirements of Catholic doctrine.) We listen avidly to a dreary procession of stale jokes and songs about dream houses and faraway places. Because of these diversions we are giving up a good part of our heritage. And we are robbing our children, too. The great classics of childhood — *Huck Finn, Tom Sawyer, Alice, Treasure Island, The Wind in the Willows* — are unopened books, unexplored lands. We have let them be supplanted by the Lone Ranger and Gorgeous George.

Living is more than watching and listening. It is *doing*. I believe in the heresy that it's more fun to kiss a pretty girl myself than to watch some shadowy figment go through the motion on a screen. I would rather bat a ball to a bunch of kids than watch Joe DiMaggio hit a homer. Evenings, I would rather paint a picture or bake a cherry pie than to sit on my calluses listening to time-worn allusions to Al Jolson's age, Jack Benny's miserliness, Bob Hope's nose.

Oh, I don't dislike spectator sports. Some of my best friends are spectators. In the course of a year I'm likely to see a couple of fights, some baseball and college football. I like them all in small doses. I refuse to let them dominate my life.

A few years ago I walked into the office of a distinguished elderly lawyer and found him reading a book of verse by an obscure 19th-century poet. Behind him were volumes on astronomy, botany and geology. When I expressed surprise at the range of his reading, he said: "Life is a corridor with many doors. I am hurrying to open as many as I can before the ultimate one is opened."

I thought of that next day when I tried in vain to hire a carpenter to screen a porch. At the library I got a book telling how to do it, and for the first time in my life I built something with my own hands. It wasn't an expert job. But I learned the thrill of doing something I'd always thought beyond me. It was a small door I opened then, but it was the first of many.

An important thing to remember is that, no matter what strange new door we plan to open, there are experts to guide us — *for free*. Want to paint a picture? There are hundreds of books to tell you how — books in which the great masters have spread out their own hard-earned knowledge. Want to build a swimming pool or a kitchen table? Want to be a sculptor in your spare time? Want to learn French or Italian? You can learn if you have enough curiosity to open a door.

One of my favorite doors opens into the world of gardening. A lot of jokes have been told about the "book" farmer. I'm a book farmer and don't care who knows it.

A neighbor of mine who had planted the same strain of corn for 50 years was inclined to look down his nose at book farmers. One day I gave him a handful of hybrid seed.

A few weeks later I stopped by. "It's the only corn that's any danged good," said my friend. Then, in reluctant capitulation, "I'd like to learn some more about them seeds."

Some people are timid about trying new things. I know one chap who'd been taking photographs for 20 years. One day, after a big local event, I asked him how his pictures came out. He looked surprised. "I won't have them back for a couple of days."

"Do you mean you don't develop and print your own pictures?"

He shook his head. "I'm afraid that's a little too technical for me."

I led him to the nearest drugstore. "Look at the label on this developer can," I said. "You can read, can't you? The manufacturer has been writing all these things for you."

He took the plunge and is now an excellent all-round photographer.

A woman I know was discouraged by the high prices of clothing during the war years. A complete novice at sewing, she found all the information she needed in manuals and pattern guides. Today, though dresses are cheaper, she continues to make her own. "Now I'm *doing* something while I listen to the radio," she explains.

I believe that doing things for yourself is the vital component for a sound personality and an exciting life. In the past two years I have done 50 or more oil paintings, most of them bad. I have written a little poetry and read a great deal more. I have baked everything from a loaf of bread to a mince pie. I have studied Spanish and geology. And because I have four children I have also fished, skated, played baseball, made snowmen, played badminton. Meanwhile I have held down a fulltime newspaper job.

I believe fervently in the idea that the hallmark distinguishing man from beast is his creative instinct. It is one of the anomalies of our civilization that the most intensive efforts to satisfy man's creative needs are made in mental hospitals.

Creative expression is not confined to "making" something. I know one middle-aged woman with a grown family who refurnished her cellar as a club for teen-agers. In a few years thousands of young boys and girls had come under her warm and pleasurable influence. Another middle-aged childless couple acted as foster parents to state wards. They kept none of the board money but put it aside for the education of these homeless waifs. They've raised dozens of children and had fun doing it.

An industrialist friend of mine started out as a song writer and then went into a factory. He has made a lot of machinery and some money. But only when he organized a neighborhood singing club did he fulfill his ambitions. "Sometimes," he says proudly, "they even sing some of the songs I wrote."

These are doors to new worlds. They are tiny declarations of independence against being made into the faceless man who sits, listens and watches.

A philosopher once observed that man lives in a prison cell lined with mirrors. Today that prison cell is lined with loudspeakers and screens. All very fine, to a degree. But for a really full life we've got to burst out of the cell — and our children with us. For them the danger of growing into a race of super-robots is greater because the conditioning has begun earlier.

Teach them, by example, to open doors. Show them the value of a wide range of interests in contrast with the narrowly grooved life, the difference between apathetic acceptance of things as they are and inquiry. The result? It is the difference between man the intelligent, creative creature and man the village videot.

Number of words 1275
See page 203 for Questions

Reading Time in Seconds _____
See page 323 for Conversion Table

SELECTION 18

Books in the Bloodstream

Norman Cousins

Cicero, who was said to spend much time in the library, declared, "To be ignorant of what happened before you were born is to be forever a child." Open a book to grow up, he seems to be saying. Drop yourself into the bloodstream of human experience.

There was a time when a library was considered the greatest of all national treasures. We can remind ourselves that Demetrius Phalereus, who superintended the great library at Alexandria, held up a large shipment of supplies to Greece — not because he wanted more money but because he insisted that Egypt be paid by Greece in original manuscripts. Phalereus held out for two folios by Aeschylus, one by Sophocles, and one by Euripides. Not even a lefthander or a switch-hitter to seal the bargain. Just a straight transaction of several dozen tons of wheat for a few pounds of manuscript.

And the importance attached to libraries in those early but otherwise advanced times may be apparent from the amount of time Cicero took away from his consulship to spend in the library. Every now and then, in fact, it became necessary for Cicero to assure the people that he was not neglecting affairs of state in the pursuit of his hobby. In more recent times, this question has come up in a somewhat different form, indicating that the distance from Publicans to Republicans may not be as great as we think.

In any event, the Greeks and the Romans had a word for their books, a good word, and they attached to their libraries the same special feelings of satisfaction and awe that a more modern generation has sometimes applied to Fort Knox. Indeed, the Latin term *thesaurus* means, quite literally, a treasure house. In any inventory

From *Saturday Review*, April 25, 1959. Reprinted by permission of Saturday Review/World.

of their national assets, the Romans counted their manuscripts even before they counted their edifices.

To be sure, a library in the old days was rather careful about the company it kept. The first question a Roman interested in a library would ask was not "How many books does it have?" or even "What did it cost?" but "What does it have that is worth providing space to keep?" The yardstick then and for a few centuries to come was not coverage so much as it was cogency. As late as the fourteenth century, in fact, one of the best libraries in Europe, the Royal Library of France, did not number more than 900 volumes, all of which knew the meaning of service.

In our time, of course, we are compelled to be comprehensive. This is inevitable. New knowledge is just as much entitled to elbow room as the old. In fact, new knowledge is being generated so fast that it can hardly be classified, let alone be fitted out for its cubicles. We must manage somehow both to pay our respects to this new knowledge and to find a place for it on the open stacks.

Even so, one wonders whether the fascination with numbers ought not to be subdued somewhat where books are concerned. The value of a library is no more represented by the number of volumes it houses than a book by the number of its pages. It is what happens to people inside the library that counts and not just the yardage of the catalogue cards. A good library should be the delivery room of the intellect for people who like to bring ideas to life. It is also, or should be, a busy thoroughfare where a reasonably curious man can rub shoulders with the interesting and provocative people of history, and, indeed, where he can get on reading terms with some original ideas. It is an exchange center for basic facts, to be sure; but there is no reason why it should not fulfill Disraeli's designation as a place which affords the consoling pleasures of the imagination.

Most important of all, however, the library in today's world offers more than incidental intelligence for a society looking for a place to go. One of the unhappy characteristics of modern man is that he lives in a state of historical disconnection. He has not put his experience to work in coping with new dangers. He has tended to segregate himself from the wisdom so slowly and painfully built up over long centuries. He has made the mistake of thinking that because there is so much that is new in the nature of contemporary crisis the past has nothing of value to say to us. But the fact that men like Socrates or Comenius or Milton or Jefferson or Lao-Tse did not have to contend with atomic weapons or intercontinental missiles does not mean that their views of life and great issues have meaning only for their own times. Similarly, the Peloponnesian Wars may be more than two thousand years in the past, but some of the basic principles emerging from that experience might be helpful today. And the story of man's own growth and his struggle to create and preserve his noble works — all this deserves our respect. At least we ought to know what it is that is now being jeopardized.

It is in this sense that the library may be able to speak to the human condition in today's world. For books serve as the natural bloodstream of human experience. They make it possible for the big thoughts of big minds to circulate in the body of history. They represent a point of contact between past and future.

There is something else that books can do. They can figure in the essential conversion operation that man now requires. For it is not enough that man has been able to develop his scientific and mechanical skills in converting things. It is not enough that man can convert the face of nature into a countenance congenial to human life. Not enough for him to convert sand, stone, and water into gleaming and wondrous towers. Not enough to convert fluids into fabrics. Not enough to convert the invisible atom into an infinity of power. Not enough to convert the rush of water into the whirling fantasy of the dynamo and thence into the magic impulses that banish darkness or turn wheels or carry images and voices over empty space.

What is most needed now is to apply the human conversion skills to those things that are now most essential for his survival. Man has to convert facts into logic, free will into purpose, conscience into decision. He has to convert historical experience into a design for a sane world. He has to convert the vast processes of education into those ideas that can make this globe safe for the human diversity. And he will have to learn how to convert the individual morality into a group ethic.

Our lack of conversion skills in these respects has converted us into paupers. The plenty produced by our scientific and physical skills has not relieved the poverty of our purposes. The only thing greater than our power is our insecurity. All our resources and all our wealth are not enough to protect us against the effects of irrational ideas and acts on the world stage. It makes little difference how magnificent are our new buildings or how impressive are our private kingdoms. If no answer is found to war, all men will die poor.

The library — and the term is used here as symbolic of the universe of knowledge, systematic and unsystematic both — the library can be a strong part of the new conversion process. It can furnish the basic materials that must go into the making of the new purposes and designs.

Some people may take the fatalistic view and say it is too late. They may say that man cannot possibly develop the comprehension necessary to deal with change in the modern world, that he will require many centuries before his conversion skills can be developed as they now need to be developed in the cause of human survival.

But there is a larger view of man, one that history is

prepared to endorse. This view holds that the great responses already exist inside man and that they need only to be invoked to become manifest. For man is infinitely malleable, infinitely perfectible, infinitely capacious. It is the privilege of anyone in a position of leadership to appeal to these towering possibilities.

Number of words 1358
See page 205 for Questions

Reading Time in Seconds _____
See page 323 for Conversion Table

Why Not Speed Up Your Reading?

Leonard A. Stevens

Slow readers are slaves to slowness. But rapid readers are not *slaves to speed. Rapid readers can easily slow down; slow readers cannot easily speed up — an important distinction. Now read on for some practical suggestions for speeding up your reading.*

For many people today, reading is no longer relaxation. To keep up with their work they must read letters, reports, trade publications, interoffice communications: a never-ending flood of words. In getting a job or advancing in one, the ability to read and comprehend quickly can mean the difference between success and failure. Yet the unfortunate fact is that most of us are poor readers.

A few months ago a man who had been promoted to a top management job came to see Dr. Emmett A. Betts, director of Temple University's Reading Clinic. The first morning on his new job he had found a huge pile of mail on his desk. He realized it would take him most of the day just to read the letters; moreover, a similar pile would confront him every morning.

A reading test showed that the executive was reading only about 160 words a minute. He was an engineer who had spent years plowing through difficult technical material. He had been forced to go slowly to get the meaning. Soon he began reading everything, even light fiction, at the same turtle's pace. Dr. Betts diagnosed the executive's reading problem as a common one — inability to "shift gears." If the subject matter were difficult, careful reading was justified; when it was easy, he should have zipped through it.

First, Dr. Betts forced the executive to read exceptionally fast some first- and second-grade material. Then he gave him increasingly difficult texts. Soon the former engineer was reading on his job at about 900 words a minute — and his problem was over.

Bad readers trudge home with brief cases bulging with material that should have been read on the job. Recently the vice-president of a large company conferred with Paul D. Leedy, adult adviser at New York University's Reading Institute. Nights and week-ends, he said, he had to catch up on reading he should have done at the office, leaving little time to devote to his family.

Leedy found that the executive was a word-by-word reader. He gave him special assignments to help him grasp whole phrases instead of individual words, and also gave him assignments on a reading accelerator. This moves a curtain down a page at a predetermined rate of speed, forcing the student to read faster to keep ahead of it. At first the executive felt he was reading only superficially. But as his speed picked up, he found he was getting more out of his reading. Soon he was reading nearly 1,200 words a minute, compared to 225 when he started.

An engineer reported graphic evidence that faster reading improves concentration. He told of working with a reading accelerator in a room outside which children were playing noisily. At first he couldn't keep up with the pace set by the accelerator because of the clatter. As an experiment he set the device to scan the pages even faster. He soon found that he was concentrating so hard on keeping up with the machine that he was no longer aware of the noise.

Most reading faults can be traced to early school training. According to Dr. Betts, two persons out of five in school were forced to read material too difficult for them to understand at the time, a frustrating experience which left them with bad reading habits.

Fortunately, almost anyone can learn to read faster and with more comprehension. Age makes little difference. According to a recent study of 138 students at The Reading Laboratory, Inc., all age groups showed a marked increase in reading rate after training — from 93 percent for the 50–59 age group to 142 percent for the 20–29. Dr. Nila Banton Smith, director of New York University's Reading Institute, says that the average adult student, in 28 training hours, nearly triples

---

From *The Reader's Digest*, January 1955. Reprinted by permission of the author.

his reading speed and boosts his comprehension by about 30 percent.

The best way to improve your reading, of course, is to enroll in a reading clinic. If there's no clinic handy or you cannot afford special training, most experts agree you can improve your reading ability yourself — provided you have no eye trouble. (If reading tires you easily or makes your eyes or head ache, you should consult a doctor.)

Here are some suggestions on how to train yourself:

If you are a lip reader, mouthing each word so you are slowed down to a snail's pace, place a finger on your lips and hold them firmly until the habit has been broken.

If your head swings as your eyes move along a line, lock your head between your hands as you read.

To break yourself of the habit of following print with your finger, grip the sides of what you are reading firmly with both hands.

Read in a quiet spot, as free from distractions as possible. But don't daydream; force yourself to concentrate on what you're reading.

If you stumble over unfamiliar words, try to guess the meaning from the context, then check the meaning in a dictionary later.

Make your eyes literally leap over lines of print and try to grasp the meaning of whole phrases at a time.

Race an alarm clock. Estimate the number of words in an article or book chapter and set a time limit on how long you should take to read it. Set the alarm for that period of time. See if you can finish before the alarm goes off. Gradually shorten your target time.

After reading a section as fast as you can, pause and summarize in your mind the author's main points. Check yourself by reviewing the section.

Don't reread. Pretend the words disappear as your eyes pass over them. You'll probably be surprised to find that you didn't miss anything important.

Try glancing only at nouns and verbs in sentences to see how much you can get out of reading this way. Underlining these key words may help you get started, but stop underlining as soon as you catch on to the technique.

Draw a line down the center of a newspaper column. Center your vision on the line and try to grasp the meaning of the words on each side as you move down the page.

The secret of success is constant practice. The payoff will be worth the effort.

Number of words 1050
See page 207 for Questions

Reading Time in Seconds _____
See page 323 for Conversion Table

SELECTION 20

Reading for A's

Gregory Cowan and Elisabeth McPherson

Reading plays many different roles in our lives. Sometimes we read for pure pleasure, sometimes for inspiration, sometimes for specific problem-solving help — and, as explained in this selection — sometimes for better grades. Exactly how is that managed to best advantage?

Where and when and what you study are all important. But the neatest desk and the best desk light, the world's most regular schedule, the best leather-covered notebook and the most expensive textbooks you can buy will do you no good unless you know how to study. And how to study, if you don't already have some clue, is probably the hardest thing you will have to learn in college. Some students can master the entire system of imaginary numbers more easily than other students can discover how to study the first chapter in the algebra

book. Methods of studying vary; what works well for some students doesn't work at all for others. The only thing you can do is experiment until you find a system that does work for you. But two things are sure: nobody else can do your studying for you, and unless you do find a system that works, you won't get through college.

Meantime, there are a few rules that work for everybody. The first is *don't get behind*. The problem of studying, hard enough to start with, becomes almost impossible when you are trying to do three weeks' work in one weekend. Even the fastest readers have trouble doing that. And if you are behind in written work that must be turned in, the teacher who accepts it that late will probably not give you full credit. Perhaps he may not accept it at all.

From *Background for Writing* by Gregory Cowan and Elisabeth McPherson. Copyright © 1967 by Elisabeth McPherson and Gregory Cowan. Reprinted by permission of Random House, Inc.

Getting behind in one class because you are spending so much time on another is really no excuse. Feeling pretty virtuous about the seven hours you spend on chemistry won't help one bit if the history teacher pops a quiz. And many freshmen do get into trouble by spending too much time on one class at the expense of the others, either because they like one class much better or because they find it so much harder that they think they should devote all their time to it. Whatever the reason, going whole hog for one class and neglecting the rest of them is a mistake. If you face this temptation, begin with the shortest and easiest assignments. Get them out of the way and then go on to the more difficult, time-consuming work. Unless you do the easy work first, you are likely to spend so much time on the long, hard work that when midnight comes, you'll say to yourself, "Oh, that English assignment was so easy, I can do it any time," and go on to bed. The English assignment, easy as it was, won't get done.

If everything seems equally easy (or equally hard), leave whatever you like best until the end. There will be more incentive at half past eleven to read a political science article that sounded really interesting than to begin memorizing French irregular verbs, a necessary task that strikes you as pretty dull.

In spite of the noblest efforts, however, everybody does get a little behind in something some time. When this happens to you, catch up. Don't skip the parts you missed and try to go ahead with the rest of the class while there is still a big gap showing. What you missed may make it impossible, or at least difficult, to understand what the rest of the class is doing now. If you are behind, lengthen your study periods for a few days until you catch up. Skip the movie you meant to see or the nap you planned to take. Stay up a little later, if you have to. But catch up.

If you are behind not just in one class but in all of them, the problem is a little different. Maybe you have had a bad bout of mumps or an attack of the general confusion common to students in their first quarter of school. Whatever your ailment was, if it has put you two weeks behind in everything, probably you cannot hope to catch up. Your best bet, in these circumstances, is to face the situation and drop a class. With one less course to worry about, you can spend both the class hours and the study time reserved for that class in catching up with your remaining classes. It's too bad to drop a course in the middle of a term, but it's a lot better to finish your first quarter with twelve hours of C than with seventeen hours of D or F.

The second rule that works for everybody is *don't be afraid to mark in textbooks.* A good student's books don't finish the term looking as fresh and clean as the day they were purchased: they look used, well used. Some sections are underlined. Notes are written down the margins. Answers to some of the questions are sketched in. In fact, the books look as though somebody had studied them.

If you are the well-brought-up product of a public school, this method of studying books may horrify you. Perhaps in kindergarten you learned that it was naughty to scribble in your books with your crayon. In grade school it was made clear that anyone who wrote in a book was headed for juvenile court. In high school you discovered that even the student who wrote on bathroom walls was more respectable than the evil character that marked in his books. And up to now there were good reasons for these restrictions. It does seem senseless and wasteful to let a child ruin a book with crayon scribbles or to let an idle student deface a book with aimless doodles or caricatures of his homeroom teacher's long nose. Besides, the school district didn't want you to produce all the answers for the student who would use the book next year.

In college your books belong to you. Even so, you are still dogged by the same advice, this time from the college bookstore: don't write in the book if you want to sell it. Of course, some students do sell their books. These students figure that books cost a lot of money, that the courses are dull anyway, and when these students finish the term, they think they never want to see those books again. These students count themselves fortunate if the manager of the bookstore offers anything at all for their books. These pseudo-students are more interested in saving a dollar or so next year than in learning much right now. On the other hand, the student who wants to make the most of his textbooks will not worry about selling them; he'll worry about keeping them and using them to the best advantage.

Let's assume that *you* plan to keep your book. First, put your name in it, in large, clear writing so that when you leave it in the coffee shop, some honest student can return it to you. Then start marking it up. We are not suggesting, of course, that you dig up your old crayons or draw cartoons of your teachers in the margins. But some kinds of marking are both useful and economically sound. To get your money's worth from your text, you must do more with it than just read it.

To begin with, when you first get a new textbook, look at the table of contents to see what material the book covers. Flip through the pages to see what study aids the author has provided: subheadings, summaries, charts, pictures, review questions at the end of each chapter. After you have found what the whole book covers, you will be better prepared to begin studying the chapter you have been asked to read.

Before you begin reading the chapter, give it the same sort of treatment. Skim through the first and last paragraphs; look with more care at the subheadings; if there are questions at the end of the chapter, read them first so you will know what points to watch for as you read. After you are thus forewarned, settle down to the actual business of reading. Read the chapter all the way through, as fast as you comfortably can. Don't mark anything this first time through except the words that are new to you. Circle them. When you have finished the chapter, find out what these unknown words mean, and write the definitions in the margin opposite the word.

Then look again at the questions, seeing whether you have found the answers to all of them. Guided by the things the questions emphasize and your knowledge of what the whole chapter covered, go rapidly through the chapter again, underlining the most important points. If the chapter falls into three major divisions, underline the three sentences that come closest to summing up the idea of each division. Number these points in the margin: 1, 2, 3. For each major point you have numbered, underline two or three supporting points. In other words, underline the sections you think you might want to find in a hurry if you were reviewing the chapter.

What happens in class the next day, or whenever this assignment is discussed, will give you some check on whether you found the important points. If the teacher spends a lot of time on a part of the text you didn't mark at all, probably you guessed wrong. Get yourself a red pencil and mark the teacher's points. You can make these changes during the study time you have set aside for comparing class notes with the textbook.

One word of warning: don't underline everything you read. If you mark too much, the important material won't stand out, and you will be just as confused as if you had not marked anything at all.

The third rule useful to everybody is *don't let tests terrify you.* If you have kept up in all your classes, if you have compared your class notes with your texts, if you have kept all your quizzes and gone over your errors, if you have underlined the important parts of each chapter intelligently, the chances are good that you can answer any questions the teacher will ask.

Being fairly sure that you can answer all the questions, however, is not the same thing as answering them. Nothing is more frustrating than freezing up during an important test, knowing all the answers but getting so excited at the sight of the test that half of what you actually know never gets written down.

Do you know the story of the lecturer who cured his stage fright by pretending that all the people listening to him were cabbages? A head of cabbage is no more capable of criticizing a lecture than cabbage soup would be. And who's afraid of a bowl of borsch? You might adapt this system to taking tests. Pretend that the test is only a game you are playing to use up an idle hour. Pretend that your test score is no more important than your score in canasta last night. But you tried to win at canasta; try for as high a test score as you can get without frightening yourself to death.

One way to insure a good score is to read the entire test before you answer any questions. Sometimes questions that come near the end will give clues to the answers on earlier questions. Even if you don't find any answers, you can avoid the error of putting everything you know into the first answer and then repeating yourself for the rest of the test.

Be careful, too, not to spend all your time on one question at the expense of the others. If you have sixty minutes to finish a test that contains ten questions, plan to spend five minutes on each question and save ten minutes at the end to read through what you have written, correcting silly mistakes and making sure you have not left out anything important. If some of the questions seem easier than others, answer the easiest first. There is no rule that says you must begin at the beginning and work straight through to the end. If you're going to leave something out, it might as well be the things you aren't sure of anyway.

Following these three suggestions, reading through the test, budgeting your time, doing the easy part first, will not guarantee A's on all your tests. To get A's on essay tests, you must be able to write well enough that your teacher is convinced you *do* understand. What following these suggestions *can* do, however, is help you make the most of what you know.

Number of words 2090
See page 209 for Questions

Reading Time in Seconds _____
See page 323 for Conversion Table

Library in Your Lap — 2075 A.D.

James Cooke Brown

The science fiction of today often creates the reality of tomorrow. In this excerpt you question one who has just returned from the world of our future — the world of 2075 A.D. As she describes her favorite invention, the love of reading comes through loud and clear.

"Myra," James asked, "what was the invention of the next hundred years that pleased you most?"

She thought for a moment, and from the frown of concentration on her face, I gathered there were some close runners in that race. Finally she looked up and smiled. "The reader," she said firmly. "Yes; I think the reader was my favorite gadget. . . . It's the next development in the long history of the book. And it may well be the last, for it's the very essence of the book. So in that Platonic sense I guess it is heavenly. The reader itself is a light, flat, plastic box with a glass screen set into the top. They come in several sizes, but the most common is about the size of a magazine. Thicker but a little lighter. It's a television receiver coupled with a radio transmitter, essentially, but since they don't use cathode ray tubes any more, and since all their electronic circuitry is grown, it's far, far lighter than you would expect for what it does. Just a few hundred grams, actually, with power cell and all.

"Along the lower edge of a typical reader is an alphanumeric keyboard. If you know the title of the book you want, you key it into the set. If the title is unique, the first page of that book will appear before you on the screen in about three seconds. Thereafter, and until you release it, you have complete control of one copy of that book as well as the TV transmitter that happens to be looking at it. For example, by using certain simple controls you can turn its pages, leaf backward or forward . . . do anything you like with it. But if the title you have asked for is not unique, the list of all works which have that title will appear on the screen before you, together with the names of their authors, brief descriptions, dates, and so on; and you can then make your choice among them. And even if you don't know the title of the book you want, you can easily get it anyway by a slightly longer search that the reader will conduct for you, provided you know something about it — nearly any scrap of information will do — and provided it exists. Every book that does exist is available to any reader at any time of day or night.

"That, I suppose, is the most astonishing fact about the reader, James. Every book that has ever been written is . . . well, simply waiting to materialize in this little box sitting in your lap. It's an eerie feeling. At first, having a reader in your hands is a little like being drunk. Then it begins to be embarrassing . . . a surfeit of riches, I suppose. Then it's simply orgiastic. That stage lasts quite a long time. During our first month at Loma Verde, Mat and Jean-Jacques and Julie and I would rush back to our rooms at the slightest provocation, and there we would have orgies of reading. Reading aloud, browsing, looking things up, challenging one another, comparing authorities, looking things up again. Sometimes we did this when we were together, sometimes we did it alone. You can't imagine what a feeling of excitement, of sheer intellectual power, it gives you to know that you can learn anything, find anything out, look anything up, simply by fiddling with a little plastic box sitting in your lap. Later, months later, you calm down. But it takes some getting used to, this knowledge that all knowledge is available to you. You get the feeling there are no secrets you cannot share . . . if only you work hard enough to puzzle them out.

"Now the technical system that stands behind this little box is as straightforward as a wish. There is one central storage area — a library, I guess you'd call it — for the whole world. It happens to be in the middle of the Australian desert but it might be anywhere. The library is in direct radio contact, through satellite relay stations, with every reader transceiver in the world. When anyone requests a book his set is immediately linked to one of the millions of miniaturized, roving scanners that inhibit the immense building where the books are stored. There are as many of these scanners — bugs, the reader people call them — as the maximum number of clients the reader service can expect to be dealing with at any one time plus a margin. So no one ever has to wait for a scanner to be free. There are, I've heard, about one hundred million of these bugs on active duty at peak periods of the day. I've also been told that each of these little robots occupies the space of a 3-centimeter cube. The design of that tiny space is, of course, the technical heart of the system.

"The documents themselves are nothing but microprinted cards. They're so finely printed, in fact, that about nine hundred book pages can be recorded on a single card. Each card is three centimeters square. There are as many copies of each document as are ever likely to be called for at one time, plus another statistically computed safety margin. So again, no one ever has to wait for a book. Now these document cards are mag-

From *The Troika Incident,* Doubleday & Company, Inc., 1970.

netically coded; and they're stored in coded racks that cover literally millions of square meters of floor space. When a reader calls for a certain document, the idle bug that happens to be closest to the address of that document is assigned to that particular reader. The first thing the bug does is go to the appropriately coded rack — never more than a few meters away — and remove a copy of the required document. Then it flashes the title page onto the distant reader's screen and awaits further orders. Thereafter, and until the user releases it, bug, document and reader are linked together in one integrated system which is completely under the user's control. Once released, the bug replaces the card and stands by ready for another call. . . ."

"I'll buy one, Myra," I said gladly. "In fact I'm not sure that I can get along without one. And you're right, such a system — in embryo at least — is technically possible right now."

Number of words 1056
See page 211 for Questions

Reading Time in Seconds _____
See page 323 for Conversion Table

SELECTION 22

Reading Is Like Skiing

Mortimer J. Adler and Charles Van Doren

Emerson put it this way — " 'Tis the good reader that makes the good book." Similarly, perhaps, it's the good skier that makes the good skiing. What is the similarity between such obviously dissimilar activities as reading and skiing? Well, you'll soon find out.

Reading is like skiing. When done well, when done by an expert, both reading and skiing are graceful, harmonious activities. When done by a beginner, both are awkward, frustrating, and slow.

Learning to ski is one of the most humiliating experiences an adult can undergo (that is one reason to start young). After all, an adult has been walking for a long time; he knows where his feet are; he knows how to put one foot in front of the other in order to get somewhere. But as soon as he puts skis on his feet, it is as though he had to learn to walk all over again. He slips and slides, falls down, has trouble getting up, gets his skis crossed, tumbles again, and generally looks — and feels — like a fool.

Even the best instructor seems at first to be no help. The ease with which the instructor performs actions that he says are simple but that the student secretly believes are impossible is almost insulting. How can you remember everything the instructor says you have to remember? Bend your knees. Look down the hill. Keep your weight on the downhill ski. Keep your back straight, but nevertheless lean forward. The admonitions seem endless — how can you think about all that and still ski?

The point about skiing, of course, is that you should not be thinking about the separate acts that, together, make a smooth turn or series of linked turns — instead, you should merely be looking ahead of you down the hill, anticipating bumps and other skiers, enjoying the feel of the cold wind on your cheeks, smiling with pleasure at the fluid grace of your body as you speed down the mountain. In other words, you must learn to forget the separate acts in order to perform all of them, and indeed any of them, well. But in order *to forget them as separate acts, you have to learn them first as separate acts.* Only then can you put them together to become a good skier.

It is the same with reading. Probably you have been reading for a long time, too, and starting to learn all over again can be humiliating. But it is just as true of reading as it is of skiing that you cannot coalesce a lot of different acts into one complex, harmonious performance until you become expert at each of them. You cannot telescope the different parts of the job so that they run into one another and fuse intimately. Each separate act requires your full attention while you are doing it. After you have practiced the parts separately, you can not only do each with greater facility and less attention but can also gradually put them together into a smoothly running whole.

All of this is common knowledge about learning a complex skill. We say it here merely because we want you to realize that learning to read is at least as complex as learning to ski or to typewrite or to play tennis. If you can recall your patience in any other learning experience you have had, you will be more tolerant of instructors who will shortly enumerate a long list of rules for reading.

The person who has had one experience in acquiring a complex skill knows that he need not fear the array of rules that present themselves at the beginning of something new to be learned. He knows that he does not have to worry about how all the separate acts in which he must become separately proficient are going to work together.

The multiplicity of the rules indicates the complexity of the one habit to be formed, not a plurality of distinct habits. The parts coalesce and telescope as each reaches the stage of automatic execution. When all the subordi-

nate acts can be done more or less automatically, you have formed the habit of the whole performance. Then you can think about tackling an expert run you have never skied before, or reading a book that you once thought was too difficult for you. At the beginning, the learner pays attention to himself and his skill in the separate acts. When the acts have lost their separateness in the skill of the whole performance, the learner can at last pay attention to the goal that the technique he has acquired enables him to reach.

Number of words 732
See page 213 for Questions

Reading Time in Seconds _____
See page 323 for Conversion Table

See page 213 for Questions

See page 323 for Conversion Table

SELECTION 23

How to Find Time to Read

Louis Shores

How many books did you read this past year? And why didn't you read more? Most people reply by saying, "I just didn't have enough time." In that case, take time right now to learn how to find time for more reading pleasure.

If you are an average reader you can read an average book at the rate of 300 words a minute. You cannot maintain that average, however, unless you read regularly every day. Nor can you attain that speed with hard books in science, mathematics, agriculture, business, or any subject that is new or unfamiliar to you. The chances are you will never attempt that speed with poetry or want to race through some passages in fiction over which you wish to linger. But for most novels, biographies, and books about travel, hobbies or personal interests, if you are an average reader you should have no trouble at all absorbing meaning and pleasure out of 300 printed words every 60 seconds.

Statistics are not always practicable, but consider these: If the average reader can read 300 words a minute of average reading, then in 15 minutes he can read 4,500 words. Multiplied by 7, the days of the week, the product is 31,500. Another multiplication by 4, the weeks of the month, makes 126,000. And final multiplication by 12, the months of the year, results in a grand total of 1,512,000 words. That is the total number of words of average reading an average reader can do in just 15 minutes a day for one year.

Books vary in length from 60,000 to 100,000 words. The average is about 75,000 words. In one year of average reading by an average reader for 15 minutes a

day, 20 books will be read. That's a lot of books. It is 4 times the number of books read by public-library borrowers in America. And yet it is easily possible.

One of the greatest of all modern physicians was Sir William Osler. He taught at The Johns Hopkins Medical School. He finished his teaching days at Oxford University. Many of the outstanding physicians today were his students. Nearly all of the practicing doctors of today were brought up on his medical textbooks. Among his many remarkable contributions to medicine are his unpublished notes on how people die.

His greatness is attributed by his biographers and critics not alone to his profound medical knowledge and insight but to his broad general education, for he was a very cultured man. He was interested in what men have done and thought throughout the ages. And he knew that the only way to find out what the best experiences of the race had been was to read what people had written. But Osler's problem was the same as everyone else's, only more so. He was a busy physician, a teacher of physicians, and a medical-research specialist. There was no time in a 24-hour day that did not rightly belong to one of these three occupations, except the few hours for sleep, meals, and bodily functions.

Osler arrived at his solution early. He would read the last 15 minutes before he went to sleep. If bedtime was set for 11:00 P.M., he read from 11:00 to 11:15. If research kept him up to 2:00 A.M., he read from 2:00 to 2:15. Over a very long lifetime, Osler never broke the rule once he had established it. We have evidence that after a while he simply could not fall asleep until he had done his 15 minutes of reading.

In his lifetime, Osler read a significant library of books. Just do a mental calculation for half a century of 15-minute reading periods daily and see how many books you get. Consider what a range of interests and variety of subjects are possible in one lifetime. Osler read widely outside of his medical specialty. Indeed, he developed from this 15-minute reading habit an avocational specialty to balance his vocational specialization. Among scholars in English literature, Osler is known as an authority on Sir Thomas Browne, seventeenth century English prose master, and Osler's library on Sir Thomas is considered one of the best anywhere. A great many more things could be said about Osler's contribution to medical research, to the reform of medical teaching, to the introduction of modern clinical methods. But the important point for us here is that he answered supremely well for himself the question all of us who live a busy life must answer: How can I find time to read?

The answer may not be the last 15 minutes before we go to sleep. It may be 15 minutes a day at some other time. In the busiest of calendars there is probably more than one 15-minute period tucked away somewhere still unassigned. I've seen some curious solutions to the problem of finding time for reading.

During army days in the last year of the war I discovered a Pfc. in my squadron who seemed unusually well-read. I found in his 201 file a remarkable civilian and military biography. His four years of service included two overseas, all meritorious but without heroics. Had all of his recommendations for promotion gone through he would have had not only his commission, but probably the rank of captain. But here he was, still a private first-class — because, despite the military emphasis on education, efficiency, loyalty, and all other criteria for determining promotion, accident plays a most important part. Every time this Pfc. had been recommended for promotion, except once, he had been transferred, or come up against a table of organization limitations, or a new change in regulations, or a superior officer who had filled out the forms incorrectly or forgotten them in his third right-hand drawer. And so he had remained a Pfc., and had taken his reward in reading. The amount he did in the army was prodigious.

I was curious about his method. And one day, before I asked him, I found a partial answer. Every day the enlisted men put in an hour of drill and formations. During that time at least one fairly long period of rest was called. Imagine my surprise on my first visit to the drill field when, at the command "rest!" I saw one man in the whole long line pull out a paper pocket book and begin to read, standing up.

When I talked with him, I found that from boyhood he had developed the habit of carrying a little book in his pocket from which he read every minute he was not doing something else. He found a book especially useful and relaxing during the periods of waiting which all of us experience daily — waiting for meals, buses, doctors, hair cuts, telephone calls, dates, performances to begin, or something to happen. There were his 15 minutes a day, or more. There were his 20 books a year — 1,000 in a lifetime.

No universal formula can be prescribed. Each of us must find our own 15-minute period each day. It is better if it is regular. Then all additional spare minutes are so many bonuses. And, believe me, the opportunity for reading bonuses are many and unexpected. Last night an uninvited guest turned up to make five for bridge. I had the kind of paper book at hand to make being the fifth at bridge a joy.

The only requirement is the will to read. With it you can find the 15 minutes no matter how busy the day. And you must have the book at hand. Not even seconds of your 15 minutes must be wasted starting to read. Set that book out in advance. Put it into your pocket when you dress. Put another book beside your bed. Place one in your bathroom. Keep one near your dining table.

You can't escape reading 15 minutes a day, and that means you will read half a book a week, 2 books a month, 20 a year, and 1,000 or more in a reading lifetime. It's an easy way to become well read.

Number of words 1300
See page 215 for Questions

Reading Time in Seconds _____
See page 323 for Conversion Table

Some Uses of Biography

Royal Bank of Canada Monthly Letter

Finding time to read, knowing how to speed your reading, getting books into your bloodstream — those are but a few of the problems. Selecting the right books to read is still another problem. Why, for example, should you select some biographies?

In Oscar Wilde's play *A Woman of No Importance,* Lord Illingworth remarks: "The Book of Life begins with a man and a woman in a garden." To this, Mrs. Allonby replies: "It ends with Revelations." It is the wealth of interesting stories that come in between that make up biography.

Autobiographies and biographies are increasingly helpful as the complexities of life multiply. How men and women faced up to challenges boldly and either won triumphantly or went down gallantly is a story pertinent to statesmen, to people in the professions and in business.

Some may say that the practical concerns of people and the patterns of society have changed so radically that it is useless to read the story of a person written even twenty years ago. Yet the values, the principles and the practices that made life worth-while in the past have not really changed. Analyse any life-story and you will find it composed of ambition, learning, work, relations with people, and awareness of the rightness and wrongness of actions.

Books that tell about the lives of people are the most valuable on one's bookshelves. One famed bookman divided his big library into two parts — biography and "all the rest." He said that he had never read a biography from which he had not learned something.

How men and women planned their lives, faced up to difficulties, and attained success, gives us a yardstick by which to measure the progress of humanity, including ourselves.

SELF-IMPROVEMENT

Reading biography is not to be thought of as a sure-fire way to attain personal success, but the attentive reader will learn much about how people did jobs, won friends, and got ahead. As Emerson remarked: "In every man there is something wherein I may learn of him, and in that I am his pupil."

A biography shows the effectiveness of self-help, of patient purpose, of resolute working, and of integrity. In reading about the life of a person you see how problems arise, are sharpened, project themselves into crises and conflict, and how they are met by action.

Sometimes a young man will discover himself, his qualities and possibilities, in a biography just as Correggio felt within him the stirring of genius on contemplating the works of Michelangelo.

This sort of study is quite different from reading rules for behaviour and prescriptions for success in a text-book. Example is one of the most potent of instructors, and here, in biographies, are examples of how to put ideas across in business or politics, and how to so live as to be worthy of remembrance. Here you see the causes of people's victories and defeats, so that you can avoid the latter and imitate the former. Even if your achievement does not quite match theirs, it will at least have a touch of it.

Reading biography is not all that is needed by an aspiring person. One has to get busy doing things. A well-written biography does not picture its subject sitting around apathetically while life flows past. Theodore Roosevelt, who campaigned for "the strenuous life," would not allow photographers to snap their shutters while he had his hands in his pockets: he showed his vitality by gesturing with them as busily as a prize-fighter.

Even to people who do not expect to get utilitarian hints from the experiences of others, biography is an inspiring study. When we read the story of a life we learn that its subject was not born a professional this or that, or a skilled craftsman or astronaut. He was born a human being and worked at becoming what has made him famous.

People who have reached the peak of success in any enterprise have passed through discouragement and hard times, but they learned that there are few things a person cannot do if he is doggedly determined. In desperate situations they masked their doubts and made a display of confidence and serenity. They refused to call any try their last try.

Every success biography emphasizes that the prevalent "something for nothing" philosophy does not stand up under examination. Everything has a price and must be earned.

Biography also dispels the idea that there is no more creative work to be done, only copying, annotating and criticizing. Every life-story reveals something that its owner found new, something fresh. It would be ridiculous for an artist today to say "All that is left for me to do is to copy the nymphs and the madonnas of the old masters."

From *Royal Bank of Canada Monthly Letter,* Vol. 54, No. 8 (August 1973). Reprinted with permission from The Royal Bank of Canada.

PRACTICAL LESSONS

Biographies of men and women in all callings tell us how they sold goods or ideas, gained support for their plans, and earned friendships. Readers may learn their principles of salesmanship: that argument is not a selling device, that one should find out what people's wants are, that it is not by showing off their own importance but by giving other people a sense of importance that they turn opponents into supporters.

Benjamin Franklin was an accomplished salesman. Seeking to win the friendship of a man who had attacked him in a speech, Franklin wrote him a note expressing the desire to read a rare book of which the man was proud to be the possessor. The man sent it; Franklin wrote a note of appreciation; they became lifelong friends.

LaSalle, the noted French explorer, gained the good-will of hostile Indians by addressing them in their own language and using their style of oratory. Emil Ludwig said of Napoleon in the Italian campaign: "Half of what he achieves is achieved by the power of words." Sometimes the general told his ragged, hungry army about the good food and comfortable lodging they would find beyond the mountains: on other occasions he pictured his soldiers returning as heroes to their home towns.

These examples from biography show how leaders paid attention to the needs and desires of those whom they wished to influence.

Aspiring people are not ashamed to draw upon the experience, thoughts and work of others for inspiration, ideas and methods. Thoreau had been gone half a century when his doctrine of civil disobedience was applied by Mahatma Gandhi in India and South Africa. Shakespeare drew the material for his plays from many biographies. It was a translation of Plutarch's *Lives* that introduced him to the great gallery of Greeks and Romans.

SOME AUTOBIOGRAPHIES

Every piece of biographical writing, whether by the subject or some other writer, increases the reader's self-reliance by demonstrating what people can be and what they can do.

Some, like John Bunyan, have set down simply the battle of the emotions that tried their souls. Vicomte de Chateaubriand, one of the most important figures in the literary history of France, gives an account of his life and thought in *Memoirs from Beyond the Grave*. In *Out of My Life and Thought* Dr. Albert Schweitzer selects bits here and there from mind and life to illustrate the *why* of what happened.

Madame de Staël's *Memoirs* are amusing. Her portraits of persons are vivid and convincing. Yet, as she said in opening her story: "If I write the record of my life, it is not because it deserves attention, but in order to amuse myself by my recollections."

Benjamin Franklin's is the greatest autobiography in American literature. He was gifted by nature with a versatility of genius unexampled by any figure known to history, with the exception, perhaps, of Leonardo da Vinci.

Sir James M. Barrie, whose dramatic fantasy *Peter Pan* is universally adored, told a story in his Rectorial Address at St. Andrews University in 1922 — a story which stands as the greatest example of courageous autobiography. "It is a letter to me from Captain Scott of the Antarctic, and was written in the tent you know of, where it was found long afterwards with his body and those of some other very gallant gentlemen, his comrades. It begins: 'We are pegging out in a very comfortless spot. . . . We are in a desperate state — feet frozen, etc., no fuel, and a long way from food, but it would do your heart good to be in our tent, to hear our songs and our cheery conversation. . . . We are very near the end. . . . We did intend to finish ourselves when things proved like this, but we have decided to die naturally without . . .'."

FAME IS NOT ALL

Biography has been described as the literature of superiority, but a person can be superior in even humble life. In fact, there are some people who believe that you learn most about the state of society by studying the lives of the little, typical figures in it.

Some of the most interesting autobiographies are by people who are not great in an absolute sense but have a story to tell and tell it interestingly. And what better bequest could men or women leave to children than the plain story of their lives, their triumphs over adversity, how they picked themselves up after a knock-down, how they progressed from point to point in understanding, always striving toward something better, and how they rejoiced when they reached a new peak.

The person who reads biography will not become mentally bankrupt. To read and to learn from what he reads is a mark of intelligence.

We learn all we can from history and biography in order to profit by the accumulated wisdom of the race. We do not have to start our own lives from the ground, but from the shoulders of the people whose lives we read.

Number of words 1574
See page 217 for Questions

Reading Time in Seconds _____
See page 324 for Conversion Table

It's Not Too Late to Learn to Read

Chester C. Bennett

Meet Mike. As you get better acquainted, do his difficulties have a familiar ring? It's never too late to learn how to deal more effectively with these funny black marks that you are looking at. Start capitalizing immediately on the practical tips that follow.

Despite its title, this paper is not for the non-reader, the illiterate, or the five year old, to whom the fact that funny black marks on paper can be made to tell stories and sing and laugh and paint pictures is still a puzzling mystery. The intriguing problems of beginning reading instruction are left to others. This discussion is really intended for people who do not read efficiently — habitually slow readers.

To clarify the problem, take a look at Mike, a veteran . . . [who is] now back at college to resume his interrupted education. He's an intelligent lad. His study habits are pretty rusty, but then, he never was very facile with books — reading was always considerable of a chore, and eternally time-consuming. Economics class is dismissed — ten o'clock. A free hour until eleven o'clock "psych" class. He'd pledged himself to get in an hour's study this morning. A group of boys drift by. "Hi, Mike, let's go to Tony's and beat the gums over a coke." With unaccustomed determination, Mike hears himself saying, "Nope, gotta study." The gang drifts on. Mike's slightly unwilling feet set off in the other direction. "Maybe I should have gone to Tony's. Can't do any solid studying till the house gets quiet at night. Never get much out of an odd hour of reading. Oh well, give it another whirl today." He stops at the drug store for a pack of cigarettes, and the usual exchange of comment: "Good game Saturday. Really gave them a trimming." Two blocks later Mike is entering his room at 10:15. He takes off his jacket, hangs it in the closet, and crosses to the small bookcase. What to study? Economics? Not after that last dull lecture. History? Too far behind; have to set an evening aside and spend all night catching up. Psychology will do. Mostly separate experiments — good for reading a few pages at a time. Picking out his psychology text Mike settles back in his easy chair. "Where was I reading last? Something about optical illusions because I called Larry in to try them out and we ended up going to play pool." Mike riffles the pages to find the diagrams and examines them again. "Tricky things. Light's bad here. Better move the chair over by the window." Settled again, Mike turns to "Chapter 5 — Learning. Introduction. As

we have seen, the human organism responds to many stimuli . . ." Mike's hand dips into his pocket, "Where are those cigarettes? Oh yes, the jacket." He crosses to the closet for the pack, goes over to the desk for a match and lights up. Settled in the chair once more, he glances at his watch — 10:25. "This is getting nowhere fast." Page 163 again. "Chapter 5 — Learning. Introduction. As we have seen, the human organism . . . ." For a time, Mike reads. Words march past his eyes in slow procession. "An ingenious experiment by Bronson proved . . . ." "That's that redhead's name — Muriel Bronson — Wonder if she'd give me a tumble for the homecoming dance. Try the movies first — casual — won't cost so much if she's a sad sack. Reminds me, gotta wire Dad for another check. . . ." Ten minutes and three pages later, the psychology of learning intrudes again upon Mike's consciousness. And with it comes the familiar realization that he has looked at every single word on those three pages and hasn't the foggiest notion what it was all about. Another glance at his watch — 10:50. Better get back to class. He considers inserting a bookmark to show the eight pages he has "read," but decides he'll have to go over it again anyway. And with the passing thought that he probably missed a good bull session at Tony's, Mike sets off for the campus.

Mike hasn't learned to read. He's not only a slow reader; he's a discouraged reader — a hopeless reader. No wonder he goes on believing an odd hour of reading isn't worth settling down for. No wonder he heaves a sigh every time the campus bookstore sells him a thick volume with 600 pages of solid pictureless text. How many months will it take to crawl through this one? How much can I skip and still get by? Why does it take so many words to get a few ideas across? Many a Mike will graduate from college still convinced that reading a serious book is arduous, interminable, and pretty futile anyway because you don't get much out of it even with a second or third rereading.

To understand Mike's problem, let's go back to elementary school. The curriculum under which most of us learned to read provided a daily period of reading instruction throughout the first four grades. We stood before the class to read our stint aloud, or we reined in impatient eyes, "keeping the place" while a slower pupil stumbled through his stint. But always words had

Abridged version of paper presented at Pennsylvania State College Annual Reading Instruction Conference, August 1946, by permission of the author.

sounds, and the sound conveyed meaning, rather than the sight. Thus for four years we learned to read. But suddenly we were on our own. Fifth graders should read to learn — and silently — without further instruction. Improvement in our reading habits would follow from unguided practice as we read to master geography, history, literature. Buswell's 1921 study of "Fundamental Reading Habits" examined the outcome of this curriculum. Through the first four grades the average pupil steadily increased his reading rate, reduced both the number of fixations per line and the frequency of regressive movements and shortened his mean fixation time. After grade four, these progress curves showed marked deceleration in all respects. The average eighth grade pupil was reading only a little more skillfully than he did as he entered grade five. A good many pupils struggled on into high school and probably into adult life with fourth grade reading ability.

The difficulty is that many of them never quite achieved the transition from oral to true silent reading. They failed in varying degree, of course. There are the mumblers, who still must hear themselves recite in order to read. There are the soundless whisperers, who shape each word with silent lips. There's an interesting group who manage to inhibit movement, but find reading leaves them with throats dry and hoarse. Finally there are the pedestrian silent readers not quite emancipated from the compulsion to look at every word and feel its auditory form before they can move on to the next. Here in the twilight zone they are still reading the sound of words, still chained to the speed of speech, still oral readers at heart. These are the grown-up fourth grade readers.

And Mike is one of them. Let's analyze his bout with "learning." In 25 minutes of actual reading time, he covered eight pages — a not unusual cruising rate of 20 pages an hour. A typical psychology text will run about 360 words to the page. Devoting three minutes to a single page, Mike is averaging just two words a second, or 120 words a minute — a typical speaking rate. Assuming normal vision, a reader of very moderate efficiency will let his eyes fall upon a line of print and take in two or three words in a single fixation lasting about ¼ of a second. Efficient readers may double this recognition span and halve the fixation time. In all probability, Mike's first glance at a paragraph does register a couple of words in a quarter of a second. What are his eyes doing with the other three fourths of the second which he devotes to the reading of those two words? More to the point, what is his mind doing with that 75 percent of surplus time? For the speed limits in reading depend on the eyes rather than the reactive facility of the mind.

In the first quick fourth of a second Mike has probably seen and mentally registered the first three words to be read. So he begins a soundless recital. His eyes dance ahead, pick up the next two or three words,

notice a polysyllabic technical term coming up in the next line — while his sub-vocal pronouncing machinery is still working on those first few words. Back go his eyes to recapture the third word, now almost forgotten, and to add two or three more for the pronouncer to be working on. Then they are off again. A pattern of interword spaces cutting a diagonal white gash through eight or ten lines of type catches the vagrant eyes. A glance at the page number arouses that discouraged getting-nowhere-fast feeling — and again the eyes take up the job for a fleeting moment. Oh, his eyes are busy enough. But it's busy work — literally looking for something to do while they wait for the plodding pronunciation of words which they have long since reported. And the eye movement habits being reenforced are best suited to watching a butterfly in flight.

If Mike's eyes wander impatiently, what of his thinking machine, which responds with even more trigger-happy abandon? Even when the reading matter is interesting, it's like trying to keep his attention on the plot of a mystery movie shown in slow motion throughout. His active mind simply refuses to wait for the lagging parade of words. Associations beckon, the environment intrudes, and his thoughts are off to "Shoes and ships and sealing wax, and cabbages and kings." Shortly Mike has a well established habit of sounding off the words, patiently and systematically — while he thinks of things completely divorced. Mothers sometimes read aloud to their children that way — while they plan tomorrow's menu. Mike's eyes, working at about 20 percent efficiency, scarcely bring his mind enough intellectual fodder to bother with. It's not because he "can't concentrate," but because he won't twiddle his mental thumbs and wait, that he gets nothing out of the slow trickle of words.

But let's watch Mike on another occasion. Ten o'clock. Economics class is dismissed and again he pauses on the steps of Burton Hall, fancy free for the next hour. Harry comes down the walk. "Hi, Mike. All set for the Psych quiz today?" "Oh-oh! Forgot all about it. See you later." With purposeful strides Mike is on his way to his room. The quiz was to cover "learning" — two chapters — or was it three? "Never did get around to reading them, but the prof has been going over this learning business for a month now. Maybe I can tie a little of it together. One hour to go." At 10:05 Mike is entering his room, stripping off his jacket. He flings it across the easy chair, pulls the psychology text from the shelf and sits at his desk. A glance at the index tells him the chapter on Learning begins on page 163 and there's a chapter on "Practice and Retention" and another called "Generalization" which ends on page 258 — 95 pages in all. Mike lays his watch on the desk. It says 10:06. Twenty minutes to a chapter and he can still make class by 11:10. " 'Introduction' — skip it. That's the usual stuff about 'We have seen. . . . We shall see. . . .' Already know this is going to be about learning.

'Learning Defined' — better have that in mind. 'Thorndike's early formulation of the Laws of Learning.' Exercise, effect — remember them." Mike is turning pages. Paragraph headings, topic sentences stand out in bold relief. He looks at his watch — 10:20 — five more minnutes on this chapter — keep moving. And Mike does, fitting what he reads to what he already knows, skipping over the familiar, fixing the important in his mind, with a fraction of his attention on probable quiz questions and another fraction on his watch. At 10:57 Mike has to speed up for a very quick skimming of 12 remaining pages, and a glance back at four or five points he feels sure he should have in mind. At 11:05 he grabs his jacket and hurries off toward the campus.

Are my stories overdrawn? I think not, and I suggest further that attributing both incidents to the same person is not at all implausible. The second presupposes an intelligent student, but the first by no means implies a stupid one. Mike is simply an habitually inefficient reader, and he may well continue so, finding in the second experience no such measure of encouragement as he finds of discouragement in the first. As a matter of fact, he may not interpret the quiz preparation as real reading at all. He is likely to call it cramming, or scanning, or to borrow that expressive military term — briefing. He will admit that he can hit the high spots pretty rapidly upon occasion and under pressure, but a person can't fly the throttle wide open all the time. Perhaps he will suggest the time-worn fallacy that what's read so quickly is soon forgotten. He views the quiz preparation as an abnormal over-exertion — something of a stunt. Reading remains a tedious chore.

Suppose we grant that Mike's review was not a typical reading situation. The motivation was urgent and specific. He was looking for highlights and missing many details. He was filling the gaps in a partial knowledge already acquired from class lectures. But isn't that a fairly adequate interpretation of the reading task? It is probably unfortunate that our reading is not more often strongly motivated. As a usual thing the informational reader is adding to a more or less adequate knowledge of the subject, and expects to retain only the gist of an author's argument or a limited amount of new information. Reading to pass a quiz may introduce an artificial goal without making the process artificial.

Did Mike's burst of speed overtax his intellectual powers? Without indulging in a discussion of "mental fatigue," I think it reasonable to suppose that Mike's review session left him less exhausted — and better able to continue intellectual activity — than did his earlier struggle with eight pages. Moreover, I'm willing to predict that two months later on a final exam, without further review, Mike will have better retention of the chapters on learning than of other chapters which he plodded through word by word.

So it's not too late for these pedestrian readers to learn to read. They will need guidance and they will need a morale injection. For their attitude is typically one of discouragement despite the fact that their own experience may occasionally demonstrate the possibilities. But they can be helped, as reading clinics and remedial programs have amply proved. When reeducation is purposefully attempted, quick improvement is the rule and dramatic progress is not uncommon. The results suggest that if they knew how to proceed many of these fourth grade readers could gain materially from a program of self instruction. Without enlarging on all the detailed hints that could be suggested, I recommend to them four basic procedures:

First: *Time your reading.* I propose this as a starting point because it is the quickest, and easiest, way to produce tangible results. The mere fact of having a watch at one's elbow and being aware of the passage of time may result in increasing the reading rate by 25 to 50 percent, or even more for a slow but intelligent reader. And nothing will contribute more to his morale. Few people have any accurate notion of how fast, or, perhaps I should say, how slowly, they do read in terms of pages per hour or words per minute. Once you know your score, it is difficult to resist the sport of racing with yourself, stepping up the pace toward a faster and faster goal.

As a corollary to timing yourself, keep a reading diary. For each session of reading, note briefly the type of material and record the pages covered and the time actually spent in reading. Better still, from a spot count of words per line, estimate your reading rate in words per minute. It is fairly safe to guarantee a slow reader, who will take the trouble to keep such a diary, that his reading will speed up appreciably. And the usual outcome of faster reading is better comprehension.

The second suggestion is: *Budget your reading.* Whenever you sit down with a book, examine the material you intend to cover and decide, in advance, how much time you will give to it. You will have to know your reading rate to make accurate estimates, but your budgeting should be qualitative as well as quantitative. It will take you longer to cover 100 pages of Whitehead's *Process and Reality* than of Carnegie's *How to Win Friends and Influence People.* Some material should be read slowly — pondered and savored. Indeed, poetry and prose of unusual beauty must sometimes be read aloud for full appreciation. On the other hand a good deal of unimportant writing should be skimmed with the least possible expenditure of time, or avoided entirely. Reading rates for fiction vary a good deal depending upon the reader's taste, and the relative importance of plot or diction to his pleasure. Perhaps your speed will prove most consistent, and your budgeting easiest for run of the mill informational reading — editorials and essays, biography, popularized science and discussions of socio-political problems. This is the reading where efficiency counts, where time saved means wider reading and more informed citizenship. Make a habit of budgeting informational reading.

Third: *Read with a purpose.* The typical adult fourth grade reader glances at the title of a volume, turns to page 1 and dives without pausing to wonder whether he'll be in over his depth or strike his head on a shallow rocky bottom. The purposeful reader examines the table of contents, reads the preface and notes the stray bits of information about the author and his intentions to be found on title page, dedication, jacket, or advertising blurb. When he turns to page 1 he knows what he is looking for. His budgeting becomes qualitative as he undertakes, not just 400 pages of print, but 400 pages of pretty heavy philosophy, or of highly biased opinion, or of documented information or of good entertaining fun. He has decided in advance whether his reading will be thorough study or a quick once over, and he continues to make such decisions paragraph by paragraph, digesting the important and tasting the trivial. Since the mind is seldom fully occupied with merely logging what the eyes report, keep it busy cataloguing and organizing, relating what is read to past experiences, filing it systematically for future reference. Sketch the author's broad outline and read to fill it in. Don't wait for him to tell you what it was after you've collected a purse full of back-of-envelope notes. Fix your own destination. Don't let the words lead you around by the nose.

Finally: *Get acquainted with your eye behavior.* Some authors have said that the efficient reader is unaware of his eye movements. On the contrary, it is the fourth grade reader who gives his eyes free rein and lets them govern the reading process for him. The concert pianist, the true artist, does not forget his technique. He has simply learned to use it without becoming its slave. Not many of us have developed sufficient artistry in reading to expect our eyes to behave themselves without supervision. Like any other psycho-physical coordination — your mashie approach or your backhand drive — your eye movements require analysis and guided practice if you would maintain peak proficiency.

There is no short cut to artistry. A little effort will bring quick results for the very slow reader but refinement of skill at more proficient levels demands persistent effort. Stepping yourself up from 80 pages an hour to 90 is more difficult than increasing a 20 page rate to 30. But any gain in rate opens the doors to wider reading, more informed living, or time for other things. And oddly enough, it usually leads to better comprehension and retention of what's read. For the secret of concentration is keeping the mind busy. Doing all the odd jobs I've described at once; keeping track of the time, analyzing and cataloguing the contents, hurrying your eyes and making them behave; you will still carry more away from your reading than you will just reading and forgetting about the process. It's not too late to try it.

Number of words 3364
See page 219 for Questions

Reading Time in Seconds _____
See page 324 for Conversion Table

The Right to Read

David Dempsey

The present relationship between reading and economic survival deserves a close, careful scrutiny. From all evidence, the reading skills, abilities, and interests that you are now developing should be of special importance in your career planning. Exercise your right to read. Make your future more satisfying.

"Millions of Americans read so poorly that they can barely read at all." This statement by the National Reading Council . . . underscores one of the country's greatest social problems. An estimated three million adults are totally illiterate. Another twenty-five million job holders have "reading deficiencies . . . serious enough to deny them advancement." Five million young people are unable to read well enough to qualify for most types of employment. Eight million school children suffer from reading disorders requiring special remedies. The council speaks of a "reading disease" of epidemic proportions, an opinion buttressed by one authority, Dr. Samuel Sava, who argues "that a figure of 25 percent for functional illiteracy for the male population at large would not be far off the mark."

The startling thing about these figures is that not only do more Americans go to school than ever before but on the average they stay in school longer. Paradoxically, as the educational level of the country has risen, so has the rate of functional illiteracy. For this, one logically blames the schools; yet, the problem is not so simple. As American industry makes increasingly so-

From *Saturday Review,* April 17, 1971. Reprinted by permission of Saturday Review/World.

phisticated demands upon even its lowest paid workers, standards of "literacy" rise, too. Today, only about 15 percent of the jobs in the United States are "unskilled" (compared to 30 percent in 1945). By the end of the decade, it is predicted that this figure will drop to 5 percent. Under these conditions, literacy takes on a new meaning, and this year's slogan for National Library Week — "You've got a right to read" — assumes a special urgency. The right to be able to read is, today, a condition of economic, to say nothing of cultural, survival.

When the National Reading Council was organized, under the chairmanship of AT&T Vice President Walter W. Straley, no single government body had ever attempted to coordinate an attack on the "reading disease" in the sense that the National Institute of Health researches and seeks cures for physical ailments. One of the council's first acts was to commission Louis Harris & Associates to measure the "survival" literacy rate in the United States — that is, the percentage of Americans lacking the practical reading skills necessary to "survive" in this country.

The test used in the survey was the ability of the respondent to fill out application forms such as those used for Social Security, public assistance, Medicaid, and a driver's license. The findings were not too surprising. Functional illiteracy is highest for big-city dwellers and for rural inhabitants, with the latter group slightly worse off than the former in the ranges measured. Fewer people who live in small towns and cities had difficulty reading the forms. Suburban residents showed up best. Geographically, the South had the highest range of illiteracy, and people in the West showed the fewest reading problems.

Practical literacy decreases in direct proportion to income. Five percent of those who earn less than $5,000 a year missed more than 30 percent of the answers, but only 1 percent of those with an income of $15,000 or higher did that poorly. Illiteracy among white respondents is about half that of blacks. Even among members of the low-income group, the range for non-whites is much higher than that for whites. The youngest age group proved to be the most literate; the oldest (fifty and over) the most deficient. Between the sexes, women surpass men slightly in reading ability, although no one is quite sure why.

Until a few years ago, it was widely assumed that the reading difficulties of many children were caused by dyslexia, a disorder supposedly the result of MBD (minimal brain damage); but this theory could hardly explain why dyslexia should be more prevalent among poor children than among their more fortunate peers. Recently, a committee of medical and reading experts appointed by the Secretary of Health, Education and Welfare concluded that MBD is a small factor in the total problem, and that not more than 2 to 5 percent of the school-age population suffers from physiological disorders that make learning how to read difficult.

The explanation, rather, lies in the cultural disorder underlying the family background of the student, the poor nutrition (a child may lack the energy level to concentrate, although he may be inherently bright), the absence of physical and social amenities. Studies indicate that the best readers come from homes that have lots of appliances and lots of rooms, but not necessarily lots of books.

From this the logical, but erroneous, conclusion might be drawn that if we should simply fill up the homes of nonreaders with dish washers and turn on the hot water, the children would necessarily be turned on to print. This might help, but it would not solve the problem. Middle-class culture is as much a symptom of achievement as a reason for it. One appliance, however, that is specifically useful is television. Today, the right to read implies the right to watch TV. As Dr. Sava points out, television stimulates reading and "supplies conceptual background or comprehension and extends interests." But this gives rise to paradox. Although television may improve reading skills, it conditions the child to an electronic mode of communication so that the immediate benefit to books may prove to be a long-term loss.

Moreover, as the poverty child grows older, his limited access to books may choke off an interest in reading. Ghetto libraries are not always geared to ghetto needs. (To the poor, a library can be just another forbidding, middle-class institution.) The very act of teaching "literacy" can discourage a desire to read. Professor Philip Ennis, of Wesleyan University, points out that "The pressure to read for practical purposes can be so heavy and . . . onerous due to the training of 'how to read a page' in school that the use of print for other motives can be endangered."

It was with this in mind that the National Book Committee, the Ford Foundation, and the National Endowment for the Humanities combined forces to set up a Books Exposure project in Fall River, Massachusetts, three years ago. Carried out in five "culturally disadvantaged" elementary schools, this experiment in motivation emphasized reading at home as well as at school, and for pleasure rather than achievement.

Fall River proved to be a good choice; as a decaying textile city, it exhibited in microcosm most of the educational problems that attend the economic and social ills of the large metropolis. The school drop-out rate was high (33 percent in high school, an even higher percentage in junior high) and 25 percent of the school population was foreign-born, chiefly Portuguese. By and large, the children came from non-reading backgrounds. Previous efforts to improve their reading skills had been "costly and generally ineffective."

The research design in this project consisted of fifteen

experimental and fifteen control classrooms, at grade levels one through five. Some fifty-seven volunteers were recruited, most of them local adults. In the experimental groups, reading sessions were held once a week, during school hours. Children were allowed to take books home, and they were given four books a year, of their own choice, as gifts. They also wrote their own poems, book reports, and stories. Emphasis was on "surrounding children with stimulating adults who encourage them to read, . . . share their excitement about books, and give them books of their own to keep."

The control groups, by comparison, were supplied with books, which the students were allowed to borrow, but there were no volunteers, no reading sessions, no writing projects, and no gift books. The results, when measured against the experimental units, were dramatically lower in the development of "reading attitudes," although both groups showed improvement over previous performance. In sum, continued exposure to books created a desire to read for pleasure, and when this was reinforced by group reading, adult stimulation, and book ownership, the children for the first time tended to prefer reading to many other forms of activity, and to "become increasingly careful in their choices."

Books Exposure is now moving on for tryouts in Boston and Minneapolis. Among older children, similar success in turning non-readers into readers has been achieved in "crash programs" such as that carried out in the nearly all-black Marshall High School on Chicago's South Side. A few years ago, Principal Henry Springs set up educational (he doesn't call it remedial) reading classes for students who wanted to catch up. "We keep these reading labs open from eight o'clock in the morning until ten at night, and the students come in," Springs told a conference organized by the National Book Committee. "The students run the bookshop, and they sell the books [primarily black-oriented] as fast as we can purchase them. . . . Some of the youngsters can't read these books, but they carry them around all the time." It is not just a matter of chance that more than 50 percent of Marshall graduates now go on to college.

The National Reading Council hopes to enlist ten million volunteer tutors by 1976 to work with children who need help. A network of training centers will be set up across the country, model tutorial programs are to be conducted in various cities, and a public relations campaign will recruit volunteers and sell the idea to local communities, with the necessary funding to come from the Office of Education and other federal agencies.

"Tutoring breaks down the unproductive teacher-class relationship and, by definition, sets up a high productive arrangement of one-to-one where concern is paramount," the council declares. In tests to date, the most effective tutors have proved to be older children. "It has been shown that such programs upgrade the reading skills of not only the pupil but the tutor as well," the council adds.

Well and good, but where do we go from here? Fortunately, public libraries are beginning to take up the challenge of the ghetto in "outreach" programs directed at non-borrowers and (in many cases) non-readers. This is sometimes done by setting up neighborhood, or storefront, centers manned by community personnel. The Brooklyn Public Library's "3 Bs" project places small collections of paperbound books in bars, beauty salons, and barber shops. A few cities run free bus service for children in the district to get them into the library. The New Haven center ties in books with handicraft, art, music, and language clubs for young people. In some libraries, phonograph records provide background music for reading sessions, as well as enticement for the rock-happy young.

All of these programs have two things in common: They direct their primary efforts at poverty areas, and, hopefully, they extend the idea of literacy beyond the merely functional. Ultimately, for the millions of marginally literate in this country, reading must become its own reward. The right to read means more than knowing how to fill out a form.

Number of words 1820
See page 221 for Questions

Reading Time in Seconds _____
See page 324 for Conversion Table

You and the Knowledge Explosion

Alvin Toffler

Accelerating change — so says Alvin Toffler — is plunging us into future shock, with all its resulting bewilderment, frustration, and disorientation. Reading may well play its most vital role in helping us cope more effectively with such dizzying change. For the reader, the knowledge explosion provides a real challenge.

The rate at which man has been storing up useful knowledge about himself and the universe has been spiraling upward for 10,000 years. The rate took a sharp upward leap with the invention of writing, but even so it remained painfully slow over centuries of time. The next great leap forward in knowledge-acquisition did not occur until the invention of movable type in the fifteenth century by Gutenberg and others. Prior to 1500, by the most optimistic estimates, Europe was producing books at a rate of 1000 titles per year. This means, give or take a bit, that it would take a full century to produce a library of 100,000 titles. By 1950, four and a half centuries later, the rate had accelerated so sharply that Europe was producing 120,000 titles a year. What once took a century now took only ten months. By 1960, a single decade later, the rate had made another significant jump, so that a century's work could be completed in seven and a half months. And, by the mid-sixties, the output of books on a world scale, Europe included, approached the prodigious figure of 1000 titles per *day*.

One can hardly argue that every book is a net gain for the advancement of knowledge. Nevertheless, we find that the accelerative curve in book publication does, in fact, crudely parallel the rate at which man discovered new knowledge. For example, prior to Gutenberg only 11 chemical elements were known. Antimony, the 12th, was discovered at about the time he was working on his invention. It was fully 200 years since the 11th, arsenic, had been discovered. Had the same rate of discovery continued, we would by now have added only two or three additional elements to the periodic table since Gutenberg. Instead, in the 450 years after his time, some seventy additional elements were discovered. And since 1900 we have been isolating the remaining elements not at a rate of one every two centuries, but of one every three years.

Furthermore, there is reason to believe that the rate is still rising sharply. Today, for example, the number of scientific journals and articles is doubling, like industrial production in the advanced countries, about every fifteen years, and according to biochemist Philip Siekevitz, "what has been learned in the last three decades about the nature of living beings dwarfs in extent of knowledge any comparable period of scientific discovery in the history of mankind." Today the United States government alone generates 100,000 reports each year, plus 450,000 articles, books and papers. On a worldwide basis, scientific and technical literature mounts at a rate of some 60,000,000 pages a year.

The computer burst upon the scene around 1950. With its unprecedented power for analysis and dissemination of extremely varied kinds of data in unbelievable quantities and at mind-staggering speeds, it has become a major force behind the latest acceleration in knowledge acquisition. Combined with other increasingly powerful analytical tools for observing the invisible universe around us, it has raised the rate of knowledge acquisition to dumbfounding speeds.

Francis Bacon told us that "Knowledge . . . is power." This can now be translated into contemporary terms. In our social setting, "Knowledge is change." . . . In the United States today the median time spent by adults reading newspapers is fifty-two minutes per day. The same person who commits nearly an hour to newspapers also spends time reading magazines, books, signs, billboards, recipes, instructions, labels on cans, advertising on the back of breakfast food boxes, etc. Surrounded by print, he "ingests" between 10,000 and 20,000 edited words per day of the several times that many to which he is exposed. The same person also probably spends an hour and a quarter per day listening to the radio — more if he owns an FM receiver. If he listens to news, commercials, commentary or other such programs, he will, during this period, hear about 11,000 preprocessed words. He also spends several hours watching television — add another 10,000 words or so, plus a sequence of carefully arranged, highly purposive visuals.

Nothing, indeed, is quite so purposive as advertising, and today the average American adult is assaulted by a minimum of 560 advertising messages each day. Of the 560 to which he is exposed, however, he only notices seventy-six. In effect, he blocks out 484 advertising messages a day to preserve his attention for other matters.

All this represents the press of engineered messages against his senses. And the pressure is rising. In an effort to transmit even richer image-producing messages at an even faster rate, communications people, artists and others consciously work to make each instant of exposure to the mass media carry a heavier informational and emotional freight.

Thus we see the widespread and increasing use of symbolism for compacting information. Today advertising men, in a deliberate attempt to cram more messages into the individual's mind within a given moment of time, make increasing use of the symbolic techniques of the arts. Consider the "tiger" that is allegedly put in one's tank. Here a single word transmits to the audience a distinct visual image that has been associated since childhood with power, speed, and force. The pages of advertising trade magazines like *Printer's Ink* are filled with sophisticated technical articles about the use of verbal and visual symbolism to accelerate image-flow. Indeed, today many artists might learn new image-accelerating techniques from the advertising men.

If the ad men, who must pay for each split second of time on radio or television, and who fight for the reader's fleeting attention in magazines and newspapers, are busy trying to communicate maximum imagery in minimum time, there is evidence, too, that at least some members of the public want to increase the rate at which they can receive messages and process images. This explains the phenomenal success of speed-reading courses among college students, business executives, politicians and others. One leading speed-reading school claims it can increase almost anyone's input speed three times, and some readers report the ability to read literally tens

of thousands of words per minute — a claim roundly disputed by many reading experts. Whether or not such speeds are possible, the clear fact is that the rate of communication is accelerating. Busy people wage a desperate battle each day to plow through as much information as possible. Speed-reading presumably helps them do this.

The impulse toward acceleration in communications is, however, by no means limited to advertising or to the printed word. A desire to maximize message content in minimum time explains, for example, the experiments conducted by psychologists at the American Institutes for Research who played taped lectures at faster than normal speeds and then tested the comprehension of listeners. Their purpose: to discover whether students would learn more if lecturers talked faster.

Even in music the same accelerative thrust is increasingly evident. A conference of composers and computer specialists held in San Francisco not long ago was informed that for several centuries music has been undergoing "an increase in the amount of auditory information transmitted during a given interval of time," and there is evidence also that musicians today play the music of Mozart, Bach and Haydn at a faster tempo than that at which the same music was performed at the time it was composed. We are getting Mozart on the run.

Number of words 1220
See page 223 for Questions

Reading Time in Seconds _____
See page 324 for Conversion Table

You Can't Get Ahead Today Unless You Read

George Gallup

"When I get a little money, I buy books; and if any is left, I buy food and clothes."
What an unusual priority! But — what an unusual man! Reading must have contributed its share, as it can still do today, according to George Gallup.

With knowledge in all fields expanding at a remarkable rate, and with competition growing keener for top positions in the business and professional world, the importance of reading must be carefully reassessed.

The cultural value of reading is well established. Likewise, the pleasures of reading have been widely extolled. These will not, therefore, be the chief concern of this article, but rather the very practical reasons why young and old should spend more time reading.

Fortunately, or unfortunately, competition starts at

an early age in our highly competitive society. There was a time in America when the accepted formula for success was hard work. Today the formula calls for a college education. This new factor is so widely recognized that nearly seven of every ten parents throughout the country want their children to go to college. And at least half of all high-school seniors have definite plans to continue their education. During the next few years this proportion is likely to increase, just as it has during the last two decades.

The desire for a college education is most laudable. The only problem is how to expand college facilities and teaching staffs to take care of the onrush of millions of high-school graduates.

From the *Ladies Home Journal*, August 1960. Reprinted by permission of the author.

The simple truth, which every parent should recognize, is that our colleges and universities will not be able to take care of all those students who are planning to go to college and that a rigorous screening process will be employed to sort out the students who are best prepared.

Already the institutions in the country with the highest academic standards are carefully selecting their students, and in some instances accepting only one of every five applicants. Since only the better-qualified students tend to apply to these colleges, parents can gain some idea of how difficult it is for their sons and daughters to obtain admittance to one of these top institutions.

Even in the universities where by law, or by policy, all graduates of accredited secondary schools are permitted to enter the freshman class, the struggle to stay in for the full four years and to emerge with a college degree has become a very tough one.

Time was when a student who demonstrated a moderate interest in his work and who spent a reasonable amount of time in study could be fairly certain of getting a bachelor-of-arts degree. But those happy-go-lucky days are gone forever. College administrators do not feel justified in providing classroom and dormitory space to laggards. There are too many young men and women knocking at the door — students who are eager to make full use of this educational opportunity.

So the problem does not end with gaining admittance to a college or university. To keep one's grades at a high enough level to stay in college and to qualify for a degree requires a high order of scholastic ability.

What has this to do with reading?

A well-established fact is that students who possess verbal facility tend to score the highest on college-entrance examinations. And verbal facility is gained almost entirely through extensive reading.

College students today complain loudly about the great amount of supplementary reading assigned them by their professors. The fast readers cover the ground easily; the slow ones just don't have the necessary time. The fast readers quite obviously get higher marks on these assignments. The slow readers stand a good chance of being flunked out.

Important to many parents who haven't the financial resources to provide a college education for their children is the opportunity to win scholarships. The cost of a college education ranges generally between $6000 and $10,000. And if present trends continue, the cost may well be 50 percent higher than this ten years from now.

The Government has instituted a lending program, and most colleges make some provision for helping needy students through loans. Even with this help, many also require scholarships. And scholarships, with rare exceptions, have to be placed on a strictly competitive basis.

Students who pass scholastic-achievement tests with the highest scores have a great advantage. Invariably the students who win scholarships are the ones who have read most in their younger days.

Many of the best professional colleges, whether they be law, medicine or engineering, now require students to have had two or more years of liberal-arts courses as a prerequisite for admittance. Some, indeed, are including courses in the humanities in their professional curricula. Verbal skills are essential if the student wishes to pass these courses.

Why is so much emphasis placed on verbal facility? One reason is that *words are the tools of thought.* Abstract thinking is carried on by word concepts. The more extensive, the more precise one's vocabulary, the more exact one's thinking.

Undoubtedly this explains why there is such a high correlation between the results of a vocabulary and intelligence or "I.Q." test. Often a simple vocabulary test can be substituted for an intelligence test when circumstances make it impossible to administer a long test.

A simple vocabulary test can also reveal to a surprising extent one's educational attainment. This statement, of course, applies to the typical person, and not to that rare individual who without benefit of college education has managed to do a great deal of reading and who has, consequently, given himself the equivalent of a college education.

To see for yourself the high degree of relationship between educational attainment and vocabulary, try out the list of words given below.

These words have been carefully selected from general-magazine articles and from newspaper editorials. They are all useful words; not one can be properly described as a "trick" word.

Go over the list carefully and check the words that you think you know. Then look up the doubtful ones in the dictionary to be sure you are right before you credit yourself.

Here is the list:

elite	plebeian	enervate
obese	inane	laconic
ostracize	sagacious	nepotism
nostalgia	plebiscite	soporific
omnipotent	surfeit	recondite
avocation	banal	panegyric

If you are a high-school graduate you should know the correct meaning of two of these words. If you attended college, but left before graduation, you should be able to define five of these words. And if you are a college graduate, you should know eight of these words to equal the college average.

When this test was given to a national sample of high-school graduates it was found that one in every three could not define a single word correctly! And indicative of the lessened attention given to reading today, the most recent graduates tested had the lowest scores of all. On the average they knew only one word in the list, and fully half of those tested were unable to define correctly a single word!

Many parents are concerned about the lack of interest in reading displayed by their children. But they have found no easy way to induce these youngsters to read more. Only thirty years ago reading was one of the chief sources of entertainment — but that was before radio and television became so widely available.

Part of the blame for today's situation must be placed on parents. In far too many homes there is a tendency for the parents to urge young Johnny or Mary to "Run off to your room and read a good book" while papa and mamma sit glued to the TV set looking at an exciting Western or mystery.

If mothers and fathers have little time to give to reading — whether it be newspapers, magazines or books — they can be absolutely certain that their example will have a powerful impact on their children.

There is mounting evidence of a decline in reading interest in America, especially on the part of high-school and college graduates. In fact, some studies have brought to light the cases of college graduates who have not read a single book in at least a year. And in one survey it was found that more than half of those who were graduated from high school had not read a book during the previous twelve months.

It is a matter of national shame that new houses are being built without any provision for books. This lack of concern for a home library would have shocked earlier generations who prided themselves on the number and quality of books available in their own homes.

Each generation, of course, has its own special likes and dislikes. Books which were exciting to parents and to their parents can be frightfully dull to young people today — a fact which should be kept in mind in trying to induce the upcoming generation to spend more time reading.

Too often the reading lists recommended by our public schools include books which are boring and unpalatable to present-day students. Requiring children to read these books is self-defeating. Often the result of forcing a child to read a book for which he is not properly prepared or psychologically attuned is to develop in him a distaste for all books.

Reading is a habit and parents should not be too much concerned as to whether critics or authorities have recommended a given book. The prime objective is to get young people to read, and obviously it is easier to get them to read what they like than to get them to read what they don't like. In the latter case it will be only a short time until they read nothing at all.

For this reason, I believe that teachers, parents and school librarians should co-operate in making up book lists, and these lists should be constantly revised. Books which students like, and books which they dislike, should be carefully identified. Equipped with this information,

librarians can be reasonably certain that the book which they put into the hands of a student is one which he will enjoy, and having read it, he will be back next week for another book.

I would make it a regular order of business in parent-teachers meetings to discuss the success which those parents present are having with this problem of reading in their own homes. This exchange of ideas could be most valuable in discovering interesting books and the most effective measures for getting students to read them. And of equal importance is the regular reading of magazines and newspapers.

Many years ago I taught a course in freshman English at the University of Iowa. My students, I discovered, had read rather few books before they entered the university to start their college careers, a situation which is common throughout the country. The English Department at that time required these freshmen to read many books which were beyond their comprehension and appreciation. The result of this forced feeding was inevitable: literary indigestion. Most of these students, I am certain, came to think of "good" books as "dull" books, a fact which may account for the generally low interest in book reading displayed today by many of our college graduates.

I am certainly not opposed to "good" books. In fact, I am so desirous that such books be read in America that I do not want the interest in all books — both good and bad — killed by policies pursued for the right ends but by the wrong methods. The only certain way to get young people to spend more time reading is to make certain that the reading they do is both interesting and rewarding. The constant reader slowly but surely cultivates a taste for the "good" books.

A few years ago I enlisted the aid of teachers in some thirty high schools in various parts of the country in a study dealing with this problem. I suggested that they ask their students to list the most interesting and rewarding books they had ever read, and the age at which they had read each of these books. The results of this study were most revealing. Some books found on the recommended lists were mentioned, but most were books not on these standard lists. On the other hand, the books the students had liked best were not "cheap" or "trashy" books. They reflected the tastes and interests of a new generation brought up in entirely different circumstances from their elders, who had made up the lists.

Why all this fuss about reading? The answer has already been given. If students increase the amount of their reading of books, magazines, newspapers, then more of them will pass the college-board examinations, more will win scholarships, more will earn degrees.

Stated another way, persons who read more write better, speak better, think better. And it goes without saying that they know more. As a result of a knowledge of the past they can think better about the present and future.

Parents who despair of the quality of education their children are receiving can take new hope. It is in their province to do something about it. They need not reform the local school system, or move to a community which has a better one. All they have to do is find a way to get their own children to read a great deal more. The deficiencies of almost any school can be remedied by a carefully planned reading program.

If reading is all-important today for children, it is equally important for their parents. Reading is the one certain way to improve oneself. In a world which grows more complex, it is almost inconceivable that any person who wishes to keep himself well informed on matters vital to himself and his children and who wishes to improve his lot can achieve these goals without spending at least *two hours each day in reading.*

Some years ago I seriously considered starting what I called the hour-for-hour club. Persons who joined this organization would agree to spend one hour in serious reading or study for each hour they spent being entertained. I still think the idea is a good one. And certainly if this country wishes to keep ahead of Russia in the future, then it will have to spend as much time as the Russians do in reading and study. We are not so much smarter than the Russians that we can spend less time than they do in these pursuits and still manage to keep ahead.

One of the great mistakes we in America so often make is to think of education almost entirely in terms of formal or school education. This view is not held in most European countries where school education is likely to end at an early age but self-education continues for many years. We need always to remember that learning is a process which begins at birth and ends only with death. There is no better way to spend some of our leisure hours — which grow in number constantly — than to devote a regular part of them to the reading of newspapers, magazines and books.

And this is not too much to ask. What we forget is that there is great excitement in learning, excitement which sometimes gets lost in our modern-day schools. We must find ways of bringing this excitement back to the learning process. We must recapture the spirit of Erasmus, who said, "When I get a little money, I buy books; and if any is left, I buy food and clothes."

Number of words 2550
See page 225 for Questions

Reading Time in Seconds _____
See page 324 for Conversion Table

Section III: On Writing

SELECTION 29

About Writing Letters

Royal Bank of Canada Monthly Letter

What kind of writing are you most likely to do, now and for the rest of your life?
Not themes, exams and term papers! No, it's more likely to be letters — letters of
all kinds, business and personal. That's why this selection is particularly relevant.

We are so busy tending our time-saving devices that we can find little time for anything else. We are so snowed under by the news and views of other people that we find little chance to express our own ideas.

This is an invitation to escape for a while from subjection to things and people, and to pass around some ideas of your own. Writing letters is fun, it is useful, it is easy.

Every letter cannot be a masterpiece worthy of being put into a printed book, but every letter can be, at the very least, a good journeyman job suited to its purpose. Its only purpose is to meet the needs of the reader.

People who write letters do not aspire to the fame reserved almost wholly in these days for writers of fiction. But writers of letters convey more thoughts to more people in a week than the fiction writers do in a year. They move more people to action. They give more people pleasure. They conduct the nation's business. For them there is no Governor General's medal or Canada Council grant. They do have, however, the sense of service and the tonic of self-expression.

A well written letter does not attract notice to itself. It has three points of focus: the writer, the message, and the reader. All you need is to have something to say, to know to whom you are going to say it, and then to write in such a way as to tell your story in a pleasing manner. This applies to both private and business letters.

Many people who think with regret of their lack of skill in talking well find relief through writing letters. Samuel Johnson said: "No man is more foolish than Goldsmith when he has not a pen in his hand, or more wise when he has." Napoleon was uncouth as a speaker, but became master of a quick, strong and lucid style which placed him among the great letter writers.

BUSINESS LETTERS

As to business letters: writing is part of your job, so why not make it a pleasant job?

Your work offers as much chance to be original, to persuade, and to apply logic, as any form of writing.

Business writing must be designed to perform a service. It must have something to say that matters. It has an instant impact; it involves both you and your reader. It has no room for airy frills.

William H. Butterfield, fruitful author of business textbooks, says in the latest edition of *Common Sense in Letter Writing* that there are seven steps to take: (1) get all the facts; (2) say what you mean; (3) don't take half a day saying it; (4) write courteously; (5) focus your message on the reader; (6) make your message sound friendly and human; (7) remember the "tact" in "contact."

Written with these points in mind, your letter may be received as a stroke of genius, which is pleasing. But you will know that it is the product of thought and work.

So, know what you are writing about. Don't depend upon starting out "Dear Sir" in the hope that the greeting will inspire you. Your reader's trust in what you say will be won only when you make it evident that you know your subject.

"Most correspondents," said Lord Chesterfield, "like most every learned man, suppose that one knows more than one does, and therefore don't tell one half what they could, so one never knows so much as one should."

Ideally, a business letter takes nothing for granted, but is written so as to be clear to any reader. It is written to accomplish a definite purpose, to explain something, or to get from its reader a definite kind of action.

No business letter should give the idea that it was written down to the twelve-year-old mental level. Give your reader the civility of treating him as if he were a cut above average.

The great merit in business writing is to be clear, and this includes using language that fits the purpose. Recall as a warning the wrath of a Queen when her prime minister addressed her "as if she were a public meeting."

If you think a letter you have dictated is stodgy or not clear, call in your secretary and read it aloud to her. Does it flow freely? Has it the right tone for your reader and your purpose? Does it cover the points you wish to make without excess words?

You must concentrate on getting your facts, but if your mind hits upon a good "angle" while you are scanning a sheaf of statistics, make a note of it quickly.

From *Royal Bank of Canada Monthly Letter,* Vol. 49, No. 3 (March 1968). Reprinted with permission from The Royal Bank of Canada.

It will likely illuminate what you have to write about the figures.

There is no reason why a touch of grace should not show itself in business letters. Some of the most potent letters are those that do not have to be written at all. They are "thank you" notes, words of praise for a job well done, good wishes on business and private anniversaries, and on fête days. Some firms, knowing the virtue in letters, have told their people to look for a timely excuse to write, even when there is no routine business object to be served.

LETTERS ARE WORDS

Someone quotes the Chinese as saying "A picture is worth a thousand words." But in a thousand words you could include the Lord's Prayer, the Sermon on the Mount, the Hippocratic Oath, a sonnet by Shakespeare, and Magna Charta — and no picture on earth can take the place of these.

In private correspondence we use good talking words, but whether business or private our letters must be made up of words which convey to the reader what is in our minds.

Saucy and audacious language unfit for the business office may be just the thing to lighten the day for a friend, while words weighty with the massive thoughts of business would add nothing to family fellowship.

When dealing with a serious subject, keep in mind that words are, after all, only nearly-correct ways of saying what we think, and try to use the best word, not its second cousin who is better known to you. A book of synonyms will help in this choice.

You do not need to have a big stock of tall opaque words, each having a great number of syllables. French shares with English the most elaborate compound: in-com-pre-hen-s-ib-il-it-y, with its root "hen" and its eight

prefixes and suffixes — and it describes and illustrates what we must not have in our letters.

ABOUT BEING BRIEF

A belief common in our age is that anything can be improved by cutting, and that the shorter a letter is the better. This does not stand scrutiny. A condensed style such as some magazines use is far more difficult to follow intelligently than is the more relaxed style of newspapers.

Many short-cuts are self-defeating. They waste the reader's time. The only honest way to write shortly in letters is to choose words that are strong and sure-footed so as to carry the reader on his way toward comprehension.

Being brief does not mean being like a miser writing a telegram. To chop things down merely for the sake of shortness reminds us of the dreadful deeds of Procrustes. He was a bandit who tied his victims on a bed. If their length was greater than that of the bed, he cut short their limbs. It is, most of the time, more important to be courteous and clear, even if it takes more words, than to be brief.

When you are writing a business letter you can give it onward movement and pressure and make its purpose plain by leaving out all that has not a bearing upon your subject.

Keep in mind that most business letters are written to tell a reader something he wants to know, but not everything about the subject. A visitor to the Swiss pavilion at Expo asked an attendant the time, and was told how a watch is made.

When you finish a letter, stop. You are not a novelist, who must round things off in the last chapter, disposing of his characters neatly. Don't strive for a tuneful hearts and flowers closing. It will only put a hurdle between the real end of your message and your name.

Number of words 1390
See page 227 for Questions

Reading Time in Seconds _____
See page 324 for Conversion Table

SELECTION 30

The Most Unforgettable Character I've Met

Henry Schindall

"Mint new coins — your own coins." For a would-be writer that advice is as good today as it was back when Wilmer T. Stone stepped into a high school English class. Sometimes it takes an unforgettable character to make such insights come through.

I remember vividly that first English class in the last term of high school. We boys (there were no girls in

From *The Reader's Digest,* October 1949. Reprinted by permission of the author.

the school) were waiting expectantly for the new teacher to appear. Before long, through the door came a tall, unimpressive-looking man of about 40. He said shyly, "Good afternoon, gentlemen."

His voice had a surprising tone of respect, almost as

if he were addressing the Supreme Court instead of a group of youngsters. He wrote his name on the blackboard — Wilmer T. Stone — then sat on the front of his desk, drew one long leg up and grasped his bony knee.

"Gentlemen," he began, "we are here this semester — your last — to continue your study of English. I know we shall enjoy learning with — and from — one another. We are going to learn something about journalism and how to get out your weekly school paper. Most important, we are going to try to feel the joy of good literature. Maybe some of us will really get interested in reading and writing. Those who do, I venture to say, will lead far richer, fuller lives than they would otherwise."

He went on like that, speaking without condescension, voicing a welcome message of friendliness and understanding. An unexpected feeling of excitement stirred in me.

During the term that followed, his enthusiasm spread through us like a contagion. He would read one of Keats's poems, for instance, and then say musingly, "I wonder whether we can say that better. Let's see." Then we'd all chip in, and voices would grow high-pitched in the melee of thoughts and phrases. Soon would come a glow of wonderment as we began to discover that there *was* no better way of saying it. By such devices he led us to an appreciation of the beauty and perfection of language and literature.

There was little formality about our sessions, but he never had to discipline us. Since he treated us with unfailing courtesy, we couldn't very well do anything except return it; approached as adults, we couldn't show ourselves childish. Besides, we were much too interested and too anxious to participate in the discussions to have time for foolishness.

We would point things out to one another, each contributing an idea, a viewpoint. We examined the subject as a child studies a new toy, turning it over in our hands, peering underneath, feeling its shape and finding out what made it go.

"Don't be afraid to disagree with me," he used to say. "It shows you are thinking for yourselves, and that's what you are here for." Warming to such confidence, we felt we had to justify it by giving more than our best. And we did.

Mr. Stone abhorred sloppy speech and lazy writing. I remember a book review in which I wrote, "At the tender age of 17, he . . . ." Back came a sharp note: " 'Tender age' was a good phrase when first used, but now it's like a worn-out sock. Mint new coins — your own coins."

Mr. Stone gave us the greatest gift a teacher can bestow — an awakening of a passion for learning. He had a way of dangling before us part of a story, a literary character or idea, until we were curious and eager for more; then he would cut himself short and say, "But I suppose you have read so-and-so." When we shook our heads, he would write the title of a book on the blackboard, then turn to us. "There are some books like this one I almost wish I had never read. Many doors to pleasure are closed to me now, but they are all open for you!"

He was a great believer in wide reading outside class. "You know," he said once, "if I had to put all my advice into a single word, it would be: *browse.* In any library you will find awaiting you the best that has been thought and felt and said in all the ages. Taste it, sample it. Peek into many books, read a bit here and there, range widely. Then take home and read the books that speak to you, that are suited to your interests.

"How would you like to live in another century, or another country?" he went on. "Why not for a while live in France at the time of the French Revolution?" He paused and wrote on the blackboard: *Tale of Two Cities* — Dickens. "Or how would you like to take part in 14th-century battles?" He wrote: *The White Company* — Doyle. "Or live for a spell in the Roman Empire?" *Ben-Hur* — Wallace. He put the chalk down. "A man who reads lives many lives. A man who doesn't, walks this earth with a blindfold."

The end of the term came much too soon. The morning before graduation day the class suddenly and spontaneously decided to give Mr. Stone a literary send-off that afternoon — a good-bye party with poems and songs concocted for the occasion.

Bernie Stamm started a poem called "Farewell." We cudgeled our brains and each put in a line here and there. Then Herb Galen suggested a parody, and we went to work on Gilbert and Sullivan's "A Policeman's Lot Is Not a Happy One," changing it to "Poor Wilmer's Lot Is Not a Happy One." After we finished the verses Larry Hinds sang it in his premature baritone, and we howled in glee.

That afternoon when Mr. Stone walked slowly into Room 318 we made him take a seat in the first row. Do you remember those old-fashioned school desks that you had to inch into from the side, with a small seat and a slightly sloping top? Mr. Stone, a tall, big-boned man, sat with his gawky legs spread out into the aisles and waited to see what would happen.

One of the boys, sitting in the teacher's chair, started off with a speech; the rest of us were grouped around him. Mr. Stone sat tight-lipped, until toward the end when he slowly turned to the right and then to the left, looking at each of us in turn as if he wanted to register the picture on his mind.

When we got to the last chorus of the parody, we saw tears rolling down Mr. Stone's high cheekbones. He didn't brush them off but just blinked hard once or twice. We sang louder so that nobody would seem to be noticing. As we came to the end, every throat had a lump in it that made singing difficult.

Mr. Stone got up and pulled out a handkerchief and

blew his nose and wiped his face. "Boys," he began, and no one even noticed that he wasn't calling us "men" any more, "we're not very good, we Americans, at expressing sentiment. But I want to tell you you have given me something I shall never forget."

As we waited, hushed, he spoke again in the gentle musing voice of the natural-born teacher. "That is one of the secrets of life — giving; and maybe it is a fitting thought to leave you with. We are truly happy only when we give. The great writers we have been studying were great because they gave of themselves fully and honestly. We are big or small according to the size of our helping hand."

He stopped and shook hands with each of us. His parting words were: "Sometimes I think teaching is a heartbreaking way of making a living." Then as he glanced down the line and saw the boys looking at him reverently, he added with a wistful smile, "But I wouldn't give it up for all the world."

Part of Wilmer Stone, I know, stays in the hearts of all of us who once faced him across the desks of Room 318.

Number of words 1330
See page 229 for Questions

Reading Time in Seconds _____
See page 324 for Conversion Table

SELECTION 31

Don't Write Epistols

Gelett Burgess

Epistles are letters. You know that. But where in the dictionary do you find the word epistols? *If your epistles bore people to death, isn't that exactly what pistols do in a more lethal way? So — write epistles, not epistols.*

"Why don't you read your letter? You haven't even opened it yet! It's from Aunt Clara, isn't it?"

Haven't you, too, sometimes received letters which, at first sight of the handwriting on the envelope, made you sigh and put it down?

"Oh, I'll read it after I've finished the newspaper."

You know what it will be like. They're always the same, dull and flat, and the first page usually filled with excuses for not having written before. "Too busy." They remind you of Juliet's reply to her nurse — "The excuse thou dost make in this delay is longer than the tale thou dost excuse."

The Samoans have a single word which means: "A company is approaching which contains neither a beautiful woman nor a brave man." There should be a word to describe a tiresome, vapid letter from some one of whom you are genuinely fond — some one who would do anything for you — except write an interesting letter. We might call them epistols. They certainly bore you to death.

"Having wonderful time. Wish you were here." That is the classic type of the empty, fatuous letter. Mere generalities, no details. Such writers seem to view everything through the wrong end of the telescope. All is vague and insignificant and far away. Travel round the world, some people could, or witness the explosion of an atomic bomb, and all they could say about it is "Marvelous!" And there are others who can write entertainingly about a toothpick. In one of John Keats' letters he wrote:

The streets here are excessively maiden-ladylike. The door knockers have a staid, serious, nay, almost an awful quietness about them. I never saw so quiet a collection of lions' and rams' heads.

During the war the GI's testified, one and all, that what they wanted in letters from home were the little details of the household. How the cat upset the five-gallon can of milk all over the kitchen floor; how grandpa gave up smoking; and how that cheeky Lester gal is still running after Bob Hale.

Snapshots, that's what people want, in these intimate, friendly letters. It's the little things of life that are interesting. Dull letters are written by persons with no sense of humor because they take everything too seriously. For when you take things too seriously you fail to notice little things, people's quirks and inconsistencies which make life amusing. Perhaps the most solemn bore, if induced to notice and enjoy these laugh-provoking trivialities might in time become a fair humorist. Even elephants, you know, have been taught to dance.

"What in the world shall I write about to Laura?" You sit down at your desk and bite the end of your pen and gaze up at the ceiling. You fish out her long-neglected letter and read it over. It is as flat as yesterday's pancake. Yet when you first tore it open you read it with avidity. You enjoyed it all. That was the time,

Reprinted by permission of the author. Part of this selection came from the condensation in *The Reader's Digest*, "The Simple Art of Writing Letters," May 1948.

when you were in that elated mood, to have answered it. Laura seemed very near to you and your reply would have been warm and spontaneous. You should have written then, yes, but not necessarily to have mailed it. Better to leave it in the desk drawer and wait a little while. Then it will arrive perfumed with your original enthusiasm, and Laura will say, "Well, she can certainly write a good letter!"

But to sit down and try to write a sprightly letter in cold blood, so to speak, that's a hard thing to do. There are so many things you had intended to say, so many things have happened which, though you cudgel your brains, you have forgotten. And yet you simply have to get it off into the mail this very night. Well, here's one way to make it easy.

Letters can be rich and entertaining if you make notes of things, happenings and thoughts that occur to you during the day. Keep a reminder pad on your desk and jot down notes of those ideas while they're hot. Then, when the time comes for you to write your letter, look over your memoranda:

> Sunday, 12th. Myra called. Purple hat. Arthur asked her if she had made it herself. Men have no tact. M. said she bought it in New York. Women are liars. I said it was ducky. Hypocrite. Bobby said it was funny. Children are brutally honest.

> Tuesday, 14th. Art brought boss home to dinner. Of course everything went wrong. Cake burnt. Bobby saved the day. Cute. Boss delighted. A. expects a raise any day now.

And so on, a little every day or so, and there's material for your letter abounding with life. You'll really enjoy expanding those notes, and you will fulfill what George Saintsbury said — that a letter must have "bite."

Or, if you wish your letter to be still more vivid, why not, like Bobby with his home work, take a few minutes every evening and write down what you have done or thought, even if it's only a paragraph. Begin with the actual letter, "Dear Fred," and keep adding to it whenever you're in the mood, instead of doing it all at once.

A narrative letter like that is all right, of course, when writing to your family or to intimate friends, but mere trivialities of gossip aren't enough to make a really interesting letter. You must give a part of yourself or your report is a mere anecdote without color or depth. A mere happening needs a sauce of personality to make it tasteful. You must have a reaction to make it alive and kicking. You must go below the surface. You must show how you feel about things.

Lady Mary Montagu, one of the most nimble-witted and ironic ladies in England of the 18th century wrote refreshing letters that are readable today. They had plenty of salt and pepper in them. See how she gave her own personality to them:

"Bridget Noel," she once wrote to her sister, "is come out Lady Willington." So much is mere news of the day.

She adds, "to the encouragement and consolation of all the coquettes in town." That is a piece of her own thinking. "And they make haste to be as infamous as possible in order to make their fortunes." That's a dash of her sarcastic self, cruel perhaps, but flashing with vigor.

It's not so hard as you may think, this getting your real self into a letter. Each one of us is mentally richer than he suspects and has hidden in his subconsciousness more interesting thoughts and fancies than he ever utters or writes down. We are apt to feel that we ought to write of what is considered important and throw away pet ideas and whims. Stretch the dullest person out on a couch and have a psycho-analyst draw forth his "free association" thoughts and they'd find plenty of material for an absorbing letter.

So you, who complain that you can't write a good letter, talk to yourself in ink about things that you imagine couldn't possibly interest anyone else. Let yourself go. You may feel silly at first, but keep it up, and soon queer little doors will open in your mind and you will discover and be amazed to find how remarkable you are. Write what you think about while you're shaving or doing up your hair. In those unconsidered moments the mind disports its vagaries; it reveals hidden truths and tickles you with odd suggestions.

And why is it that long letters are usually tiresome? For the same reason that a continuous talker is usually a bore. They may be brilliant, they may be sweet, but do you relish a third dish of terrapin? An old lady, still a prime favorite wherever she goes, once gave this rule for popularity: "As soon as you've made a hit, make an exit."

They say (whoever "they" is) that the increasing use of the typewriter has made letter writing a lost art. I don't get it. Did the phonograph kill the art of conversation? You can be just as glib and quotable on a keyboard as with a quill pen. The main difference is that you can't make an "ei" look as if you might have written "ie." Any mistakes you make in grammar, spelling or taste are magnified ten times when in type. Still, if you're friendly with your typewriter, you can let yourself out with a freedom you don't get with a fountain pen. So long as you don't type a letter of condolence or felicitate a bride, the machine will improve your style. When you see in print what you have written you get a new objective view of yourself and learn to avoid dullness. Even Henry James used to type his correspondence. But the best part of it is that your letter is easily read. An illegible letter, too, is an epistol. It's about as pleasant as a radio set full of heavy static.

It is the love letter which is the letter of letters, the only one really worth getting. What counsel, then, to the amorous swain, the yearning maid? None, absolutely none. The love letter is not amenable either to advice or criticism. It is perfect — in the judgment of the receiver, if the receiver is truly in love. For do you think it was young Romeo's honied words and rhetorical adulation that kept Juliet lingering on the balcony, that night? Not at all; it was the fire in his eyes, the light in his face that held her, rapt. A letter of the most impassioned poetry, when read aloud in a court of law elicits only ribald laughter. Why? Because neither the judge, the jury, the auditors nor the hard-boiled reporters are ever aware that the true message of a love letter, the blood of its life, flows between the lines or is written in a sympathetic ink that only the lover can read.

But, whether correspondence is easy for you or difficult, whether you wire a business letter or a *billet doux,* there are some general faults that you must avoid, if you wish to please. I call them Letter Writing Awfuls.

Don't write about the weather. I may be mildly interested in the temperature here, but not at all where you are.

Don't use pale ink or an outworn typewriter ribbon. Any colored ink, red, green or violet, is subtly annoying as an expression of egoism.

Don't, if you're a woman writing to a casual acquaintance, forget to put (Miss) or (Mrs.) before your signature so that the reply can be properly addressed.

Don't address a friend as "My dear" Jane. It is considered more formal than "Dear," though nobody knows why.

Don't underline words unless absolutely necessary. Underlining is like too violent gesticulation in talking.

Don't, oh, please don't, put slang words in quotation marks. Pay your correspondent the compliment of believing that he will recognize slang when he sees it.

Don't interject parenthetical exclamations such as ("Ugh!") or ("Ha-ha!") in your letter. This is supposed to be jaunty, but it's like poking a chap in the ribs when you've told a joke.

Although I'd like to subscribe my own letters "Yours Awfully," or "Yours Occasionally," I suppose it's safer to address even a person you hate as "My dear," and sign yourself "Yours faithfully," even to a crook.

You may say you haven't time to write letters. But isn't this usually because you think you have to write a long, newsy letter, and it's too much of an effort? Well, then, try short ones.

I know of a man whose habit it is to dash off a brief letter while he is waiting for his wife to finish dressing for a party. Short letters can be fun, if they keep popping like corn, unimportant perhaps, but lively.

I have a friend who, when he comes across, say, a good dog story in the papers, cuts it out and sends it with a short message to a dog-lover of his acquaintance. To another he will send a clipping about her latest fad. Or perhaps a cartoon. He keeps his eyes open for items that will particularly interest his friends, always accompanying them with a cheerful note. He never spends more than a few minutes on each, but they are always received with pleasure.

Short letters can keep a friendship alive and sparking if they are sent often enough.

Number of words 2090
See page 231 for Questions

Reading Time in Seconds _____
See page 324 for Conversion Table

Use Note-Writing to Spark Creativity

Alex F. Osborn

Claude Bernard once wrote, "If I had to define life in a word, it would be: Life is creation." For you, writing notes may well provide the very spark needed to set your creative powers aflame. Note and record your ideas before they disappear.

Writing can do much to train imagination. Scientific tests rate "facility in writing" as a basic index of creative aptitude. Arnold Bennett insisted that "the exercise of writing is an indispensable part of any genuine effort towards mental efficiency."

We need not be "born" writers in order to write. Every author was once an amateur. Matthew Arnold, a plodding school inspector, suddenly found himself hailed as a man of letters. Anthony Hope was a barrister named Hawkins. Joseph Conrad sailed before the mast for 16 years before he discovered he was a novelist. Conan Doyle, a physician, created Sherlock Holmes as a hobby. A. J. Cronin was likewise a family doctor, and so was Oliver Wendell Holmes. Charles Lamb clerked in India House, and started writing to overcome his boredom. Stephen Leacock taught at McGill University for many years before he found that his quill could tickle us. Longfellow was a language teacher. Anthony Trollope was a postal inspector. Herman Melville was an obscure customs official for 20 years.

Recent surveys tell us that nearly 2,500,000 Ameri-

Reprinted by permission of Charles Scribner's Sons from *Applied Imagination* by Alex Osborn. Copyright © 1963 Charles Scribner's Sons.

cans are trying to write for money. Most of them will hope for too much too soon, and will fall by the wayside — stopped by discouragement. But many others will make out well over the long run, according to A. S. Burack, editor of *The Writer*. He estimates: "For every person who hits the jackpot in writing and achieves big money and fame, there are at least 30 or 40 who make comfortable incomes or supplement their earnings by writing a few hours a day."

Some highly successful authors still stick to their regular jobs. Ed Streeter, who wrote *Dere Mabel* and *The Father of the Bride,* early became a banker, and stayed on as vice president of a New York trust company long after his writing had won wide acclaim.

If we use our imagination, rejections need not cause dejection. For one thing, we can put ourselves in the shoes of the greatest authors and realize how they kept going under a barrage of turndowns. W. Somerset Maugham began writing when he was 18; but 10 years elapsed before he could sell enough to make his keep.

Even if we never try to write professionally, there are many forms of amateur effort on which to sharpen our creative wits. Even letter-writing can provide helpful training if we go at it right.

One of my young friends practices by writing his own gag lines for magazine cartoons and sometimes tops the caption chosen by the editors. Another tears a picture from a magazine and writes a short story around it. A woman who is easily irritated by radio commercials occasionally rewrites one the way she would like to hear it.

An industrial engineer who had never written "anything" attended a course in creativity at the University of Buffalo. His instructor, Robert Anderson, asked him to write a story for children. I saw the manuscript which Boyd Payne turned out. It's a tale about a chicken — a Cinderella story entitled "Chickendrella." The scene is Coop Town. The main characters are Flossie Feathers and Brewster Rooster, who live on Cockscomb Avenue. It's a story that would delight any child. It helps prove that nearly all of us have it in us to write — even though we have never written, and have never thought we could.

We can also exercise imagination through word-play. For example, synonym-hunting can be an exciting game, as proved by a mixed group of all ages who spent an evening thinking up ways of saying "superficial." We hit upon 27 synonyms other than those listed in our thesaurus. One of the graphic words we thought up was "horseback." A "horseback survey" certainly paints more of a picture than does a "cursory survey."

That kind of game also makes a good twosome. Two of my young associates set out jointly to think up synonyms for *acumen*. They knew that a professor and I had thought up 38; so they were bent on beating that mark. They won. In three hours (on a train) they listed 72 words, phrases and figures of speech meaning acumen — 34 more than Professor Arnold Verduin and I had been able to dream up in the hour we had spent on the same project.

Another good exercise is to create figures of speech. These can be as simple as those which a group of us thought up: "As superficial as a Bikini bathing suit" . . . "As superficial as a cat's bath." Or, they can include an ironic twist, as when Dorothy Parker likened superficiality to "running the gamut from a to b." In his book, *Teaching to Think,* Julius Boraas strongly recommended as a creative exercise any such effort to think up figures of speech.

An effective way to induce imaginative effort is to *make notes.* For the purpose of moving our minds, pencils can serve as crowbars. Note-taking helps in several ways. It empowers association, it stores rich fuel that otherwise would trickle out through our "forgettery"; but, above all, note-taking of itself induces a spirit of effort. It is amazing how few of us take advantage of this device. One week I went through six conferences in which, all told, about 100 men took part. Only three of them put down any notes.

Robert Updegraff wrote a book about William H. Johns whom he called *Obvious Adams.* Although Mr. Johns was never regarded as "brilliant," the ideas he laboriously brought to American business made his creative record shine. His secret weapons were pencils; and they were so important to him that he went to great ends to choose them. He even had some of them made to his personal specifications.

Then, too, Mr. Johns considered the usual memo book too hard to pull out and too cumbersome to use. Likewise, he regarded the usual 3 × 5 cards as not "reachable" enough. So he designed a form of his own, 8" long and only 2½" wide, made of cardboard stiff enough to stand up and almost stick out of his inside pocket.

My own habits of note-taking might easily mark me as a "nut." Even while listening to a sermon, I sometimes surreptitiously make notes. Sitting in the dark on a veranda, I have often pulled out my card and scribbled without seeing what I wrote. While playing golf, I carry no note cards, but, whenever I hear or think of something that might lead to an idea, I put it down on my score card. Once, when without a score card, I caught and saved an idea on the inside cover of a match folder.

Physiologist R. W. Gerard of the University of Chicago advocates making notes of ideas, whenever and however they come, and he cites this case: "Otto Loewi, recently awarded the Nobel Prize for proving that active chemicals are involved in the action of nerves, once told me the story of his discovery. His experiments on the control of a beating frog heart were giving puzzling results. He worried over these, slept fitfully and, lying wakeful one night, saw a wild possibility and the experiment which would test it. He scribbled some notes and slept peacefully till morning. The next day was agony — he could not read the scrawl nor recall the solution, though remembering that he had had it. That night was even worse until at three in the morning lightning flashed again. He took no chances this time, but went to the laboratory at once and started his experiment."

Doctor Harry Hepner, Professor of Psychology at Syracuse University, writing of illumination as "the appearance of a good idea seemingly from nowhere," expressed himself as strongly in favor of catching each gleam and caging it as it comes: "Failure to record the flash, or to follow it through, may entail a tragic inability to do so later," was his conclusion.

Brand Blanshard, Professor of Philosophy at Yale, urges: "Seize the intimations of the unconscious when they come. . . . One should keep a notebook always ready to record them."

Graham Wallas testified that many of his best ideas have come to him while in his bathtub, and that he felt

there was need for new creative tools in the form of waterproofed pencils and waterproofed notebooks.

Ralph Waldo Emerson put the case just as strongly: "Look sharply after your thoughts. They come unlooked for, like a new bird seen on your trees, and, if you turn to your usual task, disappear."

An ingenious method of memo-making is used by a New York lawyer. He always carries a pack of government postal cards, addressed to himself. Whenever an idea hits him — whether on the subway or in the bathroom — he jots it down on one of the cards and sticks it in the mail.

As an author, Edward Streeter likewise believes that illumination calls for recording. He puts it this way: "The stream of ideas flows continuously during all our waking hours, and along this stream priceless ideas are passing. The thing to do is to try to catch them as they go by. We should make a rough note of every idea just as soon as it occurs to us, regardless of where we are. Somehow or other the very doing of this seems to stimulate kindred ideas."

Number of words 1548
See page 233 for Questions

Reading Time in Seconds _____
See page 324 for Conversion Table

SELECTION 33

On Learning How to Write

Benjamin Franklin

The allusions may be obscure, the style antiquated — after all, Franklin wrote this over 200 years ago — but it's still clear and vigorous writing. And what Franklin says about learning to write has been proved by experience, for he did work — and write — his way to fame. Why not try his method yourself?

From a child I was fond of reading, and all the little money that came into my hands was ever laid out in books. Pleased with the Pilgrim's Progress, my first collection was of John Bunyan's works in separate little volumes. I afterward sold them to enable me to buy R. Burton's Historical Collections; they were small chapmen's books, and cheap, forty or fifty in all. My father's little library consisted chiefly of books in polemic divinity, most of which I read, and have since often regretted that, at a time when I had such a thirst for knowledge, more proper books had not fallen in my way, since it was now resolved I should not be a clergyman. Plutarch's *Lives* there was in which I read abundantly, and I still think that time spent to great advantage. There was also a book of De Foe's, called an *Essay on Projects,* and another of Dr. Mather's,

called *Essays to do Good,* which perhaps gave me a turn of thinking that had an influence on some of the principal future events of my life. . . .

And after some time an ingenious tradesman, Mr. Matthew Adams, who had a pretty collection of books, and who frequented our printing-house, took notice of me, invited me to his library, and very kindly lent me such books as I chose to read. I now took a fancy to poetry, and made some little pieces; my brother, thinking it might turn to account, encouraged me, and put me on composing occasional ballads. One was called *The Lighthouse Tragedy,* and contained an account of the drowning of Captain Worthilake, with his two daughters; the other was a sailor's song, on the taking of Teach (or Blackbeard), the pirate. They were wretched stuff, in the Grub Street ballad style; and when they were printed he sent me about the town to sell them. The first sold wonderfully, the event being recent, having made a great noise. This flattered my vanity;

From Franklin's *Autobiography and Other Writings.* Russel B. Nye, ed. Boston: Houghton Mifflin, 1958.

but my father discouraged me by ridiculing my performances, and telling me verse-makers were generally beggars. So I escaped being a poet, most probably a very bad one; but as prose writing has been of great use to me in the course of my life, and was a principal means of my advancement, I shall tell you how, in such a situation, I acquired what little ability I have in that way.

There was another bookish lad in the town, John Collins by name, with whom I was intimately acquainted. We sometimes disputed, and very fond we were of argument, and very desirous of confuting one another, which disputatious turn, by the way, is apt to become a very bad habit, making people often extremely disagreeable in company by the contradiction that is necessary to bring it into practice; and thence, besides souring and spoiling the conversation, is productive of disgusts and perhaps enmities where you may have occasion for friendship. I had caught it by reading my father's books of dispute about religion. Persons of good sense, I have since observed, seldom fall into it, except lawyers, university men, and men of all sorts that have been bred at Edinburgh. . . .

About this time I met with an odd volume of the *Spectator*. It was the third. I had never before seen any of them. I bought it, read it over and over, and was much delighted with it. I thought the writing excellent, and wished, if possible, to imitate it. With this view I took some of the papers, and making short hints of the sentiment in each sentence, laid them by a few days, and then, without looking at the book, tried to complete the papers again, by expressing each hinted sentiment at length, and as fully as it had been expressed before, in any suitable words that should come to hand. Then I compared my *Spectator* with the original, discovered some of my faults, and corrected them. But I found I wanted a stock of words, or a readiness in recollecting and using them, which I thought I should have acquired before that time if I had gone on making verses; since the continual occasion for words of the same import, but of different length, to suit the measure, or of different sound for the rhyme, would have laid me under a constant necessity of searching for variety, and also have tended to fix that variety in my mind, and make me master of it. Therefore I took some of the tales and turned them into verse; and, after a time, when I had pretty well forgotten the prose, turned them back again. I also sometimes jumbled my collections of hints into confusion, and after some weeks endeavored to reduce them into the best order, before I began to form the full sentences and complete the paper. This was to teach me method in the arrangement of thoughts. By comparing my work afterwards with the original, I discovered many faults and amended them; but I sometimes had the pleasure of fancying that, in certain particulars of small import, I had been lucky enough to improve the method or the language, and this encouraged me to think I might possibly in time come to be a tolerable English writer, of which I was extremely ambitious. My time for these exercises and for reading was at night, after work, or before it began in the morning, or on Sundays, when I contrived to be in the printing-house alone. . . .

Number of words 920
See page 235 for Questions

Reading Time in Seconds _____
See page 324 for Conversion Table

No Memos, Please!

Murray Teigh Bloom

In business how does one keep from being buried under the avalanche of paper? How did one chain store get rid of 26,000,000 forms, weighing 120 tons? Think of the writing needed to complete those forms — the pens, the pencils, and the typewriters used. Yes — communication needs more creative management.

The silliest thing has happened. Britain's most successful chain of stores, noted for its efficiency in record-keeping, began tossing records out the window. It decided that people were smarter than machines, that clerks could be trusted, that the public was basically honest. In one year it eliminated 26,000,000 forms (weighing 120 tons) with these results:

1. Prices, already among the nation's lowest, were cut 18 percent.
2. Wages, already above average, were upped considerably.
3. Sales, already good, zoomed.

American business (even the U. S. Air Force) has

From the *American Weekly*, December 11, 1960. Reprinted by permission of the author.

become vitally interested in this revolt against paper work, about which a British admirer wrote the *London Times:* "They have put a premium on the perceptive and adaptable instrument, the human brain. This would appear to be the greatest single technical advance in the last 50 years."

It all happened to Marks & Spencer, a 237-store chain that covers the British Isles. In 1961 these green-and-gold-fronted stores will sell about a half billion dollars' worth of clothing, baked goods and fresh fruit. About 7,000,000 customers go through the stores every week, a seventh of the total British population. The Marks & Spencer store near London's Marble Arch takes in more money for every foot of floor space than any other shop or store of any kind in the world.

The new Marks-ian revolution got started by accident in 1957. One winter Saturday Sir Simon Marks, 72, multimillionaire head of the firm, visited his Reading store, 35 miles west of London. On this busy Saturday Sir Simon found two salesgirls working overtime completing "catalogue cards" on goods the store carried. Sir Simon knew that a million of these cards were filled out and filed every year as a means of keeping track of the stock on hand. But for the first time he wondered why his stores needed these cards in the first place. Before long, he and his aides came up with a much easier and more direct method of keeping track of goods in each branch store, and out the window went a million catalogue cards.

Having gotten his first, heady taste of greatly saved labor and costs through elimination of needless paper, Sir Simon and his aides now began to think seriously of all the accumulated practices and systems they had been using out of custom and tradition.

"Tell me," Sir Simon said one day, "why do we have time clocks in our main offices and all our branch stores? None of our employes are paid on an hourly basis."

A director cleared his throat: "Why, to keep track of our employes, to make sure they put in a full day, of course."

The boss shook his head gently. "Don't you trust our supervisors? Don't they know who's putting in a good day's work and who isn't?"

In a week the hundreds of time clocks in the Marks & Spencer empire were sold. Punctuality actually improved and the firm was able to abolish a million time cards.

Now Sir Simon moved on to another delicate area in employer-employe relations in large stores — the stockroom. When he wondered out loud why the stockroom had to be kept guarded, a blunt director said: "Thefts by employes. It's only a tiny minority. But we have to protect ourselves against them."

"In short," Sir Simon replied, "because among our 28,000 employes we have a few who might pilfer, we have to act as if every one of them is a thief. That makes no sense at all."

Within a week every one of the hundreds of stockrooms were opened wide. When salesgirls needed an item, they simply went to the stockroom to get it; and they didn't even have to make out any withdrawal forms. Pilferage — politely called "inventory losses" in most stores — was no worse than before. And millions of forms were no longer necessary.

But the stockrooms kept challenging Sir Simon. He knew that piles of forms and charts and records were based on the floating stockroom supply. Every last pair of nylons, of men's undershirts, of children's dresses, had to be listed and recorded so that stores knew exactly how much to reorder, so that the head office buyer knew how much to purchase. The data was fed into punch-card machines which supplied all the necessary information at considerable cost.

Sir Simon conducted a little test. He asked several store managers to go into their stockrooms, take a casual look and give him their estimates of how much they had left of certain goods. The approximations were remarkably close to the actual counts. Then and there a policy of "sensible approximation" was born. Several more millions of forms were no longer necessary.

Sir Simon formed a committee of eight to examine the firm's total paper work from petty cash voucher to annual report. The 237 store managers were called to London in small groups to offer their ideas on what forms could be eliminated. As one of the committee men put it later: "We'd ask ourselves: if we didn't have this form would the whole business collapse?" Before the year was out Marks & Spencer was safely able to eliminate 26,000,000 forms, weighing 120 tons.

In London recently, the Marks & Spencer sales promotion director, J. S. Sopel, told me a little apologetically:

"I know this makes us sound as if we were paper-happy before the revolution but actually management experts considered us one of the most efficient organizations in Great Britain. You can imagine what the situation is in other, less efficient, firms."

From the start Sir Simon made it clear that no one would be fired as a result of the revolution, even though the staggering paper elimination made it possible to eliminate 8,000 jobs out of 28,000. Since most of its employes are women and many of them leave to get married or have children there is a natural turnover. Marks & Spencer simply stopped replacing those who left. Others were re-trained for more needed jobs within the organization.

Store managers noticed that salesgirls who now had completely free access to the stockrooms learned stock room procedure quickly. Not only did this enable them to run their own counters more efficiently — by knowing exactly what stock was available to customers — but it gave them a greater interest in their jobs. Heretofore, salesgirls sold and stock girls stocked, but there were periods during the day when the salesgirls were overwhelmed by customers and the stockroom girls had little or nothing to do, and vice versa. Did this make sense?

The old categories for sales and stockroom employes were abolished. Even clerical help pitched in behind the sales counter during rush periods. Everyone now became "General Staff" and was trained to be able to work in any part of the store. The savings and added responsibilities were soon reflected in wages, already above average, which were raised considerably. And prices, already among Britain's lowest, were cut 18 percent.

There used to be three luncheon shifts to accommodate employes in the M&S employe lunchrooms, meticulously clean places where the company subsidized tasty, inexpensive meals. A manager with a stop watch used to ring the lunch bell twice for each shift — first to warn the shift to get ready, then to have the shift clear out.

"Ridiculous," Sir Simon concluded one day after observing the procedure. "Why can't we assume that our employes know how long they can spend at luncheon?" Accordingly, the bells were discarded.

Now employes are teamed. Employe A doesn't go to lunch until the other half of the team, Employe B, returns. They can make their own arrangements as to which goes to eat first. In most of the larger stores the women employes can have their hair set in M&S beauty parlors while a luncheon tray is brought to them. "If they're willing to help us save time and money, why can't we do as much for them?" a store executive said.

The revolution was under way a few months when several M&S executives got the same thought simultaneously: the company's whole expensive armory of paper safeguards and controls was based on the assumption that unless carefully watched everything would go wrong. "That's stupid," one of them said. "About 99% of the time everything goes *right*. Why do we have to make expensive assumptions that everything will go wrong most of the time?"

They threw out thousands of copies of the 13 thick operation manuals, the company "bibles." These continually revised volumes covered every conceivable — and several inconceivable — eventualities. Instead managers were told to use their common sense and not worry about what Rule 167, Paragraph B, Subdivision IV said. As a result the company was able to stop printing 120,000 expensive pages every year and eliminated the need for a sizeable staff of editors and writers.

If the management could trust the staff to use common sense, why couldn't they equally trust their customers? The M&S stores stopped giving receipts to customers. Each store promptly refunds or exchanges unsatisfactory goods, no matter in which branch the merchandise was bought. And, of course, there are no forms to be filled out. (Returns did *not* increase.)

Another hallowed big business idea — buy standard supplies in large quantities and save a lot of money — underwent re-examination. In one branch store, M&S found a three-year supply of toilet paper, a two-year supply of floor cleaner. All the savings that resulted from bulk buying were being lost many times over by the dead use of valuable space.

Result, a new method — each manager could keep on hand a modest supply of cleaning and office supplies. If he ran short he could pick up what he needed in neighborhood stores.

In the United States, the Marks & Spencer revolution has been noted and studied by a new and growing American profession, the paperwork and records managers. One of the most experienced in this new field is Robert A. Shiff, head of the National Records Management Council. He told me that no American firm had yet achieved the incredible degree of paper elimination won by Marks & Spencer but that several firms were taking important steps in the right direction. For example, time clocks have been eliminated for all clerical employes at Procter & Gamble and the Chrysler Corporation. The Richfield Oil Company was able to get rid of two-fifths of all its records and cut down expenditures for new file cabinets from $20,000 to $5,000 a year. CBS was able to eliminate 15,000,000 pieces of filed paper.

"Most of our corporations need similar revolutions," Mr. Shiff told me. "The electronic machines in offices do not reduce or eliminate the basic paper work problem. Instead they are creating many more paper records that have to be read and filed, just as we are beginning to discover an actual shortage of filing clerks and stenographers all over the country.

"Today the U. S. is spending about $12 billion a year to maintain records. Obviously a lot of these records should never have been started, let alone maintained.

"The Marks & Spencer revolution has shown many American firms that it is time to question many traditional business practices concerning paper work and employes."

Number of words 1870
See page 237 for Questions

Reading Time in Seconds _____
See page 324 for Conversion Table

She Hates Gobbledygook

Peter Wyden

In all your expatiations, eschew polysyllabic verbal symbols. That may be the best of advice, but you can hardly be certain until you translate it into plain everyday English. Perhaps you and Mona Sheppard share a common hatred. If so, in all your communications, avoid big words.

The chances are you'll soon get one of Mona Sheppard's letters. It could come from almost any large Government department. The letter won't carry her name, but it will bear two of her trademarks: it won't be as stuffy as many Government communications and, as a taxpayer, you will pay less for its production.

A persuasive, fast-moving Government career woman, until recently Mona Sheppard was the boss of all letter-writing for the world's most prolific correspondent: Uncle Sam. For twenty years she waged an up-hill crusade for fewer, shorter, simpler Federal letters.

Sooner or later, almost everybody writes the Government — for information, help, or to offer an opinion. And since almost everybody expects an answer, official letter writers grind out communications at the rate of 139 per second during every workday for an annual total of more than a billion. Many of them are so long-winded, hard to understand or totally unnecessary that a Hoover Commission survey team recently estimated the Government could save $75,000,000 annually by becoming a more efficient correspondent.

The survey team, headed by Emmett J. Leahy, president of Leahy & Co., leading New York management consultants, was so impressed by Mona Sheppard's remarkable efforts in Government that Leahy hired her as a vice-president. Although much of her time is now devoted to streamlining letter writing for business and industry, she still does work for the Government under contract.

Two years ago, when Miss Sheppard was summoned to the Baltimore office of the Internal Revenue Service, there was a backlog of 50,000 unanswered letters. It cost 81 cents to answer each one of them.

When she was through, the backlog had melted down to 3,000, cost of writing a letter averaged 38 cents, and daily production per typist had climbed from 55 to 120 letters. Savings in Baltimore: $157,200 and 500,000 carbon copies yearly.

Savings expected when the same system is installed in tax offices throughout the country: $5,500,000, some 30,000,000 carbons, and the wear and tear on taxpayers who no longer need to wade through letters beginning:

"Reference is made to your income tax return, Form 1040 or 1040A, for the year 1972. The return was received in this office without the required Form(s) W-2 attached to substantiate your claim as to the amount(s) withheld by your employer(s) from your wages."

Mona changed this to read: "Your withholding statements, Form W-2, from the employers named below are missing from your Federal income tax return."

When Mona Sheppard wrote her 112-page manual for Veterans Administration correspondence she ordered that a scientific term for an affliction like *pes planus* be followed by its better-known label, flat feet. But she came too late to intercept this classic of gobbledygook (also known as federalese):

"The non-compensable evaluation heretofore assigned you for your service-connected disability is confirmed and continued."

The veteran who received this gem wrote his Congressman: "What the hell does this mean?" It developed that since the GI's condition had not changed, he was not entitled to compensation for his disability.

Miss Sheppard wanted to be a woman of letters even as a child on her father's Central Mills, Alabama, cotton plantation. She majored in creative writing at the University of Alabama and then made the rounds of New York literary agents with her short stories and poems. She sold some jingles for greeting cards and wound up as a correspondence clerk for the Treasury Department in Washington.

There, her letters cost her a promotion and nearly got her fired. The trouble was that they came to the point too fast; they failed to quote laws verbatim and at length; they addressed taxpayers directly, not as "claimants," "applicants" or "suppliers."

However, she continued to fight for simple, concise letters, and rose steadily in the world of Government letters until she was appointed Organization and Methods Examiner for the National Archives. As Government's top expert in correspondence management, she went from one Government agency to another to sell bureaucrats on her correspondence system.

The system was born in the '30s when Mona was still a letter writer herself. "I've known very few people who really write a good letter," she recalls. "So I thought: why don't we ready-make them?" World War II gave her the chance, as she was by then in charge of correspondence for the War Manpower Commission and manpower, including letter writers, was scarce.

Taxpayers disliked form letters, or so Government tradition ran. Miss Sheppard refused to believe it.

"Don't be peeved by a form letter," she told taxpayers. "Chances are the Government saved 50 cents or more by not typing it."

Her successes got around in letter-writing circles and after the war she was drafted by the Veterans Administration whose correspondence had ballooned from 38,000,000 to 63,000,000 letters yearly. Stacked to the ceilings were unanswered inquiries from 200,000 ex-soldiers wondering how to keep their GI life insurance going. Some 8,000 new letters poured in daily.

Mona immediately got out a notice to each veteran urging him to pay his premiums while the VA dug itself out. She then composed dozens of form letters, including her all-time best-seller which told a veteran how to convert a term insurance policy into another type.

Since her arrival, the agency saved $10,860,000 on its letters and today its respect for mail is a monument to her toil.

Miss Sheppard deplores the fact that in Government letters officials still rarely meet; they "hold a meeting." They don't have trouble; they "encounter difficulties." They don't give anything; they "furnish" it. And almost nothing ever ends; it "comes to an expiration."

Mona had no police powers to stamp out such verbiage. As an expert dispatched by the National Archives, where she worked since 1950, she could only persuade agencies to accept her ideas. The agencies themselves had to install them.

Wayne S. Grover, Archivist of the United States and Mona's former boss, says, "You'll never reform Government correspondence 100 percent, but it's so essential for economy and public relations to get out immediate letters in plain English that the Government people will buy it. I hope." And when they do, you can thank Mona Sheppard.

Number of words 1020
See page 239 for Questions

Reading Time in Seconds _____
See page 324 for Conversion Table

SELECTION 36

Can You Read What You Write?

Robert O'Brien

Think of the many English words ending in -ology, a Greek element meaning "the science, theory, or study of." In a list of such words, what about the word graphology? *Is it true, as that word suggests: show me your handwriting and I'll read your character?*

In Washington, D. C., a truck driver misread a carelessly formed "4" for a "7" in a handwritten order and pumped 385 gallons of fuel oil through a disconnected intake — into the basement of the wrong house. In Connecticut a housewife dashed off a note asking the milkman to leave three quarts of chocolate milk. Next morning, neatly stacked at the back door were eight cartons of cottage cheese. In a New England city, a man stepped up to a bank teller's window and shoved a note under the wicket. In bold scratchwork it said, "Wug I thiie a www cxzllmnhd!" The jittery teller kicked his alarm button, bells clanged, police converged on the bank and nabbed the man. They discovered that he was a respectable businessman with laryngitis. What the note said was, "May I have a new checkbook?"

Bad handwriting doesn't always have results this bizarre. Still, illegibility on a national scale piles up astonishing statistics. An estimated million letters wound up as "dead letters" in U. S. post offices last year because of undecipherable addresses. Of some 400,000 federal income-tax refunds delayed in the spring of 1958, most were held up because Internal Revenue personnel were unable to read the handwriting of the claimants.

The Handwriting Foundation, established by the nation's leading pen and pencil manufacturers to promote better handwriting, estimates that illegible penmanship costs U. S. businessmen approximately a million dollars *a week* in scrambled orders, lost time, missent deliveries, clerical mistakes and other forms of inefficiency. Automation in business offices by no means eliminates handwritten paper work. In a regional office of a large oil company, a card-punch operator misread a poorly penned numeral and fed the wrong rate into her machine. In a twinkling, 2000 incorrect invoices shot out the other end.

Most Americans used to be pretty good penmen. What has happened? For one thing, penmanship is no longer stressed in most schools. The "push-pull" drills

From *The Reader's Digest*, August 1959. Reprinted by permission of the author.

of the old writing methods have become almost as archaic as the McGuffey Reader and the hickory switch.

For example: In a small city in Pennsylvania, an elementary-school official told me that pupils from the first through sixth grades receive an average of only fifteen to twenty minutes a week of formal instruction in penmanship. After that, he said, the students are largely on their own.

But lack of sufficient training is not the only cause of poor handwriting. Until he reached college, a friend of mine wrote a commendable script. Under pressure of high-speed note taking, it broke up into a hieroglyphic shorthand.

A hotelman told me, "You can almost trace a man's career by his signature. When he starts out in life, it's clear and legible. The higher he climbs, the worse it gets." A graphologist, an expert who reads character from handwriting, offered this explanation: At the bottom of the ladder, the man is considerate, conscientious, hard-working, anxious to make a good impression — qualities reflected in his straightforward script. In the rough-and-tumble of competitive life, however, he has less time for such basic details. As a result, his writing becomes hasty.

"Handwriting," the expert went on, "reveals your character more than you may realize. Reputable graphologists are careful not to jump to conclusions, but there are a few safe generalizations. Regular, steady handwriting, for instance, usually indicates a person of strong will. A straggling hand suggests a moody, fickle person. If your letters are rounded, you are probably generous and sympathetic. If they are sharp and pointed, you're apt to be set in your ways, perhaps a little intolerant. If your writing tilts sharply to the left, you may be repressed and introverted; if it leans sharply to the right, you're likely to be an affectionate, outgoing person."

Handwriting improvement may even lead to self-improvement. Psychologists believe, for example, that if you make a conscious effort to be more considerate of others by writing more clearly, you may find yourself acting more courteously at home, in your job, on the highway. An aunt of mine wrote such a small, indistinct hand that I had a hard time deciphering her letters. Suddenly, though she still wrote small, I could read every word. She simply had the thoughtful idea of using a finer pen point and writing more distinctly. "Now," she writes, "I must keep a desk that lives up to my handwriting. It's never been tidier. For the first time in my life, I know where everything is!"

The rewards of readable handwriting are far from intangible. In a recent Handwriting Foundation survey of several hundred personnel directors, 88 percent regarded legible handwriting as an important factor in landing a job. Twenty-nine percent used it as a standard for promotion. The employment manager of a large department store put it in practical terms. He spread eight filled-in application forms across his desk. On all eight the penmanship was slipshod. "These applicants were turned down," he said. "Their illegible sales slips would create extra work for our accounting division, cause customer complaints, destroy good will and lose business."

Four years ago, Philadelphia businessmen complained so about the deplorable handwriting of the city's high-school graduates that school officials launched a drive for better penmanship. They came up with a new look in the alphabet, called the "Philadelphia Simplified Alphabet," and prepared manuals, wall charts and teaching guides.

Much of the trouble, the educators found, was caused by fancy capital letters, so they pruned all unnecessary and potentially misleading "scrollwork." They insisted on such things as this: that *t*'s contain *no* loop and that they be clearly crossed (to avoid confusion with *l*'s); that the loop of an *e* be clearly kept open; that great care be taken to distinguish between potentially look-alike numerals such as *4*'s, *7*'s and *9*'s; *3*'s and *8*'s; *6*'s and *0*'s. They insisted that a one-letter space be left between words, that all letters slant the same way, be uniform in size and look as though they rest on a straight line whether there are lines on the page or not.

Today 75 percent of Philadelphia's public-school pupils are learning the new handwriting method. And from the samples I've seen, they're doing it well.

After seeing the difference these changes made, I went to work on my own capitals, numerals and loops. With patience and practice, I trimmed out a dozen flowery kinks that had cluttered my handwriting for years. The result was a gratifying improvement in legibility, neatness and writing speed.

During the process, incidentally, I discovered that it's a mistake to try to revamp your handwriting all at once. Tackle a single letter at a time. When you've made its improved form an integral part of your style, start on another letter.

Remedial action has also been taken in the schools of New England. The New England School Development Council, with a membership of 150 school systems, appointed a Handwriting Committee which discovered that far too many elementary- and high-school pupils did not know how to sit properly, how to hold their pens or pencils, or how to tell what was wrong with the way they wrote. The committee drafted and distributed a teacher's guide, *Handwriting Today*, which has re-vitalized penmanship programs.

"Handwriting," says Lewis Mumford, "is an art open to any amateur, for the delight he gets from it himself and the further pleasure he gives to others." With a little care all of us can write more clearly, showing that we respect the written word and, above all, the reader.

A final word of advice: when you start your improvement program, tell your bank and credit-card companies what you're up to. My bank telephoned me a few days after I'd started to brush up *my* handwriting. "Better come in," the manager said. "I think we've got a

forgery." I drove down and looked at the check. It was my new signature! The only difference between it and the old one was that you could read it.

Number of words 1320
See page 241 for Questions

Reading Time in Seconds _____
See page 324 for Conversion Table

SELECTION 37

But, Please George, Write It in English!

Muriel Beadle

Ideas can be expressed in many different ways. You can write literary English, newspaper English, scientific English, or gobbledygook. A whole new field — technical communication — is opening up now to those seeking a challenging career. This selection suggests the central problem.

Once upon a time a long time ago, I managed to satisfy my full science requirement at Pomona College by taking a lecture course in chemistry. (That's right; no lab.) I got an A on my term paper, which had to do with the use of sulfur dioxide in preserving fruit. Thirty years later, I rediscovered the paper — in a beat-up carton which also contained a desiccated corsage — and I gave it to my husband to read. He nearly died laughing.

Much had happened during those thirty years. Such faint interest as I may have had in science had vanished under the pressures of the depression, the war, marriage, motherhood, widowhood, and the necessity of making regular payments on the mortgage. I'd racked up some experience in the advertising business and, by the 1950s, was a newspaper reporter.

The literary approach to these two specialties is, by the standards of scientific writing, somewhat imprecise. In retail advertising, before the Federal Trade Commission concerned itself with the proper labeling of furs, I had thought up as many aliases for rabbit as any other imaginative copywriter; and I had mastered the art of generalization.

As for the newspaper: It was a tabloid. My editor's credo was: "Keep it gutsy!" He pruned away all tendencies on my part to use polysyllables or the passive tense, taught me to build sentences from small, strong words and keep paragraphs short.

Then, in 1953, I married a scientist.

Talk about living in an ivory tower! George W. Beadle didn't know who Marilyn Monroe was. He'd never seen a horse race. And although he talked about zygotes with diploid sets of autosomes as if he were speaking English, he'd blink and look puzzled when I

said I'd had trouble telescoping eight graphs into one in time for the bulldog lockup.

We'll, we've both learned a lot.

George is a geneticist. Within this field of science, there has recently been an explosion of knowledge comparable in significance to Mendel's discoveries about inheritance in the nineteenth century. What has been learned is of great import to the whole of society.

But all you have to do to scare my generation out of its wits is to say "deoxyribonucleic acid." It's immaterial that our *children* understand what DNA is; insofar as we oldsters are concerned, familiarity with modern molecular biology is in the same class as a complicated income tax return. We leave it to the experts and hope for the best.

Unfortunately, the experts can't (or at least *shouldn't*) make decisions for all of us on the control of radioactive fallout or the right of people with inherited diseases to reproduce as freely as people without such diseases. Whether one race has an inherited superiority to another race is no longer a purely academic question, either.

In our kind of society, the formation of intelligent opinion about such matters isn't going to occur until ordinary citizens understand the new genetics much better than they do now. Which is why my husband so often used to make speeches on the subject to any group of nonscientists who were curious enough and concerned enough to try to understand it.

He developed great skill in the art of keeping people awake long enough to learn something of what's been happening in biology since they dissected a frog back in '48. For example, our Siamese cats often shared the platform with him. (Their pigmentation illustrates an important point about genetic control of body chemistry.) Audiences also found themselves participating in George's demonstrations. And he made much use of analogies drawn from everyday life.

From *Saturday Review*, April 3, 1965. Reprinted by permission of Saturday Review/World.

It was one of these analogies, in fact, that got me into my recent difficulties.

As George told it, there was once a housewife who made such good angel food cake that many people asked for her recipe. On one occasion when she wrote it out, however, she listed thirteen egg whites instead of the twelve egg whites she should have specified. The cook who followed that copy of the recipe got a cake so light and delicate that *her* recipe for angel food cake became the one that all the members of the Ladies' Guild requested. The twelve-egg cake thus became extinct and the thirteen-egg cake survived.

The original cook's mistake when copying the recipe, George pointed out, was a mutation; and the subsequent replacement of the twelve-egg cake by the thirteen-egg cake was a perfect example of evolution by natural selection. It may have been that some of the ladies in his audiences felt that it was also a perfect example of the foolishness of sharing your recipes with anyone; but, for whatever reason, they listened.

On the evening that George first used the angel food cake analogy, I was full of praise. Riding home afterwards, I said, "That cake idea was great. So is your comparison of DNA code to Morse code. And to describe transfer RNA as a postman delivering packages. . . . Say! I'll bet there would be a market for your lectures in written form. Books that are supposedly written for 'the intelligent layman' all seem to degenerate into scientific double-talk by the third chapter. Why don't you write a really simple one?"

Telling someone in academic life that he ought to write a book is like telling a pretty girl that she ought to be in the movies. They can't resist the idea. But in this case, I oversold it. George decided that *I* ought to do the writing. His theory was that if I understood the hydrogen bonding of nucleotides well enough to describe it, *anybody* would understand it. He'd determine the content and provide the outline, of course; I'd have to do little more than substitute language for the sections where, on the speaker's platform, he waves his arms around. . . .

That was three years ago.

The publisher's jacket blurb will undoubtedly describe the book as a collaborative venture, but that's because we've kept the sordid details secret. I don't know how it is with the Overstreets or the Lockridges, but with us it hasn't been collaboration — it's been controversy and compromise every step of the way.

1. We disagreed about structure.

I wanted short paragraphs, a picture on every page, and at least one joke per chapter. George believes that you should start with a topic sentence and refrain from paragraphing until you've fully developed the thought, which is likely to be three pages later.

2. We disagreed about style.

My first draft was full of eureka-type prose. (Upon returning to the laboratory, Smith glanced at the rack of test tubes. They were cloudy. Could this be the breakthrough he had hoped for?") George had a fit. And you should have seen him wince when I wrote that something or other had been proved. According to my mentor, it's preferable to say that the analysis undertaken by several investigators was not without success.

3. We disagreed about vocabulary.

It wasn't difficult to decide on the basic scientific vocabulary that we would expect our readers to master. After all, if your subject was genes, chromosomes, and nucleic acids, you might as well name them. And we agreed on the elimination of truly exotic terminology. It cannot be disputed that there is a net gain in clarity when one refers to a T_2 phage as a virus.

But we quarreled about use of the jargon that characterizes not only genetics but every other profession, art, or craft — from the psychologists' *sibling* (for "brother or sister") to the astronauts' *mach number* (for "the ratio of the speed of a body to the speed of sound in the surrounding atmosphere"). To groups that use such terms, they are quick and precise. To groups that don't, they're incomprehensible.

Naturally, George opted for the jargon of genetics. And his reason was sound: To translate specialized terms into layman's language usually requires whole phrases that, by comparison to the original, are longwinded and cumbersome. It *is* simpler to say that a person is heterozygous for curly hair (seven words) than to explain that he has received a gene for curly hair from one parent and a gene for straight hair from the other parent (twenty-one words).

Nevertheless, I preferred the longer way home. If I said it once, I said it a thousand times: "But, George, it's more *readable* in everyday English." Sometimes, I convinced him.

4. On content, we disagreed about depth and scope.

Oddly, it was I — not George — who pressed for the inclusion of material that was too complicated for Joe Doakes.

Scientific research, I had discovered, is a highly creative process. At its best, it proceeds via great leaps of imagination into the unknown; and the elegance and sophistication of the thinking behind such leaps excited me. I therefore attempted to write excessively detailed accounts of research methods, and engaged in long forays into chemistry, mathematics, or physics.

For example, when I reached the point of writing about discoveries that had been made possible by invention of the electron microscope, I realized that to understand this instrument one should know something about the physical nature of light. So I undertook some independent research on the subject. The result was three pages in which I summarized all of twentieth-century physics.

When George read it, he said, "Honey, where did you get that stuff?"

"From the *Encyclopedia Britannica* and the *Life*

Science Library," I replied. "Furthermore, I think it's a remarkably lucid exposition of difficult material."

"Oh, it is," he agreed. "But it also happens to be wrong."

Our book is now in final draft. The manuscript will be ready to send to the publisher as soon as I do a little surgery on an addition of George's that begins, "These data would seem to confirm. . . ."

I should be happy, after all these months, to be getting rid of the heap of pages on my desk. But I'm not. Once they've gone, what on earth are we going to talk about after dinner?

Number of words 1662
See page 243 for Questions

Reading Time in Seconds _____
See page 324 for Conversion Table

SELECTION 38

Writing an Advertisement for Yourself

Caroline Donnelly

Your most important writing assignment — what is it? Writing that letter and résumé that will transform you from a job applicant into a job candidate. Properly written, a letter may indeed open the door wide to an important job. Here are the tips to make your letter a standout letter.

Because finding a good job often hangs on luck, an earnest job hunter takes pains with the details he can control. He may get a shoeshine or a haircut before a crucial interview, and he probably picks the best grade of bond paper for the letters and résumés he sends out. More important, he carefully weighs the words he puts on that paper. A stand-out letter or résumé, he knows, improves the odds that he will be in the right place at the right time.

Everyone who sets out to find a job that requires professional skill or training needs a résumé. It's wise to have an up-to-date résumé at your fingertips, even if you aren't actively looking for a job. Letters may play an important role in a job search, and résumés customarily are accompanied by introductory notes, but the résumé is the essential sales tool of the job seeker. Says John Sibbald, a vice president of the management consulting firm of Booz, Allen & Hamilton: "Drawing up a résumé is the single most important thing a person does to make a job change." A good résumé is the thin edge of the wedge that opens the door to a face-to-face meeting. It makes a job candidate out of a job applicant.

To their readers, résumés are people-screening devices. Personnel professionals tend to read résumés with a negative bias, skimming each for an excuse to throw it away. "I don't spend more than fifteen seconds on a résumé," admits executive recruiter Peter Lauer of Lauer & Holbrook, in Chicago. The obvious — but often overlooked — solution: leave out any information that would disqualify you.

There are as many opinions on what makes a good résumé as there are people reading résumés. Still, professionals and recent job seekers in various parts of the country generally agree that what you should know about résumés falls into six categories: what you should put in, what you should leave out, what form you should use, what tone you should take, what the résumé should look like and what kind of letter you should send with it. The following is a discussion of each of those points — with some specific advice.

WHAT TO PUT IN

The main ingredients of a good résumé are a comprehensive work history, a short outline of educational background and a smattering of personal data. Educational background should include degrees earned, scholarships, honors or participation in special programs. Personal data — hobbies and club memberships, for example — can add character, and some prospective employers look here for signs of leadership and community service. A résumé also ought to mention memberships in professional organizations, published books or articles, inventions or patents and fluency in foreign languages.

Some other particulars:

• Keep it short. A mid-career executive should aim for two pages. Three pages is the limit.

• Don't shorten your résumé by lopping off chunks of your career. Your work history should concentrate on your most recent jobs, but you should also describe the first six months in the mail-room — though not in detail.

WHAT TO LEAVE OUT

Too much information wastes space and risks exasperating the reader. For example, unless the writer never

Reprinted from the January 1974 issue of *Money* magazine by special permission; © 1974, Time Inc.

attended college, a résumé need not mention where or when he went to high school. Summer or part-time jobs should be included only if the applicant is a recent graduate, or if the jobs were unusual and showed gumption or ingenuity. Windy statements of career objectives waste precious space. Alan Neely, a personnel officer at the First National Bank in Atlanta, recalls that one applicant described his goal as "a challenging position leading to increased responsibility and self-actualization within a dynamic company." Says Neely: "That doesn't mean anything. The objective should be specific, like 'management trainee in the financial community.'" Many other personnel professionals advise against including any statement of objectives, no matter how terse, in a résumé since it can only limit the applicant's opportunities. Mention of religion, race or politics looks unprofessional.

While a good résumé omits or glosses over unfavorable information, the consequences of any serious distortion of facts can be dire. "There isn't one single company I know of that would not discharge someone on the spot if they learned of a lie," says Sheldon Hirsch, who heads his own executive search firm in Los Angeles. "And those things have a way of surfacing." Many companies check the facts in résumés; large companies with formalized hiring procedures and firms with government contracts are almost certain to do so. A fib that occasionally appears on résumés is a false claim to a college degree — a risky business, since such credentials are fairly easy to verify. Peter Lauer estimates that the applicant's educational background is misrepresented in 5 percent of the résumés he attempts to check.

What does a résumé writer do with potentially damaging information — a long period of unemployment owing to mental illness, for example? One New York personnel executive has some extreme advice: "I'd say lie about it. Say 'self-employed as a consultant.' But at the interview you've got to tell them, because they'll find out." A man applying for a job as an auditor sent the First National Bank in Atlanta a résumé that said: "During the past seven years I have been involved with top secret government work." A check revealed that he had done a stretch in prison for armed robbery and other crimes; that put him out of the running.

Another personnel man suggests covering an embarrassing interlude by specifying only the years, not the exact dates of employment. An alternate solution might be to send out a form letter focusing on career highlights instead of a conventional résumé. Letters offer a way to omit embarrassing facts.

Other guidelines:

• Play the coquette. Be comprehensive, but don't give every detail. That should stimulate the reader's appetite and prompt an invitation to an interview. There are exceptions, though. If you usually perform badly in interviews, a résumé packed with favorable information can take up the slack.

• Don't mention salary. Include anticipated salary in the covering letter only if you know the job and the company well enough to be sure you aren't overpricing or undervaluing yourself. Otherwise, save such delicate negotiations for the interview.

• Keep your references for the interview. Consideration for their privacy suggests that you leave their names and addresses out of your résumé and supply them only on request.

WHAT FORM TO USE

Most employers feel the same way about the information in a résumé as Constance Klages of Battalia, Lotz, a New York executive recruiting firm. She says bluntly: "I want it fast, and I want it easy." Those who do the hiring prefer résumés that outline the applicant's work history in reverse chronological order and that stick to a Western Union literary style. Since a job applicant wants to put his best foot forward, his résumé should state his strongest points first and save less important matters for later. Usually his last job is of greatest significance, but if he has, say, a graduate degree in business from a well-regarded school, he may want to give it top billing.

Form letters used instead of résumés, containing only selected details from the applicant's work record, may be helpful as a last resort. But they are unpopular with employers. Such letters tend to be aggressively self-promoting and incomplete. First cousin to the form letter is the résumé that touts the accomplishments of an individual without anchoring them to dates, places and job titles. Résumés and letters that intermingle pertinent information with puffery get low marks from most readers. Even if they work, there is a risk, says William Billington, partner in the Chicago recruiting firm of Billington, Fox & Ellis. "They appeal to impulsive individuals, small businessmen," he says. "People who impulsively hire, unfortunately, also impulsively terminate."

All the same, using résumés that are narratives of experience rather than simple listings of job descriptions may help job hunters with special problems. Besides people who want to hide a dark past, those with a history of job hopping find them useful. They are well suited to people whose careers consist of a series of projects — consultants, for example, or engineers, whose responsibilities grow over the years while their job titles remain the same. Women who reenter the job market after years of community service or charity work may find this type of résumé the most flattering way to present their unpaid work experience; those whose careers have been sidetracked can use narrative résumés to draw attention away from their most recent jobs.

WHAT TONE TO TAKE

Some personnel consultants find an inventory of job titles sterile and uninformative, and so favor résumés that tick off accomplishments — growth in company earnings, say, or savings traceable to job performance. Others are irritated by a hard-sell approach, which they feel rings false. "A résumé might say, 'During my eight years there, the company's profits grew from $2 million to $4 million.' That's great I say, but maybe if you weren't there, they would have grown from $2 million to $6 million," says Peter Lauer. The director of materials management at a Midwest firm agrees: "Anybody who puts down great glowing sales and cost savings, I figure he is kind of conning me a bit."

Other advice:

• Assume your résumé is not going to please everyone. Suit yourself. Adopt a style and tone that you are comfortable with.

• Take into the account the conventions of your profession. If you are a banker or accountant, you would probably do well to compose a conservative, bare-bones kind of résumé. For an advertising man, a touch of salesmanship might be appropriate.

WHAT IT SHOULD LOOK LIKE

Résumés should be attractive to the eye, but some job seekers go overboard, turning out résumés as elaborate as wedding cakes. Because dignity and good taste are valued in people in responsible jobs, attention-getting devices — photos or brightly colored binders, for example — can backfire. John Sibbald of Booz, Allen & Hamilton once received a job application from a product manager who attached a sample of his product — an aluminum bolt — to his letter. The gimmick caused a mild sensation among Sibbald's colleagues, but, he recalls, "None of us could remember the man's name."

A further tip:

• Stay away from the cluttered look. An inviting résumé, like many classy advertisements, includes a lot of white space.

THE COVERING LETTER

Even a first-class résumé is wasted if it is sent out without a covering note. Thomas Freyberg, who is in charge of hiring at the Cleveland headquarters of Eaton Corp., a manufacturer of car and truck parts, says his office often does not answer job applicants who send résumés without letters. The average job seeker can make do with one version of his résumé if he writes covering notes tailored to the job opportunity. They should be brief — not more than three or four short paragraphs. Covering notes give the job seeker a chance to use his charm. He can emphasize a salient virtue only touched upon in his résumé. He can indicate whether his job search is confidential, why he is looking and whether he is willing to relocate. If the writer was referred by a mutual acquaintance, the note should say so.

Most important, the note should make it clear that the applicant knows something about the company he is asking for a job. Unless he is mailing out hundreds of résumés in a blanket job search or answering a blind ad, a job seeker should do some homework on his prospective employer. Covering letters should be addressed to the individual most likely to make the hiring decision. For executive-level jobs, that decision is usually made not by the personnel department, but by supervisors or even by the head of the firm. An urgent job search may necessitate a scatter-shot approach. If a job seeker is mailing his résumé to many companies, he will probably not be able to research each one. But a covering letter should go with each résumé, and even a form letter should be addressed to a particular person. The names of company executives can be found in business directories.

A follow-up letter after an interview reminds the interviewer of the writer's qualifications, confirms his interest in the job and gently presses for further action, perhaps a second meeting. The interview gives the applicant a chance to learn what his prospective employer's needs are. The follow-up letter gives the applicant a chance to show the employer that he meets those needs. A letter showing interest in the employer's problems — volunteering solutions, even — should go over well. "Give free advice," suggests Peter Lauer. "It's the greatest thing you can do to get a job."

It's probably a good idea to have the résumé typed and printed professionally, which generally costs about $10 for 100 copies of a one-page résumé. For the job hunter who doesn't feel up to mounting a mass mailing, the Yellow Pages list letter shops, printers and résumé services that will engineer such campaigns — typing and reproducing résumés, attaching form letters, addressing and mailing envelopes. That complete service typically costs between 40¢ and 60¢ a letter. A job hunter who uses mass mailing techniques should not expect a reply rate of more than 5%.

While help with the mechanics can be worth paying for, personnel men frown on professionally written résumés, which can cost from $20 to $150. "They always seem to be a poor substitute for a person telling about himself," says John Coats, a recruiter at Raymond International, a Houston engineering and construction company. "They tend to look canned." Do it yourself, urge experienced résumé readers — and don't wait until you need it. John Sibbald recommends revising your résumé every three years as a way of taking stock. "Update your résumé as soon as you take a new job," suggests San Francisco marketing manager Thomas Parker. "That's when you feel up about yourself. If you wait until you are out looking for a job, you'll be writing while you are depressed."

Number of words 2352
See page 245 for Questions

Reading Time in Seconds _____
See page 324 for Conversion Table

Section IV: On Speaking

Simple Secrets of Public Speaking
Dale Carnegie

We spend a good share of our communication time in speaking — about 30 percent. Of course that figure includes both public and private speaking or talking. For most of us, however, public speaking is by far the more difficult. Here are some secrets to make it much less so.

I am going to let you in on a secret that will make it easy for you to speak in public immediately. Did I find it in some book? No. Was it taught to me in college? No. I had to discover it gradually, and slowly, through years of trial and error.

Stated in simple words, it is this: *Don't spend ten minutes or ten hours preparing a talk. Spend ten years.*

Don't attempt to speak about anything until you have earned the right to talk about it through long study or experience. Talk about something that you know, and you know that you know. Talk about something that has aroused your interest. Talk about something that you have a deep desire to communicate to your listeners.

To illustrate, let's take the case of Gay Kellogg, a housewife of Roselle, New Jersey. Gay had never made a speech in public before she joined my class in New York. She was terrified: she feared that public speaking might be a hidden art way beyond her abilities. Yet at the fourth session of the course she made an impromptu talk that held the classroom audience in the palm of her hand.

I asked her to speak on "The Biggest Regret of My Life." Six minutes later, the listeners could hardly keep the tears back. Her talk went like this:

"The biggest regret of my life is that I never knew a mother's love. My mother died when I was only six years old. I was brought up by a succession of aunts and relatives who were so absorbed in their own children that they had no time for me. I never stayed with any of them very long. They never took any real interest in me, or gave me any affection.

"I knew I wasn't wanted by any of them. Even as a little child I could feel it. I often cried myself to sleep because of loneliness. The deepest desire of my heart was to have someone ask to see my report card from school. But no one ever did; no one cared. All I craved as a little child was love — and no one ever gave it to me."

Had Mrs. Kellogg spent ten years preparing that talk? No. She had spent twenty years. She had been preparing herself to make that talk when she cried herself to sleep as a little child. She had tapped a gusher of memories and feelings deep down inside her. No wonder she held her audience spellbound.

Poor talks are usually the ones that are written and memorized and sweated over and made artificial. A poor speaker, like a poor swimmer, gets taut and tense and twists himself up into knots — and defeats his own purpose. But, even a man with no unusual speaking ability can make a superb talk if he will speak about something that has deeply stirred him.

Do beginning speakers know that? Do they look inside themselves for topics? No; they are more likely to look inside a magazine. Some years ago, I met in the subway a woman who was discouraged because she was making little progress in a public-speaking course. I asked her what she had talked about the previous week. I discovered that she had talked about whether Mussolini should be permitted to invade Ethiopia.

She had gotten her information from a weekly news magazine. She had read the article twice. I asked her if she had some special interest in the subject, and she said "No." I then asked her why she had talked about it.

"Well," she replied, "I had to talk about something, so I chose that subject."

I said to her: "Madame, I would listen with interest if you spoke about how to rear children or how to make a dollar go the farthest in shopping; but neither I nor anyone else would have the slightest desire to hear you try to interpret Mussolini's invasion of Ethiopia. You don't know enough about it to merit our respect."

Many students of speaking are like that woman. They want to get their subjects out of a book or a magazine rather than out of their own knowledge and convictions.

You are prepared right now to make at least a dozen good talks — talks that no one else on earth could make except you, because no one else has ever had precisely the same experiences. What are these subjects? I don't know. But you do. So carry a sheet of paper with you for a few weeks and write down, as you think of them, all the subjects that you are now prepared to talk about through experience — subjects such as "The Biggest

From "A Quick and Easy Way to Learn to Speak in Public," by Dale Carnegie, and from *Coronet*, February 1949. Reprinted by permission of *Esquire* Magazine © 1949 by Esquire Inc.

Regret of My Life," "My Biggest Ambition," and "Why I Liked (or Disliked) School." You will be surprised how quickly this list will grow.

Talking about your own experiences is obviously the quickest way to develop courage and self-confidence. But later you will want to talk about other subjects. What subjects? And where can you find them? Everywhere.

I once asked a class of executives that I was training for the New York Telephone Company to jot down every idea for a speech that occurred to them during the week. It was November. One man saw Thanksgiving Day featured in red on his calendar and spoke about the many things he had to be thankful for. Another man saw some pigeons on the street. That gave him an idea. He spent a couple of evenings in the public library and gave a talk about pigeons that I shall never forget.

But the prize winner was a man who had seen a bedbug crawling up a man's collar in the subway. He went to the library, uncovered some startling facts about bedbugs, and gave us a talk that I still remember after fifteen years.

Why don't you carry a "scribbling book"? Then, if you are irritated by a discourteous clerk, jot down the word "Discourtesy." Then try to recall two or three other striking examples of discourtesy. Pick the best one and tell us what we ought to do about it. Presto! You have a two-minute talk on Discourtesy.

Don't attempt to speak on some world-shaking problem like "The Atomic Bomb." Take something simple — almost anything will do, provided the idea gets you, instead of you getting the idea. Once you begin to look for topics for talks, you will find them everywhere — in the home, the office, the street.

Here are seven rules that will help immensely in preparing your speeches:

1. *Don't Write Out Your Talks.* Why? Because if you do, you will use written language instead of easy, conversational language; and when you stand up to talk, you will probably find yourself trying to remember what you wrote down. That will keep you from speaking with naturalness and sparkle.

2. *Never Memorize a Talk, Word for Word.* If you do, you are almost sure to forget it; and the audience will probably be glad, for nobody wants to listen to a canned speech. Even if you don't forget it, you will have a faraway look in your eyes and a faraway ring in your voice. If you are afraid you will forget what you want to say, then make brief notes and hold them in your hands and glance at them occasionally.

3. *Fill Your Talk with Illustrations and Examples.* By far the easiest way to make a talk interesting is to fill it with examples. Years ago, a congressman made a stormy speech accusing the government of wasting money by printing useless pamphlets. He illustrated what he meant by a pamphlet on "The Love Life of the Bullfrog." I would have forgotten that speech years ago if it hadn't been for that one specific illustration.

4. *Know Forty Times as Much About Your Subject as You Can Use.* The late Ida Tarbell, one of America's most distinguished biographers, told me that years ago while in London, she received a cable from McClure's Magazine asking her to write a two-page article on the Atlantic cable. Miss Tarbell interviewed the London manager of the Atlantic cable and got all the information she actually needed for a 500-word article. But she didn't stop there.

She went to the British Museum library and read articles and books about the cable, and the biography of Cyrus West Field, the man who laid it. She studied cross sections of cables on display in the British Museum; then visited a factory on the outskirts of London and saw cables being manufactured.

"When I finally wrote those two pages," Miss Tarbell said, "I had enough material to write a small book. But that vast amount of material which I had and did not use enabled me to write what I did write with confidence and clarity and interest. It gave me reserve power."

Ida Tarbell had learned through years of experience that she had to earn the right to write even 500 words. The same principle goes for speaking. Make yourself something of an authority on your subject. Develop that priceless asset known as reserve power.

5. *Rehearse Your Speech by Conversing with Your Friends.* Will Rogers prepared his famous Sunday-night radio talks by trying them out as conversation on the people he met during the week. If, for example, he were going to speak on the gold standard, he would wisecrack about it during the week. He would then discover which of his jokes went over with his listeners, which remarks elicited interest. That is an infinitely better way to rehearse a speech than trying it out with gestures in front of the bathroom mirror.

6. *Instead of Worrying about Your Delivery, Get Busy with the Causes That Produce It.* A lot of harmful nonsense has been written about delivery of a speech. The truth is that when you face an audience, you should forget all about voice, breathing, gestures, posture, emphasis. Forget everything except what you are saying.

Don't imagine that expressing your ideas and emotions before an audience is something that requires years of technical training, such as you have to devote to mastering music or painting. Anybody can make a splendid talk at home when he is angry. If somebody hauled off and knocked you down this instant, you would get up and make a superb talk. Your gestures, your posture, your facial expression would be perfect because they would be the expression of emotion.

To illustrate, a rear admiral of the Navy once took my course. He had commanded a squadron during World War I. He wasn't afraid to fight a naval battle, but he was so afraid to face an audience that he made weekly trips from his home in New Haven, Connecticut, to New York City to attend the course. Half a dozen sessions went by, and he was still terrified. So one of our instructors, Prof. Elmer Nyberg, had an idea that he felt would make the admiral forget himself and make a good talk.

There was a wild-eyed communist in this class. Professor Nyberg took him to one side and said: "Now, don't let anybody know that I told you to do this, but tonight I want you to advocate that we grab guns, march on Washington, shoot the President, seize the government and establish communism in the U. S. I want you to get the admiral angry, so he will forget himself and make a good talk."

The Bolshevik said: "Sure, I'll be glad to." He had not gone far in his speech, however, when the rear admiral leaped to his feet and shouted: "Stop! Stop! That's sedition!" Then the old sea dog gave this communist a fiery lecture on how much he owed to this country and its freedom.

Nyberg turned to the officer and said: "Congratulations, Admiral! What a magnificent speech!" The rear admiral snapped back: "I'm not making a speech; but I am telling that little whippersnapper a thing or two."

This rear admiral discovered just what you will discover when you get stirred up about a cause bigger than yourself. You will discover that all fears of speaking will vanish and that you don't have to give a thought to delivery, since the causes that produce good delivery are working for you irresistibly.

7. *Don't Try Imitating Others: Be Yourself.* Act on the sage advice that the late George Gershwin gave to a struggling young composer. When they first met, Gershwin was famous while the young man was working for $35 a week in Tin Pan Alley. Gershwin, impressed by his ability, offered the fellow a job as his musical secretary at almost three times the salary he was then getting.

"However, don't take the job," Gershwin advised. "If you do, you may develop into a second-rate Gershwin. But if you insist on being yourself, some day you'll become first-rate on your own."

The young man heeded the warning, turned down the job and slowly transformed himself into one of the significant American composers of this generation.

"Be yourself! Don't imitate others!" That is sound advice both in music and in public speaking. You are something new in this world. Never before, since the dawn of time, has anybody been exactly like you; and never again, throughout all the ages to come, will there ever again be anybody exactly like you. So why not make the most of your individuality?

Your speech should be a part of you, the very living tissue of you. It should grow out of your experiences, your convictions, your personality, your way of life. In the last analysis, you can speak only what you are. So, for better or for worse, you must cultivate your own little garden. For better or for worse, you must play your own little instrument in the great orchestra of life.

Number of words 2320
See page 247 for Questions

Reading Time in Seconds _____
See page 324 for Conversion Table

SELECTION 40

Your Voice Is Your Fortune

Paul D. Green and Cliff Cochrane

This selection poses an interesting question about the relationship between your voice and your fortune. Major speech defects are also spotlighted. In addition, you'll find suggestions from experts for improving that voice — and fortune — of yours.

When Billy Rose was launching his story-telling radio program, he listened to a transcription of his first script.

"Take it away!" he cried, aghast. "That's an impostor. It sounds like a nail file rubbing a cheese grater!"

Billy's reaction was one common to most people hearing their own voices for the first time on wire recorders. For, as Pat Kelly, supervisor of announcers

for NBC, says, "Only five persons out of a hundred are born with good voices. The rest of us have to work for one."

The important thing is, you *can* work for a good voice. And it's well worth doing. Bad speech may adversely affect your social life, your family life and your career. On the other hand, a college on Long Island kept track of scores of job-hunting graduates and established that students who had participated in college dramatics and debating, and had cultivated good voices, landed jobs much more quickly than other students.

NO PROMOTION IN 20 YEARS

An example of how important an interesting voice is to a career was given by the vice-president of a Chicago bank. "A fellow we'll call Jenkins was behind a teller's cage in this bank for twenty years. He never managed to get a promotion and he couldn't figure out why. Finally, heavy family obligations prompted him to ask for a promotion to the New Business Department.

" 'Jenkins,' the president told him, 'in this job you have to see a lot of important customers. Frankly, you sound so dispirited we're afraid to give you the chance. If you can put some snap into your voice, we'll talk about it again.'

"Well, Jenkins took his boss at his word and went to work on his voice. Within a few months he had what amounted to a new personality. He got the promotion, and in three and a half years was an officer of the bank.

"I know how much that man owes to his voice improvement," the vice-president finished. "Because you see, I'm that man."

PEOPLE STARTED LISTENING

An illustration of a different type is furnished by the middle-aged widow whose children married and moved away and who found herself facing an empty future. She had a timid, meek voice and made few friends. Largely to have something to do, she took a speech course at the local high school. Suddenly she found that people listened and were interested when she talked. She joined a couple of organizations; made a number of new friends. In a short time she was head of the Women's Auxiliary of the American Legion and became active in several other organizations. Now she leads a full and happy life — she's even found a new husband.

Of all speech defects, the commonest, according to the New York Telephone Company, is the slurring of words: "J'eat yet?" "Whyncha c'mover?" etc. Other speech sins an employer is likely to object to, according to a survey of business firms made by Dr. James F. Bender, director of the National Institute for Human Relations, include these:

Among men — mumbling, a rasp, sullenness, tonal monotony, overloud voices, stilted accents.

Among women — a whine, shrillness, nasal tones, raucous and strident voices, baby talk, affected accents.

Most important of all, perhaps, you owe it to your children to watch your speech habits. Good speech can help them learn in school, and give them a better chance later in life. Don't ridicule or punish children for bad speech — use tact and set a good example.

HOW TO HEAR YOURSELF

How can you check up on your own voice deficiencies?

A good way is to copy Billy Rose and have a transcription made. There are several other simple tricks, too. Stand in an enclosed space — a stall shower is good — and talk. Don't be misled by the resonance; tune your ears for whiny, nasal and unpleasant tones, for slurred syllables and unclear consonants. Or talk through a paper cone standing close to a wall. The sound of your voice will bounce off the wall and back to your ear. Radio announcers and concert singers cup their hands over their ears to hear themselves more accurately.

You might try merely reading aloud to the family and asking for criticism. They'll be glad to supply it. Once you've taken the measure of your voice, here are steps to improve it, according to voice experts:

1. Pick a model to imitate — an actor or radio commentator. Men should choose a person whose voice hits a good average, like Lowell Thomas or George Putnam, rather than one with a distinctive accent or intonation, like Basil Rathbone or H. V. Kaltenborn. Women would do well to pick someone like Loretta Young or Irene Dunne rather than Katharine Hepburn or Tallulah Bankhead. But don't go overboard in imitation. Keep your own personality.

2. Take regular breathing exercises to develop your lung power, remembering to push your diaphragm out when breathing in.

3. Try lowering the pitch of your voice.

4. Have a complete medical checkup on your adenoids, tonsils, larynx and sinuses.

5. Improve your speaking personality by pumping some enthusiasm into your tones. It may be difficult to greet your mother-in-law with a cheery "Good morning, Mom!" but you'll get used to it.

Don't try to convert yourself into a Winston Churchill or a Franklin D. Roosevelt. Not everyone is cut out to be a high-powered orator. Harry Truman, for example, kept Democratic strategists awake nights worrying about his flat, thin monotone. But Truman scored a vocal success by making good use of what he had. By going in heavily for informal, conversational talks, he impressed the voters with the sincerity and natural friendliness of his speaking personality.

If your voice problem is extreme, you should go to a good speech school or to an instructor. The American Speech and Hearing Association, whose offices are at the State University of Iowa, Iowa City, and at Purdue University, Lafayette, Ind., can give you a list of approved schools.

Not long ago a schoolteacher challenged a class to name a profession in which a good speaking voice would not be an aid to success. One bright lad spoke up: "Bartending." But the schoolteacher promptly reminded him of a bartender who rose to become mayor of the world's biggest city: William O'Dwyer.

Number of Words 1050
See page 249 for Questions

Reading Time in Seconds _____
See page 324 for Conversion Table

Accustomed as I Am…

J. Campbell Bruce

Experience, so they say, is the best teacher. That probably explains why there are more than 3,100 clubs to provide experience to help you speak more effectively. This selection tells you how these Toastmasters Clubs work. Find the nearest one and join it.

Suppose you *had* to make a speech and yet, like most of us, were scared silly. How would you like a small and sympathetic group of amateurs to practice on — an audience consisting of persons just as timid and inexperienced as you, and just as eager to learn to talk well?

Such a helpful setting is provided by more than 3,100 Toastmasters Clubs, whose 80,000 members meet weekly or biweekly in the United States and in 40 other countries around the world. In the past 55 years these non-profit clubs have benefited half a million men who probably never thought they would be able to make a successful speech.

What has brought and held these men together, however, is more than the chance to learn how to make a speech: it is the values gained in the process that can be carried over in all phases of their lives. In conversation, for example. In some respects every private speech is a public speech. So is the ability to give lucid directions on a job. So are commands and entreaties in the home. It is not strictly with the formal speech but with daily communication that the Toastmasters deal.

What the clubs provide is a *variety* of situations in which the members may practice. During his first year each of the 30 members of a club gets the opportunity for at least 12 speech experiences. In one, he may be heckled, or his notes may be filched ahead of his remarks, or a Klieg light may be turned on him as in a theater or television studio. Thus the cliché "Unaccustomed as I am . . ." no longer holds, and each man acquires the habit of speaking without suffering the shakes.

Only in this crucible can he learn the intangibles that the practiced speaker knows — the first thing to establish rapport quickly with an audience. A teacher or text may wisely tell him the importance of this principle, but a person must test it in action before he believes it. It is the source of all confidence before an audience of any size.

Madame Ernestine Schumann-Heink, the famous singer, used to stand quietly before she commenced her songs and repeat silently to herself the words: I love my audience, I love my audience. Her audiences loved her in turn. As Toastmasters find out, there may be other ways to reach this moment of rapport, of intimacy with an audience, but it is essential to have enough opportunities in enough kinds of situations to learn how to achieve it.

"Talk to an audience of many people as you would to one person." This is the principle stated by Ralph C. Smedley, who organized the first Toastmasters Club, at the Bloomington, Ill., Y.M.C.A. in 1905. Such advice was heresy in a day when orators bounced bombastic phrases off auditorium walls. But it proved sage with time, and it helps Toastmasters carry informality into public speech and the values of public speech into private talk.

Intangibles that often make for grace in speaking — timing, for example — are also studied. The pungent power of brevity is soon realized. As the late Franklin P. Adams once said in summing up a discussion of timing, "For one thing it means knowing when to stop. Like this." The speech that promises a terminal point, and yet goes on, irritates everyone.

The Toastmasters provide criticism by an evaluator. This club member seeks out a speaker's foibles and mannerisms, then describes them so the speaker can correct them. When a new minister-member of a Western group gave his "icebreaker" talk, the critic pointed out that the minister spent most of his time looking heavenward, little at his audience. This was doubtless natural enough for a man in his profession, the evaluator said, but it was distracting to those listening to him.

Every beginner in the study of the art of speaking is told that fluency results from careful preparation. Without preparation, a person may suffer the same stuttering inadequacy that the late Aneurin Bevan once experienced in a union meeting in South Wales as a lad of 17. A visitor said to Bevan, "You stammer in speech because you falter in thought. If you can't say it, you don't know it." Boning up hard before his next talk proved the worth of the advice.

When preparation pays off in a speech, the natural next step is to apply it to an interview, saving time while making the points sharper. When a man learns how fluency of speech carries the mind forward, he talks with fewer *ah's* and *uh's* and *but's* and *well's* in daily speech. When he learns that a firm and pleasing tone commands respect in talking with 29 others, he pays more attention to his voice when talking with just one other.

From *The Reader's Digest*, October 1960. Reprinted by permission of the author.

All sorts of questions come up in the course of the experience a club offers. There is, for instance, the question of stories and how to use them. Almost every speaker thinks he must start his remarks with an anecdote. He finds how ineffectual this device may sometimes be, and discovers that a story is good only if it is a hammer that drives home a point. If it is not appropriately used, it may only detract and distract.

Not the least important service rendered by these clubs is the chance to rehearse all sorts of talk. One of the devices used is a staged telephone conversation that is listened to and criticized by the group. In this a man tries to make a sale to a difficult client. The Toastmasters point out that a busy man speaks about 7,500 times a year (30 times a day) on the telephone, so that telephone manners and speech become an important aspect of the business of communication.

To ease the first painful steps of blocking out a speech, the Toastmasters suggest writing a letter to a friend:

Dear Bill: I am going to make a speech at our club on the subject of _____. I want to convince the audience that _____. I plan to start like this _____. Then I'll say that this point is important _____. Then I'll bring up this point _____. Then I'll end up the speech like this _____.

The device helps the beginner to come to grips with the subject. It incidentally suggests a way to get started on any hard task: begin here; block it out in a form that is familiar and easy. Dr. Frank Baxter, popular TV and college teacher, says that when students tell him they can't write a paper he asks them to write a letter telling him why they can't write a paper. This relaxes them, and usually the letter turns out to be the paper — or a real start toward it.

Toastmasters training also develops better deportment in conversation. Most of us are far too casual in our talk, presuming upon the good nature of our companions, being sloppy in what we say and the way we say it. Toastmasters experience reminds a person of the proprieties of speech that ought to be observed every day.

Even technical matters having to do with platform address help to make for a more natural person off the stage. The nagging problem of gestures must be faced by every speaker whether before an audience or in an informal group. Smedley broke down a beginner's timidity in gesturing by telling him to make a speech on Why I Can't Make Gestures. He tried it.

"I wish I could make sweeping gestures like this," he began, throwing out his arms freely to embrace the group. "Or like this," he continued, coming forward with a strong thrust of the arm and piercing the audience with his index finger. "But all I can do is to keep my hands down here at my sides, like this, or in my pockets, nonchalantly, like this."

By acting it out he loosened himself up and saw how ridiculous his fear of movement had been. And whether the Toastmaster learns movement by this means or by holding an object in his hands while he talks — a book, or a pointer, or his glasses or a pencil — he soon finds how important easy, natural motions of the hands are in making conversational points.

The inner confidence that comes from learning to face and influence an audience often gives a man backbone in his job. He discovers that what he fears is not an audience but himself. Learning to be resourceful on his feet, to handle or parry questions, he gets a new dignity.

A company president noticed that his accountant, who previously kept to himself and hardly cared to speak to anyone, had a new glint in his eye and a new lift in his shoulders. He even said Good Morning with a firm voice. Curious, the boss asked who had been feeding him meat — and discovered that learning to speak in public had spruced him up in private.

Today the Toastmasters idea has spread to persons not directly eligible for regular club membership either because they are not males, because they are not 21 years of age or because of the restrictions of some kind of institutional life. To provide a program for such circumstances, Toastmasters International organized Gavel Clubs, which embrace groups in veterans' hospitals and rehabilitation centers, and among men and women in colleges and universities. These clubs also reach down into high schools and elementary schools, giving boys and girls practice in communication that they often do not get in regular schooling.

For example, there are now 1,000 school children organized in 29 Gavel Clubs under the direction of the Bakersfield Toastmasters Club and the Kern County, Calif., superintendent of schools. The children, ages 10 to 14, meet once a week and conduct themselves as any Toastmasters Club would. But what impresses the teachers who evaluate the program is not the obvious training that students get in oral English. Their comments stress the fact that the clubs help to develop tact and judgment in criticizing others, encourage a better use of ideas, help students to rise to new situations, and stimulate general scholastic improvement.

The fealty engendered by Toastmasters Clubs indicates something of what their members get out of them. One of the Hollywood groups meets once a week at 7:15 *in the morning*. An industrial swing-shift club in Portland meets at 1 a.m.

The Toastmasters do not admit women, but 22 years ago, with headquarters' advice and consent, the first Toastmistress Club was formed. There are today 850 Toastmistress Clubs, with a total of more than 16,000 members.

Smedley, now 82, looks back with satisfaction on the growth of his idea. What began as an attempt to teach young men the simple principles of holding meetings has turned into a world-wide organization. The young men at the Bloomington Y adopted the name "Toastmasters" because it suggested a pleasant social atmosphere, free from anything like work or study. The program: short speeches, with criticism by the members.

The program still holds. "I know from experience," says Smedley, "that you can no more teach a person to be a good speaker in 10 or 12 lessons than you can teach him to swim with a $10 correspondence course. We don't give lessons. We just get the fellows to practice."

Number of words 1890
See page 251 for Questions

Reading Time in Seconds _____
See page 324 for Conversion Table

SELECTION 42

New Hope for Audiences

National Parent-Teacher

Discussion is, in a sense, a variety of public speaking. A discussion can, of course, be lively, stimulating, and purposeful. But all too often it is just the opposite. In short, discussion often needs new hope to give it new life.

The late Eduard C. Lindeman, who ended his teaching days at the New York School of Social Work and spent much of his life in conference activities, was one of the first men of our time to recognize that new ground rules are needed for small group discussions. He pointed out how much we still continue to use the "fight symbol" in all our meetings, which advertises and encourages disagreement. An audience is invited by the chairman to "go after" the speaker. Debates are prized for their pugilistic effects. Discussions are considered lively only if the line of battle is drawn.

CIRCULAR RESPONSE

Professor Lindeman saw that it was not enough merely to get people together around a table. The result might be disastrous unless there were some clearly defined purpose and some method of discussion that would help achieve this purpose. The group, in a word, must learn to think together, not merely provide a setting in which two or three members do all the talking and lambaste each other while the other members of the group sit passive and bored. So he proposed this arrangement:

The members of the group — not more than twenty and preferably fifteen — are seated in a circle. The chairman or leader proposes the question to be taken up. The discussion begins with the man or woman at his right. That person has the first opportunity to express his views. Then the person at *his* right has a chance to talk, and so on until the discussion has gone around the circle. No member of the group can speak a second time until his turn comes again.

If, for example, you are sitting fourth from the leader's right, you may express your views on the subject and also, if you must, on the opinions advanced by the leader and the three who have spoken before you. But if the person on your right says something that arouses your ire or excites your response, you have no chance to comment until the next time around.

So much for the mechanics of the circular response procedure. And the mechanics alone accomplish wonders toward remedying the bad manners and monopolistic practices that mar many a small group discussion. Extreme views belligerently presented are modified by the restraints imposed. The timid person speaks more freely when he knows that it is his natural right as a member of the group. In some places where there is a Quaker influence a member may even delay speaking and invoke a moment of silence on the part of the whole group. This is likely to improve the quality of what follows, for good discussion often needs a measure of silence.

FROM MANY VIEWS, A NEW VIEW

One special advantage of the circular response method is its suitability for mixed age groups. Students as young as fourteen have taken part in groups made up mostly of adults. When their turn comes, they speak freely and as members, not as individuals segregated because of their age.

It is not merely because of the ground rules that the young and the timid both speak more freely under this method. Another reason is to be found in the fact that circular response, by its very nature, encourages every person in the group to make his particular contribution to the problem at hand. The skillful chairman will make the most of this feature. He will visualize a common pot of experience as existing in the very center of the group and will help members to put their contributions into

Reprinted by permission from *National Parent-Teacher*.

this pot instead of throwing remarks at each other. The whole effort is to arrive at a consensus — and understanding. Naturally such an object will not always be attained, but the direction is toward creative thinking by the group, a mingling and distillation of many views, so that something new is actually brought into being.

If circular response is used in the discussion of political or economic problems — as part of a larger adult education program — the chairman and the group will of course need a certain amount of careful preparation. Circular response is not a substitute for reading and thinking or a convenient way of pooling ignorance. But it offers many blessings and benefits, regardless of the subject, for it reminds those who take part that the aim of discussion is reflection and not fireworks.

Two pages out of the literature of group dynamics may be taken and applied to circular response. One is to appoint a person whose function is to summarize the findings of the group at the end of the discussion. The other is to have another person, sitting with but not of the group, to act as observer. He is not concerned with the content of the discussion. His duty is to spend a few moments at the end of the discussion period commenting on the procedure itself and the behavior of the members, pointing out how the whole business can be carried on better next time.

ROLE PLAYING

Where the issue is one that concerns a delicate or difficult problem of human relations, the method known as role playing can be of great value. In role playing members of a group act out a real-life situation. They have no script, no set dialogue, and they make up their parts as they go along.

The situation to be acted out may be based on some clash or conflict — perhaps in the home, on the job, or in the community. But role playing need not center on conflict. It may be a practice session to put people at ease in assignments like interviewing an official, calling on a voter to remind him to register, or conferring with a school board member. However, role playing is put to its best use when it dramatizes a situation that most people in the group face and feel somewhat strongly about.

Suppose a parent education study-discussion group is exploring the age of adolescence. Most of the members are parents of teen-agers, and most of them feel quite strongly about the matter of getting home on time after a date. They can imagine a situation in a household where a fifteen-year-old girl resents the rule that she must be in by ten o'clock. So three group members volunteer to act it out, playing the roles of mother, father, and daughter.

After the parts have been decided upon, an inexperienced group might take a little time to discuss the kind of person each player is to portray. The young girl might be rebellious and quick-tempered, the mother

given to worry and nagging, and the father a strict disciplinarian. This discussion of roles, or warming-up period, may not be necessary in groups familiar with the technique.

At this point the players may need some reassurance. It is not always easy for adults to throw themselves into a part, even though all of us have some sense of drama. They may be self-conscious before a group. Or they may be reluctant to act out in public their own thoughts and feelings — or thoughts and feelings that might rightly or wrongly be construed as theirs.

To overcome these obstacles it is suggested that the leader say something like this: "Keep in mind that this is make-believe. You're playing a part. You're not going to show what *you* consider right. You're going to talk and act as you think the person you are playing would talk and act."

Once the players understand the problem and their own roles, the drama may start. It need not last long. Often two or three minutes are enough to bring out the point and show how human relations operate in such a situation.

A still further possibility is to replace some or all of the cast, thus giving other members of the group a chance at role playing.

The situation, the roles, and the solution may have to be discussed and played several times before the actors and the group feel that they have worked out a satisfactory handling of the problem. In this way each drama can mean new learning and new insight for both players and observers.

The advantages of role playing are many. It offers groups a dramatic way of calling attention to problems that involve strong emotions. It provides a way of learning the skills needed to carry out the goals of the group. It gives each player a chance to take on the personality of another human being — to enter into his feelings and for the moment to think and act from his point of view. Through it the whole group has an opportunity to see several solutions to a problem, some of them better than others. Finally, it offers practice in handling problems under two big advantages. When mistakes are made in this setting, the players are spared the penalties exacted in real life. Better still, an audience is at hand — observing, weighing, seeking along with the players better ways of coping with problems that await answers from actors and watchers alike.

REVIEWING THE ROLES

After the role playing comes discussion. The leader invites comments from the group with such questions as these: "Do you agree with the way the roles were played?" "Would you have played any of them differently?" "What would you have said or done? Why?" Or he may be more specific and ask: "What made the girl rebellious?" "Why was her mother particularly worried?" "What was at the root of the father's attitude?" "What could the girl have done to ease matters?" "How else could the father have handled the problem?" "What suggestion could the mother have made?"

When members have arrived at a new understanding of the roles and of possible solutions the whole drama may be tried again, incorporating the changes agreed upon by the group. The same members may play the same roles, thus gaining experience in trying out various ways of handling feelings. Or the same players may continue but this time take different parts. The player who had been the mother may now take the role of the girl. The one who played the girl may now be the father; and the father, the mother. This recasting of characters helps create understanding of another's feelings and point of view.

Number of words 1704
See page 253 for Questions

Reading Time in Seconds _____
See page 324 for Conversion Table

Why They Didn't Get the Job

Changing Times

You use speech in so many different situations. And in each different situation, different procedures, principles, and know-how are demanded. Take the interviewing situation. What exactly do you say to move yourself toward a job? How do you change the "why they didn't" to "why they did"?

Hunting a job is somewhat like hunting big game. Days and weeks are spent in getting ready, selecting a territory to hunt in and journeying to it, beating the bushes, stalking the game. But all that is nothing but a build-up to a few swift moments of climax when the success or failure of the chase is actually decided. The whole purpose of the preliminaries is to give the hunter his chance, to bring him face to face with the quarry and let him make his kill or miss it.

Job hunting works the same way. It might better be called interview hunting. For all the weeks spent in writing letters, answering ads, preparing resumés, visiting agencies and making phone calls are, again, really just a build-up. The objective is to bring you face to face with the quarry. The preliminaries are successful if they produce an interview. It is in the interview that you finally get your chance to win a job or lose it.

And here's another parallel: In both kinds of hunting, there is as much or more to be learned by finding out what those who missed did wrong as there is in finding out what those who succeeded did right.

Here then, from the experience of personnel men and employment counselors, are some tips on the things that job applicants most often do wrong — some of the mistakes that most commonly cost people the jobs they have been looking for, that most often cause them to muff their chances when the chances finally come.

"I WANT A JOB — ANY JOB"

A source of annoyance and extra work for hiring officials is the job seeker who doesn't know what kind of job he wants. He is not after this job or that job but just *a* job. Or he mentions some very general category — like "office work" or "outdoor work."

Take the case of Fred S., for example, whose ten years of business experience were about equally divided between sales and accounting. He had also been responsible for a good deal of general office supervision. When he went job hunting, he thought he ought to hit all possibilities — so he would ask for a job in selling *or* accounting *or* office management. Employers got an impression that he was a drifter, someone who didn't care much about what he did, whose career plans were still uncertain. Other men got the nod.

Eventually he made himself sit down and decide among the three choices. He picked selling. And when he went all out for a selling job, mentioning his accounting and supervisory experience only as extras that could increase his usefulness in sales, he got a job fast.

Betty W. applied for a job with a big national trade association. She said she didn't have any special job in mind, but she was "really very interested" in the field that the association operated in and thought it would be "terribly interesting" to work for such an organization.

That meant that the interviewer had to dig out her training and experience and aptitudes and specific interests and attempt to match them with available openings. As it happened, Betty was qualified for two jobs then available — one as a research assistant and one as a file clerk. But she didn't get either one; the employer eventually settled on two other equally qualified girls, one of whom had applied for a research position and one who had applied for a filing job.

It seldom pays to be vague or general or "ready to do anything." You can't expect the employer to choose your career for you, nor can you expect him to hire you on general principles and decide later what to do with you. You can't expect him to be eager to take a chance on someone who doesn't seem to know his own mind and may soon decide to go off and try something else.

"WHO CARES ABOUT A NECKTIE?"

It hardly seems necessary to mention this. Everyone knows enough to comb his hair and shine his shoes before keeping an appointment, doesn't he? Yes, almost everyone. But there is more to appearance than that.

Appropriateness in dress, for example. Among the young ladies who applied for the job of receptionist in a real-estate firm's main office were two who didn't stop to think of that point. A girl recently out of high school showed up in her classroom "uniform" of sweater and skirt and ankle socks and saddle shoes. Another girl, at the opposite extreme, came dressed to the teeth, wearing a fancy cocktail dress, and a feathery hat and too much make-up.

Bruce T. had always worked in establishments where sports shirts, slacks and jackets were standard dress. But he left an unfavorable impression in the employment offices of companies whose people were expected to dress more formally on the job.

A hiring official identifies two frequently encountered types of applicants that either impress him unfavorably or distract him so that he can't conduct a proper interview.

One is the slouch, who sits on the small of his back or flops into a chair as though he were relaxing in his own back yard.

The other is the fidget, who is constantly opening and closing a purse, shifting packages or a brief case around, shuffling papers, tapping a foot, or — worst of all — playing with things on the interviewer's desk.

Excessive nervousness is a commonly cited fault. An applicant may be so upset and fearful that he gets all balled up, volunteers nothing, lacks any trace of poise and self-confidence.

Lighting a cigaret without the courtesy to ask permission first and chain smoking through an interview are miscues that often bring demerits. Attempting to be too familiar is another.

"MY LAST JOB? THAT OUTFIT?"

There are three mistakes that applicants make in answering questions about a previous job, how they liked it and why they left it. By way of illustration here is the case of John R., who made all three before an employment counselor set him straight.

John was an accountant in his forties who had spent

years with a certain metalworking company. Twice during recent years a department-head post had been vacant, and twice, though John felt himself in all ways qualified and deserving, he had been passed over for promotion and an outsider brought in. When the same thing appeared about to happen a third time, he went to the boss. The upshot was a rather bitter argument, as a result of which John was fired.

The first time he was interviewed by a prospective employer, John tried to cover up his reasons for leaving. He gave the impression that there had been a reorganization of his department. That was common mistake number 1 — not telling the truth. For, of course, the employer checked.

The second time, therefore, John told the truth: He had been fired after a fight with the boss. But he didn't want it left there. He wanted his side of the story told, and he told it — with feeling. He made clear to his interviewer just exactly what he thought of the former employer and the way the business was run. And that was common mistake number 2 — running down an ex-employer. Nine times out of ten it leaves the interviewer with a bad taste in his mouth and suspicions in his mind.

The third time, having realized that he had done wrong to shoot off his mouth, John played it straight. He said simply that he had been dismissed as a result of a disagreement with the boss over promotion policies. That was essentially truthful and neither damaging to his cause nor disdainful of the former job. But the counselor with whom he later discussed things at an employment agency pointed out that he had made common mistake number 3 — failing to use the occasion as a springboard for bringing out a favorable point. And so from then on, John followed up with a remark that promotion policies were of particular interest to him because he felt that he was in a stage of his career when he was capable of filling, and could best serve an employer in, a more responsible position. And that led directly into a factual explanation, backed up by the record, of just why he felt so. His case was a perfectly good one, and the firing incident, properly handled, gave him an excellent opportunity to sum it up. After a couple more tries he landed the higher-level job he was after.

The rule for talking about the last job is this: Don't be dishonest, defensive or apologetic. Do discuss it on a positive plane and turn it to whatever advantage you can.

"WHAT DO YOU FOLKS DO?"

An astonishing number of job applicants don't bother to arm themselves with the most elementary information about the job they apply for or the company they apply to.

The retiring editor of a well-known equipment manufacturer's company newspaper was interviewing potential successors. One of them was Irving S., an experienced and competent young newspaper reporter. In the first five minutes the editor found that Irving —

• had only a vague and incomplete knowledge of the company's product line,

• did not know that it had a Canadian subsidiary and a branch plant out West,

• had never seen a copy of the company newspaper he wanted to edit,

• had not even bothered to read any of the several copies available on an anteroom table while he was waiting to keep his appointment.

An extreme case? Perhaps. But it takes only a little of that sort of thing to irritate a prospective employer and give a poor impression of an applicant's good sense.

Another type of ill-informed applicant is the one who doesn't know anything about job classifications and qualifications. When an airline sent representatives into Jane B.'s city to recruit people for several types of work, Jane read the advertisement and applied. But she didn't read the ad very carefully. As a result she took half an hour of the interviewer's time completing an application for one of the several types of jobs open. Then she discovered that the job she was applying for would involve moving to another city. The ad had stated this, but she "hadn't noticed." It was too late to back up and go after one of the other jobs.

"I MIGHT LISTEN TO AN OFFER"

Many an applicant gets passed over because of an attitude of indifference, but in most cases not much can be done about it. The person usually needs changing, not just his job-hunting technique. He strolls into the interview, looks bored, chats about this and that, makes no particular effort to get a job, lolls around waiting for the interviewer to offer him one.

But there are times when it is technique that is to blame. Harvey A. missed job after job because he has never really grasped the fact that he has to pitch into an interview and prove that he has something the potential employer needs. Instead he sits back and waits to be offered something. Gloria J. doesn't bother to pay close attention to questions — a surprisingly common fault, interviewers report — and as a result sometimes gives wrong information, often makes it necessary for the interviewer to repeat, and consistently misses her chance to drive home favorable points.

Not infrequent, either, are cases like that of Francis M., who thinks that a "big shot" technique is most effective. He tries to give the impression that he doesn't really need the job, is not at all sure he wants it, but would be glad to consider any reasonable proposition the employer might care to make.

"WELL . . . UH . . . GUESS THAT'S ALL"

Look back over the reasons why people missed jobs, and you will find that in many cases they well deserved

to lose out. That is, the very fact that they made the mistakes indicated that they were not best-grade material. But here finally is a very, very common cause for flunking interviews that is usually no real reflection on the applicant's intrinsic worth. It is the failure to recognize that he is in a competition, that he is probably one of several reasonably qualified applicants, that to come out on top, he has got to bring out and emphasize whatever special points he alone can offer to tip the balance in his favor.

In short, large numbers of job hunters miss the big chance either because they don't know their strong points or they don't make the special effort to sell their strong points.

Lucy S. is a statistician who has specialized for years in the field of international transportation. Recently she was interviewed by the head of an export-import firm who wanted to add a statistical department to his New York headquarters. It would have been a big break, a big step up in salary, prestige and future. Lucy is topnotch in her profession, attractive and pleasant. She didn't get the job — not because she wasn't as good as the others, but because she didn't convince her prospective boss that she was noticeably better than the others. She didn't sell the "extras."

In her interviews Lucy described her training, listed her experience, outlined the duties she had performed, furnished references, showed her familiarity with the work required in the new job. But here are some things that Lucy either didn't mention or didn't emphasize strongly enough:

• All those considered for the job spoke the languages and had worked with the statistical material of the countries with which the firm did its principal business. But Lucy alone had traveled extensively in them.

• Some of the statistical material was intended for use in advertising and sales presentations. Because the company staff men would adapt the data and prepare the presentations, the employer made no special point of this. But on a previous job Lucy had turned out material to be used for the same purpose, and she had been required to get it into final shape herself; her experience would have enabled her to assist in that part of the work and probably expedite and improve it.

• Lucy's college training fitted particularly well with certain important technical aspects of the job to be done. But the employer knew nothing of the technical side of statistics, and Lucy didn't think to explain.

This story has a happy ending, however. The man who got the nod didn't work out, and Lucy got a second chance. This time she made it. In the interim, she had happened to attend a lecture on job finding. And she had taken to heart this portion of the lecturer's advice:

Study both yourself and the job. List your strong points, the items on your record most favorable to you. Make another list of special qualifications, ones that others are not likely to be able to offer. Make a third list of those points where your qualifications match outstandingly with the job you're applying for. Get your lists down pat. And see to it that you get everything on them over to the interviewer, whether you are offered an occasion to do so or whether you have to make one.

Which leads back to the analogy of the hunter. It's not enough to know how to aim and when to pull the trigger. In job hunting, as in all hunting, you also have to be ready with the right kind of ammunition — and you have to use it.

Number of words 2550
See page 255 for Questions

Reading Time in Seconds _____
See page 324 for Conversion Table

SELECTION 44

Accents Are His Business

Frank Kane

Shakespeare once wrote, "Mend your speech a little, lest you may mar your fortunes." He could have written, "lest you reveal your background and regional antecedents." You may think that's an impossibility until you read about Dr. Smith's uncanny ear for accents.

The stocky young man in the back of the taxicab listened patiently while the cabby orated on every subject from the Brooklyn Dodgers to the high cost of living. Finally the young man leaned forward and said: "After coming from Hamburg, did you spend much time in Cleveland before moving to New York?"

The cab squealed to a sudden halt that threw the passenger off the back seat. Right there, Dr. Henry Lee Smith, Jr., made a mental vow never again to try his tricks on a cabby.

"How'd you know I came from Hamburg?" the driver demanded.

"By the way you talk," Dr. Smith explained. "You have some very definite traces of a Hamburg area dialect, with a Cleveland overlay that breaks through the New York characteristics."

The cabby eyed his fare with a mixture of suspicion and awe, then continued on his way — the latest of a long string of people to be amazed by Dr. Smith's knack for telling others where they come from by the way they talk.

Recently, when the editor of a Manhattan amusement magazine expressed some cynicism as to Dr. Smith's ability, the doctor agreed to accept the editor himself as a subject. After a brief conversation, the voice detective told the editor that he was a native New Yorker with a strong Boston overlay, and that in some way he had been subjected to a strong Russian influence. The editor sheepishly admitted that he had been born in New York, educated at Harvard and now was married to a Russian girl!

Although analyzing dialects started out as a hobby with Dr. Smith, it is now an important phase of his work as a linguistic scientist. After his graduation from Princeton with a Ph.D. in Oriental languages in 1938, he first joined the English Department at Barnard College, then went to Brown University, where he was placed in charge of public speaking.

Part of his technique was to have students read passages into a microphone, then analyze their speech defects and mannerisms from the record. After a time he trained himself to recognize various sectional and dialect patterns, and for his own amusement he would tell the students their backgrounds.

Smith's hobby became so well-known that a radio producer built a network show around him. Here he took members of the studio audience, listened to their pronunciation of key words, and guessed their origin with startling accuracy.

It was while conducting this program that Dr. Smith became involved in the now-famous Lord Haw Haw controversy. With both British and American intelligence services trying to determine the identity of the notorious Nazi broadcaster, Dr. Smith was invited by a radio network to try his hand at analyzing Haw Haw's background from a voice recording.

Unhesitatingly he placed Haw Haw as of Irish origin, and added: "He has also spent considerable time in the United States. German is definitely a second language." The description perfectly fitted William Joyce, the British traitor then in Germany.

A few weeks later, however, when Smith heard a direct broadcast by Haw Haw, he publicly reversed himself, saying that the speaker was a native German with British undoubtedly a second language. Promptly a former employee of the Berlin broadcasting system wrote to Dr. Smith, informing him that this description fitted Helmuth Dietz, famous German radio mimic.

Dr. Smith was vindicated on both counts when Germany fell, since records proved that both Joyce and Dietz had broadcast as Lord Haw Haw.

During the war, the voice detective found an intimate knowledge of dialects and speech characteristics of various sections of America and other countries invaluable. It was important in devising a new system of language training that makes it possible for a foreigner to learn to speak English without an accent, and for an American to learn a foreign language with no carry-over of his native dialect.

The Special Projects Division of the Army gave him a selected group of German prisoners on which to test his new system. The results were so amazing that at the end of hostilities the State Department invited Dr. Smith to head a School of Language Training in the Foreign Service Institute, utilizing his techniques exclusively.

When asked how much influence parents exercise on a child's speech habits, Dr. Smith says that although a youngster may occasionally imitate a parent's vocal mannerisms, the influence is usually negligible. However, every so often a case crops up to prove the reverse.

One of his most baffling experiences occurred recently with a young girl whose speech, to him, showed unmistakable signs of a Baltimore area dialect. Since he is himself a Baltimorean, Dr. Smith was humiliated when the girl told him that she had never been in Baltimore, that she had learned English in South America and that neither of her parents was a Baltimorean.

He felt better a few days later when the girl's aunt told him that the girl had indeed learned English in South America, but had been taught by her grandmother, who hailed from Baltimore.

In another case, Smith faced a girl who spoke a pure Cleveland dialect, yet who insisted she had never been west of the Hudson River. Subsequent questioning, however, revealed that the girl's parents hailed from Cleveland, and that each time she had come home from school with a New York expression or inflection, it had been carefully spanked out of her.

Is it always possible to identify a person's background by his speech? In about eight cases out of ten, says Dr. Smith. He has most difficulty with professional soldiers, actors, and singers with trained voices, due to the fact that when there are two or more overlays the original dialect is often wiped out.

For instance, Fred Allen, the radio comedian, has added so many overlays to his native Bostonian that little trace of it remains. On the other hand, Jack Benny is still easily identifiable as Illinois, and even an amateur can spot the North Carolina dialect in orchestra leader Kay Kyser's speech.

Recently, a would-be radio announcer was turned down by executives of a New York station on the ground that there was too much localism in his speech.

"You must get rid of all traces of regional accent," he was told. "It annoys listeners who don't happen to come from your part of the country."

The applicant indignantly denied he had any local accent, and even pointed out that he had had his voice "trained." At the suggestion of the station operator, he dropped in on Dr. Smith. The voice detective listened to the "trained" announcer, then not only told the applicant he was obviously from Philadelphia, but even told him what section of Philadelphia!

Can anyone learn to identify a person's background by the way he speaks? Yes, says Dr. Smith — very easily. The first clue lies in the pronunciation of the words "merry," "Mary" and "marry." If the subject pronounces each with its distinctive vowel sounds, he hails from east of the Alleghenies. In the Midwest and Far West, all three words rhyme, being pronounced like "merry" in the East. In coastal New England and the Tidewater South, the girl's name would be pronounced "May-ree."

The second test for East-West is pronunciation of "water" and "wash." In the East, the first word is pronounced "waw-ter," with the lips rounded, and the second, with no rounding of the vowel, becomes "wah-sh." In the Midwest, it's just the reverse — "waw-sh" and "wah-ter." In the Far West, both vowels are pronounced alike, halfway between the extremes of East and Midwest.

For North-South determination, the word "greasy" is the best test. North of a line very close to the Lincoln Highway, "greasy" is pronounced "gree-sy," while south of that line it is pronounced "gree-zy."

For those who are skeptical that speech differences can exist as closely as a town apart, Dr. Smith points out that although New York and Philadelphia are roughly in the same speech zone, the "gree-sy"-"gree-zy" line runs about halfway between Trenton and Philadelphia. On the New York and Trenton side, the word "on" is pronounced "ahn," while on the Philadelphia side it becomes "awn."

With all these variations, what is the proper speech dialect? Dr. Smith doesn't believe in any single standard. He thinks that anyone can speak his own regional speech effectively, and he does not join in the usual condemnation of the Brooklyn, Bronx, New England or "Deep South" accents, so long as they are natural and effective.

"Don't try to model your speech on some mythical standards for 'good' English," he advises. "And don't, as so many Americans do, render lip service to an artificial Oxford accent.

"Pattern your speech on the customs and culture of your own particular area. If your accent happens to be somewhat different from that of somebody across the Hudson River or below the Mason-Dixon Line, it doesn't matter."

What would the perfect voice sound like?

"There's no such thing as the perfect voice," Dr. Smith says. "However, if I were asked to create a composite of fine qualities, such a voice would have the diction, fluency and timing of Franklin Roosevelt; the authority of Raymond Gram Swing; the dramatic force of Winston Churchill; the punch of Walter Winchell; the charm of Helen Hayes; the tone of Maurice Evans; and the informality and warmth of Will Rogers.

"But," Dr. Smith adds, "it's a good thing that no human actually has such a compelling voice. If there were such a speaker, he could probably do whatever he liked with the rest of us."

Number of words 1590
See page 257 for Questions

Reading Time in Seconds _____
See page 324 for Conversion Table

SELECTION 45

Conversation Is More Than Talk

Gelett Burgess

Conversation! Is it really a lost art? What general principles, if followed, can transform conversation into that rarity — good conversation? After all, conversing is something you do far more often than public speaking. That's why it's well worth reading and thinking about.

Good talkers are common, but good conversation is rare. Yet, like good manners, conversation is an essential requisite for anyone who wishes to be friends with those people who are usually most worth while. The man or woman who understands that good conversation is a social exchange of ideas is welcome everywhere.

There is a fundamental principle underlying good conversation. It is the basis of all good manners. This principle is the avoidance of friction in social contacts — a friction caused by irritation, boredom, envy, egotism, ridicule, and such emotions.

In San Francisco I once was a member of a small group which met weekly for the purpose, we proudly claimed, of reviving the lost art of conversation. Here are some of the rules we finally adopted that guided our talks and made our conversation a delightful game.

1. *Avoid all purely subjective talk.* Don't dilate on your intimately personal affairs — your health, your troubles, domestic affairs; and never, never discuss your wife or husband.

Streams of personal gossip and egotism destroy, in any group, all objective discussion — of art, science, history, timely topics, sports, or whatever. Such monologues not only bore the listener, but, as the talker is repeating only what he or she already knows, he learns nothing from others.

2. *Don't monopolize the conversation.* One of my friends long ago was a laughing, attractive person, who told stories well, with a mixture of highbrow terms and slang that was most amusing. But his stories were too long and too many. You roared with laughter, but after a while you grew restless and yearned for a more quiet, comfortable talk with plenty of give-and-take. You couldn't help remembering what old John Dryden said about those "who think too little, and who talk too much."

3. *Don't contradict.* Flat contradiction is another conversation-stopper. You may say, "I don't quite agree with that," but conversation, to be pleasant and profitable, should never descend to the level of emotional argument.

To get the most benefit from a conversation one should instead seek to find points of agreement. In that way, the subject develops in interest with each one's contribution to the discussion, and you both advance in knowledge. I had a postal-card correspondence with a friend, once, on the subject of God. We found we had so many ideas in common that, if I were not converted to his thought, my own thinking was considerably broadened.

4. *Don't interrupt.* Of course, when you toss a few grace notes into the talk such as, "How wonderful!" or "You mean she didn't know?" it doesn't throw the train of conversation off the track. But to interpolate views of your own is not only discourteous, but leaves what the speaker has to say unfinished when he perhaps hasn't yet made his point. Conversation is like an ordered dinner where each is served in turn. It should have rhythm and tempo to be gracious and truly social.

One perfect conversational dinner party is still alive in my memory. It was given in Boston by Mrs. James T. Fields, widow of the publisher who had entertained every visiting writer from Dickens to Kipling. There were present Mr. and Mrs. Thomas Bailey Aldrich; the brilliant Mrs. Bell, daughter of Rufus Choate; Bliss Perry, then editor of The Atlantic Monthly; and myself.

Reprinted by permission of the author from *Your Life*, December 1947.

Six is the ideal number for an intimate dinner; if you have more the conversation is apt to break up into separate side dialogues. At Mrs. Fields' each of us talked and each of us listened. No one interrupted; no one contradicted; no one monologued. The affair had the charm and pleasing restfulness of music.

5. *Don't abruptly change the subject.* Some people virtually interrupt, after patiently and painfully waiting for a talker to cease, by jumping into the conversation with a new subject.

In our Conversation Club it was an unwritten rule that after one person had stopped talking there should be half a minute or so of silence in which to reflect, digest, and appreciate what had been said. It is the proper tribute to anyone who has offered an idea for consideration. I have known this pause to take place often in men's conversation, but have you ever known a group of women to desist for a second?

There is no surer way to make people like you than to pay them the compliment of interest and sympathy. Prolong their subject, ask more about it, and they expand like flowers in the sun. Yet what usually happens is that, should you venture to describe some misfortune or accident that has happened to you, they immediately narrate a similar mischance that they have suffered.

6. *Show an active interest in what is said.* You need not only your ears to listen well, but your eyes, hands, feet, and even posture. I have often tested the merits of a story or an article I have written by reading it aloud to one or two friends. What they said about it never helped me much since one often liked what another didn't.

But if their eyes went up to the ceiling, or to a picture on the wall, if their fingers moved or their feet tapped the floor or swung from a knee, I had indisputable evidence that the manuscript wasn't holding their interest and I marked the dull spots for revision.

And so in good conversation your social duty is to manifest an alert interest in what is said. It brings out the best in the speaker and it insures his confidence in your sympathy.

7. *After a diversion, return to the subject.* There is no surer test of being able to converse well than this. Often while a subject is not yet fully considered it is completely lost in some conversational detour. To reintroduce this forgotten topic is not only polite and gracious, but it is the best evidence of real interest.

If it is your own story, it is futile for you yourself to bring it back to persons who have by-passed it. Let it go, and see that you don't commit their error.

8. *Don't make dogmatic statements of opinion.* The Japanese tea ceremony, when gone through according to the old rules, was perhaps the most refined and idealistic social form ever practiced. Everything about the special tea house, every stone on the path to it, every gesture in partaking of the tea was strictly prescribed. It was a cult of simplicity and self-effacement.

One of the rules of behavior concerned conversation during the ritual. It was considered vulgar and inartistic for host or guest to make any definite, decisive statement. One might speak of anything — the symbolism of the one *kakemono* on the wall, perhaps, or the beauty of a flower arrangement — but never with an expression of finality. The remark was left up in the air, so to speak, for the next guest to enlarge upon or add to, so that no one was guilty of forcing any personal opinion upon the others.

It is a good game, but difficult; try it some time with your friends. The principle applies well to almost any conversation where opinions are concerned. You may state facts as facts; but your application of them should be tentative, with such qualifications as "In my opinion," or "It seems to me," or "Isn't it possible that . . .?"

If you associate with people of wisdom and understanding, you'll find they probably use such qualifying phrases, "with the meekness of wisdom," as St. James says, while the ignoramus is always for cut-and-dried pronouncements.

9. *Speak distinctly.* Even a bore can attain a certain consideration if he enunciates his words well, while another person with a great deal more intellect will not be listened to simply because he mumbles or whispers.

While I was a member of the executive committee of the Authors' League I was fascinated by the fact that one or two men were always listened to, while the others often had to force their way into the conversation. Those who spoke slowly dominated the meeting. High, hurried voices simply couldn't compete with Ellis Parker Butler's deliberate words, and his voice helped him maintain his leadership for years.

If you observe a group talking, you'll find that the one with a low, controlled voice always gets the most respect. The eager, temperamental contenders dash up against him like waves against a rock, and the rock always withstands them.

10. *Avoid destructive talk.* Did you ever attempt to live for a single day without saying anything destructive in tone? At a house party, long ago, I was one of half a dozen guests who agreed to try it. If one of us went to the window and said, "It looks like rain," there would be a whoop of glee, and a fine of one dollar. If you said you didn't like bananas, another dollar; and so on.

At the end of the day we agreed that nothing but optimism and Pollyanna was a good deal of a bore, and we liked a little pepper in our conversational soup; but we did realize for the first time how many quite unnecessary derogatory remarks we were all likely to make.

Evil, of course, must be condemned and opposed. But the unnecessary criticism, the desire to raise a laugh through ridicule, the general tendency to look on the unpleasant side of life, puts lines and a cynical expression in your face, and makes people shun you no matter how clever you are.

Now this little decalogue may seem simple, even axiomatic. But you will be amazed to find how often these primary rules are violated even by those who are supposed to be cultivated people, and how often their infringement causes unpleasantness.

So much for the negative side. What about the constructive view? How to create and maintain an agreeable conversation?

The secret is simple. To talk well one must think well. If you merely relate an incident that has happened — the facts in the case — it is nothing but anecdote. To make good conversation you must think underneath, above, and all around the subject.

This kind of thinking is well illustrated in the conversation of baseball enthusiasts. Are they content with telling the score, the number of base hits, errors, and home runs? Not at all. They discuss a team's potentialities, its comparison with another, the characteristics of the different players and their values, the theory and technique of the game. The same principle applies to all kinds of conversation.

Number of words 1930
See page 259 for Questions

Anyone who finds it hard to talk should learn to think about what he sees and hears and reads, and get something out of it. Ask why, and what it means. Discover what you can learn from it.

As you ponder, try to associate the subject with your own experience and observations and with ideas previously acquired.

Furthermore, if you mingle only with your own set or trade, your conversation inevitably degenerates into shop talk, or sport talk, or dress talk.

Get out of your rut and enlarge your interests by making acquaintances engaged in other pursuits. Develop a genuine curiosity about what is outside your ken, not a cheap inquisitiveness with regard to personalities. Join clubs. Join the church actively. Develop a hobby. Read up on subjects that have interested you. Study Spanish or nature or numerology — anything that has been outside your field of view.

If you fertilize and enrich your thinking in such ways you need not worry about being able to converse well. Every new experience will make your talk more interesting and more valuable.

Reading Time in Seconds _____
See page 324 for Conversion Table

SELECTION 46

How <u>Not</u> to Tell a Story

Bennett Cerf

One way to learn how to tell a story superlatively well is to learn how not to tell a story superlatively well — so says Bennett Cerf. Here's still another speech situation. Why not please your friends? Take time now to master the storytelling art.

The one thing that every introvert, extrovert, megalomaniac, Caspar Milquetoast, octogenarian and infant prodigy in America is convinced he can do superlatively well is tell a funny story. Since this state of mind — or great delusion, if you will — obviously is permanent, and since, to make matters worse, the tempo of modern life has developed in people's voices a penetrating, Orson Wellesish quality that makes you hear what they are saying whether you want to or not, it seems high time to formulate a list of elementary rules that may at least prevent our determined raconteurs from making all the possible mistakes every time they swing into action.

I feel qualified to draw up such a list on two counts. First, since editing my college funny paper almost thirty years ago I have been guilty of every one of the

common errors myself. Second, since my compilation of humorous anecdotes, Try and Stop Me, achieved success, every man, woman and child I meet seems to think that the thing in the world I desire most is to hear more witticisms of uncertain vintage along the same general lines.

I very soon discovered that the most irritating thing I could do was to admit that I had heard the story about forty times before. I learned to mask my emotions under a frozen, desperate smile, ready to burst into hollow laughter at the appropriate moment and cry, "Yes, sir, you really have given me a new one there. Use it? You bet I will!" At the same time, I began to study the things people do when they are launched upon a joke or anecdote, and the following compilation of Don'ts is based largely upon my bitter and highly involuntary experiences.

1. Don't make a story too long. The commonest and

Reprinted by permission of Mrs. Bennett Cerf from *The Saturday Evening Post*, March 6, 1948.

most fatal mistake of the amateur storyteller is to stretch his yarn beyond all reasonable limits. The audience, usually waiting only for an opportunity to get the floor itself, loses all interest. The punch line is buried in a morass of unnecessary verbiage. I have seen so magnificent a raconteur as Herbert Bayard Swope bogged down by the introduction of too many extraneous details. Mr. Swope has a trick of weaving the names of his listeners into a tale he is spinning to insure their absorbed interest. His heroine is "a beautiful girl like little Ginny here at my right." His locale is a town where "I remember seeing you doing something you shouldn't have, Marie." His time is set by a "that must have been about twenty years before young Bennett here was born" — and so on until everybody at the table has been included.

It is a device that delights a listener who appreciates a true artist at work, but even Mr. Swope sometimes carries it too far. They had a saying at the offices of the old Morning World: "If Swope can't get away with it, don't you try!" Great professional comics like Lou Holtz or Joe Laurie, Jr., can stretch out a story for ten minutes, and actually milk it for additional laughs en route. Ordinary folk cannot.

2. Don't forget your point in the middle of a story. The most pathetic spectacle in Raconteurritory is the man who suddenly slows down in the course of his narrative, scratches his head and announces sheepishly, "Good Lord, I've forgotten how it ends." He leaves his listeners with the same sense of utter frustration as an inept columnist who once provoked George S. Kaufman into declaring, "The Rationing Board is after So-and-So to find out what he's done with all the points he dropped from his stories." If you haven't got your punch line absolutely straight in your mind, don't start.

3. Don't laugh too much yourself. A character to be avoided at all costs is the man who breaks himself up in the course of a story, shaking so with imbecilic laughter that you understand little of what he's trying to tell you, and care less. A hearty laugh at the end of the story, constituting yourself a sort of cheer leader, is not only permissible but, if not carried to excess, sound strategy. While the story is in progress, however, let your audience do the laughing — if any!

4. Don't lay hands on your audience. Particularly repulsive is the bruiser who accompanies his stories with a series of pokes, jabs and punches in the tenderest parts of his victims' anatomies. I remember seeing Alfred Knopf, the publisher, cornered one day at a literary tea by one of his heftiest and most important authors. Said author had him backed into a cul-de-sac of the cocktail bar, holding him firmly with his left arm, while he punched home the point of his story with the right. Mr. Knopf was laughing bravely, but the look in his eye suggested a Hatfield watching a McCoy being chosen as the bravest man in town.

5. Don't tell your story more than once to the same audience. I have seen more than one narrator so intoxicated by the laughter that greeted his rendition of a story that he promptly repeated either the whole of it or at least the tag, usually raising his voice the second time to insure further response from his audience. Almost as disastrous is the plight of the man who allows himself to be persuaded to retell the same story more than twice in the same room. The wise artist limits his encores. It's bad enough to subject your wife to hearing your gems over and over. She is used to it — or is she? Your friends won't be so docile.

If possible, try to remember the people to whom you have told a certain story; highly though they may cherish you, you will go down in their esteem if you carol "Here's a new one I just heard today," and then launch into the same tale you told at the previous Monday's poker session! Lowell Thomas once made the mistake of telling the same story at successive Dutch Treat Club dinners.

A friend could not resist saying, "That story wasn't quite so good tonight as it was a year ago."

Thomas, no mean hand at repartee, turned the tables with a quick "Neither are you, my friend."

6. Don't give the point of the story before you begin. Many a hapless amateur has killed a good anecdote by introducing it in some such fashion as "Did you fellows ever hear the story of the softhearted Ku Klux big shot whose friends call him Kleagle Tender?" Or "Did I tell you about the wife who directed a man inquiring for her husband to a fishing camp, suggesting that he look for a pole with a worm at each end?" If his audience says "No," he begins his story without realizing he has no ammunition left. A good detective-story writer saves his solution for the last chapter!

7. Don't insist on telling a story after your victim informs you he has heard it. A dreary type indeed is the determined monologist who swings into action something like "Have you heard the one about the downhearted octopus?" and although all in the room immediately chorus "Yes," proceeds to tell it anyhow. This is one way of insuring yourself a Mickey Finnish. Oscar Wilde's comment on a bore of this ilk was, "He's been invited to all the best homes in London — once!"

8. Don't oversell your story in advance. The man who prefaces a recital with "This is the funniest story you ever heard in your life" is apt to find the burden of proof sitting too heavily on his shoulders.

9. Don't tell your stories at the wrong place. A quip that convulsed the boys in the club car can fall awfully flat at Mrs. Waxelbaum's tea for the bishop. And a tidbit that had the English professors at the Faculty Club in stitches for an hour may be just beyond the comprehension of the babe you met at Leon and Eddie's. Probably you have heard of the gentleman who told an unknown dinner partner a joke that made a monkey of the guest of honor. When he had finished, she remarked coldly, "Do you know who I am? I am the guest of honor's

wife!" "Do you know who I am?" groaned the narrator, and when the answer was "No," cried, "Thank God!" and fled from the room. You may not be so fortunate!

10. Don't tell your stories at the wrong time. The best story in the world will fall flat if it is told at an inappropriate moment. A gathering engaged in serious discussion often will resent the introduction of unseemly levity. The man who can toss off a funny story in the right spot is a wit; the oaf who is telling them all the time is a nitwit.

11. Don't always "know another version." A man who can get himself disliked very thoroughly is one who is not content to let somebody else win an uninterrupted laugh, but must always top the other's story with "Oh, I know another version of that same joke — very ancient too." If he tells his story — and to borrow from myself, try and stop him! — the result, if the similarity actually exists, is anticlimactic and painfully unproductive of merriment; if, as is more often the case, there is no similarity at all, he is shown up as a fool, and a jealous one at that.

12. Don't tell stories that depend for their humor on events or personalities never heard of by your audience. Many stories, hilarious if you know the people involved or the circumstances that provoked the original situation, are unbelievably dull to a stranger. It is stories of this type that can win you a speedy reputation as a "name dropper" or a plain, unmitigated bore. In some parts of the country you must be more careful of per-

sonality angles than in others. New Englanders, in particular, are suspicious of strangers and don't like liberties to be taken with their landmarks or prominent citizens. Remember the story of the man of ninety-three who died last summer at Nantucket. The local paper's obituary concluded: "Although not a native, Mr. Blank came to this island at the age of two."

13. Avoid dialect stories as much as possible. Dialect stories are the hardest to tell properly. The endeavor of amateurs to impersonate Scotsmen, Negroes or Hebrews is often too horrible even to think about. If you must tell stories of this type — and be sure that no supersensitive member of your audience is going to be offended — take the dialect part as much for granted as possible, and concentrate on putting over the punch line. Personally, I find it difficult to enjoy dialect even on the printed page, and have deliberately avoided many recognized classics on that account. When I hear some noisy limelight-hogger begin, "This feller Pat says to Mike, 'Begorrah, me fine buck, Oi —' " I make a dive for the radio and find actual relief in a singing commercial.

This list of Don'ts has grown more formidable than I had intended, and will probably make me self-conscious in my own joke-telling for months to come — loud cries of "Hear, hear." Further, I notice that my injunctions number thirteen. Reminds me of the man who spluttered indignantly, "Me superstitious? I should say not! I'm afraid it would bring me bad luck!"

Number of words 1910
See page 261 for Questions

Reading Time in Seconds _____
See page 324 for Conversion Table

SELECTION 47

America's Penniless Millionaire

Farnsworth Crowder

What can you do to become a millionaire? Do as Conwell did. Develop one *speech so inspiring that it will make you a fortune of five million. Then, after you've made your million, how do you make yourself a penniless millionaire? You'll soon find that out, too.*

Statistically, the most extraordinary speech of all time was a collection of two dozen true stories woven into an inspirational lecture called *Acres of Diamonds*. It had a "run" of fifty years; it was repeated no less than 6000 times to an audience of millions throughout the world. It crowded little provincial churches and packed the largest auditoriums in the biggest cities. It hypnotized gatherings of the widest diversity, from handfuls of prairie

homesteaders in crossroads school houses to metropolitan assemblies of the elect. It drew fees ranging from a chicken dinner to $9000. Its net earnings, conservatively husbanded, easily could have built for its author a fortune of five million. That it did nothing of the sort was due to the fact that, as rapidly as the money rolled in, the author gave it away. During certain long periods, though he was making tens of thousands, he would rarely have more than a hundred ready dollars of his own at one time. Russell Herman Conwell was "America's penniless millionaire."

His fabulous lecture was a defense, by means of

anecdotes, of the theme that the world is a vast acreage strewn with diamonds. The wise man snatches up the dull stone that others have been kicking around. He chips a corner to find an eye of blue-white fire looking at him and then laboriously polishes it down to the form of a splendid jewel.

Opportunity, said Conwell, is no chance visitor who knocks but once and flees. It stands, very possibly, in our own boots, wearing our own socks. It is in our own back yard. It sits on the door step beside the milk bottle, waiting to be brought in. It is here, now; not over the horizon, tomorrow. It wanders about in unlikely and forlorn and even trampish guises, while heedless people kick it aside in their frantic rush to find a spectacular golden goddess called Luck.

With respect to this particular deity, Russell Conwell was an atheist. "The most hopeless proposition in the world," he would say, "is the fellow who thinks that success is a door through which he will sometime stumble if he roams around long enough." Good Luck he would define as a product of purpose, will, training and industry; Bad Luck as a face-saving excuse rather than an explanation. Golden Apples were to him a harvest from hard work, not chance sports on neglected trees.

To support his thesis, he scarcely could have found a more pat illustration than his own life. He mined and minted his own Good Luck. It was said of him that he could see the promise and design of a mountain in a molehill and then bring the mountain into being. He uncovered opportunities on the most unexpected and discouraging sites. He could snatch up thin suggestions and develop them into monuments.

From earliest youth, he seemed to realize, with some compelling intuitive wisdom, that he must make the best of whatever raw material was under his own hat and within immediate reach of his hands. He might have to live in poverty on a Massachusetts rock pile that his father called a farm. He might have to get up at four in the morning and work like a man. There might be no well-staffed neighborhood school with a rich curriculum. But he could learn to read. He carried a book wherever he went, down the furrows, to the pasture, out to the barn. It was a habit he never broke and never ceased to advocate: "Remember, you can carry a university in your coat pocket."

He so far developed the power to read, and with it his memory, that he could fix a page in mind and later recall it, word for word, as if he held the book in his hand. The capacity of his memory became an astonishment to his friends: though he believed he had only an average memory given an extraordinary discipline.

He never allowed it to break training. He never practiced the gentle vices of loafing and wool-gathering. During his services with the Union Army, he employed idle hours to commit the whole of Blackstone. Years later, while commuting by train to and from his law offices in Boston, he learned to read five languages.

No time, no occasion, no suggestion was ever left unexploited. As a boy, he made the farm livestock his first audience. The power, as orator and preacher, which was to make him the platform peer of William J. Bryan, was first exercised in the chicken house.

By the time he entered Yale College, his habits of application and self-command enabled him to carry the academic and law courses simultaneously, while supporting himself with employment in a New Haven hotel. When the Civil War broke, it was as if he had anticipated the opportunity to become "the recruiting orator of the Berkshires." He raised and captained the Mountain Boys of Massachusetts and was later returned from the South to assemble a company of artillery.

There is an event of his military service which demonstrates his facility for laying hold of symbols, suggestions and incidents and fixing them tenaciously into the dynamic pattern of his life. A diminutive orderly, John Ring, attached to the company, became profoundly devoted to big fine-looking Captain Conwell — and to the Captain's sword, which represented, to John, both his beloved officer and all the glory of war. One day, near New Bern, a surprise Confederate advance routed the company from its position. Retreating across a river, the men fired a wooden bridge to cut off their pursuers. They had also cut off escape for their orderly: Johnnie Ring had dashed back to bring the Captain's sword. He appeared with it at last and gained the blazing bridge. But with clothes in flames he fell into the river. Dragged out and returned to consciousness, his first thought was for his Captain and the sword. He smiled to find it safe beside him, took it in his arms and died.

"When I stood over his body," Conwell recollected, "and realized that he had died for love of me, I made a vow that I would live, thereafter, not only my own life, but also the life of John Ring, that it might not be lost."

And from then on, for sixty years, Russell Conwell literally worked a double day — eight hours for himself and eight for Johnnie. And always over the head of his bed hung the sword to keep bright his extravagant vow. That he kept it, one can well believe after a glance at a mere catalogue of his activities.

Following a European interlude to recover his health, broken by war injuries, he settled down to an intensive, versatile career in Boston. He opened two law offices in Boston. He lectured. He launched the Boston Young Men's Congress. He wrote editorials for the *Traveler,* corresponded for outside newspapers and went abroad frequently to interview celebrities. He managed a political campaign. He made money in real estate. He founded the *Journal* in suburban Somerville and maintained a free legal clinic for the poor.

Conwell had lost his first wife and had married again, a woman who freshened his interest in religious work. One day, an elderly lady visited his office for legal counsel on selling a distressed church property in Lexington. To give his advice, he journeyed out to a meeting of the discouraged and pastorless congregation. There was such melancholy in the little group, some of whom had worshiped there all their lives, that Conwell was moved to blurt, "Why sell it? Why not start over again!"

They objected that the structure was too dilapidated and money too dear. But young Conwell's eye for the hidden chance was wide awake and challenged. "You can make repairs," he shouted. "I'll help you!"

On the appointed day he borrowed tools and came out. No one else showed up, but he pitched in on the rickety front steps. A livery-stable proprietor of the town paused to ask what he was going to do. "Build a new church," Conwell answered. They fell to chatting and before he left, the man had pledged $100 toward a new building.

It was all the prospect that Russell Conwell needed to set imagination and energy to working. He made the hundred-dollar kernel grow. While the new church was going up, he preached to the congregation in rented rooms. Within eighteen months he had been ordained as their minister and had built around them a flourishing institution.

From Lexington he was invited to another hapless, debt-ridden little church in Philadelphia. He accepted and, characteristically, saw great possibilities in the discouraging new scene. The salary offered him was only $800, but the trustees stipulated that every time he could double the congregation, they would match the feat with a doubled salary. Six weeks after taking charge, Conwell had done it. Within six years he was drawing $10,000. Thereafter, he mercifully excused the trustees from their agreement. Had he held them to it, his salary would have climbed to over $25,000.

The popularity of his services was soon straining the capacity of the auditorium. One Sunday, from the many being turned away, he rescued a particularly unhappy little girl and saw her to a place inside. She was so grateful for the kindness and so distressed at the smallness of the room that she resolved to save her money for a building that would be big enough. Before she had advanced far on her grand project, she died. Her father turned over her fund, just fifty-seven cents in pennies.

Conwell reported the gift to his trustees. They were touched, but he was inspired. If $100 could be the nucleus of a building fund in Lexington, fifty-seven cents could do similar duty in Philadelphia! Accordingly, he went to the owner of a certain fine lot on Broad Street. The price was $10,000. Conwell made the outrageous offer of a down payment of fifty-seven cents. It was accepted. In due time the balance was paid off and upon that property, in 1891, was dedicated the largest church auditorium of its day.

The design of Russell Conwell's achievements might be called horticultural — the discovery of a seed; an uncanny insight into its fertility; a prodigious amount of work to make it grow.

From the modest ambitions of a young man came a university. Conwell was solicited for advice by a student who wanted to better his education, but was handicapped by having little money and a mother to support. As to all such, Conwell's first admonition was: "Read. Make a traveling library of your pocket." And then he added: "Come to me one evening a week and I'll begin teaching you to be a minister myself."

The first week, the student appeared with six friends in tow. The second week, forty were in the class. More volunteer teachers had to be invited. A house was rented. By the end of the first year, 250 were studying in this informal night college. A second house was hired. Buildings rose beside the great Temple church into the physical form of Temple University. "Our aim from the first," said President Conwell, "was to give education to those unable to get it through the usual channels." He lived to see more than 100,000 such pupils take work in his school.

Similar and equally unpretentious was Conwell's founding of Philadelphia's big Samaritan Hospital. Two rented rooms, one nurse, one patient. That was all. But it was enough for a beginning. In its expansion, the Samaritan acquired Goodheart Hospital and Garretson in the industrial quarter of the city and all became affiliated with Temple University.

But the heading up of a huge institutional church, a University and three hospitals was not enough for the dual capacities of Russell Conwell-Johnnie Ring. Out of the daily stint of sixteen hours was found the time to go on the platform for more than 8000 lectures — usually *Acres of Diamonds;* to maintain contacts with scores of the leading men of his time and with hundreds of the boys and girls he was helping through school; and to write thirty-seven volumes — biographies, travel books and legal treatises. In authorship, his vast reading and disciplined memory served him like a reference library. It was told that, on the train between lecture dates, without notes or books, he dictated a best-selling biography of Charles H. Spurgeon, the eminent evangelist, in twelve days.

His famous lecture was one more work developed from a rudiment. Any number of people might have heard — did hear — the story which an Arab guide along the Euphrates River was fond of telling. They might have thought it interesting, even worthy a place in their repertoire of traveler's tales. But to Russell Conwell's ears, it was dramatically suggestive; its lesson squared with his own philosophy of success; it could be made the germinal anecdote of a strong lecture.

The Arab's story was that of the wealthy and contented farmer, Ali Hafed, who was made to feel wretchedly poor and miserable by a visitor who infected him with a passion for diamonds. So covetous did Ali become that he sold the farm, abandoned his family and set out to prospect the world. And while he found no precious stones and at last threw his spent and starving body into the sea, the man who had purchased his farm discovered along its familiar stream beds the diamond mines of Golconda. "Ali would have been better off to remain at home and dig in his own cellar."

Throughout his lecture, Conwell hammered with his massive force at that simple moral. The impact of the message on many lives was crucial. As the years went by, testimonials poured in on him from governors, mayors, teachers, merchants, engineers and professionals, thanking him for the impetus his lecture had given their lives.

And from the thousands of college young people benefited by his largess came testimonials even more gratifying. Conwell was only thirty-three, and far from rich, when he determined to devote the proceeds of his lecturing to students fighting the kind of material odds and social discriminations he had experienced at Yale. His program of donations was continued for over forty years. He always kept a list of candidates for aid, most of them recommended by college presidents. His one rigid and unvarying requirement before extending help was that a student must be trying to help himself. He wanted his gifts to be, not chance windfalls, but premiums for diligent effort already made.

When, in 1925, Russell Conwell entered his eighty-second and last year, with all his enormous work behind him, books written, institutions founded and prospering, honors, degrees, prizes and medals to his name, there was one old-man satisfaction that he could not have. He could not mull over huge bank accounts and vast accumulated investments. He had distributed his fortune as he made it. He remarked, shortly before his death, that his riches lay in the men and women he had started on the road to accomplishment and happiness; and that was all, in the way of assets, he needed now.

Number of words 2530
See page 263 for Questions

Reading Time in Seconds _____
See page 324 for Conversion Table

SELECTION 48

To Improve Telephone Manners
Don Wharton

Even if you don't make public speeches, engage in discussions, or tell funny stories, you still make phone calls. How many are important? To the person calling — every one! How aware are you of things that either diminish or enhance the effectiveness of your telephone communications?

Business firms, universities, hospitals, labor unions and police departments all over the country are getting the telephone company to help them improve their telephone manners. In New York alone 1200 banks, stores and manufacturers have skilled observers listen in regularly. Often a firm with a carefully trained receptionist out front discovers that its invisible receptionist at the switchboard is curt, indifferent, indistinct in speech.

For instance, one of New York's best-known hotels asked the phone company to overhaul the telephone habits of its employes. Operators were leaving the line without explanation, calls were transferred grudgingly, clerks were surly, receivers were banged down noisily. Sometimes room service hung up or carried on side conversations while a guest was speaking.

Armed with a headset, a telephone consultant sat in at the hotel switchboard. Later, recordings were made, based on typical calls. Then she had three-hour sessions with successive groups of employes, played the recordings to demonstrate how each employe's voice sounded over the phone, showed a movie on telephone courtesy. In the past year the movie has been shown to 1,750,000 persons.

The program, as is usually the case, resulted in marked courtesy at this hotel. Every new employe is now given telephone training.

Recently I sat in on a telephone-manners session of a large New York manufacturer. Here were six secretaries, good-looking girls, attractively dressed, poised. Each had a pleasant personality. Yet when their telephone voices were recorded and played back they sounded unpleasant or indifferent. One voice was flat, monotonous; one was a high whine; another was a tiny uncertain voice. None of the playbacks sounded friendly or helpful, yet that firm spends millions each year on ads designed to attract phone callers. The girls were crestfallen, but they stayed on to learn all they could about improving their telephone manners.

It has been said that an interested voice is like offering a warm handshake over the phone. A common failing is that voices lack color, interest, cordiality. Consultants advise secretaries and others using the phone to practice in front of a mirror — alone. The telephone company has various aids, including tests, exercises and practice sentences, for individuals who wish to improve their telephone speech. These can be obtained from the local telephone business office.

A New York department store had its telephone-order service analyzed, and the findings were startling. The operators sounded bored, made customers hang on interminably without apology, didn't offer to call back, expressed no regret if the desired item was sold out. Nearly 700 persons in this store have now received telephone training. Where order girls used to say "Hold on," they now ask: "Do you mind waiting while I check that for you?" Instead of returning to the line with an abrupt "It comes in blue," they reopen the conversation politely: "Thank you for waiting." Instead of telling callers, "You have to check with Mr. Blank," they say something like "Mr. Blank is handling that — I'll be glad to transfer you."

On the phone arbitrary expressions give an unfavorable impression: "You have to," "You must," "It's necessary," "It's required." "Will you ask Mr. Smith to call Mr. Jones, please?" doesn't sound at all like the peremptory "Tell Mr. Smith to call Mr. Jones, please."

Another phrase frowned on is "He's in conference." One telephone consultant told me that there is no way of saying these three words without sounding pompous. She advises secretaries to say "He's in a meeting," or "He's talking with someone right now," or "He's on another line." And the secretary should offer to help, should take some positive action.

The telephone company has been gradually eradicating "Hello" as a greeting in business offices. It also campaigns intensively against "Who's calling?" "Hello" is appropriate in the home but the company considers "Who's calling?" tactless anywhere. In offices, when the identity of the caller must be established, they suggest some such phrase as "May I tell him who's calling, please?" Those extra four words, "May I tell him," do a big psychological job. They get away from the implication that only persons on a preferred list get through to the boss. Further, they indicate a willingness to be of service to the person calling.

An increasing number of executives are answering their own phones without having the call go through a secretary. The head of one firm says, "There are not many inconsequential calls, and the few that are can be easily terminated. The man who will talk with anyone without first having a blueprint builds friendliness for his company."

Most telephone-company officials answer their own calls. In New York all Socony-Vacuum officials including the president do so. So also at the National Shawmut Bank in Boston and Monsanto Chemical Company in St. Louis. Many executives, out of courtesy, now call numbers themselves rather than cause waiting at the other end when a secretary gets the person being called.

The Bell System's 250,000 operators probably constitute the most courteous large working force in the nation. Operators are not polite because they have orders to be polite. Their courtesy is a reflection of the manners pervading the entire system. An operator in training encounters politeness all around her. Her instructor, supervisor, chief operator, the repairman fixing the switchboard — all show the same attitude toward the student that she is expected to show to customers.

Recently in a Philadelphia exchange I put on earphones and listened in on two student operators — 17-year-old girls just graduated from high school, in training only three days. Already they were getting a helpful, friendly tone in their voices.

Beginners are taught to be natural rather than formal. They say "I'm sorry" rather than "I am sorry," "I'll see" rather than "I shall see," "May I help you?" rather than "What information do you wish, please?" Operators used to repeat the same phrase — for instance, "One moment, please" — but now they are taught to vary the wording.

At Syracuse, N. Y., last summer I watched operators record their voices on little discs. The disc is brought out a week or two later, put on the machine and another sample taken of the girl's voice. This is done a third time. By playing back the various samples a student operator observes her progress and can hear herself as others hear her, often the key to developing a courteous, helpful, cheerful tone. These discs are being used all over central New York not only to help beginners but to keep experienced operators on their mettle. Already numerous business firms have borrowed the technique to improve the telephone manners of their employes.

The Bell System has a saying that "every call is important to the person calling." Courtesy in the telephone business began about 1880 when the rude remarks of teen-age boy operators became unbearable. They were replaced by young women — a heretical idea then. By 1890 women operated practically all Bell System daytime switchboards; with the 20th century they began working at night. The slogan "The Voice with a Smile" came in 1912.

About 160 million telephone conversations are held in this country every business day. How much pleasanter life would be if they were all conducted with the smiling voice of Bell System operators.

Number of words 1220
See page 265 for Questions

Reading Time in Seconds _____
See page 324 for Conversion Table

Section V: On Listening

SELECTION 49

The Vague Specific

Richard B. Gehman

To be understood, be specific. A listener may have no trouble with the specific but much trouble with the vague specific. The vague specific! That phrase sounds much like the ones "pretty ugly" or "a little big."
Too bad we don't also have the wife's side of this problem!

The other day my wife woke me from a nap and said, "Say, what about all those things out in the front room?"

"What things?"

"Why, you know," she said, "those things. All that stuff."

She sounded as though she supposed I knew exactly what she meant. I didn't. For all I knew, "those things" could have been the furniture, books, rugs, magazines, lamps, or the remnant of a sandwich I'd been eating. I never did find out what she meant, because just then the telephone rang and she went to answer it.

I tell this rather pointless story because it actually has a point: It refers to an American conversational peculiarity — the habit, common mainly among women, of referring vaguely to specific persons or things. I have named this the Vague Specific.

Women working together around the house are particularly addicted to this form of communication. Not long ago I copied down a conversation my wife and the maid had in the next room. It went this way:

"Here," my wife said, "you can take these."

"Where do you want them?"

"Oh, put them out there somewhere."

"With the others?"

"No," said my wife, decisively, "put them with those things behind the others."

The terrifying thing about this is that each knew exactly what the other meant. I can't explain this gift that women have, but I've analyzed it thoroughly and divided the Vague Specific into three general categories.

The first is the *Surrealist Vague Specific.* Once, from a distant room, my wife called to me:

"Say, come and do something about this box — it's rotten!"

Her words conjured up a picture reminiscent of a Salvador Dali painting: a headless torso, a melting watch, a rotten box.

"What do you mean?" I called.

"This box," she insisted, "is rotten!"

I went to investigate. The rotten box turned out to be an old window box, one that I'd been promising to fix. It was falling apart — but so far as my wife was concerned, it was rotten, so we threw it away.

This was similar to an experience suffered by a friend of mine, Arnold Uffelman, who appeared at my door one day looking haggard. "How about coming over and having a look at our washing machine?" he asked. "My wife says the thing on its side is acting funny." He sighed, and asked if I had anything to drink in the house.

After we'd fixed the washing machine — just a matter of readjusting the thing on its side — Uffelman and I fell to discussing this habit our wives have of being specifically vague. He thought of the second category: the *Vaguely Specific Individual.*

Uffelman's wife often turns to him and says something like, "What's the name of that fellow who drives the truck?"

Poor Uffelman knows of at least ten fellows who drive trucks, but he's never been able to think of the specific one his wife vaguely means.

I can sympathize with Uffelman, because all this is not unlike an announcement my wife sometimes makes to me when I get home from a tough cocktail hour at Pete's.

"The men came today," she says.

I never can tell which men she means, but I can never get up enough courage to ask. For a while, I had a system figured out to beat her at this game, but it backfired. The conversation went like this:

My wife: "The men came today."

Me: (Craftily) "What did you tell them?"

My wife: "I told them to go ahead."

The only satisfaction I got from this was the knowledge that, whatever the men had gone ahead and done, it was going to cost me money.

The third major category is the *Vaguely Specific Time.* I will list a few of these, with comments:

"Do you remember that time we were at the shore, and it rained?" (We've been to the shore 14 or 15 times; it's rained almost every time.)

"When was it that we had the Coes over?" (We've

had the Coes over 12 times in the past two years.)

"What was the name of that couple we met the time we went to the Zeamers'?" (No comment here, except to point out the neat juxtaposition of the *Vaguely Specific Individual* and the *Vaguely Specific Time*. No mean feat.)

As I was saying, I can't explain all this. I thought I was on the trail of it the other day when I was reading a book on the psychology of American women, but just as I'd got to the second chapter my wife interrupted. "The woman's here for the money," she said. I gave the woman, whoever she was, her money, and then I went back to continue my reading — but somehow I couldn't find the book.

"Say," I asked my wife, "what happened to that book I had?"

For some reason, she didn't know what I was talking about.

Number of words 820
See page 267 for Questions

Reading Time in Seconds _____
See page 324 for Conversion Table

SELECTION 50

We Quit Talking—and Now the Cupboard Is Bare

Ewart A. Autry

Ambrose Bierce, in his book The Devil's Dictionary, *defines the word* bore. *A bore is "a person who talks when you wish him to listen." That suggests that listening is the communication key to social acceptance. Here's a married couple to show you both the advantages and disadvantages of listening.*

"We're talking too much," my wife announced one morning at breakfast. "But these are the first words we've said since we sat down," I protested. "I mean when we're out in public or have company," she explained. "We carry too much of the conversation. It must bore others."

I thought it over. "Well," I finally agreed, "it's true we rarely run out of words."

"And we're always eager to get them in," she continued. "We talk so much that people learn everything about us while we're learning nothing about them. So let's do something about it."

"Tape our lips?" I suggested.

She ignored that, with reason. "Let's agree to limit our part of the conversation when others are around," she said. "We'll set up some signals. When you think I'm talking too much just touch your forehead and I'll slow down. When I think you're talking too much, I'll use the same signal."

I was skeptical but willing to try. So we did. On our very next visitor.

It wasn't a successful experiment. He was a phlegmatic neighbor who never used any more words than were absolutely necessary. That, coupled with our resolve to let guests carry most of the conversation, produced long, awkward silences. Intermittently the three of us stared into our open fire and there was little sound except the crackling of my hickory logs.

When our visitor had gone, my wife looked chagrined. "I kept hoping you'd talk," she said, "but I didn't know how to get you started. The only signal we agreed on was the one to cut down on the talking."

There was another repercussion from that fiasco. Our visitor reported to the neighbors that we weren't well and they kept calling to inquire about our health. "That's some reputation to have," I grumbled. "When we don't rattle on all the time, people think we're sick."

Most visitors, though, unknowingly cooperated with our new scheme. They kept the conversation rolling with no more than an occasional word from us. It was amazing how much some people talked. I commented on it one day after a visit from Dan and Ina Blake. "Dan was really wound up," I said. "I thought he'd never finish that story about the big bass he caught Christmas day."

"This is the first chance he's had to finish it," advised my wife. "Always before you've interrupted to tell some wild fish story of your own."

"And I noticed Ina got in the full account of her latest operation," I retorted. "Other times you've put your stitches in before she could even begin on hers."

"It takes will power to keep your mouth shut," said my wife thoughtfully. "Especially when you have something more interesting to tell than what's being told."

The signals actually worked well and we didn't have to use them too often. But sometimes we'd let our tongues get ahead of our brains. Like when I was telling Don Duke about a bass I'd hooked. The fish was weighing about nine pounds and I had him on the way to the boat when I saw my wife touch her forehead. I

Reprinted from *Minutes,* Magazine of Nationwide Insurance, Fall 1970.

immediately cut the bass down to three pounds and let him get away.

Then there's the time my wife was telling some friends about a recent vacation trip to the ocean. She was waxing poetic as she described a sunset over the water. I noticed our visitors beginning to wiggle restlessly, so I caught her eye and touched my forehead. You never saw a sun drop so quickly into the sea.

There were times when others noticed our signals. Once we were visiting friends and I was talking too much. My wife touched her forehead. When I didn't react immediately she kept touching it. In a few minutes our hostess left the room and returned with a glass of water and an aspirin. "You poor thing," she said to my wife. "You have a headache. Take this."

A few days later I had a bad crick in my neck. I went to a doctor who is a family friend. At his invitation my wife came into the consultation room. She began to tell him my various symptoms. I thought she was telling too much so I touched my forehead. The doctor noticed it immediately. "Ah, ha," he said. "Just as I thought. You have sinus trouble."

He tilted my chin and sprayed my nose with the hottest stuff I ever felt. My eyes watered for an hour.

But I must have touched the right spot. My neck was better before we got home.

Our talk curb has been in effect for a year now. We've talked less and heard more. Not all of it has been worthwhile but at least it's been as good as some of the stuff we were putting out.

And we've learned one thing for certain — talk less and you'll have more company. More people came to our house this past year than in any of the thirty we've been married. One of our regular visitors said why. "I like to visit here," he beamed. "You're interesting people to talk to."

"To." Not "with."

We have a problem though. Much of our company has been at mealtime. Sometimes our pantry has been stripped to the danger point. Right now we're trying to decide whether to buy more groceries each week or forget our conversation moratorium.

When I mention the second possibility, my wife gets an eager gleam in her eyes. And come to think of it, there are a few things I'd like to say too. So, if you're planning to come to our house, you'd better hurry. Before we start talking again.

Number of words 950
See page 269 for Questions

Reading Time in Seconds _____
See page 325 for Conversion Table

Listening Between the Lines of Conversation

Jesse S. Nirenberg

To read well, you must read both the lines and between the lines. The same is true, apparently, with listening. If our interpersonal relations are to be properly satisfying, we must understand the interplay of communication between lines of conversation.

Each line of conversation conveys several messages simultaneously. One of these messages is communicated through the meaning of the words. This is the explicit message. Other messages are transmitted *by implication*. These we shall call *implicit* messages.

The individual's implicit messages express his real feelings or the things he really wants at the moment. Therefore, to understand an individual by knowing his likes and dislikes; to cultivate a relationship with him by giving him what he really wants; to protect him from what he wants but shouldn't have; and to influence him by relating your ideas to his interests; you have to listen between the lines and deal with his intentions.

This requires cultivating the habit of continually analyzing motive. What does the speaker mean besides what he is explicitly saying? How does he feel? What does he want? And usually you have to hold up your end of the conversation while answering these questions for yourself. With practice it will become second nature and you will be much better able to achieve a meeting of minds.

Let's take an example. Suppose you are sitting on a park bench on a warm, sunny, summer day. A man who is a stranger to you shares this bench. Both of you have been sitting there silently.

Suddenly he remarks, "Beautiful day. Hardly a cloud in the sky."

The explicit message in his remark refers to the beauty of the day and the absence of clouds. But he is also communicating implicitly. For one thing he indi-

From the book *Getting Through to People*, by Jesse S. Nirenberg, Ph.D.; © 1963 by Jesse S. Nirenberg. Published by Prentice-Hall, Inc., Englewood Cliffs, New Jersey.

cates that he wants to have conversation with you. Secondly, by choosing a very conventional, impersonal opening he conveys a wish to be at least moderately proper about opening conversation with a stranger. After all, he could have opened a little more brashly with, "I had a delicious bowl of beef stew for lunch," or "What do you do for a living?" or "My name is Frank Williams, what's yours?"

You reply, "Yes, it is a beautiful day. If I had known it was this warm, I wouldn't have worn my coat."

Your explicit message communicates that you feel the day is beautiful, that you hadn't realized before coming out that it would be so warm, and that you regret wearing your coat. Beyond this is your implicit message which tells that you are willing to talk with him, and that you would like to carry the conversation even further since you introduce a more personal note, your regret about wearing your coat.

Now suppose he replies in turn, "I don't blame you for wearing it, though. It is a very good looking coat."

Beyond his explicit message that he considers your coat good looking he is also communicating the following implicit messages: he *wants you to know* that he considers it good looking, which very likely indicates that he wishes to please you; he would like to continue the conversation; and he feels that even if you knew the weather were warm you might be motivated to wear the coat because of its fine appearance.

The context of a remark determines the implicit messages it conveys. For example, in the above conversation the words themselves of his opening remark about it being a beautiful day do not imply a wish to engage you in conversation. It's only as an opening remark that they contain this intention. If instead these words were a reply to a question the implicit message would change while the explicit still remains the same.

The explicit message might be defined then as the content of a remark completely apart from its context. The implicit messages come from the total context.

To illustrate further, suppose someone in your family enters your house and seeing that you are about to go out, comments that it is raining and that you had better wear your rubbers. In addition to telling about the rain he communicates that he thinks you don't know it is raining, that he cares about keeping you from getting wet, and that he feels that he can influence you.

Implicit messages can be communicated through the pacing of ideas and the timing of pauses as well as through the words. For example, in conversation, over-elaboration or repetition, which slows the pacing, implies that the speaker is anxious that he is not getting his ideas into the mind of the listener. Ironically, his over-explaining often brings about the result he dreads — the listener's tuning out because he feels that he already knows what the speaker is saying, had grasped it the first time, and can afford to not listen to the unnecessary repetition.

Similarly, with regard to pauses, a listener may realize that he has the answer to the problem the speaker is posing, before the speaker stops. In his eagerness, the listener then replies with his answer just as the speaker finishes his last word. This gives the speaker the impression that his ideas were not thought about, carefully considered; that the listener was just waiting for him to finish so that the listener could have his say.

Generally, in conversation when ideas are being exchanged there is an instant's pause between a comment and a reply to the comment. This is part of the rhythm of talk and is the time needed for the listener to absorb the comment and formulate at least the opening of his reply. When the ideas presented are difficult to absorb the pause is longer. But when there is no pause at all, it implies a lack of thought or even of listening.

Therefore, when you reply in conversation make sure to pause for the instant even if you've already formulated your reply. This courtesy of implying that the other person's ideas deserve consideration, will help cultivate his receptivity to your ideas.

As illustrated above, we are continuously communicating through two channels — explicit and implicit. But why do we need two channels? The answer is, because we are civilized.

Living in a society requires that we abide by a whole complex of rules — legal and moral laws, family and community customs, and etiquette. Since these rules are man-made we are not born with natures that are inherently fitted to these rules. This means we must continually make compromises between what our natures want and what the rules require.

The ability to compromise, to give up part of what he wants, develops as the child grows. The little infant has no scruples. He tries to get what he wants in any way he can. As he grows older he learns that he must not kill, hurt, cheat, steal, lie, or be discourteous. He comes to know the penalties for each of these — penalties imposed not only by others but by his own conscience as well.

But human nature is alive and kicking within him. He wants, yet has to curb many of his wishes; he gets angry, and at the same time must control his temper; and he gets frightened, but hides his fear when it seems shameful.

This vital, energetic, demanding human nature won't be still. It insists on a voice. But because men's minds are atuned to the Rules this voice of primitive impulse would sound offensive and even threatening.

As a compromise, therefore, the channel of implicit communication is used. What is proper is said explicitly. What might offend is implied.

By implication we can praise and reassure ourselves; insult, reject, and derogate others; talk about the things we want but shouldn't really ask for; and tell others that we like them where shyness prevents a direct declaration. We can also attempt to control others through threat or flattery while claiming innocence of such discourtesy.

This all really comes down to the following five inter-

personal operations: 1. building up one's self; 2. attacking others; 3. making demands; 4. controlling; and 5. expressing love.

Number of words 1320
See page 271 for Questions

Reading Time in Seconds _____
See page 325 for Conversion Table

One Who Listens

Albert Edward Wiggam

One who listens is one who learns, as the following selection makes perfectly plain. One mark of an educated man is this: he listens to one who knows — listens both to experts and to experience. For that kind of listening, open ears and open mind are essential.

When I was a boy I heard a story told by a lecturer at our County Teachers' Institute in the old court-house at Vernon that I have never forgotten, a story that goes to the heart of this phase of a man's education. I have forgotten the lecturer's name, but as the story went, Old John Crosby was the best farmer in Johnson County. His corn and hogs and pumpkins always took first prize at the County Fair. The way John Crosby farmed was a model for the whole county. If he plowed and planted at a certain time or in a certain way, or bred his stock, or fattened his cattle this way or that, it must be right. It was the "Crosby way" and that was the last word among the Johnson County farmers. He believed this and his neighbors believed it. Old Crosby scorned "these scientific fellers," as he called them, "who write pieces for the agricultural papers."

"Them fellers just spin these scientific yarns out of their heads, while they are settin' in their laboratories," said Old John. "They go in one of my ears and out both. You can't teach farming in a college." And that settled it.

But his son, Young John, had gained a different notion from the high-school principal. This principal was different from the previous ones for, strange to say, he took the pupils out of the schoolroom into the fields and did a great deal of his teaching under the skies, in the wind and sunshine and even in the rain. He showed them about plants and animals and rocks and trees, where they could touch nature at its heart and feel its pulses for themselves. He was a mental kinsman of Plato and Socrates and Aristotle, of Pliny and Marcus Aurelius, of Pestalozzi and Horace Mann, of John Dewey and his educational confreres, for he tried to make his school, as all born teachers do whether they

have ever heard of these masters or not, a part of life instead of an addition to life.

This principal had inspired Young John with the notion of going to the State Agricultural College. Old Crosby, of course, pooh-poohed the idea, but finally yielded to the combined pleadings of the boy and his mother, and the lad went off to take the short winter course.

"But when you get back," warned the Old Man, "I'll give you half of the west sixty and I'll take the other half. We'll put them both in corn and then I'll show you what those fellers in college don't know about dirt farming."

When the young man came back home, Old John got a great deal of amusement out of some of the boy's "new-fangled ideas." "Wants to give the cows a 'balanced ration,'" laughed the Old Man at the village store. "Says some of 'em are just boardin' on me and are not payin' their keep. He thinks I don't know milk when I see it."

One morning, however, in the early spring, Old John said to Mother Crosby, just a bit uneasily:

"Mother, what's that boy got in his room up-stairs in the south window?"

"Oh, just some boxes o' dirt, testin' his seed corn," replied the mother cautiously.

"Huh!" snorted the Old Man. "Do you reckon I've been selectin' seed corn for forty years and can't tell a good ear from a bad one?"

But Crosby could not help noticing that the boy had scarcely any replanting to do, while nearly one-fifth of his own corn failed to come up.

And so it went all through the summer. When the dry weather set in, the boy kept right on plowing but the Old Man laid off as usual.

"He don't seem to understand," said Crosby, "that all this plowing when the ground is dry will just make the moisture evaporate."

But the boy went on plowing just the same and kept his own counsel.

Finally, in October, when the corn was cribbed, Old John proudly put in his usual seventy-five bushels per acre. But when Young John weighed in his last load the average was ninety!

The next morning the Old Man came down to breakfast in his Sunday blacks and with his satchel packed.

"Why, Father," exclaimed Mother Crosby in astonishment, "are you sick? Where are you going?"

"Oh," replied the Old Man, with a sheepish grin, *"I'm going to college."*

For all I know Old John Crosby may have gone to college for the next twenty years and may now be a professor of agricultural chemistry, but the biggest day in his education was the day when he closed his satchel, and opened his mind to listen to the voices of those who knew.

However, there is one point in this story, an extremely important point in education that we should not overlook, and that point is that Old Crosby *already knew a great deal.* His practical mind and long experience had taught him many things worth knowing. He was not by any means altogether wrong. In many respects he was eminently right. He was right when he said, "You can't make a farmer in college." You can't. Neither can you make an expert accountant, or a doctor, or lawyer, or engineer, or artist or any other finished educational product, fully fitted for the practical work of life. The best educational systems will never be able to put out a youth equipped with the whole armor of both experience and academic training, a full-fledged artist, craftsman or practitioner, as Minerva sprang full grown from the head of Jove.

You should, therefore, observe that Old Crosby was already getting seventy-five bushels per acre and the college added only fifteen. So when he got to college, I have not a particle of doubt that he had a great deal of value to tell the theoretical and experimental professors. And if those professors did not listen very carefully to Crosby's practical knowledge, I do not believe they had very much knowledge to give him in return.

They were just as much tight-minders as he was before he humbled his mind and joined the educationally converted. Crosby was wrong when he assumed the professors had nothing to tell him; and they were wrong if they assumed he had nothing to tell them. When he got back to the farm and combined his long practical experience with his theoretical and experimental knowledge, I suspect that he beat Young John about as badly as Young John had beaten him.

It is only when the schools and the practical man get together that we shall develop the best farmers, or accountants, or the best business men, or the best anything. I was deeply impressed with this line of thought as I lunched the other day with two friends, a celebrated psychologist and the manager of one of our great chain-store systems. The business man wanted the psychologist to help him in selecting his employees, and he asked him what he would do if he should come into his plant.

"Why," replied the psychologist, "my first job would be to find out *what you already know and what you have tried.* I want the benefit of your practical experience first. No scientist can get his knowledge out of the air. His first business is to get a grasp of the actual physical facts of the situation. A man might have twenty times as much knowledge of the human mind as the best psychologist now has, but he could not help you very much unless he knew the situation amid which your men work, what kind of men they now are, what kind of men you think would be better. I might select much worse men than you have, because my first duty is to know the jobs. I must first know what the jobs require before I can tell what would make a good man or a poor man to fill any one of them. It is, therefore, only by combining your experience with what theoretical knowledge I may possess that we shall be able, by our united efforts, to secure better employees."

When business men and scientists, school and industry, education and life, culture and the day's work, strike hands in this royal and loyal manner, both business and science, education and life will reap immense financial as well as humanistic rewards.

Number of words 1410
See page 273 for Questions

Reading Time in Seconds _____
See page 325 for Conversion Table

Listening Is a 10-Part Skill
Ralph G. Nichols

When you sit down by Dr. Nichols at his desk, what do you see? A sign of name-plate size that reads, "I'm listening"! For the first time you may realize the significance of listening in interpersonal relations. It's important to be listened to — and to listen.

White collar workers, on the average, devote at least 40 percent of their work day to listening. Apparently 40 percent of their salary is paid to them for listening. Yet tests of listening comprehension have shown that, without training, these employes listen at only 25 percent efficiency.

This low level of performance becomes increasingly intolerable as evidence accumulates that it can be significantly raised. The component skills of listening are known. They boil down to this:

Learning through listening is primarily an inside job — inside action on the part of the listener. What he needs to do is to replace some common present attitudes with others.

Recognizing the dollar values in effective listening, many companies have added courses in this skill to their regular training programs. Some of the pioneers in this effort have been American Telephone & Telegraph Co., General Motors Corporation, Ford Motor Company, The Dow Chemical Company, Western Electric Co., Inc., Methods Engineering Council of Pittsburgh, Minnesota Mining & Manufacturing Co., Thompson Products, Inc., of Cleveland, and Rogers Corp. of Connecticut.

Warren Ganong of the Methods Engineering Council has compared trainees given a preliminary discussion of efficient listening with those not provided such discussion. On tests at the end of the courses the former achieved marks 12 to 15 percent higher than did the latter.

A. A. Tribbey, general personnel supervisor of the Wisconsin Telephone Company, in commenting on the results of a short conference course in which effective listening was stressed, declared: "It never fails to amaze us when we see the skill that is acquired in only three days."

The conviction seems to be growing that upper-level managers also need listening skill. As Dr. Earl Planty, executive counselor for the pharmaceutical firm of Johnson & Johnson, puts it: "By far the most effective method by which executives can tap ideas of subordinates is sympathetic listening in the many day-to-day informal contacts within and outside the work place. There is no system that will do the job in an easier man-ner. . . . Nothing can equal an executive's willingness to hear."

A study of the 100 best listeners and the 100 worst listeners in the freshman class on the University of Minnesota campus has disclosed ten guides to improved listening. Business people interested in improving their own performance can use them to analyze their personal strengths and weaknesses. The ten guides to good listening are:

1. FIND AREA OF INTEREST

All studies point to the advantage in being interested in the topic under discussion. Bad listeners usually declare the subject dry after the first few sentences. Once this decision is made, it serves to rationalize any and all inattention.

Good listeners follow different tactics. True, their first thought may be that the subject sounds dry. But a second one immediately follows, based on the realization that to get up and leave might prove a bit awkward.

The final reflection is that, being trapped anyhow, perhaps it might be well to learn if anything is being said that can be put to use.

The key to the whole matter of interest in a topic is the word *use*. Whenever we wish to listen efficiently, we ought to say to ourselves: "What's he saying that I can use? What worth-while ideas has he? Is he reporting any workable procedures? Anything that I can cash in, or with which I can make myself happier?" Such questions lead us to screen what we are hearing in a continual effort to sort out the elements of personal value. G. K. Chesterton spoke wisely indeed when he said, "There is no such thing as an uninteresting subject; there are only uninterested people."

2. JUDGE CONTENT, NOT DELIVERY

Many listeners alibi inattention to a speaker by thinking to themselves: "Who could listen to such a character? What an awful voice! Will he ever stop reading from his notes?"

The good listener reacts differently. He may well look at the speaker and think, "This man is inept. Seems like almost anyone ought to be able to talk better than that." But from this initial similarity he moves on to a different conclusion, thinking "But wait a minute. . . . I'm not interested in his personality or delivery. I want to find out what he knows. Does this man know some things that I need to know?"

Essentially we "listen with our own experience." Is the conveyer to be held responsible because we are poorly equipped to decode his message? We cannot understand everything we hear, but one sure way to raise the level of our understanding is to assume the responsibility which is inherently ours.

3. HOLD YOUR FIRE

Overstimulation is almost as bad as understimulation, and the two together constitute the twin evils of inefficient listening. The overstimulated listener gets too excited, or excited too soon, by the speaker. Some of us are greatly addicted to this weakness. For us, a speaker can seldom talk for more than a few minutes without touching upon a pet bias or conviction. Occasionally we are roused in support of the speaker's point; usually it is the reverse. In either case overstimulation reflects the desire of the listener to enter, somehow, immediately into the argument.

The aroused person usually becomes preoccupied by trying to do three things simultaneously: calculate what hurt is being done to his own pet ideas; plot an embarrassing question to ask the speaker; enjoy mentally all the discomfiture visualized for the speaker once the devastating reply to him is launched. With these things going on subsequent passages go unheard.

We must learn not to get too excited about a speaker's point until we are certain we thoroughly understand it. The secret is contained in the principle that we must always withhold evaluation until our comprehension is complete.

4. LISTEN FOR IDEAS

Good listeners focus on central ideas; they tend to recognize the characteristic language in which central ideas are usually stated, and they are able to discriminate between fact and principle, idea and example, evidence and argument. Poor listeners are inclined to listen for the facts in every presentation.

To understand the fault, let us assume that a man is giving us instructions made up of facts A to Z. The man begins to talk. We hear fact A and think: "We've got to remember it!" So we begin a memory exercise by repeating "Fact A, fact A, fact A. . . ."

Meanwhile, the fellow is telling us fact B. Now we have two facts to memorize. We're so busy doing it that we miss fact C completely. And so it goes up to fact Z. We catch a few facts, garble several others and completely miss the rest.

It is a significant fact that only about 25 percent of persons listening to a formal talk are able to grasp the speaker's central idea. To develop this skill requires an ability to recognize conventional organizational patterns, transitional language, and the speaker's use of recapitulation. Fortunately, all of these items can be readily mastered with a bit of effort.

5. BE FLEXIBLE

Our research has shown that our 100 worst listeners thought that note-taking and outlining were synonyms. They believed there was but one way to take notes — by making an outline.

Actually, no damage would be done if all talks followed some definite plan of organization. Unfortunately, less than half of even formal speeches are carefully organized. There are few things more frustrating than to try to outline an unoutlineable speech.

Note-taking may help or may become a distraction. Some persons try to take down everything in shorthand; the vast majority of us are far too voluminous even in longhand. While studies are not too clear on the point, there is some evidence to indicate that the volume of notes taken and their value to the taker are inversely related. In any case, the real issue is one of interpretation. Few of us have memories good enough to remember even the salient points we hear. If we can obtain brief, meaningful records of them for later review, we definitely improve our ability to learn and to remember.

The 100 best listeners had apparently learned early in life that if they wanted to be efficient note-takers they had to have more than one system of taking notes. They equipped themselves with four or five systems, and learned to adjust their system to the organizational pattern, or the absence of one, in each talk they heard. If we want to be good listeners, we must be flexible and adaptable note-takers.

6. WORK AT LISTENING

One of the most striking characteristics of poor listeners is their disinclination to spend any energy in a listening situation. College students, by their own testimony, frequently enter classes all worn out physically; assume postures which only seem to give attention to the speaker; and then proceed to catch up on needed rest or to reflect upon purely personal matters. This faking of attention is one of the worst habits afflicting us as a people.

Listening is hard work. It is characterized by faster heart action, quicker circulation of the blood, a small rise in bodily temperature. The overrelaxed listener is merely appearing to tune in, and then feeling conscience-free to pursue any of a thousand mental tangents.

For selfish reasons alone one of the best investments we can make is to give each speaker our conscious attention. We ought to establish eye contact and maintain it; to indicate by posture and facial expression that the occasion and the speaker's efforts are a matter of real concern to us. When we do these things we help the speaker to express himself more clearly, and we in turn profit by better understanding of the improved communication we have helped him to achieve. None of this necessarily implies acceptance of his point of view or favorable action upon his appeals. It is, rather, an expression of interest.

7. RESIST DISTRACTIONS

The good listeners tend to adjust quickly to any kind of abnormal situation; poor listeners tend to tolerate bad conditions and, in some instances, even to create distractions themselves.

We live in a noisy age. We are distracted not only by what we hear, but by what we see. Poor listeners tend to be readily influenced by all manner of distractions, even in an intimate face-to-face situation.

A good listener instinctively fights distraction. Sometimes the fight is easily won — by closing a door, shutting off the radio, moving closer to the person talking, or asking him to speak louder. If the distractions cannot be met that easily, then it becomes a matter of concentration.

8. EXERCISE YOUR MIND

Poor listeners are inexperienced in hearing difficult, expository material. Good listeners apparently develop an appetite for hearing a variety of presentations difficult enough to challenge their mental capacities.

Perhaps the one word that best describes the bad listener is "inexperienced." Although he spends 40 percent of his communication day listening to something, he is inexperienced in hearing anything tough, technical, or expository. He has for years painstakingly sought light, recreational material. The problem he creates is deeply significant, because such a person is a poor producer in factory, office, or classroom.

Inexperience is not easily or quickly overcome. However, knowledge of our own weakness may lead us to repair it. We need never become too old to meet new challenges.

9. KEEP YOUR MIND OPEN

Parallel to the blind spots which afflict human beings are certain psychological deaf spots which impair our ability to perceive and understand. These deaf spots are the dwelling place of our most cherished notions, convictions, and complexes. Often, when a speaker invades one of these areas with a word or phrase, we turn our mind to retraveling familiar mental pathways crisscrossing our invaded area of sensitivity.

It is hard to believe in moments of cold detachment that just a word or phrase can cause such emotional eruption. Yet with poor listeners it is frequently the case; and even with very good listeners it is occasionally the case. When such emotional deafness transpires, communicative efficiency drops rapidly to zero.

Among the words known thus to serve as red flags to some listeners are: mother-in-law, landlord, redneck, sharecropper, sissy, pervert, automation, clerk, income tax, communist, Red, dumb farmer, pink, "Greetings," antivivisectionist, evolution, square, punk, welsher.

Effective listeners try to identify and to rationalize the words or phrases most upsetting emotionally. Often the emotional impact of such words can be decreased through a free and open discussion of them with friends or associates.

10. CAPITALIZE ON THOUGHT SPEED

Most persons talk at a speed of about 125 words a minute. There is good evidence that if thought were measured in words per minute, most of us could think easily at about four times that rate. It is difficult — almost painful — to try to slow down our thinking speed. Thus we normally have about 400 words of thinking time to spare during every minute a person talks to us.

What do we do with our excess thinking time while someone is speaking? If we are poor listeners, we soon become impatient with the slow progress the speaker seems to be making. So our thoughts turn to something else for a moment, then dart back to the speaker. These brief side excursions of thought continue until our mind tarries too long on some enticing but irrelevant subject. Then, when our thoughts return to the person talking, we find he's far ahead of us. Now it's harder to follow him and increasingly easy to take off on side excursions. Finally we give up; the person is still talking, but our mind is in another world.

The good listener uses his thought speed to advantage; he constantly applies his spare thinking time to what is being said. It is not difficult once one has a definite pattern of thought to follow. To develop such a pattern we should:

Try to anticipate what a person is going to talk about. On the basis of what he's already said, ask yourself: "What's he trying to get at? What point is he going to make?"

Mentally summarize what the person has been saying. What point has he made already, if any?

Weigh the speaker's evidence by mentally questioning it. As he presents facts, illustrative stories and statistics, continually ask yourself: "Are they accurate? Do they come from an unprejudiced source? Am I getting the full picture, or is he telling me only what will prove his point?"

Listen between the lines. The speaker doesn't always put everything that's important into words. The changing tones and volume of his voice may have a meaning. So may his facial expressions, the gestures he makes with his hands, the movement of his body.

Not capitalizing on thought speed is our greatest single handicap. The differential between thought speed and speech speed breeds false feelings of security and mental tangents. Yet, through listening training, this same differential can be readily converted into our greatest asset.

Number of words 2490
See page 275 for Questions

Reading Time in Seconds _____
See page 325 for Conversion Table

Listen, Doctor!

Milton Silverman

Your very life may depend on how well your doctor has kept up with modern medical advances. For one thing, 90 percent of the drugs used today did not even exist thirty years ago. Has your doctor kept up? To learn we use three channels — reading, listening, and observing. Listen, Doctor!

In a small Midwestern hospital, a newborn baby girl lay dying with a mysterious combination of symptoms that defied diagnosis.

"I couldn't figure this one," her doctor said. "The baby was vomiting continually, she wouldn't gain weight and she seemed to be a little constipated."

Ordinarily, such signs point to an intestinal obstruction, but X-ray studies had shown that the intestinal tract was clear. It might have been an infection somewhere in the body, or even a brain hemorrhage, but these were ruled out by all the usual tests.

"The only thing we knew for sure," he said, "was that the baby was nearly dead."

Late one night, still completely baffled by the case, the doctor came home, glumly greeted his wife and went to bed. His eyes were so reddened and tired that he was unable to keep them open, let alone attempt to read any of the medical books and magazines piled high on his bureau — a pile which had been accumulating there for weeks. With his eyes closed, however, the doctor managed to turn on a tape recorder which stood on his bedside table.

What he heard was no ordinary program. There was no Beethoven symphony or Tchaikovsky concerto or even an appropriate lullaby by Brahms.

Instead, the doctor began to listen to a pleasant, well-modulated voice describing the latest advances in the diagnosis and treatment of diseases of the adrenal glands.

Halfway through the program, he heard a few phrases which instantly had him wide awake: ". . . symptoms starting soon after birth . . . failure to maintain normal weight gain . . . bowel action reduced . . . insufficiency of adrenal cortical hormones. . . ."

The doctor snapped off the machine. "Good Lord!" he said. "That must be it!"

His wife stared at him. "What in the world are you talking about?" she asked.

"Adrenal insufficiency of the newborn," he said as he started to dress again. "That's the trouble with the Hastings baby. Call the hospital and tell 'em I'm on my way."

Within an hour, he had begun injections of a powerful adrenal-gland extract. In six hours, the dreadful vomiting had stopped, and in twelve hours the little girl was declared out of danger. A few weeks later she was apparently cured.

"I suppose I should have known about the disease," the doctor said afterward. "It had all been reported in a medical journal. It had been described at a medical convention. But I was too busy with my patients to go to the convention, and I didn't have a chance even to read the journal."

A similarly taped medical report, prepared by a remarkably enterprising group of workers in Los Angeles, was used with equal effect on a patient being treated in a New England town.

"This poor woman wasn't dying," her physician said. "She just wished she were dead. She had a weird, terrifying anxiety that wasn't controlled by any standard psychiatric treatment. Her husband was afraid she would kill herself."

One morning while the doctor was shaving — practically the only time of day when he was not coping with patients or telephone calls — he turned on a new tape and heard the reports on mental patients treated successfully with an odd native remedy imported from India, a remedy later used in this country under the name of Rauwolfia.

"My patient and her husband both thought I was a little odd myself when I suggested such an exotic drug," he said. "But I made them listen to the tape themselves. They agreed to let me try. We got some of the medicine and tried it, and it worked brilliantly."

Other physicians have adopted the custom of listening to the new tapes regularly at their breakfast tables, or in hospital dining rooms. One North Dakota doctor carries his tape recorder in his airplane. A Utah surgeon takes his recorder on fishing trips and listens to new advances in surgery while he ties trout flies at night in his Snake River fishing lodge. Groups of doctors listen together in American military hospitals in Germany and Japan, in medical outposts in the Aleutians and the South Pacific, in oil-refinery hospitals in Saudi Arabia and Venezuela, and in medical-mission stations in the Belgian Congo and Ghana.

"This new kind of medical education," state the editors of one distinguished medical journal, "could easily become the most important form of postgraduate training within the next decade."

Known simply as Audio-Digest, this form of keeping doctors up-to-date is aimed at smashing what has become one of the most dangerous bottlenecks in modern medicine — the inability of physicians to keep up with the almost incredible flood of new medical discoveries. Medical advances are now being reported in the staggering total of some 6000 different technical journals every month.

It has been noted by various critics that not all these technical reports are worth reading. Some of the articles are highly unscientific, repetitive, outmoded or pure medical gobbledygook. It has also been noted that some physicians who bitterly bewail their lack of time to study are likely to be making such complaints while playing bridge, pursuing a golf ball or checking the action at European ski resorts. But even those doctors who sincerely want to keep up-to-date have been facing an impossible situation.

"No practicing physician can find the time to read even one percent of these reports," a medical official stated a few years ago. "The busier the doctor, the less are his chances to keep up with medical progress. Accordingly, it is inevitable that he will fail to save some patients even though the cure for their disease may have been announced — somewhere, by somebody — many months before."

Major credit for finding a solution to this deadly problem goes to a tall, slim public-speaking instructor, radio announcer, avocado grower and onetime airline pilot named Jerry Pettis, now public-relations counsel of the Los Angeles County Medical Association and the American Medical Association. Late one afternoon in 1951, shortly after he had gone to work for the California Medical Association, he visited the offices of one of the busiest and most successful physicians in California.

"Be with you in two minutes," said the doctor. "I've got one more patient in the examining room. Sit over there at my desk and make yourself comfortable."

Nearly an hour later the doctor came back into the office. "That took a little longer than I expected," he said, "Now let's get out of here and pick up a sandwich. I have to be at the hospital in twenty minutes."

"Wait a moment," said Pettis.

He pointed to a towering stack of magazines on the desk — medical journals, surgical journals, special journals on allergy, hormones, arthritis and heart disease, and even journals which condensed the articles in other journals. Some dated back six months or more. Many had obviously never been opened.

"That's a mighty imposing file of literature," he said. "When do you read it?"

The doctor shook his head. "It's tough," he said. "I keep hoping I'll find time to catch up one of these days. But whenever I think I've found a few extra minutes, there's another patient or another consultation or another committee meeting or — well, that's the practice of medicine for you."

"What do other men do?"

"Most of us are in the same boat." And he added, "Jerry, if anybody could lick this one for us, it'd be as good as discovering a couple of more wonder drugs."

In the next few months, working nights and weekends, Pettis attacked the problem. He wrote to nearly 100 physicians and asked them, "When do you have time to yourself?" A few answered, "Never!" and one doctor retorted, "How can I have any spare time when I have to reply to dam-fool questions like this?" But some said, "At breakfast," "In the bathroom," or, "In bed, when I'm too tired to read," while several said, "In my car, on the way to the office."

The ex-pilot was intrigued by that last answer. "That's where we'll start," he told his wife, Shirley. "We've got to get a tape recorder that'll work in a doctor's automobile, and then make tape recordings of the most important medical reports every week."

The Pettises first presented their idea to one of their friends, Dr. Robert L. Marsh, a Glendale surgeon. "It's marvelous," he said. "It might even work. Sure, I'll help with it." Next they enlisted Claron Oakley, a young science writer, to write and narrate the scripts and eventually to serve as editor. Oakley had a pleasing voice and a familiarity with medical terms, and, in addition, was willing to gamble time and energy on the new project. "He sounds like a doctor," one physician said later, "and not like some actor reading a television commercial."

Then they looked for a recording studio. "This posed a few difficulties," Pettis recalls. "We didn't have enough money to rent a regular commercial studio. Luckily we were able to borrow the studio of a local radio preacher."

Thereafter, for some weeks, the studio was utilized on Sundays for messages on the saving of souls, and the rest of the week for instructions on the saving of tonsils, spleens, gall bladders and other portions of the body.

At the same time, work commenced on adapting a standard tape-recording machine and converter for use in a car. It quickly appeared that none of the available commercial models could work properly from the battery in a moving automobile. When the car accelerated, slowed to a stop or bounced across a bump in the road, the sound from the machine would be garbled by strange wheezes, squawks and outright screeches. This problem was solved by a new converter modified by the second tenor in the radio preacher's church quartet who happened to be an electronics engineer.

Some consideration was given to the possibility that a physician driving his car while engrossed in one of these tape recordings — for example, on the surgical repair of automobile-accident victims — might himself become a menace to highway safety. It was decided, however, that listening to such a program would not be much more dangerous than listening to a rock-and-roll program on the car radio.

Finally, to manufacture copies of the first trial tapes,

Pettis took on Clifford Whenmouth, a former sound engineer for an Australian tape-recording company. Whenmouth made the duplicates in his own living room after his wife and children had gone to bed, working from midnight until dawn. It was slow work — in those days it took one hour to duplicate an hour's tape — but by March, 1953, the first tapes were ready for demonstration.

These first recordings were presented at a small medical meeting in Los Angeles. The results were hardly exciting.

"We got thirty-six doctors to agree to subscribe for one tape a week for a year," Pettis said. "It wasn't enough for us to break even, but we were sure we had something."

Officials of the California Medical Association, quietly watching these early developments, likewise felt that Pettis had something. Late in 1953, they made arrangements to take over the program, setting up the Audio-Digest Foundation under Dr. Edward C. Rosenow, Jr., of Los Angeles, head of the C.M.A.'s postgraduate-education department. Under the new plan, Pettis served as the producer and directed the mechanics of preparing the tapes as selected by the medical men. All profits were to be turned over to the support of the nation's medical schools.

In a few months, due in large part to Doctor Rosenow's co-operation and influence among his fellow doctors, the prospects seemed to be somewhat brighter. Distinguished medical leaders at Harvard, Ohio State, the Mayo Clinic, the Lahey Clinic and other medical centers agreed to serve as a nationwide board of editors. Among these leaders was Maj. Gen. Silas B. Hays, soon to be named Surgeon General of the Army.

"You're darn right I'll help!" said General Hays. "Our doctors out in Guam aren't getting the latest information they want. We need this stuff in Tokyo and Nuremberg. The Air Force and the Navy will certainly want it. You get busy and produce those tapes. We'll buy them."

The ice had finally broken. Orders for the new tapes came pouring in, and Pettis and his co-workers — now with the full backing of the medical societies — began to produce them. They started with approximately 600 medical journals a month, written in English, French, German, Italian and other languages — the journals considered to be the most valuable among the world's medical publications. From these they selected the scientific articles which would presumably be of most use to practicing physicians. Final selection was made by Doctor Rosenow, on the advice of his committee of medical authorities. Each of these articles was then translated, if necessary, condensed by a trained writer, checked for accuracy by a medical expert and finally recorded.

Along with these article digests were recordings of special medical-school lectures on new drugs and surgical techniques, panel discussions on such controversial topics as the treatment of stomach ulcers or the prevention of heart disease, and even up-to-the-minute accounts of new discoveries announced at medical conventions.

"We could move so fast," says Pettis, "that when an important new discovery came without warning, we could report it through Audio-Digest many days or even weeks before the official reports came out in the medical journals."

One vital step in getting this speed was the use of new electronic duplicating devices, which now make it possible to make ten high-fidelity copies of a one-hour sound track in less than two minutes.

Another important advance came when Audio-Digest augmented the original series of weekly tape recordings, intended for doctors in general practice, with four bi-weekly series designed for specialists in internal medicine, surgery, obstetrics and gynecology, and pediatrics. Each tape, costing the subscriber $2.75 for a one-hour program, remained the property of the doctor and could be filed in his tape collection. By using an index accompanying each reel of tape, and an indicator on the recording machine, he could listen to the whole program or to any portion he desired. The doctor could use his own home tape-recording device or purchase a special machine costing as little as fifty dollars.

By last year it was abundantly clear that Audio-Digest had made good. With almost 4000 subscribers, it was estimated that the reports were being heard each week by between 15,000 and 20,000 doctors, ranging from top specialists in the greatest medical centers to general practitioners working in the most remote areas of the world. A number of county medical societies are purchasing the tapes as a free service for their members, who borrow them like library books or use them in the society's reading rooms.

Interestingly, it was observed, the new tapes were found to be serving as an aid rather than as a competitor to the standard medical journals. Alerted by Audio-Digest reports, physicians were turning to the appropriate journal for a complete account of the discoveries which concerned their patients. Many a physician gave credit to the recordings for letting him rediscover the pleasures of reading. Accordingly, medical editors from coast to coast were almost unanimous in praising Audio-Digest as a major advance in medical education.

Perhaps the finest tribute, however, was paid by a physician practicing alone in an isolated lumber town in Northern California. "For the first time in twenty-three years," he said, "I feel that once again I'm practicing modern medicine and giving my patients the best that modern research can offer. I thank you and, more important, my patients thank you."

Number of words 2600
See page 277 for Questions

Reading Time in Seconds _____
See page 325 for Conversion Table

Listen to This, Dear

James Thurber

At times, according to Thurber, reading and listening come into sharp conflict.
Ideally each should supplement, not negate, the other. Listening attentively to
another establishes a close personal relationship. Reading attentively is different.
That involves a close relationship, but to a book, not to a person.

It is a commonplace that the small annoyances of the marriage relationship slowly build up its insupportabilities, as particles of sediment build up great deltas. And yet I have never seen, even among the profundities of our keenest researchers into divorce, a competent consideration of the problem that is created by the female's habit of interrupting the male when he is reading. It is, indeed, more than a habit; I believe it is a law of woman's behaviorism as deeply rooted as her instinct to attract the male. And it causes almost as much trouble.

In the early ages of mankind, woman's security, and hence her contentment, were assured by the activity of the male and jeopardized by his inactivity. The male rampant — killing animals for food and for clothing, digging out caves, and putting up huts, driving off enemies — early came to be associated in the mind of the elemental female with warmth, well-being, safety, and the kindred creature comforts. Lying down, or even sitting down, the male was a symbol of possible imminent disaster: famine, exposure, capture and servitude, even death. Any masculine posture of relaxation or repose, therefore, became a menace which must be removed.

The reasonable dismay of the primeval female at the sight of her mate doing nothing was so powerful that it remains ineradicable in the mind and the heart of the female of today, although logical motivation for her original dread has largely disappeared with the shaping up of our civilization. The softer centuries, it is true, have reduced her primal terror to a kind of hazy uneasiness, just as they have tempered the violence of her protest, but the instinct to prod the inert male into action nevertheless persists. Where once woman shook man, or struck him with a rock, or at least screamed imprecations at him, when he sat down to draw pictures on the walls of the cave, she now contents herself with talking to him when he is reading. The male's ability to lose himself in the printed page brings back to the female, from vanished wildernesses, the old, dim fear of masculine inertia.

"I must tell you what happened to the base of the Spencers' child's brain," a wife will begin when her husband has just reached the most exciting point in the sports extra's account of a baseball game or a prizefight, and she will proceed to go into details which, although interesting, or even horrific, lack the peculiar excitement of competitive competition to which the husband has adjusted his consciousness. Or she will say, "I want you to listen to this, dear," and she will read him a story from her section of the evening paper about a New Jersey dentist who tried to burn up his wife and collect her insurance. Telling the plots of plays, and speculating as to why a certain couple were drawn together, or drifted apart — as the case may have been — are other methods a wife frequently uses to interrupt her husband's reading.

Of the various ways of combating this behavior of the female, open resentment, manifested by snarling or swearing or throwing one's book or newspaper on the floor in a rage, is the worst, since nine times out of ten it will lead to quarrels, tears, slamming of doors, and even packing of suitcases, and the disruption of family life. The husband may gain, by this method, the privacy of his club, but he will no longer be in the proper frame of mind for quiet reading. He will find himself wondering where his wife is, whether she has gone home to her mother, whether she has taken veronal (I am dealing, of course, with those high-strung, sensitive couples who make up such a large percentage of present-day families). He will then fall to recalling miserably the years of their happiness, and end up by purchasing a dozen roses for his wife, and five or six rye highballs for himself, after which he must still face the ordeal of patching things up, a business made somewhat easier perhaps by the fact of the roses, but correspondingly harder by the fact of the highballs. This whole method of protest, in a word, takes a great deal out of a man and is not to be recommended.

The best way of dealing with a wife who tells long stories of the day's happenings, or reads accounts of murders aloud when her husband has settled down to his book or journal, is to pretend to listen but not really to listen at all. To the uninitiated this may seem simple, but the husband who has perfected the method knows that it calls for a unique bifurcation of the faculty of attention, and a remarkable development of the power of concentration. In order to go right on with his own reading while his wife is talking, the husband must deaden his mind to the meaning of her words and at the same time remain conscious of the implications of her inflections. Thus he will be able, at the proper places in her recitation, to murmur an interested "Yes?" or an incredulous "No!," although not following her narrative at all and still getting the sense of what he is reading. "Um," "Hm," and "Um hm" should also be freely used, but never "Hm?" for it denotes a lapse of attention. Exclamations of astonishment or high interest, such as "You don't say!" are extremely dangerous and should be interjected only by the oblivious husband who is so sensitive to the tempo and pitch of his wife's voice that he can be positive when she has reached some (to her) important climax in whatever she is relating.

This form of deception is, of course, fairly easy to practice when the female is reading aloud, for her eyes must naturally be upon the printed page before her. It is not so easy when she is relating an occurrence, or a chain of occurrences, for her eyes are then likely to be upon the male. In this case he should contrive, as soon as she begins, to drop his magazine or newspaper on his knee, as if he had abandoned it — all the time, however, keeping the type within range. I know of one husband who drops his newspaper on the floor before him and then bends over it with his hand to his brow, shielding his eyes, his elbow on his knee, as if he were intent upon his wife's words. He continues to read right along, however.

A defense against forward passes, as they say in football, must also be carefully built up by the inattentive husband. By forward passes, I mean sudden and unexpected questions which the wife is likely to fling at any minute, such as, for example, "Would you think Hilda Greeb capable of a thing like that?" In building up a defense against this trick play, the husband must keep a little corner of his consciousness alert, like the safety man on a defensive football team, for all sentences beginning with "would," "should," "are," "have," "can," and the like. In this way he can spot a question coming in time to have some sort of response ready. In the case of the question we have already cited, "Would you think Hilda Greeb capable of a thing like that?" it is probable that either a "Yes" or "No" would see the husband safely by the crisis. If he says "Yes," the wife will probably say, "Well, of course I would, knowing her as well as I do." However, each particular husband, knowing the twists and turns of his particular wife's mind, must work out his own system of defense against forward passes. The greatest care should be taken by every husband, however, to answer only those questions which are directed to him. He must, I mean, be on guard against "inner-quote queries." For example, if a wife should say, in the course of whatever she is telling, "So I asked her, 'what time is it?'" the husband is lost if he is caught off guard and replies, "About a quarter after eight, I think." This is bound to lead to accusations, imprecations, quarrels, tears, slamming of doors, etc.

I know a few husbands who simply evade the whole problem by giving up reading. They just don't read anything any more. It seems to me that this is cowardly.

Number of words 1400
See page 279 for Questions

Reading Time in Seconds _____
See page 325 for Conversion Table

SELECTION 56

Women Are Good Listeners

John Mason Brown

As a speaker, John Mason Brown draws on his first-hand experience with both men and women to tell us about them as listeners. And in the process, he reveals himself as a forerunner of the women-as-people appreciators.

On the island of Martha's Vineyard is a women's club called the "I Want To Know Club." This name, so ungarnished and lacking in self-consciousness, is a favorite of mine. In the frankest possible manner it tells why men and women are willing to subject themselves to lectures.

More than fifty years ago in England a young man, who was growing a scraggly mustache at the time, spoke at a political meeting. His name was Winston Churchill. When he was through, a woman (who never would have qualified for the Martha's Vineyard club) said, "Young man, I care for neither your mustache nor your opinions." "Madam," replied Churchill, "you are as unlikely to come into contact with the one as with the other."

Few speakers today sport mustaches, but all of us who lecture do have opinions. It is because men and women *do* want to come into contact with these opinions that they go to lectures.

There are, of course, other reasons. One is the herd

From *McCall's,* July 1953. Reprinted by permission from *McCall's.*

instinct — the universal need, born, no doubt, of loneliness, to enjoy the feeling of companionship which comes from being part of an audience. Another is escape — the simple, natural and urgent desire to get away from home, to break the routine of daily living, to see and be seen, perhaps to be taken into a new world. Even so, the chief reason people gather together in the sight of a lecturer is, I believe, that they too "want to know."

Americans, however, have surrendered to an odd myth when it comes to public speaking. It is a widespread belief that there is something silly about an audience of women listening to a lecture, and something equally silly about anyone, especially a man, lecturing to a group of women.

"Going out to bring culture to the girls?" or "Off on the chicken-patty circuit?" friends in New York often say, smiling with a mixture of pity and condescension, when I tell them I am starting on a lecture trip. Those who fancy themselves sophisticates or intellectuals are particularly apt to indulge in this kind of talk. They think it funny. I don't. I wouldn't lecture to women's clubs if I thought it was silly.

Most people agree that the dignity of a professor is beyond challenge when he is holding forth to a class of young people whose reading and experience may be very limited, who may or may not be listening, and whose attendance is compulsory. There is a kind of Roman grandeur, we feel, about a Senator orating, although only four or five of his confreres may be present and none of them is paying attention.

Similar prestige is attached to addressing men's business and professional clubs, conventions, and societies dedicated to the study of such varied subjects as local history or foreign affairs, birds or Browning. Even after-dinner speaking is esteemed, if not always enjoyed, and appearances before community forums are taken with fair seriousness — providing the meetings are held at night and men are present.

But let a sizable number of females unescorted by males assemble to hear a lecture, and quicker than you can say "Kinsey" the business of speaking, like the business of listening, is assumed by most men (and not a few traitorous women) to become faintly absurd. This is one of the most popular of American fallacies. Every lecturer who has ever spoken before women's clubs has encountered it. The majority of lecturers, no matter how much they resent it or how false they know it to be, are on the defensive because of it. And, unfortunately, some lecturers — to their own discredit and that of their profession — lecture to women as if they believe the myth to be true.

Some years back in a movie called *The Gracie Allen Murder Case*, Grace Allen was, as usual, spilling words as if they were seeds being scattered by a canary. In her torrent of talk she let slip an important clue to a grateful and surprised detective. "What's that you said, Gracie?"

he asked. "How should I know?" replied Miss Allen. "I wasn't listening."

As someone who has traveled up and down this country for twenty-five years speaking before every kind of audience, I have had to listen not only to myself lecturing but, between lectures, to sneering comments about audiences supposedly stupid because unblessed by the presence of men. These attacks make no more sense than Miss Allen's prattle. More surprising than anything else is the contemptuous attitude toward women which they betray, in this of all countries.

Let's face the facts. The United States is a land where men govern but women rule. With cause, its male citizens sometimes wonder if they are not living in a matriarchy instead of a democracy. The domination exerted by American women is as firm as it is subtle, unobtrusive and amiable. In fact, women in America appear to have won every right except the right to be taken seriously while listening to a lecture attended only by women. In this case the right of assembly is not denied them but they expose themselves to ridicule when they exercise it.

Mention a women's club audience to almost any American man and instantly one of Helen Hokinson's famous cartoons comes to his mind. Her fatuous matrons were a delectable crew, far more intrigued with what covered their heads than with what filled them. Her "girls" were females of a certain vintage, who, in spite of having grown stout, had never grown up. Clubwomen were Miss Hokinson's dish, a dish which she made everyone's delight. It was she who showed a plump program chairman boasting to a hall filled with equally plump dowagers that for next season she had Clifton Fadiman, Dorothy Thompson and the Vatican Choir "in the hollow of my hand." It was Miss Hokinson who had a treasurer announce, "I'm sorry, Madam President. There won't be any treasurer's report this month, because we have a deficit."

Far be it from me to deny that some women who attend lectures in the company of other women do look and think like Helen Hokinson girls. They resemble them as surely as some men resemble those silver-haired and popeyed old roués who whoop it up at hot spots or sleep away the hours at their clubs in Peter Arno's cartoons. But this I do know. There have been very few of Miss Hokinson's girls in any women's club that I have ever spoken to.

Although unconvoyed women who attend morning or afternoon lectures in present-day America may or may not be matrons, they belong to a different generation and a different breed from Miss Hokinson's. The majority of them are far from idle. They are younger women, and are apt to be college graduates. If they do not have jobs away from their homes they have very definite jobs waiting for them there. Most are refugees for a few snatched hours from their washing machines, their dishes, their housecleaning or their children. They are lean, not plump, and intellectually curious rather than curious intellectually.

They may be local women hungering for something denied them in the small towns in which they live. They may be women brought up in large cities, whose husband's business or military service has taken them to towns where they miss ready-made stimulation. Or they may be women in the most sizable sophisticated of cities, who are guilty of no other impulse than the very human and universal wish to keep in touch with things. But, however diverse they are as individuals or in background, they all blend to form audiences which, North or South, East or West, are anxious to learn something — and hope, quite rightly, to be entertained in the process.

I do not mean to maintain for a moment that all women who go to lectures are mental giants. Many of them are no better equipped mentally than their husbands or the person addressing them. To picture every feminine assembly as a congress composed exclusively of the counterparts of George Eliot, Madame de Stael, Jane Welsh Carlyle, Emma Willard, Rebecca West or the Hamiltons, Edith and Dr. Alice, would be as absurd as to pretend that every male conclave, Rotarian, legal or academic, is attended only by the twin brothers of Plato, Socrates, Francis Bacon, Voltaire, Shaw and the two Alberts, Schweitzer and Einstein.

That women are different from men has, since the creation, been one of the most welcome of God's blessings from the point of view of both sexes. The differences between them are not only physical, they are intellectual too, and are the result of the different demands made upon them by life. Naturally this means that many of their interests are also different. Yet, from a lecturer's experience, it is interesting to observe how little these differences matter when it comes to the reactions of an audience.

After a lecture at the Detroit Town Hall, a woman in an audience composed almost entirely of women sent me a written question which undergraduates would identify as "a stinker." The question was: "Do you think that women as a group suffer from a lack of intelligence?"

My answer was an emphatic "Of course not." It was an honest answer, made with no desire to curry favor or to indulge in the magnoliaed phrasing of a bogus chivalry.

I did, however, feel honor bound to add certain reservations. Had I been asked if women suffer individually from a lack of intelligence, I confessed I would have to say of them — as anyone would have to say with equal truth about men — it depends upon the individual. I could not resist pointing out that all women are no more born bright than are all men. And, just as surely as a man is not wise merely because he is a man, a woman is not foolish simply because she is a woman. Truth forced me to admit that some women who take scrupulous care

of their figures are tempted, with the passing years, to let their minds go; that most women lack the discipline for sustained thinking which work forces on most men; and that there are women who, in spite of being college graduates, lead such disjointed lives because of the daily pressure of small duties and small concerns that they tend to lose the habit of consecutive thought.

As an illustration I could have offered the instance of the wife of a friend of mine. She had spent the whole summer in the company of her young children, thinking only of their needs. On her return to New York in the early fall she went for the first time in many months to an adult dinner party. To her horror she discovered that, to start conversation with the distinguished man sitting next to her, she turned to him and said automatically, "I bet I can finish my soup sooner than you can."

But the question I was asked at Detroit concerned the intelligence of women as a group, and as a group, let me repeat, they are certainly the equals in intelligence of men. Audiences, young or old, male, female or mixed, are unexpectedly similar in their basic pattern. One may be quicker in its reactions than another, one colder, one warmer. A college audience may be less restrained and more eager than an elderly group. Male listeners may release laughs which are wonderfully deep-toned and thunderous compared to the lighter laughter of women. Yet, in spite of these surface differences, as Danny Kaye has observed, "Once you scrape the veneer, audiences are the same all over the world."

I do not know about theater audiences the world over. But I do know something about lecture audiences in this country and the special world of women's clubs. Knowing these audiences as I do, I have long realized that each one, regardless of sex, presents the same challenge to the speaker. Each listens to the serious portions of the same lecture in an identical manner; each laughs at the same points; and all of them ask very much the same questions.

The questions have changed over the years. They have kept pace with the altered concerns of more serious times. Women are now as interested as men in hoping to find answers to these graver questions. Inevitably every question period brings forth its questions which are duds. The lady who asks, "Why must we read or see anything sad when the world is so sad?" is, I begin to suspect, a soft-pated darling who in some way gets hold of my itinerary, accompanies me on my travels without my knowing it, and bobs up in almost every audience, much to my regret.

A sister of hers must be the woman who, with considerable show of resentment, asked me last winter why, instead of talking about some books, plays and films which had their sordid aspects, I had not recommended a few cheerful and innocent works which she could share with her twenty-two-year-old daughter.

I had to reply, "Madam, I haven't had the privilege of meeting your daughter. I must say, on the basis of what you have said, that if she has not encountered these themes before in her reading she must be unacquainted with the world's finest literature, including its greatest tragedies. If at twenty-two your daughter has never heard about these things I can only say she must be a sad case of arrested development."

Once a man at the University of Cincinnati asked me my pet question. I had been describing with enthusiasm Carmen Miranda, the Brazilian songstress, when she first conquered New York. Though I spoke under academic auspices, the man's question was, "By any chance do you know Carmen Miranda's telephone number?"

I think it only fair to point out that no women have ever asked me the telephone numbers of Tyrone Power, Sir Laurence Olivier or Alfred Lunt. But they have asked me almost everything else.

When, for example, a novel appears such as Edna Ferber's *Giant,* which is laid in the Lone Star State, naturally Texas women are interested in an outsider's reaction to it. Other listeners show the same interest in books dealing with their localities. Since the war — and especially since the Korean war — women everywhere ask questions about the draft, about the possible future of their sons, about the presence of Communists in universities and, of course, about McCarthy. But because they know that by profession I am a critic who writes of books and plays, the overwhelming majority of their questions have to do with literature and the theater.

I dwell upon the interest of women in the arts for a very definite reason. If they were not actively interested in them I tremble to think what would happen to the theater, to writers, musicians, painters and sculptors in this country. It is women who, in the smallest towns no less than the largest cities, keep up with the news and reviews of plays, books, exhibitions, ballets, concerts and the opera. It is women who do most of the reading in America.

It is women who serve as a kind of "steering committee" in the realm of the arts, advising their husbands what to see, hear and read, and often dragging them against their wills to so-called "cultural" events. Without women, poets would be thinner than they now are, very few novels would enjoy the circulation of present-day best-sellers, many works of nonfiction would achieve only a fraction of their contemporary sales, and that famous "Fabulous Invalid," the theater, would really be on its deathbed.

This takes me back to the popular fallacy which maintains that women become silly when they listen to lectures in the company of other women, and that men are silly when they lecture to them. With all my heart I believe lecturing is a means of communication every bit as respectable as writing. I happen to be a writer as well as a lecturer, and I have equal respect for both means of expression. When it comes to audiences, I have the same respect for audiences made up of women as I have for male audiences.

Nonlecturing writers are incredibly inconsistent. They make fun of talking to women's clubs and sneer at women as listeners, yet they welcome these same women when they are purchasers and readers of their books.

Women's clubs, like men's clubs, have their laughable features. But the time seems to me long overdue to stop laughing at women as listeners and recognize the all-important part they play in preserving and widening the culture we have as a people.

Number of words 2780
See page 281 for Questions

Reading Time in Seconds _____
See page 325 for Conversion Table

SELECTION 57

The Romance of Words
Wilfred Funk and Norman Lewis

Words are not dead things. They are born, they mature — they even die. Take the
word ducemptologist. *It's just now born and not in a single dictionary. It means*
"salesman." After all, a salesman practices the science (ology) *of leading* (ducere)
us to buy (emere). *There is romance in words.*

From now on we want you to look at words intently, to be inordinately curious about them and to examine them syllable by syllable, letter by letter. They are your tools of understanding and self-expression. Collect them. Keep them in condition. Learn how to handle them. Develop a fastidious, but not a fussy, choice. Work always towards good taste in their use. Train your ear for their harmonies.

We urge you not to take words for granted just because they have been part of your daily speech since childhood. You must examine them. Turn them over and over, and see the seal and superscription on each one, as though you were handling a coin. *We would like you actually to fall in love with words.*

Words, as you know, are not dead things. They are fairly wriggling with life. They are the exciting and mysterious tokens of our thoughts, and like human beings, they are born, come to maturity, grow old and die, and sometimes they are even re-born in a new age. A word, from its birth to its death, is a process, not a static thing.

Words, like living trees, have roots, branches and leaves.

Shall we stay with this analogy for a few moments, and see how perfect it is?

The story of the root of a word is the story of its origin. The study of origins is called *etymology,* which in turn has *its* roots in the Greek word *etymon* meaning "true" and the Greek ending — *logia* meaning "knowledge." So *etymology* means the true knowledge of words.

Every word in our language is a frozen metaphor, a frozen picture. It is this poetry behind words that gives language its overwhelming power. And the more intimately we know the romance that lies within each word, the better understanding we will have of its meaning.

For instance, on certain occasions you will probably say that you have "calculated" the cost of something or other. What does this term "calculate" really mean? Here is the story. Years ago, ancient Romans had an instrument called a *hodometer,* or "road measurer," which corresponds to our modern taximeter. If you had hired a two-wheeled Roman vehicle to ride, say, to the Forum, you might have found in the back a tin can with a revolving cover that held a quantity of pebbles. This can was so contrived that each time the wheel turned the metal cover also revolved and a pebble dropped through a hole into the receptacle below. At the end of your trip you counted the pebbles and *calculated* your bill. You see the Latin word for pebble was *calculus,* and that's where our word "calculate" comes from.

There are, of course, many words with much simpler histories that this. When you speak of a "surplus," for instance, you are merely saying that you have a *sur* (French for "over") *plus* (French for "more") or a *sur-plus.* That is, you have an "over-more" than you need.

Should you be in a snooty mood for the nonce, and happen to look at someone rather haughtily, your friends might call you *supercilious,* a word which comes from the Latin *supercilium,* meaning that "eyebrow" you just raised. That person you are so fond of, who has become your companion, — [*cum* (Latin for "with") and *panis* (Latin for "bread")] — is simply one who eats bread with you. That's all. Again, "trumps" in bridge is from the French "triomphe" or triumph, an old-time game of cards. In modern cards one suit is allowed to triumph over, or to "trump" the other suits. And still again, in the army, the *lieutenant* is literally one who takes the place of the captain when the latter is not around. From the French *lieu* (we use it in "in lieu of") and *tenir,* "to hold." The captain, in turn, derives from the Latin word *caput* (head); colonel comes from *columna* (the "column" that he leads).

If, by any chance, you would like to twit your friend, the Wall Street broker, just tell him that his professional title came from the Middle English word *brocour,* a *broacher,* or one who opens, or broaches, a cask to draw off the wine or liquor. We still employ the same word in the original sense when we say "he broached (or opened up) the subject." Finally the broacher, or broker, became a salesman of wine. Then of other things, such as stocks and bonds.

These are the roots of words. We next come to the

From *30 Days to a More Powerful Vocabulary,* by Wilfred Funk and Norman Lewis, by permission of Funk & Wagnalls Publishing Co., Inc.

branches. The branches of our language tree are those many groups of words that have grown out from one original root.

Let's take an example. The Latin term *spectare* which means "to see" contains the root *spec,* and from this one root have sprouted more than 240 English words. We find the root hidden in such words as *spec*-tacles, those things you "see" through; in re*spect,* the tribute you give to a person you care to "see" again; in*spect,* "to see" into; disre*spect* (*dis* — unwilling; *re* — again; *spec* — to see) therefore, when you treat someone with disrespect, you make it plain that you do not care to see him again; intro*spec*tion, looking or seeing within; *spec*tator, one who "sees" or watches.

Turning to the Greek language, which has so largely enriched our own, we discover the root appearing in English as *graph.* This means "to write" and has been a prolific source of words for us. We have tele*graph,* which literally means "far writing"; phono*graph,* "sound-writing"; photo*graph,* "light-writing"; steno*grapher,* one who does "condensed writing"; a *graphic* description, one that is just as clear and effective as though it had been written down; mimeo*graph,* "to write a copy or imitation."

We have in our language a host of roots such as these. There is the Latin *spirare,* meaning "to blow or breathe," from which we get such English words as in*spire* (breathe into); ex*pire* (breathe out); per*spire* (breathe through); re*spir*ation (breathing again or often). And there is also our word "liable" that comes from the Latin *ligare,* "to bind." This fascinating root *lig* has branched out into ob*lige* and ob*lig*ate (to bind to do something); *lig*ature (bandage or binding); *lig*ament (something that ties two things together); and, with the root no longer so obvious, "league" (those nations or other organizations that are bound together);

and even the word "ally" which is from *ad* and *ligare,* to bind to one another.

These, then, are the branches. We turn now to the leaves. If the roots are the origins of words and the branches are the word families that stem out of them, the leaves of this language tree would be the words themselves and their meanings.

Each given word, in its beginning, had, no doubt, only one meaning. But words are so full of life that they are continually sprouting the green shoots of new meanings.

Shall we choose just one word as an instance of the amazing vitality of language? The simple three letter word *run,* up to this moment of writing, has more than 90 dictionary definitions. There is the *run* in your stocking and the *run* on the bank and a *run* in baseball. The clock may *run* down but you *run* up a bill. Colors *run.* You may *run* a race or *run* a business or you may have the *run* of the mill, or, quite different, the *run* of the house when you get the *run* of things. And this little dynamic word, we can assure you, is not yet through with its varied career.

Is it any wonder that our unabridged dictionaries contain as many as 600,000 living and usable words, words sparkling with life, prolific in their breeding, luxuriant in their growth, continually shifting and changing in their meanings?

Words even have definite personalities and characters. They can be sweet, sour, discordant, musical. They can be sweet or acrid; soft or sharp; hostile or friendly.

From this time on, as we enter our word studies, try to become self-conscious about words. Look at them, if possible, with the fresh eyes of one who is seeing them for the first time. If we have persuaded you to do this, you will then be on the way to the success that can be won with a more powerful vocabulary.

Number of words 1380
See page 283 for Questions

Reading Time in Seconds _____
See page 325 for Conversion Table

Words That Laugh and Cry

Charles A. Dana

Mark Twain sensed the physical power of words when he wrote: "A powerful agent is the right word. Whenever we come upon one of those intensely right words in a book or a newspaper the resulting effect is physical as well as spiritual, and electrically prompt."

Did it ever strike you that there was anything queer about the capacity of written words to absorb and convey feelings? Taken separately they are mere symbols with no more feeling to them than so many bricks, but string them along in a row under certain mysterious conditions and you find yourself laughing or crying as your eye runs over them. That words should convey mere ideas is not so remarkable. "The boy is fat," "the cat has nine tails," are statements that seem obviously enough within the power of written language. But it is different with feelings. They are no more visible in the symbols that hold them than electricity is visible on the wire; and yet there they are, always ready to respond when the right test is applied by the right person. That spoken words, charged with human tones and lighted by human eyes, should carry feelings, is not so astonishing. The magnetic sympathy of the orator one understands; he might affect his audience, possibly, if he spoke in a language they did not know. But written words: How can they do it! Suppose, for example, that you possess remarkable facility in grouping language, and that you have strong feelings upon some subject, which finally you determine to commit to paper. Your pen runs along, the words present themselves, or are dragged out, and fall into their places. You are a good deal moved; here you chuckle to yourself, and half a dozen lines farther down a lump comes into your throat, and perhaps you have to wipe your eyes. You finish, and the copy goes to the printer. When it gets into print the reader sees it. His eye runs along the lines and down the page until it comes to the place where you chuckled as you wrote; then he smiles, and six lines below he has to swallow several times and snuffle and wink to restrain an exhibition of weakness. And then some one else comes along who has no feelings, and swaps the words about a little, and twists the sentences; and behold the spell is gone, and you have left a parcel of written language duly charged with facts, but without a single feeling.

No one can juggle with words with any degree of success without getting a vast respect for their independent ability. They will catch the best idea a man ever had as it flashes through his brain, and hold on to it, to surprise him with it long after, and make him wonder that he was ever man enough to have such an idea. And often they will catch an idea on its way from the brain to the pen point, turn, twist, and improve on it as the eye winks, and in an instant there they are, strung hand in hand across the page, and grinning back at the writer: "This is our idea, old man; not yours!"

As for poetry, every word that expects to earn its salt in poetry should have a head and a pair of legs of its own, to go and find its place, carrying another word, if necessary, on its back. The most that should be expected of any competent poet in regular practice is to serve a general summons and notice of action on the language. If the words won't do the rest for him it indicates that he is out of sympathy with his tools.

But you don't find feelings in written words unless there were feelings in the man who used them. With all their apparent independence they seem to be little vessels that hold in some puzzling fashion exactly what is put into them. You can put tears into them, as though they were so many little buckets; and you can hang smiles along them, like Monday's clothes on the line, or you can starch them with facts and stand them up like a picket fence; but you won't get the tears out unless you first put them in. Art won't put them there. It is like the faculty of getting the quality of interest into pictures. If the quality exists in the artist's mind he is likely to find means to get it into his pictures, but if it isn't in the man no technical skill will supply it. So, if the feelings are in the writer and he knows his business, they will get into the words; but they must be in him first. It isn't the way the words are strung together that makes Lincoln's Gettysburg speech immortal, but the feelings that were in the man. But how do such little, plain words manage to keep their grip on such feelings? That is the miracle.

Number of words 800
See page 285 for Questions

Reading Time in Seconds _____
See page 325 for Conversion Table

The Trouble with Man Is Man

James Thurber

"We have met the enemy, and they are ours." So a military victory was once announced. "We have met the enemy, and he is us" may contain a more important truth. Is Thurber saying much the same thing when he says — "The Trouble with Man Is Man"?

Man has gone long enough, or even too long, without being man enough to face the simple truth that the trouble wih Man is Man. For nearly three thousand years, or since the time of Aesop, he has blamed his frailties and defects on the birds, the beasts, and the insects. It is an immemorial convention of the writer of fables to invest the lower animals with the darker traits of human beings, so that, by age-old habit, Man has come to blame his faults and flaws on the other creatures in this least possible of all worlds.

The human being says that the beast in him has been aroused, when what he actually means is that the human being in him has been aroused. A person is not pigeon-toed, either, but person-toed, and what the lady has are not crow's-feet but woman-wrinkles. It is our species, and not any other, that goes out on wildcat strikes, plays the badger game, weeps crocodile tears, sets up kangaroo courts. It is the man, and not the shark, that becomes the loan shark; the cat burglar, when caught, turns out not to be a cat but a man; the cock-and-bull story was not invented by the cock and the bull; and the male of our species, at the height of his arrogant certainties, is mansure and not cocksure, just as, at his most put-upon, he is woman-nagged and not hen-pecked.

It is interesting to find in one dictionary that "cowed" does not come from "cow" but means, literally, "with the tail between the legs." I had naturally assumed, too, that Man blamed his quailing, or shrinking with fear, on the quail, but the dictionary claims that the origin of the verb "to quail" is uncertain. It is nice to know that "duck" meaning to avoid an unpleasant task, does not derive from our web-footed friend but from the German verb *"tauchen,"* meaning "to dive." We blame our cowardice, though, on poultry, when we say of a cringing man that he "chickened out."

Lest I be suspected by friends and colleagues, as well as by the F.B.I. and the American Legion, of wearing fur or feathers under my clothing, and acting as a spy in the midst of a species that is as nervous as a man and not as a cat, I shall set down here some of the comparatively few laudatory phrases about the other animals that have passed into general usage. We say, then, that a man has dogged determination, bulldog tenacity, and is the watchdog of this or that public office, usually the Treasury. We call him lionhearted, or as brave as a lion, as proud as a peacock, as lively as a cricket, as graceful as a swan, as busy as a bee, as gentle as a lamb, and we sometimes observe that he has the memory of an elephant and works like a beaver. (Why this should make him dog-tired instead of beaver-tired I don't know.)

As I sit here, I suddenly, in my fevered fancy, get a man's-eye view, not a bird's-eye view, of a police detective snooping about a brownstone house, back in the prohibition days. He has been tipped off that the place is a blind tiger that sells white mule, or tiger sweat, and he will not believe the denials of the proprietor, one Joe, whose story sounds fishy. The detective smells a rat and begins pussy-footing around. He is sure that this is a joint in which a man can drink like a fish and get as drunk as a monkey. The proprietor may be as wise as an owl and as slippery as an eel, but the detective is confident that he can outfox him.

"Don't hound me. You're on a wild-goose chase," insists Joe, who has butterflies in his stomach, and gooseflesh. (The goose has been terribly maligned by the human being, who has even gone so far as to pretend that the German jack-boot strut is the goose step. Surely only the dog, the cat, and the bug are more derogated than the goose.) "You're as crazy as a loon," Joe quavers.

"Don't bug me," says the cop, and the bloodhound continues his search. Suddenly he flings open a door, and there stands the proprietor's current mouse, a soiled dove, as naked as a jay bird. But the detective has now ferreted out a secret panel and a cache of currency. "There must be ten thousand clams here," he says. "If you made all this fish legitimately, why do you hide it? And don't try to weasel out."

"In this rat race it's dog eat dog," the proprietor says, as he either is led off to jail or pays off the cop.

The English and American vocabularies have been vastly enlarged and, I suppose, enriched by the multitudinous figures of speech that slander and libel the lower animals, but the result has been the further inflation of the already inflated human ego by easy denigration of the other species. We have a thousand disparaging nouns applicable only to human beings, such as scoundrel, rascal, villain, scalawag, varlet, curmudgeon, and the like, but an angry person is much more apt to use, instead of one of these, such words as jackal, jackass, ape, baboon, gorilla, skunk, black sheep, louse, worm, lobster, crab, or shrimp. Incidentally, the word "curmudgeon" seems to derive from the French *"cœur méchant,"* so that an old curmudgeon is nothing worse than an old naughty heart.

The female of our species comes out of slight, slur, insult, and contumely wearing more unfavorable tags and labels than the male. The fishwife, for example, has no fishhusband. The word "shrew" derives from the name of a small furred mammal with a malignant reputation, based on an old, mistaken notion that it is venomous. Shrews are, to be sure, made up of both males and females, but the word is applied only to the female human being. Similarly, "vixen," meaning an ill-tempered person, was originally applied to both sexes (of human beings, not of foxes), but it is now aimed only at the woman. When a man, especially a general or other leader, is called a fox, the word is usually employed in a favorable sense.

Both "shrew" and "vixen" are rarely used any more in domestic altercations. For one thing, neither implies mental imbalance, and our species is fond of epithets and invective implying insanity. The list of such slings and arrows in Roget's Thesaurus contains, of course, such expressions as "off one's rocker" and "off one's

trolley," but once again the lower forms of life are accused of being "disturbed," as in "mad as a March hare," "bats," "batty," "bats in the belfry," "crazier than a bedbug," and so on. (My favorite phrase in this Roget category gets away from bugs and bats, and rockers and trolleys; it is "balmy in the crumpet.")

Every younger generation, in its time and turn, adds to our animalistic vocabulary of disparagement. A lone male at a dance is no longer a stag turned wolf when he dogs the steps of a girl; he's a bird dog. And if the young lady turns on him, she no longer snaps, "Get lost!" or "Drop dead!" but, I am told, "Clean out your cage!" Since I heard about this two years ago, however, it may well be old hat by now, having given way to something like "Put your foot back in the trap!" or "Go hide under your rock!" or "Crawl back into the woodwork!"

I am afraid that nothing I can say will prevent mankind from being unkind to catkind, dogkind, and bugkind. I find no record of any cat that was killed by care. There are no dogs where a man goes when he goes to the dogs. The bugs that a man gets out of his mechanisms, if he does get them out, are not bugs but defects caused by the ineptitude, haste, or oversight of men.

Let us all go back to counting sheep. I think that the reason for the prevalent sleeplessness of Americans must be that we are no longer counting sheep but men.

Number of words 1366
See page 287 for Questions

Reading Time in Seconds _____
See page 325 for Conversion Table

SELECTION 60

How to Improve Your Vocabulary

Edgar Dale

It's not enough just to recognize the importance of word power. The next step is much more important. Exactly how do you improve your vocabulary? In this selection you'll find seven specific suggestions. Put them to immediate use and start enjoying the added confidence that follows.

The best readers usually have the best vocabularies. No really good reader has a poor one. A good reader is word-conscious, word-sensitive; he knows that words are an excellent way to share ideas and feelings. So one way to improve our reading is to improve our vocabulary, and vice versa.

What is an improved vocabulary? Certainly it is larger and broader. But also it has greater depth and precision. What can we do to develop a richer vocabulary?

Let's look first at the difference in size between an

inadequate, poverty-stricken vocabulary and the rich vocabulary of an able, mature reader. About how many words are known by the average eighth-grader, the high-school graduate, the college graduate? How many does the ablest reader know?

There are about 600,000 words in a big, unabridged dictionary such as *Funk and Wagnalls New College Standard* or *Webster's New International*. *Webster's New Collegiate Dictionary* has more than 125,000 entries, and the 896-page *Thorndike-Barnhart Comprehensive Desk Dictionary* includes over 80,000.

The big, unabridged dictionaries, however, contain many forms of the same word, as well as many rare and obsolete words, and names of thousands of places, persons, rivers, and towns. So I find it more useful to think in terms of the 80,000-word Thorndike-Barnhart dictionary.

The average eighth-grader knows at least 10,000 of these words, the average high-school graduate about 15,000, and the average college graduate not fewer than 20,000. But even college graduates have trouble with such words as *adumbrate, attenuate, avuncular, deprecate, egregious, germane, ingenuous, jejune, plethora, temerity, unconscionable, unctuous.* An able reader increases his vocabulary well beyond the college graduate's 20,000 words.

The best way to improve your vocabulary is through firsthand experiences. If you have had experience in cooking, you know such words as *dredge, sear, draw, marinate, parboil, sauté, braise, frizzle, coddle.* A sports fan will know baseball terms, such as *fungo, Texas leaguer, infield fly.* You don't usually learn such vocabularies by reading books or magazines. But cooks and sports fans do read in these fields and thereby increase the range and depth of their vocabularies.

So a first rule in improving your vocabulary is to improve the range and depth of your experiences. Visits to museums, art exhibits, the legislature, or Congress bring increased vocabulary. So do working with the Community Chest, a nature hike, political activity, or a visit to the seashore. Think of the terms that sailing may bring into your active vocabulary: *scupper, topsail, dinghy, starboard, luff.*

A second suggestion is to work at your vocabulary a little every day. You can do this in several ways. Underline in pencil the hard words you run across in magazines, books, or newspapers. You need not even look them up. Just fix your attention on them, guess their meaning, and go right ahead with your reading. The next time you see one of these words, test your previous guess about its meaning. Maybe your guess fits now, and maybe it doesn't. Check it with your desk dictionary. You might also note its origin and get an additional memory hook on which to hang this word. If you check the pronunciation and say the word aloud, you get another boost in remembering it. You can also check on words you may mispronounce, such as *acclimate, archipelago, niche, orgy, schism, succinct.*

Third, you can sharply improve your vocabulary by reading more. You will see the hard words more often and in a variety of contexts. Of the many ways to increase your vocabulary by indirect experience, reading is the best.

Fourth, start using some of your "new" words in ordinary conversation.

Fifth, read aloud. Years ago, when I started to read "Penrod and Sam" to a seventh-grade class, I discovered that my speaking vocabulary was way behind my reading vocabulary. I did not know how to pronounce such words as *conversant, dolorous, primordial, flaccid, solaced.*

Sixth, you can increase your word power by becoming conscious of key roots and important suffixes and prefixes. A root such as *folium,* meaning *leaf,* gives us *foil, cinquefoil, foliaceous, foliage, foliate, folio, portfolio, trefoil.*

Do you know the prefixes *crypto-, hyper-, hypo-, neo-?* They appear in words like *cryptocommunist, cryptograph, hyperbole, hypertension, hypertrophy, hypochondriac, neoclassic, neologism, neophyte.*

A single root such as the Greek *nym,* meaning name, yields *antonym, homonym, acronym, pseudonym, synonym, anonymous. Nom,* from the Latin *nomen,* also meaning name, gives us *nominate, nominative, nomination, denomination, nomenclature, nominee.*

A seventh way to improve your vocabulary is to develop an interest in the origins of words. Thus you learn that a *nightmare* is not a night horse but an evil spirit formerly supposed to cause bad dreams. A *nasturtium* is a nose twister. *Recalcitrant* means kicking back. *Excoriate* means to take the hide off. The *devil* in "between the devil and the deep blue sea" is a part of a boat.

Finally, it will help if you become conscious of the four stages by which vocabulary grows.

In the first stage, you see a word and are certain you have never seen it before. You never saw *shug* and *bittles,* hence don't know them. They are not words at all; I just made them up.

But you probably have seen words like *lethargic, lissome, serendipity.* If so, you may be in the second stage and may say, "I've seen these before, but I haven't any notion what they mean."

In the third stage, you are able to place the word in a broad classification. You may say, "I know that *lethargic* is an unfavorable word, that *lissome* and *serendipity* are attractive, favorable words, but I don't know exactly what they mean."

You are in the final stage when you know the word accurately.

Many of us have a large number of words in stage three, the twilight zone between words being known and yet not known. Are some of the following words in your twilight zone: *lares and penates, abscond, garrulous, dolorous, ingenuous, friable, tedium, savant, sedulous, sine qua non?*

Also, you may move a word toward a more scientific definition. You may have used *respiration* as a synonym for breathing; later you may learn it is the name for the body's process of absorbing oxygen and giving off carbon dioxide and water. A child may think of a *whale* as a fish, but the adult thinks of it as a mammal that nurses its young. A *spider* is not an insect. A *star* is not a planet. Botanically, a *tomato* is a fruit.

And there is precision of vocabulary — Wordsworth's "choice word and measured phrase." A tree isn't just a tree; it is a *cryptomeria,* a *locust,* a *white pine,* a *yellow poplar.* The ground may be *moist, sodden, arid,* or *parched.* Is a person *sulky, petulant,* or perhaps *bilious?* Why not learn the difference between a *jackanapes* and a *jackal,* a *winch* and a *wench, pretentious* and *portentous?* The educated person is one who sees life with increasingly finer discriminations. And certainly this applies to his discrimination about the words he uses in speech and recognizes in reading.

Sometimes we may say, "Why should I study words before I need to use them? If I meet them in my reading, I'll look them up." But, curiously, a brief acquaintance with a word may cause us to see it later. Haven't you ever looked up an unusual or rare word and then suddenly found it in later reading?

Once, to illustrate an article, I chose four words from a list — *alb, valerian, periwinkle,* and *fichu.* I didn't know what they meant, but within three months I had "accidentally" seen and learned all of them. *Alb* appeared on a label in an exhibit of religious garments; *fichu* on a label describing the neckerchief worn by a young woman in a painting. I saw *valerian* in a display at the old country drugstore in the Farmers' Museum in Cooperstown, New York. And the color *periwinkle* blue turned up in the film *Artists and Models.*

I can draw two conclusions. First, just looking carefully at an unknown word and noting its spelling, as I suggested earlier, may cause us to be ready to see it later. And second, exhibits, galleries, and museums are good places to improve our vocabularies. Just looking sharply at an unknown word can thus be the cause of further experience as well as a result. A chance acquaintance with words sometimes brings them into our vocabulary. We become restless when we don't know what a *pied piper* is, the difference between a *monogram* and a *monograph,* between a *connoisseur* and a *dilettante,* between *ingenious* and *ingenuous.*

The best way of all to improve your vocabulary is to get fun out of words. I enjoy collecting interesting misuses and mispronunciations, such as: "He stepped on the exhilarator." "We are studying jubilant delinquency." "I don't deserve all this oolagoozing." "I don't like to sing solo; I like to sing abreast." "Minch pie." "My boy can't come to school. He has indolent fever."

If we accept the late John Erskine's theory that we have a moral obligation to be intelligent, we should improve our vocabularies. Then, we can read magazines and books that wake us up mentally. We can "argue" with the authors. We can discuss what we have read, improve our dinner-table conversation, be more interesting people.

Your vocabulary gives you away. It may suggest that you are a person with a rich and varied experience, for it tells where you have been, what you have read, talked about, reflected upon. And it tells how far you have traveled along the road to intellectual maturity and discriminating living.

Number of words 1600
See page 289 for Questions

Reading Time in Seconds _____
See page 325 for Conversion Table

SELECTION 61

My Alma Mater

Malcolm X

Have you ever observed, personally, a man who commanded total respect with his words? Malcolm X once did. That started him on a word-building program without parallel. The heart of his program was the dictionary. Here's what he did with it.

The first man I met in prison who made any positive impression on me whatever was a fellow inmate, "Bimbi." I met him in 1947, at Charlestown. He was a light, kind of red-complexioned Negro, as I was; about my height, and he had freckles. Bimbi, an old-time burglar, had been in many prisons. In the license plate shop where our gang worked, he operated the machine that stamped out the numbers. I was along the conveyor belt where the numbers were painted.

Bimbi was the first Negro convict I'd known who didn't respond to "What'cha know, Daddy?" Often, after we had done our day's license plate quota, we would sit around, perhaps fifteen of us, and listen to Bimbi. Normally, white prisoners wouldn't think of listening to Negro prisoners' opinions on anything, but guards, even, would wander over close to hear Bimbi on any subject.

He would have a cluster of people riveted, often on odd subjects you never would think of. He would prove to us, dipping into the science of human behavior, that the only difference between us and outside people was that we had been caught. He liked to talk about histori-

From *The Autobiography of Malcolm X,* by Malcolm X and Alex Haley. Copyright © 1965 by Alex Haley and Betty Shabazz. Reprinted by permission of Grove Press, Inc.

cal events and figures. When he talked about the history of Concord, where I was to be transferred later, you would have thought he was hired by the Chamber of Commerce, and I wasn't the first inmate who had never heard of Thoreau until Bimbi expounded upon him. Bimbi was known as the library's best customer. What fascinated me with him most of all was that he was the first man I had ever seen command total respect . . . with his words.

Bimbi seldom said much to me; he was gruff to individuals, but I sensed he liked me. What made me seek his friendship was when I heard him discuss religion. I considered myself beyond atheism — I was Satan. But Bimbi put the atheist philosophy in a framework, so to speak. That ended my vicious cursing attacks. My approach sounded so weak alongside his, and he never used a foul word.

Out of the blue one day, Bimbi told me flatly, as was his way, that I had some brains, if I'd use them. I had wanted his friendship, not that kind of advice. I might have cursed another convict, but nobody cursed Bimbi. He told me I should take advantage of the prison correspondence courses and the library.

When I had finished the eighth grade back in Mason, Michigan, that was the last time I'd thought of studying anything that didn't have some hustle purpose. And the streets had erased everything I'd ever learned in school; I didn't know a verb from a house. . . .

Many who today hear me somewhere in person, or on television, or those who read something I've said, will think I went to school far beyond the eighth grade. This impression is due entirely to my prison studies.

It had really begun back in the Charlestown Prison, when Bimbi first made me feel envy of his stock of knowledge. Bimbi had always taken charge of any conversation he was in, and I had tried to emulate him. But every book I picked up had few sentences which didn't contain anywhere from one to nearly all of the words that might as well have been in Chinese. When I just skipped those words, of course, I really ended up with little idea of what the book said. So I had come to the Norfolk Prison Colony still going through only book-reading motions. Pretty soon, I would have quit even these motions, unless I had received the motivation that I did.

I saw that the best thing I could do was get hold of a dictionary — to study, to learn some words. I was lucky enough to reason also that I should try to improve my penmanship. It was sad. I couldn't even write in a straight line. It was both ideas together that moved me to request a dictionary along with some tablets and pencils from the Norfolk Prison Colony school.

I spent two days just riffling uncertainly through the dictionary's pages. I'd never realized so many words existed! I didn't know which words I needed to learn. Finally, just to start some kind of action, I began copying.

In my slow, painstaking, ragged handwriting, I copied into my tablet everything printed on that first page, down to the punctuation marks.

I believe it took me a day. Then, aloud, I read back, to myself, everything I'd written on the tablet. Over and over, aloud, to myself, I read my own handwriting.

I woke up the next morning, thinking about those words — immensely proud to realize that not only had I written so much at one time, but I'd written words that I never knew were in the world. Moreover, with a little effort, I also could remember what many of these words meant. I reviewed the words whose meanings I didn't remember. Funny thing, from the dictionary first page right now, that "aardvark" springs to my mind. The dictionary had a picture of it, a long-tailed, long-eared, burrowing African mammal, which lives off termites caught by sticking out its tongue as an anteater does for ants.

I was so fascinated that I went on — I copied the dictionary's next page. And the same experience came when I studied that. With every succeeding page, I also learned of people and places and events from history. Actually the dictionary is like a miniature encyclopedia. Finally the dictionary's A section had filled a whole tablet — and I went on into the B's. That was the way I started copying what eventually became the entire dictionary. It went a lot faster after so much practice helped me to pick up handwriting speed. Between what I wrote in my tablet, and writing letters, during the rest of my time in prison I would guess I wrote a million words.

I suppose it was inevitable that as my word-base broadened, I could for the first time pick up a book and read and now begin to understand what the book was saying. Anyone who has read a great deal can imagine the new world that opened. Let me tell you something; from then until I left that prison, in every free moment I had, if I was not reading in the library, I was reading on my bunk. You couldn't have gotten me out of books with a wedge. Between Mr. Muhammad's teachings, my correspondence, my visitors — usually Ella and Reginald — and my reading of books, months passed without my even thinking about being imprisoned. In fact, up to then, I never had been so truly free in my life. . . .

As you can imagine, especially in a prison where there was heavy emphasis on rehabilitation, an inmate was smiled upon if he demonstrated an unusually intense interest in books. There was a sizable number of well-read inmates, especially the popular debaters. Some were said by many to be practically walking encyclopedias. They were almost celebrities. No university would ask any student to devour literature as I did when this new world opened to me, of being able to read and *understand*.

I read more in my room than in the library itself. An inmate who was known to read a lot could check out more than the permitted maximum number of books. I preferred reading in the total isolation of my own room.

When I had progressed to really serious reading, every night at about ten P.M. I would be outraged with the "lights out." It always seemed to catch me right in the middle of something engrossing.

Fortunately, right outside my door was a corridor light that cast a glow into my room. The glow was enough to read by, once my eyes adjusted to it. So when "lights out" came, I would sit on the floor where I could continue reading in that glow.

At one-hour intervals the night guards paced past every room. Each time I heard the approaching footsteps, I jumped into bed and feigned sleep. And as soon as the guard passed, I got back out of bed onto the floor area of that light-glow, where I would read for another fifty-eight minutes — until the guard approached again. That went on until three or four every morning. Three or four hours of sleep a night was enough for me. Often in the years in the streets I had slept less than that.

I have often reflected upon the new vistas that reading opened to me. I knew right there in prison that reading had changed forever the course of my life. As I see it today, the ability to read awoke inside me some long dormant craving to be mentally alive. I certainly wasn't

seeking any degree, the way a college confers a status symbol upon its students. My homemade education gave me, with every additional book that I read, a little bit more sensitivity to the deafness, dumbness, and blindness that was afflicting the black race in America. Not long ago, an English writer telephoned me from London, asking questions. One was, "What's your alma mater?" I told him, "Books." You will never catch me with a free fifteen minutes in which I'm not studying something I feel might be able to help the black man. . . .

Every time I catch a plane, I have with me a book that I want to read — and that's a lot of books these days. If I weren't out here every day battling the white man, I could spend the rest of my life reading, just satisfying my curiosity — because you can hardly mention anything I'm not curious about. I don't think anybody ever got more out of going to prison than I did. In fact, prison enabled me to study far more intensively than I would have if my life had gone differently and I had attended some college. I imagine that one of the biggest troubles with colleges is there are too many distractions, too much panty-raiding, fraternities, and boola-boola and all of that. Where else but in prison could I have attacked my ignorance by being able to study intensely sometimes as much as fifteen hours a day?

Number of words 1720
See page 291 for Questions

Reading Time in Seconds _____
See page 325 for Conversion Table

SELECTION 62

A Master-Word Approach to Vocabulary

James I. Brown

A master-word is like a master key. An ordinary key unlocks only one or two doors. A master key for a building may unlock over a hundred doors. Master-words provide that same kind of comprehensive help in unlocking word meanings — not one word but hundreds.

How would you like a way of getting acquainted with words, a thousand at a time?

A few minutes with each of the following fourteen words will help you master well over 14,000 words. These words, the most important in the language to speed you along a superhighway toward vocabulary and success, do even more. They furnish invaluable background for further word study and give you a technique, a master key, which has endless possibilities.

You see, most of our English words are not English at all, but borrowings from other languages. Eighty percent of these borrowed words come to us from Latin

and Greek and make up approximately sixty percent of our language.

Since this is so, the most important of these classical elements offer amazingly useful short cuts to a bigger vocabulary. The words in the list at the end of this article contain twelve of the most important Latin roots, two of the most important Greek roots, and twenty of the most frequently used prefixes. Over 14,000 relatively common words, words of collegiate dictionary size, contain one or more of these elements (or an estimated 100,000 words of unabridged dictionary size).

Now, how to put these words to work, converting them into keys to the meanings of thousands of related words?

First, look up each of the fourteen words in the dic-

Adapted from *Word Study,* May 1949.

tionary, noticing the relationship between derivation and definition. For example, take the word "intermittent." Let's chop it in two and chase it back to its birthplace. The two halves you come up with are a Latin prefix "inter-," which means "among" or "between," and a root word "mittere," which to a Roman meant "to send." "To send between!"

That does it. That drags the ghosts out of the Latin closet and arranges their bones so you can tell what goes on. An *intermittent* sound is one that is "sent between" periods of silence. Maybe those Romans had something, when you dust away the cobwebs caused by a dislike of high-school Latin. Now compare that derivational meaning, "to send between," with the dictionary definition, "coming or going at intervals."

This step develops an understanding of the many relationships existing between derivation and definition, relationships from almost exact agreement — as with *prefix*, by derivation and definition meaning "to fix before," — to varied extensions and restrictions of the derivational meaning.

Next, look up each prefix. When you look up "pre-," for example, you'll find five somewhat different specific meanings, all denoting priority — priority in time, space, or rank. The dictionary entry will fix those meanings in mind and will often indicate assimilative changes.

The third step is to list at least ten words containing the prefix, checking each with the dictionary to avoid mistakes. You'll find some prefixes as changeable as chameleons. *Offer* is really *ob-fer*, but *offer* is easier to say. And there's the word *cooperation*, "to operate or work together." But doesn't *com-* mean "together?" Yes, but *comoperation* is awkward to say, so we say *cooperation*. This prepares you for the changes that occur when *com-* is combined with *-stant*, *-relation*, *-laboration*, and *-cil* to make *constant*, *correlation*, *collaboration*, and *council*. There's your background for recognizing similar chameleon-like changes of *ob-*, *ad-*, *ex-*, and others.

Finally, list at least ten words containing the root, checking each carefully with the dictionary. A few examples are listed for each root which should suggest others. Try to discover less common forms by some intelligent guessing.

Take the root *plicare*, "to fold" — the one that's part of *complication*. First of all, you'll think of *application*, *implication*, and *duplication*. *Duplication* may suggest *duplex* as well as *perplex* and *complex*. *Complex* may open the way to *comply*, which may in turn remind you of *apply*, *imply*, *pliant*, *supply*, *deploy*, and *employ*. Each discovery you make of a variant form adds that much to your background and understanding of the large family of words for which that root is key. Your dictionary will keep your guesses in line with the facts.

So much for method. Now, just how useful is your newly acquired knowledge of roots and prefixes?

Suppose you see the strange word *explication*. You know *ex-* means "out" and you know *plicare* means "to fold" — "to fold out." With the help of the sentence — "his explication was confused and difficult to follow" you see that explication refers to an unfolding

THE FOURTEEN WORDS

KEYS TO THE MEANINGS OF OVER 14,000 WORDS

	WORDS	PREFIX	COMMON MEANING	ROOT	COMMON MEANING
1.	*Precept*	pre-	(before)	capere	(take, seize)
2.	*Detain*	de-	(away, from)	tenere	(hold, have)
3.	*Intermittent*	inter-	(between)	mittere	(send)
4.	*Offer*	ob-	(against)	ferre	(bear, carry)
5.	*Insist*	in-	(into)	stare	(stand)
6.	*Monograph*	mono-	(alone, one)	graphein	(write)
7.	*Epilogue*	epi-	(upon)	legein	(say, study of)
8.	*Aspect*	ad-	(to, towards)	specere	(see)
9.	*Uncomplicated*	un-	(not)	plicare	(fold)
		com-	(together with)		
10.	*Nonextended*	non-	(not)	tendere	(stretch)
		ex-	(out of)		
11.	*Reproduction*	re-	(back, again)	ducere	(lead)
		pro-	(forward)		
12.	*Indisposed*	in-	(not)	ponere	(put, place)
		dis-	(apart from)		
13.	*Oversufficient*	over-	(above)	facere	(make, do)
		sub-	(under)		
14.	*Mistranscribe*	mis-	(wrong)	scribere	(write)
		trans-	(across, beyond)		

or folding out of meaning — or an explanation, in other words. Sometimes knowing only part of the word is enough. A student reading of a man's *predilection* for novels need only notice the *pre-* to assume that the man places novels "before" other books, that he has a "preference" or "partiality" for novels. Take another example. Is a *precocious* child one who has matured before or later than the average child? Again the prefix is your key to the meaning.

This procedure puts certain psychological laws of learning to work for you overtime. It forces you to discover meaningful relationships between derivation and definition. It stimulates you to use your knowledge to analyze strange words and understand familiar words better. It leads you to discover important principles of language development. In short, it forces you to take the initiative necessary to speed toward vocabulary and success.

And spelling is easier. If you continually misspell *prescription*, spelling it with a *per-*, you have only to remember the meanings of the prefixes. Since a prescription is written *before* being filled, you'll have to spell it with a *pre-*. You'll also know how to spell such demons as *misspell* or *misstep*, for you know they're combinations of *mis-* with *spell* and *step*. And what about someone who migrates into this country? Is he an *immigrant* or *emigrant*? Since he's coming *into* the country, he is an *in-migrant* or by assimilation an *immigrant*.

In this way you begin to understand the intricacies of our language. At first you'll have trouble spotting the root *facere* in such a word as *benefactor*. But soon you'll be a regular Sherlock Holmes, able to ferret out that root in such varied disguises as *artifice, affair, feature, affection, facsimile, counterfeit, fashion, facilitate*. You'll soon have no trouble finding the prefix *ex-* in *effect*, or *in-* in *illiterate*, or *dis-* in *differ*.

And best of all, you'll have a master key to unlock the meanings of thousands of other words, a technique to use with other classical elements. Yours is the magic touchstone, curiosity about derivations, which will bring words to life and lead you eventually to an awareness and understanding of words reached by relatively few.

Number of words 1090
See page 293 for Questions

Reading Time in Seconds _____
See page 325 for Conversion Table

The Discipline of Language

Royal Bank of Canada Monthly Letter

New words or new meanings for old words help you read, write, speak, and listen more effectively. They also change you — make you a somewhat different human being — so semanticists remind us. Discipline is the key to endowing words with their special power.

There is magic in words properly used, and to give them this magic is the purpose of discipline of language.

Some quite intelligent people have been lured into thinking that a concern for words is out of date. Others allow themselves to believe that to speak and write sloppily is somehow an emblem of the avant-garde.

The truth is that in no other time in history was it so important to use the right words in the right place in the right way to convey what we have in our minds. We need the proper use of language to impose form and character upon elements in life which have it in them to be rebellious and intractable.

A glance at our environment will show that our high standard of living, brought about by our mastery of science and technology, is menaced by the faulty use of signals between men, between ideologies and between nations. By misinterpreting signals (which is all that words are) we create disorder in human affairs.

Communication of ideas is an important human activity. When we invented writing we laid the foundation-stone of civilization. In the beginning the power of words must have seemed like sorcery, and we are compelled to admit that the miracles which verbal thinking have wrought justified the impression.

Words underlie our whole life, are the signs of our humanity, the tools of our business, the expressions of our affections, and the records of our progress. As Susanne Langer says in *Philosophy in a New Key*: "Between the clearest animal call of love or warning or anger, and a man's least, trivial word, there lies a whole day of creation — or, in modern phrase, a whole chapter of evolution."

This language has such transcendent importance that we must take pains with its use.

In business there is no inefficiency so serious as that which arises from poverty of language. The man who

From *Royal Bank of Canada Monthly Letter*, Vol. 45, No. 7 (July 1964). Reprinted with permission from The Royal Bank of Canada.

does not express himself meaningfully and clearly is a bungler, wasting his time and that of his associates.

The key word in all use of language is communication. Thoughts locked up in your own breast give no profit or pleasure to others, but just as you must use the currency of the country in which you are travelling, so you need to use the right currency in words if you are going to bring your thoughts into circulation. Many centuries ago Paul the Apostle wrote in these cautionary terms to one of his churches: "Except ye utter by the tongue words easy to be understood, how shall it be known what is spoken? . . . ye shall speak into the air."

IMPORTANCE IN BUSINESS

The workmen engaged in building the Tower of Babel were craftsmen, skilled in their trades. Take away their tools: they will replace them. Take away their skills: they will learn anew. But take away their means of communication with one another and the building of the Tower has to be abandoned.

How serious the problem of communication is in business may be revealed in this sentence: your letter's only justification is the critical three minutes when it must stand, naked and unexcused, fighting the boredom and inattention of the reader.

The environment of your letter — up-to-date letterhead with embossed symbol, double weight paper, deckle edges — these do not amount to much. Sour notes in music do not become sweet because the musician is in white tie and black tails.

What counts is simply this: to say what you mean with precision and accuracy in plain language. A true definition of style is "proper words in proper places with the thoughts in proper order." A scrupulous writer will ask "What am I trying to say? Do these words express it?" A word does not serve well which does not excite in the reader the same idea which it stands for in the mind of the writer.

There is no easy way of choosing words. They must not be so general in meaning as to include thoughts not intended, nor so narrow as to eliminate thoughts that are intended. Let the meaning select the word.

A word is ambiguous when the reader is unable to choose decisively between alternative meanings, either of which would seem to fit the context.

A great deal of unclear writing results from the use of too many broad, general words, those having so many possible meanings that the precise thought is not clear. The more general the words are, the fainter is the picture; the more special they are, the brighter.

Socrates pointed the way toward clarity in the use of language when he demonstrated to his disciples that they would get nowhere in their dispute about justice unless they agreed upon clear definitions of the words they used. He made sure that they were talking about the same things.

If you look back over the past week's differences of opinion expressed in conferences, memos and letters, you will be surprised by the number of times you said, or someone else said: "Why didn't he say that in the first place?" That refrain is monotonous in business offices and workshops.

There is only one way to make sure of the communication of ideas: to demand that what is being said to you shall be said in terms understandable to you, and to discipline your own language so that it says what you want it to say.

If you are just beginning to write, make it your first rule to be plain. If nature means you to be a fancy writer, a composer of odes or a trail-blazing author like Joyce or Stein, she will force you to it, but whatever of worth you turn out even then will be based upon your developed skill with words.

Meantime, say what you have to say, or what you wish to say, in the simplest, most direct and the most exact words. Someone who has no better employment may pick holes in every third sentence of your composition, but you have written in such a way as to satisfy the common sense of those who read to find meaning.

The plain way of writing conceals great art. By avoiding pomposity, ambiguity and complexity you attain simplicity, which is the greatest cunning because it conveys your meaning into the mind of another straight away, without effort on his part. It carries with it, too, a feeling of sincerity and integrity, for who can be suspicious of the motives of a person who speaks plainly?

WHAT WORDS ARE

Words are the only currency in which we can exchange thought even with ourselves. It is through words, which are the names for things and actions, that we perceive the events of the world.

Because of this universal importance, we need to be as clear-cut as we can in their use. Inexactness to some degree is inevitable, because thought can never be precisely or adequately expressed in verbal symbols. Words are not like iron and wood, coal and water, things we see and touch. Words are merely indicators, but they are the only sensible signs we have, enabling us to describe things and think about them. In the darkness of night we talk about the sun, knowing that the word "sun" presents a picture to our hearer; we write about the "sparkling ripples" caused by the stone we cast into a pool, knowing that our description presents a motion picture to our reader.

What we need to do is keep our thinking and speaking language under the discipline of meaning. We cannot shape ideas and develop an argument without choosing and ordering our words. Many people have far better ideas than anyone knows: their thoughts either beat about in their heads, finding no communication package in which to emerge, or they come out distorted and in fragments.

A BIG VOCABULARY

Knowledge of words is not burdensome. Words are pleasant companions, delighting in what they can do for you whether in earnest or in fun, in business or in love. The true dimension of your vocabulary is not, however, the number of words you can identify but the number of words you can use, each with its appropriate area of meaning.

With an adequate vocabulary you are equipped to express every shading of thought. Too often in the ordinary intercourse of life we let this wealth of words lie inert and unemployed. We work a limited number of words to death. We exist in voluntary word poverty. We do coarsely what might be done finely.

One road to language mastery is the study of synonyms, words that are similar yet not identical in meaning. Two words that seem to be the same may have very much in common, but also have something private and particular which they do not share with each other, some personality natural to the word or acquired by usage.

Everyone recognizes the difference between child and urchin, hand and fist, mis-statement and lie. There is an overtone of meaning which causes a mother to resent your calling her child "puny" instead of "delicate." People persist in confusing "instruction" with "education" when discussing our school system. The former is furnishing a child with knowledge and facts and information; the latter is a drawing forth from within, opening up fountains already in his mind rather than filling a cistern with water brought from some other source.

Study the different shades of meaning expressed by the synonyms of a general word like "said." When should you use "maintained"? Under what conditions would "claimed" be more appropriate? Look at the different effects produced in your mind by substitution of these and other words for "said" in this sentence: "He said (asserted, implied, assumed, insisted, suggested) that the police were doing a good job." And try the substitutes for "looked" in the sentence "John looked at Mary" . . . glared, gazed, leered, glanced.

We may use "arrogant," "presumptuous," and "insolent" almost interchangeably in loose talk, but when we examine them with care we find three distinct thoughts: claiming the homage of others as his due; taking things to himself before acquiring any title to them; breaking the recognized standard of social be-

haviour. There is a world of difference between the meanings of misconduct, misbehaviour and delinquency, and between vice, error, fault, transgression, lapse and sin.

This discrimination may appear trifling to some and tiresome to others. The writer who wishes to think clearly and express his thoughts clearly — and is there anyone who will admit that he wishes to be a bungler in thought and speech? — will see its virtues.

THE NEEDS OF THE DAY

A youth may fail in mathematics or economics, which means only that he is deficient in those subjects, but if he fails in language he is fundamentally uneducated.

Yet the current passion for pictures and sounds, and the growing aversion to reading, have produced a generation of students who are finding it difficult to speak and write with sufficient accuracy to meet modern job requirements.

Afraid of loading children with too much learning, the fourth grade teacher in the United States uses a primer with some 1,800 words. A Russian child has a primer of 2,000 words in the first grade and of 10,000 words in the fourth. He is, moreover, reading Tolstoy in the first grade while his opposite number in the United States is working his way through a book entitled "A Funny Sled." This charge is made in an article in *Horizon*.

Add to that the fact of multiple-choice examination papers which toady to our natural desire to avoid work. All the pupil need do is put an "X" in the appropriate square. He avoids all intellectual effort involved in marshalling his thoughts and expressing them coherently.

Some teachers go so far as to deny any standards of "right" or "wrong" in the few essays they give their pupils. They put this anarchical philosophy into the phrase: "Correctness rests upon usage." They are followers of the Humpty Dumpty school: "When I use a word it means just what I choose it to mean."

We are in danger of falling into the terrible plight of having a high technology unsupported by people who can discuss it or operate it understandingly — a sophisticated savagery.

Language goes deeper than technical literacy. It is not only being able to read newspapers. It has to do with forming us as human beings, with the qualities of civilization. Without discipline, language declines into flabby permissiveness, into formlessness and mindlessness. It deteriorates into what the late James Thurber called "Our oral culture of pure babble."

Number of words 2090
See page 295 for Questions

Reading Time in Seconds _____
See page 325 for Conversion Table

Do You Know How Words Can Make You Rich?

Morton Winthrop

To earn more money, learn more words! That pretty well sums up the following selection. You can even determine your probable top salary by trying the vocabulary test that follows. If you're disappointed, just give yourself a raise! Increase your vocabulary, beginning right now.

If you are not earning enough money, perhaps it's because you don't know the meanings of enough words.

More than any other single factor yet known, vocabulary predicts financial success!

This is the finding of the Human Engineering Laboratory, a leading nationwide psychological testing service, which has been exploring the aptitudes and careers of people for the last 38 years.

Now, with a short 20-word test developed for *This Week* by the Laboratory, you can fairly accurately predict your top income.

Don't leap to the conclusion that a large vocabulary by itself — and a good score on our quiz — will guarantee you success. Vocabulary, which is really a measure of your potential — must be linked with good work habits, initiative and responsibility.

DIZZY DEAN SPEAKS UP

As Dizzy Dean, baseball's master of malapropism (need to look that one up?) said: "There's a lot of guys that know how to read and write but that ain't making a living."

All the same, 30,000 vocabulary tests given each year by the Human Engineering Laboratory prove that big incomes and big vocabularies go together — and the same goes for small ones.

The Laboratory was founded in 1922 by a Harvard philosophy major named Johnson O'Connor. The Lab's first home was at the West Lynn, Mass., plant of General Electric, where O'Connor was in charge of selecting capable engineers. So successful was he in matching the man with the job through a battery of carefully developed tests that high-school students began asking to take them for career guidance. As these requests multiplied, O'Connor began giving tests evenings and Saturdays. Eventually the Laboratory expanded to the present huge, independent, non-profit outfit with branches in major cities throughout the country. It has developed dozens of tests to help a person find where his abilities lie, but the single most important is the vocabulary test, similar to that on these pages.

Husbands and wives taking our test needn't be surprised if their scores come close to matching. The Laboratory has discovered that married couples tend to know the same words because of the similarity of their educations, interests and backgrounds.

Men tend to marry girls with similar-sized vocabularies. So women who aren't married yet can fairly accurately predict the earning power of their husbands-to-be by word-testing themselves.

Vocabulary is an indication of precise as well as broad knowledge, and does not depend solely upon education but upon wide reading and wide experience as well.

"I once tested the president of a coal-mining company in Pennsylvania," says O'Connor. "He was a man who had worked his way up from the pits and his grammar was terrible. Yet, in all the vocabulary tests, he got only two words wrong. The best score that any college graduate in that town could make was thirteen words wrong."

A 40-year-old woman tested recently in Chicago had only gone through the eighth grade, yet she scored extremely high in laboratory vocabulary tests. She is an avid reader, interested in philosophy, semantics and logic. For the past five years she has headed a group of 60 accountants, although she is not an accountant herself.

Even among college graduates, vocabulary differences can be startling. In 1955, a group of college seniors selected by a large industrial plant as executive material was hired by the company to go to work after graduation.

The men were given a group of vocabulary tests. At work, each man was shifted around so that he had an equal opportunity to learn and to assume responsibility. *By last June, all of those men who had been tested in the top 10 percent in vocabulary had become executives. Not a single man who had tested in the bottom 25 percent is an executive!*

If you should score poorly on our test, all is not lost. According to Mr. O'Connor, you can work at building your vocabulary — and with it your chances for a larger income. Wide reading is an invaluable aid. The following techniques will pay off for you:

1. Set a goal of at least one serious book a month.
2. When you read, have a dictionary at hand. When you meet a difficult word, look it up.
3. Examine carefully how you heard or saw the

From *This Week* Magazine, October 30, 1960. Reprinted by permission of the author.

word used. As O'Connor says, "People often try to use terribly difficult words and, of course, they wind up using them wrong. Other people laugh and the incentive to learn more new words is often lost."

No matter how you choose to build your vocabulary — through crossword puzzles, books, or reading the dictionary — *the point is you should do it!*

Not only is the reward a much greater possible income, but greater insight and confidence in yourself and what you can do.

Number of words 790
See page 297 for Questions

Reading Time in Seconds _____
See page 325 for Conversion Table

This 20-word test will give you a fairly accurate idea of what your top income will be. Circle one of the five words which comes closest to the meaning of the first word in italic type. Be sure to read all five choices and, where you have no idea, guess. After you finish the test, turn to page 298 for the answers and your future top income.

1. Did you see the *clergy?* / funeral / dolphin / churchmen / monastery / bell tower

2. Fine *louvers.* / doors / radiators / slatted vents / mouldings / bay windows

3. Like an *ellipse.* / sunspot / oval / satellite / triangle / volume

4. *Dire* thoughts. / angry / dreadful / blissful / ugly / unclean

5. It was the *affluence.* / flow rate / pull / wealth / flood / bankruptcy

6. Discussing the *acme.* / intersection / question / birth mark / perfection / low point

7. How *odious.* / burdensome / lazy / hateful / attractive / fragrant

8. This is *finite.* / limited / tiny / precise / endless / difficult

9. Watch for the *inflection.* / accent / mirror image / swelling / pendulum swing / violation

10. The *connubial* state. / marriage / tribal / festive / spinsterly / primitive

11. See the *nuance.* / contrast / upstart / renewal / delinquent / shading

12. Where is the *dryad?* / water sprite / fern / dish towel / chord / wood nymph

13. Will you *garner* it? / dispose of / store / polish / thresh / trim

14. A sort of *anchorite.* / religious service / hermit / marine deposit / mineral / promoter

15. *Knurled* edges. / twisted / weather beaten / flattened / ridged / knitted

16. Is it *bifurcated?* / forked / hairy / two wheeled / mildewed / joined

17. Examining the *phthisis.* / cell division / medicine / misstatement / dissertation / tuberculosis

18. *Preponderance* of the group. / absurdity / heaviness / small number / foresight / majority

19. Ready to *expound.* / pop / confuse / interpret / dig up / imprison

20. Staring at the *relict.* / trustee / antique table / corpse / widow / excavation

See page 298 for answers

The Semantic Environment in the Age of Advertising

Henryk Skolimowski

We live in a world of words, we wrap our ideas in words, we waste words, we worry over words — right words and wrong words. That explains the phrase "semantic environment." An advertising man has to know, as you will soon know, exactly what words are most powerful.

David Ogilvy is a very successful advertising man. In addition, Mr. Ogilvy has turned out to be a successful writer. His book, *Confessions of an Advertising Man,* was a best-seller. His confessions are in fact intimate whisperings of one adman to another. These whisperings, however, turned out to be interesting enough to make his book one of the most readable and lucid stories of advertising ever written. What is so fascinating about this book is not the amount of linguistic contortions which he advocates, but the amount of truth which is expressed there incidentally. There is nothing more comforting than to find truth accidentally expressed by one's adversary. *Confessions of an Advertising Man* provides a wealth of such truths.

Mr. Ogilvy tells us that "the most powerful words you can use in a headline are FREE and NEW. You can seldom use FREE," he continues, "but you can always use NEW — if you try hard enough." It is an empirical fact that these two words have a most powerful influence upon us. This fact has been established by scientific research. Whenever these words appear, they are used deliberately — in order to lull and seduce us.

The word FREE is especially seductive. Whether we are aware of this or not, it has an almost hypnotic effect on us. Although we all know "nothing is for nothing," whenever the word FREE appears, it acts on us as the light of a candle acts on a moth. This is one of the mysteries of our language. And these mysteries are very skillfully exploited by advertising men.

Apart from the words FREE and NEW, other words and phrases "which make wonders," as Mr. Ogilvy's research has established, are: "HOW TO, SUDDENLY, NOW, ANNOUNCING, INTRODUCING, IMPORTANT, DEVELOPMENT, AMAZING, SENSATIONAL, REVOLUTIONARY, STARTLING, MIRACLE, OFFER, QUICK, EASY, WANTED, CHALLENGE, ADVICE TO, THE TRUTH ABOUT, COMPARE, BARGAIN, HURRY, LAST CHANCE." Should we not be grateful to Mr. Ogilvy for such a splendid collection? Should we not learn these "miraculous" phrases by heart in order to know which

Reprinted from *Etc.: A Review of General Semantics,* Vol. XXV, No. 1 (March 1968). By permission of the International Society for General Semantics.

particular ones drive us to the marketplace? To this collection I should like to add some of the phrases which I found: SIMPLE, SAVE, CONVENIENT, COMFORT, LUXURY, SPECIAL OFFER, DISTINCTIVE, DIFFERENT, RARE.

Having provided his collection, Ogilvy comments upon these words that make wonders (and this comment is most revealing): "Don't turn up your nose at these cliches. They may be shopworn, but they work." Alas! They work on us. What can we do about their merciless grip? Nothing. Language and its workings cannot be controlled or altered through an act of our will. The cumulative process of the development of language used as the instrument of tyranny or as the bridge to God through prayers; as a recorder of everyday trivia or as a clarion trumpet announcing new epochs in human history; as an expression of private feelings of single individuals or as a transmitter of slogans to the masses — this process has endowed some words with incredible subtleties and others with irresistible power. The only thing we can do about the influence of language on us is to become aware of it. This awareness may diminish the grip language has on us.

It is very gratifying to know that nowadays advertising is so punctilious, so systematic, and so scientific in its approach to the customer. Mr. Ogilvy in *Confessions* relentlessly repeats that "research has shown" so and so, "research shows" this and that, "research suggests" that, "research has established" that, etc. This constant reference to research is not an advertising humbug. It is through systematic research that we are "hooked" more and more thoroughly. With perfect innocence Ogilvy informs us that "Another profitable gambit is to give the reader helpful advice or service. It hooks about (was this a slip of the tongue, or intentional, plain description?) 75 percent more readers than copy which deals entirely with the product."

Madison Avenue has, above all, established that through words we may be compelled to perform certain acts — acts of buying. This conclusion is not to be found in Ogilvy. Whether it is an historical accident or not, it is a rather striking fact that, independent of semanticists and logicians and linguistic philosophers, advertising men have made some important discoveries about language. And they have utilized these discoveries with amazing success. They are probably not aware of the theoretical significance of their discoveries and are no doubt little interested in such matters.

J. L. Austin, one of the most prominent linguistic philosophers at Oxford during the 1950's, developed a theory of what he called *performative utterances*. He observed that language is systematically employed not only for stating and describing but also for performing actions. Such utterances as "I warn you to . . ." or "I promise you x" are performances rather than descriptions. They function not only on a verbal level, but also as deeds, as concrete performances through words. The discovery and classification of performative utterances is an important extension of ordinary logic — that is, logic concerned with declarative utterances. On the other hand, it is an important finding of the hidden force of language in shaping our social and individual relationships.

Quite independently, advertising men have developed and successfully applied their own theory of performative utterances. They may be oblivious to the logical subtleties involved; however, they are not oblivious to the power of their medium — that is, the verbal utterances through which they induce our acts of buying. Again, there is very little we can do about it. This is the way language works. We can only recognize this fact. But once we recognize it, we acquire some immunity.

Now, we all know that advertising messages are conveyed in words. Usually, there are not only words, but pictures and images which suggest appropriate associations to the person reading the words. The images are projected to be psychologically appealing. Psychologically appealing images are those which appeal to our seven deadly sins: sexual urges, vanity, snobbery, gluttony, greed, etc.

Many analyses of advertising have shown the mechanism of psychological associations built into the ad message. In particular they showed that the level of most of these appeals is that of sheer brutes, of ultimate halfwits whose only desire is to satisfy their most rudimentary biological urges. However, not many analyses of advertising, if any at all, show how frail the link is between the picture set to evoke emotional reactions and the linguistic utterance which, in the final analysis, is the message of the ad. We must remember that it is the verbal message which ultimately draws us to the marketplace.

My thesis is that the semantic environment has a more profound influence on our behavior and our attitudes than we are aware. If this thesis is correct, it may throw some light on the phenomenon which we usually attribute to the population explosion and the mechanization of our lives; namely, the depersonalization of human relations. I should like to suggest that perhaps a transfer of attitudes through the change of the semantic environment has taken place. Previously, highly emotional expressions were applied to human beings. Nowadays, they are constantly and massively applied by the admen to objects. We have thus developed loving fondness for objects which we worship. Dehumanizing of human relations seems to be the other part of this process. It is quite natural that when we become more and more emotionally involved with objects, we tend to be less and less involved with people. As a consequence, attitudes traditionally reserved for objects are now displayed toward people. In love, in friendship, and in the multitude of other human relations, detachment, lack of interest, and coldness seem to prevail. Human beings are treated like objects.

To summarize, the success of advertising and our failure to defend ourselves against it result mainly from our obliviousness to some of the functions of language. We think that language is a tool, an indifferent piece of gadgetry which simply serves the process of communication and that the only relation we have to language is that *we use language*. We do indeed use it. But this is only part of the story. The other part, which is usually overlooked, is that *language uses us* — by forming our personal and emotional habits, by forming our attitudes. Language is thus not only our servant; it is also our master. No one knows this better than the adman!

The relation between language and us is more complicated than we usually are prepared to admit. To escape the tyranny of language, we have to recognize the double role of language in human relations, (1) as a carrier of messages we send, and (2) as a shaper of the content of human relations. We cannot reduce or nullify the influence of language on us by simply denying the existence of this influence. The only reasonable thing we can do is to recognize the force of language: its strength, the way it works, its theater of operations. By identifying the traps of language, by identifying the linguistic strategies of the admen and other propagandists, we shall be able to cope with the semantic environment much more effectively than we have done hitherto.

Number of words 1532
See page 299 for Questions

Reading Time in Seconds _____
See page 325 for Conversion Table

Section VII: Current Problems

SELECTION 66

Your Mind Can Keep You Well

John A. Schindler

Fifty percent of all people going to the doctors in the United States are victims of one *disease. What treatment might be expected — hydrotherapy, physiotherapy, electrotherapy? Strangely enough, what might be called bibliotherapy might be best. Read this article. It's excellent bibliotherapy.*

As a doctor I know that there are a thousand different ailments that this human clay is heir to, and one of them is as common as the other 999 put together. Fifty percent of all the people going to doctors in the United States today are victims of this one disease. Many would put the figure higher. At one well-known clinic in the South a report was published reviewing 500 consecutive admissions to that institution; of those, 386 — or 77 percent — were sick with this one disease. Persons of any age, in any walk of life, can contract it. Furthermore, it is a terrifically expensive disease to diagnose and treat.

I hesitate to give you its name because immediately you will get a lot of misconceptions. The first will be that it is not a real disease. But don't kid yourself. It used to be called psychoneurosis. Now it is known as psychosomatic illness. And it is *not* a disease in which the patient just *thinks* he is sick. The pain you get is often just as severe as the pain you get with a gall-bladder colic.

Psychosomatic illness isn't produced by a bacterium, or by a virus, or by a new growth. It is produced by the circumstances of daily living. I have tried to find one word for it, but it takes three, each meaning about the same thing but in different degrees. They are: *cares, difficulties, troubles.* Whenever one has such a thick, impenetrable layer of c.d.t. that he can't get up above it into a realm of joy and pleasure occasionally, he gets a psychosomatic illness.

There are three general groupings of people who suffer from c.d.t. In the first group are the people who are habitually crabby. I drove past a friend's farm one summer day and I thought to myself, "Those oats ought to make Sam happy." So I drove in and I said, "Sam, that's a wonderful field of oats," and Sam said, "Yes, but the wind will blow it down before I get it cut." He got it cut all right, he got it threshed, and he got a good price for it. Well, I saw him one day and I said, "Sam, how did the oats turn out?" And he said, "Oh, it was a good crop, and I guess the price was all right, but you know a crop like that sure takes a lot out of the soil."

People like Sam invariably get a psychosomatic illness, and get it hard. As a rule they are invalids for the rest of their lives. There is nothing you can do about it.

The second group, where most of us belong, are the people who all day long manage to be concerned, to be anxious, to be worrying about something. If there's nothing around home or the business, they worry about Mrs. Smith down the street. Why doesn't she get her daughter in before 11 o'clock at night? Something is going to happen to her!

The third group is made up of those who have an acute case of c.d.t. Maybe they have gotten themselves into some kind of mess, financial or domestic. They are usually easier to treat than those in the second group, who are certainly easier to treat than those in the first group.

How does this c.d.t. bring on illness? To understand that, we must consider what thinking is and what emotion is. Thinking is not something that goes on solely in the brain: it involves the entire body in a series of correlated nerve impulses that center in the brain. Particularly is this true when an emotion colors our thinking. The psychologist Williams James gave us the best definition that we have of emotion when he said that it is the state of mind that manifests itself by a perceptible change in the body.

One emotion we all recognize is anger. You don't have to be told when a man is angry. His face either gets white or it gets red; his eyes widen; his muscles tighten up so that he trembles. That is the state of mind manifesting itself by a perceptible change in the body.

Another emotion is embarrassment. A person who blushes certainly doesn't have a disease of the skin. In his case embarrassment produces a dilation of the blood vessels in the face.

A third example in the group of unpleasant emotions is the man or woman who vomits or faints at the sight of blood. The sight of blood leads to such painfully disagreeable thinking that the stomach does the things that result in vomiting. Or the heart and the blood vessels leading to the brain do the things that result in fainting.

Now, how does all this bring about a disease? Very simply. Most of our disagreeable emotions produce

From *The Reader's Digest,* November 1960.

muscle tightness. Suppose that all day long your thinking is acutely disagreeable. You are tightening up muscles. Take your fist and hold it loosely; it doesn't hurt; but hold it tight for a long time and it begins to hurt. The squeeze produces pain.

One of the first places to show tension is the group of muscles at the back of the neck. Another group that come into play very early are the muscles at the upper end of the esophagus. When they squeeze down you feel a lump. It is difficult to swallow. If the muscles in the lower esophagus contract, then it's more serious. Much more commonly the stomach is involved. And when the muscles of the stomach begin to squeeze down you are conscious of a heavy, disagreeable pressure inside. When the muscles squeeze down hard, then it hurts, just as bad as any ulcer. In our town we had a grocer with a competitive business, a nagging wife, a wayward son — and he had this pain most of the time. Doctors assured him he had no ulcer. He finally began to believe them when he noticed that every time he went fishing the pain disappeared. And it didn't come back again until he was almost home.

This same kind of muscle spasm can occur in any part of the colon. Many persons who complain of a pain exactly like gall-bladder pain don't have gall-bladder trouble at all. They're dissatisfied, and the upper colon is squeezing down. And believe me, their suffering is real. If the pain happens to be lower down, it will seem just like appendicitis. And then it takes a very smart doctor not to open that abdomen.

Other muscles also respond to emotional stimuli, particularly the muscles of the blood vessels. A good many of the people who go to a doctor with a severe headache have that ache because some blood vessel inside or outside the skull is squeezing down so hard from nervous excitation that it produces pain.

And a third of all skin diseases treated by dermatologists are produced by blood vessels in the skin reacting to anxiety, worry, disgust and so on. Each time certain individuals become upset or irritated or peeved, serum is actually squeezed out through the wall of the blood vessel and into the skin. The tissue becomes thickened. Finally the serum is pushed up through the surface of the skin where it becomes scaly, crusty and itchy, and the patient has a neurodermatitis.

One favorite place for nervous tension is in the muscles in the upper left part of the thorax. People rarely come to see us doctors because they have a pain on the right side. It's almost always on the left. If it's on the right — pshaw! — it doesn't amount to anything. If it's on the left — ah! — could be heart trouble! Then they start watching for it. And merely watching for it can bring on the pain.

Muscle tension is just one way in which the symptoms are produced in a psychosomatic illness. Another is the effect that the emotion has on the endocrine system. Most of you have driven down a street in an automobile too fast when suddenly somebody has come out from a side street. You started to breathe deeply, your heart began to pound and you got a little faint. Acute fear in your mind produces these bodily changes. An impulse is sent to the adrenal glands, which squeeze adrenaline into the blood stream. When that adrenaline hits the heart, the heart starts to thump. When it hits the respiratory center in the brain, you start to gasp. When it hits the blood vessels going into the brain, they narrow down and you feel woozy.

There are other organic effects of psychosomatic illness. If it happens to be the blood vessels on your heart that squeeze down every time you get excited or angry, it is serious. John Hunter, the English physiologist, had that kind of heart, and he always said, "The first scoundrel that gets me angry will kill me." And that's exactly what happened. He got up in a medical meeting one time to refute something that he didn't like, and his anger produced such a contraction of the blood vessels on his heart that he fell dead.

Many victims of psychosomatic illness are up and around. Many are in hospitals. Thousands have been in bed at home for years. To avoid psychosomatic illness, we must learn how to make our attitude and thinking as pleasant and cheerful as possible. It would be idiotic for me to tell you that you can be pleasant and cheerful all the time. Of course you can't. But I can offer certain suggestions which will help you to think right about yourself.

First, quit looking for a knock in your motor. Don't be analyzing your feelings all the time, looking for trouble.

Second, learn to like to work. To get any place in this world you've got to work. One thing you will escape, if you learn to like it, is work tension, the tension that comes to those who look upon work as something to be gotten over with.

Third, have a hobby. A hobby is an important element in getting your mind off work tension. During the day when you are hurrying and worrying, just relax for thirty seconds by thinking briefly about that thing you're making in the basement, that community project you're interested in or that fishing trip you're taking next week-end.

Fourth, learn to like people. Carrying a grudge or dislike can have disastrous bodily effects. We had a man in the hospital who got there because he had to work in an office with a man he didn't like. He said, "I don't like the way he combs his hair, the way he whistles through his teeth, the way he always starts a sentence with 'Listen!'" On questioning the patient I found that he never liked anybody — his mother or his father or any other member of his family. But you've got to live with people, so learn to like them.

Fifth, learn to be satisfied when the situation is such that you can't easily change it. A young lady was in a hospital with a psychosomatic illness because she had become dissatisfied with her life. She had been a secretary, had held a war job in Washington. There she married an Army captain. After the war she found herself living in a trailer, raising three children. She didn't like to live in a trailer, didn't like to raise children in a trailer, wasn't sure that she liked to live with her husband in a trailer. She wanted to be a secretary, back in Washington. I didn't tell her what her trouble was. I just advised her to read the four Pollyanna books. She did, and she returned to live in the trailer and like it. She had learned that it is just as easy under most conditions to be satisfied as it is to be dissatisfied, and it is much more pleasurable.

Sixth, learn to accept adversity. In this life you're going to meet some adversity. You may meet a lot, but don't let it bowl you over. I had a patient who hadn't worked for a year. Then his wife died. A month later his son was killed. And he sat around thinking, "How unfortunate I am — why did this have to happen to *me!*" He became very sick. A lot of people start a psychosomatic illness after an adversity.

Seventh, learn to say the cheerful, humorous thing. Never say the mean thing, even if you feel like doing so. In the morning, look at your wife or your husband and, even if it isn't so, say, "My dear, you look good this morning." It will make both of you feel better.

Finally, learn to meet your problems with decision. About the worst thing to do is to have a problem and to mull it over and over in your mind. If you have a problem, decide what you are going to do about it and then quit thinking about it.

These are some of the things you have to learn if you want to escape the most common disease of all. The key is: *I'm going to keep my attitude and my thinking as pleasant and as cheerful as possible.* There isn't any better way to happiness.

Number of words 2210
See page 301 for Questions

Reading Time in Seconds _____
See page 325 for Conversion Table

SELECTION 67

How to Live 24 Hours a Day

Arthur Gordon

To live fully is, of course, a major problem. A Gallup Poll asked, "Do you find life exciting, pretty routine, or dull?" Of the 1,521 questioned, 51 percent found life "dull" or "routine." Going to college makes the most difference; only 24 percent of the college-bred replied "dull" or "routine." What else helps twenty-four hours a day?

Like several million other people, my wife is a faithful reader of a lady columnist who gives advice on all subjects. Pretty good advice, too, most of the time. But the other night I noticed the faithful reader frowning over the newspaper. "Here," she said, "take a look at this."

In the column, a married woman in her mid-30s was voicing a wistful complaint. She got on well with her husband, they had three well-adjusted children, there were no great health or financial problems. But something was wrong. There was busyness in her life, but no fulfillment. There was a coping with day-to-day problems, but no sense of adventure or joy. She had every reason to be contented, but she felt only half alive. What should she do? What *could* she do? She signed herself, *The Unenviable Mrs. Jones.*

In reply, the columnist urged the woman to be satisfied with what she had. Other people, she pointed out, had far more serious difficulties. "Count your blessings," she advised . . . and moved on to the next problem.

"The trouble with that reply," my wife said, "is that it doesn't answer the question. And the question needs to be answered, because it's just about the most important one there is. I know exactly how that woman feels. She wants to overcome her sense of futility. She wants somebody to tell her how to escape from ordinariness and start living — really be alive — 24 hours a day."

"Can anyone," I said skeptically, "really be alive every single hour?"

"Oh," said my wife impatiently, "you know what I mean. In terms of time we all live 24 hours a day, but that's just horizontal living. In terms of emotions, people live vertically. At least, they should. That's what this Mrs. Jones is groping for: Depth in living and feeling. Intensity — that's the word, I guess. If you ask me, the main enemy in most marriages today isn't cruelty or infidelity or poverty or alcoholism. It's monotony. And frustration. I feel very sorry for Mrs. Jones."

"So do I," I said.

"Well," my wife said, "why don't you *do* something about it? In your work you meet all sorts of people who are supposed to be experts in the field of human behavior. Surely they'd have something to offer that would be helpful. Why don't you pick a psychiatrist and a minister and ask them what they'd say if Mrs. Jones came to them with her problem?"

"I might talk to Herb Smith about it," I said, "the next time we go fishing. He's about as good a psychiatrist as I know. And the next time I go to New York I could ask Norman Peale what he would say."

"Do that," my wife replied. "This is a tough question. People need some answers."

"It's a very widespread thing," Dr. Herbert D. Smith said, "this nagging uneasiness, this feeling that life is hiding from you, that you've lost the capacity to enjoy or appreciate the ordinary pleasures of existence. I think women are more susceptible to it than men — partly because men tend to be absorbed in their work, partly because, being more emotional, women can become emotionally starved more easily.

"Now, what would I say to Mrs. Jones? I think I'd start by trying to reassure her a little. I'd tell her that her feelings are understandable, that many people have similar ones, that it takes courage to admit that you're dissatisfied with your life.

"Next, I'd try to inject some realism into her thinking. I'd say, 'Mrs. Jones, let's talk for a moment about something called acceptance. It's important, because unless you start with a degree of acceptance, you're going to go right on being discontented no matter what I say to you. We all have certain limitations in our lives. We all yearn for more excitement and pleasure than we have. There are times when I wish I were an explorer or an astronaut, but I'm just a doctor, you're just a housewife, and I can't radically change my circumstances any more than you can. What I *can* change — if I work at it — is my attitude toward these circumstances, and, to some degree, my performance within those circumstances.'

"Finally, I'd give Mrs. Jones three specific suggestions to follow. She's really in a prison, partly of her own making. These three suggestions are designed to help her break out. Here they are:

"1. *Pay more attention to people.* Attention is a dialogue, and a dialogue is an escape from self. You can't be totally self-imprisoned when you pay deep attention to what another person feels, or says, or is.

"It doesn't matter who the other person is. Let's say your neighbor Martha drops in from next door for a cup of coffee. You're fond of Martha, but you take her completely for granted, and at times you feel she's a bit of a trial because she's always complaining about something.

"But take a new look at Martha. Why is she the way she is? What is she trying to say to you that she doesn't know how to say in words? What needs does she have that you might possibly supply? Ask yourself, 'Who is this person?' On the surface she may seem like the same old Martha, complaining this time because her feet hurt or her husband snores. But actually, you have, right there in your kitchen, sitting at your table, a creature so fantastically complex that all the psychiatrists in the world couldn't fully explain her to you — or to herself.

"And don't limit yourself to Martha. Learn to observe and study all kinds of people. It's endlessly fascinating — and it will take your mind off yourself.

"2. *Give your emotions more elbowroom.* You can't expect them to have much vitality if you're constantly overcontrolling them. Too many of us are hesitant about expressing affection — we're afraid it may be misinterpreted or even rejected. Too many of us are ashamed of flashes of anger even when there's a valid cause. Too many of us have forgotten how to roar with laughter. These stifled emotions fence us in, cut us off from life and people. If Mrs. Jones would let herself go occasionally, instead of mutely enduring her frustrations, she might be a lot better off.

"3. *Start a one-woman rebellion against routine.* This is the greatest single cause of emotional numbness: The unvarying repetition of basically uninteresting tasks. Life tries to clamp a pattern down on all of us, and it's not easy to fight back. But it's imperative to try, even in small things. I remember I once ordered a man to drive to work by a different route every day, no matter how much extra time it consumed. He thought this was foolish, but it wasn't. He was encrusted with old, stale habits. We had to start somewhere.

"So I would say to Mrs. Jones, 'When routine begins to stifle you, look for new ways of doing things. Even with chores that have to be done, try to dramatize them somehow. Set new performance goals. Try to cut your shopping time or your vacuuming time in half; compete with yourself.

" 'Force yourself to do something unexpected now and then. Walk in the summer rain without an umbrella or a raincoat. Get up before dawn and watch a sunrise. Strike up a conversation with a stranger. Write a letter without using the words *I* or *me, my* or *mine*. In a restaurant, order a meal consisting exclusively of things you have never tasted before.

" 'In other words, Mrs. Jones, fight deadening routine as if it were your mortal enemy. Because it is.'

"If Mrs. Jones or anyone like her will take those suggestions seriously," Dr. Smith concluded, "I think she'll find that her problems grow less."

"What this Mrs. Jones is suffering from," Norman Vincent Peale said thoughtfully, "is a form of soul-sickness that is a peculiarly modern disease. Part of it,

I think, is the result of a kind of emotional isolation. One or two generations ago, children grew up in large families with uncles and aunts scattered up and down the block and grandparents readily available. There wasn't so much shifting around; people knew and counted on their neighbors. But now we tend to live in tight family units — two antagonistic generations crowded together with all the interpersonal strains concentrated relentlessly day after day. Just parents and kids, no buffer personalities at all. No wonder people feel stifled and depressed.

"As for Mrs. Jones, I would make a few suggestions designed to get her into better alignment with the universe that surrounds her. I'd try to keep them practical, not pious. And I'd try to make them short.

"I'd say to her, 'Mrs. Jones, one of the things you need most is a heightened sense of awareness. This is not a gift that anyone can hand you; you must develop it yourself. You must make a conscious and deliberate effort to become more sensitized to the beauty and mystery and magic of things. Take life to pieces and what do you have? Miraculous fragments of reality. Not one of them is really commonplace. It's our reactions to them that grow dull if we let them.

" 'Learn to look beyond the obvious. If, let's say, you see a furry caterpillar walking on your windowsill, you must sometimes — not always, but *sometimes* — regard it not just as an unwelcome intruder that deserves to be squashed, but as a manifestation of the life force that in its own way is just as remarkable as you are.'

"I knew a woman once who had a serious illness followed by a long convalescence. Day after day she lay in bed, weak and listless. Her doctors were very concerned; the vital spark seemed almost to have flickered out. Then, suddenly, she began to improve dramatically.

"Later, when asked about her recovery, she pointed to a magnifying glass, small but powerful. 'This has a lot to do with it,' she said. 'When a friend brought it to me, I had almost lost interest in living. But when I began to look through it, commonplace things became astonishing. You have no idea what you can see in a simple flower, or a leaf, or a piece of cloth. I believe that something in me decided that this world was too beautiful to leave — and so I began to get well.'

"I would say to Mrs. Jones that this kind of discovery is available to all of us. Not everyone can be a Thoreau, perhaps, and live by a remote lake with no companionship but his own thoughts. But it should be possible for each of us to find his own small wilderness in a garden or a seashore or even a cramped backyard — any place where things grow and the seasons change and small creatures exist in their own tiny worlds. Even a city dweller can go up on the roof at night, or out into the street and stare at the stars and think about the incomprehensible distances and magnitudes involved. I remember once being told by an astronomer about one star so huge that if a creature existed on it in the same proportion to his star as we are to our Earth, he could swallow our sun without burning his throat. 'Ponder that, Mrs. Jones, and feel your mind reel — as it should!'

"What else can you do to develop a sense of wonder? All sorts of mental tricks! Imagined scarcity, for example. Suppose the common alley cat you see crossing the road were the *only* cat in existence. What a fabulous creature it would be considered — beautiful, sinuous, superb and priceless. Or suppose this were the last time you could ever see a sunset, or hear great music, or tuck your child into bed. Just a supposition, sure — but it creates a sense of wonder and gratitude.

"I would also advise Mrs. Jones to align herself with goodness now and then. I know that's what a preacher is expected to say, but there's more to it than that. 'This is an ethical universe,' I'd say. 'You are part of it, Mrs. Jones. Therefore it's important to put yourself in tune with those powerful unseen forces.'

"How do you do this? It's simple. Visit a sick friend. Take on some worthwhile civic responsibility. Help someone less fortunate. Give somebody an unexpected gift. Put yourself out when you'd much rather not. Do these things as often as you can.

"What does this have to do with intensity of living? Just this: The person who is bored or unfulfilled is almost always the person who is uninvolved. And often he's uninvolved because his self-esteem and, consequently, his self-confidence are low. Performing a kindness; helping another person makes you like yourself better. And the more you like yourself, the more outgoing and unbored you are going to be.

"Finally," the minister said, "I'd talk to Mrs. Jones about love, because this is the key that will open the doors that she feels are closed to her. I'd probably talk to her mainly about married love, which someone has called 'the persistent effort of two persons to create for each other conditions under which each can become the person God meant him to be.' If a woman — or a man, for that matter — can even come close to this ideal, *everything* is going to be colored by it. Every one of the 24 hours in a day is going to be richer and brighter.

"I rather suspect that if Mrs. Jones ever had this kind of relationship, it has become dimmed by the dust of daily living. That's what's at the heart of her discontent. And so I would recommend that she and her husband find a quiet place and quiet time and ask themselves three basic questions. Perhaps they could think them over alone at first.

" '1. In the life that you are leading today, what gives you most satisfaction, what seems most worthwhile? Is it sex, religion, children, work, some form of recreation? Do you agree, between yourselves, as to what it is? Do you share it — or does it separate you? Don't try in one sitting to solve the problems the question may raise. Just look at them honestly.

" '2. Thirty years from now, when you look back at your life as it is today, how will you feel about the way you are investing your time? Will you think some of your activities were unnecessary and meaningless? Will you wish you had used the priceless days of hours differently? Sit quietly — and discuss — and think.

" '3. If you could change just one thing in your husband-wife relationship, if each of you had one magic wish that could be instantly granted, what would that wish be? Listen carefully to what your partner says, because in it may lie a clue to your own happiness — or to what is keeping you from it.'

"And that," Dr. Peale concluded, "is approximately what I'd say to the unhappy Mrs. Jones."

"Well," I said later, when I had put their thoughts on paper and showed them to my wife, "what do you think?"

"They're good answers," she said. "But it's still an enormous question."

"Of course it is," I said. "People have been wrestling with it since the beginning of time."

"Maybe," she said, "maybe there are no complete blueprints. Maybe each of us has to grope and struggle and find the answers for ourselves as we go along."

"Perhaps," I said.

"I think your minister friend came closest when he said that the central love-relationship is the main thing. If that's right, everything else will follow. If it's wrong, everything else will be in shadow."

"So we sit here in the sunshine counting our blessings, eh?"

She laughed. "As a matter of fact," she said, "sometimes I do."

Number of words 2654
See page 303 for Questions

Reading Time in Seconds _____
See page 325 for Conversion Table

SELECTION 68

How to Be an Employee

Peter F. Drucker

Almost everyone fits into the employee category at one time or another. Further-more, for most people the major part of life is spent as an employee. This selection is one that carries major significance for living, for women as well as for men. How do you like Drucker's advice?

Most of you graduating today will be employees all your working life, working for somebody else and for a pay check. And so will most, if not all, of the thousands of other young Americans graduating this year in all the other schools and colleges across the country.

Ours has become a society of employees. A hundred years or so ago only one out of every five Americans at work was employed, i.e., worked for somebody else. Today only one out of five is not employed but working for himself. And where fifty years ago "being employed" meant working as a factory laborer or as a farmhand, the employee of today is increasingly a middle-class person with a substantial formal education, holding a professional or management job requiring intellectual and technical skills. Indeed, two things have characterized American society during these last fifty years: the middle and upper classes have become employees; and middle-class and upper-class employees have been the fastest-growing groups in our working population

— growing so fast that the industrial worker, that oldest child of the Industrial Revolution, has been losing in numerical importance despite the expansion of industrial production.

This is one of the most profound social changes any country has ever undergone. It is, however, a perhaps even greater change for the individual young man about to start. Whatever he does, in all likelihood he will do it as an employee; wherever he aims, he will have to try to reach it through being an employee.

Yet you will find little if anything written on what it is to be an employee. You can find a great deal of very dubious advice on how to get a job or how to get a promotion. You can also find a good deal on work in a chosen field, whether it be metallurgy or salesmanship, the machinist's trade or bookkeeping. Every one of these trades requires different skills, sets different standards, and requires a different preparation. Yet they all have employeeship in common. And increasingly, especially in the large business or in government, employeeship is more important to success than the special professional knowledge or skill. Certainly more people fail because they do not know the requirements of being an employee than because they do not adequately possess the skills of their trade; the higher you climb the ladder, the more you get into administrative or executive work, the greater the emphasis on ability to work within the organization rather than on technical competence or professional knowledge.

Being an employee is thus the one common characteristic of most careers today. The special profession or skill is visible and clearly defined; and a well-laid-out sequence of courses, degrees, and jobs leads into it. But being an employee is the foundation. And it is much more difficult to prepare for it. Yet there is no recorded information on the art of being an employee.

THE BASIC SKILL

The first question we might ask is: what can you learn in college that will help you in being an employee? The schools teach a great many things of value to the future accountant, the future doctor, or the future electrician. Do they also teach anything of value to the future employee? The answer is: "Yes — they teach the one thing that it is perhaps most valuable for the future employee to know. But very few students bother to learn it."

This one basic skill is the ability to organize and express ideas in writing and in speaking.

As an employee you work with and through other people. This means that your success as an employee — and I am talking of much more here than getting promoted — will depend on your ability to communicate with people and to present your own thoughts and ideas to them so they will both understand what you are driving at and be persuaded. The letter, the report or memorandum, the ten-minute spoken "presentation" to a committee are basic tools of the employee.

If you work as a soda jerker you will, of course, not need much skill in expressing yourself to be effective. If you work on a machine your ability to express yourself will be of little importance. But as soon as you move one step up from the bottom, your effectiveness depends on your ability to reach others through the spoken or the written word. And the further away your job is from manual work, the larger the organization of which you are an employee, the more important it will be that you know how to convey your thoughts in writing or speaking. In the very large organization, whether it is the government, the large business corporation, or the Army, this ability to express oneself is perhaps the most important of all the skills a man can possess.

Of course, skill in expression is not enough by itself. You must have something to say in the first place. The popular picture of the engineer, for instance, is that of a man who works with a slide rule, T square, and compass. And engineering students reflect this picture in their attitude toward the written word as something quite irrelevant to their jobs. But the effectiveness of the engineer — and with it his usefulness — depends as much on his ability to make other people understand his work as it does on the quality of the work itself.

Expressing one's thoughts is one skill that the school can really teach, especially to people born without natural writing or speaking talent. Many other skills can be learned later — in this country there are literally thousands of places that offer training to adult people at work. But the foundations for skill in expression have to be laid early: an interest in and an ear for language; experience in organizing ideas and data, in brushing aside the irrelevant, in wedding outward form and inner content into one structure; and above all, the habit of verbal expression. If you do not lay these foundations during your school years, you may never have an opportunity again.

If you were to ask me what strictly vocational courses there are in the typical college curriculum, my answer — now that the good old habit of the "theme a day" has virtually disappeared — would be: the writing of poetry and the writing of short stories. Not that I expect many of you to become poets or short-story writers — far from it. But these two courses offer the easiest way to obtain some skill in expression. They force one to be economical with language. They force one to organize thought. They demand of one that he give meaning to every word. They train the ear for language, its meaning, its precision, its overtones — and its pitfalls. Above all they force one to write.

I know very well that the typical employer does not understand this as yet, and that he may look with suspicion on a young college graduate who has majored, let us say, in short-story writing. But the same employer will complain — and with good reason — that the young men whom he hires when they get out of college do not know how to write a simple report, do not know how to tell a simple story, and are in fact virtually illiterate. And he will conclude — rightly — that the young men are not really effective, and certainly not employees who are likely to go very far.

The next question to ask is: what kind of employee should you be? Pay no attention to what other people tell you. This is one question only you can answer. It involves a choice in four areas — a choice you alone can make, and one you cannot easily duck. But to make the choice you must first have tested yourself in the world of jobs for some time.

Here are the four decisions — first in brief outline, then in more detail:

1. Do you belong in a job calling primarily for faithfulness in the performance of routine work and promising security? Or do you belong in a job that offers a challenge to imagination and ingenuity — with the attendant penalty for failure?

2. Do you belong in a large organization or in a small organization? Do you work better through channels or through direct contacts? Do you enjoy more

being a small cog in a big and powerful machine or a big wheel in a small machine?

3. Should you start at the bottom and try to work your way up, or should you try to start near the top? On the lowest rung of the promotional ladder, with its solid and safe footing but also with a very long climb ahead? Or on the aerial trapeze of "a management trainee," or some other staff position close to management?

4. Finally, are you going to be more effective and happy as a specialist or as a "generalist," that is, in an administrative job?

Let me spell out what each of these four decisions involves:

The decision between secure routine work and insecure work challenging the imagination and ingenuity is the one decision most people find easiest to make. You know very soon what kind of person you are. Do you find real satisfaction in the precision, order, and system of a clearly laid-out job? Do you prefer the security not only of knowing what your work is today and what it is going to be tomorrow, but also security in your job, in your relationship to the people above, below, and next to you, and economic security? Or are you one of those people who tend to grow impatient with anything that looks like a "routine" job? These people are usually able to live in a confused situation in which their relations to the people around them are neither clear nor stable. And they tend to pay less attention to economic security, find it not too upsetting to change jobs, etc.

There is, of course, no such black-and-white distinction between people. The man who can do only painstaking detail work and has no imagination is not much good for anything. Neither is the self-styled "genius" who has nothing but grandiose ideas and no capacity for rigorous application to detail. But in practically everybody I have ever met there is a decided leaning one way or the other.

The difference is one of basic personality. It is not too much affected by a man's experiences; he is likely to be born with the one or the other. The need for economic security is often as not an outgrowth of a need for psychological security rather than a phenomenon of its own. But precisely because the difference is one of basic temperament, the analysis of what kind of temperament you possess is so vital. A man might be happy in work for which he has little *aptitude;* he might be quite successful in it. But he can be neither happy nor successful in a job for which he is *temperamentally* unfitted.

You hear a great many complaints today about the excessive security-consciousness of our young people. My complaint is the opposite: in the large organizations especially there are not enough job opportunities for those young people who need challenge and risk. Jobs

in which there is greater emphasis on conscientious performance of well-organized duties rather than on imagination — especially for the beginner — are to be found, for instance, in the inside jobs in banking or insurance, which normally offer great job security but not rapid promotion or large pay. The same is true of most government work, of the railroad industry, particularly in the clerical and engineering branches, and of most public utilities. The bookkeeping and accounting areas, especially in the larger companies, are generally of this type too — though a successful comptroller is an accountant with great management and business imagination.

At the other extreme are such areas as buying, selling, and advertising, in which the emphasis is on adaptability, on imagination, and on a desire to do new and different things. In those areas, by and large, there is little security, either personal or economic. The rewards, however, are high and come more rapidly. Major premium on imagination — though of a different kind and coupled with dogged persistence on details — prevails in most research and engineering work. Jobs in production, as supervisor or executive, also demand much adaptability and imagination.

Contrary to popular belief, very small business requires, above all, close attention to daily routine. Running a neighborhood drugstore or a small grocery, or being a toy jobber, is largely attention to details. But in very small business there is also room for quite a few people of the other personality type — the innovator or imaginer. If successful, a man of this type soon ceases to be in a very small business. For the real innovator there is, still, no more promising opportunity in this country than that of building a large out of a very small business.

BIG COMPANY OR SMALL?

Almost as important is the decision between working for a large and for a small organization. The difference is perhaps not so great as that between the secure, routine job and the insecure, imaginative job; but the wrong decision can be equally serious.

There are two basic differences between the large and the small enterprise. In the small enterprise you operate primarily through personal contacts. In the large enterprise you have established "policies," "channels" of organization, and fairly rigid procedures. In the small enterprise you have, moreover, immediate effectiveness in a very small area. You can see the effect of your work and of your decisions right away, once you are a little bit above the ground floor. In the large enterprise even the man at the top is only a cog in a big machine. To be sure, his actions affect a much greater area than the actions and decisions of the man in the small organization, but his effectiveness is remote, indirect, and elusive. In a small and even in a middle-sized business you are normally exposed to all kinds of experiences, and expected to do a great many things without too much help or guidance. In the large organization you are normally taught one thing thoroughly. In the small one the danger is of becoming a jack-of-all trades and master of none. In the large one it is of becoming the man who knows more and more about less and less.

There is one other important thing to consider: do you derive a deep sense of satisfaction from being a member of a well-known organization — General Motors, the Bell Telephone System, the government? Or is it more important to you to be a well-known and important figure within your own small pond? There is a basic difference between the satisfaction that comes from being a member of a large, powerful, and generally known organization, and the one that comes from being a member of a family; between impersonal grandeur and personal — often much too personal — intimacy; between life in a small cubicle on the top floor of a skyscraper and life in a crossroad gas station.

START AT THE BOTTOM, OR . . .?

You may well think it absurd to say that anyone has a choice between beginning at the bottom and beginning near the top. And indeed I do not mean that you have any choice between beginner's jobs and, let us say, a vice presidency at General Electric. But you do have a choice between a position at the bottom of the hierarchy and a staff position that is outside the hierarchy but in view of the top. It is an important choice.

In every organization, even the smallest, there are positions that, while subordinate, modestly paid, and usually filled with young and beginning employees, nonetheless are not at the bottom. There are positions as assistant to one of the bosses; there are positions as private secretary; there are liaison positions for various departments; and there are positions in staff capacities, in industrial engineering, in cost accounting, in personnel, etc. Every one of these gives a view of the whole rather than of only one small area. Every one of them normally brings the holder into the deliberations and discussions of the people at the top, if only as a silent audience or perhaps only as an errand boy. Every one of these positions is a position "near the top," however humble and badly paid it may be.

On the other hand the great majority of beginner's jobs are at the bottom, where you begin in a department or in a line of work in the lowest-paid and simplest function, and where you are expected to work your way up as you acquire more skill and more judgment.

Different people belong in these two kinds of jobs. In the first place, the job "near the top" is insecure. You are exposed to public view. Your position is ambiguous; by yourself you are a nobody — but you reflect the boss's status; in a relatively short time you may even speak for the boss. You may have real power and influence. In today's business and government organization the hand that writes the memo rules the committee; and the young staff man usually writes the memos, or at least the first draft. But for that very reason everybody is jealous of you. You are a youngster who has been admitted to the company of his betters, and is therefore expected to show unusual ability and above all unusual discretion and judgment. Good performance in such a position is often the key to rapid advancement. But to fall down may mean the end of all hopes of ever getting anywhere within the organization.

At the bottom, on the other hand, there are very few opportunities for making serious mistakes. You are amply protected by the whole apparatus of authority. The job itself is normally simple, requiring little judgment, discretion, or initiative. Even excellent performance in such a job is unlikely to speed promotion. But one also has to fall down in a rather spectacular fashion for it to be noticed by anyone but one's immediate superior.

SPECIALIST OR "GENERALIST"?

There are a great many careers in which the increasing emphasis is on specialization. You find these careers in engineering and in accounting, in production, in statistical work, and in teaching. But there is an increasing demand for people who are able to take in a great area at a glance, people who perhaps do not know too much about any one field — though one should always have one area of real competence. There is, in other words, a demand for people who are capable of seeing the forest rather than the trees, of making over-all judgments. And these "generalists" are particularly needed for administrative positions, where it is their job to see that other people do the work, where they have to plan for other people, to organize other people's work, to initiate it and appraise it.

The specialist understands one field; his concern is with technique, tools, media. He is a "trained" man; and his educational background is properly technical or professional. The generalist — and especially the administrator — deals with people; his concern is with leadership, with planning, with direction giving, and with coordination. He is an "educated" man; and the humanities are his strongest foundation. Very rarely is a specialist capable of being an administrator. And very rarely is a good generalist also a good specialist in a particular field. Any organization needs both kinds of people, though different organizations need them in different ratios. It is your job to find out, during your apprenticeship, into which of those two job categories you fit, and to plan your career accordingly.

Your first job may turn out to be the right job for you — but this is pure accident. Certainly you should not change jobs constantly or people will become suspicious — rightly — of your ability to hold any job. At the same time you must not look upon the first job as the final job; it is primarily a training job, an opportunity to analyze yourself and your fitness for being an employee.

THE IMPORTANCE OF BEING FIRED

In fact there is a great deal to be said for being fired from the first job. One reason is that it is rarely an advantage to have started as an office boy in the organization; far too many people will still consider you a "green kid" after you have been there for twenty-five years. But the major reason is that getting fired from the first job is the least painful and the least damaging way to learn how to take a setback. And whom the Lord loveth he teacheth early how to take a setback.

Nobody has ever lived, I daresay, who has not gone through a period when everything seemed to have collapsed and when years of work and life seemed to have gone up in smoke. No one can be spared this experience; but one can be prepared for it. The man who has been through earlier setbacks has learned that the world has not come to an end because he lost his job — not even in a depression. He has learned that he will somehow survive. He has learned, above all, that the way to behave in such a setback is not to collapse himself. But the man who comes up against it for the first time when he is forty-five is quite likely to collapse for good. For the things that people are apt to do when they receive the first nasty blow may destroy a mature man with a family, whereas a youth of twenty-five bounces right back.

Obviously you cannot contrive to get yourself fired. But you can always quit. And it is perhaps even more important to have quit once than to have been fired once. The man who walks out on his own volition acquires an inner independence that he will never quite lose.

WHEN TO QUIT

To know when to quit is therefore one of the most important things — particularly for the beginner. For on the whole young people have a tendency to hang on to the first job long beyond the time when they should have quit for their own good.

One should quit when self-analysis shows that the job is the wrong job — that, say, it does not give the security and routine one requires, that it is a small-company rather than a big-organization job, that it is at the bottom rather than near the top, a specialist's rather than a generalist's job, etc. One should quit if the job demands behavior one considers morally indefensible, or if the whole atmosphere of the place is morally corrupting — if, for instance, only yes men and flatterers are tolerated.

One should also quit if the job does not offer the training one needs either in a specialty or in administration and the view of the whole. The beginner not only has a right to expect training from his first five or ten years in a job; he has an obligation to get as much training as possible. A job in which young people are not given real training — though, of course, the training need not be a formal "training program" — does not measure up to what they have a right and a duty to expect.

But the most common reason why one should quit is the absence of promotional opportunities in the organization. That is a compelling reason.

I do not believe that chance of promotion is the essence of a job. In fact there is no surer way to kill a job and one's own usefulness in it than to consider it as but one rung in the promotional ladder rather than as a job in itself that deserves serious effort and will return satisfaction, a sense of accomplishment, and pride. And one can be an important and respected member of an organization without ever having received a promotion; there are such people in practically every office. But the organization itself must offer fair promotional opportunities. Otherwise it stagnates, becomes corrupted, and in turn corrupts. The absence of promotional opportunities is demoralizing. And the sooner one gets out of a demoralizing situation, the better. There are three situations to watch out for:

The entire group may be so young that for years there will be no vacancies. That was a fairly common situation in business a few years back, as a result of the depression. Middle and lower management ranks in many companies were solidly filled with men in their forties and early fifties — men who were far too young to be retired but who had grown too old, during the bleak days of the Thirties, to be promotable themselves. As a result the people under them were bottled up; for it is a rare organization that will promote a young man around his older superior. If you find yourself caught in such a situation, get out fast. If you wait it will defeat you.

Another situation without promotional opportunities is one in which the group ahead of you is uniformly old — so old that it will have to be replaced long before you will be considered ready to move up. Stay away from organizations that have a uniform age structure throughout their executive group — old or young. The only organization that offers fair promotional opportunities is one in which there is a balance of ages.

WHO GETS PROMOTED?

And finally there is the situation in which all promotions go to members of a particular group — to which you do not belong. Some chemical companies, for instance, require a master's degree in chemistry for just about any job above sweeper. Some companies promote only engineering graduates, some government agencies only people who majored in economics, some railroads only male stenographers, some British insurance companies only members of the actuaries' association. Or all the good jobs may be reserved for members of the family.

There may be adequate promotional opportunities in such an organization — but not for you.

On the whole there are proportionately more opportunities in the big organization than in the small one. But there is very real danger of getting lost in the big organization — whereas you are always visible in the small one. A young man should therefore stay in a large organization only if it has a definite promotional program which ensures that he will be considered and looked at. This may take several forms: it may be a formal appraisal and development program; it may be automatic promotion by seniority as in the prewar Army; it may be an organization structure that actually makes out of the one big enterprise a number of small organizations in which everybody is again clearly visible (the technical term for this is "decentralization").

But techniques do not concern us here. What matters is that there should be both adequate opportunities and fair assurance that you will be eligible and considered for promotion. Let me repeat: to be promoted is not essential, either to happiness or to usefulness. To be considered for promotion is.

YOUR LIFE OFF THE JOB

I have only one more thing to say: to be an employee it is not enough that the job be right and that you be right for the job. It is also necessary that you have a meaningful life outside the job.

I am talking of having a genuine interest in something in which you, on your own, can be, if not a master, at least an amateur expert. This something may be botany, or the history of your county, or chamber music, cabinet-making, Christmas-tree growing, or a thousand other things. But it is important in this "employee society" of ours to have a genuine interest outside of the job and to be serious about it.

I am not, as you might suspect, thinking of something that will keep you alive and interested during your retirement. I am speaking of keeping yourself alive, interested, and happy during your working life, and of a permanent source of self-respect and standing in the community outside and beyond your job. You will need such an interest when you hit the forties, that period in which most of us come to realize that we will never reach the goals we have set ourselves when younger — whether these are goals of achievement or of worldly success. You will need it because you should have one area in which you yourself impose standards of performance on your own work. Finally, you need it because you will find recognition and acceptance by other people working in the field, whether professional or amateur, as individuals rather than as members of an organization and as employees.

This is heretical philosophy these days when so many companies believe that the best employee is the man who lives, drinks, eats, and sleeps job and company. In actual experience those people who have no life outside their jobs are not the really successful people, not even from the viewpoint of the company. I have seen far too many of them shoot up like a rocket, because they had no interests except the job; but they also come down like the rocket's burned-out stick. The man who will make the greatest contribution to his company is the mature person — and you cannot have maturity if you have no life or interest outside the job. Our large companies are beginning to understand this. That so many of them encourage people to have "outside interests" or to develop "hobbies" as a preparation for retirement is the first sign of a change toward a more intelligent attitude. But quite apart from the self-interest of the employer, your own interest as an employee demands that you develop a major outside interest. It will make you happier, it will make you more effective, it will give you resistance against the setbacks and the blows that are the lot of everyone; and it will make you a more effective, a more successful, and a more mature employee.

You have no doubt realized that I have not really talked about how to be an employee. I have talked about what to know before becoming an employee — which is something quite different. Perhaps "how to be an employee" can be learned only by being one. But one thing can be said. Being an employee means working with people; it means living and working in a society. Intelligence, in the last analysis, is therefore not the most important quality. What is decisive is character and integrity. If you work on your own, intelligence and ability may be sufficient. If you work with people you are going to fail unless you also have basic integrity. And integrity — character — is the one thing most, if not all, employers consider first.

There are many skills you might learn to be an employee, many abilities that are required. But fundamentally the one quality demanded of you will not be skill, knowledge, or talent, but character.

Number of words 5180
See page 305 for Questions

Reading Time in Seconds _____
See page 325 for Conversion Table

If London Cleans Its Air and Water, Why Can't Our Large Cities?

Donald Gould

Pollution! It's a growing contemporary problem of worldwide scope. What does it take to give our antipollution efforts proper momentum? This story about London could help. It provides a possible pattern plus some needed encouragement.

A few days ago I was walking down Fleet Street in the city of London on a Saturday afternoon so hot that my feet flinched each time I put one down on the burning sidewalk. Fleet Street is almost empty on a Saturday, so I was bound to notice two American matrons hobbling wearily toward me in the heat, and I was bound to overhear one complain to the other about the fellow from whom they had asked directions. He had told them to plod on if they wanted to see St. Paul's Cathedral, but he must have been fooling, for there was still no sign of anything like a cathedral.

Just then they rounded a half bend, and there suddenly, huge and glowing, was Wren's great stone anthem, alive and alight in the summer sunshine, filling and shaping and commanding the entire scene.

These two good, tired, disgruntled ladies simply stopped in their tracks and said, "Oh, my!"

A few years ago this wouldn't have happened. St. Paul's was not a glowing monument, but a soot-black hulk, hardly to be distinguished from its equally grimy surroundings. Like everything else in London, Wren's cathedral was thickly coated with greasy filth which millions of chimneys daily poured into the sky — a filth which for generations fell softly in a malignant mist on all the lovely shapes of columns, spires, porticoes and gables of the town, so that the richness of the place was smothered into a dirty mass.

London suffered the full impact of the garbage of the new industrial age. Her air was poisoned and her river stank. Two happy accidents have been responsible for stimulating today's vigorous corrective measures. First is the fact that the Houses of Parliament stand alongside the Thames.

A river can tolerate some organic waste without turning sour. It contains bacteria which break down dead plant and animal matter into inoffensive substances. But to do this job, bacteria need oxygen.

A certain amount of oxygen from the air becomes dissolved in river water. If a lot of rubbish must be dealt with, the bacteria will get more oxygen by breaking down nitrates and so releasing nitrogen, a bland gas

which makes up something like 80 percent of the air we breathe. However, if the quantity of organic rubbish is so large that neither dissolved oxygen, nor oxygen from nitrates, can deal with it, the bacteria will start breaking down sulfates.

When you take oxygen away from a sulfate, you are left with the foul-smelling gas, hydrogen sulfide — the stuff that rotten eggs smell of. It is also a highly aggressive chemical which likes combining with other materials, and can therefore do a lot of damage.

About a century ago the load of organic waste in the Thames became so large that hydrogen sulfide began to rise from the river. Riverside citizens became accustomed to the permanent whiff of stale eggs, but sometimes the stench grew so great that parliamentary sittings were adjourned. This, of course, focused official attention wonderfully upon the problem.

The second lucky accident for London happened more recently and concerned the Englishman's curious regard for animals. The English country gentleman will get on his horse, and go out and harass foxes, but he would, on the whole, feel easier after beating his wife than his dog. We show, indeed, an enormous kindness to animals, except those which may be ritually destroyed. But our national conscience in this matter got a tremendous jolt in the winter of 1952.

London had long been accustomed to its own ugly brand of winter fog, which inspired the term "smog," for it resulted from a dreadful mixture of smoke and water droplets. During the foul British winters, water would condense in tiny globules around specks of soot, and the water would also contain dissolved sulfur dioxide (a major component of chimney gases). So London smogs consisted of countless billions of tiny specks of tarry dust encapsulated in small globules of dilute sulfuric acid — exactly the type of chemical weapon which the generals would be happy to pay some imaginative scientist a handsome sum to invent.

Smog killed people quite effectively. Every time London was subjected to attack by one of these miasmas the death rate showed a sharp peak spiking above the normal for the time of year. Most victims were old and nobody bothered a great deal.

Smogs also caused chaos on roads and railways, but Londoners are used to that, so it caused small reaction.

In truth, many of us rather enjoyed our smogs. They were something extra to grumble about, and they broke up the grim routine of the winter working day.

Then came the terrible smog of December 1952. An unfortunate duck, flying blind, crashed through the glass roof of Victoria Station and fell at the feet of passengers bravely waiting for trains which were quite unable to move. A performance of *La Traviata* ended when the singers could no longer see the conductor. In cinemas only front-seat customers could follow what was happening on the screen. Yet Londoners enjoyed the same feeling of togetherness that they had achieved during the blitz. Then the really shocking news began to spread around town.

The Smithfield Show was in progress — an annual festival of butchers, where live animals, raised for the table, are awarded prizes before they go to slaughter. When the smog struck, many died before they could be judged or butchered. About 4,000 Londoners also died as a result of that particular smog. But I believe it was the death of a few steers which made people decide that enough was enough. We are accustomed to the idea of people dying, but when you bring a great mass of beef into the center of your city, and it lies down and dies, then you begin to sense that something might be seriously wrong.

Anyway, the smog of 1952 convinced Londoners that something had to be done about their poisonous air, and only four years later the first effective Clean Air Act was passed.

It was hardly ahead of its time. At the beginning of this century just under 400 tons of soot settled on each square mile of London every year. Between the wars, this continuing inky blizzard eased off slightly, dropping to around 300 tons. This was simply the result of the growing use of fuels like anthracite, coke, oil, gas and electricity.

The cost of living with all this filth was incalculable. Even a recent estimate has put the annual national bill for air pollution damage at around $850 million. Chief material victims are buildings and engineering works. Steel and bricks are attacked by acids formed from sulfur gases escaping from chimneys in homes and factories using fossil fuels — coal or oil. Far graver is the damage done to people.

The commonest result of breathing smoke is chronic bronchitis. This amounts to a slow destruction of the lungs. In Britain the disease kills an estimated 30,000 people every year, and makes many more into virtual cripples who struggle, coughing and breathless, through each night and day. The huge total of 35 million working days is lost annually by sufferers. All this makes clean air a sound economic proposition.

The British Clean Air Act of 1956 was so relatively modest a measure that some American experts claimed it couldn't possibly impinge upon so prickly a problem.

Principally, it gave to local authorities the power to designate smokeless zones. Here citizens are not allowed to burn smoky fuels in their grates. Local authorities meet 70 percent of the cost of changing over household equipment to burn smokeless fuel.

This simple measure has worked miraculously well, particularly in London, where boroughs applied their powers with enthusiasm. Some 80 percent of London's smoke came from domestic chimneys, so that smoke suppression in an entire area could be achieved simply by telling a few merchants to sell only smokeless fuel. Any reluctant householder would soon change his heating system and accept his 70 percent subsidy once he could no longer buy the coal to burn in his old smoky grate.

Since the Clean Air Act, London has become a wonderfully brighter city. Graceful structures like Admiralty House, the National Gallery, and the Guildhall were built of a mellow stone which has been hidden under layers of soot for generations. Only within the past decade has it become worthwhile to scrape off the grime and show these places as their architects meant them to be seen.

Now that much of the cleaning has been done, Londoners delight in new beauty, but to begin with there was some uneasiness. We had become so accustomed to the blackness of our great buildings that many people felt that this was their proper state. When the dean and chapter of St. Paul's decided that the new purity of the London air justified the huge expense of cleaning the cathedral stone, they asked the public to subscribe the necessary money. For many weeks afterwards letters appeared in the *Times* protesting the sacrilege. How dare anyone wreak such a change on the dear familiar blackness of St. Paul's! There were even claims that Sir Christopher Wren, knowing what happened to buildings in the London air, had meant his cathedral to be black, and had designed it with that color in mind.

But the protests have disappeared in the face of the rejuvenated stone. London is a more exciting place to move around in now than it has been for many years.

More birds are moving into town. London has always been a wonderful aviary — on the line of a number of migration routes, but recently birds which have not been seen here for a long time have been nesting in the city. We now have swifts, house martins and even swallows — insect-eating birds. Ornithologists at the London Natural History Society believe that our cleaner air has encouraged the return of insects that don't care for soot.

Measurements made by the meteorological office show that since the passing of the Act of 1956, the amount of winter sunshine enjoyed by Londoners has increased by 50 percent. The frequency of what are officially described as "dense" fogs has fallen by about 80 percent, and of "thick" fogs by 75 percent. The killer smogs have gone completely.

The same kind of success has marked efforts to clean up the Thames. The Thames doesn't stink any more. We have yet to see salmon making their way through the London docks toward spawning grounds in the Berkshire hills. But there is now no part of the river which is absolutely starved of oxygen. Freshwater fish are venturing farther down toward the sea, and sea fish are moving farther in. There are anglers on the river bank at Hammersmith after silver and scarlet roach which are busying the water there. Elvers — young eels — which used to be a favorite dish of Londoners, are coming upstream again.

Wordsworth, gazing from Westminster Bridge more than 150 years ago, saw his city "like a garment, wear the beauty of the morning. . . ." Then industrial man spewed his garbage upon it, and all that beauty began to suffocate. But at last the sickness is being cured. London is living again, thanks importantly to the quiet cooperation of local borough governments. Perhaps there is a lesson here for all the world's sick cities.

Number of words 1898
See page 307 for Questions

Reading Time in Seconds _____
See page 325 for Conversion Table

SELECTION 70

Too Many Divorces, Too Soon

Margaret Mead

"Let me not to the marriage of true minds
Admit impediments. Love is not love
Which alters when it alteration finds. . . ."

From Shakespeare on, marriage has been a favorite subject. What about divorce — the other side of the coin? Why the shift of attention?

In our generation divorce has become part of the American way of life.

We have not stopped believing in marriage. We are still among the most married people in the world, and increasingly Americans are willing to try a second, a third and even a fourth marriage. But over the past 30 years the proportion of women whose first marriage has broken down in divorce has continued to increase and in the last ten years alone the total annual number of divorces has risen steeply.

What has changed is not our belief that a good marriage is the most important adult relationship, but our expectation about the durability of marriage. We no longer deeply believe that two people who once have made the choice to marry necessarily should try to weather the storms that shake any vital, intimate relationship. Instead, and more and more, our answer to a difficult marriage is: Try it again — with someone else. And marriages are dissolved even though in reality, for too many people — particularly young mothers with children to care for and nowadays young fathers with children to rear — divorce means going it alone.

It is true that many young people in their 20s are deciding to remain single or are experimenting with alternatives to marriage. As yet we cannot know whether they will succeed in setting new styles in relationships between men and women or what the consequences will be for the kind of fragile marriage we now have.

One thing we do know is that these experiments with new styles have not yet reached down to a still younger age group — to the adolescents who fall in love and want to establish an exclusive pair relationship. For them marriage remains the answer they prefer — indeed, the only answer that promises freedom from parental control and the right always to be together. Equally important, it is the only solution — aside from breaking off the relationship — that most parents will tolerate. Whatever their reservations may be, where their adolescent sons and daughters are concerned, parents usually accept marriage with the idea that it may help — or force — the young pair to "settle down." And if it doesn't work out, they can always get divorced.

Certainly this is not the point of view of two young people deeply in love for the first time. They enter marriage, however hurriedly, with the happy conviction that it will work, that they are different from those who fail. Some of them *are* different and *do* succeed magnificently in growing into adulthood and parenthood serene and confident.

But many do not — too many, especially when there are children who later are shuffled about from one parent to the other. Especially when a second marriage with a second baby or a third does not work either — and unsuccessful second marriages tend to have a shorter life span than the first. Especially when the young mother does not find a new partner and, totally inexperienced and saddened, must both work and try, alone, to do what it has always taken two parents to do well, and then often with the help of other adults — to bring up children to be full human beings.

Knowing that the proportion of early marriages has dropped, many people simply shrug off the problems of early marriage and divorce. But the fact is that in absolute numbers teen-age marriages are increasing. The children of the "baby boom" are growing up and very many of them are marrying early. By ignoring their problems we are creating new difficulties, I think, for their generation and the next as well.

For their marriages are the most fragile of all. Compared to the marriages of young people in their 20s, statistics show, the marriages of teen-agers are of shorter duration and end in the catastrophe of divorce more than twice as frequently. And even when such marriages survive for many years, they carry a high risk. After ten years and 20 years, the likelihood that they will end in divorce remains twice as high as the marriages of young people who were only a few years older when they married.

Whatever we may think about divorce in general, I believe it is crucially important that we think very hard about the fate of the thousands of young people whose marriages falter and fail before they reach their mid-20s. It is not enough to say: They were too immature to make so important a decision, too inexperienced to handle their problems. This may well be true — in our society. But need it be?

Statistics tell part of the story of the hazards in early marriage:

Marriage and early pregnancy are the main reasons today why girls drop out of school, perhaps never to return. In most communities there is no place in the high-school system for a young married woman, let alone for a young mother. Often, too, young husbands fail to go on with their education. The freedom gained by leaving home and school becomes the obligation to work — to be self-supporting and, for a young father, to support a family. Lack of education in turn means that a very large proportion of the very young married live at the poverty level without any reserves to fall back on or any hope of getting out of poverty and debt by getting jobs that require greater skills and practice in using those skills.

There are, of course, young families that are supported by parents. Sometimes this works out happily, particularly when parents are furthering the education of their married children so that they can better make their own way. But mere financial support can mean a prolongation of parental control and childhood dependence and lead to resentment that invades all the family relationships.

In young marriages there is also the problem of health for mothers and their babies. Childbirth can be very safe today. But for many mothers under 20 there are still heavy risks in carrying and bearing a child. And the chances for that baby to be well born are far less than for those whose mothers are only a few years older. Today 25 percent of the low-birth-weight babies are born to mothers in their teens. We know this, and yet it is very difficult for teen-aged adults to get the counseling they need or the medical care and support young mothers especially should have.

But such statistics can tell only part of the story of why so many young marriages end up as young divorces.

More significant is the dull and frightening sense of isolation that so often takes the place of feelings of freedom and the delight in being alone with a loved partner. Married and living alone, the young husband and wife no longer move among older adults, whose concerns they no longer share, and they have no place among their unmarried peers. All the social supports of their lives fall away in their total dependence on each other.

In most societies in which there is teen-age marriage, the young couple are given a great deal of time to find themselves in their new life. The young wife goes back and forth between her parents' home and her own, and when the first baby comes she is in the center of a group of mothering women while she gains her own experience of motherhood. The young husband too can count on help and companionship.

But with our insistence that marriage, as an adult relationship, means living in and fending for one's own home, the high price of early marriage too often is unprotected isolation and extreme loneliness. Unprepared for parenthood, two young people who have become very close may see the new baby as an interloper. Or if they are already restless, the baby may become just one more obstacle to pleasure and freedom. The mother is permanently stuck at home. The father is almost equally confined — or goes out alone. There is no money now for pleasure and almost nowhere the young couple can go for amusement with the baby.

Then our current belief that a speedy divorce is the way out of the dilemma begins to take effect. From the time a young wife gets pregnant, fear of divorce hangs over her. Will he stay with her? Will he help take care of the baby? Will he still love her? Or will he, like so many other young fathers, throw up his responsibilities because the load is too heavy, the future too bleak? And her anxieties feed his. Looking around, she becomes much more aware of the fatherless families she knows about; looking around, he sees the defecting fathers who are going their own way. And each accuses the other of things they both fear and long for — freedom from responsibility, a chance to get away, longing for better opportunities in life, a way out of their unhappy situation.

But is the divorce that so often follows the only solution? For a marriage that has irretrievably failed, it may be. But need it have failed?

The greatest enemy of young marriages, I believe, is the fact that from the beginning we anticipate their failure. Almost no one — neither the friends of the young couple nor their parents, teachers and employers — expects a very young marriage to grow in stability and happy mutuality. When it does fail, most people say: "I told you so!" And the failure is the more poignant because of this ultimate rejection.

Where primitive peoples waited for young married couples to attain some maturity before they settled down, we all too often use marriage as the means of getting young people to settle down — the girl safely in her home, the boy firmly tied to his job. Since they are married, we expect them to behave as adults. But at the same time, because they are so young and inexperienced, we expect them to fail.

It is this ambivalence in our social attitudes toward young marriage that sets it apart from other marriages and compounds the problems of early-marriage failure and early divorce. It is also this ambivalence that prevents us from considering in all seriousness what can be done to protect these marriages while a young husband and wife are growing each other up, are learning to become parents before they are fully adult and are searching for a significant place for themselves in a world they have only begun to explore.

We shall not solve the problems of early marriage and early divorce until the climate of opinion about marriage and divorce in general changes. This may involve a much stronger feeling that it is valuable to remain single in the years in which a man and a woman are finding themselves as individuals. It may include a fresh appreciation of friendship as a basic adult relationship. Almost certainly, as we continue to value marriage we shall realize that a good marriage — and a good divorce too — does take a lot of devotion and hard work.

All that will help. But for young marriages it will not be enough.

Looking at young people who are trying to make a go of it, the thing that is most obvious is that they exist in a kind of limbo. They are treated neither as full adults nor as children. They are accorded neither the full rights that go with adult responsibilities nor the protections that go with childhood dependence. So they are left without the major sources of support provided in our kind of society.

Communities, educators, counselors and families all can contribute to providing a legitimate place in life for those who enter marriage early. They need to live where they can keep in touch with their peers, married and single, and where they have some continuing communication with older adults. Group living — as married students live close together during their college years — can keep them in touch with each other and give some unmarried young people a way to try out living away from home. Facilities for continuing their education and access to the kinds of education that will help them find their way as young adults are essential, both for their future and to keep them moving with their peers. The right to family counseling and medical care — without adult intervention — can ease many of their difficulties.

But above all they need opportunities to belong — to have the support of small groups of their own choice. They need to know that other people, young and not so young, have trouble getting adjusted to each other; they need to learn how to talk things out. Consciousness-raising for young couples is a much safer and more constructive enterprise than consciousness-raising for one sex, where women — or men — talk about their spouses who aren't present until often they are turned into monsters. They need to know what their spouses are troubled about as a first step in reaching out to help each other. And they need ideas — things to think about and things to do together outside the narrow walls of their marriage.

Young couples need a chance to continue to become persons. Some will grow together; some will grow apart. But whatever the outcome for the marriage, they will have had a *good* experience of being and living with a growing human person.

Number of words 2225
See page 309 for Questions

Reading Time in Seconds _____
See page 325 for Conversion Table

On Seeking a Hero for the White House

Time Magazine

You've heard of the divine right that protected kings. The king was placed in his throne by God to serve God's will. In our country, there's a President, not a king. The problem of getting the right man into the White House deserves thoughtful scrutiny.

If the task of finding the ideal President were turned over to an executive recruiting agency, its scouts would find the U.S. full of men of extraordinary ability. They would be dazzled by all the bright lawyers, economists and scientists, the able mayors who run cities more populous than states. The country teems with brilliant managers of great organizations, including virtuosos who shift effortlessly between corporations, foundations and Government service. Quite a few such men know more about the nation's besetting problems than any visible presidential candidate.

The age cries out for greatness in the White House. The trouble is not only that so many talented Americans shun politics, but also that no sort of accomplishment in other fields necessarily qualifies a man for the extraordinary demands of the presidency. Solemn reformers will doubtless one day propose a special Presidential Academy with a faculty of hundreds. Enrollment would be for a decade, the curriculum immense and open-ended. With his power over nuclear war or peace, the American President can do no less than strive to be the world's most rational man; a philosophy degree might help, at least a little. Surely he also needs degrees in law, economics, political science and military strategy, to say nothing of personnel management.

MORALITY PLAY

Alas, no amount of schooling is likely to produce the philosopher-king who could truly handle a job that may be getting too big for one individual. And even the present system may not be so bad as it often seems. The electoral machinery is ramshackle, the campaigns absurdly long, and yet they train the survivors in many skills that are as necessary to governing as they are to getting elected: the skills of compromise, of horse trading, of creating coalitions.

Far more than all that, a President has to establish moral authority based on public trust. Indeed, the whole art of governing a democracy lies in mustering popular consent on a vast scale. A President must have convictions, a vision of where the nation should travel; he must summon the national mood and push it in the right direction. If he fails to give his people a sense of partici-

pation in crucial decisions, his politics may be doomed from the start. "A President," says Political Scientist James MacGregor Burns, "must be both preacher and politician."

The President must really assume a role in a morality play, a ritual drama in which Americans expect him to slay evil. That idea goes back to the founders' exultant belief that America was truly God's country, the nation charged with the task of proving that a free society could thrive. This belief lingers, and it is not confined to assertive patriots. Consciously or unconsciously, it is shared by the country's harshest critics, including the New Left, whose very anger is based partly on the assumption that the U.S. should be near-perfect, a working utopia.

The great American morality play, the acting out of American goodness in the world, used to be comparatively simple. It could be accomplished by isolation, by existing as an uncontaminated example to other nations. Later, it could be accomplished by forceful intervention against evil, as in both World Wars and Korea. It is the special bitterness of the Viet Nam war that it has put into sharp question just how the U.S. can continue its role of working for good in the world. At home the dilemma is parallel. There, American goodness was first based on self-reliance, then, in the 20th century, on a growing sense of social justice, always surrounded by a belief in steady progress. Suddenly, the emergence of the militant civil rights movement, and the redefinition of poverty as an outrage, undermined the basic American belief in gradual, beneficial improvement.

Not only will the next President have to go on combating foreign and domestic violence; he will have to cope with some critics who insist that he renounce force while others demand force so repressive as to threaten the very values of U.S. life. He faces a combustible era of hope, hunger and hatred, of challenges to authority everywhere, of fractioned ideologies and aggressive nationalisms. He will have to cope with race, crime, the moon and nearly a billion Chinese. He will have to show that he understands why youth is restless. He will have to be a conciliator of unprecedented ability, uniting the nation's angry have-nots with the affluent majority. Above all, he will need to master the art of making people surpass themselves — their fears, selfish desires, corrosive group interests.

All these demands make clear what voters should

more than ever seek. It is the quality at once most obvious and most elusive: character. To vote wisely for a presidential candidate is basically to judge his strength of character — shorthand for the classic moral virtues of courage, justice and prudence. Equally significant is a man's self-confidence, a quality of inner assurance. Mere arrogance is not self-confidence, and oratorical skill is not a sign of it. More revealing is a capacity for growth, a virtue necessary to every good President. Those who grow acquire a sense of history, a feeling that the right moment has come for the right innovation — and the confidence to forge ahead even when the people are not quite ready.

All these qualities create the incalculable gift of moral authority. Presidents who have attained such leadership have somehow managed to appear larger than life, yet not so large as to frighten their fellow countrymen. They have not feared to make enemies. They have not feared to admit error — perhaps the most attractive trait that men in power can display. They have accepted personal responsibility for their administrations, whether it was Truman declaring that "the buck stops here," or Kennedy taking the blame for the Bay of Pigs fiasco by forthrightly announcing: "I am the responsible officer."

THE GREATEST ASSET

They have earned consent by acts of visible integrity amid temptations; a refreshing few have also deflated themselves with self-depreciating laughter. They have appealed to the best in people by uttering the right words at the right time, words that form a kind of national chorus: "With malice toward none . . . World safe for democracy . . . Only thing we have to fear is fear . . . Ask not what your country . . ." The lines are clichés now, but that very fact is a kind of tribute.

If these lines were good theater, they were also intensely believable. The next President will find a greater skepticism, a greater resistance to words, no matter how ringing. He will find the moral authority of the U.S., and of the presidency itself, considerably diminished. Yet he may also find that this moral authority can be quickly restored. His greatest asset, perhaps, will be that the world *wants* the U.S. to be great, or at least inspiring (if nothing else, John Kennedy demonstrated that). Similarly, Americans *want* their President to be great, or at least admirable. For all the dissent and despair, Americans are not yet cynics, and have not yet lost their capacity for enthusiasm. Voters are looking for a presidential hero, a figure who will not only accept the U.S. assumption that one man is equal to the task, but who will also be responsive to the people as well as responsible for them.

Will they find him? If the present field does not look brilliant, history proves that Presidents, like monarchs, show their true qualities only once they are in power. At any rate, in seeking the ideal man for the White House, or at least an approximation of the ideal, the electorate can ultimately rely only on a little reason, much instinct, and a great deal of luck — which is sometimes known as destiny.

Number of words 1280
See page 311 for Questions

Reading Time in Seconds _____
See page 325 for Conversion Table

SELECTION 72

Seven Keys to the Puzzle of Coping with Life

Dr. Roy Menninger

Coping with life happens to be a universal problem. A psychiatrist is perhaps especially well qualified to share with us insights that will provide significant help. Menninger gets us back to the basics. As the Greeks put it — "Know thyself." Menninger adds — in seven ways.

In this incredibly complex world each of us needs to examine ourselves — our motivations, our goals. As a search for a clearer idea of what we stand for, toward what we are headed, and what we think is truly important, this kind of continuing self-scrutiny can help to stabilize us in a world of explosive change. A close look at ourselves contributes to that sought-after capacity for autonomy, and gives us greater ability to make wise and useful choices, to exert some control over our own destiny.

It is never easy for any of us to look closely at ourselves — the ancient aphorism of "physician, heal thyself" notwithstanding. Most of us do so only when forced by crisis, anxiety, or a blunt confrontation with reality. Some of us have spouses or friends who help us look at the sore spots within, the personal rough spots which cause us and others pain. But for most of us, it is far easier to look outside, to look at others, whether to

From *The Menninger Perspective*, Vol. 3, No. 4 (June/July 1972).

admire or to find fault, whether to seek guidance or to castigate.

As important as this self-knowledge is, the daily pressures to act, to do, to decide make it difficult to stop and think, to consider, to examine one's life goals, one's directions, one's priorities — the basic choices one faces in managing his own world. Indeed, it is more than probable that few of us would pause to undertake such a vital inventory unless someone else said, as I am saying now, "Stop! Think about these issues for a while; defer those other 'important' things that pre-empt your daily routine!"

How are we to go about this? I ask you to focus on several rhetorical questions — rhetorical because the answers are to be offered to yourself, not to the public scene. The questions are intended to be a framework around which you may organize ideas about yourself and your relationships with your environment. Though they are questions which focus on the inner world, though they are here raised by a psychiatrist, and though they might be considered a kind of "mental health check-up," they will unquestionably strike you as rather nonmedical and perhaps even more philosophic than scientific. But pre-eminently they are intended to provoke honest thought — never an easy task in relation to one's self.

I

The first of these questions is perhaps the most global for it invites a review of your basic life direction: What are your goals in life? Put otherwise, toward what objectives are you aiming and how realistic are they? How well do they incorporate what is *really* important to you, and how well do they accurately express your values? Are they for real, or only for show?

The network of queries arising from the central question provokes several observations. In an era when planning and setting objectives are bywords for every organization, it is ironic to see how few people have adopted the same strategy for themselves. Perhaps only in late middle-age does the lack of a clear sense of direction and the absence of specific goals become an appalling reality. Many people reach that point in life with a bitter sense of loss and regret, wondering where time and opportunity have gone. The lack of intrinsic value in the materialistically oriented goals some people adopt is obvious when they helplessly wonder what to do next with their lives, now that they have the million dollars they planned to make. The acquisition of a bigger house, a bigger car, and a bigger boat, plus all the status that money will buy has taken on the appearance of a logical goal for many — but would that truly represent your central values?

One cannot think about one's own life goals without asking still other difficult questions: To what purposes do you dedicate your efforts and your lives? What are your personal priorities, and how well does your life's work reflect those priorities? Most of us find such difficult questions easy to avoid, presuming that time will answer them — as indeed it will, though not necessarily to our ultimate satisfaction. A close, comfortable, and accepting relationship with another person — a spouse, a colleague, a friend, or even a psychotherapist — can be of great help in considering such questions. The dilemma is, will you find such an opportunity?

II

Closely related to the question about goals is one which bears on your use of time and energy: Does your use of your vital resources truly reflect your priorities? Without much thought most of you would certainly answer "yes," failing to appreciate that for 90 percent of us the answer is almost assuredly "no." Executives with broad responsibilities are presumed to use their time for the things that are important — such things as planning, policy preparation, and the "big" decisions. With a consistency that is hard to believe, studies have repeatedly shown that this is rarely true, and that much more often the busy executive is spending 90 percent of his time on matters that could better be done by others, are simply a part of the daily routine, and have limited relation to the vital responsibilities which he carries.

Most of us will recognize in a moment of more somber thought that the "important things" in our lives are frequently deferred with some comforting but self-deceiving assumption that there will always be time tomorrow.

From yet another perspective, there is a high probability that your use of time and energy reflects serious imbalances within the life space of each of you. In spite of public protestations about the importance of the family, about the needs of the community, about the troubles in our world, most of us devote the smallest proportion of our time to these areas. Indeed, it could be fairly said of many of you that you are married to your jobs, not your husbands or wives, that you are invested in your colleagues, not your children, that you are committed to your business, not your society. The point is not that these imbalances are wrong, but that it is quite probable that they are decidely inconsistent with your own statements about what is important and what constitute your personal priorities.

It is this inconsistency which produces a subtle but corrosive tension as your conscience cries out for one commitment while your activities express another. At times this reflects a distorted conception of responsibility, at times an impulsive response to the demands of others, but most often it is the outcome of unthinking behavior, the consequence of a general failure to consider your goals, your priorities, and your plans for reaching them.

Nowhere is the imbalance in the use of time and energy more obvious than in regard to ourselves. Executives are dedicated people, and for many this dedication implies and finally comes to mean considerable self-sacrifice. Time for one's self is discouraged, pleasure is deemed to be selfish, and one's own needs come last.

Again drawing upon information from a study of executives, I can report that less than 40 percent of some 4,000 executives studied had an avocational pursuit. They appeared to have had few sources of personal gratification and gave themselves few opportunities for fulfilling personal pursuits. Why do they not think better of themselves than that, and are they so different from you?

III

The third question is to ask if your sense of responsibility is also out of balance. In its extreme forms, it is easy to find examples of those who will assume no more responsibility for anything than absolutely necessary; certainly the fragmentation of our contemporary culture encourages us to restrict our efforts to smaller and smaller sectors of the human community. Executives demonstrate that same pattern, pointing out that the quality of information is so great that fragmented specialization is inevitable and even advisable. And perhaps it is, but are we guilty of hiding an unduly narrow concept of our responsibility to others behind that rationalization?

Considerably more common in the field of industry is a pattern that reflects the other extreme: an excessive sense of responsibility that keeps us moving like a driven animal. Again, the needs of our organization and the endless call for our services make it hard to define a sense of responsibility which simultaneously expresses our commitment to our organization, to ourselves, and to our family and world as well. Failing to do so exposes us to the ravages of guilt feelings and failure, and of all the feelings known to the human psyche, guilt is probably the most painful.

It is easy to confuse a concept of responsibility with a command for action, connecting a notion of obligation with a need to do something about it. When one begins to discover how big the problem is about which he is worrying, his growing sense of helplessness leads him to turn away, disconnect, and assume that someone else will worry instead.

A more difficult but more effective concept of responsibility is an acknowledgement of the importance of continuing to think about problems and dilemmas, neither turning away in frustration nor hurling one's self forward into them under the pressure of guilt. Continuing to think about the problems of delinquency in one's community, the need for better school programs for the limited as well as the gifted, and the hundreds of other things for which responsible concern is needed is a way of staying engaged, remaining open to alternatives and opportunities, and being ready to respond when the occasion permits.

In more personal terms, the concept of balanced responsibility implies a willingness to accept the responsibility for one's own attitudes, feelings, failures and prejudices, forsaking the easier and unfortunately more frequent tendency to project or displace these feelings and attitudes onto persons or forces external to one's self. It is worth asking: Do each of you demonstrate a readiness to acknowledge your anger, your bias, or your limitations — at least to yourself, and to others when this is germane to the situation?

IV

My fourth query is to ask about your courage — not the sort more commonly associated with the battlefield, challenging or embarrassing situations or the like — important though that is. I refer to the courage we need to face the internal foe, for we are in most cases our own worst enemies. In the inimitable words of Pogo, "We have met the enemy — and they is us." This kind of courage is exemplified in an ability to look at yourself honestly and fairly — an expression of the responsibility I noted earlier. It is not easy to entertain the questions I am posing without fluctuating wildly between extremes of excessive personal criticism and total denial that these thoughts have any bearing on you at all.

It is this courage which enables us to face, to articulate, and finally to accept our disappointments and losses — one of the most difficult tasks the human psyche faces.

Perhaps this is not so apparent until one stops to realize that life itself is a succession of losses — beginning with the loss of the warmth and comfort of the uterus which nurtured us for the first nine months of our existence; progressing through childhood and its many losses: dependent infant status, our favorite childhood toys, our privileged status; the loss of the family as adolescence separates us from childhood; the loss of irresponsible pleasures of youth with the advent of maturity; the loss of jobs, or positions, or self-esteem, money, opportunity; the loss of one's friends with advancing age; these and a million others, and finally the ultimate loss of life itself. It is something to ponder how extensive the experience of each of us is with loss, big and small, and to note that these are experiences with profound effects upon our mental health. Even as losses vary in their impact upon us, our psychic structure varies in its capacity to handle them, and not all of us do it with equal success.

It has been said that the quality which distinguishes a great man from another otherwise like him is his capacity to manage disappointment and loss. One thinks of the experiences of Winston Churchill and the crushing disappointments of his early career, or those of Franklin Roosevelt with a disabling onslaught of polio, and begins to realize the wisdom in that observation.

Accepting loss is to accept the reality of it, to allow one's self to feel the pain and anguish of it. One can then come to terms with its meaning. Doing so is vital if the spirit is to continue to grow, and in some cases even to survive. It is relevant to note that the successful rehabilitation of a person newly blind depends upon his first having accepted the painful reality of his loss of vision, in a process of mourning akin to grieving the loss of a loved one.

It brings me to ask: What can you say about your courage to face and to accept the anguish of loss?

V

The fifth query is to ask you to examine the consistency and the quality of your personal relationships. Most of us accept the truism that people are important to people, yet we fail to perceive how often human relationships are superficial, meager, and unrewarding. Is this true of your own? Which of your relationships can you say has a quality of involvement with the other, expressing a depth of emotional investment which is real and mutually experienced? It is again too easy to explain that the pressures of our lives and the demands upon us, the superficial materialism of the age and all the rest are what account for a deep sense of poverty in our relationships with others. To call again upon that element of courage to which I earlier referred, can we examine the quality of the relationships of those who are closest to us to question how honest, how open, how real they are?

It is clear that the capacity to establish close, significant emotional ties with others is characteristic of emotional maturity. It is clear, moreover, that the work, the effort, and sometimes the pain of doing so is quite enough to discourage many, especially when the trends in our society are moving in the same direction. And yet we are still disdainful of the empty superficiality of the cocktail party, even when lessened by the illusion of intimacy which alcohol can provide.

The phenomenon of parallel play in the nursery school — two children in close physical contact with each other but playing entirely alone — is expectable at the age of 2 or 3. When it can be said to characterize a pattern of living at the age of 20 to 40, it hints at relationships eroded by infantile expectations and a lack of mutual commitment. Relationships which show a depth of emotional involvement require a willingness to engage, to share, to listen, to give. What can you say about these qualities in your human relationships?

VI

Not unrelated to a question about your human relationships is a query about sources of your emotional support: From whom do you receive it and to whom do you give it? I have referred to the lack of fulfilling avocation in the lives of many executives — the absence of a rewarding investment in art, in music, in physical activity, in stamp collecting, or a hundred others. Does this also describe you?

It is also clear that many people who are imbued with an especially strong sense of responsibility have great difficulty in seeking or accepting support from others. For some, this is reminiscent of a profoundly unpleasant sense of helplessness from an earlier phase of life. For some it is an unacceptable admission of weakness, of inadequacy; for some it is a contradiction of one's sense of strength and commitment to help others. Ironically, those whose careers lead to increasing responsibility to others must therefore provide increasing support for others at the very moment when they are progressively more isolated, less able to fend for help for themselves, and less able to receive it when it is available. Greater responsibility generates greater personal need — and greater obstacles to receiving it.

VII

Lastly, any survey of your mental health must ask about the role of love in your lives. For most of us the very use of this word threatens a deluge of sentimentality. It is a word which too readily conjures images of Technicolor Hollywood and cow-eyed adolescents. But it is a respectable feeling. I use it to refer to a capacity to care. Perhaps we are not fully aware that it implies a willingness to invest ourselves in others, to be involved with them, to listen to them — in short, to care about them. It should therefore be a hallmark of all our relationships with others. This is the true sense of helping, for it is the only antidote to hate we know, and it is also the foundation stone for that indispensable pillar of good human relationships — trust. Both are always in short supply.

Without intending to promote egocentricity, I would have to ask how truly and how well you love yourself — not in irrational or narcissistic and overblown terms, but as an object of pride and self-esteem, a thing of value, a person of worth. As one can love himself in this mature and realistic way, so he is able to extend the help of love to others in ways which are not demeaning, not controlling, not condescending or patronizing, but respectful and genuinely caring.

Your relationships to others do indeed mirror your relationship to yourself. How well you deal with others may depend upon your success in managing yourself in relation to the provocative and difficult questions I have posed for you today. No one has suggested these questions are easy; in some sense they may be unanswerable. But they do need to be thought about by each of you, talked about with those you love and are close to, and examined repeatedly in the months and years ahead.

Number of words 3010
See page 313 for Questions

Reading Time in Seconds _____
See page 325 for Conversion Table

Education for More Than One Career

Sidney P. Marland, Jr.

*With life expectancy moving into the seventies, training for "a single vocation is
obsolete." Use reading to open additional career doors and interests. Parallel your
major vocational thrust with one or two other reading-centered possibilities. When
it's time to change, the transition should be relatively easy.*

For fifteen years, Anthony Morley was a clergyman, his
parish an inner-city neighborhood. Today he is a fulltime graduate student in school administration at the
City University of New York. He is working on ways to
humanize the computer for classroom instruction. He's
also looking at ways to reform school finance. When his
training program is completed, he hopes to work in a
State Department of Education because, he says, that's
where power and responsibility for reform in our schools
are lodged.

Why change careers in midstream? Morley says, "In
my ministry, I felt I was nibbling away at the fringes of
social problems. Given my particular interest and abilities, I felt I could do more and enjoy it more inside the
educational system. It reaches every child."

Anthony Morley is one of a small number of people,
successful in other fields, who are preparing for new
careers in education with the financial help of the U.S.
Office of Education. This program is one federal response, and there are others, to the fast-growing need in
this country for educating people for more than a single
career in one lifetime.

Others in the Educational Leadership Program have
equally interesting backgrounds. Tom McCollough of
Columbus, Ohio, is former vice president of a large
pharmaceutical laboratory. Matthew Prophet, Fort
Sheridan, Illinois, was a regular Army lieutenant colonel.
A. W. Larson of Baldwin, New York, served as president of a management consulting firm. Lila Carol, New
Rochelle, New York, was an executive assistant to the
Mayor of that city. Mostly in their early forties, these
people obviously took a hard look at their lifestyles and
family commitments and decided that for them a career
change was in order.

It is too early to know what the extent will be of the
U.S. government's direct involvement in continuing
education; but there can be no question of the importance we in the Office of Education attach to career
education on all levels.

Let me mention another Office of Education program: offering a career to people who have never had
one. This year more than 8,000 men and women are
working part-time in neighborhood schools as classroom
or library aides. All come from low-income circumstances and work with disadvantaged children they
know and understand. Many are Vietnam veterans who
might otherwise have landed on the streets. While working as aides, all participants are enrolled in teacher-
preparation or related programs in local colleges and
universities. Many will undoubtedly earn a degree, become certified teachers, and enter a professional world
otherwise closed to them.

New careers are not necessarily tied to paying jobs.
The volunteer movement, especially for mature citizens,
is a growing phenomenon, particularly when the volunteer possesses specific skills or competencies, and brings
to his work all the necessary self-discipline and integrity
that attaches to conventional employment.

One of the most remarkable men I know is Howard
Bede, of Highland Falls, Illinois. Thirteen years ago he
retired as vice president of a major advertising and publishing firm in Chicago. By that time, he had already
done more than most of us envision in a lifetime. As a
young man, Bede had wanted to become an architect,
but lacked the money for college. He started with the
next best option, as draftsman in an architectural firm.
Recognizing the limitations of that job, he took his
growing knowledge of architectural principles into the
construction field and ultimately found his niche in
publishing, initially with construction-related journals.
Along the way, Bede became an amateur geologist and
photographer. On world tours incidental to his business
he managed to photograph and collect data on every
major volcano. When he retired, he had no idea of retreating from the mainstream of living usefully.

At that time, I was superintendent of schools in
nearby Winnetka, looking for ways to motivate third-
and fourth-grade youngsters who were capable of doing
much better academic work than their tests indicated.
Our principals and teachers agreed that mature people
who would volunteer to come to the classrooms and
share their knowledge and experience might be just
what we needed. We felt they would bring fresh ideas
and motivations to children with learning problems, as
well as to youngsters who were exceptionally gifted.

Bede was one of those early volunteers and is still at
it, along with 2,000 other people of all ages, most of
whom he inspired. The program now reaches twenty-
one towns in the Chicago area. What does he talk to
young people about? Publishing, of course, and writing

Abridged from *World*, July 18, 1972. Reprinted by permission
of Saturday Review/World.

and volcanoes and how to set up a darkroom to develop pictures in school or at home. When the children ask, he also talks about what life was like in the Depression; many of their teachers are themselves too young to remember. Most of all, he asks students what they want to do with their lives and how they intend to get there. He asks them to think ahead, to consider the options, and then to chart a realistic career education, intuitively, without formal curriculums.

Bede sums up his second "career" by saying, "I have gained more than I have given the children — the satisfaction in being constructively active." Further, Bede looks and behaves as young as he did thirteen years ago when the program started.

Janet Freund, the energetic and highly capable professional who serves in the Chicago area as coordinator between the schools and volunteers, believes there are really two periods of quiet crisis for most of us: when we are young and trying to find our way into a complex and confusing adult world, and when we retire from the challenges and pace of the working world and feel that society scarcely notices our withdrawal.

A very distinguished New York banker retired from his vocation four years ago, and has since been working full time as a volunteer and a leader of other successful businessmen-volunteers to help manage and renew the city that he helped build and that has treated him well. He keeps longer hours now and probably works more desperately and harder than he did at his bank. He has a new career of his own choosing. He didn't need career education for his own renewal, for he is one of those who does not depend on the system to help him break the lockstep. Most of us do not possess that initiative, talent, or instinct for unaided self-direction.

As we look at America's priorities in the closing years of the century, I think it's clear that we have the technology and know-how to conquer our present-day problems and make life more livable. The real question is whether we have the social and political attitudes to put our knowledge and resources to work in bringing about a better life.

One of the first places to start, in my view, is with the shibboleths that confine a versatile human being to a single career path just because that's the way our schools and colleges, our corporate structures, our labor organizations, our work ethic, and our social patterns have developed. At a time when life expectancy is moving into the seventies, the notion that a person should be trained for a single vocation or profession is costly and obsolete. Nothing is more wasteful than human energies and talents — regardless of the age of the person involved — that are not being utilized.

New forms of education for meeting these needs are now taking shape. The "University Without Walls" experiment, sponsored by the U.S. Office of Education, is beginning to give substance to the idea that adults with varied backgrounds and career interests need to be served in non-traditional ways. It provides opportunities for independent study, coupled with new courses, innovative teaching methods, and differing time/space dimensions. Offices may be used as classrooms, and social service agencies may be the target of study and improved performance.

. . . .

The adults in this country constitute a work force of about eighty-one million employed people, of whom only twenty-seven million possess a marketable skill as a result of conscious career development. The remaining two-thirds of the work force, not counting five million unemployed, have managed to enter a livelihood of sorts, without special skills or experience. During a forty-six-year employed life, these individuals will hold twelve different jobs, for the most part unrelated to each other. Only one man in five in this group remains in the same general occupational category during his working years. There is nothing wrong with changing careers, provided the individual is acting upon his own choice. However, it is doubtful that many in this group have much choice.

The five million unemployed Americans are perhaps the most serious challenge to the goals of career education, since most of them are beyond the immediate range of conventional educational institutions. Further, a great many of these individuals not only lack salable skills but need training in those basic communication skills essential to the comprehension of career opportunities and increasing responsibilities in the world of work. Often, the disadvantaged adult does not trust the system, since he has experienced repeated failure in it. Career education is searching for new ways to reach out to such individuals and to facilitate their re-entry into a system of career development that will include basic academic instruction as well as skill training. Career guidance, counseling, and assistance in initial job placement and follow-up constitute a very crucial component of the career education structure for this segment of our society.

Currently, about two and a half million young people a year leave high school or college, with or without degrees or diplomas and with no idea of what to do with their lives. Heaven only knows how many mature job-holders of all ages are underemployed, unhappy in their work, and unable to break the lockstep. Many students complete their education according to clearly defined career goals, including those of bricklayer, cosmetologist, newspaper reporter, or surgeon. Perhaps they had good guidance from school or family, or possessed more than ordinary qualities for taking charge of their own lives, but I estimate that upwards of 50 percent of our young people now in school or college have no real goals toward which to aim, and that they have very little information or help for establishing those goals and pursuing them systematically.

There may have been a time when we could afford

the luxury of twelve or sixteen or more years of formal education without work-related purpose. The swiftly moving technological and social evolution no longer has a place for the unskilled or unschooled. More students enter college and leave than graduate, and not for reasons of academic failure. About 40 percent of our high school students are enrolled in the general curriculum, which frequently leads neither to higher education nor a job.

There are unfilled jobs all over the country. Yet, 17 percent of our under-twenty age group are unemployed, many of them on welfare. More than 30 percent of our minority young people of this age group were unemployed in 1971. Virtually none of these young people had the benefits of career education or the traditional vocational-technical education available in many schools. Is it any wonder that student unrest is the result of the unchanging institutional codes that have failed to make learning useful or meaningful for those who now want more realistic teaching and learning than the system offers?

Education, I repeat, is not solely a matter of equipping students for jobs. The heart of the learning process involves sciences. It is the way a man's mind works, and not just what he can do with his hands, that gives quality and purpose to life. But I see no conflict between the virtues of liberal education and career development. In fact, our neglect of career development in recent years has done damage to the total educational needs of both the individual and the nation.

Number of words 2108
See page 315 for Questions

Reading Time in Seconds _____
See page 325 for Conversion Table

SELECTION 74

Is the Work Ethic Going Out of Style?

Time Magazine

Work! That's so important that there are over 200 quotations listed in Bartlett's Familiar Quotations *under* work *or* works. *For example, Carlyle said "work is alone noble," and he meant all work. What do today's workers say about the work ethic?*

In the pantheon of virtues that made the U.S. great, none stands higher than the work ethic. One politician said in a nationwide radio address: "The work ethic holds that labor is good in itself; that a man or woman at work not only makes a contribution to his fellow man but becomes a better person by virtue of the act of working." He then warned ominously: "We are faced with a choice between the work ethic that built this nation's character — and the new welfare ethic that could cause the American character to weaken." . . .

Is the work ethic really in trouble?

There are signs aplenty that the ethic is being challenged, and not just by welfare recipients. In offices and factories, many Americans appear to reject the notion that "labor is good in itself." More and more executives retire while still in their 50s, dropping out of jobs in favor of a life of ease. People who work often take every opportunity to escape. In auto plants, for example, absenteeism has doubled since the early 1960s, to 5% of the work force; on Mondays and Fridays it commonly climbs to 15%. In nearly every industry, employees are increasingly refusing overtime work; union leaders explain that their members now value leisure time more than time-and-a-half.

Beyond that, an increasing number of Americans see no virtue in holding jobs that they consider menial or unpleasant. More and more reject such work — even if they can get no other jobs. Though unemployment is a high 5.5% of the labor force, shortages of taxi drivers, domestic servants, auto mechanics and plumbers exist in many places.

Young adults are particularly choosy; many have little interest in the grinding routine of the assembly line or in automated clerical tasks like operating an addressing machine or processing a payroll. The nation's 22.5 million workers under 30, nursed on television and still showing their Spock marks, may in fact be too educated, too expectant and too anti-authoritarian for many of the jobs that the economy offers them. Affluence, the new rise in hedonism, and the antimaterialistic notions expressed in Charles Reich's *The Greening of America* have turned many young people against their parents' dedication to work for the sake of success.

More than the youth are uneasy. A Gallup poll of workers of all ages last year showed that 19% were displeased with their jobs, up from 13% in 1969. Observes Psychiatrist Robert Coles: "Working people with whom I have talked make quite clear the ways they feel cornered, trapped, lonely, pushed around at work and confused by a sense of meaninglessness."

These developments should not come as too much of a surprise, considering that only fairly recently in human development has man — or woman — had anything but contempt for work. The Greeks, who relied on slaves for their work, thought that there was more honor in leisure — by which they meant a life of contemplation — than in toil. As Aristotle put it: "All paid employments absorb and degrade the mind." Christianity finally bestowed a measure of dignity on work. Slaves and freemen are all one in Christ Jesus, said St. Paul, adding: "If any one will not work, let him not eat." For the medieval monks, work was a glorification of God; the followers of St. Benedict, the father of Western monasticism, set the tone in their rule: *"Laborare est orare"* — to work is to pray. During the Reformation, John Calvin asserted that hard-earned material success was a sign of God's predestining grace, thus solidifying the religious significance of work. Around Calvin's time, a new, commerce-enriched middle class rose. Its members challenged the aristocracy's view that leisure was an end in itself and that society was best organized hierarchically. In its place they planted business values, sanctifying the pursuit of wealth through work.

The Puritans were Calvinists, and they brought the work ethic to America. They punished idleness as a serious misdemeanor. They filled their children's ears with copybook maxims about the devil finding work for idle hands and God helping those who help themselves. Successive waves of immigrants took those lessons to heart, and they aimed for what they thought was the ultimate success open to them — middle-class status. They almost deified Horatio Alger's fictional heroes, like Ragged Dick, who struggled up to the middle class by dint of hard work.

During the Great Depression, the work ethic flourished because people faced destitution unless they could find something productive to do. World War II intensified the work ethic under the banner of patriotism. While the boys were on the battlefront, the folks on the home front serenaded Rosie the Riveter; a long day's work was a contribution to the national defense. In sum, the American work ethic is rooted in Puritan piety, immigrant ambition and the success ethic; it has been strengthened by Depression trauma and wartime patriotism.

Not much remains of that proud heritage. Today, in a time of the decline of organized churches, work has lost most of its religious significance. Horatio Alger is camp. Only a minority of workers remember the Depression. Welfare and unemployment benefits have reduced the absolute necessity of working, or at least made idleness less unpleasant.

Automation has given many people the ethic-eroding impression that work may some day be eliminated, that machines will eventually take over society's chores. Says John Kenneth Galbraith: "The greatest prospect we face is to eliminate toil as a required economic institution."

Do all these changes and challenges mean that Americans have lost the work ethic? There is considerable evidence that they have not. After all, more than 90% of all men in the country between the ages of 20 and 54 are either employed or actively seeking work — about the same percentage as 25 years ago. Over the past two decades, the percentage of married women who work has risen from 25% to 42%. Hard-driving executives drive as hard as they ever did. Even welfare recipients embrace the work ethic. In a recent study of 4,000 recipients and non-recipients by Social Psychologist Leonard Goodwin, those on welfare said that, given a chance, they were just as willing to work as those not on welfare.

Despite signs to the contrary, young people retain a strong commitment to work. A survey of college students conducted by the Daniel Yankelovich organization showed that 79% believe that commitment to a career is essential, 75% believe that collecting welfare is immoral for a person who can work, and only 30% would welcome less emphasis in the U.S. on hard work.

What is happening is that the work ethic is undergoing a radical transformation. Workers, particularly younger ones, are taking work *more* seriously, not less. Many may have abandoned the success ethic of their elders, but they still believe in work. Young and old are willing to invest more effort in their work, but are demanding a bigger payoff in satisfaction. The University of Michigan Survey Research Center asked 1,533 working people to rank various aspects of work in order of importance. "Good pay" came in a distant fifth, behind "interesting work," "enough help and equipment to get the job done," "enough information to do the job," and "enough authority to do the job."

Indeed in labor contract negotiations expected to begin early next summer, the United Auto Workers intend to make a major point of its demand for increased participation by workers in decision-making within plants. "People look at life in different ways than they used to," says Douglas Fraser, a U.A.W. vice president. "Maybe we ought to stop talking about the work ethic and start talking about the life ethic."

The trouble is that this new humanistic, holistic outlook on life is at odds with the content of many jobs today. Most white collar work involves elemental, mind-numbing clerical operations. Factory work is usually dull and repetitive, and too often dirty, noisy, demeaning and dangerous as well. It is a national scandal that last year on-the-job accidents killed 14,200 U.S. workers. In most auto assembly plants, a worker must even get permission from his foreman before he can go to the bathroom. The four-day week offers no real prospect for humanizing work; doing a boring job for four days instead of five is still an empty experience. Charles Reich says: "No person with a strongly developed aesthetic sense, a love of nature, a passion for music, a desire for reflection, or a strongly marked independence could possibly be happy in a factory or white collar job."

A few enlightened employers have concluded that work, not workers, must change. Says Robert Ford, personnel director at American Telephone & Telegraph: "We have run out of dumb people to handle those dumb jobs. So we have to rethink what we're doing." In restructuring work, corporate experimenters have hit on a number of productive and promising ideas. Among them:

Give workers a totality of tasks. In compiling its telephone books, Indiana Bell used to divide 17 separate operations among a staff of women. The company gradually changed, giving each worker her own directory and making her responsible for all 17 tasks, from scheduling to proofreading. Results: work force turnover dropped, and errors, absenteeism and overtime declined.

Break up the assembly line. A potentially revolutionary attempt at change is under way in the Swedish auto industry. Volvo and Saab are taking a number of operations off the assembly line. Some brakes and other subassemblies are put together by teams of workers; each performs several operations instead of a single repetitive task. In the U.S., Chrysler has used the work team to set up a conventional engine-assembly line; two foremen were given complete freedom to design the line, hand-pick team members and use whatever tools and equipment they wanted.

Permit employees to organize their own work. Polaroid lets its scientists pursue their own projects and order their own materials without checking with a supervisor; film assembly workers are allowed to run their machines at the pace they think best. A T & T eased supervision of its shareholder correspondents and let them send out letters to complainants over their own signatures, without review by higher-ups. Absenteeism decreased and turnover was practically eliminated. Syntex Corp. allowed two groups of its salesmen to set their own work standards and quotas; sales increased 116% and 20% respectively over groups of salesmen who were not given that freedom.

Let workers see the end product of their efforts. Chrysler has sent employees from supply plants to assembly plants so they can see where their parts fit into the finished product. The company has also put assembly-line workers into inspection jobs for one-week stints. Said one welder: "I see metal damage, missing welds and framing fits that I never would have noticed before."

Let workers set their own hours. In West Germany, some 3,500 firms have adopted "sliding time." In one form of the plan, company doors are open from 7 a.m. until 7 p.m., and factory or office workers can come in any time they like, provided that they are around for "core time," from 10 a.m. to 3 p.m., and they put in a 40-hour week. Productivity is up, staff turnover is down, and absenteeism has fallen as much as 20%.

Treat workers like mature, responsible adults. A few firms are attempting to give workers more status and responsibility. In its Topeka, Kans., plant, for example, General Foods has eliminated reserved parking spaces for executives, banished time clocks, made office size dependent not on rank but on need, abandoned the posting of in-plant behavior rules and put the same carpeting in workers' locker rooms as in executives' offices.

The work ethic is alive, though it is not wholly well. It is being changed and reshaped by the new desires and demands of the people. "The potential of the work ethic as a positive force in American industry is extremely great," says Professor Wickham Skinner of the Harvard Business School. "We simply have to remove the roadblocks stopping individuals from gaining satisfaction on the job. The work ethic is just waiting to be refound."

In the new ethic, people will still work to live, but fewer will live only to work. As Albert Camus put it: "Without work all life goes rotten. But when work is soulless, life stifles and dies." It will be a long while, if ever, before men figure out ways to make the work of, say, a punch-press operator or a file clerk soul-enriching. While waiting for that millennium — which may require entirely new forms of work — bosses who expect loyalty from their employees should try to satisfy their demands for more freedom, more feeling of participation and personal responsibility, and more sense of accomplishment on the job.

Number of words 2122
See page 317 for Questions

Reading Time in Seconds _____
See page 325 for Conversion Table

The End of American Independence

Lester R. Brown

About two centuries ago the Declaration of Independence established this country as the land of the free. In what sense are we coming to the end of our cherished independence? And what can be done to regain that independence so dear to our hearts?

Throughout its two centuries of existence, the United States has enjoyed an uncommon degree of national independence, in part because two vast oceans have isolated it from political conflicts in Europe and elsewhere and in part because it has been an essentially self-sufficient continental storehouse of energy fuels and raw materials.

Suddenly, this is beginning to change, and very rapidly. As recently as 1970 we were importing only a small fraction of our petroleum and only a few of the important minerals. By 1985 we will be importing well over half of our petroleum and will be primarily dependent on imports for nine of the thirteen basic minerals required by a modern industrial economy. The import bill for energy fuels and minerals, which totaled $8 billion in 1970, is projected to multiply severalfold by 1985. Within a fifteen-year span, scarcely half a generation, we will make the transition from being an essentially self-sufficient country to — at least in terms of raw materials — a have-not country. We do not yet appreciate the economic, social, and political consequences of this historically abrupt transition.

One new problem is the question of access to these raw materials abroad. We have always assumed that once our own supply of a given raw material was exhausted, we could move into the world market and buy whatever we needed. We now find that this assumption is not universally shared.

The world energy market has been transformed within a few years from a buyer's to a seller's market. We have seen the exporting countries organize to bargain collectively, and do so very effectively. The first round of negotiations centered on the price and the share of proceeds from exports that went to exporting countries. The second round focused on control of the subsidiaries of international oil companies in the exporting countries; those negotiations were concluded by an agreement signed in September 1972.

The ink was scarcely dry before a possible new phase in the negotiating strategy of the exporting countries was unveiled, in a speech given in Washington by Sheik Ahmed Yamani, Saudi Arabia's minister of petroleum. It was summed up in one sentence, in which Sheik Yamani said, "The government of Saudi Arabia is prepared to guarantee an uninterrupted flow of petroleum to the United States in exchange for the opportunity to invest in petroleum refining and distributing facilities down to the service-station level."

We have little choice but to take the proposal seriously. Since several oil-rich nations have few people and little domestic use for additional income at the present time, they may be unwilling to expand their production in response to U.S. needs unless they can find something "interesting" and profitable to do with the additional income.

If there ever was a sector of our economy that seemed invulnerable, it was the capacity of U.S. agriculture to provide an adequate supply of low-cost food to American consumers.

But the skyrocketing food prices of 1973 have made us aware for the first time that this may not always be the case. Like it or not, this year we are sharing a decreased food supply with 248 million Soviet consumers. We have no real choice but to do so. Some political leaders have suggested that we limit our food exports in order to keep prices down at home. However, anyone who proposes severe limits on U.S. farm exports must also be prepared for a rigorous program of gasoline rationing, for it is with expanding farm exports that we are hoping to pay the rapidly rising energy bill.

Global food supplies may fall short of demand with increasing frequency in the decades ahead, with the result that international prices of food commodities can be expected to continue rising over the long term. The United States will not be able to isolate itself from such trends.

Our efforts to expand the world food supply, particularly the supply of high-quality protein, are hampered in three important areas. One is world fisheries. Beginning in 1950 the world fish catch increased for eighteen consecutive years, expanding an average of about 6 percent each year. But in 1969, for the first time in nearly two decades the world's fish catch dropped, and since then it has been fluctuating unpredictably. Many marine biologists now feel that the global catch of table-grade fish (as distinct from fish meal for poultry and pig feed) may be very close to the maximum sustainable level. Unless we move toward a cooperative global approach in the management of our finite marine resources, we can expect depleted stocks, declining catch, soaring food prices, and intense com-

From *Saturday Review/World*, December 18, 1973. Reprinted by permission of Saturday Review/World.

petition among countries for available supplies in the years ahead. And the added pressures on land-based protein sources that would result from a falloff in fish production would drive up food prices even further.

A second problem area is beef production. Part of the problem here is that the carrying capacities of grazing lands around the world are limited and in many cases fully utilized. More importantly, we have not been able to devise a commercially satisfactory way of getting more than one calf per cow per year. For every animal that goes into the production process, we must maintain one adult animal for one year.

The third area in which we have not been successful is in raising soybean yield per acre. Soybeans are an extremely important global source of high-quality protein, but since 1950 soybean yields in the United States have increased only about 1 percent a year (compared with 4 percent a year for corn). To my knowledge, no experts expect any sort of breakthrough in the foreseeable future. The crucial role of soybeans as a global protein source and the additional economic importance of soybeans to the United States are underlined by the fact that soybeans constituted our greatest single export item in dollar value in 1972.

As world demand for meat products continues to rise, prices for protein products can be expected to rise as well. We may be in the early stages of a transformation of the world protein market from a buyer's to a seller's market, not unlike the recent transformation of the world energy market.

One of the questions that is coming into focus as we face growing scarcity of resources of many kinds is how to divide finite resources among countries. In the international development community, the conventional wisdom has been that the 2 billion people living in poor countries could never aspire to the standard of living that most of us in North America enjoy, simply because the world does not contain enough iron ore, protein, petroleum, and so on. At the same time, we in the United States have continued to pursue superaffluence as though there were no limits on how much we could consume; one car per family, or two, or three — at least one TV set or, perhaps, two or three. We make up 6 percent of the world's people; yet we consume one-third of the world's resources.

As long as the resources we consumed each year came primarily from within our own boundaries, this was largely an internal matter. But as our resources come more and more from the outside world, "outsiders" are going to have some say over the rate at which and terms under which we consume. We will no longer be able to think in terms of "our" resources and "their" resources, but only of *common* resources. Everyone now wants to use the energy resources in the Middle East, or the protein from oceanic fisheries, or the soybeans that we produce.

As Americans consuming such a disproportionate share of the world's resources, we have to question whether or not we can continue our pursuit of superaffluence in a world of scarcity. We are now reaching the point where we must carefully examine the presumed link between our level of well-being and the level of material goods consumed. In the early stages of society's consumption, the two were closely related. If you have only one crust of bread and get another crust of bread, your well-being is greatly enhanced. But if you have a loaf of bread, then an additional crust of bread doesn't make that much difference. In the eyes of most of the world today, Americans have their loaf of bread and are asking for still more. People elsewhere are beginning to ask why. That is the question we're going to have to answer, whether we're trying to persuade countries to step up their exports of oil to us or trying to convince them that we ought to be permitted to maintain our share of the world fish catch.

The prospect of a scarcity of, and competition for, the world's resources requires that we re-examine our own lifestyles. The technologies underlying our economic system evolved in a situation of relative abundance of energy, water, land, food minerals, and other resources. Now we need to find ways of cutting back on resource consumption. In most cases we can do so without necessarily reducing our level of well-being. For example, we could reduce the size of automobiles from 4500–5000 pounds to 2500 pounds without seriously reducing our well-being. Such a step would automatically strengthen the dollar, reduce our political vulnerability in the Middle East, and cut air pollution. Our overall mobility would be increased since adoption of smaller cars would, in effect, increase parking facilities by half.

It is ironic that as we Americans prepare to celebrate the two-hundredth anniversary of our national independence, we discover that we are losing much of that independence. We see that our important national problems — the environmental crisis, the energy crisis, inflation, spreading drug addiction, aerial hijacking — do not have national solutions. Increasingly we find that our day-to-day well-being is dependent on the resources and cooperation of other countries. We can no longer protect the value of our currency without the assistance of other governments. Even our daily weather may be influenced by activities beyond our boundaries.

For the United States this means rethinking the way in which we relate to the rest of the world. It means a major reordering of national priorities. A foreign-affairs budget of nearly $85 billion — of which $82 billion is for military expenditures and $3 billion for economic, food, and technical assistance — does not reflect a genuine sense of concern for the problems of the rest of mankind. Declining U.S. economic assistance, trade policies that discriminate against the poor countries, and a military budget bloated out of all proportion to national security needs have alienated and embittered many of the poor countries on whose resources and cooperation our future well-being depends. We cannot expect people in these countries to concern themselves with our worsening energy and food shortages or spreading drug addiction unless we demonstrate some concern for the hunger, illiteracy, and disease that are diminishing life for them.

Number of words 1812
See page 319 for Questions

Reading Time in Seconds _____
See page 325 for Conversion Table

Part Two

COMPREHENSION AND VOCABULARY CHECK QUESTIONS AND EXERCISES

Perhaps the best measure of reading comprehension is your ability to reexpress with a minimum of loss or distortion what you have just read. That is, however, a very time-consuming process and does not lend itself to easy objective evaluation. The ten objective COMPREHENSION CHECK QUESTIONS are intended to provide a quick, convenient approximation or supplement to any such re-expression.

Your score on the first five questions will suggest how well you note details and is spoken of as *Receptive Comprehension*. Your score on the last five questions will suggest how well you get the central idea, draw inferences, reach conclusions, note relationships, and recognize pattern and organization. These last five questions come under the heading of *Reflective Comprehension*. The sixth question is always on the central idea. Indicate your answer by entering the number of the correct choice in the space following the question. When you have finished, check your answers with the key on page 337.

The VOCABULARY CHECK QUESTIONS are meant to encourage increased attention to context. In a general way they parallel the twofold division of the COMPREHENSION CHECK QUESTIONS. The distinction here is between knowing a word without further study, and having to depend upon a reflective analysis of context in order to arrive at an accurate understanding of its meaning. Low comprehension, in both reading and listening, is often attributable to inadequate vocabulary (Column I score) or to inability to make effective use of contextual clues in arriving at word meanings (Column II score).

Without looking back at the selection, you are to enter a set of answers in Column I, headed *without context*. This provides a measure of your word knowledge without the help of context. Next, turn back to the selection containing the words, find the word, and study it in its full context to see if you can arrive at a better understanding of its meaning. Use Column II, headed *with context,* for entering your second set of answers. When you have completed both sets, check your results by using the key on page 337 or by referring to your dictionary.

If you are as skilled as you should be in using contextual clues to word meanings, your scores in the second column should be almost perfect. If they are low, you have particular reason for developing added skill with context to facilitate your mastery of new words and improve comprehension. In the first few selections you read, if your answers in Column I are all correct, you may wish to omit working through the items a second time with the help of context. In that case, take 20 off for each mistake to get your WORD COMPREHENSION SCORE.

A careful record of your performance as you work through the various tests should do much to hasten your progress. Enter all your test results on the PROGRESS RECORD at the end of the book, pages 328 following.

The seventy-five EXERCISES on the reverse side of the Check Questions provide for added practice, reinforcement, and extension of reading and study-related skills. The ten exercises for the ten selections in Section VII are, for example, focused on writing skills. The format is based on Franklin's method, described in Selection 23, but modified here to make it more objective for easier checking. For specific matters of style, usage, diction, grammar, and the like, refer to a standard handbook of English, such as *The Heath Handbook of Composition,* 10th edition.

INDEX OF EXERCISES

SECTION VII.   Writing-Related Exercises

NAME_____ DATE_____ READING RATE_____ W.P.M.

COMPREHENSION CHECK QUESTIONS

1. One tool specifically mentioned was (1) a screwdriver; (2) a thermometer; (3) an auger; (4) a can opener.   1. *2*

2. The author speaks of (1) a physician; (2) a dentist; (3) an aviator; (4) a mechanic.   2. *1*

3. Our present numerical system came originally from (1) India; (2) Greece; (3) Rome; (4) England.   3. *1*

4. Language is viewed here as a (1) communication tool; (2) magic tool; (3) brain tool; (4) social tool.   4. *3*

5. What is *not* discussed? (1) increasing your vocabulary; (2) studying diacritical marks; (3) studying etymology; (4) comparing languages.   5. *2*

Receptive Comprehension _____

6. This selection is intended primarily to explain (1) the function of language; (2) how to use language more effectively; (3) the dependence of tool and user; (4) the limitations of language.   6. *1*

7. The opening paragraphs about a certain tool were intended to point up the tool's (1) range of uses; (2) limitations; (3) relationship to the user; (4) all of the preceding points.   7. *4*

8. The reference to the exact third of a meter was to show (1) that tools have limitations; (2) the advantages of the metric system; (3) how tools increase brain power; (4) that skilled users improve tool efficiency.   8. *1*

9. Learning a new language was mentioned to show how (1) we tend to think in English; (2) a foreign vocabulary is mastered; (3) a tool increases thinking power; (4) tool and user form a complex unit.   9. *4*

10. The style of this article is best described as (1) concise; (2) amusing; (3) elevated; (4) conversational.   10. *4*

(10 off for each mistake)   *Reflective Comprehension* _____

TOTAL READING COMPREHENSION SCORE _____

VOCABULARY CHECK QUESTIONS

			without context I	*with context* II
1. *cope*	(1) confine; (2) work together; (3) cook; (4) contend; (5) accompany.		*4*	
2. *cumbersome*	(1) cumulative; (2) curative; (3) antiquated; (4) gaunt; (5) clumsy.		*5*	
3. *shackles*	(1) shanties; (2) rags; (3) shambles; (4) restraints; (5) goals.		*4*	
4. *competence*	(1) ability; (2) complacency; (3) compulsion; (4) obedience; (5) compliment.		*1*	
5. *advocate*	(1) confess; (2) favor; (3) advise; (4) oppose; (5) speak.		*2*	

(10 off for each mistake)   *Word Comprehension* without *contextual help* (I) _____

Word Comprehension with *contextual help* (II) _____

TOTAL WORD COMPREHENSION SCORE _____

EXERCISES

1. *Reading sentences and paragraphs:* As a reader, one of your problems is recalling details — the type of problem tested in the first five comprehension check questions for all the articles in this text. Usually details are supporting evidence leading to a conclusion or generalization. That means that as you read you should not only note details but also see what they add up to.

Take these details: With a hammer you (1) drive nails; (2) pull nails; (3) split a board; (4) break stones; (5) bang someone on the head; (6) and so forth.

What do those details add up to? What do you conclude? (1) that many things can be done with a hammer? (2) that many things cannot be done with a hammer?

Now take another set of details. With a hammer you cannot (1) saw a piece of wood; (2) drive a screw; (3) bore a hole.

What do those details add up to? (1) that many things can be done with a hammer? (2) that many things cannot be done with a hammer?

Fit both sets of details into one paragraph and what central idea do you have? (1) that many things can be done with a hammer? (2) that many things cannot be done with a hammer? (3) that many things can and cannot be done with a hammer?

Now turn back to the article and reread the first paragraph to review the common relationship between details and generalizations.

2. As a reader you will usually find that ideas of similar weight are in constructions of a similar kind. As an example, try reading the following sentence where this principle is violated:

The automobile gives us the seven-league boots of fairy tales; wings come to us from the airplane; if we want the muscular strength of a Titan, it can be obtained from the hydraulic press.

Now look at the same sentence as it originally appeared, constructed so as to put parallel ideas into parallel form:

The automobile gives us the seven-league boots of fairy tales, the airplane gives us wings, the hydraulic press gives us the muscular strength of a Titan.

See how helpful parallel form is, both to reader and writer!

Improve the parallelism of the following sentence:

You cannot saw a piece of wood; driving a screw is impossible; or to bore a hole cannot be done.

Revision: _____

_____

_____

When you have finished, compare your version with the original on page 3.

3. Alertness to parallelism pays off nicely, helping you see relationships more easily. As a further example, turn back to the article to look for four consecutive paragraphs where the author uses parallelism in the first few words. See if you can identify those paragraphs, entering the first two words in each paragraph in the spaces below:

A. _____   C. _____

B. _____   D. _____

Each paragraph begins with a question. In the first paragraph the answer is *no*. The parallel form suggests what about the answer to the questions in the next three paragraphs? Sharpen your awareness of parallel form. It helps.

NAME————————————————— DATE———————— READING RATE—————— W.P.M.

COMPREHENSION CHECK QUESTIONS

1. The author says his mind is like (1) an empty pail; (2) a butterfly net; (3) alphabet soup; (4) a steel sieve.   1. *4*

2. When he is introduced to someone, he (1) looks him in the eye; (2) smiles; (3) throws his chest out; (4) repeats the name of the person forcefully.   2. *1*

3. When he is buying a shirt, what figure sticks in his mind? (1) 36; (2) 25; (3) 18; (4) 9.   3. *1*

4. He refers to (1) the Jabberwocky; (2) Kubla Khan; (3) the Ancient Mariner; (4) Mandalay.   4. *3*

5. The telephone exchange mentioned was (1) Parkway; (2) Midway; (3) Ocean; (4) Federal.   5. *3*

Receptive Comprehension ————

6. This is primarily to (1) help us remember better; (2) illustrate the problems posed by a poor memory; (3) reveal the author's personal troubles in remembering; (4) poke fun at memory books.   6. *3*

7. The chief purpose is to (1) amuse; (2) clarify; (3) moralize; (4) convince.   7. *1*

8. The bit about Mr. Garden was intended to (1) illustrate the value of associations; (2) demonstrate the author's foggy memory; (3) ridicule the association technique; (4) explain how association works. 8. *2*

9. In style, this is best described as (1) humorous; (2) conversational; (3) witty; (4) farcical.   9. *4*

10. The idea is presented largely through (1) narrative bits; (2) details; (3) comparisons; (4) analysis of difficulties.   10. *1*

(10 off for each mistake)   *Reflective Comprehension* ————

TOTAL READING COMPREHENSION SCORE ————

VOCABULARY CHECK QUESTIONS

		without context I	with context II
1. *furtive*	(1) useless; (2) mad; (3) sharp; (4) rapid; (5) stealthy.	1. *5*	————
2. *well-feigned*	(1) well-timed; (2) friendly; (3) well-pretended; (4) tired; (5) well-fed.	2. *3*	————
3. *sporadic*	(1) occasional; (2) spontaneous; (3) playful; (4) sparkling; (5) germlike.	3. *1*	————
4. *verbatim*	(1) spoken; (2) word for word; (3) idiotic; (4) talkative; (5) part of speech.	4. *2*	————
5. *veritable*	(1) valuable; (2) vernacular; (3) skilled; (4) true; (5) springlike.	5. *4*	————

(10 off for each mistake)   *Word Comprehension* without *contextual help* (I) ————

Word Comprehension with *contextual help* (II) ————

TOTAL WORD COMPREHENSION SCORE ————

EXERCISES

1. Spotting the central idea: The good reader is one who is able to see past all the details and development to grasp the central or topic idea of a paragraph. Try this with some of the paragraphs in this selection, expressing the topic idea below in a word or phrase. Just turn back to the selection, find the paragraph in question, read it over rapidly, then summarize the topic idea briefly.

Example: the paragraph beginning, "Frankly, I've got . . . ," is chiefly about

his sievelike mind
_____

A. The paragraph beginning, "Maybe I don't . . . ," is chiefly about

_____

B. The paragraph beginning, "It's hard enough . . . ," is chiefly about

_____

C. The paragraph beginning, "I have the . . . ," is chiefly about

_____

D. The paragraph beginning, "I'm no good . . . ," is chiefly about

_____

E. The paragraph beginning, "It isn't that . . . ," is chiefly about

_____

2. Putting the association method to work in spelling: For example, if you are not certain whether it is *indispen*sable or *indispen*sible, just remember that an *able* man is indispens*able*. That associaton should help fix the right spelling in mind. And is it *attendence, attandance,* or *atendence?* If you are not sure, remember that a good time to start an evening of dancing is ten — *at-ten-dance.*

List below five words that you tend to misspell, then make up some association or mnemonic for each, to help you remember the correct form.

Word	Association or Mnemonic
1.	
2.	
3.	
4.	
5.	

3. Levels in the cognitive domain: The cognitive domain is the domain of intellect, of intellectual development. Ideally, comprehension check questions should touch on all levels of cognition in order to provide maximum stimulus for the reader's intellectual development. Only recently have levels of cognition been rather clearly delineated. Seven levels deserve particular attention.

(1) Memory (remembering what was expressly said)
(2) Translation (putting what was said into other words or form)
(3) Interpretation (noting unstated relationships)
(4) Application (applying a principle recognized)
(5) Analysis (breaking a subject down into its parts for examination)
(6) Synthesis (fusing parts into a whole)
(7) Evaluation (formulating a standard and using it to judge the worth of something)

Now how are you going to remember those seven levels? Just remember this sentence:

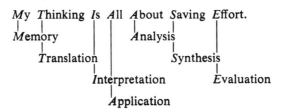

My Thinking Is All About Saving Effort.

174

NAME————————————————————— DATE——————————— READING RATE——————————— W.P.M.

COMPREHENSION CHECK QUESTIONS

1. If the author ran a creative writing school, he said, the main course would be on (1) observing; (2) writing sentences; (3) keeping a daily journal; (4) listening.   1. ————

2. What made Merrill's horse uncontrollable? (1) a new jacket; (2) some new chaps; (3) a new poncho; (4) some jangling spurs.   2. ————

3. In the brush one afternoon the author saw what? (1) some deer; (2) a moose; (3) some rabbits; (4) a fox.   3. ————

4. Specific reference was made to (1) Shelley; (2) John Keats; (3) Byron; (4) Charles Dickens.   4. ————

5. Mention was made of the excitement of looking at (1) the Milky Way; (2) a fiery comet; (3) the Southern Cross; (4) an eclipse of the sun.   5. ————

Receptive Comprehension ————

6. The main purpose of the article is to show (1) the importance of making discoveries; (2) how to make discoveries; (3) the role of chance in making discoveries; (4) the need for new things in stimulating discoveries.   6. ————

7. Mention of the rose-colored snow was primarily to show the (1) importance of art; (2) relationship between art and nature; (3) effect of sun on snow; (4) need to look closely at our surroundings.   7. ————

8. The story of Merrill's horse was to illustrate the importance of (1) observing; (2) habitual routine; (3) the sense of smell; (4) similarities between man and animal.   8. ————

9. The anecdote about the philosopher and his pipe was to show (1) how we learn from others; (2) the importance of practical knowledge; (3) the uselessness of formal education; (4) the need to learn something new.   9. ————

10. The writer's attitude toward life is best described as (1) questioning; (2) positive; (3) challenging; (4) objective.   10. ————

(10 off for each mistake)   *Reflective Comprehension* ————

TOTAL READING COMPREHENSION SCORE ————

VOCABULARY CHECK QUESTIONS

		without context I	*with context* II
1. *verification*	(1) confirmation; (2) greenness; (3) regulation; (4) change; (5) dizziness.	1. ————	————
2. *docile*	(1) devoted; (2) domestic; (3) foolish; (4) obedient; (5) uncertain.	2. ————	————
3. *immobile*	(1) movable; (2) motor-driven; (3) unmoving; (4) noisy; (5) crowded.	3. ————	————
4. *antipodes*	(1) islands; (2) opposites; (3) poisons; (4) stories; (5) similarities.	4. ————	————
5. *comatose*	(1) lively; (2) lethargic; (3) healthy; (4) humorous; (5) dignified.	5. ————	————

(10 off for each mistake)   *Word Comprehension* without *contextual help* (I) ————

Word Comprehension with *contextual help* (II) ————

TOTAL WORD COMPREHENSION SCORE ————

EXERCISES

Noting sequence of events: In arranging material, three sequential patterns are usually used — chronological, spatial, or expository. In practice, almost all writing is a combination of these patterns, in which case it is classified according to the predominant pattern.

An effective reader feels sufficiently at home with such patterns to follow them almost instinctively. This involves anticipating what comes next as well as making accurate deductions, both of which come under the heading *interpretation.*

To develop added effectiveness in dealing with the chronological pattern, try to rearrange the following jumbled sentences into a coherent paragraph, as found in the original article. To make the exercise more demanding, a sentence from an adjoining paragraph has been included. Through inference you are to determine which sentence does not belong with the others; then rearrange the remaining sentences into proper chronological order. If you have a well-developed sense for such a pattern through the unstated relationships present, you should come up with the exact sequence found in the original.

Here are the sentences you are to rearrange. Enter the numbers in the blanks following the sentences.

(1) One coldish morning a year or so later, Richard Merrill, his wife, and her visiting sister proposed riding horseback to a mountain several miles away from the ranch.

(2) The only way to mount him, Merrill said, was either to tie him up like a freshly caught mustang and blindfold him or take off the leggin's.

(3) Many years ago a ranchman named Richard Merrill told me about a one-man horse he had owned and ridden.

(4) He took them off.

(5) The horse would allow nobody but his owner to mount him.

(6) Before mounting him, Merrill pulled on his new leggin's.

(7) He was strong, intelligent, enduring.

(8) The next morning he saddled his horse for the purpose of riding out in a pasture.

(9) Upon being approached by the fresh, smelly leather, the horse became frantic, uncontrollable.

(10) The horse was docile as usual.

(11) One evening Merrill brought a new pair of leggin's (called chaps in some parts of the West) home from town.

Enter here the proper order of the sentences: Sen. 1 _____, Sen. 2 _____, Sen. 3 _____, Sen. 4 _____, Sen. 5 _____, Sen. 6 _____, Sen. 7 _____, Sen. 8 _____, Sen. 9 _____, Sen. 10 _____.

Enter the number of the sentence belonging in another paragraph: Sen. _____.

When you have rearranged the sentences, find one example of a sentence with a pronoun as one of the first two words, the pronoun antecedent being in the preceding sentence. This is a common device to connect sentences.

_____   _____
(antecedent)   (pronoun)

Repetition is still another device to make chronology more obvious. Find one example of a word toward the end of one sentence repeated toward the beginning of the next.

_____   _____
(word)   (word repeated)

A third way to make chronology apparent is by use of a word, such as "afterward," that indicates a time sequence. List three such words from the sentences you rearranged.

(1) _____

(2) _____

(3) _____

NAME———————————————————— DATE—————————— READING RATE——————————— W.P.M.

COMPREHENSION CHECK QUESTIONS

1. Franklin sometimes sat up all night reading (1) *Pilgrim's Progress;* (2) Plutarch's *Lives;* (3) *Paradise Lost;* (4) *Gulliver's Travels.*   1. ————

2. Darwin's father sent him to the University of Glasgow to study (1) medicine; (2) music; (3) for the ministry; (4) for government service.   2. ————

3. Mozart attempted to strike harmonious intervals on the clavier at the age of (1) three; (2) four; (3) five; (4) six.   3. ————

4. One of the following was *not* mentioned: (1) Napoleon; (2) Mozart; (3) Goethe; (4) Shakespeare.   4. ————

5. "Men of genius," when compared with ordinary men, are (1) quite different; (2) more imaginative; (3) essentially the same; (4) more temperamental.   5. ————

Receptive Comprehension ————

6. The purpose of this selection is to suggest the (1) importance of hard, sustained effort; (2) role of deep and ardent curiosity; (3) significance of flashes of inspiration; (4) special insights of men of genius.   6. ————

7. The author implies that Franklin learned to write chiefly because he (1) was urged to write; (2) read so widely; (3) practiced so hard; (4) wanted to so much.   7. ————

8. By implication good speaking probably results from (1) intelligent practice; (2) strong desire; (3) hard work; (4) wide reading.   8. ————

9. In selecting reading for an anthology, the author would probably favor most strongly getting the reactions of (1) the teachers using the book; (2) the students using the book; (3) well-known writers and critics; (4) literary figures and reviewers.   9. ————

10. The author implies that in selecting reading material the most important consideration would be (1) difficulty; (2) literary merit; (3) timeliness; (4) personal appeal.   10. ————

(10 off for each mistake)   *Reflective Comprehension* ————

TOTAL READING COMPREHENSION SCORE ————

VOCABULARY CHECK QUESTIONS

		without context I	*with context* II
1. *scant*	(1) limited; (2) rapid; (3) frightening; (4) colorful; (5) designed.	1. ————	————
2. *fervor*	(1) search; (2) intensity; (3) charm; (4) fete; (5) sickness.	2. ————	————
3. *verdant*	(1) colorful; (2) populated; (3) golden; (4) verbal; (5) green.	3. ————	————
4. *propensity*	(1) liking; (2) scheme; (3) propellent; (4) hatred; (5) expression.	4. ————	————
5. *sundry*	(1) bright; (2) various; (3) costly; (4) warm; (5) sullen.	5. ————	————

(10 off for each mistake)   *Word Comprehension* without *contextual help* (I) ————

Word Comprehension with *contextual help* (II) ————

TOTAL WORD COMPREHENSION SCORE ————

EXERCISES

Dealing with synthesis and analysis: The good reader is one who is familiar with a variety of ways of organizing material. In the same way, a good driver is one who is familiar with a wide variety of highway signs and markers and can travel with a minimum of error. Synthesis and analysis are patterns of organization that should be well known.

Suppose we look more closely at each. Synthesis is essentially a fitting together of parts or ideas to form a whole — a generalization or thesis. For example, when you add the prefix *in-* to the prefix *de-* to the root *pend* to the suffix *-ence,* you get the word *independence,* formed from a synthesis of language elements. Analysis is just the opposite. You start with a whole and break it down into its parts so as to understand it better. With *independence,* that would mean breaking the word down into the two prefixes, root, and suffix forming the word.

Now think back to the article on interest. Notice how the author turns to three careers, synthesizing from each the parts that can be put together to form a single generalization or thesis. Look back to see exactly what words he uses as road markers to call attention to a new thought division. Write the first six words of each paragraph that marks the beginning of his treatment of another individual. Use the following spaces.

(1) _____

(2) _____

(3) _____

To pull together the threefold pattern, the elements to be synthesized, the author uses what might be called a summary statement serving as a transition leading on to his generalization. The paragraph that serves this important function begins with what fourteen words? Enter them below.

_____

_____

What generalization comes from the synthesis of these three careers — the truth to be distilled as a matter of major concern? Enter the statement of that truth below.

_____

_____

_____

The remaining paragraphs lead on to a somewhat modified final truth, growing out of the additional development. State that final truth below, underlining the portion added to the initial generalization synthesized from the three careers.

_____

_____

_____

Examining your reading interests: Analyze your own reading interests below, listing two conclusions — one focused on a major strength, one on a major weakness.

A. _____

_____

B. _____

_____

NAME——————————————— DATE————————— READING RATE————————— W.P.M.

COMPREHENSION CHECK QUESTIONS

1. To kill the dragons Gawaine used a (1) sword; (2) lance; (3) battle-ax; (4) spear.   1. ————

2. When Gawaine is first told he is to kill dragons, he asks for (1) an enchanted cap; (2) a magic word; (3) more training; (4) some other job.   2. ————

3. After killing a dragon, Gawaine would always bring back (1) the claws; (2) a lock of hair; (3) a tooth; (4) the ears.   3. ————

4. Gawaine said he thought some of the dragons were (1) 50 feet long; (2) 100 feet long; (3) 200 feet long; (4) 500 feet long.   4. ————

5. The dragon that finally killed Gawaine was (1) a small one; (2) a fair-sized one; (3) a large one; (4) of unknown size.   5. ————

Receptive Comprehension ————

6. This story illustrates the importance of (1) training; (2) courage; (3) attitude; (4) magic.   6. ————

7. Gawaine's record of fifty killings was primarily attributable to (1) his skill; (2) his assurance; (3) his training; (4) none of those factors.   7. ————

8. You would infer that the Headmaster regarded Gawaine (1) highly; (2) with some aversion; (3) as likable but a mediocre student; (4) as a capable but lazy student.   8. ————

9. The humor of this article is best described as (1) mildly satiric; (2) rather obvious; (3) farcical; (4) stilted.   9. ————

10. You would infer from this that to read well one should be (1) well educated; (2) interested in books; (3) confident; (4) experienced.   10. ————

(10 off for each mistake)   *Reflective Comprehension* ————

TOTAL READING COMPREHENSION SCORE ————

VOCABULARY CHECK QUESTIONS

		without context I	*with context* II
1. *restive*	(1) subdued; (2) limited; (3) nervous; (4) respected; (5) happy.	1. ————	————
2. *versatile*	(1) upright; (2) dizzy; (3) visible; (4) competent; (5) vested.	2. ————	————
3. *impetuously*	(1) rudely; (2) furiously; (3) impassively; (4) imperfectly; (5) fairly.	3. ————	————
4. *indulgently*	(1) slowly; (2) ravishingly; (3) with lenience; (4) with a smile; (5) honestly.	4. ————	————
5. *debauch*	(1) outlet; (2) rubbish; (3) collapse; (4) dissipation; (5) evening.	5. ————	————

(10 off for each mistake)   *Word Comprehension* without *contextual help* (I) ————

Word Comprehension with *contextual help* (II) ————

TOTAL WORD COMPREHENSION SCORE ————

EXERCISES

Interpreting what you read: The difference between what is stated and what is unstated focuses on the difference between receptive questions — those among the first five — and reflective questions — those among the last five. To see that difference more clearly, take a typical question on "The Fifty-first Dragon." Find in that article the actual statement answering the following question:

"The dragon that finally killed Gawaine was (1) a small one; (2) a fair-sized one; (3) a large one; (4) of unknown size."

Enter the exact stated words from the article that answer the question:

_____

In answering such questions the reader must read and remember a stated fact.

Now take a typical question from among the last five, which demand interpretation. Here it is often a matter of drawing inferences or conclusions based on certain relevant evidence. To understand the problem, examine the article closely for evidence bearing on each of the four choices. Enter the exact words under the appropriate choice to see what evidence supports each possibility.

Here is the question. Space is given under each choice for entering relevant evidence.

"You would infer that the Headmaster regarded Gawaine (1) highly; (2) with some aversion; (3) as likable but a mediocre student; (4) as a capable but lazy student."

(1) highly _____

_____

(2) with some aversion _____

_____

(3) as likable but a mediocre student _____

_____

(4) as a capable but lazy student _____

_____

Try still another question from the last five. This time, imagine that you are arguing with someone, not only about which is the right answer but about why you think the other answers are wrong. List under each of the four choices the specific evidence you would use in making your point. Here is the question.

"Gawaine's record of fifty killings was primarily attributable to (1) his skill; (2) his assurance; (3) his training; (4) none of those factors."

(1) his skill _____

_____

(2) his assurance _____

_____

(3) his training _____

_____

(4) none of those factors _____

_____

NAME_____ DATE_____ READING RATE_____ W.P.M.

COMPREHENSION CHECK QUESTIONS

1. What animals were said to produce signs? (1) moose; (2) loons; (3) prairie dogs; (4) rabbits.   1. _____

2. At one point, man is pictured in some detail as a (1) cave dweller; (2) purely sign-using animal; (3) success-worshipping animal; (4) maker and user of tools.   2. _____

3. The author refers specifically to (1) stream of thought; (2) lack of thought control; (3) stream of consciousness; (4) mental diseases.   3. _____

4. The article discusses (1) sexual drives; (2) survival of the fittest; (3) proper management of learning; (4) dreaming.   4. _____

5. What is called a necessary and elementary process for man? (1) observation; (2) memorization; (3) articulation; (4) conception.   5. _____

Receptive Comprehension _____

6. This is mainly to explain (1) the difference between symbols and signs; (2) how man differs from other animals; (3) why man developed language; (4) the importance of symbolizing for man.   6. _____

7. According to this article, man apparently lives primarily for his (1) pleasures; (2) rights and property; (3) ideas; (4) social position.   7. _____

8. The most significant difference between sign and symbol is that between (1) a real and mental image; (2) nearness and distance of reference; (3) purposeful vs. random acts; (4) thinking vs. dreaming.   8. _____

9. The statement "I can make nothing of it," was used to call attention to our (1) instinctive behavior; (2) need to understand; (3) need for action; (4) learned behavior.   9. _____

10. You would infer that language resulted primarily from man's (1) biological need; (2) intelligence; (3) special talent for speech; (4) physical speech-making equipment.   10. _____

(10 off for each mistake)   *Reflective Comprehension* _____

TOTAL READING COMPREHENSION SCORE _____

VOCABULARY CHECK QUESTIONS

		without context I	*with context* II
1. *unequivocal*	(1) equal; (2) spaced; (3) musical; (4) questioning; (5) clear.	1. _____	_____
2. *imminence*	(1) fame; (2) height; (3) stature; (4) coming; (5) position.	2. _____	_____
3. *figment*	(1) net; (2) thread; (3) fabrication; (4) appetite; (5) diet.	3. _____	_____
4. *mongering*	(1) feeling; (2) resting; (3) dealing; (4) checking; (5) recording.	4. _____	_____
5. *fiat*	(1) fate; (2) purchase; (3) appearance; (4) fault; (5) decree.	5. _____	_____

(10 off for each mistake)   *Word Comprehension* without *contextual help* (I) _____

Word Comprehension with *contextual help* (II) _____

TOTAL WORD COMPREHENSION SCORE _____

EXERCISES

Getting the main ideas: If, in reading a paragraph or entire article or chapter, you get the main idea, you have what is needed to draw the best possible assumptions about the details used to develop that idea. To sharpen your awareness of such relationships between main idea and development, read the following paragraph. When you have finished, write what you think would be the most appropriate statement of the main idea — the topic sentence for the paragraph.

Here is the paragraph, with space provided for your topic sentence to be added. When you have finished, compare your written version with the original, noting any differences. There were only eight words in the original.

To them as well as to us sounds and smells and motions are signs of food, danger, the presence of other beings, or of rain or storm. Furthermore, some animals not only attend to signs but produce them for the benefit of others. Dogs bark at the door to be let in; rabbits thump to call each other; the cooing of doves and the growl of a wolf defending his kill are unequivocal signs of feelings and intentions to be reckoned with by other creatures.

For the next paragraph, reverse the procedure. Read the topic sentence, then check all those sentences after it that actually develop that topic idea. Sentences are included that develop still other ideas, so not all should be checked.

Here is the topic sentence:

Dreaming is apparently a basic function of human brains, for it is free and unexhausting like our metabolism, heartbeat, and breath.

Which of the following six sentences develops that topic idea? Check only those which do.

(1) Words, pictures, and memory images are symbols that may be combined and varied in a thousand ways.　———

(2) The symbolic character of dreams is fairly well established.　———

(3) If we bear in mind this all-important craving for expression we get a new picture of man's behavior; for from this trait spring his powers and his weaknesses.　———

(4) Symbol mongering, on this ineffectual, uncritical level, seems to be instinctive, the fulfillment of an elementary need rather than the purposeful exercise of a high and difficult talent.　———

(5) It is easier to dream than not to dream, as it is easier to breathe than to refrain from breathing.　———

(6) Language is the highest and most amazing achievement of the symbolistic human mind.　———

Now check back to the original to see how well developed your sense of main idea and development is.

Anticipating the next words: The good reader is alert enough so that when certain definite clues are present, he can actually skip the next words, so sure he is that he knows what they are. Take this sentence:

"It is easier to dream than not to dream, as it is easier to breathe ————————————————————————." Finish the sentence, then compare it with the original. Even if the wording is not exactly the same, the sense should be — which is the important thing for the reader.

NAME——————————————————— DATE————————— READING RATE——————— W.P.M.

COMPREHENSION CHECK QUESTIONS

1. The article mentions (1) astrology; (2) geometry; (3) metaphysics; (4) graphology.   1. ————

2. Appropriateness is a principle of language now (1) fully accepted by dictionaries; (2) not yet accepted by dictionaries; (3) just beginning to be accepted by them; (4) accepted in theory but not in practice.   2. ————

3. Usage is said to be divided into how many levels? (1) not given; (2) two; (3) three; (4) four.   3. ————

4. The author mentions (1) *The Reader's Digest;* (2) *Harper's;* (3) *The Atlantic Monthly;* (4) *Vogue.*   4. ————

5. The new emerging grammar is predicted to be more (1) dull; (2) difficult; (3) useful; (4) interesting.   5. ————

Receptive Comprehension ————

6. This is mainly about (1) whether the linguists will succeed; (2) the concept of difficulty levels; (3) the effects of the change on teaching English; (4) the relative nature of correctness.   6. ————

7. According to linguists, "Ain't you coming?" is (1) logically unacceptable English; (2) correct English; (3) incorrect English; (4) sometimes correct, sometimes not.   7. ————

8. The best statement about criteria of correctness is that they are (1) quite complex; (2) absolute; (3) nonexistent; (4) dependent upon dictionary authority.   8. ————

9. The concept of levels of usage is particularly useful in (1) avoiding prescriptive grammar; (2) teaching writing; (3) teaching descriptive grammar; (4) preparing a dictionary.   9. ————

10. We are asked to analyze a page of English so as to appreciate the (1) complexity of language; (2) failure of traditional grammar; (3) value of grammar as a discipline; (4) importance of well-established grammatical distinctions.   10. ————

(10 off for each mistake)   *Reflective Comprehension* ————

TOTAL READING COMPREHENSION SCORE ————

VOCABULARY CHECK QUESTIONS

		without context I	*with context* II
1. *criteria*	(1) complaints; (2) standards; (3) wrinkles; (4) credits; (5) keys.	1. ————	————
2. *strata*	(1) clouds; (2) streaks; (3) levels; (4) wanderers; (5) strains.	2. ————	————
3. *nuances*	(1) shades; (2) strings; (3) annoyances; (4) numbers; (5) proofs.	3. ————	————
4. *fluently*	(1) irregularly; (2) correctly; (3) highly; (4) smoothly; (5) cleverly.	4. ————	————
5. *tangible*	(1) confused; (2) hopeful; (3) breakable; (4) false; (5) definite.	5. ————	————

(10 off for each mistake)   *Word Comprehension* without *contextual help* (I) ————

Word Comprehension with *contextual help* (II) ————

TOTAL WORD COMPREHENSION SCORE ————

EXERCISES

Using the topic sentence survey: The average person would not think of making an extended auto trip without first consulting some road maps. On the other hand, few individuals think of surveying a book or chapter before reading it. Yet traveling through print in a direct, meaningful way is usually much more difficult than traveling through countryside. If maps are useful to drivers, surveys are even more useful to readers.

Since that is so, just how do you go about surveying a chapter, article, or book? The best survey should bring you a maximum of information in a minimum of time. Furthermore, it should bring you the most important information. With these things in mind, suppose we try to survey this informative article, using the topic sentence survey type.

Here are the two essential steps:

1. Read the title, getting yourself properly oriented to its implications.
2. Read the first sentence of each paragraph in the article. Since, in expository writing, that is usually the topic sentence, you should be getting most of the ideas of key importance.

Now suppose we see what a survey of this article would bring us, either as a preliminary to reading or as a review of reading:

THE FUTURE OF GRAMMAR

The last few decades have witnessed an amiable but spirited battle between linguistic scientists and defenders of traditional ways of teaching English. . . . .

Our purpose here is not to discuss when or whether the transition will take place but rather to suggest what its effects on English teaching are likely to be.

Some effects there have been already, and not all of them are good. . . . .

Logic has nothing to do with it. . . . .

All this is old stuff. . . . .

One thing that the idea of relativity of correctness does *not* mean is that it doesn't matter how we talk or write. . . . .

Certainly it matters how you say a thing. . . . .

This is what the growing heaps of linguistic information, like the Linguistic Atlas and the dialect dictionaries, are showing ever more clearly. . . . .

So far we have tried to meet this difficulty with the concept of "levels of usage," dividing usage into several strata, usually three — standard, colloquial, vulgate. . . . .

The alternative is to abandon the prescriptive idea altogether, to give up the notion of bringing the student to a fore-determined pattern of usage, and to seek other results entirely. . . . .

Experiments in this direction are already underway in many schools throughout the country. . . . .

Along with this must go a quiet revolution in our techniques for describing language. . . . .

But probably the most discouraging thing about traditional grammar is the set of tautologies in which it wanders: "a noun is a name," "a verb is an action," "an interrogative sentence is a sentence which asks a question." . . . .

Somebody will have to do something about this, and many people are already trying — seeking to look at the language and see what's there and find ways of describing it. . . . .

As you can see, this look at a tenth part of the original article does bring you into contact with most of the major points developed and discussed, giving you an ideal background for rereading the article with much more intelligence.

It also suggests a potential weakness. If the first sentence is *not* the topic sentence, your survey is to that degree somewhat short of bringing you all the important ideas. Note how often the topic sentence comes first.

Check further by turning to the article to see which sentence is the topic sentence. Enter the number below; then re-examine all paragraphs to see if there is some typical clue in the first sentence that suggests the topic sentence is still to come. Enter a zero if no topic sentence is found.

Paragraph   Number of topic sentence

Paragraph #1: Topic sentence is #_____   Paragraph #8: Topic sentence is #_____

Paragraph #2: Topic sentence is #_____   Paragraph #9: Topic sentence is #_____

Paragraph #3: Topic sentence is #_____   Paragraph #10: Topic sentence is #_____

Paragraph #4: Topic sentence is #_____   Paragraph #11: Topic sentence is #_____

Paragraph #5: Topic sentence is #_____   Paragraph #12: Topic sentence is #_____

Paragraph #6: Topic sentence is #_____   Paragraph #13: Topic sentence is #_____

Paragraph #7: Topic sentence is #_____   Paragraph #14: Topic sentence is #_____

Compare the topic sentence survey type with the short survey type on page 188.

NAME_____ DATE_____ READING RATE_____ W.P.M.

COMPREHENSION CHECK QUESTIONS

1. When Ali started home after his University experience, he came on (1) a jackass; (2) foot; (3) a spirited Arabian; (4) a camel.

    1. _____

2. How many years did Ali study at the University of El-Azhar? (1) two; (2) four; (3) six; (4) eight.

    2. _____

3. At his first stop in the village, Ali found the Khatib preaching about the (1) prophetic powers of Mohammed; (2) miraculous deeds of Mohammed; (3) nature of God as revealed by Mohammed; (4) punishment of sinners and unbelievers as described by Mohammed.

    3. _____

4. What indignity was *not* suffered by Ali at the hands of the villagers? (1) stoning; (2) imprisonment; (3) beating; (4) destruction of his diploma.

    4. _____

5. When Ali came to the village of the Khatib a second time, (1) he was dressed in silks and satins; (2) he was dressed in the coarse raiment of a scholar; (3) he was dressed in the garb of a foreigner; (4) no mention was made of his dress.

    5. _____

Receptive Comprehension _____

6. The purpose of this selection is to show the need for (1) wordly wisdom; (2) book learning; (3) tact and cleverness; (4) a well-rounded development.

    6. _____

7. The selection was intended primarily to (1) entertain; (2) persuade; (3) describe; (4) explain.

    7. _____

8. When Ali and the Khatib first met, (1) Ali was apparently in the right in their argument; (2) the Khatib was apparently in the right; (3) both were mistaken; (4) both were equally well informed about Mohammed.

    8. _____

9. You would infer from Ali's first experience with the Khatib that in an argument the deciding factor is most likely to be (1) the truth; (2) tact; (3) authority; (4) personality.

    9. _____

10. You would judge from this that the best way of convincing someone is to (1) cite direct evidence; (2) contradict the opposite viewpoint; (3) appeal to authority; (4) present your case indirectly without seeming to disagree.

    10. _____

(10 off for each mistake)

Reflective Comprehension _____

TOTAL READING COMPREHENSION SCORE _____

VOCABULARY CHECK QUESTIONS

		without context I	*with context* II
1. *aphorisms*	(1) insects; (2) drugs; (3) peaks; (4) visitors; (5) sayings.	1. _____	_____
2. *raiment*	(1) beams; (2) surface; (3) curve; (4) parapet; (5) garments.	2. _____	_____
3. *credulous*	(1) easily convinced; (2) critical; (3) shy; (4) apt; (5) worthy of praise.	3. _____	_____
4. *boon*	(1) log; (2) sound; (3) structure; (4) favor; (5) fate.	4. _____	_____
5. *meticulously*	(1) hurriedly; (2) decisively; (3) very carefully; (4) actually; (5) quite gayly.		

(10 off for each mistake)

Word Comprehension without *contextual help* (I) _____

Word Comprehension with *contextual help* (II) _____

TOTAL WORD COMPREHENSION SCORE _____

EXERCISES

Reading for imagery: One of the important differences between reading exposition and narration is in savoring the mental pictures typical of narration. These demand a special response by the reader to the sense impressions provided — a vicarious enjoyment of things seen, heard, tasted, felt, or smelled.

As a means of sharpening your awareness of such sense impressions, make a list of from three to ten specific sensory images in each of the following five categories. For example, "black coffee" is primarily a sight impression, but if you are reading imaginatively it should also be listed under *taste* or *smell*.

Sights	Tastes	Smells	Feels	Sounds

Look back over each of the quoted word or phrases listed; then concentrate your full attention on each, imagining as vividly as possible what is described. How well did you imagine the taste of "black coffee"? Did you think of it as deliciously hot, pleasantly warm as it ran down your throat? Did you imagine its aroma? Did you visualize the steam slowly rising from the cup? In short, did you imaginatively bring together the whole range of sensory impressions found in "black coffee"?

Developing an idea: Actually, as a reader, when you get the main idea, you strip away the author's development of a thesis or point to get the kernel. To understand the process better, look at it from the writer's point of view. Starting with a main idea, the writer then goes on to develop it fully.

See how this works with a single sentence. Contrast the sentence "Ali then took a hair from the Khatib's beard" with the original passage describing that act. How does an author develop parts of a narrative and bring them to life?

Getting the main idea: This is a story told to illustrate a general principle. Write the thesis or central idea developed, using the author's phrasing. To be truly educated, one should

NAME————————————————————— DATE——————————— READING RATE——————————— W.P.M.

COMPREHENSION CHECK QUESTIONS

1. This selection mentions the Institute for Propaganda (1) Analysis; (2) Evaluation; (3) Security; (4) Appraisal.   1. ————

2. How many techniques were discussed? (1) eight; (2) seven; (3) six; (4) five.   2. ————

3. Specific mention was made of a new-model (1) color TV set; (2) car; (3) refrigerator; (4) speed boat.   3. ————

4. What did one salesman do? (1) hand out free pens; (2) wear unpressed pants; (3) use bad grammar; (4) do some back slapping.   4. ————

5. Still other persuasion techniques were said to be found in what book? (1) *Persuasion Tips;* (2) *General Speech;* (3) *Winning Your Listeners;* (4) *Basic Speech Techniques.*   5. ————

Receptive Comprehension ————

6. The main idea is to help us (1) identify propaganda; (2) prepare propaganda; (3) fight propaganda; (4) understand propaganda.   6. ————

7. This selection seems to be addressed primarily to the (1) speaker; (2) salesman; (3) consumer; (4) listener.   7. ————

8. To call someone "God-fearing" would be an example of (1) name calling; (2) card stacking; (3) transfer; (4) glittering generalities.   8. ————

9. The cigarette sales anecdote was to illustrate what technique? (1) testimonial; (2) band wagon; (3) transfer; (4) card stacking.   9. ————

10. The chief purpose was to (1) entertain; (2) explain; (3) persuade; (4) convince.   10. ————

(10 off for each mistake)   *Reflective Comprehension* ————

TOTAL READING COMPREHENSION SCORE ————

VOCABULARY CHECK QUESTIONS

		without context I	*with context* II
1. *devastatingly*	(1) hopefully; (2) helplessly; (3) rightly; (4) destructively; (5) largely.	1. ————	————
2. *illuminate*	(1) solidify; (2) suggest; (3) leave out; (4) clarify; (5) stretch.	2. ————	————
3. *proposition*	(1) part of speech; (2) advantage; (3) sermon; (4) application; (5) proposal.	3. ————	————
4. *sway*	(1) influence; (2) disturb; (3) express; (4) facilitate; (5) repeat.	4. ————	————
5. *adverse*	(1) empty; (2) unfavorable; (3) additional; (4) strong; (5) inconclusive.	5. ————	————

(10 off for each mistake)   *Word Comprehension* without *contextual help* (I) ————

Word Comprehension with *contextual help* (II) ————

TOTAL WORD COMPREHENSION SCORE ————

EXERCISES

Using the short survey: There are several different ways to survey just as there are different ways to read. One survey type is based on the likelihood that topic sentences usually come first. The short survey is based on the idea that the first paragraph and last paragraph are most revealing about what goes in between. The first paragraph normally points ahead so that the reader is aware of what is coming. The last paragraph either summarizes what has been said, points up its significance, or extends the coverage somewhat. Those points of major importance in between are often highlighted by headings in italics or heavier type.

With these things in mind, note the essential steps in making a short survey to get maximum information in minimum time.

1. Read the title, getting yourself properly oriented to its implications.
2. Read the first paragraph in entirety and not just the first sentence.
3. Read any headings or italicized portions.
4. Read the last paragraph in its entirety.

See what kind of overview you would get by using this type of survey on Selection 9, as follows:

DETECTING PROPAGANDA

Most techniques of propaganda have been well defined by the Institute for Propaganda Analysis. The institute calls them "propaganda techniques," perhaps somewhat inaccurately according to the dictionary definition of the word "propaganda." However, the techniques are used by persuasive talkers, both in the trained-speaker category and in the conversational, person-to-person category. The institute has identified seven techniques and given them titles:

1. Name calling.
2. Glittering generalities.
3. Transfer.
4. Testimonial.
5. Plain folks.
6. Card stacking.
7. Band wagon.

In addition to these seven devices there are, of course, other techniques used in oral persuasion. In their book, *General Speech,* A. Craig Baird and Franklin H. Knower point out a number of other things that persuasive talkers use or play upon to their advantage: "flattery; appeals to fear, hate, anger, frustration or discontent growing out of lack of opportunity or misfortune; the creation of devils on which to place blame; repetition and more repetition; wishful thinking, rationalization, rumor, distrust; identification with the great, the beautiful and the good; prophecies and positive suggestion."

Compare the short survey with the topic sentence survey introduced on page 184. They make ideal pre-reading techniques or review aids.

NAME————————————————— DATE————————— READING RATE————————— W.P.M.

COMPREHENSION CHECK QUESTIONS

1. The author refers to (1) Gray's "Elegy in a Country Churchyard"; (2) Shakespeare's *Julius Caesar;* (3) Coleridge's *Ancient Mariner;* (4) Pope's *Essay on Man.*   1. ————

2. The good reader is likened to a (1) miner; (2) musician; (3) prospector; (4) chemist.   2. ————

3. Who was spoken of as a most charming writer of informal essays? (1) Garrick; (2) Lamb; (3) Goldsmith; (4) Dr. Johnson.   3. ————

4. About what percent of his time is a college freshman said to spend in talking? (1) 25; (2) 40; (3) 60; (4) no percentage figures given.   4. ————

5. Words are specifically mentioned as they relate to the (1) engineer; (2) historian; (3) physicist; (4) professional man.   5. ————

Receptive Comprehension ————

6. The main idea of this selection was to (1) prove that we think with words; (2) show the value of the dictionary; (3) persuade the reader to study words; (4) indicate the importance of vocabulary in getting grades.   6. ————

7. How is the material primarily arranged? (1) in a chronological order; (2) around a question and answer pattern; (3) from most to least importance; (4) by analysis.   7. ————

8. He discussed radio and television largely to show their (1) stimulating effect on vocabulary growth; (2) help in establishing proper pronunciation; (3) widespread use; (4) detrimental effect on word development.   8. ————

9. Of the four communication skills, which does the author seem to consider most difficult to develop? (1) writing; (2) listening; (3) spelling; (4) reading.   9. ————

10. The words *rigamorole, twelth, maintainance,* and *modren* were mentioned to call attention to problems of (1) meaning; (2) derivation; (3) pronunciation; (4) spelling.   10. ————

(10 off for each mistake)   *Reflective Comprehension* ————

TOTAL READING COMPREHENSION SCORE ————

VOCABULARY CHECK QUESTIONS

		without context I	*with context* II
1. *commensurate*	(1) mental; (2) certain; (3) corresponding; (4) valuable; (5) vocal.	1. ————	————
2. *lexicon*	(1) study guide; (2) harp; (3) dictionary; (4) bounty; (5) textbook.	2. ————	————
3. *jaded*	(1) spiritless; (2) oriental; (3) carved; (4) eroded; (5) enameled.	3. ————	————
4. *impeccable*	(1) careless; (2) imprecise; (3) sharp; (4) engraved; (5) faultless.	4. ————	————
5. *onus*	(1) honor; (2) reason; (3) blame; (4) purpose; (5) ornament.	5. ————	————

(10 off for each mistake)   *Word Comprehension* without *contextual help* (I) ————

Word Comprehension with *contextual help*   (II) ————

TOTAL WORD COMPREHENSION SCORE ————

189

EXERCISES

Seeing words as road signs: A good reader is one who has developed a keen awareness of specific words that point direction and content. For example, the words *to illustrate* let the reader know that a general statement has been made and is about to be developed by use of an illustration.

Think in terms of the article "Why Word Study Is Necessary," quoting specific portions of that article to answer the questions that follow.

1. Why does the author say that word study is necessary?

Because_____

_____

_____

_____

2. Subheadings are like major highway signs, marking major changes in direction or content. List the subheadings below in the order found:

    1. _____

    2. _____

    3. _____

    4. _____

    5. _____

    6. _____

3. One pattern used in surveying an article involves reading *only* the first and last paragraphs for an overview. Often the first paragraph will indicate the plan and ordering of the material. Does the first paragraph of this selection prepare you for the six main divisions that follow? Quote below the specific words functioning in that way:

4. Often the last paragraph provides a summary of the material covered along with a review of the sequence of presentation. Is this true of the last paragraph in this selection? Quote the specific words functioning in that way:

5. Suppose the subheadings in this article were all eliminated. When and how would you know that a new division was being introduced? For example, if the subheading *Vocabulary and Reading* were eliminated, you would find the word *reading* to be the thirteenth word in the paragraph dealing with that main division. Enter evidence below for each of the six subheadings, as done for the first one.

    (1) "Probably the most rewarding of all . . . is reading. . . ."

    (2) _____

    (3) _____

    (4) _____

    (5) _____

    (6) _____

NAME————————————————— DATE————————— READING RATE————————— W.P.M.

COMPREHENSION CHECK QUESTIONS

1. According to the Duke of Wellington, habit is what? (1) stronger than nature; (2) ten times nature; (3) nature personified; (4) our hidden nature.   1. ————

2. The critical age period for forming intellectual habits was said to be (1) between twenty and thirty; (2) below twenty; (3) the first ten years; (4) the first six years.   2. ————

3. The writer quotes (1) Goethe; (2) Shakespeare; (3) the Bible; (4) Alexander Pope.   3. ————

4. The author says there is no more contemptible type of character than the (1) agitator; (2) drifter; (3) dreamer; (4) exploiter.   4. ————

5. The article refers specifically to (1) Robinson Crusoe; (2) Rip Van Winkle; (3) Shylock; (4) Samson.   5. ————

Receptive Comprehension ————

6. The primary purpose of this selection is to (1) suggest the key role of habit in education; (2) prove that habit is our best friend; (3) explain the difficulties of habit formation; (4) contrast habit with thought.   6. ————

7. The story about the discharged veteran and the practical joker was to show (1) the thoroughness of military training; (2) how absent-minded the veteran was; (3) our natural tendency to obey; (4) the strength of habit.   7. ————

8. Apparently the best way to break the smoking habit would be to (1) stop abruptly; (2) taper off gradually; (3) first cut down to only two cigarettes a day; (4) stay away from other smokers.   8. ————

9. You would conclude that a tendency to act comes primarily from (1) motivation; (2) reasoning; (3) willing; (4) doing.   9. ————

10. You would infer that the author would particularly favor (1) meeting things as they come; (2) avoiding too rigid a schedule; (3) relaxing during the weekends; (4) following a weekly schedule.   10. ————

(10 off for each mistake)   *Reflective Comprehension* ————

TOTAL READING COMPREHENSION SCORE ————

VOCABULARY CHECK QUESTIONS

		without context I	*with context* II
1. *ordinance*	(1) statement; (2) reputation; (3) movement; (4) established custom; (5) new publication. 1.	————	————
2. *inanition*	(1) ridicule; (2) anger; (3) worry; (4) growth; (5) exhaustion. 2.	————	————
3. *squalid*	(1) nasty; (2) flat; (3) worn; (4) sober; (5) exhaustion. 3.	————	————
4. *concomitants*	(1) references; (2) rules; (3) accompaniments; (4) contradictions; (5) plots. 4.	————	————
5. *gratuitous*	(1) useful; (2) meaningful; (3) casual; (4) unnecessary; (5) grateful. 5.	————	————

(10 off for each mistake)   *Word Comprehension* without *contextual help* (I) ————

Word Comprehension with *contextual help* (II) ————

TOTAL WORD COMPREHENSION SCORE ————

EXERCISES

Reading paragraphs: Each paragraph should have a single central idea. If it is expressed in a sentence, the sentence is called a topic sentence and may come at the beginning, middle, or end of the paragraph. But at times the main idea is not expressed — only implied.

Analyze the specified paragraphs from the article on habit. If the paragraph contains a topic sentence, write it in the space provided below. If the main idea is implied, try to compose an appropriate topic sentence for the paragraph, writing it in the space provided below.

For example, reread the first paragraph in the article. Check the appropriate choice.

Is the topic idea expressed   _____

                     or implied?   _____

If the topic idea is expressed, enter the exact words that express it:

If the topic idea is implied, express it in a sentence that you devise and write here:

It seems to be expressed in the phrase — "habit is ten times nature." The words, "degree to which this is true" lead on to the example of the soldier who, by years of discipline and the ingraining of habit, is fashioned "completely over again."

Now take the next paragraph and analyze it in similar fashion.

Paragraph 2:

Is the topic idea expressed   _____

                     or implied?   _____

If the topic idea is expressed, enter the exact words that express it:

If the topic idea is implied, express it in a sentence that you devise and write here:

Paragraph 3:

Is the topic idea expressed   _____

                     or implied?   _____

Notice how much of the paragraph deals with "domestic beasts." How much deals with "men"? How much with wild animals?

If the topic idea is expressed, enter the exact words that express it:

If the topic idea is implied, express it in a sentence that you devise and write here:

Paragraph 4:

Is the topic idea expressed   _____

                     or implied?   _____

What is the function of the single word *it*, which is used to begin the six sentences immediately following the first sentence? Does this help you in your analysis?

If the topic idea is expressed, enter the exact words that express it:

If the topic idea is implied, express it in a sentence that you devise and write here:

NAME————————————————— DATE——————— READING RATE————————— W.P.M.

COMPREHENSION CHECK QUESTIONS

1. William James estimated that we function at less than what percent of our capacity? (1) 5; (2) 10; (3) 20; (4) 25.   1. ————

2. In an emergency a middle-aged California woman (1) swam across a river; (2) climbed a cliff; (3) lifted a car; (4) ran more than three miles.   2. ————

3. The Japanese Suzuki taught children between what ages to play violin concertos? (1) between four and six; (2) between five and seven; (3) between six and eight; (4) no specific age given.   3. ————

4. Specific mention was made of (1) Einstein; (2) Will Rogers; (3) Beethoven; (4) Grandma Moses.   4. ————

5. Research on human potential has been conducted at the University of (1) Denver; (2) Utah; (3) Chicago; (4) Minnesota.   5. ————

Receptive Comprehension ————

6. This is mainly focused on what aspect of human potential? (1) the need to use it; (2) its relationship to creativity; (3) the need to understand it; (4) its relationship to the media.   6. ————

7. Quotes from such well-known scientists as Margaret Mead were used to show what about human potential? (1) the strong current interest; (2) the lack of agreement; (3) the range of available research; the small amount being tapped.   7. ————

8. The discussion of man's sense of smell was intended primarily to show (1) how to develop it; (2) the effect of pollution on it; (3) the typical individual differences in it; (4) the need to develop it.   8. ————

9. The attitude of the writer toward hypnosis is best characterized as (1) suspicious; (2) accepting; (3) unscientific; (4) doubtful.   9. ————

10. The writer looks on the mass media (1) favorably; (2) critically; (3) with mixed feelings; (4) as essential to modern life.   10. ————

(10 off for each mistake)   *Reflective Comprehension* ————

TOTAL READING COMPREHENSION SCORE ————

VOCABULARY CHECK QUESTIONS

			without context I	with context II
1. *succumb*	(1) help; (2) prosper; (3) search; (4) sue; (5) yield.	1.	————	————
2. *latent*	(1) tardy; (2) peaceful; (3) inactive; (4) sideways; (5) favorable.	2.	————	————
3. *inimical*	(1) unfriendly; (2) exceptional; (3) beginning; (4) unjust; (5) wrong.	3.	————	————
4. *estrangement*	(1) estimate; (2) alienation; (3) fragrance; (4) influence; (5) different.	4.	————	————
5. *discrete*	(1) silent; (2) unhappy; (3) safe; (4) separate; (5) visible.	5.	————	————

(10 off for each mistake)   *Word Comprehension* without *contextual help* (I) ————

Word Comprehension with *contextual help* (II) ————

TOTAL WORD COMPREHENSION SCORE ————

EXERCISES

Noting structure and meaning: A writer attempts to organize his material so as to express his thesis or central idea as effectively as possible. The reader has the reverse problem. He attempts to discover the plan of organization so as to determine with accuracy the central idea expressed. Suppose we examine rather closely this article on human potentiality within this framework of reference.

Sometimes it is useful to look at an article from a basic plan of organization, as indicated in the divisions that follow. After each division put the number of the paragraphs you would assign to each category. Number the twenty-one paragraphs in the article and use that numbering in the following exercises.

Basic plan

Introduction: ————————————————————— (enter paragraph numbers)

Body: ————————————————————— (enter paragraph numbers)

Conclusion: ————————————————————— (enter paragraph numbers)

Check more closely to see if there are any main divisions in the body of the article. If so, how many would you list?

If you were to group together paragraphs 3 through 13 and paragraphs 14 through 19, what would you use as headings to focus on the major emphasis in each group? Enter your headings below.

Heading to be used after paragraph 2:

Heading to be used after paragraph 13:

Paragraph 3 refers to "indicators." How many different indicators are discussed? Check and then list them.

List of indicators

Does paragraph 14 discuss an indicator, or does it turn to another major division? What single word expresses the focus of the paragraph?

To what words would you point to prove that paragraph 13 is a continuation of a point or division that goes back several paragraphs?

Notice the very first word in the title. List below at least ten words in the article specifically emphasizing further that key portion of the main idea being developed.

1. ———————————————— 6. ————————————————

2. ———————————————— 7. ————————————————

3. ———————————————— 8. ————————————————

4. ———————————————— 9. ————————————————

5. ———————————————— 10. ————————————————

Repetition is one way to make certain a main idea is coming through.

NAME———————————————— DATE———————— READING RATE———————— W.P.M.

COMPREHENSION CHECK QUESTIONS

1. Pfungst was spoken of as a (1) linguistic scientist; (2) psychologist; (3) horse trainer; (4) writer.   1. ————

2. The selection specifically refers to television (1) talent contests; (2) interviews; (3) panel discussions; (4) word games.   2. ————

3. Filmed sequences showed that trained experimenters (1) treated both sexes alike; (2) varied question wording depending on sex of subject; (3) sat closer to subjects of the opposite sex; (4) took longer with subjects of the opposite sex.   3. ————

4. One experiment involved training rats (1) to trip a lever for food; (2) to learn a simple sequence of two actions; (3) to push a button to avoid a shock; (4) to run a maze.   4. ————

5. Specific mention was made of (1) the University of California; (2) Princeton; (3) Harvard University; (4) San Diego State College.   5. ————

Receptive Comprehension ————

6. This is mainly about (1) bias in interviewing; (2) animal intelligence; (3) nonverbal communication; (4) development of I.Q.   6. ————

7. In the title "In Other Words," the word *words* is used in what sense? (1) literal; (2) unimaginative; (3) figurative; (4) limited.   7. ————

8. The Clever Hans illustration was used to show (1) how observant horses are; (2) how important body language is; (3) how uniformly people act; (4) how easily the horse's behavior should be explained.   8. ————

9. This selection discusses behavior that is primarily (1) obvious; (2) unsophisticated; (3) unconscious; (4) mechanical.   9. ————

10. From this selection you would infer that it is most important that (1) others think that you can succeed; (2) you think you can succeed; (3) tests show that you can succeed; (4) your initial efforts show that you can succeed.   10. ————

(10 off for each mistake)   *Reflective Comprehension* ————

TOTAL READING COMPREHENSION SCORE ————

VOCABULARY CHECK QUESTIONS

		without context I	with context II
1. *uncanny*	(1) free; (2) common; (3) serious; (4) wise; (5) limited.	1. ————	————
2. *imperceptible*	(1) undesirable; (2) unnoticeable; (3) imperfect; (4) unexpected; (5) self-conscious.	2. ————	————
3. *inadvertently*	(1) unintentionally; (2) helpfully; (3) daringly; (4) admittedly; (5) foolishly.	3. ————	————
4. *elicit*	(1) glide over; (2) draw out; (3) raise; (4) trap; (5) steal.	4. ————	————
5. *blatantly*	(1) glaringly; (2) frequently; (3) noisily; (4) soundly; (5) criminally.	5. ————	————

(10 off for each mistake)   *Word Comprehension* without *contextual help* (I) ————

Word Comprehension with *contextual help* (II) ————

TOTAL WORD COMPREHENSION SCORE ————

EXERCISES

1. Developing skill in interpretation: Interpretation is one of the important cognitive levels, focusing on how effectively you deal with *unstated relationships*. As an alert reader you will want to develop maximum skill in anticipating what will either be stated or implied.

Take this sentence from another article on nonverbal communication: "Anyone who owns a cat, a dog, or a baby is well aware that certain meanings can be clearly expressed without the use of words." After such a generalization, what would you anticipate next? Can you make a supposition?

The next sentence actually begins: "The cat sits up politely for a morsel of turkey, the _____?" What specific word do you anticipate next? Hopefully, as you looked back at the series, "a cat, a dog, or a baby," you were led to anticipate the word *dog.* If you did, congratulate yourself. You anticipated well. The next word is *dog.*

Suppose we go a step further. Which of the following choices would best fit your anticipation? The dog (1) sleeps on the floor; (2) sniffs the air; (3) scratches on the door. If you selected the third choice, you are again anticipating well, for that was the phrase used.

For further practice, see if you can supply the missing words exactly in the following passage. Every fifth word of the original is omitted. By anticipating and reasoning, fill in all the blanks. Then check back to the original to see how accurate you were. A score of 15 out of 17 exactly right would be good.

Early in this century, _____ horse named Hans amazed _____ people of Berlin by _____ extraordinary ability to perform _____ calculations in mathematics. After _____ problem was written on _____ blackboard placed in front _____ him, he promptly counted _____ the answer by tapping _____ low numbers with his _____ forefoot and multiples of _____ with his left. Trickery _____ ruled out because Hans' _____, unlike owners of other _____ animals, did not profit _____ — and Hans even performed _____ feats whether or not _____ owner was present.

2. Think over the day. What examples of nonverbal communication do you remember? List some examples below:

3. How would you communicate nonverbally the following ideas?

A. I'm tired

B. I'm sleepy

C. I'm thirsty

D. I'm a friend

NAME———————————————— DATE———————— READING RATE———————— W.P.M.

COMPREHENSION CHECK QUESTIONS

1. The mass media habit was specifically likened to (1) a tonic; (2) a security blanket; (3) a sleeping pill; (4) an addiction.

    1. ————

2. The author refers to the portable (1) radio; (2) TV set; (3) record player; (4) cassette player.

    2. ————

3. What program is mentioned by name? (1) I Love Lucy; (2) Sesame Street; (3) The F.B.I.; (4) Maude.

    3. ————

4. As a sedative for children, the article mentions (1) warm milk; (2) paregoric; (3) poppy juice; (4) a pacifier.

    4. ————

5. The author quotes from the writings of (1) Freud; (2) Bacon; (3) Thoreau; (4) McLuhan.

    Receptive Comprehension ————

6. This is mainly about (1) suggestions for measuring happiness; (2) the effects of the mass media; (3) evaluating life quality; (4) the difference between present and past cultures.

    6. ————

7. The author's attitude toward the mass media is best described by what word? (1) critical; (2) objective; (3) hopeful; (4) beneficial.

    7. ————

8. In his discussion of values, what seemed to be rated as most important? (1) our privacy; (2) our experience; (3) our security; (4) our intelligence.

    8. ————

9. The purpose of discussing soap operas and comic strips was to show (1) how strongly they appeal; (2) how they confuse actuality with fiction; (3) how they give people an escape from reality; (4) how they interfere with the experiencing of life.

    9. ————

10. Violence and delinquency were blamed primarily on (1) human nature; (2) television and comic books; (3) peer influence; (4) lack of parental guidance.

    10. ————

(10 off for each mistake)   *Reflective Comprehension* ————

TOTAL READING COMPREHENSION SCORE ————

VOCABULARY CHECK QUESTIONS

		without context I	*with context* II
1. *diffuse*	(1) satisfied; (2) concentrated; (3) infrequent; (4) shy; (5) widespread.	1. ————	————
2. *cliché*	(1) sudden noise; (2) hiss; (3) order; (4) common expression; (5) argument.	2. ————	————
3. *motility*	(1) intention; (2) liveliness; (3) saying; (4) terrain; (5) group.	3. ————	————
4. *disparate*	(1) unlike; (2) important; (3) healthy; (4) vanishing; (5) prompt.	4. ————	————
5. *ineluctable*	(1) irregular; (2) attractive; (3) tasty; (4) inevitable; (5) chosen.	5. ————	————

(10 off for each mistake)   *Word Comprehension* without *contextual help* (I) ————

Word Comprehension with *contextual help*   (II) ————

TOTAL WORD COMPREHENSION SCORE ————

EXERCISES

Noting transitional and connective devices: The efficient reader is alert to any words or phrases that let him follow with increased ease the path set by the writer. When a skilled reader reads, "To go back now to our general maxims. . . ," he knows he should look on the preceding development as somewhat of a digression from the main outline and the following paragraph as a return to another main division. Other words suggest cause, result, comparison, repetition, and the like, used in developing the subject. Enhance your alertness by classifying the following words and phrases taken from this selection, using the following divisions:

1. Addition	3. Repetition	6. Emphasis
2. Example	4. Comparison	7. Cause-effect
	5. Contrast	

(*Example:* "furthermore" would be classed as #1 — Addition)

a. "We have already stressed. . ." _____

b. "Further. . ." _____

c. "Even the most profound. . ." _____

d. "is thus weakened. . ." _____

e. "Sometimes it is argued. . ." _____

f. "For instance. . ." _____

g. "It seems more likely. . ." _____

h. "After all. . ." _____

i. "It is not so much an escape but. . ." _____

j. "Besides. . ." _____

k. "But mass media. . ." _____

Answers: *a.* 3; *b.* 1; *c.* 6; *d.* 7; *e.* 4 or 5; *f.* 2; *g.* 6; *h.* 6; *i.* 5; *j.* 1; *k.* 5.

NAME———————————————— DATE——————— READING RATE——————— W.P.M.

COMPREHENSION CHECK QUESTIONS

1. Under a bluff reef there is a (1) tree branch; (2) submerged log; (3) wreck; (4) sand-bar.   1. ———

2. Mr. Higgins left Mark Twain but was hiding (1) below; (2) in the engine room; (3) behind a chimney; (4) behind a door.   2. ———

3. In the emergency, Twain (1) bumped against the shore; (2) yelled for Mr. Bixby; (3) rang the bell; (4) left the wheel.   3. ———

4. A reference was made to (1) Victoria Falls; (2) the Missouri River; (3) the Grand Canyon; (4) Niagara.   4. ———

5. The navigation of the Mississippi was for how many miles? (1) eight hundred; (2) eleven hundred; (3) twelve hundred; (4) fourteen hundred.   5. ———

Receptive Comprehension ———

6. This is chiefly about (1) learning to pilot a boat; (2) problems of understanding the river; (3) training a pilot; (4) the changing nature of the river.   6. ———

7. This would be classified primarily as (1) description; (2) narration; (3) exposition; (4) persuasion.   7. ———

8. To describe Mr. Bixby, which word seems best? (1) competent; (2) impatient; (3) easy-going; (4) excitable.   8. ———

9. To pilot a boat well, what seems to be most important? (1) intelligence; (2) calm nerves; (3) constant attention; (4) careful observation.   9. ———

10. What dictionary definition seems closest to the meaning of *read* as used in this selection? (1) interpret; (2) utter; (3) foretell; (4) acquire information.   10. ———

(10 off for each mistake)   *Reflective Comprehension* ———

TOTAL READING COMPREHENSION SCORE ———

VOCABULARY CHECK QUESTIONS

		without *context* I	*with* *context* II
1. *vaingloriously*	(1) helplessly; (2) bravely; (3) boastfully; (4) sadly; (5) openly.	1. ———	———
2. *prodigiously*	(1) generously; (2) smartly; (3) profanely; (4) marvelously; (5) properly.	2. ———	———
3. *imminent*	(1) famous; (2) impending; (3) imperishable; (4) steadfast; (5) manageable.	3. ———	———
4. *blandly*	(1) blankly; (2) tranquilly; (3) blamelessly; (4) loudly; (5) brightly.	4. ———	———
5. *void*	(1) vicious; (2) lacking; (3) complete; (4) victorious; (5) varied.	5. ———	———

(10 off for each mistake)   *Word Comprehension* without *contextual help* (I) ———

Word Comprehension with *contextual help*   (II) ———

TOTAL WORD COMPREHENSION SCORE ———

EXERCISES

TREAT CAUSES, NOT SYMPTOMS

When you step into a doctor's office with a splitting headache, you expect more than an aspirin. That headache is usually a symptom of something that needs attention — something that is causing discomfort. A doctor, if he is to be genuinely helpful, must treat causes, not symptoms.

It helps to look at reading from this same vantage point. Suppose a student comprehends poorly and goes to a clinician for help. It will take more than the admonition, "Try to comprehend better" to bring results.

Poor comprehension is really a symptom — a symptom of what? That's the question which must be answered. Unfortunately the answer is likely to be complex, not simple. Many causes, not one, have to be examined.

For example, if a student reads that "Elizabeth is taciturn," he may not comprehend the statement because of a vocabulary deficiency. That's one important cause to check.

Sometimes a student may read a whole page or chapter and get very little. Why? Frankly because he was bored — had no real interest in it. Lack of interest, then, is another cause of poor comprehension.

Difficulty is still another factor accounting for low comprehension. The Flesch Reading Ease Score provides one method of determining difficulty, rating reading matter on a scale from 0 to 100 or from very easy to very difficult. Both word length and sentence length are used to determine difficulty.

A well-trained mechanic can often just listen to motor sounds and diagnose engine difficulties. He has had sufficient background and experience to do what one lacking that background would find impossible. In reading, also, low comprehension may be caused by inadequate background in a subject matter area.

And of course your reading rate affects comprehension. Reading either too rapidly or too slowly may affect comprehension adversely. For most students there is usually a "just-right" speed which provides maximum comprehension.

Lack of concentration is still another reason for low comprehension. Some readers have never developed proper techniques for dealing successfully with distractions, have never disciplined themselves to give concentrated attention to anything for any length of time. In this day of commercials, station breaks, and coffee breaks, we may be losing the ability to concentrate for extended periods of time.

This does not exhaust the list of causes, although those certainly deserve major attention. Other factors need to be kept in mind — temperature, noise, and movement, for example. Then there are the mechanics of reading — fixation patterns, regression patterns, vocalizings, word-for-word habits.

What does this add up to? Look closely and carefully at each of these possible causes. Try to decide which factor or combination of factors probably explains your low comprehension. Fortunately, without exception, you can do something about each of them. So set up a program for dealing with the causes underlying your symptoms. Then and only then can you begin to see good results.

From James I. Brown, *Guide to Effective Reading*, D. C. Heath and Co., 1966.

(500 words)

COMPREHENSION CHECK QUESTIONS

1. The article specifically mentions (1) a dentist; (2) a doctor; (3) an intern; (4) a receptionist.   1. _____

2. Poor comprehension is spoken of as (1) a symptom; (2) a disease; (3) a cause; (4) an accident.   2. _____

3. The Reading Ease Score mentioned was developed by (1) Flesch; (2) Fischer; (3) Flexner; (4) Garrison.   3. _____

4. The article mentions (1) a well-trained mechanic; (2) an experienced teacher; (3) a pilot; (4) a trouble-shooter.   4. _____

5. The article mentions (1) wage hikes; (2) coffee breaks; (3) bonus gifts; (4) hypos.   5. _____

6. The central idea is to get you to (1) discover symptoms; (2) deal with causes; (3) improve comprehension; (4) check vocabulary deficiency.   6. _____

7. The allusion to station breaks was primarily to suggest (1) the importance of variety; (2) their effect on habits of concentration; (3) their encouragement of vocalization; (4) the importance of visual aids.   7. _____

8. A student who comprehends poorly (1) is reading too rapidly; (2) is not really interested; (3) is not concentrating; (4) may be doing none of these things.   8. _____

9. If your reading speed is not increasing, you should apparently try to (1) find out how to increase it; (2) try a new method; (3) discover why not; (4) work harder.   9. _____

10. Apparently, the most helpful move to insure progress is (1) careful self-analysis; (2) extensive practice; (3) a higher goal; (4) more work on vocabulary.   10. _____

SCORE _____

Answers: 1.2; 2.1; 3.1; 4.1; 5.2; 6.2; 7.2; 8.4; 9.3; 10.1.

NAME_____ DATE_____ READING RATE_____ W.P.M.

COMPREHENSION CHECK QUESTIONS

1. The author specifically speaks of feeding the mind (1) candy bars; (2) bonbons; (3) chocolate pudding; (4) sugar-plums.   1. _____

2. The article mentions eating at one sitting two or three (1) loaves of bread; (2) heads of lettuce; (3) cauliflowers; (4) beefsteaks.   2. _____

3. Specific reference is made to what kind of mind? (1) lean; (2) elegant; (3) fat; (4) mechanical.   3. _____

4. In the selection, mention was made of (1) Emerson's *Essays;* (2) Shakespeare's *King Lear;* (3) Gray's *Elegy;* (4) Pope's *Dunciad.*   4. _____

5. A specific rule was given for determining whether someone was (1) wise or foolish; (2) young or old; (3) educated or uneducated; (4) rich or poor.   5. _____

Receptive Comprehension _____

6. This is mainly about (1) reading a properly balanced fare; (2) selecting a varied reading fare; (3) thinking over what you have read; (4) spacing reading activities properly.   6. _____

7. The opening paragraphs were primarily to make us think about (1) the care lavished on our bodies; (2) the care we give to our mind; (3) how forgetful we are; (4) how important both body and mind are.   7. _____

8. The illustration of the thirsty haymaker was intended to remind us of the importance of (1) sufficient reading; (2) a wide variety of reading; (3) not reading too many kinds at once; (4) not reading too many of one kind of book.   8. _____

9. In essence, by "ticketing," the author means (1) buying; (2) using; (3) reading extensively; (4) labeling.   9. _____

10. His example of a "mental bun" suggested a way to test a person's (1) depth of reading interests; (2) mental health; (3) ability to concentrate; (4) taste for culture.   10. _____

(10 off for each mistake)   *Reflective Comprehension* _____

TOTAL READING COMPREHENSION SCORE _____

VOCABULARY CHECK QUESTIONS

		without context I	*with context* II
1. *ensue*	(1) enter; (2) take action; (3) follow; (4) charge; (5) report.	1. _____ _____	
2. *propensity*	(1) property; (2) fault; (3) statement; (4) inclination; (5) reason.	2. _____ _____	
3. *mastication*	(1) slicing; (2) chewing; (3) overcoming; (4) swallowing; (5) ruling.	3. _____ _____	
4. *impetus*	(1) search; (2) solution; (3) force; (4) method; (5) move.	4. _____ _____	
5. *ascertain*	(1) lead; (2) help out; (3) assert; (4) find out; (5) keep on.	5. _____ _____	

(10 off for each mistake)

Word Comprehension without *contextual help* (I) _____

Word Comprehension with *contextual help* (II) _____

TOTAL WORD COMPREHENSION SCORE _____

EXERCISES

Exploring factors affecting comprehension: After reading the preceding short selection, "Treat Causes, Not Symptoms," look at yourself more closely. Try to determine your major problems, then move toward solving them. Standardized test scores are particularly helpful if they are available. But this text is laid out to provide fairly complete evidence for helping you diagnose and assess most problems.

Under each of the following headings, record any concrete evidence available. Then, on the basis of your evaluation, look at the suggestions for dealing with the problem.

Vocabulary. Is this a major problem? To see, get some of the evidence down, as follows:

A. Enter the number you did correctly on the 20-item vocabulary test, p. 134. ⎯⎯⎯⎯
   Enter the salary expectation figure from p. 298. ⎯⎯⎯⎯
B. When you have completed any ten of the five-item Vocabulary Check Questions (a total of fifty items), enter the number you did correctly out of the fifty. ⎯⎯⎯⎯
C. Turn to p. 129 and cover the column of words to the right of the column heading PREFIX. Try to supply the common meaning for each of the twenty prefixes listed. Check your answers by uncovering the column. Enter the number you did correctly out of the twenty. ⎯⎯⎯⎯
D. Take your comprehension scores on the first ten selections read, average them, and enter the *average* score here. An average below 70 percent suggests vocabulary deficiency. ⎯⎯⎯⎯

Now, looking over the evidence you have accumulated for rating your vocabulary, check one of the following three choices: No problem ⎯⎯⎯⎯ Minor problem ⎯⎯⎯⎯ Major problem ⎯⎯⎯⎯.

Now what can you do to improve? Here are some suggestions. Check each when you have completed it.

1. Read the short selection "Context — Key to Meaning," p. 204, noting and applying relevant portions.
2. Read with particular emphasis the nine selections in Section VI on vocabulary for pertinent suggestions.
3. Complete the five-item Vocabulary Check Questions for each selection. Discover all unknown words and work them into your active vocabulary. Build added skill with context by using the first column (*without context*), then scanning the article to see how each word is used in context, putting a second set of answers in the column headed *with context*.
4. Read the article "A Master-Word Approach to Vocabulary," p. 128, and follow all suggestions given.
5. Do the dictionary improvement exercises, pages 286, 292, 294, 298, and 300.
6. For additional help, order the pocket-size vocabulary building game from Telstar, 366 North Prior Avenue, St. Paul, Minn. 55104. It provides a visualizing aid to unlock the meanings of over 30,000 common English words.

Interest. Is this a major problem? Again, check by getting some of the evidence down.

A. Look at the personal interest rating scale mentioned on p. 328. Use this scale with the first twenty selections you read, then average your ratings. If your average is above 2, interest should be no problem. If it is below 3, it looks like a major problem.
B. Check the relationship between your interest rating and comprehension. Does interest seem to make a consistent difference? Data from some 200 students using selections from an earlier edition of *Efficient Reading* should permit you to make meaningful comparisons. Notice that as articles are more difficult, interest tends to drop. If the drop is more pronounced with you, build stronger interests.

READING EASE GROUPING	AVERAGE INTEREST RATING	YOUR INTEREST RATING (AVERAGE)
Easy	2.109	⎯⎯⎯
Fairly Easy	2.299	⎯⎯⎯
Standard	2.346	⎯⎯⎯
Fairly Difficult	2.359	⎯⎯⎯
Difficult	2.381	⎯⎯⎯
Very Difficult	2.454	⎯⎯⎯

Looking back over this evidence, how would you rate interest? No problem ⎯⎯⎯⎯ Minor problem ⎯⎯⎯⎯ Major problem ⎯⎯⎯⎯.

Now what can you do to improve interest level? Here are some specific suggestions. Check each when completed.

1. Read "The Importance of Being Interested" (Sel. 4, p. 8. ⎯⎯⎯⎯
2. Apply the suggestions in the selection "Building Specific Interests," p. 206. ⎯⎯⎯⎯
3. Keep rating each selection read for interest, averaging each set of ten to see if there is improvement. ⎯⎯⎯⎯

Difficulty. Is this a major problem? Look at the evidence.

A. Using the Flesch Reading Ease Score on page 327, figure your average comprehension for the first twenty selections read.
B. Compare your average with those from some 200 students who used an earlier edition of *Efficient Reading.*

READING EASE GROUPING	AVERAGE COMPREHENSION	YOUR AVERAGE COMPREHENSION
Fairly Easy	68.5	⎯⎯⎯
Standard	67.5	⎯⎯⎯
Fairly Difficult	65.2	⎯⎯⎯
Difficult	67.4	⎯⎯⎯

The relationship between ease and comprehension is not perfectly consistent, suggesting that other factors may be more important than difficulty. If, however, for you the relationship is consistent and the differences in comprehension are more pronounced, you know difficulty is a problem. Rate yourself as before: No problem ⎯⎯⎯⎯ Minor problem ⎯⎯⎯⎯ Major problem ⎯⎯⎯⎯.

Now what can you do to deal with difficult material effectively?

Read the selection "Reading for Exams," p. 208, and "Organization — Your Reading Satellite," p. 210.

Explorations of *rate,* as suggested on page 212, of *background,* of *concentration,* and *mechanical difficulties* — such as vocalizing, regressing, and perceiving — lend themselves to similar analysis.

NAME_____ DATE_____ READING RATE_____ W.P.M.

COMPREHENSION CHECK QUESTIONS

1. Television is spoken of as the logical conclusion of a process that began (1) a decade ago; (2) two decades ago; (3) three decades ago; (4) four decades ago.   1. _____

2. The title for this article grew out of a talk with a (1) lawyer; (2) carpenter; (3) farmer; (4) photographer.   2. _____

3. The writer of this article calls himself a (1) nature lover; (2) book farmer; (3) student; (4) self-made philosopher.   3. _____

4. It is said that man may be distinguished from beast by his (1) ability to communicate; (2) social nature; (3) intelligence; (4) creative instinct.   4. _____

5. The author fears that our children will grow into super-robots because now the conditioning (1) has begun earlier; (2) has been more complete; (3) has been more concentrated; (4) has been more subtle.   5. _____

Receptive Comprehension _____

6. The purpose of this article is to suggest the (1) danger of television; (2) need for creative expression; (3) dangers of spectator living; (4) need for active participation.   6. _____

7. Of the following educational methods, which would the writer consider the most effective? (1) the lecture method; (2) the discussion method; (3) the laboratory method; (4) the socialized-recitation method.   7. _____

8. Of the following the least likely to be considered as "opening a door" is (1) taking pictures; (2) baking a cake; (3) reading a book; (4) driving a car.   8. _____

9. The story about the farmer who used hybrid seeds is intended to suggest the value of (1) reading; (2) listening; (3) neighbors; (4) experimentation.   9. _____

10. The article implies that learning to read could best be done by (1) studying the research in the field; (2) taking a course in the theory of reading; (3) practicing new techniques of reading; (4) drilling on exercise material designed to improve reading.   10. _____

(10 off for each mistake)   *Reflective Comprehension* _____

TOTAL READING COMPREHENSION SCORE _____

VOCABULARY CHECK QUESTIONS

		without context I	*with context* II
1. *atrophy*	(1) assail; (2) fasten; (3) repel; (4) waste away; (5) enchant.	1. _____	_____
2. *avidly*	(1) eagerly; (2) viciously; (3) well; (4) reluctantly; (5) truly.	2. _____	_____
3. *capitulation*	(1) comparison; (2) repulsion; (3) impulse; (4) surrender; (5) captivation.	3. _____	_____
4. *novice*	(1) nurse; (2) beginner; (3) fiction writer; (4) new star; (5) priest.	4. _____	_____
5. *anomalies*	(1) annoyances; (2) abnormalities; (3) additions; (4) opponents; (5) expectations.	5. _____	_____

(10 off for each mistake)   *Word Comprehension* without *contextual help* (I) _____

Word Comprehension with *contextual help* (II) _____

TOTAL WORD COMPREHENSION SCORE _____

EXERCISES

CONTEXT — KEY TO MEANING

When you come to an unknown word in your reading, what should you do? Eighty-four percent of the students in one college class answered — "look it up in the dictionary."

Take a closer look at that answer. Suppose you see the word *extenuate*. You consult the dictionary and find what? Not *the* meaning of *extenuate* but *four* meanings! Furthermore, the dictionary can never tell you exactly which meaning is intended.

Or take the common word *fast*. What does it mean? You answer — "quickly or rapidly," and you're quite right. But you're equally right if you say "firmly fastened." As a matter of fact, the one word *fast* is really not one word but twenty-one, all rolled into one. It has twelve meanings as an adjective, five as an adverb, two as a verb, and two as a noun. And that's talking in terms of the relatively small collegiate-size dictionary.

So — what does *fast* mean? You have to say *it all depends* — depends on the context, on the way the author used the word. To be sure, a dictionary should list all the different meanings. Even when a word is used in a new sense, that new meaning should eventually get into the dictionary, if it is used enough to become established. But unless the word has only one definition, we must always rely on context, not the dictionary, for its exact meaning. When you remember that the 500 most commonly used words have a total of 14,070 separate meanings, an aver-age of 28 per word — you can see why context must come first.

Furthermore, individuals vary widely in their ability to use contextual clues to arrive at accurate word meanings. In one class, for example, students took a difficult vocabulary test — first without any context to help, then a second time with sentence contexts for each word. Two students made identical scores of 30 the first time through. On the second time through one moved up to 40 but the other jumped up to 90. He had developed uncanny skill in getting word meanings through context. Obviously, that is a skill which deserves top priority. Research by Holmes accents its importance. He discovered that *vocabulary in context* contributed more to reading power than any other first-order factor isolated — 37 percent.

One sure way of developing that skill is to keep away from your dictionary until you have inferred a meaning from context alone. Then, and only then, should you turn to the dictionary for confirmation. If you go to the dictionary first you, by that move, discourage the development of the very skills and insights you need. Furthermore you'll find your interest is whetted by putting context first. You become more eager and alert to check your inference.

So — from now on — when you spot a strange word, look first at the context, formulate a tentative definition, *then* check it with the dictionary. You'll remember those new words much longer with that treatment. You'll also insure better comprehension.

(500 words)

From James I. Brown, *Guide to Effective Reading*, D. C. Heath and Co., 1966.

COMPREHENSION CHECK QUESTIONS

1. Specific mention is made of (1) a high school class; (2) a college class; (3) a TV class; (4) an English class. 1. _____

2. *Fast* has how many different meanings? (1) 5; (2) 12; (3) 16; (4) 21. 2. _____

3. The author specifically mentions (1) a collegiate-sized dictionary; (2) the *Oxford Dictionary;* (3) the Webster's dictionary; (4) a dictionary of slang. 3. _____

4. In the use of contextual clues, individuals were said to (1) be about the same; (2) vary widely; (3) vary with I.Q.; (4) improve with age. 4. _____

5. When first meeting a strange word, you are told to (1) look it up; (2) note any familiar prefix or root; (3) infer its meaning from context; (4) skip it and come back to study it later. 5. _____

6. This is chiefly about (1) the relationship between context and meaning; (2) multiple word meanings; (3) kinds of context; (4) developing skill with context. 6. _____

7. Primary emphasis is on (1) when context should be used; (2) how context should be used; (3) why context deserves priority; (4) what context includes. 7. _____

8. The discussion of *extenuate* and *fast* illustrated (1) two different points; (2) somewhat the same point; (3) different kinds of dictionary entries; (4) how dictionaries differ. 8. _____

9. You would infer from this that going to the dictionary first is most like (1) diving into deep water; (2) beginning a race; (3) using a crutch; (4) climbing a mountain. 9. _____

10. You were most strongly cautioned against (1) consulting the dictionary first; (2) guessing at word meanings; (3) neglecting common words; (4) relying solely on context. 10. _____

SCORE _____

Answers: 1.2; 2.4; 3.1; 4.2; 5.3; 6.1; 7.3; 8.2; 9.3; 10.1.

NAME_____ DATE_____ READING RATE_____ W.P.M.

COMPREHENSION CHECK QUESTIONS

1. Mention was made of the library at (1) Athens; (2) Cairo; (3) Alexandria; (4) Rhodes.

    1. _____

2. The Royal Library of France was said to number about how many volumes? (1) 700; (2) 900; (3) 1500; (4) 1800.

    2. _____

3. The author says that in our time, with libraries, we are compelled to be (1) comprehensive; (2) selective; (3) arbitrary; (4) practical.

    3. _____

4. A reference was made to the (1) Gallic Wars; (2) Battle of the Bulge; (3) Battle of Waterloo; (4) Peloponnesian War.

    4. _____

5. The only thing greater than our power was said to be our (1) insecurity; (2) lack of understanding; (3) complacency; (4) immorality.

    5. _____

Receptive Comprehension _____

6. The central idea is to (1) contrast ancient and modern views toward libraries; (2) suggest that libraries are now too large; (3) explain how libraries link past and future; (4) suggest that libraries need comprehensive coverage.

    6. _____

7. The author shows most concern over (1) scientific discoveries; (2) personal problems; (3) war; (4) development of practical skills.

    7. _____

8. This selection mainly reflects (1) pessimism; (2) fatalism; (3) optimism; (4) uncertainty.

    8. _____

9. The material in this selection is arranged primarily (1) on a cause-effect basis; (2) from least to most importance; (3) on a question-answer basis; (4) from the general to the specific.

    9. _____

10. Man's greatest problem, according to the author, is apparently in the area of (1) technical know-how; (2) social continuity; (3) economic control; (4) moral values.

    10. _____

(10 off for each mistake)   *Reflective Comprehension* _____

TOTAL READING COMPREHENSION SCORE _____

VOCABULARY CHECK QUESTIONS

		without context I	*with context* II
1. *folios*	(1) folders; (2) manuscripts; (3) archives; (4) plays; (5) indexes.	1. _____	_____
2. *edifices*	(1) churches; (2) buildings; (3) warnings; (4) factors; (5) aids.	2. _____	_____
3. *cogency*	(1) fairness; (2) information; (3) theory; (4) bigness; (5) relevancy.	3. _____	_____
4. *congenial*	(1) agreeable; (2) intuitive; (3) innate; (4) exasperating; (5) constructive.	4. _____	_____
5. *malleable*	(1) compact; (2) artificial; (3) disposable; (4) tractable; (5) hopeful.	5. _____	_____

(10 off for each mistake)   *Word Comprehension* without *contextual help* (I) _____

Word Comprehension with *contextual help* (II) _____

TOTAL WORD COMPREHENSION SCORE _____

EXERCISES

BUILDING SPECIFIC INTERESTS

Frank complained that he could not remember chemical symbols or formulas. Still he could reel off detailed information about big-league baseball for hours. How come? The secret, of course, was his strong interest in baseball.

Obviously, if you can build a fairly strong interest in any subject matter field, your mastery of it is greatly facilitated. Churchill divided people into two categories — "those whose work is work and whose pleasure is pleasure, and secondly, those whose work and pleasure are one." Interest makes the difference. Why not take full advantage of this in dealing with difficult subjects?

Suppose, for example, that you are taking chemistry but find it dull and uninteresting. This probably means you will avoid studying it and will be likely to do poorly or fail — unless you can develop an interest.

Try these positive suggestions to stimulate added interest in any subject.

First, cultivate the acquaintance of genuinely interested students. After a chemistry lecture, listen for a student who is talking with some enthusiasm and interest about a point raised in class. Fall into step with him or her. Suggest a cup of coffee. You'll be pleasantly surprised how soon some of that enthusiasm will rub off on you. Take the student who drew a bird-watcher for a roommate. At first he smiled to hear all the talk about birds. Two months later, however, he had bought binoculars and bird books and was himself going on early morning trips to identify birds. Fortunately, interest is contagious.

Second, read popular books on the subject. A man with no interest in art read Stone's book, *Lust for Life,* a biography of Vincent van Gogh. When he finished he amazed his wife by suggesting a visit to an art museum. Stefansson, the arctic explorer, traced his life-long interest in exploring to the reading of one book. Henri Fabre, famous French entymologist, is another whose life was changed by a book. Take the book *Crucibles: The Story of Chemistry,* by Jaffe. Read about the chemist Lavoisier, who lost his head on the guillotine. "It took but a moment to cut off that head, although a hundred years perhaps will be required to produce another like it." So said a contemporary. Such personal glimpses should take you back to your textbook with new zest and interest.

Third, spend extra time on dull, difficult subjects. The more you know about something, the more interested you become. If you know nothing about football you're not likely to be as interested as one who has watched many games and knows both players and rules.

Fourth, watch for educational TV shows or movies in the area of your low interest. The movie "Tom Jones" has stimulated many to read the book. In the same way, a movie about Pasteur can stimulate added interest in chemistry.

Now, get busy! Develop interest in specific subjects. More than anything else, this can change your outlook, can turn study from work to pleasure, can turn a potential *D* into a *B.*

(500 words)

From James I. Brown, *Guide to Effective Reading,* D. C. Heath and Co., 1966.

COMPREHENSION CHECK QUESTIONS

1. Frank was said to be interested in (1) baseball; (2) tennis; (3) football; (4) the Olympics. 1. _____

2. Which of the following was quoted? (1) Kennedy; (2) Stevenson; (3) Churchill; (4) Roosevelt. 2. _____

3. Reference was made to (1) a physicist; (2) a biologist; (3) an entymologist; (4) a sculptor. 3. _____

4. You were told to (1) listen to hi-fi; (2) collect stamps; (3) travel; (4) watch TV. 4. _____

5. How many specific suggestions were given? (1) none; (2) two; (3) three; (4) four. 5. _____

6. This dealt chiefly with (1) why interest should be cultivated; (2) how to develop interests; (3) the why and how of developing interests; (4) what specific interest should be developed. 6. _____

7. The quotation about "work and pleasure" was intended to point up (1) individual differences; (2) how interesting work really is; (3) the importance of interest; (4) how work stimulates interest. 7. _____

8. To develop interest in nuclear physics, which of the following books would be most helpful? (1) *College Physics;* (2) *Nuclear Physics;* (3) *The Atomic Structure of the Universe;* (4) *Our Friend the Atom.* 8. _____

9. Other things being equal, you would assume from this that the best grades are made by students who (1) are most interested; (2) study hardest; (3) are most intelligent; (4) have developed the most effective study habits. 9. _____

10. You would expect the writer to favor (1) a special hour for review; (2) two hours of preparation for every class hour; (3) provision for more leisure time; (4) less preparation time for interesting subjects. 10. _____

SCORE _____

Answers: 1.1; 2.3; 3.3; 4.4; 5.4; 6.3; 7.3; 8.4; 9.1; 10.4.

NAME————————————————— DATE———————— READING RATE——————— W.P.M.

COMPREHENSION CHECK QUESTIONS

1. One executive's pile of mail would take him (1) most of the day just to read; (2) half a day to read; (3) all day to read; (4) all day to read and answer.   1. ————

2. That executive's reading rate was how many words a minute? (1) 138; (2) 160; (3) 180; (4) 205.   2. ————

3. Part of his reading training was with (1) first-grade material; (2) the tachistoscope; (3) *Reader's Digest* material; (4) LEX-O-GRAM vocabulary cards.   3. ————

4. The article does *not* mention (1) Dr. Betts; (2) Paul D. Leedy; (3) Henry B. Paulu; (4) Dr. Nila Banta Smith.   4. ————

5. The fastest reading rate mentioned is about (1) 600 wpm; (2) 800 wpm; (3) 1,000 wpm; (4) 1,200 wpm.   5. ————

Receptive Comprehension ————

6. This is intended primarily to (1) explain common reading difficulties; (2) point up the importance of reading; (3) show what poor readers we are; (4) help us read better.   6. ————

7. The story about the man using the accelerator is used to show how rapid reading improves (1) comprehension; (2) eye movements; (3) word grouping habits; (4) concentration.   7. ————

8. The chief cause of reading faults in schools is (1) too poor instruction; (2) too little practice; (3) too uninteresting reading; (4) too difficult reading.   8. ————

9. The age group figures are used to show that (1) younger students improved more; (2) age makes no difference; (3) older students improved more; (4) age makes little difference.   9. ————

10. The best way to improve your reading is by (1) racing an alarm clock; (2) glancing only at nouns and verbs; (3) enrolling in a reading clinic; (4) forcing heightened concentration.   10. ————

(10 off for each mistake)   *Reflective Comprehension* ————

TOTAL READING COMPREHENSION SCORE ————

VOCABULARY CHECK QUESTIONS

		without *context* I	*with* *context* II
1. *confront*	(1) confuse; (2) expect; (3) agree; (4) face; (5) visit.	1. ————	————
2. *trudge*	(1) plod; (2) hasten; (3) loiter; (4) plunge; (5) walk.	2. ————	————
3. *conferred*	(1) admitted; (2) arranged; (3) wrote; (4) lectured; (5) talked.	3. ————	————
4. *superficially*	(1) studiously; (2) casually; (3) with difficulty; (4) well; (5) sensibly.	4. ————	————
5. *graphic*	(1) energetic; (2) monolithic; (3) realistic; (4) static; (5) easily grasped.	5. ————	————

(10 off for each mistake)   *Word Comprehension* without *contextual help* (I) ————

Word Comprehension with *contextual help* (II) ————

TOTAL WORD COMPREHENSION SCORE ————

EXERCISES

READING FOR EXAMS

Remember the dejected student wandering through the bookstore, complaining about grades? A clerk picked up a *How-to-Study* guide and said, "Here's a book that will do half your work for you." The student brightened up immediately. "Fine! I'll take . . . I'll take *two*."

Sounds like another musical, doesn't it — *How to Succeed in College without Really Trying?* Yes, if it weren't for those ubiquitous quizzes, mid-quarters, and finals, it might be that easy. Even these, however, with the right approach, should pose no problems.

Faced with an important exam, most students cram. Frantically, the night before the test, they start studying, washing down chapter after chapter with strong black coffee. By exam time the next day their eyes burn, their heads throb, and their brains refuse to marshall the pertinent details into anything like order and clearness. In short, their so-called preparation turns that hoped-for *B* into an unwanted *D*.

You, of course, want a plan that insures *B*'s or better, not *C*'s or worse. And here it is.

Start preparing for exams the first day of class by doing each assignment on time. After all, a head start should mean a winning race. If no specific assignments are made, divide the text or texts by the number of weeks and read accordingly. At the end of each week, make a rapid review a routine step. Skim along at top speed for a quick backward look over the ground covered. This lays an ideal foundation for the next moves.

From James I. Brown, *Guide to Effective Reading,* D. C. Heath and Co., 1966.

Then, when an exam is announced, use these five steps to insure maximum results.

(1) Get a broad overview by reading the introductory paragraph or paragraphs and noting any subheadings in heavy type or italics. This gives you an aerial view of the ground to be covered, revealing meaningful broad interrelationships. Take a minute or so to think back over the chapter. Then, if one is given, read the summary at the end to reinforce the learning of main points.

(2) Next, read your lecture notes and any supplementary materials that should be included. With the broad overview, it is much easier to pigeonhole this added material.

(3) Then read the textbook carefully for details — your one and only reading. Some students reread the text, but studies indicate that that produces only slightly better results — so slight that your time is much better spent in the other ways indicated.

(4) When you finish reading a chapter or unit, ask yourself what specific details seem most important. See if you can supply the figures, names, dates, or details that you feel are important. You'll be interested in seeing how many of these appear on the exam — a tribute to your insights.

(5) Finally, think of a probable essay-type question or so over each chapter. Answer each orally, evaluating them in terms of clear organization and attention to details that demonstrate your competence.

Obviously, it's the exceptional student who prepares with this thoroughness. That's another reason for its effectiveness. Try it. Start enjoying better results right now.

(500 words)

COMPREHENSION CHECK QUESTIONS

1. The article mentions a (1) How-to-Study guide; (2) reading improvement text; (3) How-to-Spell-it guide; (4) book on writing better exams.

   1. _____

2. Faced with an important exam, most students were said to (1) panic; (2) cram; (3) get interested; (4) begin concentrating.

   2. _____

3. You were told to start preparing for exams by (1) drawing up a study schedule; (2) doing each assignment on time; (3) checking the course bibliography; (4) getting copies of old exams.

   3. _____

4. How many readings are you advised to make of the text when preparing for an exam? (1) one; (2) two; (3) several, depending upon the subject; (4) number was not specified.

   4. _____

5. The final step is to (1) think of essay-type questions over the material; (2) review all notes; (3) get some well-earned rest; (4) make sure you have pen, pencil, and eraser.

   5. _____

6. This is mainly about (1) planning your reading; (2) preparing for exams; (3) developing key reading skills; (4) establishing proper study procedures.

   6. _____

7. Which of the following inferences is *least* well supported by the opening story? That the student (1) is lazy; (2) has just come from his advisor; (3) considers books helpful; (4) has poor study habits.

   7. _____

8. That opening story was intended primarily to (1) get you to act; (2) arouse your interest; (3) stress the importance of reading; (4) suggest a solution to the low-grade problem.

   8. _____

9. The last half of the selection is organized on what basis? (1) general-to-specific preparations; (2) specific-to-general preparations; (3) immediate-to-preliminary steps; (4) preliminary-to-immediate steps.

   9. _____

10. From this selection you would infer what to be most important? (1) what to read; (2) when to read it; (3) how to read it; (4) where to read it.

    10. _____

SCORE _____

Answers: 1,1; 2,2; 3,2; 4,1; 5,1; 6,2; 7,2; 8,2; 9,4; 10,3.

NAME—————————————————— DATE——————— READING RATE——————— W.P.M.

COMPREHENSION CHECK QUESTIONS

1. It was said that (1) there is a single proven study method; (2) what works well with some students doesn't for others; (3) you need a different method for every subject matter area; (4) a how-to-study book is indispensable.   1. ————

2. If you get behind, you are advised to (1) get notes covering the missed material from another student; (2) skip to the material currently being covered; (3) skim over missed material; (4) catch up.   2. ————

3. At your first reading you are told to (1) underline main points; (2) circle unknown words; (3) make marginal notes; (4) use color-coded checks.   3. ————

4. When beginning a test, (1) outline each question before writing; (2) start right in on question 1; (3) start on the most difficult question; (4) read it through completely first.

5. How many rules are discussed at some length? (1) one; (2) two; (3) three; (4) four.   5. ————

Receptive Comprehension ————

6. The main idea is to (1) keep you from falling behind; (2) get you to mark your books; (3) help you do better on tests; (4) help you do better in school.   6. ————

7. Strongest emphasis is placed on (1) where to study; (2) proper management of study; (3) needed study aids and supplies; (4) the best time to study.   7. ————

8. The chief purpose of this selection was apparently to (1) guide; (2) clarify; (3) persuade; (4) evaluate. 8. ————

9. You would infer from this selection that the writers (1) were too unrealistic; (2) knew students well; (3) were too idealistic; (4) did not understand student problems.   9. ————

10. The tone of the selection is best described as (1) formal; (2) humorous; (3) straightforward; (4) imaginative.   10. ————

(10 off for each mistake)   *Reflective Comprehension* ————

TOTAL READING COMPREHENSION SCORE ————

VOCABULARY CHECK QUESTIONS

		without context I	*with context* II
1. *virtuous*	(1) brave; (2) truthful; (3) youthful; (4) righteous; (5) extraordinary. 1.	————	————
2. *incentive*	(1) encouragement; (2) reluctance; (3) distraction; (4) fine; (5) happening. 2.	————	————
3. *bout*	(1) bottle; (2) spell; (3) raft; (4) marker; (5) strike. 3.	————	————
4. *caricatures*	(1) pen drawings; (2) critical statements; (3) models; (4) falsified images; (5) ludicrous likenesses. 4.	————	————
5. *pseudo-students*	(1) sham students; (2) star students; (3) former students; (4) self-made students; (5) grad students. 5.	————	————

(10 off for each mistake)   *Word Comprehension* without *contextual help* (I) ————

Word Comprehension with *contextual help* (II) ————

TOTAL WORD COMPREHENSION SCORE ————

EXERCISES

NAPL. What does that mean? You don't know? No wonder — those letters need to be organized before they make PLAN. Now you see the important role of organization.

Organizing and reading must go hand-in-hand, if reading is to be truly effective. It helps to remember that reading is the reverse of writing; the writer sends, the reader receives. Fortunately, most writers try to organize their remarks carefully enough to insure clear, accurate communication. The reader, by trying to discover the writer's plan, gets as close as possible to his original meaning. Comprehension is thereby increased.

How is organization revealed? As a reader, you should become more sensitive to three kinds of special devices — typographical, rhetorical, and verbal. To make certain parts stand out, a writer may resort to CAPITAL LETTERS, **boldface type,** or *italics.* Or he may turn to such rhetorical devices as repetition, parallelism, or balance. Repeating a key word or phrase helps the reader fit what is said into a more orderly pattern. When Lincoln spoke of government "of the people, by the people, and for the people," he used parallelism to accent the three-fold pattern he wanted to emphasize. And Patrick Henry's "give me liberty or give me death," used balance to heighten the two-fold nature of that choice. Finally, verbal devices help the reader mark transitions, note methods of development, and discover outline form. The word *another,* for example, suggests a transition. *Consequently* suggests a development based on cause-and-effect relationships. And such words as *first* or *finally*

are most useful indicators of outline form. All these devices, like road signs, help the reader keep on the track.

The other way is through noting paragraph structure. Major thought units are marked off by paragraphs. Each paragraph has a topic sentence, expressed or implied, plus supporting details. In outlining any article, rely heavily on paragraphing to make the plan clear.

What does organization contribute? When you have developed real skill in noting organization, the benefits fall into two categories — a sharpened awareness of certain key factors as well as improved ability in two areas.

A sharpened awareness of the thesis or main idea is one important benefit. Getting the main idea of this 500-word selection, for example, is greatly simplified by reducing the 500 words to a manageable skeleton — or outline. Organization also brings added awareness of the interrelationships between parts. Subordinate parts are seen as exactly that, their relationship to major divisions being more obvious.

Finally, organization improves both understanding and remembering. Knowledge and understanding are, in a sense, different. It is possible to know the facts but not understand what they mean. Organization helps here. And it contributes added retention. It is much easier to remember details if you have an outline as a frame of reference. It is easier, for example, to remember CAPITALS, **boldface type,** and *italics,* when they are grouped under the heading *Typographical devices.*

So, make organization a concomitant to reading. It can turn NEMAGIN into MEANING, the obscure into the obvious.

(500 words)

From James I. Brown, *Guide to Effective Reading,* D. C. Heath and Co., 1966.

COMPREHENSION CHECK QUESTIONS

1. You were told to keep organizing and reading (1) as separate activities; (2) as consecutive steps; (3) hand-in-hand; (4) apart.   1. _____

2. Reading is spoken of as (1) the reverse of writing; (2) the spark for comprehension; (3) easier than writing; (4) the road to outlining.   2. _____

3. Reference was made to (1) Franklin; (2) Washington; (3) Monroe; (4) Lincoln.   3. _____

4. The special devices discussed were likened to (1) keys; (2) road signs; (3) timetables; (4) road maps.   4. _____

5. Parallelism is classed as a (1) typographical device; (2) verbal device; (3) rhetorical device; (4) paragraph device.   5. _____

6. This is mainly about (1) how organization is revealed; (2) what organization contributes to reading; (3) outlining techniques; (4) the role of organization in reading.   6. _____

7. The opening reference to NAPL (PLAN) was intended to show (1) how to organize; (2) the simplicity of good organization; (3) the importance of organization; (4) how slight changes make big differences.   7. _____

8. Two of the main divisions are marked off by (1) boldface type; (2) headings; (3) italics; (4) capital letters.   8. _____

9. The phrase, "make organization a concomitant to reading," apparently means to make it (1) a supplement; (2) an aid; (3) an end; (4) an accompaniment.   9. _____

10. Most attention is given to (1) how to organize; (2) what purpose it has; (3) when to organize; (4) what organization is.   10. _____

SCORE _____

Answers: 1, 3; 2, 1; 3, 4; 4, 2; 5, 3; 6, 4; 7, 3; 8, 3; 9, 4; 10, 2.

NAME_____ DATE_____ READING RATE_____ W.P.M.

COMPREHENSION CHECK QUESTIONS

1. The reader was said to be about the size of a (1) magazine; (2) spiral-bound notebook; (3) ream of typing paper; (4) city telephone directory.   1. _____

2. The reader's weight was given in (1) ounces; (2) grams; (3) pounds; (4) kilograms.   2. _____

3. To get a book, you use (1) an electronic code; (2) a simple voice command; (3) an electronic title-finder; (4) an alphanumeric keyboard.   3. _____

4. The central storage area for this world library was located where? (1) Mt. McKinley; (2) Australian desert; (3) Brussels; (4) Egypt.   4. _____

5. The microprinted cards on which all documents are stored can take about how many book pages per single card? (1) 300; (2) 600; (3) 900; (4) not specified.   5. _____

Receptive Comprehension _____

6. This selection mainly (1) explains why the reader was developed; (2) describes its appearance; (3) points up its value; (4) explains its workings.   6. _____

7. The chief purpose is apparently to (1) entertain; (2) clarify; (3) stimulate; (4) evaluate.   7. _____

8. Points are developed largely through use of (1) definitions; (2) analogies; (3) personal examples; (4) specific details.   8. _____

9. The best word for describing the organization of this part of the story is (1) special; (2) analytical; (3) logical; (4) chronological.   9. _____

10. Apparently the most important thing about the reader is its (1) lightness; (2) efficiency; (3) mental stimulus; (4) ease of operation.   10. _____

(10 off for each mistake)   *Reflective Comprehension* _____

TOTAL READING COMPREHENSION SCORE _____

VOCABULARY CHECK QUESTIONS

			without context I	*with context* II
1. *eerie*	(1) high-pitched; (2) restrained; (3) loud; (4) soothing; (5) unsettling.	1.	_____	_____
2. *surfeit*	(1) sufficient; (2) scarcity; (3) application; (4) excess; (5) factory.	2.	_____	_____
3. *orgiastic*	(1) musical; (2) eccentric; (3) producing unrestrained activity; (4) calm; (5) noisy.	3.	_____	_____
4. *provocation*	(1) training; (2) stimulation; (3) lying; (4) working; (5) opening.	4.	_____	_____
5. *robots*	(1) controls; (2) thieves; (3) towers; (4) automatons; (5) keys.	5.	_____	_____

(10 off for each mistake)   Word Comprehension without *contextual help* (I) _____

Word Comprehension with *contextual help* (II) _____

TOTAL WORD COMPREHENSION SCORE _____

EXERCISES

Exploring your rate-comprehension relationship: One of your first and most important moves in improving your reading is to explore the relationship between reading rate and comprehension. Such an exploration will let you know how important a factor rate is and, by implication, how important such matters as vocabulary, concentration, interest, and background are.

Beginning at about 100 words per minute, read ten selections of comparable difficulty (see Index According to Order of Difficulty, p. 327). Try to read each one about 60 wpm faster than you read the previous one. Then check your comprehension on each selection, plotting your results on the graph below. Keep increasing rate until comprehension drops to the 40 percent level or below, even if you have to call your activity skimming instead of reading. The resulting graph will provide evidence for a more intelligent approach to your reading improvement efforts. Specifically, it should answer the following three questions:

(1) Is it true that the slower you read, the better you comprehend?
(2) What is your present optimum speed for comprehension?
(3) What is your present best practice speed?

Generally speaking, the faster you read, within limits, the better you comprehend. Is this so with you? If it is, what are the limits? For most students, optimum comprehension comes at speeds somewhat above their slowest rates. A rapid drop-off as rate is increased indicates that rate is indeed of primary importance as a factor. A gradual drop-off or rather lengthy plateau area suggests that other factors are probably more important.

Further analysis of your graph record will suggest what those factors may be. For example, if comprehension never rises above a 60 or 70 percent level, despite wide variations in rate, you have reason to consider vocabulary as a possible limiting factor. If you do not drop below the 40 percent level, you have reason to conclude that you have an excellent general background and are able to pick up additional information even at extremely high rates. If your record is quite erratic, this suggests that differences in difficulty, background, or interest are more important than differences in rate, and should be explored further.

When you have completed your exploration, you should have definite answers to all three questions.

(1) Was your best comprehension score achieved at your slowest rate?
(2) At what specific rate or rates did you get your best comprehension, whether 70, 80, 90, or 100 percent?
(3) Finally, what is your present best practice speed? Your answer to this question depends on your answer to the preceding one. Your best present practice speed must be faster than the speed at which you now get best comprehension. After all, you don't want to waste precious time practicing what you already do well. No — you want to develop the skill to get that same comprehension but at speeds from 300 to 600 wpm faster than present speeds. To do that with maximum effectiveness, use the procedure described in "Swing Three Bats" (p. 216).

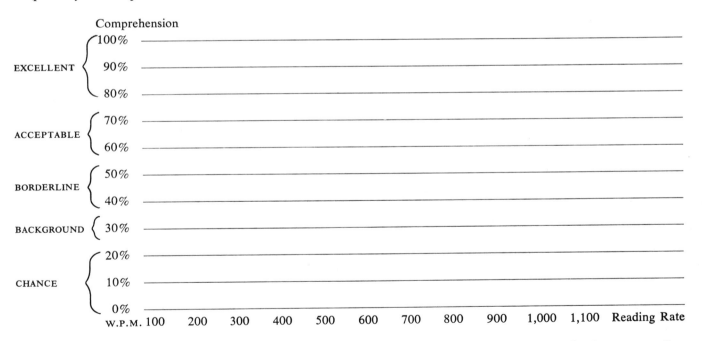

When graphing your results, identify your first reading by the figure *1*. Then connect the dot for each subsequent reading with the preceding one by a line, to indicate the order in which it was read. Results for a group of 100 students, following these directions with ten readings, show the following average changes: 197, 293, 359, 305, 306, 350, 411, 406, 432 and 467 wpm. Can you achieve a better than average range? Try a slower beginning rate as well as a faster final rate than indicated in the averages given above.

NAME_____ DATE_____ READING RATE_____ W.P.M.

COMPREHENSION CHECK QUESTIONS

1. Reading and skiing are specifically spoken of as what kind of activities? (1) graceful and harmonious; (2) daring and exciting; (3) exacting and demanding; (4) fast and tiring.   1. _____

2. When one first puts skis on, he is said to look and feel like a (1) neophyte; (2) fool; (3) penguin; (4) duck out of water.   2. _____

3. An instructor says you must remember to (1) try easy turns first; (2) bend your knees; (3) keep a sharp lookout for boulders; (4) hold your ski poles away from your legs.   3. _____

4. Learning to read was said to be at least as complex as learning to play (1) golf; (2) tennis; (3) handball; (4) baseball.   4. _____

5. Specific reference was made to tackling (1) an expert run; (2) a steep slope; (3) a tricky jump; (4) a flag-marked run.   5. _____

Receptive Comprehension _____

6. The central idea of this selection is to (1) tell us how to read better; (2) indicate how alike reading and skiing are; (3) suggest the need for instruction; (4) reveal the complexity of the reading process.   6. _____

7. This selection was developed largely by (1) illustration; (2) analogy; (3) description; (4) contrast.   7. _____

8. You would assume that, following this discussion, the next aspect of reading to be treated would cover (1) practice exercises; (2) an enumeration of rules; (3) basic principles; (4) the defining of criteria for good reading.   8. _____

9. The tone of this selection is best described as (1) conversational; (2) forceful; (3) humorous; (4) critical.   9. _____

10. The chief purpose of this is to (1) clarify; (2) entertain; (3) stimulate; (4) convince.   10. _____

(10 off for each mistake)   *Reflective Comprehension* _____

TOTAL READING COMPREHENSION SCORE _____

VOCABULARY CHECK QUESTIONS

		without context I	with context II
1. *admonitions*	(1) cautions; (2) attitudes; (3) comments; (4) applications; (5) descriptions. 1.	_____	_____
2. *anticipating*	(1) aging; (2) arguing; (3) foreseeing; (4) suggesting; (5) concluding. 2.	_____	_____
3. *fluid*	(1) effortless; (2) fixed; (3) open; (4) customary; (5) forced. 3.	_____	_____
4. *coalesce*	(1) unite; (2) inhabit; (3) light; (4) change; (5) grasp. 4.	_____	_____
5. *array*	(1) statement; (2) orderly group; (3) catalog; (4) haphazard collection; (5) dictionary. 5.	_____	_____

(10 off for each mistake)

Word Comprehension without *contextual help* (I) _____

Word Comprehension with *contextual help* (II) _____

TOTAL WORD COMPREHENSION SCORE _____

EXERCISES

THE GOAL? ADAPTABILITY

What's a good car? One that's speedy? Easy to handle? Well designed? What about low initial cost, economy of operation, roominess, low maintenance, or riding ease? Perhaps you'll agree that no *one* factor provides a completely satisfying answer.

What's a good reader? Here, too, no one factor is enough. Speed isn't everything; neither is comprehension. More important than either one is the *ability to adapt* — to adapt rate to purpose and to a wide variety of reading materials. Adaptability, then, is the true mark of a good reader.

How do you measure adaptability? How better than by actually putting yourself into different reading situations to see how well you adapt? For example, using three articles of comparable difficulty, check your performance when reading normally, thoroughly, and rapidly.

To discover your normal leisure reading habits, read an article neither faster nor slower than you ordinarily do when you have some leisure and want to settle down comfortably with a magazine. Don't try to comprehend more or less than usual in that situation. When you have finished and taken the test, determine your reading rate and comprehension. Next, see how well you adapt yourself to the problem of getting meaning. In reading the next article, your purpose is to get as much comprehension as possible in a single reading. Keep track of reading time, but remember that it's comprehension you're after. With the last article, your purpose is to cover ground rapidly. Read it at your top rate. Although speed is your primary concern, check comprehension to see what price you ordinarily pay for haste.

These three sets of rate and comprehension scores provide a useful composite index of adaptability, a three-dimension picture of yourself as a reader. Careful analysis of these scores should reveal information of importance in directing future practice efforts and achieving maximum results. As Kettering once said: "A problem well-stated is a problem half-solved." In reading, that might well be paraphrased: "A problem *well-identified* is a problem half-solved."

For example, what about the range of reading rates at your command? Subtract your slowest rate from your top rate for that figure. Is it 200 wpm or more? If so, you're among the top 20 percent of adults *before* training in reading. If that figure is 50 wpm or less, you'll want to overcome your tendencies toward one-speed reading.

When reading at top speed, a rate under 300 wpm probably means vocalizing and regressing.

Did you get comprehension when that was your purpose? And did you get details as well as main ideas and inferences? Was comprehension consistently good or did it vary considerably? Consistently good comprehension without considerable range in rate may indicate an unwillingness to recognize the importance of both depth and breadth as you read, an overlooking of Bacon's dictum: "Some books are to be tasted, others to be swallowed, and some few to be chewed and digested."

Such an analysis touches significant facets of this thing called *adaptability,* so important in defining a good reader.

(500 words)

COMPREHENSION CHECK QUESTIONS

1. The good reader is likened to a good (1) car; (2) motor; (3) driver; (4) model.   1. _____

2. You were told to use articles of comparable (1) column width; (2) difficulty; (3) length; (4) subject matter.   2. _____

3. Mention was made of (1) Byron; (2) Ford; (3) Lamb; (4) Kettering.   3. _____

4. Reference was made to (1) stuttering; (2) word-for-word reading; (3) the tachistoscope; (4) one-speed reading.   4. _____

5. A speed range of 200 wpm or more was said to put you among the top (1) 60 percent; (2) 40 percent; (3) 20 percent; (4) 5 percent.   5. _____

6. The primary purpose of this selection is to (1) define what is meant by a good reader; (2) define adaptability; (3) explain how to measure adaptability; (4) explain how to identify vocalizing difficulties.   6. _____

7. The emphasis in this selection is on (1) wisdom is power; (2) knowing thyself; (3) reading maketh a full man; (4) the reading man is the thinking man.   7. _____

8. The threefold check is intended to (1) eliminate reading difficulties; (2) identify reading difficulties; (3) test reading improvement; (4) determine reading potential.   8. _____

9. A vocabulary deficiency would be suggested by (1) consistently low comprehension; (2) consistently slow rate; (3) a drop in comprehension as rate is increased; (4) an increase in comprehension as rate is decreased.   9. _____

10. Difficulty with concentration would be suggested if (1) rapid reading brought better comprehension; (2) rapid reading did not affect comprehension; (3) normal rate brought better comprehension; (4) comprehension remained fairly constant.   10. _____

SCORE _____

Answers: 1.1; 2.2; 3.4; 4.4; 5.3; 6.1; 7.2; 8.2; 9.1; 10.1.

214

NAME——————————————————— DATE——————— READING RATE——————— W.P.M.

COMPREHENSION CHECK QUESTIONS

1. An average reader was said to read an average book at about what word-per-minute rate? (1) 300 wpm; (2) 250 wpm; (3) 200 wpm; (4) 150 wpm.

  1. ————

2. At that rate, reading for fifteen minutes a day would enable you to read how many books in a year? (1) ten; (2) fifteen; (3) twenty; (4) twenty-five.

  2. ————

3. Sir William Osler was said to have how many occupations? (1) one; (2) two; (3) three; (4) four.

  3. ————

4. Osler was an authority on (1) Sir Edmund Spencer; (2) William Caxton; (3) Samuel Johnson; (4) Sir Thomas Browne.

  4. ————

5. You were told specifically that the only requirement for being well-read is (1) the will to read; (2) careful planning; (3) keeping a book handy; (4) setting a definite schedule.

  5. ————

Receptive Comprehension ————

6. The central focus is on (1) finding an opportunity to read; (2) proving how much can be read in fifteen minutes a day; (3) showing how reading contributes to accomplishment; (4) providing a universal formula for being well-read.

  6. ————

7. You would infer that the author would advise reading (1) rapidly; (2) at a natural rate; (3) at a variety of rates; (4) at a slow, careful rate.

  7. ————

8. The Osler illustration was intended to get us to (1) read the last fifteen minutes of the day; (2) think in terms of fifteen minutes a day; (3) see how much Osler accomplished; (4) find a time to read.

  8. ————

9. This was addressed primarily to (1) busy people; (2) students; (3) professional men; (4) executives.

  9. ————

10. The Pfc. illustration was to show us how (1) he found opportunities to read; (2) unfortunate he was; (3) carefully he planned; (4) much he read.

  10. ————

(10 off for each mistake)   *Reflective Comprehension* ————

TOTAL READING COMPREHENSION SCORE ————

VOCABULARY CHECK QUESTIONS

		without context I	*with context* II
1. *attain*	(1) dress; (2) reach; (3) buy; (4) try; (5) explain.	1. ————	————
2. *avocational*	related to (1) work; (2) routine; (3) apprenticeship; (4) salaries; (5) hobbies.	2. ————	————
3. *meritorious*	(1) praiseworthy; (2) salable; (3) practical; (4) original; (5) ordinary.	3. ————	————
4. *criteria*	(1) credits; (2) criticisms; (3) standards; (4) crimes; (5) notes.	4. ————	————
5. *prodigious*	(1) free; (2) enormous; (3) fraternal; (4) profound; (5) reckless.	5. ————	————

(10 off for each mistake)   *Word Comprehension* without *contextual help* (I) ————

Word Comprehension with *contextual help* (II) ————

TOTAL WORD COMPREHENSION SCORE ————

EXERCISES

SWING THREE BATS

Suppose you are a 200-word-a-minute reader. Realizing the distinct advantage of increased reading efficiency, you immediately set to work. Your goal? Double your present rate with the same or better comprehension.

Now, how do you go about reaching that goal? Well, how do you learn to play golf — or the piano? For one thing, by practicing. Paderewski once said: "I practice faithfully every day. If I miss one day, I notice it. If I miss two days, the critics notice it. And if I miss three, my audience notices it."

But that is hardly specific enough to be helpful. Take Henry Smith, freshman. Henry was one of those 200-word-a-minute readers, struggling to keep up in an assignment-filled world. His English teacher, sensing his problem, encouraged him to work on improving his reading. After three weeks of determined "practice," Henry reported disconsolately back to his teacher — *no real progress.*

Records of his practice session showed that only once — his second session — had he tried reading faster than 300 words a minute. But comprehension fell to a low of 30 percent, so for the remaining sessions he dropped back to his usual rate. To be sure, as he continued to practice, his comprehension rose from an initial 80 to 90 percent. But Henry's real need was for improvement in rate, and three weeks of fairly conscientious practice had not brought results.

But what had he been practicing? Suppose a hunt-and-peck typist wanted to improve her typing efficiency. Would she expect to master the touch system by practicing hunt-and-peck methods? And Henry — could he expect to master rapid reading by practicing slow reading?

Again, how to develop reading efficiency? What is best — a gradual increase in rate of about twenty-five words a minute every week or an immediate jump to double your present rate?

At first thought, a gradual increase might seem best. Yet that approach tends to reinforce old habits more than establish new ones. It may never provide the momentum needed for overcoming the inertia of long-established habits. Furthermore, since nothing succeeds like success, this method may result in loss of interest and discouragement. Jumping immediately to double your present rate has the advantage of a clean break with old habits. But failure to adjust immediately to this difficult new level often means frustration and discouragement.

There is still a third possibility, one which student records suggest is best. It is a zigzag pattern, embodying a rather sharp break from old habits with moves that reduce the accompanying frustration. Watch a batter swing three bats, throw two down, then step up and knock a homer. That one bat feels much lighter and easier to handle after swinging three. Try the same psychology in reading. Jump from your customary 200-word-a-minute rate to 300 words a minute before dropping back to 250. If 250 is your top speed, it will always seem uncomfortably fast. If 300 is top speed, 250 will soon seem much slower and easier reading.

Swing three bats!

(500 words)

COMPREHENSION CHECK QUESTIONS

1. Critics noticed a difference when Paderewski missed practicing for (1) one day; (2) two days; (3) three days; (4) four days.

    1. _____

2. Henry was encouraged to work on reading by (1) an English teacher; (2) a psychology teacher; (3) a counselor; (4) a high-school teacher.

    2. _____

3. Henry's initial comprehension was (1) 80 percent; (2) 60 percent; (3) 40 percent; (4) not specifically mentioned.

    3. _____

4. Jumping immediately to double one's present rate was said to have the advantage of (1) eliminating needless frustration; (2) giving one a feeling of immediate success; (3) making a clean break with old habits; (4) heightening interest.

    4. _____

5. Before reporting back Henry practiced (1) two weeks; (2) three weeks; (3) four weeks; (4) five weeks.

    5. _____

6. The chief purpose of this selection is to (1) suggest how improvement may best be made; (2) establish the importance of practice; (3) discuss the reasons for failure and discouragement; (4) stress the importance of rate.

    6. _____

7. The Paderewski story was used to (1) stress the importance of swinging three bats; (2) emphasize the importance of practice; (3) explain Henry's failure; (4) stress the importance of daily effort.

    7. _____

8. The analogy to the hunt-and-peck typist was intended to suggest (1) that Henry had been practicing the wrong things; (2) that Henry had not been working long enough to see results; (3) that reading is like typing; (4) that mechanical aids are particularly helpful.

    8. _____

9. You would infer from this selection that reading efficiency depends largely upon (1) a series of intensive practice sessions; (2) strong motivation and interest; (3) intelligence; (4) a specified practice procedure.

    9. _____

10. As used in this selection, swing three bats means (1) work energetically; (2) coordinate your efforts; (3) look on practice as a game; (4) work beyond the desired level.

    10. _____

'SCORE _____

Answers: 1, 2; 2, 1; 3, 1; 4, 3; 5, 2; 6, 1; 7, 4; 8, 1; 9, 4; 10, 4.

NAME——————————————————— DATE——————— READING RATE——————— W.P.M.

COMPREHENSION CHECK QUESTIONS

1. In this selection there is a quotation from (1) Mark Twain; (2) Artemus Ward; (3) Oscar Wilde; (4) Ogden Nash. 1. ————

2. Correggio felt the stirring of genius upon contemplating the works of (1) Michelangelo; (2) Leonardo da Vinci; (3) Raphael; (4) Andrea del Sarto. 2. ————

3. Franklin made a man his friend by (1) doing him a favor; (2) loaning him some money; (3) inviting him out to a fine dinner; (4) borrowing a rare book from him. 3. ————

4. LaSalle gained the goodwill of some Indians by (1) bringing them gifts; (2) smoking the peace pipe with them; (3) letting them use some grazing land; (4) addressing them in their own language. 4. ————

5. Specific mention is made of (1) John Smith; (2) Sir James M. Barrie; (3) George Washington; (4) Sir Winston Churchill. 5. ————

Receptive Comprehension ————

6. This selection is primarily to (1) indicate what biographies to read; (2) distinguish between biography and autobiography; (3) categorize types of biography; (4) suggest reasons for reading biography. 6. ————

7. By inference this selection was written primarily for (1) college students; (2) women; (3) adults; (4) business personnel. 7. ————

8. The quoted portion of Captain Scott's letter was to illustrate what about biography? (1) how courage is revealed; (2) how interesting it is; (3) the difference between letters and autobiography; (4) the difference between biography and autobiography. 8. ————

9. Reference to the bookman who divided his big library into biography and "all the rest" was primarily to show (1) the nature of his library; (2) the importance of biography; (3) his special reading tastes; (4) his special book classification system. 9. ————

10. The author apparently feels *what* to be the chief reason for reading biography? (1) to attain personal success; (2) to profit from the lives of others; (3) to find ourselves; (4) to increase self-reliance. 10. ————

(10 off for each mistake) *Reflective Comprehension* ————

TOTAL READING COMPREHENSION SCORE ————

VOCABULARY CHECK QUESTIONS

		without context I	*with context* II
1. *integrity*	(1) honor; (2) value; (3) productivity; (4) bias; (5) inventiveness.	1. ————	————
2. *apathetically*	(1) sincerely; (2) sadly; (3) listlessly; (4) passionately; (5) regretfully.	2. ————	————
3. *utilitarian*	(1) ordinary; (2) literal; (3) useful; (4) exact; (5) illegal.	3. ————	————
4. *annotating*	(1) adding explanatory notes; (2) following directions; (3) attempting; (4) disagreeing; (5) converting.	4. ————	————
5. *bequest*	(1) basic law; (2) trial; (3) search; (4) something handed down; (5) request.	5. ————	————

(10 off for each mistake) *Word Comprehension* without *contextual help* (I) ————

Word Comprehension with *contextual help* (II) ————

TOTAL WORD COMPREHENSION SCORE ————

EXERCISES

Developing specialized reading skills: Surveying: Rapid reading is a necessity in light of our present knowledge explosion. But to keep from being inundated we need additional help from some specialized reading skills. Take surveying, for one. What is it, how does it work, and when should you use it?

Surveying is a technique for getting a general overall picture of an article, chapter, or book in the shortest possible time. It is designed to bring you the essence with a minimal investment of time. You can survey ten to forty articles or chapters in the time it takes to read just one.

It is based on certain general characteristics of written communication. Usually, for example, the title of an article provides the most concise indication of its content. Then, normally, the first paragraph points the direction to be taken. Major divisions are often marked off with headings. Italics, graphs, and tables stress other important facets. Finally the last paragraph usually summarizes or reiterates essentials.

To survey, just translate those characteristics into action, as follows:

(1) Read the title.
(2) Read the first paragraph in entirety.
(3) Read all headings, italicized words, graphs, or tables.
(4) Read the last paragraph in entirety.

This technique focuses attention on those few parts most likely to provide the best possible overview. Try it now yourself. The parts are all laid out here for your attention.

Uses of Biography

"In Oscar Wilde's play *A Woman of No Importance*, Lord Illingworth remarks: 'The Book of Life begins with a man and a woman in a garden.' To this, Mrs. Allonby replies: 'It ends with Revelations.' It is the wealth of interesting stories that come in between that make up biography." (first paragraph)

Self-Improvement   (heading)

Practical Lessons   (heading)

Some Autobiographies   (heading)

Memoirs from Beyond the Grave. . .Out of My Life and Thought. . .Memoirs. . .Peter Pan (italicized words)

Fame Is Not All   (heading)

"We learn all we can from history and biography in order to profit by the accumulated wisdom of the race. We do not have to start our own lives from the ground, but from the shoulders of the people whose lives we read." (last paragraph)

Using those few words as clues, notice the perspective you have on the entire article. Reading only about 7 percent of the article lets you know, generally, what to expect in the remaining 93 percent. Furthermore, surveying lets you cover fourteen articles of similar length in the time that it would normally take to read only one.

Sometimes an overview is all that you need. But be sure not to overlook the fringe benefits. First, surveying speeds up your reading. Just as you can drive a familiar road more rapidly than a strange one, so when you read after a survey you read more rapidly because you know the ground to be covered. Second, surveying tends to sharpen your awareness of main ideas. After all, the main ideas stand out sharply in a survey. Finally, surveying helps you remember essentials more easily.

So, next time you open your chemistry text, don't start reading. Survey the chapter first. You will read it a bit more rapidly afterward, will have a stronger grasp of main points, and will remember them better. Make this a routine procedure and enjoy the resulting advantages.

Developing specialized reading skills — Skimming: A second most useful technique is that of skimming. Use it either as a preliminary to reading or as a review. Here's how it works. Like surveying, it is based on known characteristics of written communication.

In a sense, skimming is an overlay on surveying. It is exactly like surveying except that you skim all the paragraphs between the first and last paragraphs (which are skipped completely when making a survey).

If the paragraphs are short, skim them by reading the first sentence only; then, shifting into high gear, note all key words and phrases in the remainder of the paragraph. Follow that same procedure with all paragraphs up to the last, which is read in entirety. With long expository paragraphs, you may want to read both the first and last sentence, noting key words and phrases between.

Try it now with the article "Uses of Biography," turning back to page 49. You get a much more complete picture from your select reading of those portions most likely to contain the substance of the article. Familiarize yourself with both superspeed techniques, substituting them for normal reading whenever appropriate. They will add immeasurably to your reading flexibility.

NAME————————————————————— DATE————————— READING RATE————————— W.P.M.

COMPREHENSION CHECK QUESTIONS

1. Mike's first "study" session is with (1) economics; (2) psychology; (3) history; (4) English.   1.————

2. Most people have had training in reading through the (1) 4th grade; (2) 6th grade; (3) 8th grade; (4) high school.   2.————

3. Mike's word-per-minute reading rate for his first "study" session was given as (1) 75 wpm; (2) 96 wpm; (3) 120 wpm; (4) 163 wpm.   3.————

4. For a program of self-instruction the author recommends (1) one basic procedure; (2) two basic procedures; (3) three basic procedures; (4) four basic procedures.   4.————

5. Mike's burst of speed probably (1) left him mentally exhausted; (2) resulted in poor retention; (3) was a waste of time; (4) resulted in better retention.   5.————

Receptive Comprehension ————

6. The purpose of this selection is to suggest (1) the effectiveness of self-instruction in reading; (2) a specific weakness in our educational system; (3) ways of helping slow-reading adults; (4) the importance of speed in the reading process.   6.————

7. You would infer that motivation is a factor of (1) no importance; (2) little importance; (3) some importance; (4) particular importance.   7.————

8. Particular emphasis is placed on (1) timing your reading; (2) keeping a reading diary; (3) practicing on newspapers; (4) using a tachistoscope.   8.————

9. This article reflects particular concern over (1) recreational reading; (2) informational reading; (3) all kinds of reading; (4) the reading of literature.   9.————

10. You would infer that the best competition is with (1) yourself; (2) another individual of the same general ability; (3) the class average; (4) another individual slightly better than yourself.   10.————

(10 off for each mistake)   *Reflective Comprehension* ————

TOTAL READING COMPREHENSION SCORE ————

VOCABULARY CHECK QUESTIONS

		without context I	*with context* II
1. *facile*	(1) difficult; (2) quarrelsome; (3) witty; (4) broken; (5) effortless.	1. ————	————
2. *arduous*	(1) zealous; (2) luxurious; (3) parched; (4) hard; (5) fragrant.	2. ————	————
3. *stint*	(1) stench; (2) pain; (3) color; (4) loop; (5) share.	3. ————	————
4. *inhibit*	(1) suppress; (2) live in; (3) encourage; (4) damage; (5) begin.	4. ————	————
5. *tangible*	(1) confused; (2) tasty; (3) definite; (4) open; (5) hypothetical.	5. ————	————

(10 off for each mistake)   *Word Comprehension* without *contextual help* (I) ————

Word Comprehension with *contextual help* (II) ————

TOTAL WORD COMPREHENSION SCORE ————

EXERCISES

Developing specialized reading skills: Scanning: To function effectively, a mechanic needs many different tools. After all, he doesn't use a file to loosen a bolt or a wrench to tighten a screw. Similarly, to read and study effectively you need many different techniques, not just one.

Scanning is the technique to use when you want to find one small bit of information within a relatively large body of printed material. It fits the proverbial needle-in-the-haystack situation. It can and should be the fastest of the specialized reading speeds. The survey provides a quick, high-level view, skimming provides a lower-level view to bring more details into sight, and scanning zooms you in for a close, sharp view of only one detail.

With practice, you should scan accurately at from 10,000 to 15,000 wpm. Students in the Efficient Reading classes at the University of Minnesota scan initially, on the average, at about 1,500 wpm. After practice the class average moves up to about 15,000 wpm.

This text is laid out to help you make enviable progress toward that top-level performance. Your first move is to check both the speed and accuracy with which you now can scan. Use the following table to get your approximate rate. You can use it as it is with articles of approximately 2,000 words in length, such as Selections 13, 45, and 46. Then, dividing the figure in the time column by 2, you can also use it with selections of approximately 1,000 words in length, such as Selections 19, 21, and 35.

Scanning Time	Wpm Rate		Scanning Time	Wpm Rate
10 sec. —	12,000 wpm		60 sec. —	2,000 wpm
15 sec. —	8,000 wpm		80 sec. —	1,500 wpm
20 sec. —	6,000 wpm		90 sec. —	1,333 wpm
30 sec. —	4,000 wpm		100 sec. —	1,200 wpm
40 sec. —	3,000 wpm		120 sec. —	1,000 wpm
50 sec. —	2,400 wpm		140 sec. —	855 wpm

Sample scanning problem based on Selection 13, "In Other Words": Keeping an accurate count of your scanning time, scan this entire selection, "In Other Words," as rapidly as you can to find the answer to this question: How many times was the proper name *Pfungst* mentioned in the article? Determine your present scanning rate and accuracy.

A few weeks later, after additional practice, recheck your performance to see how much improvement you have made. For this recheck use the same selection, but try to answer this question: How many times does the abbreviation *IQ* appear? Again determine your rate and accuracy.

Scanning makes an ideal review technique in preparation for mid-terms or finals. It lets you check important details in the material to be covered. Perhaps even more important is the contribution that scanning makes to your development of vocabulary and comprehension. Here are suggestions for those uses.

Scan-checking to improve vocabulary: The five-item vocabulary tests for each selection are designed to help you make better use of context in arriving at word meanings. Getting word meaning from context is a rather specialized skill of the utmost importance. Use scanning to develop that skill. Take each five-item vocabulary test, putting your answers in the first column, headed *without context.* Then scan the selection rapidly, underlining each of the five words when you find them. Examine the context for clues to word meaning, changing any answers by entering revised answers in the second column, headed *with context.* If you make effective use of context, the answers in that second column should be perfect. If vocabulary is not a major problem, scan for only one word in each five-item test — the most difficult or strangest of the five. This will help you to become a more rapid and accurate scanner as well as to improve word mastery.

Scan-checking to improve receptive or reflective comprehension: If a certain type of math problem tends to give you difficulty, you need to work through some of that type very carefully, rethinking the problem until it is clear. This rethinking is equally useful in improving comprehension.

Here's how it works. Read a selection and finish the test as usual. Before checking the answers with the key in the back, select one or two questions — ones you feel least sure about — reread each and then scan through the selection as rapidly as possible until you find the exact place where the question is answered. In short, you check the accuracy, not by consulting the key but by returning to the article itself.

When you are dealing with one of the reflective-type questions, scanning is not quite so simple. With them you will seldom be able to find any one statement that answers the question. Here you need to scan for all bits of relevant evidence. Then by weighing one bit with another you can finally arrive at a tenable conclusion as to the best answer.

Such rethinking of difficult questions should eliminate or lessen present difficulties in handling similar questions, thus improving comprehension. For example, you may notice that the term *exposition* poses difficulties that will be cleared up as you notice the problem and check meaning.

Here are some sample general statements for use with any and all of the selections.

(1) Take any comprehension check question, reread it, then scan rapidly to find the exact spot where the question is answered.

(2) Take the most difficult reflective-type question. Reread it, then scan the entire selection for all relevant information. Weigh the evidence for and against each of the four choices before deciding which is best. You may want to imagine that you are in a debate, forced to prove to an unwilling believer that your answer is indeed the best.

NAME_____ DATE_____ READING RATE_____ W.P.M.

COMPREHENSION CHECK QUESTIONS

1. One authority believes what percent of the male population is functionally illiterate? (1) 30; (2) 25; (3) 20; (4) 10.   1. _____

2. To test "survival" literacy level, use was made of (1) newspaper paragraphs; (2) standard signs and warnings; (3) application forms; (4) paragraphs from a driver's manual.   2. _____

3. One Book Exposure project was set up in (1) Fall River; (2) St. Paul; (3) Washington, D.C.; (4) Detroit.   3. _____

4. The Book Exposure project used (1) volunteer helpers; (2) regular teachers; (3) specially trained clinicians; (4) graduate students.   4. _____

5. From the all-black Marshall High School in Chicago, what percent of their graduates now go on to college? (1) about 20; (2) about 30; (3) about 40; (4) about 50.   5. _____

Receptive Comprehension _____

6. This is mainly to (1) underscore the need to attack the problem of illiteracy; (2) indicate how serious the problem is; (3) show the relationship between reading ability and income level; (4) discuss the cause of illiteracy.   6. _____

7. For best results, emphasis should apparently be on reading (1) for practical ends; (2) to achieve success; (3) for pleasure; (4) to solve personal problems.   7. _____

8. To be a good reader, apparently where is the best place to be brought up? (1) in a big city; (2) in a rural community; (3) in a small town; (4) in a suburb.   8. _____

9. From this selection you would assume what to be most important? (1) an interest in reading; (2) the ability to read; (3) proper instruction in reading; (4) the availability of books.   9. _____

10. In discussing the relationship of dyslexia and reading difficulties, chief weight was given to (1) differences between rich and poor children; (2) carefully controlled studies; (3) illiteracy figures; (4) geographic differences.   10. _____

(10 off for each mistake)   *Reflective Comprehension* _____

TOTAL READING COMPREHENSION SCORE _____

VOCABULARY CHECK QUESTIONS

		without context I	with context II
1. *paradoxically*	(1) effectively; (2) aimlessly; (3) fixedly; (4) incredibly; (5) beautifully. 1.	_____	_____
2. *dyslexia*	(1) dizziness; (2) short-sightedness; (3) eye disease; (4) brain disorder; (5) word-study. 2.	_____	_____
3. *peers*	(1) equals; (2) plagues; (3) sights; (4) superiors; (5) inferiors. 3.	_____	_____
4. *amenities*	(1) finalities; (2) corrections; (3) changes; (4) pleasantries; (5) formalities. 4.	_____	_____
5. *onerous*	(1) honorable; (2) ominous; (3) restful; (4) powerful; (5) burdensome. 5.	_____	_____

(10 off for each mistake)

Word Comprehension without *contextual help* (I) _____

Word Comprehension with *contextual help* (II) _____

TOTAL WORD COMPREHENSION SCORE _____

EXERCISES

USE THE SSQ FORMULA

Before a new pitcher heads for the mound, he takes time to warm up. Before you begin reading, you too should do some warming up — some preparing.

When you sit down to study, those first few minutes are not too productive. Interest and **concentration cannot be switched on** and **off,** as a light switch. **Unrelated thoughts** have to be **pushed out** gradually, as you begin a new activity. Can you **shorten this** warm-up process? **Yes** — by the following formula.

Survey: This first step gives you the best possible overview in the shortest possible time. To survey an article or chapter, **read** the **title,** the **first paragraph,** all **headings, italicized words,** and the **last paragraph.** You should then have the **bare essentials.**

To illustrate, note the underlined parts here. They are what you would **read in** your **survey.** If you can **read** the entire 500-word **selection in two minutes,** it will take only **twelve seconds to survey** it. Or take a **longer chapter** from an anthropology text. **Surveying** the 7,650-word chapter means reading only 350 words — **over twenty-one times faster** than normal reading. This diving in headfirst — this sudden immersion — **forces** almost immediate **concentration.**

Skim: Skimming builds up an even stronger foundation. For this, **read** the **title** and **first paragraph,** as in the survey. **Then** read the **first sentence** and **key words in** all the following **paragraphs, plus** any **headings, heavy-type** or **italicized words.** When you reach the **last paragraph,** read

it completely. As you see, this means rereading all parts covered in the survey, but taking an important next step. **This** selective **reading** of from 20 to 40 percent of the material, **takes** only **about a fifth** to a **third** your **usual** reading **time. Note** the **parts** in **heavier type** on this page. **It** marks what you would **cover** in skimming. Instead of two minutes, it should take only fifty-two seconds.

Question: Generally, a faster-than-comfortable reading speed means better-than-usual concentration. One **student,** however, slipped into an **unfortunate habit,** while trying to develop added concentration. He **tried** so hard to **finish** a certain number of pages **in a limited time** that he was **not actually reading** — just **going through** the **motions. To break himself** of this habit, he used this third step — **raising questions.**

More than anything else, a question is likely to drive unwanted thoughts out of mind. This tends to **shorten** the needed **warming-up** period. **Raise questions** both after surveying and after skimming the material. For example, take the reader who reads the title and consciously asks — "What does SSQ stand for?" He will obviously **read with** much **more purpose** than one who has not evidenced such curiosity. Naturally, **when** you **survey** and **skim, much is missed.** In a sense, however, this **tends** to **encourage** more **questions** than in normal reading, making this dynamic third step an almost automatic consequence of the first two.

So — use these prereading steps. Survey the material. **Skim it rapidly. Then raise questions — ideal preparation for the reading to follow.**

From James I. Brown, *Guide to Effective Reading,* D. C. Heath and Co., 1966.

(500 words)

COMPREHENSION CHECK QUESTIONS

1. The article mentions (1) a catcher; (2) a curve ball; (3) a fly; (4) a pitcher. 1. _____

2. The first few minutes of study were said to be (1) crucial; (2) important; (3) unimportant; (4) unproductive. 2. _____

3. Surveying this article was said to take (1) six seconds; (2) twelve seconds; (3) twenty seconds; (4) thirty-six seconds. 3. _____

4. Skimming is spoken of as (1) speed reading; (2) a useful substitute for reading; (3) useful only with textbook material; (4) selective reading. 4. _____

5. One student was said to (1) read too fast; (2) concentrate poorly; (3) go through the motions of reading; (4) spend too much time in skimming. 5. _____

6. This selection focuses mainly on (1) explaining the formula; (2) describing its origin; (3) encouraging its use; (4) pointing up its advantages. 6. _____

7. Major attention is placed on (1) the actual reading; (2) the selection of appropriate approaches; (3) the proper sequence of steps; (4) preparation for reading. 7. _____

8. The mention of the troubled student was to point up primarily the (1) need for a warm-up period; (2) danger in too much reading speed; (3) importance of concentration; (4) usefulness of questions. 8. _____

9. In the allusion, "diving in headfirst," the water is analogous to (1) meaning; (2) print; (3) the act of reading; (4) preparation for reading. 9. _____

10. You would infer that the reference to SSQ in the title was primarily to (1) aid memory; (2) summarize; (3) arouse interest; (4) save space. 10. _____

SCORE _____

Answers: 1,4; 2,4; 3,2; 4,4; 5,3; 6,3; 7,4; 8,4; 9,2; 10,3.

NAME————————————————————— DATE————————— READING RATE——————————— W.P.M.

COMPREHENSION CHECK QUESTIONS

1. Book output on a world scale is now close to (1) 70,000 titles a year; (2) 160,000 titles a year; (3) 1,000 titles a week; (4) 1,000 titles a day.   1. ————

2. The author specifically mentions (1) Galileo; (2) Columbus; (3) Plato; (4) Gutenberg.   2. ————

3. Who said, "Knowledge . . . is power"? (1) Pope; (2) Emerson; (3) Bacon; (4) Aristotle.   3. ————

4. In the U.S., adults spend about how many minutes per day reading newspapers? (1) twenty-three; (2) thirty-one; (3) fifty-two; (4) seventy-one.   4. ————

5. In advertising today increasing use is made of (1) color; (2) photography; (3) symbols; (4) multi-media.   5. ————

Receptive Comprehension ————

6. The central idea is to explain the (1) knowledge explosion; (2) time required to deal with the knowledge explosion; (3) growth of speed-reading courses; (4) speed at which knowledge and its communication is growing.   6. ————

7. The author's attitude toward change might best be described as (1) matter-of-fact; (2) concerned; (3) cynical; (4) receptive.   7. ————

8. You would infer that in another ten years (1) reading would be less important; (2) we will reach an upper limit on publications; (3) the TV medium will begin to supersede print; (4) reading will be even more important.   8. ————

9. In the discussion of speed reading, the author seems (1) impartial; (2) disinterested; (3) convinced; (4) open-minded.   9. ————

10. He developed the points largely by (1) analogy; (2) repetition; (3) quotes from experts; (4) details.   10. ————

(10 off for each mistake)   *Reflective Comprehension* ————

TOTAL READING COMPREHENSION SCORE ————

VOCABULARY CHECK QUESTIONS

		without context I	with context II
1. *unprecedented*	(1) without example; (2) hopeful; (3) preliminary; (4) without approval; (5) helpless.	1. ————	————
2. *dissemination*	(1) disappearing; (2) spreading; (3) growing; (4) making unlike; (5) association.	2. ————	————
3. *median*	(1) strip; (2) metallic object; (3) fresh; (4) meditative; (5) middle.	3. ————	————
4. *ingests*	(1) takes in; (2) inherits; (3) happens; (4) converts; (5) engineers.	4. ————	————
5. *allegedly*	(1) hopefully; (2) supposedly; (3) happily; (4) graphically; (5) alluringly.	5. ————	————

(10 off for each mistake)   *Word Comprehension* without *contextual help* (I) ————

Word Comprehension with *contextual help*   (II) ————

TOTAL WORD COMPREHENSION SCORE ————

EXERCISES

Perceptual development: College and adult readers without special training habitually perceive words one at a time. Obviously one way to improve reading rate is to train yourself to take in two or more words at a quick look.

By using a 3 × 5 card and a daily paper, you can develop added perceptual span and accuracy. Just cover a headline in a column of print with the 3 × 5 card. Then jerk the card rapidly down and back to expose for a few seconds the first line of the headline. Repeat if necessary to get the complete line. Do the same thing with the next line and so on through the first paragraph of the news story.

For additional perceptual training, practice on the three-division and two-division lines below. Use the 3 × 5 card to cover the print, leaving only the black dot visible. Jerk the card quickly down and back to expose the phrase below for a few seconds. Try to read the entire phrase at one quick look. Ordinarily practice of this kind is provided by a tachistoscope. The procedure just described, however, is a close approximation and should show comparable results.

Three-Division

•
Carl Sandburg
    •
    has often said
        •
       that every student
 •
should learn how
    •
   to read a newspaper
      •
     The other day
•
I heard a
   •
  noted publisher declare
     •
    that many college graduates
•
lack that ability.

Two-Division

First, the newspaper should
   •
carry out our daily
  •
and seller of
   •
in touch with
 •
the mutual advantage

       •
      and does help us
       •
      business. It puts the buyer
      •
    groceries, appliances, automobiles
       •
      each other, to
      •
    of both.

Leaning on key details to formulate main ideas: Daily newspapers provide ideal exercise material for developing added skill in getting main ideas. Just cover the headline for any story, read the story — at least the first paragraph — , then write a headline that captures the essence in just four to six words. As an aid, think in terms of six key questions: Who? What? Why? When? Where? and How? Once you have answered those questions about the news story, ask yourself one more question. Of those six, which one or two seems most important? In this way you can decide which main idea or ideas deserve to dominate the headline.

Try this with the following brief paragraph of a news story:

> Farmers in central Minnesota reported serious crop damage yesterday as a result of an early morning frost combined with an unseasonably cold weekend.

Answer the six questions by looking back at that paragraph; then star the two you consider most important.

Who? _____   When? _____

What? _____   Where? _____

When? _____   How? _____

Finally, which of the following do you think actually appeared as headline for that story?

(1) CENTRAL MINNESOTA FARMERS   (3) SERIOUS CROP DAMAGE
   SUFFER FROM BAD FROST   FOLLOWS EARLY FROST

(2) CROP DAMAGE CAUSED   (4) FROST CAUSES CROP
   BY EARLY FROST   DAMAGE FOR FARMERS

(Headline #3 was actually used.)

NAME——————————————————————— DATE——————— READING RATE——————— W.P.M.

COMPREHENSION CHECK QUESTIONS

1. How many parents in the U.S. want their children to go to college? Nearly (1) 50 percent; (2) 60 percent; (3) 70 percent; (4) 80 percent.   1. ————

2. The average high school graduate should know how many words from the short vocabulary quiz provided? (1) eight; (2) five; (3) two; (4) none.   2. ————

3. On the vocabulary test, the most recent high school graduates (1) showed a wide range of ability; (2) scored about average; (3) scored higher than the others; (4) had the lowest scores of all.   3. ————

4. The author speaks of teaching (1) political science; (2) freshman English; (3) literature; (4) economics.   4. ————

5. How much time each day should be spent in reading? At least (1) four hours; (2) two hours; (3) one hour; (4) forty-five minutes.   5. ————

Receptive Comprehension ————

6. The value of reading receiving most attention in this selection is the (1) practical; (2) recreational; (3) cultural; (4) intellectual.   6. ————

7. Vocabulary is stressed largely because words are (1) basic to all communication; (2) tools of thought; (3) useful socially; (4) helpful in getting good grades.   7. ————

8. The first consideration in encouraging one to read more is to provide (1) suitable instruction; (2) interesting reading; (3) additional incentives; (4) more "good" books.   8. ————

9. The survey of reading habits was mentioned largely to illustrate (1) the good taste of some students; (2) how reading interests change; (3) the value of pocket books; (4) the reason for decline in reading.   9. ————

10. To get children to read, parents should rely mostly on (1) direct advice; (2) example; (3) magazines; (4) book lists.   10. ————

(10 off for each mistake)   *Reflective Comprehension* ————

TOTAL READING COMPREHENSION SCORE ————

VOCABULARY CHECK QUESTIONS

		without context I	*with context* II
1. *extolled*	(1) extracted; (2) praised; (3) spoke out; (4) rang; (5) released.	1. ————	————
2. *laudable*	(1) praiseworthy; (2) laughable; (3) helpful; (4) harmful; (5) singable.	2. ————	————
3. *rigorous*	(1) athletic; (2) tremendous; (3) moral; (4) strict; (5) relaxed.	3. ————	————
4. *correlation*	(1) correspondence; (2) confirmation; (3) correction; (4) figure; (5) average.	4. ————	————
5. *induce*	(1) order; (2) refer; (3) try; (4) persuade; (5) lessen.	5. ————	————

(10 off for each mistake)   *Word Comprehension* without *contextual help* (I) ————

Word Comprehension with *contextual help*   (II) ————

TOTAL WORD COMPREHENSION SCORE ————

WORD GROUPING EXERCISES

Can you read this?

THESE LINES ARE JUST AN EYE-CATCHING WAY
CHANGING THAT REALIZE TO YOU HELPING OF
YOUR PERCEPTUAL HABITS MAY SEEM DIFFICULT,
SOON VERY WILL INSIGHT AND PRACTICE BUT
BRING MASTERY OF THE CHANGES. READ THESE
WAY NEW THE IN — NOW AGAIN ONCE LINES FEW
SEE HOW QUICKLY YOU LEARN TO CHANGE?

Practice moving your eye down the middle of the column as you read.

Prove for yourself
why reading by phrases
aids comprehension
and is better than
word-for-word reading.
Notice what happens
when you read
one
word
at
a
time
or take time to
divide a word
into
syl-
-la-
-bles
as you read.

"Some books
are to be tasted,
others to be swallowed,
and some few
to be chewed
and digested;
that is, some books
are to be read
only in parts,
others to be read
but not curiously,
and some few
to be read wholly
and with diligence
and attention . . .
Reading maketh a full man,
conference a ready man,
and writing
an exact man." Bacon

Now try reading some square span.

Your eyes don't see	in narrow horizontal lines	but see an area	on all sides of the place	where they are focused.	Andrews, a student editor	at Southern Methodist University,	devised Square Span,
a way of modifying	the printed page	to fit man's natural	eye habits much better	than the ordinary arrangement	of printed words.	Tests show that	a majority of readers
could read it	with greater speed than	they could read	conventional printed matter.	At least it offers	an exercise in the grouping	of words that should	serve to discourage word-for-word tendencies.
Try a few more lines	just for additional	practice in grouping words	and in developing a rhythmic	eye movement across the page.	Adapting your reading speed	to the material	is the main thing
in reading.	It is as foolish	to speed through a	poem by Keats as it is	to slow to a snail's pace	in reading material obviously designed	to be read in a hurry.	
Experimental flashes with the tachistoscope	reveal that it is possible	to see five or six words	strung out in this manner	when flashed on a screen			
at 1/100 of a second.	Are you developing	suitable word-grouping habits?					

NAME————————————————— DATE————————— READING RATE—————————— W.P.M.

COMPREHENSION CHECK QUESTIONS

1. A well-written letter was said to have how many points of focus? (1) one; (2) two; (3) three; (4) four.   1. ————

2. Specific reference was made to (1) Samuel Johnson; (2) Shelley; (3) Wellington; (4) Walt Whitman.   2. ————

3. A prime minister was said to have addressed his queen as if she were (1) a commoner; (2) an equal; (3) an institution; (4) a public meeting.   3. ————

4. Mention is made of (1) the Lord's Prayer; (2) the Declaration of Independence; (3) the Gettysburg Address; (4) the Presidential Oath of Office.   4. ————

5. Procrustes was spoken of as a (1) prophet; (2) bandit; (3) merchant; (4) beggar.   5. ————

Receptive Comprehension ————

6. This selection is primarily to (1) explain how business and personal letters differ; (2) suggest how to write better letters; (3) discuss reasons for writing effective letters; (4) show the importance of word choice in letters.   6. ————

7. The introductory comment about labor-saving devices was to suggest that (1) they take time away from letter-writing; (2) they provide more time for letter-writing; (3) they should help us streamline letter-writing efforts; (4) they illustrate the rapidity of change.   7. ————

8. The reference to *incomprehensibility* was to suggest the (1) need for short words; (2) usefulness of long words; (3) way words are built; (4) need for the right word.   8. ————

9. The illustration of Procrustes was intended primarily to make what point? (1) be brief; (2) be exact; (3) don't be too exact; (4) don't be too brief.   9. ————

10. Apparently the chief concern in writing a business letter is to be (1) brief; (2) clear; (3) tactful; (4) interesting.   10. ————

(10 off for each mistake)   *Reflective Comprehension* ————

TOTAL READING COMPREHENSION SCORE ————

VOCABULARY CHECK QUESTIONS

		without context I	with context II
1. *uncouth*	(1) unhappy; (2) unsocial; (3) disobedient; (4) uncultured; (5) normal.	1. ————	————
2. *lucid*	(1) readily understood; (2) badly tangled; (3) fortunate; (4) glittering; (5) luxurious.	2. ————	————
3. *stodgy*	(1) impassive; (2) full; (3) alert; (4) sharply outlined; (5) dull.	3. ————	————
4. *audacious*	(1) daring; (2) quiet; (3) memorable; (4) hopeful; (5) customary.	4. ————	————
5. *opaque*	(1) clear; (2) obscure; (3) reflective; (4) opposite; (5) peaceful.	5. ————	————

(10 off for each mistake)   *Word Comprehension* without *contextual help* (I) ————

Word Comprehension with *contextual help* (II) ————

TOTAL WORD COMPREHENSION SCORE ————

BE A PERFECT SPELLER IN 30 MINUTES
Norman Lewis

Can you become a perfect speller? Yes — if you are willing to memorize a few intriguing rules and give your memory a stimulating jolt. I have demonstrated again and again in my adult classes at the City College of New York that anyone who possesses normal intelligence and has had an average education should have no trouble in becoming a perfect speller in 30 minutes or even less!

What makes the task so easy and rapid?

1. Investigations have proved that 95 percent of our spelling mistakes occur in just 100 words. Not only do we all seem to misspell the same words, but we usually misspell them in just about the same way.
2. Correct spelling depends entirely on memory, and the most effective way I know of to train your memory is by means of association — or by *mnemonics* (pronounced *nemonics*).

If you are a poor speller, the chances are that you've developed a complex because you misspell some or all of the 100 words with which this article deals. When you have mastered this list by means of association and memory, 95 percent of your spelling difficulties will vanish.

So let's start with the 25 troublesome words listed below. In addition to the correct spelling of each of the words, you will find the simple mnemonic that will enable you to fix that correct spelling indelibly in your memory.

All right
> Two words, no matter what it means. Keep in mind that it's the opposite of all wrong.

Repetition
> The first four letters are the same as those in repeat.

Irritable, Inimitable
> Think of allied forms, irritate and imitate.

Recommend
> Commend, which is easy to spell, plus the prefix *re-*.

Ridiculous
> Think of the allied form, ridicule, which is usually spelled correctly, thus avoiding rediculous.

Despair
> Again think of another form — desperate — and so avoid dispair.

Stationery
> The word that means paper; notice the *er* in paper.

Stationary
> This means standing, so notice the *a* in stand.

Superintendent
> The superintendent in an apartment house collects the rent — thus you avoid superintendant.

Coolly
> You can spell cool — simply add the adverbial ending *-ly*.

Separate, Comparative
> Look for a rat in both words.

Supersede
> The only word in the language ending in *-sede*.

Succeed
Proceed
Exceed
> The only three words in the language ending in *-ceed*. In the order given here the initial letters form the first 3 letters in spell.

Cede, Recede,
Precede, etc.
> All other words with a final syllable sounding similar end in *cede*.

Procedure
> One of the double e's in proceed moves to the end in procedure.

Absence
> Think of the allied form absent, and you will not be tempted to misspell it abscence.

Conscience
> Science, plus the prefix *con-*.

Anoint
> Think of an ointment, hence no double n.

Ecstasy
> To *sy* (sigh) with ecstasy.

Analyze, Paralyze
> The only two non-technical words in the language ending in *-yze*.

Whether or not you have faith in your ability as a speller you will need only 30 seconds to overcome your difficulties with each of the 25 words in the list, or 12½ minutes all told. And as you probably misspell only some of the words, not the entire 25, you should be able to eliminate your errors in even less time. Just try spending 30 seconds, now, on each of the words you're doubtful about — then put your new-found learning to the test by filling in the missing letters in the same list of words which follows. To your delight, you'll find that it's not at all difficult to make a perfect score. Try it and see for yourself.

A—RIGHT	SUPER—
REP—TITION	SUC—
IRRIT—BLE	PROC—
INIMIT—BLE	EXC—
RE—O—MEND	PREC—
R—DICULOUS	PROC—DURE
D—SPAIR	AB—ENCE
STATION—RY (paper)	CON—NCE
STATION—RY (standing)	A—OINT
SUPERINTEND—NT	ECSTA—Y
COO—Y	ANAL—E
SEP—RATE	PARAL—E
COMPAR—TIVE	*(continued on page 230)*

(continued on page 230)

Reprinted from *Coronet,* February 1946. Copyright, 1946, by Esquire, Inc.

NAME_____ DATE_____ READING RATE_____ W.P.M.

COMPREHENSION CHECK QUESTIONS

1. The teacher's name was (1) Stamm; (2) Steele; (3) Stone; (4) Smith.   1. _____

2. Mention is made of reading a poem by (1) Keats; (2) Shelley; (3) Burns; (4) Byron.   2. _____

3. The teacher stirred their imagination by asking them how they would like to live in (1) England during the reign of Elizabeth; (2) Italy during the Renaissance; (3) Greece at the height of its glory; (4) France at the time of the French Revolution.   3. _____

4. For the good-bye party the boys prepared a (1) eulogy; (2) gift; (3) parody; (4) play.   4. _____

5. The class met in Room (1) 308; (2) 318; (3) 288; (4) 280.   5. _____

Receptive Comprehension _____

6. The purpose of this article is to (1) tell about an unusual character; (2) describe how he taught English; (3) suggest the importance of wide reading; (4) help us feel an appreciation for this character.   6. _____

7. The teacher's comment on the phrase "tender age" was (1) one of approval; (2) not given; (3) one suggesting lazy writing; (4) one suggesting a specific revision.   7. _____

8. His attempts to get them to see if they could improve on a poem were intended to lead to (1) a better understanding of the poem; (2) a better appreciation of literature; (3) an improvement in writing and speaking; (4) improvement of discussion techniques.   8. _____

9. His most important piece of advice was to (1) study; (2) work; (3) browse; (4) read.   9. _____

10. The article implies that we should read things of (1) personal interest; (2) recognized merit; (3) current interest; (4) literary worth.   10. _____

(10 off for each mistake)   *Reflective Comprehension* _____

TOTAL READING COMPREHENSION SCORE _____

VOCABULARY CHECK QUESTIONS

		without context I	*with context* II
1. *condescension*	(1) condemnation; (2) grief; (3) control; (4) insulation; (5) air of superiority.	1. _____	_____
2. *melee*	(1) combining; (2) confused mass; (3) melting; (4) maturing; (5) orderly plan.	2. _____	_____
3. *abhorred*	(1) clung to; (2) hated; (3) wandered; (4) gave up; (5) assumed.	3. _____	_____
4. *bestow*	(1) give; (2) assign; (3) beset; (4) beg; (5) elevate.	4. _____	_____
5. *concocted*	(1) finished; (2) exploded; (3) devised; (4) seasoned; (5) drank.	5. _____	_____

(10 off for each mistake)   *Word Comprehension* without *contextual help* (I) _____

Word Comprehension with *contextual help* (II) _____

TOTAL WORD COMPREHENSION SCORE _____

Mere repetitious drill, however, will not teach you to spell correctly. If you drive a car or sew or do any familiar manual work, you know how your hands carry on automatically while your mind is far away. So if you hope to learn how to spell by filling pages with a word, about all you'll get for your trouble will be writer's cramp.

The only way to learn to spell the words that now plague you is to devise a mnemonic for each one.

If you are never sure whether it's *indispensible* or *indispensable*, you can spell it a thousand or a million times — and the next time you have occasion to write it you'll still wonder whether to end with *ible* or *able*. But if you say to yourself just once that *able* men are generally indispens*able*, you've conquered another spelling demon.

In the test below are another 25 words from the list of 100, each presented in both the correct form and in the popular misspelling. Go through the list quickly, checking what you consider the proper choices. In this way you will discover which of the 25 would stump you in a spelling test. Then devise a personal mnemonic for each word you failed to get right, writing your result in the margin of the page.

Don't be alarmed if some of your mnemonics turn out to be silly — the sillier they are, the easier to recall them in an emergency. One of my pupils, who could never remember how many *l*'s to put into tranquillity (or is it *tranquility?*), came up with this: "In the old days life was more tranquil, and people wrote with *quills* instead of fountain pens. Hence — *tranquillity!*" That is the preferred form, though either is correct.

Another pupil, a girl, who always chewed her nails over *irresistible* before deciding whether to end it with *ible* or *able*, suddenly realized that a certain brand of lipstick was called "*Irresistible*," the point being that the only vowel in *lipstick* is *i* — hence, *ible*! Silly, mnemonics, aren't they? But they work. Now tackle the test and see how clever — or silly — you can be.

Do These Words Stump You?

Listed below are the correct and incorrect spellings of 25 words commonly misspelled. Check a or b, whichever you think is correct. Then look at the answers to see how well you did.

1. (a) supprise,
   (b) surprise
2. (a) inoculate,
   (b) innoculate
3. (a) definitely,
   (b) definately
4. (a) priviledge,
   (b) privilege
5. (a) incidently,
   (b) incidentally
6. (a) predictible
   (b) predictable
7. (a) embarassment,
   (b) embarrassment
8. (a) descriminate,
   (b) discriminate
9. (a) description,
   (b) discription
10. (a) pronounciation,
    (b) pronunciation
11. (a) occurence,
    (b) occurrence
12. (a) developement,
    (b) development
13. (a) arguement,
    (b) argument
14. (a) assistant,
    (b) asisstant
15. (a) grammer,
    (b) grammar
16. (a) parallel,
    (b) paralell
17. (a) drunkeness,
    (b) drunkenness
18. (a) suddeness,
    (b) suddenness
19. (a) dissipate,
    (b) disippate
20. (a) weird,
    (b) wierd
21. (a) baloon,
    (b) balloon
22. (a) noticeable,
    (b) noticable
23. (a) truely,
    (b) truly
24. (a) vicious,
    (b) viscious
25. (a) insistent,
    (b) insistant

By now you're well on the way to developing a definite superiority complex about your spelling. Remember: you want to spell correctly so that in correspondence you will not give your reader the impression your education has been sadly neglected. The conquest of the 100 words most commonly misspelled is not guaranteed to make you top man in a spelling bee, but it's certain to improve your writing and do a lot to bolster your ego.

So far you have worked with 50 of the 100 spelling demons. The remainder of the list appears below. Test yourself, and discover which words are your Waterloo. Study each one you miss, observe how it's put together, then devise whatever association pattern will fix the correct form in your mind.

Once you've mastered this list, you are a good speller. And — if you've truly applied yourself — your goal has been achieved in 30 minutes or less!

How Good Are You Now?

Here are fifty words which also frequently stump the expert speller. See how quickly you can master them by finding a simple association for each.

misspelling	vacillate	possesses
conscious	oscillate	professor
indispensable	forty	category
disappear	dilettante	rhythmical
disappoint	changeable	vacuum
corroborate	accessible	benefited
sacrilegious	accommodate	committee
persistent	license	grievous
exhilaration	panicky	judgment
newsstand	seize	plebeian
desirable	leisure	tariff
irresistible	receive	sheriff
tranquillity	achieve	connoisseur
dilemma	holiday	necessary
perseverance	existence	sergeant
until	pursue	irrelevant
tyrannize	pastime	

Answers: 1–b, 2–a, 3–a, 4–b, 5–b, 6–b, 7–b, 8–b, 9–a, 10–b, 11–b, 12–b, 13–b, 14–a, 15–b, 16–a, 17–b, 18–b, 19–a, 20–a, 21–b, 22–a, 23–b, 24–a, 25–a.

230

Name————————————————— Date——————— Reading Rate————————— w.p.m.

COMPREHENSION CHECK QUESTIONS

1. A quotation is given from a letter by (1) Shelley; (2) Byron; (3) Keats; (4) Burns.   1. _____

2. Mention is made of (1) Lady Jane Worthington; (2) Lady Esther Cavendish; (3) Lady Mary Montagu; (4) Lady Laura Lawrence.   2. _____

3. The writer speaks of certain faults to avoid, calling them Letter Writing (1) Don'ts; (2) Awfuls; (3) Illiteracies; (4) Sins.   3. _____

4. George Saintsbury said a letter must have (1) color; (2) snap; (3) brevity; (4) bite.   4. _____

5. The author seems most excited when he cautions against (1) underlining words; (2) putting slang in quotations; (3) writing about the weather; (4) using colored ink.   5. _____

Receptive Comprehension _____

6. The purpose of this article is to (1) suggest things to avoid in writing letters; (2) suggest the importance of letters in keeping friendships alive; (3) suggest how to write more interesting letters; (4) suggest how even simple things may be made interesting.   6. _____

7. You would infer that excuses for not having written sooner are (1) appropriate; (2) necessary; (3) tedious; (4) discourteous.   7. _____

8. The last two letter writers are mentioned to illustrate the value of (1) short letters; (2) long, newsy letters; (3) getting yourself into a letter; (4) using cheerful detail.   8. _____

9. You would infer that the best advice for the would-be writer is to be (1) clear; (2) specific; (3) witty; (4) coherent.   9. _____

10. Apparently letter writing is most important as a means of (1) making friends; (2) conducting business effectively; (3) developing powers of observation; (4) developing writing ability.   10. _____

(10 off for each mistake)   *Reflective Comprehension* _____

Total Reading Comprehension Score _____

VOCABULARY CHECK QUESTIONS

		without context I	with context II
1. *vapid*	(1) steamy; (2) proud; (3) changeable; (4) lifeless; (5) superior.	1. _____	_____
2. *avidity*	(1) eagerness; (2) dryness; (3) aversion; (4) average; (5) strength.	2. _____	_____
3. *vagaries*	(1) stupidity; (2) voids; (3) tramps; (4) doubts; (5) caprices.	3. _____	_____
4. *illegible*	(1) not easily readable; (2) illiterate; (3) not legal; (4) secret; (5) untrue.	4. _____	_____
5. *amenable*	(1) improved; (2) submissive; (3) treated; (4) opposed; (5) harmful.	5. _____	_____

(10 off for each mistake)   *Word Comprehension* without *contextual help* (I) _____

Word Comprehension with *contextual help* (II) _____

Total Word Comprehension Score _____

EXERCISES

1. Substituting details for generalities: Good writing, as well as good letter writing, demands more than mere generalities. Make each of the following general statements come to life by the addition of concrete details. Compare with the originals.

A. Her letters are interesting.

B. Keep your friends by writing short letters often.

C. Avoid writing overly long letters.

D. Be sure to include your personal reactions when you tell some anecdote.

E. Don't use parenthetical exclamations.

2. Correcting serious sentence errors: Unintentional fragmentary sentences and comma faults are the two most serious sentence errors. Some of the following sentences need to be revised in order to eliminate such faults. Be prepared to explain why changes were made. Check with the text. Does degree of formality or informality perhaps make a difference?

A. You know what it will be like, they're always the same.

B. Having wonderful time. Wish you were here.

C. We might call them epistols, they certainly bore you to death.

D. Snapshots, that's what people want, in these intimate, friendly letters.

E. But to sit down and try to write a sprightly letter in cold blood, so to speak. That's a hard thing to do.

F. Letters can be rich and entertaining. If you make notes of things, happenings and thoughts that occur to you during the day.

G. It's not so hard as you may think. This getting your real self into a letter.

H. You must go below the surface, you must show how you feel about things.

I. It is the love letter which is the letter of letters. The only one really worth getting.

J. To another he will send a clipping about her latest fad. Or perhaps a cartoon.

NAME————————————————— DATE——————— READING RATE————————— W.P.M.

COMPREHENSION CHECK QUESTIONS

1. Conan Doyle, creator of Sherlock Holmes, was a (1) teacher; (2) clerk; (3) physician; (4) sailor.   1. ————

2. In the children's story mentioned, one character is (1) Flirty Gertie; (2) Rudy Rooster; (3) Brewster Rooster; (4) Adelaide Egsofen.   2. ————

3. Synonym-hunting was practiced on (1) *salient;* (2) *superlative;* (3) *aggressive;* (4) *acumen.*   3. ————

4. The secret weapons for Mr. Johns' creative record in business, were said to be (1) 3 × 5 cards; (2) pencils; (3) dreams; (4) coffee-hour contacts.   4. ————

5. Specific reference is made to which author? (1) Edward Streeter; (2) Ernest Hemingway; (3) Oscar Wilde; (4) Stevenson.   5. ————

Receptive Comprehension ————

6. This selection is mainly to show (1) the importance of note-taking; (2) different ways of note-taking; (3) the value of illumination; (4) how to develop creativity in word choice.   6. ————

7. The paragraph mentioning a number of famous writers was intended to show that (1) anyone can write; (2) you needn't start as a writer; (3) writing trains imagination; (4) relatively few succeed as writers.   7. ————

8. The reference to W. Somerset Maugham was largely to (1) point up writing difficulties; (2) encourage us in our writing efforts; (3) show the need for rewriting; (4) reveal his outstanding talent.   8. ————

9. What was apparently the chief purpose of synonym-hunting? (1) to develop a more useful vocabulary; (2) to develop increased creativity; (3) to develop added language facility; (4) to turn waiting time into thinking time.   9. ————

10. The dream illustration was primarily to support the idea of (1) sleeping on a problem; (2) making notes; (3) tapping the subconscious; (4) remembering dreams.   10. ————

(10 off for each mistake)   *Reflective Comprehension* ————

TOTAL READING COMPREHENSION SCORE ————

VOCABULARY CHECK QUESTIONS

		without context I	*with context* II
1. *acclaim*	(1) haste; (2) greeting; (3) fine; (4) control; (5) approval.	1. ————	————
2. *acumen*	(1) appetite; (2) flaw; (3) idea; (4) shrewdness; (5) accuracy.	2. ————	————
3. *surreptitiously*	(1) rapidly; (2) noticeably; (3) forcefully; (4) boldly; (5) stealthily.	3. ————	————
4. *entail*	(1) cause; (2) begin; (3) approach; (4) fail; (5) seek.	4. ————	————
5. *kindred*	(1) effective; (2) strange; (3) related; (4) fearful; (5) pleasant.	5. ————	————

(10 off for each mistake)   *Word Comprehension* without *contextual help* (I) ————

Word Comprehension with *contextual help* (II) ————

TOTAL WORD COMPREHENSION SCORE ————

EXERCISES

1. Look out your window or take a walk down the street. Observe closely the first person you see. Then write a little story about where he has come from and where he is going, using your imagination freely. (Make it a habit in the future to look for extraordinary elements in ordinary events. Jot down the best of these in your notebook.)

2. Write a children's story in which the usual child-pet relationship is reversed — for example, a dog giving a child supper, or a cat taking a sick preschooler to the doctor.

3. List as many synonyms as you can for the word *original*.

4. Imagination has been defined as the ability to see similarities in apparently different things, as opposed to judgment, which is the ability to see differences in apparently similar things. Using your imagination, complete the following statements, comparing each phrase to something uniquely different from it.

(EXAMPLE: The girl washed her hands like *a nun saying prayers.*)

A. A ball of yarn fell to the floor, looking like ——————————————————————

——

B. Her diamond ring was as big as ——————————————————————————

C. Her laughter sounded like ——————————————————————————————

D. Time is ——

E. The sky that Saturday morning was like ————————————————————————

——

F. Waves of hair sprinkled each side of her forehead, like ——————————————————

——

G. People who live in the city are like ——————————————————————————

——

H. The locker room was as quiet as ——————————————————————————————

I. The malted milk was as thick as ——————————————————————————————

J. The professor got himself trapped in his own sentences, like ——————————————————

——

5. Cut seven pieces of cardboard or heavy paper to a size you can carry easily in pocket or purse. Each day this week take one with you, jotting down ideas and impressions. At the end of the week, transfer the best ones to your notebook.

NAME⸺⸺⸺⸺⸺⸺⸺⸺⸺ DATE⸺⸺⸺⸺⸺ READING RATE⸺⸺⸺⸺⸺ W.P.M.

COMPREHENSION CHECK QUESTIONS

1. Which book did Franklin have? (1) *Robinson Crusoe;* (2) *Gulliver's Travels;* (3) *Pilgrim's Progress;* (4) *Swiss Family Robinson.*   1. ⸺⸺⸺

2. His father's library contained mostly (1) religious books; (2) literary works; (3) novels; (4) practical volumes.   2. ⸺⸺⸺

3. Who was said to have discouraged Franklin from his verse-making? (1) his brother; (2) his friend; (3) his readers; (4) his father.   3. ⸺⸺⸺

4. Franklin attempted to imitate the prose found in (1) Plutarch's *Lives;* (2) Defoe's *Essays;* (3) Stevenson's *Essays;* (4) the *Spectator.*   4. ⸺⸺⸺

5. In comparing his version with the original, Franklin said he discovered (1) punctuation difficulties; (2) a vocabulary deficiency; (3) spelling problems; (4) sentence problems.   5. ⸺⸺⸺

Receptive Comprehension ⸺⸺⸺

6. This selection is chiefly to (1) explain his love of books; (2) tell why he decided to write prose, not poetry; (3) explain why he wanted to learn to write; (4) tell about the procedure he adapted to improve his writing.   6. ⸺⸺⸺

7. You would conclude that the chief reason for Franklin's turning away from writing poetry was (1) its difficulty; (2) its poor reception; (3) its poor financial return; (4) its lack of prestige.   7. ⸺⸺⸺

8. As a self-critic, Franklin was apparently (1) fairly accurate; (2) overly critical; (3) fairly generous; (4) quite unrealistic.   8. ⸺⸺⸺

9. The part about John Collins, another bookish boy, was mainly to indicate (1) how Franklin got interested in writing; (2) why one should avoid argumentation; (3) the value of arguing; (4) the influence of reading certain books.   9. ⸺⸺⸺

10. The primary purpose of the article was to (1) teach; (2) describe; (3) moralize; (4) evaluate.   10. ⸺⸺⸺

(10 off for each mistake)   *Reflective Comprehension* ⸺⸺⸺

TOTAL READING COMPREHENSION SCORE ⸺⸺⸺

VOCABULARY CHECK QUESTIONS

			without context I	*with context* II
1. *ingenious*	(1) naive; (2) frank; (3) mechanical; (4) trusting; (5) clever.	1.	⸺⸺	⸺⸺
2. *confuting*	(1) predicting; (2) storing; (3) denying; (4) joining; (5) confounding.	2.	⸺⸺	⸺⸺
3. *disputatious*	(1) argumentative; (2) displeasing; (3) productive; (4) stingy; (4) concerned.	3.	⸺⸺	⸺⸺
4. *enmities*	(1) preliminaries; (2) foes; (3) laxatives; (4) antagonisms; (5) encouragements.	4.	⸺⸺	⸺⸺
5. *amended*	(1) complained; (2) changed; (3) corrected; (4) added; (5) suggested.	5.	⸺⸺	⸺⸺

(10 off for each mistake)   *Word Comprehension* without *contextual help* (1) ⸺⸺⸺

Word Comprehension with *contextual help* (II) ⸺⸺⸺

TOTAL WORD COMPREHENSION SCORE ⸺⸺⸺

EXERCISES

1. Select from the following subjects five on which you have a strong opinion. Then write a sentence about each in which you express that opinion, either positively or negatively. (EXAMPLE: All people who use hard drugs should be imprisoned for a minimum of five years.)

   A. Drugs
   B. Welfare programs
   C. Pornography
   D. Mercy killing
   E. Sex education in the public schools
   F. Smoking
   G. Violence on television
   H. Freeways
   I. Abortion
   J. Homosexuality

   Now write a paragraph on each of the five subjects you chose in which you defend the *opposite* opinion from the one expressed in your sentence. Try to clear your mind of all prejudices and to present the case as convincingly and as objectively as you can.

2. Consider the effectiveness of the prose in the following brief passage from Frederick Jackson Turner's *The Frontier in American History:*

   > American democracy was born of no theorist's dream. It was not carried in the *Susan Constant* to Virginia, nor in the *Mayflower* to Plymouth. It came stark and strong and full of life out of the American forest, and it gained new strength each time it touched a new frontier.

   Now jot down in as few words as possible the basic idea in each sentence. (EXAMPLE: Democracy not of theoretical origin.) Put your notes aside for a few days. When you return to them, try writing the passage in complete sentences without looking at the original. Compare your version to Turner's. In what ways is your version weaker than, or superior to, his?

   Do the same thing with any other piece of writing you admire.

NAME―――――――――――――――――――――― DATE――――――――― READING RATE――――――――― W.P.M.

COMPREHENSION CHECK QUESTIONS

1. These changes made possible a price cut of (1) 5 percent; (2) 9 percent; (3) 14 percent; (4) 18 percent.   1. ――――

2. Time clocks were (1) all sold; (2) eliminated for over half the employees; (3) reduced in number; (4) scrapped.   2. ――――

3. Forms were eliminated that weighed (1) 26,000 pounds; (2) 40 tons; (3) 80 tons; (4) 120 tons.   3. ――――

4. In the M & S employee lunchrooms (1) a system of bells was used; (2) employees checked in and out at the door; (3) time clocks were used; (4) a loud-speaker was used.   4. ――――

5. Which U. S. company is beginning to make similar moves? (1) Minnesota Mining; (2) IBM; (3) Procter & Gamble; (4) Ford Motor Co.   5. ――――

Receptive Comprehension ――――

6. This is primarily concerned with (1) a way of cutting prices; (2) improving business efficiency by eliminating unnecessary paper work; (3) cutting down on paper work; (4) making better use of employee time.   6. ――――

7. You would infer that most forms are (1) largely a matter of custom and tradition; (2) necessary; (3) helpful but not essential; (4) are created by employees wanting more work.   7. ――――

8. The story of the girls working overtime on "catalogue cards" is told to illustrate (1) how this revolution got started; (2) the time-consuming nature of paper work; (3) how paper-happy M & S was; (4) how much employees hated paper work.   8. ――――

9. Apparently employees are most likely to be happy when they (1) have less paper work; (2) don't have to consult operation manuals; (3) don't have to punch time clocks; (4) have more variety and responsibility on the job.   9. ――――

10. Most emphasis here is on the (1) where; (2) why; (3) how; (4) when.   10. ――――

(10 off for each mistake)   *Reflective Comprehension* ――――

TOTAL READING COMPREHENSION SCORE ――――

VOCABULARY CHECK QUESTIONS

		without context I	*with context* II
1. *perceptive*	(1) alert; (2) percussive; (3) transitive; (4) heartening; (5) profitable.	1. ――――	――――
2. *pilfer*	(1) pester; (2) steal; (3) support; (4) guide; (5) refer.	2. ――――	――――
3. *access*	(1) words; (2) oversupply; (3) admittance; (4) stock; (5) weight.	3. ――――	――――
4. *meticulously*	(1) systematically; (2) extremely; (3) merrily; (4) merely; (5) casually.	4. ――――	――――
5. *incredible*	(1) not culpable; (2) increasing; (3) constant; (4) unbelievable; (5) reassuring.	5. ――――	――――

(10 off for each mistake)

Word Comprehension without *contextual help* (I) ――――

Word Comprehension with *contextual help* (II) ――――

TOTAL WORD COMPREHENSION SCORE ――――

EXERCISES

Parallelism: Effective communication often depends upon the appropriate use of parallel construction. Patrick Henry realized that when he said, "Give me liberty or give me death." Abraham Lincoln realized that when he spoke of "government of the people, by the people, and for the people."

Every theme you write, every speech you make should provide an opportunity for effective use of parallelism.

List five examples of parallelism from a newspaper or magazine:

1.

2.

3.

4.

5.

Improve the parallelism in the following sentences; then check back to the original text:

A. It decided that people were smarter than machines, that those who clerked could be trusted, that honesty is basically characteristic of the public.

B. Prices, already among the nation's lowest, were cut 18 percent.
Above-average wages were upped considerably.
Zooming sales instead of good sales.

C. When a salesgirl needed an item, she simply went to the stockroom to get it; and one didn't even have to make out any withdrawal forms.

D. Every last pair of nylons, all men's undershirts, dresses for children, had to be listed and they were recorded so that stores knew exactly how much to reorder, so that the quantity for purchasing by the head office buyer could be determined.

E. A manager with a stop watch used to ring the lunch bell twice for each shift — first to warn the shift to get ready, then for having the shift clear out.

F. "Why, to keep track of our employes, making sure they put in a full day, of course."

When you have worked over the sentences and checked back, study the versions carefully to see why and when parallel constructions are used most appropriately.

NAME—————————————————— DATE—————— READING RATE—————— W.P.M.

COMPREHENSION CHECK QUESTIONS

1. Mona Sheppard worked for the Government for (1) ten years; (2) fifteen years; (3) twenty years; (4) twenty-five years.

   1. ————

2. Every workday the Government writes communications at a rate of how many per second? (1) 9; (2) 61; (3) 93; (4) 139.

   2. ————

3. For a time Mona Sheppard worked in an office of the (1) Internal Revenue Service; (2) Department of Agriculture; (3) Civil Service Department; (4) Department of the Interior.

   3. ————

4. Mention is made of (1) flat feet; (2) polio; (3) measles; (4) hyperopia.

   4. ————

5. At one time Mona's boss was (1) Herbert Hoover; (2) John A. Mills; (3) Wayne S. Grover; (4) Archibald K. Stewart.

   5. ————

   Receptive Comprehension ————

6. This is mainly about Mona's (1) personal success as a writer; (2) letter-writing reforms; (3) defense of simple English; (4) use of form letters.

   6. ————

7. Mention of her university major in creative writing is to show (1) her early interest in writing; (2) the source of her originality; (3) the value of formal training; (4) her impractical side.

   7. ————

8. The growing acceptance of her letters in Government was largely due to her skill and (1) authority; (2) initiative; (3) interest; (4) persistence.

   8. ————

9. Which of the following stylistic characteristics would she probably put first? (1) forcefulness; (2) brevity; (3) interest; (4) informality.

   9. ————

10. This article is slanted largely toward (1) adults in general; (2) students; (3) would-be writers; (4) Government employees.

    10. ————

(10 off for each mistake)   *Reflective Comprehension* ————

TOTAL READING COMPREHENSION SCORE ————

VOCABULARY CHECK QUESTIONS

		without context I	*with context* II
1. *prolific*	(1) productive; (2) prohibitive; (3) frank; (4) wasteful; (5) sketchy.	1. ————	————
2. *substantiate*	(1) lower; (2) confirm; (3) substitute; (4) take away; (5) press.	2. ————	————
3. *compensation*	(1) loss; (2) compliance; (3) discount; (4) remuneration; (5) increase.	3. ————	————
4. *concise*	(1) detailed; (2) curved; (3) brief; (4) carefully done; (5) sharp.	4. ————	————
5. *verbiage*	(1) narrative; (2) sentences; (3) wordiness; (4) outcries; (5) criticism.	5. ————	————

(10 off for each mistake)   *Word Comprehension* without *contextual help* (I) ————

Word Comprehension with *contextual help* (II) ————

TOTAL WORD COMPREHENSION SCORE ————

EXERCISES

1. Practice translating difficult technical or semitechnical paragraphs into conversational or standard English. Psychologists emphasize this rephrasing of the words of a textbook or lecture into *your own language* as an excellent way of improving learning efficiency. Try it as part of your regular study routine.

   In the space below, enter a difficult yet fairly short passage from one of your textbooks. Then, immediately after, translate the passage into simple English:

   Text version:

   Your version:

2. Select some technical term or process and attempt to explain it orally to someone who lacks your technical background (for example, *photosynthesis, osmosis, valence, denotation, connotation, malapropism, spoonerism, euphemism*).

3. You can say "Eschew polysyllabic verbal symbols" or "Avoid big words." Perhaps the single most useful spelling rule is the "Final Consonant Rule." In a handbook you may find it expressed in this way: "Monosyllabic words and words accented on the last syllable, when ending in a single final consonant, preceded by a single vowel, double the consonant when a termination beginning with a vowel is added."

   Translate that rule into language you would use in explaining it to a high school freshman:

   Revised form: _____

   _____

4. Translate this bit of federalese into the kind of language Miss Sheppard would prefer:

   "The noncompensable evaluation heretofore assigned you for your service-connected disability is confirmed and continued."

   Revised form: _____

   _____

NAME———————————————— DATE———————— READING RATE———————— W.P.M.

COMPREHENSION CHECK QUESTIONS

1. The note to the bank teller asked for (1) a new checkbook; (2) the monthly statement; (3) all available cash; (4) a safety box application.　　　　　　　　1. ———————

2. Illegibility costs U. S. businessmen about how many dollars a week? (1) ten thousand; (2) sixty thousand; (3) a million; (4) six million.　　　　　　　　2. ———————

3. Reference is made to the (1) Palmer System; (2) McFadden style; (3) McGuffey Reader; (4) Riverside Readers.　　　　　　　　3. ———————

4. Rounded letters are said to indicate (1) generosity; (2) moodiness; (3) intolerance; (4) introversion.　　4. ———————

5. Pupils are getting help with their handwriting in (1) Chicago; (2) Washington; (3) Pittsburgh; (4) Philadelphia.　　　　　　　　5. ———————

Receptive Comprehension ———————

6. This is intended primarily to (1) help improve your handwriting; (2) show the importance of your handwriting; (3) point up reasons for illegibility; (4) show the relationship between handwriting and personality.　　　　　　　　6. ———————

7. The fuel oil story is used to illustrate the (1) carelessness of the truck driver; (2) relationship between education and handwriting; (3) need for legibility; (4) similarity of *4* and *7*.　　7. ———————

8. Chief reason for poor penmanship is apparently (1) increasing use of typewriters; (2) personality factors; (3) automation; (4) lack of formal instruction.　　　　　　　　8. ———————

9. The mention of slipshod writing on application forms is to show how (1) important handwriting is in landing a job; (2) illegibly some write; (3) illegibility destroys customer good will; (4) character is revealed by handwriting.　　　　　　　　9. ———————

10. The writer tends to look upon the graphologist's ideas (1) as acceptable within limits; (2) with suspicion; (3) with uncertainty; (4) as being ridiculous.　　10. ———————

(10 off for each mistake)　　　　　　　*Reflective Comprehension* ———————

TOTAL READING COMPREHENSION SCORE ———————

VOCABULARY CHECK QUESTIONS

		without context I	with context II
1. *bizarre*	(1) remote; (2) fashionable; (3) festival; (4) sale; (5) odd.	1. ———	———
2. *archaic*	(1) bent; (2) erected; (3) efficient; (4) old-fashioned; (5) chilly.	2. ———	———
3. *intangible*	(1) honest; (2) intolerant; (3) vague; (4) permanent; (5) suitable.	3. ———	———
4. *deplorable*	(1) behaved; (2) permissible; (3) fragrant; (4) unfortunate; (5) judged.	4. ———	———
5. *integral*	(1) numerical; (2) essential; (3) able; (4) proud; (5) concentrated.	5. ———	———

(10 off for each mistake)　　　*Word Comprehension* without *contextual help* (I) ———————

Word Comprehension with *contextual help* (II) ———————

TOTAL WORD COMPREHENSION SCORE ———————

EXERCISES

1. Using longhand, write an account of how illegible writing was once a source of confusion or embarrassment to you.

2. Make a careful written analysis of your own handwriting, based upon the specific suggestions in the article and upon the additional information below.

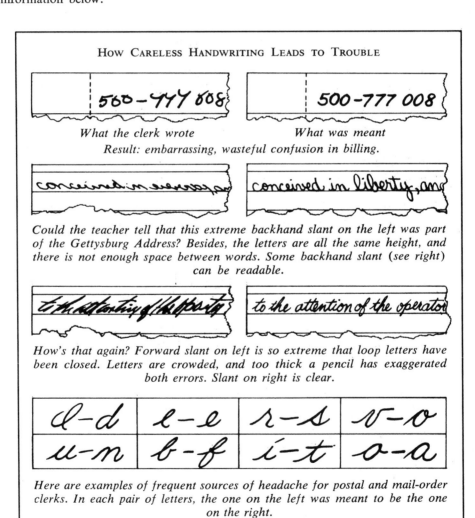

How Careless Handwriting Leads to Trouble

What the clerk wrote   *What was meant*
Result: embarrassing, wasteful confusion in billing.

Could the teacher tell that this extreme backhand slant on the left was part of the Gettysburg Address? Besides, the letters are all the same height, and there is not enough space between words. Some backhand slant (see right) can be readable.

How's that again? Forward slant on left is so extreme that loop letters have been closed. Letters are crowded, and too thick a pencil has exaggerated both errors. Slant on right is clear.

Here are examples of frequent sources of headache for postal and mail-order clerks. In each pair of letters, the one on the left was meant to be the one on the right.

3. Have five individuals rate your writing on a 5-point scale:
    1. — very legible
    2. — moderately legible
    3. — average legibility
    4. — moderately illegible
    5. — very illegible

NAME————————————————— DATE———————— READING RATE——————— W.P.M.

COMPREHENSION CHECK QUESTIONS

1. The author attended what college? (1) Vassar; (2) Tarkio College; (3) Pomona College; (4) Park College.   1. ————

2. George is a (1) biologist; (2) chemist; (3) psychologist; (4) geneticist.   2. ————

3. One of George's illustrations was about (1) an angel food cake; (2) a magnet; (3) baking bread; (4) hybrid seed corn.   3. ————

4. Who was said to share the platform with George on occasion? (1) his wife; (2) their Siamese cats; (3) their dachshund; (4) his publisher.   4. ————

5. In writing the book, the author got some material from the (1) *World Encyclopedia;* (2) *Encyclopedia Britannica;* (3) *Syntopicon;* (4) *The Intelligent Man's Guide to Science.*   5. ————

Receptive Comprehension ————

6. This article was written essentially to (1) point up the need for popularizing science; (2) provide help in selecting an appropriate vocabulary; (3) describe the couple's stylistic differences; (4) suggest basic principles of effective writing.   6. ————

7. George's wife was most interested in making their book (1) popular; (2) accurate; (3) readable; (4) original.   7. ————

8. The reference to her advertising experience was intended primarily to explain (1) her background; (2) her interest in science; (3) her marriage; (4) her interest in practical matters.   8. ————

9. In this collaboration, apparently (1) each had an equal voice; (2) George supplied all content, his wife the form; (3) both content and form were matters of joint concern; (4) George probably had the final say about both content and form.   9. ————

10. You would infer that the finished book would have (1) rather long paragraphs; (2) no jokes; (3) a topic sentence to start each paragraph; (4) fairly short paragraphs.   10. ————

(10 off for each mistake)   *Reflective Comprehension* ————

TOTAL READING COMPREHENSION SCORE ————

VOCABULARY CHECK QUESTIONS

		without context I	*with context* II
1. *desiccated*	(1) dried out; (2) worn; (3) reckless; (4) removed; (5) torn up.	1. ————	————
2. *credo*	(1) small opening; (2) necktie; (3) depression; (4) statement of belief; (5) plume.	2. ————	————
3. *mutation*	(1) cut off; (2) pirate; (3) dumbness; (4) change; (5) principle.	3. ————	————
4. *opted*	(1) decided; (2) opened; (3) optical check; (4) lined up; (5) acted.	4. ————	————
5. *lucid*	(1) clear; (2) beautiful; (3) layoff; (4) level; (5) observant.	5. ————	————

(10 off for each mistake)   *Word Comprehension* without *contextual help* (I) ————

Word Comprehension with *contextual help* (II) ————

TOTAL WORD COMPREHENSION SCORE ————

EXERCISES

Some of the following sentences are too literary — too elaborate — for the average newspaper or magazine reader. Others contain words and phrases that are too pompous or too stiff for the occasion. Revise all of them to your taste.

1. To the extent that an emancipated woman consumes more than a domesticated one (buying dresses, shoes, cosmetics, purses and all the paraphernalia needed for a life in society), it is necessary for a consumer-oriented economy to free its women.

2. I transported her to her destination on the protruding extremities of my bicycle.

3. A Christian will tell you that evil had its beginning in the Garden of Eden, while a Deist claims evil is brought about through man's will, but Voltaire — Ah! the great Voltaire — says simply of the matter: "I don't know."

4. One must insist that, technocrats and industrialists to the contrary, technology is going to destroy two thousand years of human values.

5. Every evening before submitting myself to sleep I brush my teeth with a good dentifrice.

6. If men take wives because possession is not possible without marriage, then women take husbands because marriage is not possible without possession.

7. Man, one must insist, is the least equipped of the animals to cope with the environment; indeed, man must alter the environment to survive.

8. To feel Italy's sirocco wind blow across your face is to be reminded of far-off Libya, its source.

9. To be overwhelmingly successful in business, it would seem, is to be utterly unsuccessful in marriage.

10. In the wee hours of the morning (six is wee compared to ten, isn't it?) I sit at my microscope — eyes crossed, back hunched, fists clenched — manipulating the lives of countless yeasties.

NAME_____ DATE_____ READING RATE_____ W.P.M.

COMPREHENSION CHECK QUESTIONS

1. One executive recruiter says he doesn't spend more than how much time in going over a résumé? (1) fifteen seconds; (2) one minute; (3) three minutes; (4) six minutes.   1. _____

2. Mention of religion, race, or politics was said to (1) be advised; (2) look unprofessional; (3) be advisable for an administrative position; (4) be a matter of individual taste.   2. _____

3. One applicant — a product manager — attached what to his application letter? (1) an aluminum bolt; (2) a bronze buckle; (3) a plastic knob; (4) an enameled steel screw.   3. _____

4. In a résumé you were specifically directed to adopt a style and tone (1) that suits the reader; (2) that reflects your educational level; (3) that you are comfortable with; (4) that reads well aloud.   4. _____

5. A professionally written résumé was said to cost from (1) $500 to $800; (2) $300 to $700; (3) $150 to $350; (4) $20 to $150.   5. _____

Receptive Comprehension _____

6. This is primarily to show you (1) how to get a job; (2) what to put in your résumé; (3) how to write an effective letter of application; (4) how to prepare a good résumé.   6. _____

7. The selection is organized essentially on what basis? (1) most-to-least important; (2) question-to-answer; (3) cause-effect; (4) analytical.   7. _____

8. The points are supported largely by (1) analogy; (2) statistical evidence; (3) personal examples; (4) authorities from business.   8. _____

9. The stated goal — "a challenging position leading to . . . self-actualization within a dynamic company" — was to show (1) the advantage of a personalized statement; (2) how to use praise of a company to advantage; (3) the need to show a career objective; (4) the need for a more specific statement of objective.   9. _____

10. When looking for a job, what would seem most important? (1) your appearance; (2) your interview; (3) your résumé; (4) your follow-up letter.   10. _____

(10 off for each mistake)   *Reflective Comprehension* _____

TOTAL READING COMPREHENSION SCORE _____

VOCABULARY CHECK QUESTIONS

		without context I	*with context* II
1. *terse*	(1) extended; (2) descriptive; (3) final; (4) concise; (5) dreadful.	1. _____	_____
2. *interlude*	(1) intervening time; (2) intrusion; (3) interpretation; (4) postponement; (5) act of playing.	2. _____	_____
3. *touts*	(1) informs; (2) attempts; (3) prepares; (4) praises; (5) blows.	3. _____	_____
4. *conning*	(1) caring; (2) tricking; (3) collecting; (4) helping; (5) writing.	4. _____	_____
5. *salient*	(1) modest; (2) prominent; (3) moral; (4) obscure; (5) savage.	5. _____	_____

(10 off for each mistake)   *Word Comprehension* without *contextual help* (I) _____

Word Comprehension with *contextual help*   (II) _____

TOTAL WORD COMPREHENSION SCORE _____

EXERCISES

1. The first paragraph of a letter of application should tell how the applicant learned of the position open and should state explicitly that he wants to be considered a candidate for the job. Which of the following opening paragraphs are most effective? Why? Which are ineffective? Why?

   A. The University of Minnesota College Placement Bureau has just informed me of the position of junior high home economics instructor, which is now vacant at your school. This position sounds fascinating, so I hope I can meet your qualifications.

   B. Recently I was informed by Professor A. R. Jones, University of Washington School of Forestry, that you will have a position open in your organization this spring for a qualified graduate in forest management. I would appreciate your consideration of my qualifications for this position.

   C. I was informed that there is a job opening for an aquatic biologist on Lake Michigan, by Dr. Philip Waters, Entomology Department, University of Illinois. Please consider me an applicant for this position.

   D. I understand you have an opening for an assistant county agent in Morrison County. I am interested in this position as I will be graduating from the University of Arizona on March 15.

   E. It has been called to my attention that there exists in the St. Louis Public School System openings for a qualified home economics instructor. I should like to make application for this position.

2. The final paragraph of a letter of application should express the candidate's desire for an interview. Which of the following paragraphs do that well? Why? Which do it badly? Why?

   A. If an interview would be advisable, I would be available at your earliest convenience.

   B. I do hope you will consider me for your position which is now open. I will be available for an interview any of the next four Saturday mornings. If you are not able to meet with me any of these times, please let me know the best time for you.

   C. Interview time at the University is near. I am interested in talking to you when you are here.

   D. If, after reviewing my qualifications, you are interested in further information or an interview with me, I will be available at your earliest convenience.

   E. I would appreciate hearing from you as soon as possible. If you are interested, perhaps an interview can be arranged.

NAME———————————————————————— DATE———————— READING RATE———————— W.P.M.

COMPREHENSION CHECK QUESTIONS

1. Carnegie says that he learned his secret of easy public speaking (1) from a book; (2) in college; (3) in a public speaking course; (4) from experience.   1. ————

2. Gay Kellogg was from (1) New Jersey; (2) New York; (3) New Concord; (4) New Haven.   2. ————

3. The article contains (1) three rules; (2) five rules; (3) seven rules; (4) ten rules.   3. ————

4. The late Ida Tarbell was spoken of as a distinguished (1) novelist; (2) biographer; (3) journalist; (4) lecturer.   4. ————

5. The struggling young composer whom Gershwin met was working for (1) $35 a week; (2) $45 a week; (3) $55 a week; (4) $65 a week.   5. ————

Receptive Comprehension ————

6. The purpose of this article is to (1) make us more effective speakers; (2) suggest how to organize and deliver an effective speech; (3) reveal the secret of effective public speaking; (4) explain where to find appropriate speech subjects.   6. ————

7. The story about Ida Tarbell was used to illustrate the importance of (1) using illustrations; (2) rehearsing a speech; (3) knowing more about a subject than you need; (4) being yourself instead of imitating someone else.   7. ————

8. The story about Gay Kellogg was used to illustrate the importance of (1) writing out the speech; (2) speaking from experience; (3) being yourself; (4) using illustrations.   8. ————

9. The author implies that the difference between written and spoken English is (1) negligible; (2) important; (3) largely in subject matter; (4) largely in slanting for a specific audience.   9. ————

10. The article suggests that if you are frightened when you make a speech (1) you are naturally shy; (2) you have not had enough speaking experience; (3) you have not prepared carefully enough; (4) you have not chosen a subject of real interest to yourself.   10. ————

(10 off for each mistake)   *Reflective Comprehension* ————

TOTAL READING COMPREHENSION SCORE ————

VOCABULARY CHECK QUESTIONS

		without context I	*with context* II
1. *craved*	(1) wished; (2) unbalanced; (3) moved slowly; (4) desired intensely; (5) drugged.	1. ————	————
2. *taut*	(1) tense; (2) ridiculed; (3) awkward; (4) very tall; (5) active.	2. ————	————
3. *elicited*	(1) explained; (2) escaped; (3) eliminated; (4) hurried; (5) drew forth.	3. ————	————
4. *irresistibly*	(1) regularly; (2) not compatible; (3) compellingly; (4) irrelevantly; (5) indecisively.	4. ————	————
5. *sage*	(1) useful; (2) wise; (3) tangy; (4) bitter; (5) crafty.	5. ————	————

(10 off for each mistake)   *Word Comprehension* without *contextual help* (I) ————

Word Comprehension with *contextual help*   (II) ————

TOTAL WORD COMPREHENSION SCORE ————

EXERCISES

Remembering what you read: In this selection you are given seven rules to help in preparing a speech. What are they? How many can you remember without looking back at the selection? List all you can think of in the spaces below.

1.

2.

3.

4.

5.

6.

7.

Unless you are one in a million you did not list all seven with perfect accuracy. As a reader, what can you do to remember what you read more effectively? For one thing you can devise a learning or remembering aid.

For example, when daylight saving time starts in the spring, which way do you set your watch — ahead or back? Most people start a long process of reasoning that will eventually provide an answer. Others will use a mnemonic device or memory aid. Just think — *spring ahead, fall back* — and you will have little more trouble with remembering.

Can you name the five Great Lakes? If you have trouble thinking of them, try still another type of mnemonic device. Just think of the word *HOMES*. It will help you remember Huron, Ontario, Michigan, Erie, and Superior.

Take still another type of mnemonic device, one used often by doctors and medical students. How do they remember the twelve cranial nerves? They have a sentence that helps. The key is the first letter in each word. Here is the sentence: *On old Olympus' towering top, a fat-assed German viewed a hop.* How else does one remember *olfactory, optic, oculomotor, trochlear, trigeminal, abducens, facial, acoustic, glossopharyngeal, vagus, accessory, hypoglossal!*

Now, going back to the seven rules, try to work out some mnemonic device. Can you select a single letter to remind you of each — ones that would make one seven-letter word or two shorter words?

Write the word or words here and explain:

If that doesn't work out easily, try a seven-word sentence — each word to help you recall one of the seven points or rules. Write the sentence here:

Actually your efforts to manufacture a mnemonic device will do wonders in helping you remember, whether you come up with a device or not. Compare notes with other students to see what others devised.

Substituting narration for exposition: You may explain something by relying almost entirely on rather pure expository techniques, or you may lean very heavily on narration to make your explanation both interesting and clear.

Take some of the following topic ideas and explain them orally or in writing by using a narrative form:

A. Use illustrations to make your ideas interesting and clear.
B. Narration and exposition are different in several important respects.
C. Efficient reading is extremely important for the student (or businessman, or professional man).
D. Your voice is your fortune.
E. Background is important.

NAME———————————————————— DATE——————— READING RATE——————— W.P.M.

COMPREHENSION CHECK QUESTIONS

1. Speaking of people out of a hundred born with good voices, Pat Kelly, NBC, places the number at (1) five; (2) ten; (3) twenty; (4) fifty.   1. ————

2. Compared with other students, those who had participated in college dramatics and debating were said to (1) get better paying positions; (2) land jobs more quickly; (3) get better grades in school; (4) be more popular.   2. ————

3. According to the telephone company, the commonest speech fault is (1) nasal tone; (2) lisping; (3) substitution of one sound for another; (4) slurring of words.   3. ————

4. Men and women (1) have identical voice problems; (2) have different voice problems; (3) are not treated separately in this article; (4) are considered together.   4. ————

5. Which of the following suggestions for checking up on voice deficiencies was not made? (1) make a recording of your voice; (2) talk in an enclosed space; (3) cup your hands over your ears; (4) get an oscillograph voice vibration picture.   5. ————

Receptive Comprehension ————

6. The purpose of this article is to suggest (1) the value of a good voice; (2) common voice deficiencies; (3) methods of improving your voice; (4) methods of checking up on voice characteristics.   6. ————

7. The story about Billy Rose illustrated (1) the value of an excellent voice; (2) his dissatisfaction with his voice; (3) a common reaction to hearing one's voice; (4) how voice training leads to promotions.   7. ————

8. The story about the bank official was used to illustrate (1) how important an interesting voice is to a career; (2) how easy it is to remake your voice; (3) what methods of voice training are most helpful; (4) that your voice can be improved by work.   8. ————

9. Apparently the most important suggestion for improving your voice is (1) breathing exercises; (2) lowering the pitch; (3) imitating a model; (4) getting a medical checkup.   9. ————

10. You would infer that the author is thinking primarily in terms of (1) public speaking; (2) radio announcing; (3) stage performance; (4) general conversation and discussion.   10. ————

(10 off for each mistake)   *Reflective Comprehension* ————

TOTAL READING COMPREHENSION SCORE ————

VOCABULARY CHECK QUESTIONS

		without context I	*with context* II
1. *transcription*	(1) violation; (2) transformation; (3) recording; (4) change; (5) letter.	1. ————	————
2. *aghast*	(1) nimble; (2) open; (3) agreed; (4) horrified; (5) stirred up.	2. ————	————
3. *adversely*	(1) favorably; (2) harmfully; (3) trustfully; (4) proudly; (5) daringly.	3. ————	————
4. *strident*	(1) strict; (2) harsh; (3) sick; (4) tall; (5) striped.	4. ————	————
5. *intonation*	(1) intolerance; (2) inflection; (3) voice; (4) closure; (5) system.	5. ————	————

(10 off for each mistake)   *Word Comprehension* without *contextual help* (I) ————

Word Comprehension with *contextual help*   (II) ————

TOTAL WORD COMPREHENSION SCORE ————

EXERCISES

Checking your voice: Make copies of the appropriate rating scale provided on this sheet. Have several persons who know you well rate you on all six points — points specifically mentioned in the article.

For Men

	Quite pronounced	More than average	Average	Less than average	Not noticeable
1. Mumbling	_____	_____	_____	_____	_____
2. Rasping	_____	_____	_____	_____	_____
3. Sullenness	_____	_____	_____	_____	_____
4. Tonal monotony	_____	_____	_____	_____	_____
5. Overloud	_____	_____	_____	_____	_____
6. Stilted accent	_____	_____	_____	_____	_____

For Women

	Quite pronounced	More than average	Average	Less than average	Not noticeable
1. Whining	_____	_____	_____	_____	_____
2. Shrillness	_____	_____	_____	_____	_____
3. Nasal tones	_____	_____	_____	_____	_____
4. Raucous and strident	_____	_____	_____	_____	_____
5. Baby talk	_____	_____	_____	_____	_____
6. Affected accents	_____	_____	_____	_____	_____

Self-analysis: Read aloud the first seven or eight paragraphs of this selection, using a cassette recorder to record your voice. Playing it back several times, make a personal evaluation of yourself. Ask others in your family to do the same, noting both good and bad characteristics.

Plan a definite program for improving your voice, using current radio or television personalities. The article "Accustomed As I Am. . . ," page 85, will suggest another way to develop added assurance and eliminate voice problems.

Surveying objectional habits: You may wish to check further on those speech habits or defects that seem most objectionable. To do so, make an informal survey of students or faculty to see what they consider the six most objectionable speech characteristics. Is there agreement with the six specifically mentioned in the article?

NAME——————————————————————— DATE——————————— READING RATE——————————— W.P.M.

COMPREHENSION CHECK QUESTIONS

1. Toastmasters is what kind of organization? (1) international; (2) national; (3) regional; (4) local.   1. ————

2. One minister speaker spent most of his time looking (1) at his notes; (2) heavenward; (3) out the window; (4) at the chairman.   2. ————

3. How many times a day does a busy man speak on the telephone? (1) 15; (2) 30; (3) 40; (4) 45.   3. ————

4. The Toastmasters idea has been spread by the organizing of (1) Parliamentary Clubs; (2) Gavel Clubs; (3) Discussion Clubs; (4) Junior Toastmasters Clubs.   4. ————

5. The man who started Toastmasters was (1) Smedley; (2) Bloomberg; (3) Adams; (4) Bevan.   5. ————

Receptive Comprehension ————

6. This deals chiefly with what about Toastmasters? (1) its history and growth; (2) details about its meetings; (3) its usefulness in telephone effectiveness; (4) its value to participants.   6. ————

7. You would infer that good speaking is largely a matter of (1) formal instruction; (2) experience; (3) interest; (4) native ability.   7. ————

8. Reference to Madame Schumann-Heink is to illustrate (1) the best way to get audience rapport; (2) the importance of audience rapport; (3) a technique used in Toastmasters; (4) why she was so well received.   8. ————

9. The story about the stuttering Bevan is a reminder that we should (1) prepare fully; (2) practice more; (3) take special voice training; (4) get psychiatric aid.   9. ————

10. Most emphasis in this article is placed on (1) everyday speaking situations; (2) public speaking; (3) telephone speech; (4) conference techniques.   10. ————

(10 off for each mistake)   *Reflective Comprehension* ————

TOTAL READING COMPREHENSION SCORE ————

VOCABULARY CHECK QUESTIONS

		without context I	*with context* II
1. *lucid*	(1) fortunate; (2) profitable; (3) clear; (4) absurd; (5) clumsy.	1. ————	————
2. *filched*	(1) arranged; (2) sliced; (3) swiped; (4) spun; (5) occupied.	2. ————	————
3. *cliché*	(1) trite saying; (2) clue; (3) client; (4) comment; (5) rude remark.	3. ————	————
4. *rapport*	(1) scarcity; (2) container; (3) counsel; (4) harmony; (5) swiftness.	4. ————	————
5. *foibles*	(1) leaves; (2) pages; (3) people; (4) followers; (5) faults.	5. ————	————

(10 off for each mistake)   *Word Comprehension* without *contextual help* (I) ————

Word Comprehension with *contextual help* (II) ————

TOTAL WORD COMPREHENSION SCORE ————

EXERCISES

1. If possible, attend a meeting of your nearest Toastmasters or Toastmistresses Club and write a detailed report of the session. To obtain the address of the nearest club, write to the Executive Director, Toastmasters International, 2200 Grand Ave., Santa Ana, Calif. 92705.

2. The good speaker or writer leads his listeners or readers carefully from one sentence or paragraph to the next. Toward that end he must make certain that at least one word in every sentence relates back to the preceding sentence.

The five common ways of insuring this continuity are by (1) using the same subject or a synonym or pronoun relating to the subject; (2) repeating a key word; (3) using a pronoun referring to a word or phrase in the preceding sentence; (4) using such conjunctions or adverbs as *however, since, and, moreover,* and *by contrast;* (5) using parallel construction.

Look at the opening three sentences in this selection:

Suppose you *had . . . .*

How would you like a *. . . .*

Such a helpful setting is *. . . .*

Analyze the following passage, underlining those words and phrases that have as a chief function the providing of a smooth continuity of thought from sentence to sentence:

The Toastmasters provide criticism by an evaluator. This club member seeks out a speaker's foibles and mannerisms, then describes them so the speaker can correct them. When a new minister-member of a Western group gave his "icebreaker" talk, the critic pointed out that the minister spent most of his time looking heavenward, little at his audience. This was doubtless natural enough for a man in his profession, the evaluator said, but it was distracting to those listening to him.

Every beginner in the study of the art of speaking is told that fluency results from careful preparation. Without preparation a person may suffer the same stuttering inadequacy that the late Aneurin Bevan once experienced in a union meeting in South Wales as a lad of 17. A visitor said to Bevan, "You stammer in speech because you falter in thought. If you can't say it, you don't know it." Boning up hard before his next talk proved the worth of the advice.

When preparation pays off in a speech, the natural next step is to apply it to an interview, saving time while making the points sharper. . . .

3. Use clues of this kind in rearranging the sentences in the jumbled paragraph which follows so that you have a smooth continuity:

All sorts of questions come up in the course of the experience a club offers.

If it is not appropriately used, it may only detract and distract.

Almost every speaker thinks he must start his remarks with an anecdote.

There is, for instance, the question of stories and how to use them.

He finds how ineffectual this device may sometimes be, and discovers that a story is good only if it is a hammer that drives home a point.

Obviously, when you read these five sentences in this jumbled order, you are somewhat confused. There is no continuity. Rearrange them below, giving the ideas the relationship that they need to be easily understood. Check the original for a confirmation of your reordering.

NAME——————————————————— DATE——————— READING RATE——————— W.P.M.

COMPREHENSION CHECK QUESTIONS

1. The preferred number for a discussion group as mentioned was (1) twenty-five; (2) twenty; (3) fifteen; (4) ten.   1. ————

2. Specific reference is made to (1) a timekeeper; (2) a Quaker influence; (3) the Supreme Court; (4) a devil's advocate.   2. ————

3. One role mentioned was that of a girl (1) getting home after a date; (2) asking for the family car; (3) interviewing for a job; (4) caught smoking in her room.   3. ————

4. Immediately after the role playing was said to come a (1) taped replay; (2) discussion; (3) replay with role changes; (4) written evaluation by participants.   4. ————

5. The advantages of role playing were said to be (1) one; (2) two; (3) many; (4) immeasurable.   5. ————

Receptive Comprehension ————

6. This article is mainly about how to (1) improve small group discussions and role playing; (2) solve delicate problems in human relations, (3) arrange new ground rules for small group discussions; (4) clarify purposes for discussions.   6. ————

7. What method of developing ideas does the author tend to use? (1) anecdotes; (2) exaggeration; (3) details; (4) statements of authorities.   7. ————

8. The purpose of this selection is primarily to (1) persuade; (2) describe; (3) evaluate; (4) explain.   8. ————

9. The chief purpose of the circular response pattern is to (1) create orderly discussion; (2) encourage the timid; (3) eliminate bad manners; (4) encourage more complete participation.   9. ————

10. In role playing, emphasis on make-believe is intended to get people to (1) sense problems; (2) be more relaxed; (3) feel the conflicts; (4) get rid of self-consciousness.   10. ————

(10 off for each mistake)   *Reflective Comprehension* ————

TOTAL READING COMPREHENSION SCORE ————

VOCABULARY CHECK QUESTIONS

		without context I	*with context* II
1. *pugilistic*	(1) snub-nosed; (2) talkative; (3) eloquent; (4) heavy-set; (5) belligerent.	1. ————	————
2. *lambaste*	(1) make fun of; (2) denounce; (3) cripple; (4) wail; (5) press together.	2. ————	————
3. *ire*	(1) irritation; (2) anger; (3) pain; (4) fault; (5) event.	3. ————	————
4. *consensus*	(1) general agreement; (2) action; (3) vote; (4) survey; (5) house-to-house canvass.	4. ————	————
5. *construed*	(1) sorted; (2) touched; (3) interpreted; (4) used up; (5) seized.	5. ————	————

(10 off for each mistake)

Word Comprehension without *contextual help* (I) ————

Word Comprehension with *contextual help* (II) ————

TOTAL WORD COMPREHENSION SCORE ————

EXERCISES

Reading paragraphs: Increased awareness of paragraph structure is an important step toward intelligent adjustment of rate to material. Just as a driver who sees a clear, straight stretch of highway ahead can accelerate without fear of consequences, so the reader who makes effective use of a topic sentence can shift into high for the remainder of the paragraph. A topic sentence is, in a sense, a highway marker to facilitate our attempts to follow the writer's thoughts.

Analyze the following four paragraphs to determine (a) whether the topic idea is expressed or implied, (b) if expressed, what it suggests by way of development. If the topic idea is implied, skip (b) and (c).

EXAMPLE: Paragraph beginning "One special. . . ." (Skim through the selection until you find the paragraph, then go ahead with the analysis.)

(a) Expressed _____ or implied _____

(b) The topic sentence is the first in the paragraph.

(c) It suggests that the rest of the paragraph will deal more specifically with its suitability for mixed age groups.

Paragraph beginning "If, for example, you. . . ."

(a) Expressed _____ or implied _____

(b) The topic sentence is the _____ in the paragraph.

(c) It suggests that the rest of the paragraph _____

Paragraph beginning "It is not merely. . . ."

(a) Expressed _____ or implied _____

(b) The topic sentence is the _____ in the paragraph.

(c) It suggests that the rest of the paragraph _____

Paragraph beginning "After the parts have. . . ."

(a) Expressed _____ or implied _____

(b) The topic sentence is the _____ in the paragraph.

(c) It suggests that the rest of the paragraph _____

Paragraph beginning "The advantages of role playing. . . ."

(a) Expressed _____ or implied _____

(b) The topic sentence is the _____ in the paragraph.

(c) It suggests that the rest of the paragraph _____

Compare your conclusions with those of other students; discuss any differences in an attempt to resolve them.

NAME_____ DATE_____ READING RATE_____ W.P.M.

COMPREHENSION CHECK QUESTIONS

1. It was said that job hunting might better be called (1) approval seeking; (2) interview hunting; (3) stalking a job; (4) aiming for success.

    1. _____

2. Specific mention was made of the (1) slouch; (2) gum-chewer; (3) throat-clearer; (4) shifty-eyed.

    2. _____

3. In answering questions about a person's previous job, how many mistakes were discussed? (1) one; (2) two; (3) three; (4) four.

    3. _____

4. One case mentioned was that of (1) a public relations man; (2) an accountant; (3) an airline hostess; (4) a realtor.

    4. _____

5. Lucy S. had specialized for years in what field? (1) chainstore marketing; (2) consumer relations; (3) advertising; (4) international transportation.

    5. _____

    Receptive Comprehension _____

6. This article is mainly about how to (1) get the job you want; (2) avoid common job-hunting mistakes; (3) deal properly with questions about a previous job; (4) organize your job-hunting efforts.

    6. _____

7. The example of Fred S., with ten years of business experience in sales, accounting, and office management, was to remind you to (1) aim for a specific job; (2) keep all possibilities open; (3) discover what is most needed; (4) keep abreast of change.

    7. _____

8. Points are developed largely through (1) details; (2) comparison and contrast; (3) reasoning; (4) series of examples.

    8. _____

9. The style of this selection is best described as (1) concise; (2) straightforward; (3) witty; (4) forceful.

    9. _____

10. What statement best summarizes this selection? (1) a stitch in time saves nine; (2) think before acting; (3) wise men learn from other men's mistakes; (4) experience is the best teacher.

    10. _____

(10 off for each mistake)   *Reflective Comprehension* _____

TOTAL READING COMPREHENSION SCORE _____

VOCABULARY CHECK QUESTIONS

			without context I	*with context* II
1. *muff*	(1) catch; (2) cover; (3) harm; (4) bungle; (5) assure.	1.	_____	_____
2. *miscues*	(1) blunders; (2) variations; (3) attempts; (4) strikes; (5) pains.	2.	_____	_____
3. *demerits*	(1) small cups; (2) opinions; (3) delays; (4) benefits; (5) black marks.	3.	_____	_____
4. *intrinsic*	(1) unusual; (2) uncertain; (3) inherent; (4) not valid; (5) private.	4.	_____	_____
5. *interim*	(1) beginning; (2) meantime; (3) event; (4) companion; (5) illness.	5.	_____	_____

(10 off for each mistake)   *Word Comprehension* without *contextual help* (I) _____

Word Comprehension with *contextual help* (II) _____

TOTAL WORD COMPREHENSION SCORE _____

EXERCISES

Organizing ideas: Thinking and reading are inseparable. The writer must organize his ideas coherently or the reader is in trouble. On the other hand, the alert reader must constantly check for himself the relationships and interrelationships as he reads, so that he may evaluate and understand more accurately.

To encourage more thoughtful, active reading, here are some jumbled paragraphs to be reordered and rethought. Try arranging the following groups of sentences into the most coherent paragraph unit. In each paragraph there is one sentence from an adjoining paragraph, which is somewhat out of place. First, decide which numbered sentence does not belong, entering its number in the blank indicated. Then rearrange the remaining sentences in their most coherent order. Finally, check the accuracy of your thinking by referring to the original paragraph.

A. 1. The whole purpose of the preliminaries is to give the hunter his chance, to bring him face to face with the quarry and let him make his kill or miss it.
    2. A source of annoyance and extra work for hiring officials is the job seeker who doesn't know what kind of job he wants.
    3. Hunting a job is somewhat like hunting big game.
    4. But all that is nothing but a build-up to a few swift moments of climax when the success or failure of the chase is actually decided.
    5. Days and weeks are spent in getting ready, selecting a territory to hunt in and journeying to it, beating the bushes, stalking the game.

The sentence that violates paragraph unity is # _____.

The remaining four sentences should be arranged in this order:

_____,   # _____,   # _____,   # _____.

B. 1. He made clear to his interviewer just exactly what he thought of the former employer and the way the business was run.
    2. But he didn't want it left there.
    3. Nine times out of ten it leaves the interviewer with a bad taste in his mouth and suspicions in his mind.
    4. Excessive nervousness is a commonly cited fault.
    5. The second time, therefore, John told the truth: He had been fired after a fight with the boss.
    6. He wanted his side of the story told, and he told it — with feeling.
    7. And that was common mistake number 2 — running down an ex-employer.

The sentence that violates paragraph unity is # _____.

The remaining six sentences should be arranged in this order:

_____,   # _____,   # _____,   # _____,   # _____,   # _____.

C. 1. Get your lists down pat.
    2. Study both yourself and the job.
    3. It's not enough to know how to aim and when to pull the trigger.
    4. List your strong points, the items on your record most favorable to you.
    5. Make a third list of those points where your qualifications match outstandingly with the job you're applying for.
    6. Make another list of special qualifications, ones that others are not likely to be able to offer.
    7. And see to it that you get everything on them over to the interviewer, whether you are offered an occasion to do so or whether you have to make one.

The sentence that violates paragraph unity is # _____.

The remaining six sentences should be arranged in this order:

_____,   # _____,   # _____,   # _____,   # _____,   # _____.

NAME—————————————————— DATE————————— READING RATE————————— W.P.M.

COMPREHENSION CHECK QUESTIONS

1. Dr. Smith took his Ph.D. from (1) Harvard; (2) Yale; (3) Barnard; (4) Princeton.   1. ————

2. For Dr. Smith, analyzing dialects (1) started out as a hobby; (2) grew out of his teaching of public speaking; (3) was his Ph.D. dissertation problem; (4) was stimulated by the Lord Haw Haw controversy. 2. ————

3. Dr. Smith was invited to analyze Haw Haw's voice by (1) the Army Intelligence service; (2) the British Intelligence service; (3) a radio network; (4) Brown University.   3. ————

4. It is possible to identify a person's background by his speech in about (1) five cases out of ten; (2) six cases out of ten; (3) seven cases out of ten; (4) eight cases out of ten.   4. ————

5. Which of the following words was *not* mentioned as offering a clue to background? (1) merry; (2) wash; (3) on; (4) carry.   5. ————

Receptive Comprehension ————

6. The purpose of this selection is to reveal how (1) your speech tells others where you come from; (2) to identify a person's background by the way he speaks; (3) to acquire a better speaking voice; (4) Dr. Smith analyzes and comments on speech accents.   6. ————

7. The opening story about the cabby was used to illustrate Dr. Smith's (1) interest in speech accents; (2) analysis techniques; (3) ability to analyze; (4) interest in speech analysis.   7. ————

8. The story of the girl whose speech showed unmistakable signs of a Baltimore accent was used to show how negligible, usually, is the influence of (1) parents; (2) early environment; (3) early formal schooling; (4) teachers.   8. ————

9. If you wanted to get along in a community where everyone said *tote* instead of *carry,* you would infer that you should (1) say *carry;* (2) say *tote;* (3) use some synonym; (4) pay no attention to community provincial usages.   9. ————

10. You would infer that your accent is most largely influenced by your (1) parents; (2) close friends; (3) community; (4) geographic location.   10. ————

(10 off for each mistake)   *Reflective Comprehension* ————

TOTAL READING COMPREHENSION SCORE ————

VOCABULARY CHECK QUESTIONS

		without context I	with context II
1. *cynicism*	(1) attitude; (2) difficulties; (3) philosophy; (4) tiredness; (5) distrustfulness.	1. ————	————
2. *vindicated*	(1) conquered; (2) cheated; (3) judged; (4) upheld; (5) feared.	2. ————	————
3. *negligible*	(1) sheer; (2) negative; (3) slight; (4) close; (5) salable.	3. ————	————
4. *humiliated*	(1) hindered; (2) humbled; (3) moistened; (4) tricked; (5) humane.	4. ————	————
5. *mythical*	(1) positive; (2) classical; (3) hypothetical; (4) imaginary; (5) secret.	5. ————	————

(10 off for each mistake)   *Word Comprehension* without *contextual help* (I) ————

Word Comprehension with *contextual help* (II) ————

TOTAL WORD COMPREHENSION SCORE ————

EXERCISES

How to Pronounce a Word
Norman Lewis

No matter how carefully you try to conceal certain facts about yourself, your pronunciation gives you away. Only under the most unusual circumstances could an error cost you your job, your friends or your social standing, as some speech missionaries absurdly proclaim. But under ordinary circumstances an expert can draw from your pronunciation a number of interesting conclusions about your geographical background, your education, your cultural environment and your personality.

For instance, if you say something approaching *ahl* for all or *pak* for park, you are advertising that you grew up in or around Boston. If you call the city *Shi-kaw-go*, you are probably a native of the city, while if you say *Shi-kah-go*, you are more likely from the East.

Greezy for greasy may indicate that you have Southern or Western speech habits; a sharp *r* in *park* will similarly identify you with the Western part of the country, and the complete omission of the *r* in the same word will indicate your background as the Eastern seaboard. Explode your *t's* (*wett, hurtt*) or click your *ng's* (*singg ga songg, Longg gIsland*) and you almost reveal the street on which you live in the Bronx; or pronounce the three words *Mary, marry, merry,* and you name the section of the country in which you formed your linguistic habits — the West if you say these words almost identically, the East if the words are distinctly different in sound.

Your pronunciation of certain other words, for example *either, aunt, athletic, film, grimace, comparable* and *verbatim,* will reveal to the experienced ear more secrets than you may realize. By taking a few simple tests, we can arrive at a fairly accurate analysis of the impression your speech habits give to the world.

Do You Use Illiterate Forms?

Check in each case, in the test below, the form of the word which you habitually and naturally use. As this is not a test of knowledge but of speech patterns, you should be guided solely by what you believe you say, not by what you think is correct.

In the test, the first choice in each case is the illiterate form, the second choice the accepted or educated pronunciation. If you checked form (*b*) right down the line, or did not wander from this straight path more than a couple of times, you may feel assured your speech bears no stigma of illiteracy. If, however, you made several unfortunate choices, consider this a danger signal. As a further check on pronunciation habits, ask yourself whether you are guilty of saying *axed* for asked, *myoo-ni-SIP-'l* for municipal, *lyeberry* for library, *fasset* for faucet, *rassle* for wrestle, *drownd-ded* for drowned, or *lenth* and *strenth* for length and strength.

1.	Aviator	(*a*) AVV-ee-ay-ter	(*b*) AY-vee-ay-ter
2.	Bronchial	(*a*) BRON-ikle	(*b*) BRON-kee-al
3.	Radiator	(*a*) RADD-ee-ay-ter	(*b*) RAY-dee-ay-ter
4.	Vanilla	(*a*) vi-NELL-a	(*b*) va-NILL-a
5.	Modern	(*a*) MOD-ren or MAR-den	(*b*) MOD-urn
6.	February	(*a*) FEB-yoo-ar-y	(*b*) FEB-roo-ar-y
7.	Mischievous	(*a*) mis-CHEE-vee-us	(*b*) MISS-chi-vus
8.	Attacked	(*a*) at-TACK-ted	(*b*) at-TACKT
9.	Athletic	(*a*) ath-a-LET-ic	(*b*) ath-LET-ic
10.	Elm, Film	(*a*) ellum, fillum	(*b*) elm, film
11.	Genuine	(*a*) JEN-yoo-wyne	(*b*) JEN-yoo-in
12.	Zoology	(*a*) zoo-OL-o-gy	(*b*) zoe-OL-o-gy
13.	Comparable	(*a*) com-PAR-able	(*b*) COM-par-able
14.	Bouquet	(*a*) boe-KAY	(*b*) boo-KAY
15.	Human	(*a*) YOO-man	(*b*) HYOO-man
16.	Robust	(*a*) ROE-bust	(*b*) ro-BUST
17.	Garage	(*a*) ga-RAHDJ	(*b*) ga-RAHZH
18.	Clandestine	(*a*) CLAN-de-styne	(*b*) clan-DESS-tin
19.	Preferable	(*a*) pre-FER-able	(*b*) PREF-er-able
20.	Plebeian	(*a*) PLEE-bee-an	(*b*) ple-BEE-an

Reprinted with the permission of the author from *Coronet,* November 1946.

(*continued on page 260*)

NAME————————————————— DATE———————— READING RATE——————— W.P.M.

COMPREHENSION CHECK QUESTIONS

1. The author specifically alludes to the conversation of (1) baseball enthusiasts; (2) artists; (3) families; (4) movie fans.   1. ————

2. The author lists (1) five rules; (2) eight rules; (3) ten rules; (4) twelve rules.   2. ————

3. The author belonged to (1) a conversation club; (2) a bridge club; (3) a dinner club; (4) an artist colony.   3. ————

4. Mention is made of (1) Eugene Field; (2) Ellis Parker Butler; (3) Edna St. Vincent Millay; (4) Alexander Pope.   4. ————

5. When the author read something aloud to get criticisms, he said he was helped most by (1) individual comments; (2) answers to specific questions; (3) watching their eyes or fingers; (4) noticing when they laughed.   5. ————

Receptive Comprehension ————

6. The purpose of this selection is to (1) help us become better conversationalists; (2) tell us what to avoid when we converse; (3) give us some necessary rules to guide our conversation; (4) suggest appropriate subjects for conversation.   6. ————

7. Apparently the secret of talking well is (1) reading widely; (2) thinking well; (3) listening intently; (4) talking distinctly.   7. ————

8. When a good conversationalist hears someone tell about running into another car, he will (1) narrate some similar story from his own experience; (2) ask about some of the details; (3) shift the conversation to less subjective matters; (4) make no comment until a more appropriate subject is introduced.   8. ————

9. The Japanese tea ceremony is used to illustrate the rule: (1) don't monopolize the conversation; (2) don't make dogmatic statements of opinion; (3) show an active interest in what is said; (4) avoid all purely subjective talk.   9. ————

10. The story about the guests who tried not to say anything destructive in tone for a day illustrated the need for (1) a Pollyanna attitude; (2) a limited amount of destructive talk; (3) eliminating unnecessary critical remarks; (4) looking on both the pleasant and unpleasant sides of life.   10. ————

(10 off for each mistake)   *Reflective Comprehension* ————

TOTAL READING COMPREHENSION SCORE ————

VOCABULARY CHECK QUESTIONS

		without context I	*with context* II
1. *dilate*	(1) hint; (2) expand; (3) refer; (4) close; (5) suffer.	1. ————	————
2. *interpolate*	(1) pronounce; (2) insert; (3) converse; (4) meet; (5) tempt.	2. ————	————
3. *desist*	(1) lose hope; (2) intend; (3) begin; (4) wish; (5) cease.	3. ————	————
4. *futile*	(1) useless; (2) old-time; (3) continuous; (4) easy; (5) easily fused.	4. ————	————
5. *self-effacement*	(1) pride; (2) confidence; (3) righteousness; (4) modesty; (5) egotism.	5. ————	————

(10 off for each mistake)

Word Comprehension without *contextual help* (I) ————

Word Comprehension with *contextual help* (II) ————

TOTAL WORD COMPREHENSION SCORE ————

EXERCISES

How to Pronounce a Word (*continued*)

Do You Avoid Affected Speech?

Check, as before, the forms you habitually use in the test below.

1. AGAIN	(*a*) a-GAYNE	(*b*) a-GEN
2. EITHER	(*a*) EYE-ther	(*b*) EE-ther
3. VASE	(*a*) vahz	(*b*) vayze or vayse
4. TOMATO	(*a*) to-MAH-to	(*b*) to-MAY-to
5. CHAUFFEUR	(*a*) SHO-fer	(*b*) sho-FURR
6. AUNT	(*a*) ahnt	(*b*) ant
7. SECRETARY	(*a*) SEC-re-tree	(*b*) SEC-re-terry
8. RATHER	(*a*) rah-ther	(*b*) ra-ther (rhyme with *gather*)
9. PROGRAM	(*a*) pro-grum	(*b*) pro-gramm
10. ASK	(*a*) ahsk	(*b*) ask

Except for certain sections of New England and parts of the South, the second alternative offered in the above test is in every case the popular, current and standard form. Therefore, the greater the number of *b* pronunciations you checked, the more natural and unaffected will listeners consider your speech.

If you generally mix in social, business or geographical groups in which *ahnt, tomahto* and *eyether* are accepted pronunciations, you are relatively safe in using some or all of the *a* forms in the test. Nevertheless, you should bear in mind that these are not the pronunciations common to the majority of Americans and that you may occasionally run the risk of being thought "snooty" or supercilious by your more earthy listeners.

The third and last analysis, which appears below, is just for fun, and will serve to prove that we cannot become too fussy about "correct" pronunciation. These are "catch" words; that is, you are expected to get most of them

wrong. They are, with one exception, bookish words rarely used in everyday speech — thus there is no reason why you should be familiar with the dictionary pronunciations.

Most people taking this test will make seven or more errors. If you get more than three right, you may credit yourself with unusual language gifts. If you manage to come anywhere near a perfect score, you are absolutely phenomenal. To see how well you did, check with the inverted answers below the test itself.

In your own pronunciation, you are following the wisest course if you avoid uneducated forms and silly affectations. As an aid to improving pronunciation, you can consult the dictionary, study the simple rules of speech, observe and adopt the good pronunciation habits used by literate people.

The time you spend in improving your pronunciation will pay generous dividends. Actions, we are often told, speak louder than words. But the world bases its first impression of you on what you say — and *how* you say it.

1. FINIS (the end) (*a*) FIN-iss, (*b*) fee-NEE, (*c*) FYE-niss

2. EIGHTH (the number) (*a*) ayt-th, (*b*) ayth

3. SECRETIVE (concealing) (*a*) SEEK-re-tive, (*b*) se-KREE-tive

4. CEREBRUM (portion of the brain) (*a*) SER-e-brum, (*b*) se-REE-brum

5. DOUR (stern, forbidding) (*a*) rhyme with *poor*, (*b*) rhyme with *sour*

6. CONGERIES (a heap) (*a*) CON-je-reez, (*b*) con-JEER-ee-eez

7. IGNOMINY (disgrace) (*a*) IG-no-mi-ny, (*b*) ig-NOM-i-ny

8. GRAMERCY! (a Shakespearian exclamation) (*a*) GRAM-er-see, (*b*) gra-MUR-see

9. VAGARY (whim) (*a*) VAG-a-ree, (*b*) VAY-ga-ree, (*c*) va-GARE-ee

10. QUAY (a wharf) (*a*) kway, (*b*) kay, (*c*) key

Answers: 1—c, 2—a, 3—b, 4—a, 5—a, 6—b, 7—a, 8—a, 9—b, 10—c.

Remember — pronunciations change — dictionaries vary!

260

NAME——————————————————— DATE—————————— READING RATE—————————— W.P.M.

COMPREHENSION CHECK QUESTIONS

1. Cerf says he was once (1) an editor of his college funny paper; (2) a feature columnist; (3) a humorous lecturer; (4) a faculty member.   1. ————

2. Which of the following characters is *not* specifically mentioned? (1) Caspar Milquetoast; (2) Herbert Bayard Swope; (3) Edgar Bergen; (4) Lowell Thomas.   2. ————

3. In what part of the country must you be especially careful of personality angles? (1) the South; (2) rural areas; (3) the Far West; (4) New England.   3. ————

4. Another rule is: (1) don't overwork dialect stories; (2) avoid dialect stories completely; (3) avoid them as much as possible; (4) use dialect in writing rather than telling stories.   4. ————

5. The list of don'ts numbers (1) ten; (2) eleven; (3) twelve; (4) thirteen.   5. ————

Receptive Comprehension ————

6. The purpose of this article is to tell us (1) how to tell stories more effectively; (2) how to select entertaining stories; (3) what things to avoid in telling stories; (4) specific stories to practice on.   6. ————

7. Cerf apparently believes that most people (1) tell stories reasonably well; (2) very poorly; (3) superlatively well; (4) somewhat poorly.   7. ————

8. The illustration of the storyteller who always introduced the names of his listeners into his recital is to remind us not to (1) make a story too long; (2) forget the point somewhere in the middle of the story; (3) repeat the story to the same audience; (4) tell the story in the wrong place.   8. ————

9. The story about the fishing pole with a worm at each end is used to remind us not to (1) lay hands on our listener; (2) forget the point in the middle of a story; (3) tell another version of a story just heard; (4) give the point away before we begin.   9. ————

10. Apparently the most important single rule is: (1) don't make a story too long; (2) don't lay hands on your audience; (3) don't oversell the story in advance; (4) don't tell your stories at inappropriate times. 10. ————

(10 off for each mistake)   *Reflective Comprehension* ————

TOTAL READING COMPREHENSION SCORE ————

VOCABULARY CHECK QUESTIONS

		without context I	with context II
1. *raconteurs*	(1) storytellers; (2) merchants; (3) race horses; (4) cogs; (5) wheels.	1. ————	————
2. *compilation*	(1) courtesy; (2) competition; (3) gathering together; (4) discussion; (5) cutting out.	2. ————	————
3. *verbiage*	(1) wordiness; (2) foliage; (3) greenness; (4) truth; (5) judgment.	3. ————	————
4. *inept*	(1) clumsy; (2) inactive; (3) disgraceful; (4) tired; (5) sharp.	4. ————	————
5. *docile*	(1) positive; (2) tractable; (3) generous; (4) young; (5) vague.	5. ————	————

(10 off for each mistake)   *Word Comprehension* without *contextual help* (I) ————

Word Comprehension with *contextual help* (II) ————

TOTAL WORD COMPREHENSION SCORE ————

EXERCISES

1. *Substituting narration for persuasion or exposition:* Macaulay called narration "the mighty engine of argument." The next time you are to explain something or persuade someone of something, try using an anecdote or story to make your point.

It is possible, for example, to explain that Coleridge was famous as a talker by mentioning that his London landlord offered him free quarters if he would stay on and talk, or by mentioning details of his success as a lecturer. The same point could also be made by a story. Coleridge once found Lamb hastening along a busy street and, drawing him into a doorway by a button, closed his eyes as was his habit, and started talking. Lamb, who was in a great hurry, cut off the button and left him. Hours later, so the story goes, Lamb found him in the same spot, holding the button and talking. True or not, the story serves well to remind us that Coleridge was a talker.

Taking any of the following ideas (or others that may be suggested), make a point through use of a story you know or invent for the purpose:

Vocabulary brings success.	Your voice is your fortune.
Haste makes waste.	Knowledge is power.
Practice makes perfect.	Reading pays off.

2. *Preparing a story speech:* Using the suggestions in this selection as a basis of criticism, prepare a speech to fit the following situation. Find a story that would be appropriate whenever you happen to be called upon unexpectedly to "say a few words." Be prepared to tell it before the class at any time for their critical evaluation. Be sure to provide a transition from situation to story and another transition that will get you gracefully back into your seat. Here is a sample. Find or make up another to serve the same purpose.

Friends, the last time anyone called upon me to make a speech, a man stopped afterward, gravely shook hands, then said, "Whoever told you you could speak?"

I replied a bit sharply, "I'll have you know I've spent $800 in speech lessons."
He thought for a minute, then said, "I'd like you to meet my brother."
"Why? Is he a speech teacher?"
"No. He's a lawyer. He'll get your money back for you."
I think you can see now why I make no more speeches and again take my seat!

3. Go to the library to find a book of stories or anecdotes. List the titles of two such books below.

1. _____

2. _____

4. Review the book for the class, telling the funniest story you found, observing the thirteen Don'ts in the article by Cerf. Notice how the stories are grouped and what aids are provided for finding an appropriate one for a given situation.

NAME_____ DATE_____ READING RATE_____ W.P.M.

COMPREHENSION CHECK QUESTIONS

1. The title of Conwell's lecture was (1) *America's Penniless Millionaire;* (2) *Acres of Diamonds;* (3) *The Story of Ali Hafed;* (4) *Opportunity Knocks But Once.*　　　　　　　1. _____

2. Conwell lived his early life (1) on a farm; (2) in a city; (3) in a small town; (4) in New Haven.　　2. _____

3. In the Civil War Conwell was (1) an orderly; (2) a lieutenant; (3) a captain; (4) a major.　　3. _____

4. Conwell was directly instrumental in the building of (1) a new church; (2) two new churches; (3) three new churches; (4) four new churches.　　　　　　　4. _____

5. Conwell delivered his famous lecture about (1) 1,000 times; (2) 2,000 times; (3) 4,000 times; (4) 6,000 times.　　　　　　　5. _____

Receptive Comprehension _____

6. The purpose of this article is to (1) explain the importance of cultivating your own back yard; (2) tell us about a famous speech; (3) tell us about Conwell; (4) suggest the importance of reading.　　6. _____

7. The story of John Ring is used to demonstrate Conwell's ability to (1) command; (2) lay hold of symbols and fit them into his life; (3) keep an extravagant vow; (4) understand human nature and motives.　7. _____

8. Conwell apparently considered the most important communication skill to be (1) writing; (2) speaking; (3) listening; (4) reading.　　　　　　　8. _____

9. Conwell would probably agree that a man's success depends primarily on (1) the contacts he makes; (2) his environment; (3) being at the right place at the right time; (4) making the most of his opportunities.　　　　　　　9. _____

10. You would infer that the most effective exposition is (1) narrative; (2) descriptive; (3) humorous; (4) witty.　　　　　　　10. _____

(10 off for each mistake)　　　　　　　　　　　*Reflective Comprehension* _____

TOTAL READING COMPREHENSION SCORE _____

VOCABULARY CHECK QUESTIONS

		without context I	*with context* II
1. *diversity*	(1) category; (2) deity; (3) pleasure; (4) variety; (5) popularity.	1. _____	_____
2. *guises*	(1) plants; (2) guides; (3) secrets; (4) aspects; (5) creeds.	2. _____	_____
3. *intuitive*	(1) inborn; (2) intrusive; (3) useless; (4) fickle; (5) unwilling.	3. _____	_____
4. *tenaciously*	(1) temptingly; (2) temporarily; (3) moderately; (4) persistently; (5) quietly.	4. _____	_____
5. *stipulated*	(1) dotted; (2) paid; (3) drew; (4) estimated; (5) specified.	5. _____	_____

(10 off for each mistake)　　　　　*Word Comprehension* without *contextual help* (I) _____

Word Comprehension with *contextual help*　(II) _____

TOTAL WORD COMPREHENSION SCORE _____

EXERCISES

1. Noting subtle degrees of emphasis: Many different shades of emphasis are reflected in the way that ideas are coordinated or subordinated in a sentence. An idea may be given added importance by being put into an independent clause, where it can stand alone as a complete statement or sentence. It can be given slightly less importance by putting it into a dependent clause, which cannot stand alone. If it deserves even less emphasis, the verb can be removed and the idea expressed in phrase form, either prepositional or verbal. Finally, if the idea deserves minimal emphasis, it can sometimes be boiled down to a single word.

Take this sentence: *A man was digging a ditch, and he had a big nose.* This contains two independent clauses connected with an *and*. In essence this suggests that the writer considered the two ideas of exact equal importance, putting them both into independent clauses. If the action is to get slightly more emphasis, the second clause could be made a dependent clause as follows: *The man who had a big nose was digging a ditch.*

For even less emphasis, see how the sentence reads when the dependent clause is made a phrase. *The man having a big nose was digging a ditch.* Finally, it is possible to move from a phrase to a single word, the sentence now reading: *The big-nosed man was digging a ditch.* In this rather subtle way a writer may communicate degrees of emphasis on ideas he is expressing — emphasis that you, the reader, should be aware of.

To develop that awareness more fully, try expressing shades of emphasis in the following sentence, using the patterns suggested in the model.

Conway's speech was fascinating, and *it could have made him a millionaire.*

Put the idea expressed in the first independent clause into a dependent clause.

_____

Now subordinate it further, making it a phrase of some kind.

_____

As a last move, boil the idea in the first clause into a single word.

_____

2. Getting proper emphasis through subordination: Revise the following sentences as directed, noting how proper subordination improves each one. When you have finished, check back to the original.

    A. Subordinate by changing the italicized portion from an independent clause to a dependent clause, making any other changes necessary:

EXAMPLE: *He was making tens of thousands,* and he would rarely have more than a hundred ready dollars of his own.
          Though he was making tens of thousands, he would. . . .
          (The dependent clause emphasizes the causal relationship present.)

    A. 1. There is an event of his military service, and *it demonstrates his facility for laying hold of symbols.* . . .

       2. *The Civil War broke,* and it was as if he had anticipated the opportunity to become "the recruiting orator of the Berkshires."

    B. Subordinate by changing the italicized portion from an independent clause to a verbal phrase, making any other changes necessary:
       1. He chips a corner, *and he finds an eye of blue-white fire* looking at him. . . .

       2. It stands, very possibly, in our own boots, *and it wears our own socks.*

    C. Subordinate by changing the italicized portion from a clause to a phrase of some kind, making any other changes necessary:
       1. *It was the appointed day,* and he borrowed tools and came out.

       2. *Eighteen months passed,* and he had been ordained their minister. . . .

NAME _____ DATE _____ READING RATE _____ W.P.M.

COMPREHENSION CHECK QUESTIONS

1. People from all over the country are getting help with the improvement of telephone manners from (1) psychologists; (2) receptionists; (3) public relations officials; (4) telephone company consultants.   1. _____

2. In the past year a movie on telephone courtesy has been shown to (1) 50,000 people; (2) 750,000 people; (3) 1,750,000 people; (4) 2,750,000 people.   2. _____

3. An interested voice is *specifically* compared to a (1) warm handshake; (2) friendly nod; (3) contagious grin; (4) hearty pat on the back.   3. _____

4. An increasing number of executives are (1) working to improve their own telephone manners; (2) answering their own phones; (3) having their secretaries handle more of their calls; (4) training their secretaries to use better telephone manners.   4. _____

5. In the training of telephone operators use is made of (1) drill materials; (2) disc recordings; (3) classroom practice; (4) listening training.   5. _____

Receptive Comprehension _____

6. The purpose of this article is to explain (1) techniques for improving telephone manners; (2) the importance of telephone manners; (3) present efforts to improve telephone manners; (4) the background and history of present efforts to improve telephone manners.   6. _____

7. The matter of careful, distinct enunciation was (1) stressed; (2) not specifically mentioned; (3) treated somewhat casually; (4) considered of about average importance.   7. _____

8. Which of the following would be most acceptable? (1) you're required to make a formal application; (2) you're to make a formal application; (3) will you please make a formal application? (4) please make a formal application.   8. _____

9. You would infer that business affairs are usually carried on at (1) rather formal levels; (2) a variety of levels; (3) rather informal levels; (4) too informal levels.   9. _____

10. For business calls (1) slang is acceptable; (2) contractions should not be used; (3) contractions are encouraged; (4) *who* and *whom* distinctions should be dropped.   10. _____

(10 off for each mistake)   *Reflective Comprehension* _____

TOTAL READING COMPREHENSION SCORE _____

VOCABULARY CHECK QUESTIONS

		without context I	*with context* II
1. *curt*	(1) evil; (2) civil; (3) curving; (4) abrupt; (5) cowardly.	1. _____	_____
2. *interminably*	(1) endlessly; (2) periodically; (3) internally; (4) relaxingly; (5) sharply.	2. _____	_____
3. *peremptory*	(1) perpetual; (2) dictatorial; (3) perfect; (4) disturbing; (5) scornful.	3. _____	_____
4. *eradicating*	(1) cutting down; (2) improving; (3) clearing; (4) leading; (5) eliminating.	4. _____	_____
5. *inconsequential*	(1) trivial; (2) inconsistent; (3) variable; (4) crude; (5) unbelievable.	5. _____	_____

(10 off for each mistake)   *Word Comprehension* without *contextual help* (I) _____

Word Comprehension with *contextual help*   (II) _____

TOTAL WORD COMPREHENSION SCORE _____

EXERCISES

1. *Reading punctuation:* What do you read? Words! Yes, but you also read the punctuation marks that help you make sense out of the words. For example, try reading the following familiar words in a meaningful way:

Bill where Jim had had had had had had had had had had the approval of the language experts.

Without the help of punctuation that sentence is probably meaningless. Try reading the same sentence, this time *with* punctuation:

Bill, where Jim had had "had had," had had "had"; "had had" had had the approval of the language experts.

Punctuation does indeed make for easier, more meaningful reading.

Try the following matching exercise to sharpen your awareness of some of the most common meanings of punctuation marks. Enter the most appropriate word or words from the right in the space after each mark of punctuation on the left.

Matching Exercise

1. ? _____   a. namely

2. ! _____   b. stop

3. " " _____   c. startling, isn't it

4. , _____   d. and

5. : _____   e. said

6. . _____   f. stop-and-go

7. ; _____   g. who, what, when, where, how

Rewrite this sentence to get rid of the italicized words:

Business firms *and* universities *and* hospitals *and* labor unions and police departments are getting help.

_____

_____

When you are reading two or more word-groups of like grammatical form and similar function, you are reading what is known as a series. Business firms and universities are not alike; but if the writer wants you to think of them together, he can tell you by using the proper punctuation.

Rewrite this series of three with no *and* connective, getting rid of the italicized words:

The receptionist is curt *and* indifferent *and* indistinct in speech.

_____

_____

Once you are aware that you are dealing with a series as a reader, you can anticipate what is coming next in a sentence. In the following sentence add the missing words that the punctuation suggests belong:

Operators were leaving the line without explanation, calls were transferred grudgingly, clerks _____ surly, receivers _____. (If you didn't use the same words as those in paragraph 2 of the selection to finish the sentence, you should at least have added a detail that indicated a bad telephone manner!)

2. Make some business telephone calls, keeping a record of the conversation insofar as possible. Write a brief report on each call, noting any discourtesy or particular courtesy. Check on the formality or informality of the clerk or secretary.

3. Make a telephone call to some of your friends. Rate the pleasantness of their voices and evaluate the impression the voice would likely make on some total stranger.

4. Use a tape recorder or microphone to work on developing a friendly, helpful tone.

Name———————————————————— Date———————— Reading Rate——————————— w.p.m.

COMPREHENSION CHECK QUESTIONS

1. The author mentions a (1) sleepy Siamese cat; (2) compact car; (3) bridge table; (4) remnant of a sandwich.   1. ————

2. He discusses the Vague Specific (1) as a single entity; (2) under two categories; (3) under three categories; (4) under four categories.   2. ————

3. One of his friends was (1) Salvador Dali; (2) Bernard Coe; (3) Arnold Uffelman; (4) Bill Zeamer.   3. ————

4. The piece of equipment that had broken down was (1) a toaster; (2) an electric drier; (3) a mixer; (4) a washing machine.   4. ————

5. He speaks of going to the (1) mountains; (2) movies; (3) shore; (4) Rose Bowl game.   5. ————

Receptive Comprehension ————

6. This article principally does what with respect to the Vague Specific? (1) defines it; (2) explains it; (3) clarifies it; (4) evaluates it.   6. ————

7. The chief purpose of the selection is to (1) warn; (2) entertain; (3) convince; (4) inform.   7. ————

8. The ending — the writer asking for "that book" — is to (1) provide a humorous twist to finish with; (2) show how men like to tease women; (3) ridicule his wife's vagueness; (4) try to teach her a lesson.   8. ————

9. The conversation between wife and maid is primarily to show that women (1) speak vaguely only to men; (2) use the Vague Specific with each other; (3) of all classes use the Vague Specific; (4) understand each other's vagueness.   9. ————

10. You would assume that the Surrealist variety usually relates to (1) things; (2) events; (3) conversations; (4) friends.   10. ————

(10 off for each mistake)   *Reflective Comprehension* ————

Total Reading Comprehension Score ————

VOCABULARY CHECK QUESTIONS

			without context I	with context II
1. *remnant*	(1) cure; (2) remorse; (3) small amount; (4) cutting; (5) left-over part.	1.	————	————
2. *addicted*	(1) confused; (2) stolen; (3) devoted; (4) changed; (5) combined.	2.	————	————
3. *conjured*	(1) joined; (2) summoned; (3) hid; (4) wed; (5) conspired.	3.	————	————
4. *haggard*	(1) short; (2) sleepy; (3) worn; (4) quiet; (5) quarrelsome.	4.	————	————
5. *juxtaposition*	(1) closeness; (2) transfer; (3) correctness; (4) distance; (5) justice.	5.	————	————

(10 off for each mistake)   *Word Comprehension* without *contextual help* (I) ————

Word Comprehension with *contextual help*   (II) ————

Total Word Comprehension Score ————

EXERCISES

Listening and grades: What is the most important thing that education can do for you? This was one of the questions raised in a recent nationwide survey of the goals of education, as reported in the magazine *Phi Delta Kappan.* Results showed that the very first goal in order of importance, as indicated by those surveyed, was to "develop skills in reading, writing, speaking, and listening." The goal second in importance was to "develop pride in work and a feeling of self-worth."

Obviously reaching the second goal depends in large part on how well the first goal is achieved. The better you read, write, speak, and listen, the stronger your feelings of positive self-worth, security, and self-assurance. It is with these goals in mind that all the exercises in this text are designed expressly: to hasten your achievement in these areas of primary importance.

Actually the two assimilative skills of reading and listening can and should work most closely together, attention to one providing significant insights of importance to the other. Your academic success is dependent in large part on how skilled you are in assimilating by eye and ear.

The Commission on the English Curriculum points to the fact that "pupils from pre-school through college learn more frequently by listening than by any other means." Three separate studies made at Stephens College indicate that listening is more important than reading for success in 38 to 42 percent of the college courses taken by freshmen.

Additional evidence of the significance of listening comes from research based on the first standardized test of listening ability, the *Brown-Carlsen Listening Comprehension Test,* published by Harcourt Brace Jovanovich, Inc. Research findings based on that test indicate that for a group of university sophomores grade point averages are somewhat more closely related to listening, than to reading, ability.

Evidence such as this suggests how important it is to know both what kind of reader and what kind of listener you are as you face problems of effective assimilation of information at the college and adult levels. Use this text for that purpose, in case you do not have standardized test scores providing specific percentile figures.

Use six selections — three that you read, three that are read aloud to you. For each, take the comprehension test and begin to note any differences between the reading and listening channels. A total of the three scores in each area, while not so reliable as standardized test scores, will still provide relevant evidence.

Listening Comprehension Scores	Reading Comprehension Scores
Selection #_____	Selection #_____
Selection #_____	Selection #_____
Selection #_____	Selection #_____
Total: _____	Total: _____

Are you about equally good as reader and listener? Are you a better listener than reader or a better reader than listener? The sooner you begin to find out, the sooner you can make desired adjustments. As a further aid, look more closely at the figures. Are the differences in performances caused by differences in difficulty, length, or interest?

For example, when forty-four students were given two short selections, one to be read silently, the other to be listened to, the average comprehension was slightly better in the reading situation. The average was 66 percent in reading, 58 percent in listening. Yet among the forty-four tested, one scored 80 percent in reading and only 20 percent in listening. On the same two selections, another student scored 50 percent in reading and 100 percent in listening.

NAME_____ DATE_____ READING RATE_____ W.P.M.

COMPREHENSION CHECK QUESTIONS

1. To cut down on talking, the husband suggested (1) chewing gum vigorously and constantly; (2) taping their lips; (3) using a word-rationing system; (4) taking turns talking with visitors.   1. _____

2. Specific mention was made of their (1) color TV; (2) open fire; (3) sunny patio; (4) stereo.   2. _____

3. Dan Blake told a long story about the (1) deer he shot; (2) accident he had; (3) train trip he took; (4) big bass he caught.   3. _____

4. The agreed signal to stop talking was to (1) touch the lips; (2) pull an ear; (3) touch the forehead; (4) clear the throat.   4. _____

5. The doctor diagnosed the husband as having (1) eye trouble; (2) sinus trouble; (3) hearing problems; (4) allergy problems.   5. _____

Receptive Comprehension _____

6. The chief purpose of this selection is to (1) entertain; (2) instruct; (3) explain; (4) stimulate.   6. _____

7. Which of the following statements is closest to the idea developed in this selection? (1) good listening makes good friends; (2) listen well to learn well; (3) good listening pays; (4) he who listens well, eats well.   7. _____

8. Which of the two seemed to take the leadership in their decision? (1) the husband, primarily; (2) both equally; (3) the wife, primarily; (4) first one, then the other.   8. _____

9. This selection would be most accurately classified as (1) exposition; (2) persuasion; (3) narration; (4) description.   9. _____

10. In style, you would call this selection (1) informal; (2) verbose; (3) humorous; (4) intimate.   10. _____

(10 off for each mistake)   *Reflective Comprehension* _____

TOTAL READING COMPREHENSION SCORE _____

VOCABULARY CHECK QUESTIONS

		without context I	*with* context II
1. *phlegmatic*	(1) small; (2) unemotional; (3) lively; (4) flattering; (5) show.	1. _____	_____
2. *chagrined*	(1) amused; (2) transformed; (3) pleased; (4) thanked; (5) humiliated.	2. _____	_____
3. *repercussion*	(1) blow; (2) sound; (3) repair; (4) rebounding; (5) censure.	3. _____	_____
4. *fiasco*	(1) authorization; (2) betrothed person; (3) complete failure; (4) conclusion; (5) award.	4. _____	_____
5. *moratorium*	(1) deferment; (2) burial; (3) bad situation; (4) payment; (5) inclination.	5. _____	_____

(10 off for each mistake)

Word Comprehension without *contextual help* (I) _____

Word Comprehension with *contextual help* (II) _____

TOTAL WORD COMPREHENSION SCORE _____

EXERCISES

Checking up on yourself as a listener: Suppose you try an experiment to see how you rate as a listener. Begin by taking the following twelve-item spelling quiz to see how many of the words you know how to spell accurately. To each of the following twelve words, you are to add an *-ing,* spelling the resulting combination on the line following the word, in the column headed *Initial Spelling.*

Spelling Quiz

Words	*Initial Spelling* (before listening)	*Final Spelling* (after listening)
1. din + ing	_____	_____
2. shine + ing	_____	_____
3. begin + ing	_____	_____
4. quiz + ing	_____	_____
5. unfurl + ing	_____	_____
6. occur + ing	_____	_____
7. label + ing	_____	_____
8. man + ing	_____	_____
9. droop + ing	_____	_____
10. equip + ing	_____	_____
11. profit + ing	_____	_____
12. defer + ing	_____	_____

When you have finished, do not check your answers. At this time you are to hand this text to someone else, asking him to read the rule that follows, while you listen carefully. Ask him to read it slowly twice, to make sure you understand the rule. After listening, spell the same twelve words, using the column headed *Final Spelling* and trying to apply the rule perfectly. If you understood and applied the rule, you should have a perfect score in the last column. This becomes, in a sense, a measure of your listening ability.

Here is the rule that is to be read aloud to you twice as you listen:

FINAL CONSONANT RULE: Words ending in a single final consonant, preceded by a single vowel, double the final consonant when a suffix beginning with a vowel is added and when the last syllable is accented. (Repeat the rule.)

Respell the words, using the column headed Final Spelling, applying the rule as accurately as possible. Now check both columns to see how many you got right.

What do your findings mean? Your scores for the two trials will put you into one of three categories. When ninety-two university students followed the same procedure, twenty-three were either slightly confused after listening to the rule or thoroughly confused, scoring from one to six points *lower* after listening to the rule. One student, for example, who scored 11 right the first time, spelled only 5 right in the second column.

Then nineteen of the ninety-two did not change at all after hearing the rule. One student scored 7 right the first time and 7 right after listening to the rule. This suggests a strong mind set that interfered with learning through listening.

Finally, the remaining fifty improved from one to five points after listening to the rule. One student improved from 7 to 12, a perfect score after listening to the rule.

Coming back to your own results, if you improved by one point, you have a somewhat better listening ability than found in the ninety-two students tested. If you improved to a perfect 12 in the second column, even if you moved up only from 11 to 12, you improved as much as possible.

If you scored any less than 12 right in the last column, ask yourself why. One student, in answering that question, wrote that he "didn't know what a consonant was." Word meaning was apparently part of his problem. Do you have a clear, accurate concept of what a syllable is, or a suffix, a vowel, or an accent? Any one of those may be a potential stumbling block.

Answers: 1, dinning; 2, shining; 3, beginning; 4, quizzing; 5, unfurling; 6, occurring; 7, labeling; 8, manning; 9, drooping; 10, equipping; 11, profiting; 12, deferring.

NAME————————————————————— DATE——————————— READING RATE——————————— W.P.M.

COMPREHENSION CHECK QUESTIONS

1. Words themselves were said to carry what meaning? (1) implicit; (2) hidden; (3) varied; (4) explicit. 1. ————

2. Specific mention is made of a what? (1) park bench; (2) playground; (3) picnic table; (4) zoo. 2. ————

3. Someone is told to (1) wear rubbers; (2) carry an umbrella; (3) take a raincoat; (4) wear boots. 3. ————

4. The author specifically discusses (1) rising and falling inflection; (2) eye contact; (3) conversational pauses; (4) loudness and softness of voice. 4. ————

5. The author mentions (1) control of temper; (2) effect of poverty; (3) influence of color; (4) role of vocabulary size. 5. ————

Receptive Comprehension ————

6. For the reader, this selection is primarily to (1) provide awareness of implicit and explicit messages; (2) help in building up of self-image; (3) establish underlying reasons for conversational moves; (4) point up the dominant role of manmade social customs and rules. 6. ————

7. As used in this selection, the word *listening* means (1) listening to words; (2) listening for meaning; (3) consciously hearing things; (4) attending closely. 7. ————

8. When a husband tells his wife, "You should have heard the fellows laugh at the story I told last night," he is really (1) making a demand; (2) attacking others; (3) controlling; (4) building up self. 8. ————

9. The goal of this article is primarily to get us to (1) believe; (2) predict; (3) act; (4) enjoy. 9. ————

10. In this selection, chief emphasis is on what? (1) the implicit; (2) the explicit; (3) both equally; (4) human nature. 10. ————

(10 off for each mistake) *Reflective Comprehension* ————

TOTAL READING COMPREHENSION SCORE ————

VOCABULARY CHECK QUESTIONS

		without context I	with context II
1. *explicit*	(1) skilled; (2) intended; (3) strange; (4) hidden; (5) outspoken.	1. ————	————
2. *brashly*	(1) fairly; (2) rapidly; (3) rashly; (4) carefully; (5) youthfully.	2. ————	————
3. *formulate*	(1) express; (2) correct; (3) despair; (4) complete successfully; (5) unravel.	3. ————	————
4. *scruples*	(1) beliefs; (2) ethical objections; (3) inspections; (4) manuscript scrolls; (5) struggles.	4. ————	————
5. *derogate*	(1) open; (2) depend; (3) support; (4) belittle; (5) tranquillize.	5. ————	————

(10 off for each mistake) *Word Comprehension* without *contextual help* (I) ————

Word Comprehension with *contextual help* (II) ————

TOTAL WORD COMPREHENSION SCORE ————

EXERCISES

1. *Listening vs. reading:* In the spaces below list the important advantages and disadvantages of learning through listening and learning through reading.

    A. Advantages:

Of listening	Of reading
1.	1.
2.	2.
3.	3.
4.	4.
5.	5.
6.	6.

    B. Disadvantages:

Of listening	Of reading
1.	1.
2.	2.
3.	3.
4.	4.
5.	5.
6.	6.

2. Write a fully developed paragraph of at least 125 words in which you try to prove which assimilative skill is more important — listening or reading.

NAME———————————————————— DATE——————————— READING RATE——————————— W.P.M.

COMPREHENSION CHECK QUESTIONS

1. Old John's son became interested in college through the efforts of his (1) pastor; (2) neighbor; (3) principal; (4) teacher.   1. ———

2. When dry weather came, (1) Old Crosby kept on plowing; (2) Young John kept on plowing; (3) neither one kept on plowing; (4) both kept on plowing.   2. ———

3. Wiggam reports a conversation between a psychologist and a (1) college dean; (2) professor; (3) department-store employee; (4) chain-store manager.   3. ———

4. Young John harvested (1) 50 bushels an acre; (2) 75 bushels an acre; (3) 90 bushels an acre; (4) 105 bushels an acre.   4. ———

5. Young John suggested that his father (1) rotate the crops; (2) control erosion factors; (3) feed the cows a balanced ration; (4) use hybrid seed.   5. ———

Receptive Comprehension ———

6. The purpose of this selection is to suggest the importance of (1) an education; (2) practical experience; (3) scientific farming; (4) listening to one who knows.   6. ———

7. Young John's high school education seems best described as (1) life-centered; (2) school-centered; (3) reading-centered; (4) listening-centered.   7. ———

8. Wiggam implies that learning to read better would depend primarily on (1) a grasp of basic theories; (2) practical experience with books; (3) a combination of experience and theory; (4) proper training.   8. ———

9. Suppose you are not reading up to capacity or not progressing as you should. You would infer that your first move is to analyze (1) what others have tried; (2) what you have tried; (3) what you want to do; (4) what methods are available.   9. ———

10. Old Crosby's use of the word *scientific,* in his phrase "scientific fellers," implies (1) awe; (2) approval; (3) disparagement; (4) objectivity.   10. ———

(10 off for each mistake)   *Reflective Comprehension* ———

TOTAL READING COMPREHENSION SCORE ———

VOCABULARY CHECK QUESTIONS

			without context I	*with context* II
1. *confreres*	(1) opponents; (2) employees; (3) farmers; (4) associates; (5) students.	1.	———	———
2. *satchel*	(1) opening; (2) cotton cloth; (3) planet; (4) small bag; (5) critic.	2.	———	———
3. *eminently*	(1) fearfully; (2) shapely; (3) poorly; (4) freely; (5) notably.	3.	———	———
4. *converted*	(1) transformed; (2) disputed; (3) controlled; (4) sentenced; (5) compared.	4.	———	———
5. *assumed*	(1) stated; (2) expected; (3) supposed; (4) convinced; (5) persuaded.	5.	———	———

(10 off for each mistake)

Word Comprehension without *contextual help* (I) ———

Word Comprehension with *contextual help* (II) ———

TOTAL WORD COMPREHENSION SCORE ———

EXERCISES

Using the radio to improve your listening: To develop improved concentration, accuracy, and skill in listening, put your radio to work. In the morning listen carefully to a fifteen-minute newscast, noting each story with a one- to five-word identifying phrase. When the broadcast is over, count the number of stories covered, turn your notes over, and see how many you can remember. Put a check after each story remembered. Record your results below.

Newscast	Stories remembered	Details remembered
1. _____	_____	_____
2. _____	_____	_____
3. _____	_____	_____
4. _____	_____	_____
5. _____	_____	_____
6. _____	_____	_____
7. _____	_____	_____
8. _____	_____	_____
9. _____	_____	_____
10. _____	_____	_____
11. _____	_____	_____
12. _____	_____	_____
13. _____	_____	_____
14. _____	_____	_____
15. _____	_____	_____

With practice you should develop the ability to listen with enough skill to remember each story covered. The next step is to fill in the third column, headed *Details remembered.* See how many specific facts you can add for each story. When this is done for two or three weeks, improvement will be seen both in the second and third columns.

This practice lends itself well to class or group activity and works even better if the newscast is recorded and can be played back on a tape recorder or cassette. The entire group can listen, not even keeping a tally. After the newscast, the leader or teacher can give them the total number of stories covered, asking them to list the stories and to add as much factual information as possible.

The group can compare notes, try to resolve any differences in factual statement or opinion, and then listen again to the newscast. Such an exercise should also develop added awareness of details met in reading.

NAME——————————————————— DATE——————— READING RATE——————— W.P.M.

COMPREHENSION CHECK QUESTIONS

1. White collar workers are said to devote what percent of their working time to listening? (1) no figure given; (2) 40; (3) 25; (4) 12.   1. ————

2. One company mentioned as providing training in listening is (1) IBM; (2) Ford Motor Co.; (3) Remington-Rand; (4) Monsanto Chemical.   2. ————

3. The worst listeners thought that note-taking was synonymous with (1) summarizing; (2) noting main ideas; (3) noting facts; (4) outlining.   3. ————

4. One of the ten suggestions was to (1) get the facts; (2) sit toward the front; (3) exercise your mind; (4) involve your emotions.   4. ————

5. We are told that we live in a (1) "mechanized age"; (2) "noisy age"; (3) "jet age"; (4) "wordy age."   5. ————

Receptive Comprehension ————

6. This focuses mainly on (1) how to listen better; (2) reasons for poor listening; (3) the importance of listening; (4) the value of listening training.   6. ————

7. This is addressed primarily to (1) business people; (2) students; (3) women; (4) adults in general.   7. ————

8. By inference, an interesting speech should particularly stress the (1) novel; (2) unique; (3) useful; (4) colorful.   8. ————

9. The most important suggestion is apparently to (1) keep your mind open; (2) be flexible; (3) capitalize on thought speed; (4) hold your fire.   9. ————

10. The list of "red-flag" words was to develop the point that you should (1) resist distractions; (2) judge content, not delivery; (3) keep your mind open; (4) find areas of interest.   10. ————

(10 off for each mistake)   *Reflective Comprehension* ————

TOTAL READING COMPREHENSION SCORE ————

VOCABULARY CHECK QUESTIONS

		without context I	*with context* II
1. *component*	(1) constant; (2) comrade; (3) complex; (4) partial; (5) constituent.	1. ————	————
2. *tactics*	(1) silences; (2) ideas; (3) taboos; (4) methods; (5) battles.	2. ————	————
3. *inept*	(1) awkward; (2) crude; (3) erratic; (4) motionless; (5) infallible.	3. ————	————
4. *recapitulation*	(1) summary; (2) statement; (3) analogy; (4) energy; (5) inflection.	4. ————	————
5. *transpires*	(1) raises; (2) happens; (3) sees through; (4) changes; (5) snares.	5. ————	————

(10 off for each mistake)

Word Comprehension without *contextual help* (I) ————

Word Comprehension with *contextual help* (II) ————

TOTAL WORD COMPREHENSION SCORE ————

EXERCISES

Rating yourself as a listener: Here are ten questions based on Dr. Nichols's research in the area of listening — questions that will serve nicely as an informal rating device. Check up on yourself. Without referring to the article, answer each question with a *yes* or *no*.

1. Science says you think four times faster than a person usually talks to you. Do you use this excess time to turn your thoughts elsewhere while you are keeping general track of a conversation?   1. _____

2. Do you listen primarily for facts, rather than ideas, when someone is speaking?   2. _____

3. Do certain words, phrases, or ideas so prejudice you against the speaker that you cannot listen objectively to what is being said?   3. _____

4. When you are puzzled or annoyed by what someone says, do you try to get the question straightened out immediately — either in your own mind or by interrupting the speaker?   4. _____

5. If you feel that it would take too much time and effort to understand something, do you go out of your way to avoid hearing about it?   5. _____

6. Do you deliberately turn your thoughts to other subjects when you believe a speaker will have nothing particularly interesting to say?   6. _____

7. Can you tell by a person's appearance and delivery that he won't have anything worthwhile to say?   7. _____

8. When somebody is talking to you, do you try to make him think you're paying attention when you're not?   8. _____

9. When you're listening to someone, are you easily distracted by outside sights and sounds?   9. _____

10. If you want to remember what someone is saying, do you think it a good idea to write it down as he goes along?   10. _____

If you answer "NO" to all these questions, then you are that rare individual — the perfect listener. Every "YES" answer means that you are guilty of a specific bad listening habit.

Now you should know what habits, if any, need changing to make yourself a better listener, a move that will mean improved understanding, closer friendships, and increased general efficiency.

Comparing listening and reading time: Some years ago Paul T. Rankin made a survey of the time spent in communicating. Selecting sixty-eight adults, he asked them to keep a careful record, every fifteen minutes, of the amount of time spent in talking, reading, writing, and listening. Data collected over a two-month period led to the discovery that 70 percent of his subjects' waking day was spent in verbal communication. Of that communication time, listening made up 45 percent, reading 16 percent. But that was back in 1929.

What is true today with you? Make a survey of the time you spend in listening and reading during an average day. Compare your findings with those reported by Dr. Rankin.

NAME_____ DATE_____ READING RATE_____ W.P.M.

COMPREHENSION CHECK QUESTIONS

1. Which symptom is *not* mentioned for the newborn baby? (1) vomiting; (2) constipation; (3) irregular breathing; (4) no weight gain.
   1. _____

2. One doctor took his tape recorder (1) to the barbershop; (2) on hikes; (3) on fishing trips; (4) to the beach.
   2. _____

3. Technical journals in the medical fields number about (1) 900; (2) 1,900; (3) 3,200; (4) 6,000.   3. _____

4. Major credit for the development of Audio-Digest goes to (1) Bill Hastings; (2) Jerry Pettis; (3) Bob Marsh; (4) Dr. Rosenow, Jr.
   4. _____

5. The number of subscribers to Audio-Digest is mentioned as almost (1) 4,000; (2) 5,000; (3) 6,000; (4) 7,000.
   5. _____

Receptive Comprehension _____

6. This selection is mostly to (1) tell how the idea of the Audio-Digest started and was developed; (2) show how difficult it is for doctors to keep up; (3) point up the value of the Audio-Digest; (4) suggest how slowly new ideas catch on.
   6. _____

7. The opening two anecdotes are intended to emphasize the importance of (1) listening; (2) the Audio-Digest; (3) keeping up; (4) chance factors.
   7. _____

8. This is largely (1) persuasive; (2) narrative; (3) descriptive; (4) expository.   8. _____

9. After the introduction, this is organized (1) logically; (2) chronologically; (3) into divisions and sub-divisions; (4) by classification into problems.
   9. _____

10. Perhaps the most important advantage the Audio-Digest has over medical journals is (1) interest; (2) speed; (3) brevity; (4) convenience.
    10. _____

(10 off for each mistake)   *Reflective Comprehension* _____

TOTAL READING COMPREHENSION SCORE _____

VOCABULARY CHECK QUESTIONS

		without context I	*with context* II
1. *exotic*	(1) excessive; (2) cure-all; (3) enlarged; (4) foreign; (5) meager.	1. _____	_____
2. *intrigued*	(1) stopped; (2) strengthened; (3) fascinated; (4) hinted; (5) forced.	2. _____	_____
3. *engrossed*	(1) puzzled; (2) cut; (3) absorbed; (4) promised; (5) continued.	3. _____	_____
4. *augmented*	(1) heard; (2) tested; (3) drilled; (4) enlarged; (5) memorized.	4. _____	_____
5. *abundantly*	(1) absurdly; (2) amply; (3) largely; (4) costly; (5) abruptly.	5. _____	_____

(10 off for each mistake)   *Word Comprehension* without *contextual help* (I) _____

Word Comprehension with *contextual help* (II) _____

TOTAL WORD COMPREHENSION SCORE _____

EXERCISES

1. Dr. Nichols has devised a special Listening Index for use in analyzing your bad listening habits. Check up on yourself, but be honest!

How Well Do You Listen?

How often do you indulge in ten almost universal bad listening habits? Check yourself carefully on each one, tallying your score as follows:

For every "Almost always" checked, give yourself a score of   2
For every "Usually" checked, give yourself a score of   4
For every "Sometimes" checked, give yourself a score of   6
For every "Seldom" checked, give yourself a score of   8
For every "Almost never" checked, give yourself a score of   10

Habit	Almost Always	Usually	Some-times	Seldom	Almost Never	Score
1. Calling the subject uninteresting	——	——	——	——	——	——
2. Criticizing the speaker's delivery	——	——	——	——	——	——
3. Getting *over*stimulated by some point within the speech	——	——	——	——	——	——
4. Listening only for facts	——	——	——	——	——	——
5. Trying to outline everything	——	——	——	——	——	——
6. Faking attention to the speaker	——	——	——	——	——	——
7. Tolerating or creating distractions	——	——	——	——	——	——
8. Avoiding difficult expository material	——	——	——	——	——	——
9. Letting emotion-laden words arouse personal antagonism	——	——	——	——	——	——
10. Wasting the advantage of thought speed	——	——	——	——	——	——

TOTAL ——————

Total Score Interpretation: Below 70 — You need training. From 70 to 90 — You listen well. Above 90 — You are extraordinarily good.

NAME——————————————————————— DATE——————————— READING RATE——————————— W.P.M.

COMPREHENSION CHECK QUESTIONS

1. The author likens the building up of small annoyances to the (1) straw that broke the camel's back; (2) drops that make a flood; (3) particles that dug the Grand Canyon; (4) particles that build up great deltas.   1. —————

2. The wife reads him a bit about a New Jersey (1) dentist; (2) lawyer; (3) teacher; (4) policeman.   2. —————

3. To patch up the quarrel the husband buys (1) a dozen roses; (2) a box of candy; (3) some jewelry; (4) her a dinner out.   3. —————

4. A comparison is made to (1) basketball; (2) baseball; (3) football; (4) volleyball.   4. —————

5. One suggestion made is to (1) give up reading; (2) read in the office; (3) read in the bath; (4) turn up the hi-fi to drown out interference.   5. —————

Receptive Comprehension —————

6. This is mainly to (1) explain the reason for this behavior; (2) help the husband deal with the problem; (3) warn couples to act wisely; (4) suggest the need for deception at times.   6. —————

7. You would infer that females would be next most disturbed to see their males (1) playing bridge; (2) looking at TV; (3) fishing; (4) eating.   7. —————

8. Women interrupt largely as a matter of (1) habit; (2) thoughtlessness; (3) interest; (4) instinct.   8. —————

9. This is addressed largely to (1) wives; (2) adults in general; (3) husbands; (4) marriage counselors.   9. —————

10. The suggestions are designed mainly to keep (1) both wife and husband happy; (2) the wife happy; (3) the husband happy; (4) the wife fooled.   10. —————

(10 off for each mistake)   *Reflective Comprehension* —————

TOTAL READING COMPREHENSION SCORE —————

VOCABULARY CHECK QUESTIONS

		without context I	*with context* II
1. *rampant*	(1) embankment; (2) slope; (3) breathless; (4) violent; (5) frightened.	1. —————	—————
2. *imprecations*	(1) impressions; (2) waves; (3) hints; (4) barriers; (5) curses.	2. —————	—————
3. *inertia*	(1) awkwardness; (2) inactivity; (3) inequality; (4) weight; (5) tension.	3. —————	—————
4. *manifested*	(1) manufactured; (2) kept; (3) revealed; (4) ordered; (5) filled out.	4. —————	—————
5. *bifurcation*	(1) twofold division; (2) every two years; (3) strain; (4) display; (5) secret.	5. —————	—————

(10 off for each mistake)   *Word Comprehension* without *contextual help* (I) —————

Word Comprehension with *contextual help* (II) —————

TOTAL WORD COMPREHENSION SCORE —————

EXERCISES

Effective listening depends in part on attitude, in part on actions. Here is another special Listening Index devised by Dr. Nichols to help you evaluate your listening habits and develop improved insights. For this one, think in terms of the more common face-to-face situations for listening.

ARE YOU A GOOD LISTENER?

	Almost Always	Usually	Occasionally	Seldom	Almost Never
Attitudes					
1. Do you like to listen to other people talk?	5	4	3	2	1
2. Do you encourage other people to talk?	5	4	3	2	1
3. Do you listen even if you do not like the person who is talking?	5	4	3	2	1
4. Do you listen equally well whether the person talking is man or woman, young or old?	5	4	3	2	1
5. Do you listen equally well to friend, acquaintance, stranger?	5	4	3	2	1
Actions					
6. Do you put what you have been doing out of sight and out of mind?	5	4	3	2	1
7. Do you look at him?	5	4	3	2	1
8. Do you ignore the distractions about you?	5	4	3	2	1
9. Do you smile, nod your head, and otherwise encourage him to talk?	5	4	3	2	1
10. Do you think about what he is saying?	5	4	3	2	1
11. Do you try to figure out what he means?	5	4	3	2	1
12. Do you try to figure out why he is saying it?	5	4	3	2	1
13. Do you let him finish what he is trying to say?	5	4	3	2	1
14. If he hesitates, do you encourage him to go on?	5	4	3	2	1
15. Do you restate what he has said and ask him if you got it right?	5	4	3	2	1
16. Do you withhold judgment about his idea until he has finished?	5	4	3	2	1
17. Do you listen regardless of his manner of speaking and choice of words?	5	4	3	2	1
18. Do you listen even though you anticipate what he is going to say?	5	4	3	2	1
19. Do you question him in order to get him to explain his idea more fully?	5	4	3	2	1
20. Do you ask him what the words mean as he uses them?	5	4	3	2	1

TOTAL SCORE ———————

If your score is 75 or better, you are a *Good Listener.*
If your score is 50–75, you are an *Average Listener.*
If your score is below 50, you are a *Poor Listener.*

NAME―――――――――――――――――― DATE―――――――― READING RATE―――――――― W.P.M.

COMPREHENSION CHECK QUESTIONS

1. Specific mention is made of (1) Martha Washington; (2) Dwight Eisenhower; (3) Frankenstein; (4) Winston Churchill.

    1. ―――――

2. Miss Hokinson is (1) a writer; (2) a cartoonist; (3) a lecturer; (4) an actress.

    2. ―――――

3. The author speaks of lecturing in (1) Pittsburgh; (2) Columbus; (3) Chicago; (4) Detroit.

    3. ―――――

4. A reference is made to (1) Sinclair Lewis's *Main Street;* (2) John P. Marquand's *Wickford Point;* (3) Edna Ferber's *Giant;* (4) A. B. Guthrie's *The Way West.*

    4. ―――――

5. The author is, by profession, (1) a lecturer; (2) a playwright; (3) a critic; (4) an actor.

    5. ―――――

Receptive Comprehension ―――――

6. This is chiefly about (1) the quality of women listeners; (2) why women attend lectures; (3) why women are good listeners; (4) the changing nature of female audiences.

    6. ―――――

7. The most emphasized reason for attending lectures is the desire (1) to escape; (2) to know; (3) for companionship; (4) for prestige.

    7. ―――――

8. He refers to the lady who asked why read anything sad to show how (1) much women love cheerfulness; (2) thoughtful some women are; (3) many poor questions are asked; (4) inappropriate some questions are.

    8. ―――――

9. The author's generalizations about audiences suggest that (1) women are more interested than men; (2) men are more interested than women; (3) they are both very much the same; (4) they are quite different.

    9. ―――――

10. The author seems most thankful to women for their interest in (1) current problems; (2) being entertained; (3) the arts; (4) pleasing the men.

    10. ―――――

(10 off for each mistake)   *Reflective Comprehension* ―――――

TOTAL READING COMPREHENSION SCORE ―――――

VOCABULARY CHECK QUESTIONS

		without context I	*with context* II
1. *condescension*	(1) conviction; (2) seasoning; (3) compactness; (4) contention; (5) patronizing air.	1. ―――	―――
2. *confreres*	(1) associates; (2) relatives; (3) children; (4) guests; (5) churchmen.	2. ―――	―――
3. *fatuous*	(1) plump; (2) inane; (3) deadly; (4) favorable; (5) dignified.	3. ―――	―――
4. *conclave*	(1) conclusion; (2) family; (3) meeting; (4) tour; (5) letter.	4. ―――	―――
5. *curry*	(1) discourage; (2) carry; (3) curl; (4) cultivate; (5) heal.	5. ―――	―――

(10 off for each mistake)   *Word Comprehension* without *contextual help* (I) ―――――

Word Comprehension with *contextual help* (II) ―――――

TOTAL WORD COMPREHENSION SCORE ―――――

EXERCISES

Using note-taking to improve your listening: Taking notes as you listen is often a desired move. What you want, however, is maximum time for listening and minimum time for writing. According to research done at Michigan State University, "students who take notes are more consistent both in comprehension and in retention than those who do not." But at the same time the research points up the fact that the difference between a trained and untrained notetaker is crucial.

Since, while you're writing, your effectiveness as a listener is diminished, keep your notes brief and clear and be sure to review them later on. You should develop a systematic approach, made so habitual that it permits you to concentrate more fully on what is said.

One of the most useful systems is what might be called abstracting or précis writing. Here you summarize in a short sentence what has been said for a two- or three-minute segment of the talk. A lecture usually has units or segments followed by, or preceded by, an idea to be developed or summarized. The abstracting sentence will express the generalization being developed.

To see more clearly how this is done, turn back to the article "Women Are Good Listeners," listing below what you consider to be five generalizations. Under each enter the story, illustration, or details supporting that generalization. For example, one generalization may be that here "men govern, women rule." With that generalization you might mention such details as "matriarchy, women's rights, right of assembly."

Turn back to the article now and write down five generalizations, each with supporting details, illustration, or story.

1. (Generalization) ——

   (Supporting evidence) ————————————————————————————————————

   ——

2. (Generalization) ——

   (Supporting evidence) ————————————————————————————————————

   ——

3. (Generalization) ——

   (Supporting evidence) ————————————————————————————————————

   ——

4. (Generalization) ——

   (Supporting evidence) ————————————————————————————————————

   ——

5. (Generalization) ——

   (Supporting evidence) ————————————————————————————————————

   ——

NAME_____ DATE_____ READING RATE_____ W.P.M.

COMPREHENSION CHECK QUESTIONS

1. Words are specifically likened to (1) families; (2) trees; (3) personalities; (4) seeds.   1. _____

2. *Calculate* comes from a Latin word meaning (1) "cover"; (2) "hodometer"; (3) "vehicle"; (4) "pebble."   2. _____

3. From the Latin verb *spectare* have come English words to the number of about (1) 60; (2) 180; (3) 240; (4) 310.   3. _____

4. The word *companion* means literally one who (1) eats bread with you; (2) farms with you; (3) drinks with you; (4) walks with you.   4. _____

5. Specific mention is made of the Greek word appearing in English as (1) *ology;* (2) *graph;* (3) *philos;* (4) *phobia.*   5. _____

Receptive Comprehension _____

6. The purpose of this selection is to demonstrate the (1) importance of dictionary study; (2) fascination of words; (3) interesting role of Latin and Greek in our language; (4) close relationship between vocabulary and success.   6. _____

7. The one word that perhaps best illustrates the amazing vitality of language is the word (1) supercilious; (2) inspect; (3) inspire; (4) run.   7. _____

8. The authors emphasize (1) using the dictionary daily; (2) looking at words analytically; (3) falling in love with words; (4) studying classical elements.   8. _____

9. The discussion of the Latin verbs *spectare* and *spirare* is intended to suggest the importance of (1) roots; (2) definitions; (3) literal meanings; (4) Latin.   9. _____

10. You would conclude from this selection that vocabulary study time should be spent with (1) unknown words; (2) known words; (3) modern words; (4) all kinds of words.   10. _____

(10 off for each mistake)   *Reflective Comprehension* _____

TOTAL READING COMPREHENSION SCORE _____

VOCABULARY CHECK QUESTIONS

		without *context* I	*with* *context* II
1. *inordinately*	(1) recently; (2) excessively; (3) openly; (4) impatiently; (5) evenly.	1. _____	_____
2. *fastidious*	(1) fascinating; (2) fashionable; (3) dressy; (4) popular; (5) critical.	2. _____	_____
3. *static*	(1) motionless; (2) dynamic; (3) sharp; (4) bright; (5) dull.	3. _____	_____
4. *contrived*	(1) crushed; (2) restrained; (3) devised; (4) denied; (5) compared.	4. _____	_____
5. *prolific*	(1) powerful; (2) fruitful; (3) helpful; (4) favorable; (5) meager.	5. _____	_____

(10 off for each mistake)   *Word Comprehension* without *contextual help* (I) _____

Word Comprehension with *contextual help* (II) _____

TOTAL WORD COMPREHENSION SCORE _____

EXERCISES

1. Sensing the power of words: Some years ago the *New York Times* carried an editorial headed "Vocabulary and Marks," which began by asking if there was any magic formula for getting high marks in college. The president of Stevens Institute, was quoted as saying that those students who worked on vocabulary their freshman year "were thereby enabled to do relatively better work in all their sophomore courses than their fellow classmen did. Those who improved most in vocabulary averaged three or four places nearer the top of their class during their sophomore year than during their freshman year. Conversely, all the men that did not improve at all in vocabulary averaged 7.5 places nearer the bottom of their class during the sophomore year." Apparently a new word a day keeps the low grades away!

Those results suggested the need to check the relationship between frequency of dictionary use and success in a single class, such as in a University of Minnesota Efficient Reading class. Since all students in such classes take a standardized reading test at the beginning and end of the course, any differences could be noted exactly. On the last day of class students were asked how frequently they had used their dictionary during the quarter. Those who said they had used a dictionary once a week or less improved on the pre- and post-test standardized score 11 percent. By comparison, those who said they had used a dictionary once a day or more improved 26 percent or 136 percent more than those who used a dictionary less frequently. In a reading improvement course, a new word a day keeps the low grades away also. Academically speaking, a student's best friend looks like the dictionary. Keep it handy. Use it frequently. It will pay off well. Don't underestimate the power of words.

2. The selecting of words: Building a better background in any subject matter area is very much a matter of mastering the key technical terms. Often the scanning of the index in a scientific text will reveal pertinent evidence. Some words, for example, are followed by four or five separate page references or subheadings, others by only one.

Seven students at the University of Minnesota used a somewhat modified approach in an attempt to discover the twenty most important technical terms in the field of general botany. They first prepared individual lists, getting help from students who had just finished the course, from the text index and frequency of use in the text, and from old examination papers. They then met together and prepared a composite list from the various individual lists. That listing of forty-one words was then checked by two professors who taught the course. The following list is marked to indicate how many students selected the word as being important enough to include on their lists and whether one or both of the two professors checked the word as important.

	A	B			A	B
1. assimilate	7	1	15. morphology		3	2
2. autotrophic	3	1	16. osmosis		4	2
3. calyx	1	1	17. photosynthesis		7	2
4. chloroplast	1	2	18. pistil		4	1
5. chromosome	3	1	19. plasmolysis		5	0
6. corolla	2	1	20. pollination		1	2
7. cytology	2	1	21. protoplasm		5	1
8. cytoplasm	4	1	22. pteridophyte		3	2
9. digestion	5	1	23. spermatophyte		3	2
10. ecology	2	2	24. stamen		3	1
11. genetic	2	1	25. stomata		1	1
12. meiosis	1	2	26. taxonomy		4	2
13. metabolism	5	2	27. thallophyte		3	2
14. mitosis	4	2	28. transpire		3	1

Column A gives the number of students who included the word on their initial listing. Column B gives the number of teachers who checked the word as being one of the "twenty most important words" in general botany.

Work out similar lists for other subject matters, particularly for difficult science subjects.

NAME_____ DATE_____ READING RATE_____ W.P.M.

COMPREHENSION CHECK QUESTIONS

1. Words, taken separately, are likened to (1) building stones; (2) bricks; (3) windows; (4) arrows.   1. _____

2. The article refers to (1) an orator; (2) a politician; (3) an actress; (4) a minister.   2. _____

3. The article compares (1) the pen and the sword; (2) the thinker and the dreamer; (3) newsmen and news-makers; (4) spoken and written words.   3. _____

4. Words are said to have (1) glamour; (2) independent ability; (3) egotism; (4) picturesque origins.   4. _____

5. Mention is made of (1) Washington; (2) Lincoln; (3) Mark Twain; (4) Plato.   5. _____

Receptive Comprehension _____

6. This is mostly about how words (1) improve on our ideas; (2) absorb and convey feeling; (3) reflect personal feelings; (4) must be selected with care.   6. _____

7. The sentence "The boy is fat" is used to illustrate how (1) easily words communicate ideas; (2) well words express feelings; (3) readily words can be made into sentences; (4) important the human element is.   7. _____

8. Apparently the best advice to the would-be-writer is to (1) expand your vocabulary; (2) study great literature; (3) take a course in writing; (4) care about your subject.   8. _____

9. Most emphasis is on the (1) when; (2) how; (3) who; (4) where.   9. _____

10. The tone of the essay is (1) humorous; (2) colloquial; (3) lively; (4) matter-of-fact.   10. _____

(10 off for each mistake)   *Reflective Comprehension* _____

TOTAL READING COMPREHENSION SCORE _____

VOCABULARY CHECK QUESTIONS

		without context I	with context II
1. *convey*	(1) guide; (2) carry; (3) drive; (4) change; (5) collect.	1. _____	_____
2. *symbols*	(1) feelings; (2) groups; (3) syllables; (4) representations; (5) instruments.	2. _____	_____
3. *respond*	(1) regard; (2) decorate; (3) react; (4) continue; (5) breathe.	3. _____	_____
4. *duly*	(1) properly; (2) keenly; (3) gloomily; (4) lastly; (5) simply.	4. _____	_____
5. *competent*	(1) profitable; (2) intricate; (3) contestant; (4) poetic; (5) able.	5. _____	_____

(10 off for each mistake)   *Word Comprehension* without *contextual help* (I) _____

Word Comprehension with *contextual help* (II) _____

TOTAL WORD COMPREHENSION SCORE _____

EXERCISES

1. Words that smile and snarl: Our words usually reflect our attitudes. If a boy meets a thin girl and is favorably impressed, he is likely to use the word *slender* to describe her. If he is not impressed, the word *skinny* may slip out. They both mean the same thing; yet one has a favorable, the other an unfavorable, connotation. Yes, he can say she's a vision, but not she's a sight.

In the following sentences, express the italicized observation in such a way as to show it in both a more favorable and less favorable light, keeping as close to the original word meaning as possible.

Observations	Favorable	Unfavorable
EXAMPLE: She is *thin.*	slender	skinny
1. He is *fat.*		
2. He *asked for* a favor.		
3. He made a *long speech.*		
4. She *spends money carefully.*		
5. Her hat was *different.*		

2. Words that walk and live: Some words in common use today are actually mythological characters still living on in our language. Use your dictionary to discover the character behind each of the following words and the characterizing detail that gives the word its meaning.

Words	Characters	Characterizing Details
EXAMPLE: *herculean*	Hercules	strength (to do the difficult)
1. *tantalize*		
2. *procrustean*		
3. *panic*		
4. *venereal*		
5. *odyssey*		

3. Words that fit: Many words can be used as more than one part of speech. In the following exercise, compose sentences for each part of speech indicated by the label. You may want help from your dictionary for this, distinctions of this kind being quite important.

Words	Sentences
EXAMPLE: *like* (as adj.)	You must pay a like sum to the other party.
1. *round* (as adj.)	
2. *round* (as noun)	
3. *round* (as v.t.)	
4. *round* (as prep.)	
5. *round* (as adv.)	
6. *flat* (as adj.)	
7. *flat* (as adv.)	
8. *flat* (as noun)	
9. *flat* (as v.t.)	
10. *flat* (as v.i.)	

286

NAME———————————————— DATE———————— READING RATE——————— W.P.M.

COMPREHENSION CHECK QUESTIONS

1. Specific mention is made of (1) Franklin; (2) Irving Berlin; (3) Aesop; (4) Cicero.   1. ————

2. Reference is made to the (1) French Foreign Legion; (2) the Mafia; (3) the C.I.A.; (4) the F.B.I.   2. ————

3. Our word *duck*, meaning "to avoid an unpleasant task," derives from (1) our web-footed friend; (2) the German verb *tauchen;* (3) *toucan* — a fruit-eating bird; (4) a variant of *docke*, meaning "dock."   3. ————

4. When the detective burst down the door, he found what? (1) some diamonds; (2) a cache of LSD; (3) gold bullion; (4) currency.   4. ————

5. The author mentioned finding the phrase "balmy in the crumpet" in (1) *Roget's;* (2) *Webster's;* (3) *Bartlett's;* (4) *Funk and Wagnall's.*   5. ————

Receptive Comprehension ————

6. The main idea of this selection is to get us to (1) see ourselves honestly; (2) recognize where words come from; (3) avoid words about animals; (4) appreciate how we mistreat animals.   6. ————

7. The detective episode was intended largely to show how (1) animal names reflect bad qualities; (2) many animal references there are; (3) colorful such references are; (4) much slang is found in animal references.   7. ————

8. According to the author, the chief reason for language that slanders animals is to (1) express our fear of them; (2) make ourselves feel superior; (3) express ourselves more vividly; (4) reveal the brutish nature of animals.   8. ————

9. Thurber, in this selection, (1) ridicules mankind; (2) reveals a deep concern for mankind; (3) shows dislike of animals; (4) is just being entertaining.   9. ————

10. To develop his points, the author relies chiefly on (1) definition; (2) contrast; (3) details; (4) expert opinion.   10. ————

(10 off for each mistake)   *Reflective Comprehension* ————

TOTAL READING COMPREHENSION SCORE ————

VOCABULARY CHECK QUESTIONS

		without context I	*with context* II
1. *laudatory*	(1) poisonous; (2) audible; (3) sad; (4) praiseworthy; (5) slow.	1. ————	————
2. *tenacity*	(1) fault; (2) softness; (3) persistence; (4) largeness; (5) example.	2. ————	————
3. *denigration*	(1) defamation; (2) desire; (3) application; (4) appetite; (5) poverty.	3. ————	————
4. *disparaging*	(1) self-seeking; (2) controlling; (3) displaying; (4) shouting; (5) belittling.	4. ————	————
5. *altercations*	(1) changes; (2) quarrels; (3) prisons; (4) religious principles; (5) gifts.	5. ————	————

(10 off for each mistake)   *Word Comprehension* without *contextual help* (I) ————

Word Comprehension with *contextual help* (II) ————

TOTAL WORD COMPREHENSION SCORE ————

EXERCISES

Learning and using suffixes: Do you use four or five words to express an idea when one would do it more effectively? If so, put suffixes to work. For example, "capable of being read" boils down neatly into the word *readable* when you utilize the right suffix. Using the twenty suffixes listed below, enter the appropriate one in the blank in the right-hand column.

Suffixes: *-able, -al, -ate, -dom, -er, -esque, -ess, -ful, -ile, -ish, -ive, -less, -ly, -ock, -ory, -ose, -tion, -trix, -ule, -ulent.*

Phrases

1. A small hill or mound is a   hill_____.

2. The state of being wise is called   wis_____.

3. Of or pertaining to an infant is   infant_____.

4. Full of or characterized by fraud is   fraud_____.

5. One who is young is   youth_____.

6. A woman aviator is an   avia_____.

7. Something capable of being retracted is   retract_____.

8. If someone works without tiring, he is   tire_____.

9. A situation that lends itself to remedy is   remedi_____.

10. One who helps is a   help_____.

11. Something in the manner or style of a picture is called   pictur_____.

12. To cause something to become antique is to   antiqu_____.

13. A female lion is a   lion_____.

14. Something pertaining to a book is   book_____.

15. A minute globe is a   glob_____.

16. Having the nature of a commendation means   commendat_____.

17. To act toward instigating something is to   instiga_____ it.

18. A scheme full of grandeur is   grandi_____.

19. Action tending toward a conclusion is   conclus_____.

20. An object moved in the direction of heaven moves in a   heaven_____ direction.

Answers: 1) hillock, 2) wisdom, 3) infantile, 4) fraudulent, 5) youthful, 6) aviatrix, 7) retractable, 8) tireless, 9) remedial, 10) helper, 11) picturesque, 12) antiquate, 13) lioness, 14) bookish, 15) globule, 16) commendatory, 17) instigate, 18) grandiose, 19) conclusive, 20) heavenly.

NAME————————————————— DATE——————— READING RATE——————— W.P.M.

COMPREHENSION CHECK QUESTIONS

1. The author prefers to think in terms of what dictionary? (1) *Funk and Wagnalls;* (2) *Webster's New International;* (3) Thorndike-Barnhart; (4) *Webster's New World.*   1. ———

2. The article lists some words brought into our vocabulary by (1) playing the piano; (2) star gazing; (3) gardening; (4) sailing.   2. ———

3. Specific mention is made of the root (1) *auto;* (2) *nym;* (3) *lex;* (4) *floris.*   3. ———

4. The devil in "between the devil and the deep blue sea" is (1) a reference to a myth; (2) Satan; (3) a cliff overhanging the water; (4) a part of a boat.   4. ———

5. One of the rare words mentioned is (1) *alb;* (2) *podagra;* (3) *manubrium;* (4) *volute.*   5. ———

Receptive Comprehension ———

6. The main idea is to (1) help you improve your vocabulary; (2) stimulate interest in vocabulary development; (3) show how vocabulary grows; (4) describe four stages of vocabulary development.   6. ———

7. Most emphasis is on (1) firsthand experience; (2) daily effort; (3) frequent use; (4) attention to key roots and prefixes.   7. ———

8. Particular stress is on (1) reading aloud; (2) getting fun out of words; (3) correct pronunciation; (4) reading more.   8. ———

9. Mention of *nasturtium* and *nightmare* is to get us to (1) be more precise in definition; (2) develop interest in word origins; (3) pronounce words carefully; (4) notice spelling difficulties.   9. ———

10. Most of the main points are developed by (1) analogies; (2) stories; (3) specific details; (4) generalities. 10. ———

(10 off for each mistake)   *Reflective Comprehension* ———

TOTAL READING COMPREHENSION SCORE ———

VOCABULARY CHECK QUESTIONS

		without context I	*with context* II
1. *obsolete*	(1) colloquial; (2) stubborn; (3) worn out; (4) evident; (5) out of date.	1. ———	———
2. *recalcitrant*	(1) unruly; (2) hard; (3) reciprocal; (4) reassuring; (5) calculation.	2. ———	———
3. *lethargic*	(1) healthy; (2) lively; (3) dull; (4) deadly; (5) elevated.	3. ———	———
4. *lissome*	(1) lazy; (2) lisping; (3) irregular; (4) nimble; (5) messy.	4. ———	———
5. *alb*	(1) bird; (2) robe; (3) excuse; (4) holder; (5) powder.	5. ———	———

(10 off for each mistake)   *Word Comprehension* without *contextual help* (I) ———

Word Comprehension with *contextual help* (II) ———

TOTAL WORD COMPREHENSION SCORE ———

Around 1000 B.C. the Phoenicians and other Semites of Syria and Palestine began to use a graphic sign in the forms (1,2). They gave it the name hē and used it for the consonant h. After 900 B.C. the Greeks borrowed the sign from the Phoenicians, gradually simplifying it and reversing its orientation (3,4,5,6). They also changed its name to ē and used it for the vowel e. Later they renamed the sign epsilon, "the short e," to differentiate it from ēta, which was reserved for the long ē. The Greek forms passed unchanged via Etruscan to the Roman alphabet (7,8). The Roman Monumental Capital (9) is the prototype of our modern capital, printed (12) and written (13). The written Roman form (8) developed into the late Roman and medieval Uncial (10) and Cursive (11), replacing linear with rounded shapes. These are the bases of our modern small letter, printed (14) and written (15).

e, E (ē) *n., pl.* **e's** or *rare* **es, E's** or **Es. 1.** The fifth letter of the modern English alphabet. See **alphabet. 2.** Any of the speech sounds represented by this letter.

e, E, e., E. *Note:* As an abbreviation or symbol, *e* may be a small or a capital letter, with or without a period. Established forms for these generally preferred precede the definition. When no form is given, all four forms are in general use in that sense. **1. E** earl. **2. E** Earth. **3.** east; eastern. **4. e** electron. **5. e., E.** engineer; engineering. **6. E, E.** English. **7. e, e.** *Baseball.* **8. E** excellent. **9. e** *Mathematics.* The base of the natural system of logarithms, having a numerical value of approximately 2.718... . **10.** The fifth in a series. **11. E** *Music.* **a.** The third tone in the scale of C major, or the fifth tone in the relative minor scale. **b.** The key or a scale in which E is the tonic. **c.** A written or printed note representing this tone. **d.** A string, key, or pipe tuned to the pitch of this tone.

each (ēch) *adj. Abbr.* **ea.** One of two or more persons, objects, or things considered individually or one by one; every: *Each man cast a vote.* —*pron.* Every one of a group of objects, persons, or things considered individually; each one. Usually regarded as singular: *Each presented his gift.* —*adv.* For or to each one; apiece: *ten cents each.* [Middle English *ech, ælc,* Old English *ælc, æghwile.* See **līk-** in Appendix.*]

Usage: *Each* (pronoun), employed as subject, takes a singular verb and related pronouns or pronominal adjectives in formal usage: *Each has his own job to perform.* This is true also when *each* is followed by *of* and a plural noun or pronoun: *Each of the boys has his own job.* Informally, especially in speech, such sentences sometimes take the form *Each . . . have their own job.* The plural construction is especially common when *each* refers to members of a group of men and women or boys and girls, and *their* is consequently felt to be more appropriate than *his.* On a formal level, however, a singular verb is required: *Each of them has a large following.* The alternative, *Each have large followings,* is termed unacceptable by 95 per cent of the Usage Panel. When *each* occurs after a plural subject with which it is in apposition, the verb is usually plural: *We each require much attention.* *O'Brien and Loeb each have large followings.* In examples involving compound subjects, such as the second, however, a singular verb sometimes occurs. Thus, the alternative construction, *O'Brien and Loeb each has a large following,* is acceptable to 69 per cent of the Panel, though most grammarians prescribe a plural verb. The phrase *each and every* is redundant and preferably replaced by either *each* or *every,* used singly. When it is used, however, *each and every* governs a singular verb and related words: *Each and every girl has an obligation to do her share.* See Usage note at **between.**

each other. 1. Each the other. Used as a compound reciprocal

eagle
Haliaeetus leucocephalus
Bald eagle

pronoun: *They met each other* (each met the other). **2.** One another. See Usage note.

Usage: *Each other* occurs most often when the reference is to only two persons or things. Some grammarians recommend its restriction to such examples and prescribe *one another* in examples where more than two are involved. The distinction is not observed rigidly, however. Thus, the following is acceptable to 55 per cent of the Usage Panel: *The four partners regarded each other with suspicion.* Similarly, the construction *husband and wife should confide in one another* is acceptable to 54 per cent. The possessive forms are invariably written *each other's* (not *others'*) and *one another's.*

Eads (ēdz), **James Buchanan.** 1820–1887. American civil engineer and inventor.

ea·ger¹ (ē'gər) *adj.* **-gerer, -gerest. 1.** Intensely desirous of something; impatiently expectant: *an eager search for a familiar face in the crowd.* **2.** *Obsolete.* Tart; sharp; cutting. —See Usage note at **anxious.** [Middle English *egre,* sharp, keen, eager, from Old French *aigre,* from Latin *ācer.* See **ak-** in Appendix.*] —**ea'ger·ly** *adv.* —**ea'ger·ness** *n.*

Synonyms: *eager, avid, keen, anxious, earnest, fervid, zealous.* These adjectives describe a condition of mind marked by great interest, desire, or concern, or a manifestation of such a condition. *Eager* primarily suggests strong interest or desire. *Avid,* an intensification of *eager,* implies enthusiasm and unbounded craving. *Keen* suggests acuteness or intensity of interest or emotional drive. *Anxious* applies to interest or desire tinged by concern or fear. *Earnest* stresses seriousness of purpose and sincerity of motivation. *Fervid* emphasizes intensity of interest or desire, expressed in behavior that may be compulsive or overwrought. *Zealous* makes an even stronger implication of unbridled enthusiasm or concern, sometimes verging on fanaticism and unrestrained behavior.

ea·ger². Variant of **eagre.**

eager beaver. *Informal.* An industrious, overzealous person.

ea·gle (ē'gəl) *n.* **1.** Any of various large birds of prey of the family Accipitridae, including members of the genera *Aquila, Haliaeetus,* and other genera, characterized by a powerful hooked bill, long broad wings, and strong, soaring flight. **2.** A representation of an eagle used as an emblem, insignia, seal, or the like. **3.** A former gold coin of the United States having a face value of ten dollars. **4.** *Golf.* A score of two below par on any hole. [Middle English *egle,* from Old French *egle, aigle,* from Latin *aquila†.*]

ea·gle-eyed (ē'gəl-īd') *adj.* Having keen eyesight.

eagle owl. A large Eurasian owl, *Bubo bubo,* having brownish plumage and prominent ear tufts.

Eagle Scout. The highest rank in the Boy Scouts.

ea·glet (ē'glĭt) *n.* A young eagle.

ea·gre (ē'gər, ā'-) *n.* Also **eag·er.** A tidal flood, a bore (see). [Perhaps ultimately from Old English *ēagor,* flood tide. See **akwā-** in Appendix.*]

Ea·kins (ā'kĭnz), **Thomas.** 1844–1916. American painter.

eal·dor·man (ôl'dər-mən) *n., pl.* **-men** (-mĭn). The chief magistrate of a shire in Anglo-Saxon England. [Old English *ealdormann,* prince. See **alderman.**]

Ea·ling (ē'lĭng). A borough of London, England, comprising the former administrative divisions of Acton, Ealing, and Southall. Population, 300,000.

-ean. Indicates of or pertaining to or derived from. Used chiefly with proper names; for example, **Caesarean, Tyrolean.** [Variant of **-IAN.**]

ear¹ (îr) *n.* **1.** *Anatomy.* **a.** The vertebrate organ of hearing,

---

ă pat/ā pay/âr care/ä father/b bib/ch church/d deed/ĕ pet/ē be/f fife/g gag/h hat/hw which/ĭ pit/ī pie/îr pier/j judge/k kick/l lid/
needle/m mum/n no, sudden/ng thing/ŏ pot/ō toe/ô paw, for/oi noise/ou out/o͝o took/o͞o boot/p pop/r roar/s sauce/sh ship, dish/

NAME——————————————————————— DATE——————— READING RATE——————— W.P.M.

COMPREHENSION CHECK QUESTIONS

1. Bimbi was spoken of as (1) a safe blower; (2) an old-time burglar; (3) a second-story man; (4) a dope pusher.   1. ————

2. The author said he didn't know a verb from a (1) noun; (2) book; (3) hole in the ground; (4) house.   2. ————

3. The author felt that he should try to improve his (1) speech; (2) arithmetic; (3) grammar; (4) penmanship.   3. ————

4. How many words did he think he wrote while in prison? (1) two million; (2) a million; (3) half a million; (4) amount not specified.   4. ————

5. Lights out came at what time? (1) nine P.M.; (2) ten P.M.; (3) eleven P.M.; (4) no exact time given.   5. ————

Receptive Comprehension ————

6. The main focus is on how (1) Bimbi inspired Malcolm X; (2) Malcolm X developed his reading abilities and interests; (3) he developed his vocabulary; (4) strongly he was motivated.   6. ————

7. Malcolm X apparently felt that Bimbi was respected, largely for what reason? (1) age; (2) experience; (3) words; (4) personality.   7. ————

8. What subject of discussion attracted Malcolm X most strongly to Bimbi? (1) the science of human behavior; (2) Thoreau; (3) religion; (4) historical events and figures.   8. ————

9. Copying the dictionary seemed to please Malcolm X primarily because he (1) could remember the words easily; (2) improved his handwriting greatly; (3) learned words he didn't know existed; (4) found he could use them frequently.   9. ————

10. Of the following words, which best characterizes Malcolm X? (1) tough; (2) clever; (3) persistent; (4) sociable.   10. ————

(10 off for each mistake)   *Reflective Comprehension* ————

TOTAL READING COMPREHENSION SCORE ————

VOCABULARY CHECK QUESTIONS

			without context I	*with context* II
1. *quota*	(1) query; (2) figure; (3) proportional share; (4) large quantity; (5) pursuit.	1.	————	————
2. *expounded*	(1) crushed; (2) explained; (3) investigated; (4) transported; (5) tried.	2.	————	————
3. *emulate*	(1) hire; (2) sooth; (3) antagonize; (4) hinder; (5) imitate.	3.	————	————
4. *riffling*	(1) occurring frequently; (2) shooting; (3) opening; (4) leafing rapidly; (5) guessing.	4.	————	————
5. *dormant*	(1) sleeping; (2) uniformed; (3) worn; (4) carefully planned; (5) sympathetic.	5.	————	————

(10 off for each mistake)   *Word Comprehension* without *contextual help* (I) ————

Word Comprehension with *contextual help* (II) ————

TOTAL WORD COMPREHENSION SCORE ————

EXERCISES

Reading the dictionary: Dictionaries pack a tremendous amount of information into very compact form. For that reason they have to be read in a special way. To understand the problem and to move toward improving your mastery of the dictionary, check each of the following statements with the sample dictionary page on page 290 of this text. If the statement is in accord with the preferred usage sanctioned by the dictionary, mark it with a +. If it is *not* in accord, mark it with a —.

You consult the dictionary for information about plurals, spelling, hyphenation, word division, capitals, pronunciation, usage, derivation, synonyms, grammar, and abbreviations. See how effectively you read the dictionary with statements involving each of these headings.

Plurals

    1. Two eaglet were in the nest.   1. _____

Spelling

    2. How many e's are in *feed?*   2. _____

Capitals

    3. I know that he's an eagle scout.   3. _____

Hyphenation

    4. See that eagle-stone?   4. _____

Word Division

    5. The word *eaglet* should be divided after the *g.*   5. _____

Pronunciation

    6. The first syllable in *ealdorman* should be pronounced to rhyme with *eel.*   6. _____

Usage

    7. They hurt one another's feelings.   7. _____

    8. Each of the candidates has a large following.   8. _____

Derivation

    9. The word *eagle* is derived originally from the Old French.   9. _____

    10. The word *each* comes directly from Middle English.   10. _____

Synonym

    11. *Anxious* is the appropriate synonym of *eager* for the sentence: He is quite anxious to please his demanding and difficult constituency.   11. _____

Grammar

    12. Each and every book should be read completely.   12. _____

Abbreviations

    13. In baseball the abbreviation for *error* is er.   13. _____

Check your answers below. If you miss any items, you know that you have things to learn about reading the dictionary with accuracy.

The dictionary also serves as a miniature encyclopedia, as the following questions suggest. Answer them from the dictionary page.

    14. Where is Ealing?   14. _____

    15. What is the population of Ealing?   15. _____

    16. Who was Eakins?   16. _____

    17. What did Eads do?   17. _____

    18. What suffix is listed?   18. _____

    19. What is the technical name for an eagle owl?   19. _____

    20. Who reversed the orientation of E?   20. _____

Answers: 1. —, 2. +, 3. —, 4. —, 5. —, 6. —, 7. —, 8. +, 9. —, 10. +, 11. +, 12. —, 13. —, 14. London, 15. 300,000, 16. painter, 17. civil engineering, 18. -ean, 19. *Bubo bubo,* 20. the Greeks.

NAME————————————————————————— DATE——————————— READING RATE——————————— W.P.M.

COMPREHENSION CHECK QUESTIONS

1. This selection lists (1) ten master words; (2) twelve master words; (3) fourteen master words; (4) sixteen master words.　　　　　　　　　　　　　　　　　　　　　　　　　　　　　　　　　　　　　1. ———————

2. The Latin verb *plicare* means to (1) play; (2) fold; (3) place; (4) tease.　　　　2. ———————

3. In our language, words derived from the Latin and Greek make up approximately (1) 20 percent; (2) 40 percent; (3) 60 percent; (4) 80 percent.　　　　　　　　　　　　　　　　　　　　3. ———————

4. The relationship between the derivation and common definitions of a word is (1) identical; (2) remote; (3) varied; (4) close.　　　　　　　　　　　　　　　　　　　　　　　　　　　　4. ———————

5. One of the following words is *not* discussed: (1) predilection; (2) explication; (3) cooperation; (4) prevarication.　　　　　　　　　　　　　　　　　　　　　　　　　　　　　　　　　5. ———————

Receptive Comprehension ———————

6. The purpose of this selection is to (1) encourage vocabulary building; (2) suggest the importance of Latin and Greek elements in our language; (3) describe a technique for improving one's vocabulary; (4) suggest how knowledge of certain classical elements makes spelling easier.　　　　　　　　　　　6. ———————

7. You would infer that *prescience* means (1) modern; (2) foreknowledge; (3) quietness; (4) intelligence.　7. ———————

8. Our common word *affect* probably contains an assimilated form of the prefix (1) a-; (2) abs-; (3) ad-; (4) af-.　　　　　　　　　　　　　　　　　　　　　　　　　　　　　　　　　　　　　8. ———————

9. If you wished to build a vocabulary quickly, several words at a time, probably the most useful part of a dictionary entry would be the (1) definitions; (2) derivation; (3) synonyms; (4) examples of words in contexts.　　　　　　　　　　　　　　　　　　　　　　　　　　　　　　　　　　　　　9. ———————

10. The phrase "vocabulary is a concomitant to success" probably means that vocabulary (1) results from success; (2) leads to success; (3) is unrelated to success; (4) goes along with success.　　10. ———————

(10 off for each mistake)　　　　　　　　　　　　　　　　　　　　　*Reflective Comprehension* ———————

TOTAL READING COMPREHENSION SCORE ———————

VOCABULARY CHECK QUESTIONS

		without context I	*with context* II
1. *invaluable*	(1) cheap; (2) ordinary; (3) fairly valuable; (4) very valuable; (5) useless.	1. ———————	———————
2. *converting*	(1) reflecting; (2) carrying; (3) conversing; (4) meeting; (5) transforming.	2. ———————	———————
3. *partiality*	(1) bias; (2) portion; (3) speck; (4) follower; (5) partner.	3. ———————	———————
4. *intricacies*	(1) plans; (2) origins; (3) complexities; (4) peculiarities; (5) pledges.	4. ———————	———————
5. *touchstone*	(1) criticism; (2) hope; (3) diet; (4) criterion; (5) failure.	5. ———————	———————

(10 off for each mistake)　　　　　　　　　　　*Word Comprehension* without *contextual help* (I) ———————

Word Comprehension with *contextual help* (II) ———————

TOTAL WORD COMPREHENSION SCORE ———————

EXERCISES

Using the master-word approach. What does it mean to *know* the twenty prefixes and fourteen roots in the master-word approach? Actually it means mastery of four kinds or levels of knowing — (1) memorization; (2) identification; (3) application; and (4) generalization.

Memorization. The first step of level of knowing is relatively easy. It means learning the common meaning or meanings of each prefix and root element listed in the table on page 129. Memorizing those meanings will not take long. Just cover the answers in the Common Meaning columns, check to see how many meanings you know, then memorize the others perfectly. To review, turn to the table, cover the meaning column in order to supply the meanings yourself, and uncover the answers for an immediate check.

Since things learned by rote tend to be easily forgotten, work out a mnemonic aid to link each element meaningfully with its common meaning. Take the prefix *epi-*. What does it mean, commonly? Help yourself remember its meaning by thinking of a familiar word containing that prefix — a word where the meaning "upon" is so obvious that you no longer have to memorize. The association remembers for you. For example, you know perfectly well what an *epi*taph is. It's the inscription carved "upon" a tombstone. Take another example. You know what your epidermis is. It's the outermost layer of your skin — the "upon" layer, so to speak. Such words serve as mnemonic aids to link the prefix *epi-* with the meaning "upon," thus helping you remember.

Now devise a mnemonic aid for each prefix and root element in the table to insure a mastery of the first step in knowing — knowledge of common meanings.

Identification. It is not enough, however, to know the prefix or root meaning. You must also be able to identify the presence of an element as it appears in a word — otherwise knowing its meaning is useless. Most of the time the elements are rather easily spotted, but sometimes there are real difficulties. To see the problem more clearly, try the following quiz, dealing with one of the most difficult prefixes of all to identify.

Look at the following words, checking only the ones which you can identify as containing the prefix *ad-*:

1. accuse	___	8. associate	___
2. afferent	___	9. attract	___
3. agglutinate	___	10. ascend	___
4. allude	___	11. aspire	___
5. annex	___	12. astringent	___
6. acquire	___	13. agnate	___
7. arrive	___	14. adynamia	___

How well did you identify the prefix in question 14 — the prefix *ad-*? You should have checked all but the last one. All but the last contain a form of the prefix *ad-*. To be sure, this is perhaps the most difficult of all prefixes to identify. It is a reminder of the importance of knowing at the second level and of using the dictionary as a help in mastering this second step.

Look at the following dictionary entry for the prefix *ad-*. It should prepare you for the variant forms in the quiz.

> **ad–.** Indicates motion toward; for example, *adsorb.* [Latin, from *ad,* to, toward, at. See *ad-* in Appendix.* In borrowed Latin compounds *ad-* indicates: 1. Motion toward, as in *advent.* 2. Proximity, as in *adjacent.* 3. Addition, increase, as in *accrue.* 4. Relationship, dependence, as in *adjunct.* 5. Intensified action, as in *accelerate.* Before *c, f, g, l, n, q, r, s,* and *t, ad-* is assimilated to *ac-, af-, ag-, al-, an-, acq-, ar-, as-,* and *at-;* before *sc sp, st,* and *gn,* it is reduced to *a-.*]

Roots also show wide variations in form. Since it is important to relate prefix and root closely to the words containing those elements, suppose for the next exercise that you start with the variant forms of a root and come up with certain words containing those forms. In the preceding exercise you started with words and were to note those containing the prefix.

Take the root *facere,* meaning "to make or do." English words derived from that source are likely to have one of the following five forms: *fac, fic, fea, fec,* and *fas.* In the following exercise, for each of the phrase definitions supply a single word containing one of the five forms and fitting the definition. For example, what would you call "a building where things are made"? You would call it a *factory.* The word, derived from *facere,* does contain one of the five forms, the form *fac.* And it does fit the definition. Go ahead with the exercise.

Definitions	Words
1. not easily done	_____
2. made by hand or machinery	_____
3. a notable act or deed	_____
4. to make it easy to do	_____
5. tender attachment	_____
6. evil doer	_____
7. blemish or fault	_____
8. something without flaw	_____
9. conquer or overcome	_____
10. accepted style of doing	_____

(*Exercise continued on page 296*)

Answers: 1, difficult; 2, manufacture or fashion; 3, feat; 4, facilitate; 5, affection; 6, malefactor; 7, imperfection or defect; 8, perfect; 9, defeat; 10, fashion or fashionable.

NAME————————————————————— DATE——————————— READING RATE——————————— W.P.M.

COMPREHENSION CHECK QUESTIONS

1. Words are spoken of as (1) signals; (2) cues; (3) stimuli; (4) all the preceding.   1. ————

2. The selection contains a quotation from what apostle? (1) Paul; (2) Matthew; (3) John; (4) Luke.   2. ————

3. The author specifically defines (1) *context;* (2) *style;* (3) *metaphors;* (4) *analogies.*   3. ————

4. Reference is made to what author? (1) Joyce; (2) Hemingway; (3) Pope; (4) Steinbeck.   4. ————

5. Elementary education in this country is compared with that in (1) England; (2) France; (3) Yugoslavia; (4) Russia.   5. ————

Receptive Comprehension ————

6. This selection is intended mainly to help us do what with respect to language? (1) understand its complexities; (2) use it more effectively; (3) enjoy using it; (4) appreciate the relationship between language and technology.   6. ————

7. Which dictionary definition seems closest to the meaning of discipline, as used here? (1) a branch of knowledge; (2) acceptance of authority; (3) training that develops orderliness; (4) a system of rules.   7. ————

8. The purpose of the quotation from Susanne Langer, referring to "a whole day of creation," was intended primarily to show (1) God's creative power; (2) the difference between man and animals; (3) different ways of communicating; (4) degrees of complexity.   8. ————

9. The most important advice about the use of language is apparently to be (1) concrete; (2) unique; (3) plain; (4) interesting.   9. ————

10. The study of synonyms was advocated largely to contribute (1) variety; (2) vividness; (3) individuality; (4) exactness.   10. ————

(10 off for each mistake)   *Reflective Comprehension* ————

TOTAL READING COMPREHENSION SCORE ————

VOCABULARY CHECK QUESTIONS

		without context I	*with context* II
1. *avant-garde*	(1) followers; (2) guards; (3) vanguard; (4) predecessors; (5) elite.	1. ————	————
2. *intractable*	(1) unexpected; (2) arranged; (3) unruly; (4) disjointed; (5) executed.	2. ————	————
3. *transcendent*	(1) lifting; (2) rising; (3) glittering; (4) surpassing; (5) scheming.	3. ————	————
4. *pomposity*	(1) modesty; (2) lightness; (3) thoughtfulness; (4) self-importance; (5) partiality.	4. ————	————
5. *aversion*	(1) talent; (2) dislike; (3) devotion; (4) fanaticism; (5) liveliness.	5. ————	————

(10 off for each mistake)   *Word Comprehension* without *contextual help* (I) ————

Word Comprehension with *contextual help* (II) ————

TOTAL WORD COMPREHENSION SCORE ————

EXERCISES

Application. To a mathematician such words as *abscissa, exponential,* and *asymptote* are common. To a botanist, *mitosis, meiosis,* and *stomata* are equally so. But to a student just beginning to study higher mathematics or botany, such technical words are probably meaningless. One student during his first week in college came across the words *ebracteate* and *exospore* in a botany text and *extravasate* in geology; he heard a medical doctor use the word *exostosis.* Then in his general reading he came across the others listed below. How many of them do you know? Try the following quiz to see. Enter the answers in the column headed I.

		I	II
1. *ebracteate*	(1) with bracts; (2) without bracts; (3) rounded bracts; (4) pointed bracts; (5) stiff bracts.	1. ___	___
2. *exospore*	(1) core; (2) source; (3) middle layer; (4) outer spore layer; (5) stem.	2. ___	___
3. *extravasate*	(1) melt; (2) shrink; (3) solidify; (4) crack; (5) erupt.	3. ___	___
4. *exostosis*	(1) outgrowth; (2) leg bone; (3) paralysis; (4) joint; (5) scab.	4. ___	___
5. *ebullition*	(1) bruise; (2) boiling out; (3) seeping in; (4) repair; (5) warmth.	5. ___	___
6. *elicit*	(1) draw forth; (2) make illegal; (3) hide; (4) prove; (5) close.	6. ___	___
7. *expunge*	(1) dive in; (2) soak; (3) erase; (4) swim; (5) save.	7. ___	___
8. *effete*	(1) worn out; (2) strong; (3) difficult; (4) shut in; (5) wealthy.	8. ___	___
9. *exhume*	(1) moisten; (2) work; (3) put in; (4) pay for; (5) dig out.	9. ___	___
10. *evulsion*	(1) hatred; (2) rotation; (3) lotion; (4) extraction; (5) description.	10. ___	___

TOTAL SCORES: ___ ___

Before checking your answers, think back to what you did. Did you notice, for example, that all ten words began with an *e* — five of them with an *ex-*? Do you know what the prefix *ex-* commonly means? In short, did you apply some knowledge of prefixes as you took the test? If you did, your score should reflect that fact.

Now retake the same test, using column II for your answers. Consciously apply one additional bit of information — that all ten words contain a prefix meaning "out." Lean heavily on that prefix meaning as you retake the test. Check both sets of answers with the key.

You can see more clearly how this approach works. Once you know what a prefix or root means and can identify it accurately in a word, you are ready for the pay-off step — application. A group of seventy-eight adults tried the test without being encouraged to lean on prefix meaning. They were then told, as you were, that each word contained a prefix meaning "out." That knowledge improved their average score 36 percent.

A perfect score in the second column means that you applied your knowledge well. With the adults, while improvement was general, some scored only 70 or 80 the second time through. Since even a desk-size dictionary contains over a thousand words with a prefix meaning "out," the dramatic usefulness of this shortcut seems apparent.

Generalization. Even when you develop enviable ability with the first three steps, be sure not to overlook the fourth and last step — generalization. For example, by studying only twenty prefixes you can still learn things about all the other prefixes — if you know how.

Take the prefix *ad-*. See what happens when it combines with *lude* to make *allude*. Can you now generalize about another prefix — the prefix *com-*? If *com-* were to be added to *lude*, would the resulting word be *comlude, colude,* or *collude*? How accurately can you generalize?

Take still another kind of generalization. In a sense, you know the meaning of most prefixes — but you don't know that you know. For example, you may say you don't know exactly what the prefix *re-* means. Try some generalizing with this pattern. If to *reread* is "to read again" and *reheat* is "to heat again," you have reason to conclude that a common meaning of *re-* is "again." Generalizing on the basis of that sample, you now have a formula for discovering the meaning of any prefix or root.

Take the prefix *omni-*. What does it mean? Think of some words with *omni-*, such as *omnipresent, omnipotent,* or *omnivorous*. Use the formula to generalize. If *omnipresent* means "present in all places" and *omnipotent* means "all-powerful," apparently one meaning of *omni-* is "all." Finding the meaning common to any given prefix is like finding a common denominator in a math problem. Some generalizations are, of course, more complex and difficult than others. But as you develop improved insights, you develop the skill to handle much more difficult problems, just as in mathematics.

Answers: 1, 2; 4, 3, 5; 4, 1; 5, 2; 6, 1; 7, 3; 8, 1; 9, 5; 10, 4.

NAME———————————————— DATE———————— READING RATE———————— W.P.M.

COMPREHENSION CHECK QUESTIONS

1. This was written by someone in the field of (1) testing; (2) English; (3) industry; (4) teaching.   1. ————

2. The Human Engineering Laboratory was founded by (1) Martin Johnson; (2) Thomas O'Brien; (3) Lynn Sabini; (4) Johnson O'Connor.   2. ————

3. Each year the Laboratory is said to administer how many vocabulary tests? (1) 10,000; (2) 20,000; (3) 30,000; (4) no figure given.   3. ————

4. A vocabulary test was given to the president of (1) an oil company; (2) a mail-order company; (3) a coal-mining company; (4) a milling company.   4. ————

5. We are cautioned against (1) crossword puzzles; (2) misusing words; (3) poor dictionary habits; (4) using slang.   5. ————

Receptive Comprehension ————

6. This selection is primarily to show (1) how vocabulary and success are related; (2) how to improve your vocabulary; (3) how to measure your word power; (4) how important the dictionary is.   6. ————

7. Dizzy Dean's comment is used to point up the need for (1) something beyond vocabulary; (2) a good vocabulary; (3) proper opportunities; (4) intelligence.   7. ————

8. You would infer that the best estimate of a man's vocabulary would come from a (1) look at his I.Q.; (2) look at his wife's vocabulary score; (3) check on years of formal education; (4) check on his reading habits.   8. ————

9. Which should come *first?* (1) finding a good job; (2) building a good vocabulary; (3) developing a good personality; (4) reading widely.   9. ————

10. The style of this selection is (1) forceful; (2) conversational; (3) witty; (4) formal.   10. ————

(10 off for each mistake)   *Reflective Comprehension* ————

TOTAL READING COMPREHENSION SCORE ————

VOCABULARY CHECK QUESTIONS

		without context I	with context II
1. *potential*	(1) intelligence; (2) power; (3) drive; (4) latent ability; (5) training.	1. ————	————
2. *initiative*	(1) punishment; (2) restraint; (3) brain power; (4) heritage; (5) enterprise.	2. ————	————
3. *malapropism*	(1) word misuse; (2) sickness; (3) mistake; (4) support; (5) awkwardness.	3. ————	————
4. *avid*	(1) careless; (2) old; (3) eager; (4) advanced; (5) clumsy.	4. ————	————
5. *incentive*	(1) desire; (2) gift; (3) position; (4) salary; (5) bonus.	5. ————	————

(10 off for each mistake)   *Word Comprehension* without *contextual help* (I) ————

Word Comprehension with *contextual help* (II) ————

TOTAL WORD COMPREHENSION SCORE ————

EXERCISES

Answers to the 20-Word Quiz on page 134. Check your answers, then find your age group in the columns below, and you'll learn your probable peak future income. Don't be discouraged if you didn't score well — read the article for tips on how you can improve your vocabulary and your income potential.

1. *churchmen*	6. *perfection*	11. *shading*	16. *forked*
2. *slatted vents*	7. *hateful*	12. *wood nymph*	17. *tuberculosis*
3. *oval*	8. *limited*	13. *store*	18. *majority*
4. *dreadful*	9. *accent*	14. *hermit*	19. *interpret*
5. *wealth*	10. *marriage*	15. *ridged*	20. *widow*

Figure your top income by looking up the number of correct words under your age heading.

Age 30 and Up

Score	
20–19	$36,500 and up
18–17	$24,300–$36,500
16–15	$16,200–$24,300
14–13	$12,200–$16,200
12–11	$ 8,500–$12,200
10–7	$ 6,500–$ 8,500
Below 7	Under $6,500

Age 21–29

Score	
20–17	$36,500 and up
16–15	$24,300–$36,500
14–13	$16,200–$24,300
12–11	$12,200–$16,200
10–5	$ 6,500–$12,200
Below 5	Under $6,500

Age 17–20

Score	
20–15	$36,500 and up
14–13	$24,300–$36,500
12–11	$16,200–$24,300
10–9	$12,200–$16,200
8–7	$ 8,500–$12,200
6–3	$ 6,500–$ 8,500
Below 3	Under $6,500

Age 13–16

Score	
20–12	$36,500 and up
11–10	$24,300–$36,500
9–8	$16,200–$24,300
7–6	$12,200–$16,200
5–4	$ 8,500–$12,200
3–2	$ 6,500–$ 8,500
Below 2	Under $6,500

Age 9–12

Score	
20–10	$36,500 and up
9–8	$24,300–$36,500
7–6	$16,200–$24,300
5–4	$12,200–$16,200
3–2	$ 8,500–$12,200
1	$ 6,500–$ 8,500
0	Under $6,500

Vocabulary improvement through contextual clues: Wide reading was said to be an invaluable aid to vocabulary development. This is particularly true if you sharpen your awareness of contextual clues by noting the following three common situations, so helpful in dealing with new and strange words.

(1) Words used in pairs, either similar or opposite pairs.
(2) Words surrounded by illustrative details that suggest meaning.
(3) Words followed or preceded by "remote synonyms" that make meaning clear.

For example, suppose you don't know what the word *octogenarian* means. If you find it in the following context of opposite pairs, meaning will be clarified: "Man or woman, millionaire or pauper, octogenarian or infant — all are affected by this new regulation." Or if you don't know the meaning of *lexicographers,* the meaningful details in the following context should help: "Lexicographers worked through the file marked 'new words' in an attempt to determine which words to include in the new desk dictionary." Such details strongly suggest that lexicographers are dictionary makers. As a last example, lean on a remote synonym to get the meaning of *lave:* "You must lave the area four times daily. The only way you can hope to alleviate the pain is by such regular bathing with warm water."

In the textbooks that you are studying, find two clearly defined illustrations of each of these three situations. Enter them below.

(1) Illustrations of word pairs:

    (a) _____

    (b) _____

(2) Illustrations of meaningful details:

    (a) _____

    (b) _____

(3) Illustrations of "remote synonyms":

    (a) _____

    (b) _____

Name_____ Date_____ Reading Rate_____ w.p.m.

COMPREHENSION CHECK QUESTIONS

1. One book mentioned had the title *Confessions of* (1) *a Public Relations Man;* (2) *a People Manipulator;* (3) *a Slogan Writer;* (4) *an Advertising Man.*   1. _____

2. *Free* and *new* are called most (1) useful words; (2) helpful words; (3) powerful words; (4) dynamic words.   2. _____

3. J. L. Austin was spoken of as a (1) linguistic philosopher; (2) pollster; (3) logician; (4) semanticist.   3. _____

4. How many deadly sins are there supposed to be? (1) three; (2) five; (3) seven; (4) nine.   4. _____

5. Language was spoken of as (1) a tool; (2) a servant; (3) a master; (4) all of the preceding.   5. _____

Receptive Comprehension _____

6. The main idea is to explain (1) what words influence us most; (2) the depersonalization of human relations; (3) the contributions of linguistic research; (4) the tyranny of language.   6. _____

7. Which of the following statements seems best labeled a "performative utterance"? (1) I give you a discount; (2) I am tired; (3) I drink a lot; (4) I left you a check.   7. _____

8. The author's attitude toward admen is perhaps best described as (1) interested; (2) disturbed; (3) satisfied; (4) matter-of-fact.   8. _____

9. The effectiveness of an ad is apparently most dependent on (1) the pictures; (2) the words; (3) color; (4) layout.   9. _____

10. The chief way of coping with our semantic environment is through (1) understanding it; (2) changing it; (3) controlling it; (4) accepting it.   10. _____

(10 off for each mistake)   *Reflective Comprehension* _____

Total Reading Comprehension Score _____

VOCABULARY CHECK QUESTIONS

		without context I	with context II
1. *empirical*	(1) based on observation; (2) based on theory; (3) ethical; (4) powerful; (5) without purpose.	1. _____	_____
2. *clichés*	(1) chirps; (2) commonplace expressions; (3) noises; (4) solid masses; (5) questions.	2. _____	_____
3. *punctilious*	(1) casual; (2) piercing; (3) practical; (4) very exact; (5) beaten.	3. _____	_____
4. *gambit*	(1) extravagance; (2) rarity; (3) maneuver; (4) resemblance; (5) failure.	4. _____	_____
5. *nullify*	(1) change; (2) step down; (3) poke gently; (4) compress; (5) make void.	5. _____	_____

(10 off for each mistake)   *Word Comprehension* without *contextual help* (I) _____

Word Comprehension with *contextual help* (II) _____

Total Word Comprehension Score _____

EXERCISES

1. Extending the generalization step: To reinforce and extend the generalization suggestions treated on page 296, explore in even more detail the thinking road to mastery of prefix, root, and suffix elements.

As a reminder of how this approach works, take the prefix *pre-*. Suppose you do not know what it means. You can, of course, consult the dictionary, but it is far better to use the thinking road. Start thinking of some common words containing that prefix, defining each, then seeing what meaning is common to all. For example, you might think of *preview*, *prepare*, and *precede*, meaning "to view before," "to make ready before," and "to go before." Obviously the meaning common to all probably belongs to the prefix common to all.

To develop added skill with this approach, do the following exercises with prefix, root, and suffix elements.

1. If *commingle* means to mingle —————

   and *compress* means to press or squeeze —————,

   the prefix *com-* probably means —————.

2. If *descend* means to come —————

   and *depress* means to press —————,

   the prefix *de-* probably means —————.

3. If *depart* means to go —————

   and *deprive* means to take —————,

   the prefix *de-* probably also means —————.

4. If *obstruct* means to work ————— something

   and *object* means to protest ————— something,

   the prefix *ob-* probably means —————.

5. If *hyperactive* means ——-active

   and *hypercritical* means —————ly critical,

   the prefix *hyper-* probably means —————.

6. If *portable* means able to be carried

   and *transport* to carry across,

   the root *portare* probably means —————.

7. If *attract* means to draw to

   and *extract* to draw out,

   the root *trahere* probably means —————.

8. If *tangible* means something that can be touched

   and *tangent* means touching,

   the root *tangere* probably means —————.

9. If *statuesque* means like a statue

   and *picturesque* means like a picture,

   the suffix *-esque* probably means —————.

10. If a *kitchenette* is a little kitchen

    and a *statuette* a little statue,

    the suffix *-ette* probably means —————.

2. Discovering variant forms: Some prefixes have several variant forms. If you are to put your prefix knowledge to full use, you must know all these forms well. That means, for example, recognizing *com-* in *collaborate* as well as in *compare*. Using your dictionary, find as many variant forms as possible for each of the following prefixes, the most changeable to be found.

Prefixes   *Variant Forms*

1. *ab-*   —————————————————

2. *ad-*   —————————————————

3. *in-*   —————————————————

4. *com-*   —————————————————

5. *sub-*   —————————————————

6. *ob-*   —————————————————

7. *syn-*   —————————————————

8. *trans-*   —————————————————

9. *ex-*   —————————————————

10. *dis-*   —————————————————

NAME———————————————————— DATE———————— READING RATE——————— W.P.M.

COMPREHENSION CHECK QUESTIONS

1. In a Southern clinic what percent of the admissions had psychosomatic illnesses? (1) 38; (2) 47; (3) 66; (4) 77.　　　1. ————

2. The article talks about (1) c.d.t.; (2) p.t.d.; (3) c.p.d.; (4) t.p.d.　　　2. ————

3. The article suggests (1) raising your hand above your head; (2) holding your breath; (3) holding your fist tight; (4) gritting your teeth.　　　3. ————

4. Dr. John Hunter was killed by (1) fear; (2) nerves; (3) anger; (4) high blood pressure.　　　4. ————

5. The doctor advised one patient to read (1) *The Power of Positive Thinking;* (2) the Pollyanna books; (3) the Bible; (4) *The Catholic Digest.*　　　5. ————

Receptive Comprehension ————

6. This is mainly to explain what about psychosomatic illness? (1) its nature and suggestions for avoiding it; (2) the causes; (3) the cures; (4) its widespread incidence.　　　6. ————

7. The mention of Sam is to show (1) the type of person who got psychosomatic illness; (2) how unhappy some men are; (3) how worry tends to become habitual; (4) which type needs medical attention.　　　7. ————

8. The article mentions blushing to indicate how (1) mind influences body; (2) habitual certain responses are; (3) emotions bring perceptible body changes; (4) differently people react.　　　8. ————

9. The mention of a close call when driving is to point up the effect of (1) muscle tensions; (2) surprise; (3) shock; (4) glands.　　　9. ————

10. The chief purpose of this selection is to (1) predict; (2) explain; (3) describe; (4) evaluate.　　　10. ————

(10 off for each mistake)　　　　　　　　　　　　　　　*Reflective Comprehension* ————

TOTAL READING COMPREHENSION SCORE ————

VOCABULARY CHECK QUESTIONS

		without context I	*with context* II
1. *manifests*	(1) increases; (2) shows; (3) treats; (4) varies; (5) tightens.	1. ————	————
2. *perceptible*	(1) striking; (2) intact; (3) discernible; (4) great; (5) masterful.	2. ————	————
3. *dilation*	(1) enlarging; (2) constricting; (3) change; (4) sweating; (5) fainting.	3. ————	————
4. *refute*	(1) reject; (2) protest; (3) admit; (4) respond; (5) disprove.	4. ————	————
5. *adversity*	(1) enemy; (2) advance; (3) praise; (4) misfortune; (5) capability.	5. ————	————

(10 off for each mistake)　　　　*Word Comprehension* without *contextual help* (I) ————

Word Comprehension with *contextual help* (II) ————

TOTAL WORD COMPREHENSION SCORE ————

EXERCISES

With such matters as style, usage, punctuation, diction, spelling, and sentence structure in mind, make the best possible choices in the groupings that follow, circling your preference.

       (a) doctor   (a) is   (a) different (a) ailments that

As a   I know that there   a thousand   this human clay is heir

       (b) Doctor   (b) are   (b) different (b) ailments, that

(a) to, and (a) one is   (a) 999 put (a) together (a) , fifty percent

                     as common as the other   of all the

(b) to. And (b) one of them is   (b) 999, put (b) together (b) . Fifty percent

(a) people going   (a) united states   (a) is   (a) desease (a) , many

             to doctors in the   today   victims of this one

(b) people, going   (b) United States (b) are   (b) disease (b) . Many

                     (a) well known   (a) south (a) a report

would put the figures higher. At one   clinic in the   was

                     (b) well-known   (b) South (b) , a report

(a) published reviewing   (a) 500   (a) consecative   (a) the (a) institution,

                                       admissions to   of

(b) published, it reviewed (b) five hundred (b) consecutive   (b) that (b) institution;

(a) them, (a) 386 or 77   (a) was

                     percent —   sick with this one disease.

(b) those, (b) 386 — or 77   (b) were

When you have finished, check your version with the original at the beginning of Selection 66. Consult your dictionary or an English handbook to clear up any problems.

NAME_____ DATE_____ READING RATE_____ W.P.M.

COMPREHENSION CHECK QUESTIONS

1. The unenviable Mrs. Jones was (1) in her mid-30's; (2) in her mid-40's; (3) in her late 20's; (4) of unmentioned age.

   1. _____

2. Herb Smith was a (1) psychiatrist; (2) minister; (3) social worker; (4) medical doctor.

   2. _____

3. One specific bit of advice was to pay more attention to (1) people; (2) books; (3) appearance; (4) political and social issues.

   3. _____

4. Mention was made of a (1) large ant; (2) butterfly; (3) robin; (4) furry caterpillar.

   4. _____

5. Norman Vincent Peale spoke of his own advice as (1) pious; (2) innovative; (3) practical; (4) religious.   5. _____

Receptive Comprehension _____

6. This selection is mainly about how to (1) avoid monotony; (2) live fully; (3) find love; (4) discover goodness.

   6. _____

7. The phrase "horizontal living" apparently means (1) routine living; (2) intense living; (3) sustained and satisfying living; (4) intellectual living.

   7. _____

8. The point of the story about Martha was to suggest the need to (1) give emotions full rein; (2) take our mind off ourselves; (3) develop a problem-solving attitude; (4) look at life more realistically.

   8. _____

9. Writing a letter without an *I, me,* or *my,* was intended primarily to help (1) fight self-centeredness; (2) fight deadening routine; (3) set and meet challenges; (4) develop a different writing style.

   9. _____

10. The magnifying glass episode was intended to show the need to (1) generate interest in living; (2) find beauty; (3) escape monotony; (4) get close to nature.

    10. _____

(10 off for each mistake)   *Reflective Comprehension* _____

TOTAL READING COMPREHENSION SCORE _____

VOCABULARY CHECK QUESTIONS

		without *context* I	*with* *context* II
1. *futility*	(1) stuffiness; (2) success; (3) prospect; (4) enthusiasm; (5) uselessness.	1. _____	_____
2. *valid*	(1) venturesome; (2) accurate; (3) sound; (4) relaxing; (5) varied.	2. _____	_____
3. *mutely*	(1) silently; (2) markedly; (3) uniformly; (4) strongly; (5) stealthily.	3. _____	_____
4. *imperative*	(1) improper; (2) urgent; (3) hopeless; (4) unnecessary; (5) constructive.	4. _____	_____
5. *incomprehensible*	(1) obscure; (2) without feeling; (3) compressed; (4) extended; (5) feeble.	5. _____	_____

(10 off for each mistake)   *Word Comprehension* without *contextual help* (I) _____

Word Comprehension with *contextual help*   (II) _____

TOTAL WORD COMPREHENSION SCORE _____

EXERCISES

With such matters as style, usage, punctuation, diction, spelling, and sentence structure in mind, make the best possible choices in the groupings that follow, circling your preference.

(a) "It's   (a) wide-spread   (a) said, "this nagging   (a) uneasyness,

a very   thing," Dr. Herbert D. Smith

(b) "Its   (b) widespread   (b) said. "This nagging   (b) uneasiness,

(a) Life   (a) you, that   (a) we've   (a) capability to   (a) enjoy,

this feeling that   is hiding from   lost the

(b) life   (b) you; that   (b) you've   (b) capacity to   (b) enjoy

(a) existence. I   (a) think,   (a) susceptable

or appreciate the ordinary pleasures of   women are more

(b) existance. I   (b) think   (b) susceptible

(a) men;   (a) men tend to be   (a) their work,   (a) partly because,

to it than   partly because   absorbed in

(b) men —   (b) men, tend to be   (b) one's work, (b) since,

(a) could   (a) hungry   (a) easier.

being more emotional, women   become emotionally

(b) can   (b) starved (b) more easily.

(a) say,   (a) Jones?   (a) commence   (a) a little,

"Now, what would I   to Mrs.   I think I'd   by trying to reassure her

(b) say   (b) Jones.   (b) start   (b) a little.

(a) tell   (a) understandible. . . ."

I'd   her that her feelings are

(b) inform   (b) understandable. . . ."

When you have finished, check your version with the original in Selection 67. Consult your dictionary or an English handbook to clear up any problems.

NAME———————————————————— DATE——————— READING RATE——————— W.P.M.

COMPREHENSION CHECK QUESTIONS

1. This is addressed to (1) adults in general; (2) graduating seniors; (3) businessmen; (4) personnel directors.

   1. ———

2. The basic skill is spoken of as (1) reading; (2) listening; (3) persuading; (4) expressing ideas.

   2. ———

3. To determine what kind of employee to be involves how many decisions? (1) one; (2) two; (3) three; (4) four.

   3. ———

4. A job "near the top" is said to be (1) well paid; (2) insecure; (3) difficult to find; (4) unpleasant.

   4. ———

5. Which subject is *not* discussed in this article? (1) when to quit; (2) being fired; (3) union membership; (4) specializing.

   5. ———

Receptive Comprehension ———

6. This is primarily to help in (1) picking the right job; (2) understanding employeeship; (3) developing basic employee skills; (4) preparing for successful employment.

   6. ———

7. Apparently the most important course to take is one in (1) novel and short story; (2) written composition; (3) salesmanship; (4) business administration.

   7. ———

8. In picking a job you should, above all, (1) get vocational counseling; (2) analyze the companies being considered; (3) analyze yourself; (4) take a battery of aptitude tests.

   8. ———

9. In deciding on a job, your most important consideration is (1) aptitude; (2) training; (3) temperament; (4) creativity.

   9. ———

10. Most emphasis in this selection is placed on (1) preparation; (2) know-how; (3) character; (4) personality.

   10. ———

(10 off for each mistake) *Reflective Comprehension* ———

TOTAL READING COMPREHENSION SCORE ———

VOCABULARY CHECK QUESTIONS

		without context I	*with* context II
1. *dubious*	(1) twofold; (2) precise; (3) stupid; (4) involved; (5) questionable.	1. ———	———
2. *rigorous*	(1) absent; (2) righteous; (3) direct; (4) strict; (5) helpless.	2. ———	———
3. *innovator*	(1) student; (2) worker; (3) changer; (4) artist; (5) mechanic.	3. ———	———
4. *elusive*	(1) vivid; (2) eloquent; (3) slippery; (4) impersonal; (5) exalted.	4. ———	———
5. *liaison*	(1) slanderous; (2) likely; (3) free; (4) military; (5) coordinating.	5. ———	———

(10 off for each mistake)

Word Comprehension without *contextual help* (I) ———

Word Comprehension with *contextual help* (II) ———

TOTAL WORD COMPREHENSION SCORE ———

EXERCISES

With such matters as style, usage, punctuation, diction, spelling, grammar, and sentence structure in mind, make the best possible choices in the groupings that follow, circling your preference.

The first question we might ask

(a) is what
(b) is: what

can

(a) be taught
(b) you learn

in

(a) college
(b) college,

that will help

(a) one
(b) you

in being an

(a) employee.
(b) employee?

The schools teach

(a) a lot of things
(b) a great many things

of value to the future

(a) accountant,
(b) accountent,
(c) acountant,

the future

(a) doctor or
(b) doctor, or

(a) electrician.
(b) the future electrician.

(a) Does it
(b) Do they

also teach

(a) things
(b) anything

of value to

(a) future employees?
(b) the future employee?

The answer

(a) is: "Yes —
(b) is yes —

(a) it teaches
(b) they teach

the one

(a) thing
(b) thing,

that it is perhaps most

(a) valuable
(b) valuable,

for the future employee to

(a) know. But
(b) know, and

very few students bother to learn

(a) it.
(b) it".
(c) it."

This one basic skill

(a) is
(b) consists of

the ability

(a) of organizing and expressing
(b) to organize and express

ideas in

(a) writing
(b) writting

and

(a) speech.
(b) in speaking.

As

(a) a
(b) an

employee

(a) you work
(b) one works

with and through other

(a) people.
(b) folks.
(c) human beings.

When you have finished, check your version with the original in Selection 68. Check your dictionary or an English handbook to clear up any problems.

NAME————————————————————— DATE————————— READING RATE——————————— W.P.M.

COMPREHENSION CHECK QUESTIONS

1. The two American matrons were looking for (1) Westminster Abbey; (2) the Tower; (3) St. Paul's Cathedral; (4) the Houses of Parliament.   1. ————

2. Nitrogen was said to make up about what percent of the air we breathe? (1) 40; (2) 60; (3) 80; (4) amount not given.   2. ————

3. The terrible smog that hit London came in (1) October; (2) November; (3) December; (4) January.   3. ————

4. Specific mention was made of (1) *Punch;* (2) the *Manchester Guardian;* (3) the *Times;* (4) the *London Daily News.*   4. ————

5. What were said to be coming upstream in the Thames once again? (1) salmon; (2) elvers; (3) cod; (4) mackerel.   5. ————

Receptive Comprehension ————

6. Chief emphasis is on the (1) economic costs of pollution; (2) causes and control of pollution; (3) changed appearance of London; (4) special English regard for animals and the location of the Houses of Parliament.   6. ————

7. The opening episode about the American matrons was intended primarily to (1) arouse interest; (2) show the fresh beauty of London; (3) indicate the amount of pollution in London; (4) show typical tourist reactions.   7. ————

8. The discussion of the chemistry involved in organic waste in the Thames was to show how (1) long it takes to pollute a river; (2) complex the problem is; (3) difficult it is to stop; (4) the smell came about.   8. ————

9. The author is apparently (1) an American; (2) a Canadian; (3) an Australian; (4) an Englishman.   9. ————

10. The primary purpose is apparently to (1) convince; (2) arouse to action; (3) entertain; (4) evaluate.   10. ————

(10 off for each mistake)   *Reflective Comprehension* ————

TOTAL READING COMPREHENSION SCORE ————

VOCABULARY CHECK QUESTIONS

		without context I	with context II
1. *malignant*	(1) overly large; (2) magnificent; (3) harmful; (4) soothing; (5) sore.	1. ————	————
2. *harass*	(1) harmonize; (2) protect; (3) hasten; (4) torment; (5) attempt.	2. ————	————
3. *miasmas*	(1) floods; (2) storms; (3) antidotes; (4) headaches; (5) vapors.	3. ————	————
4. *impinge*	(1) touch on; (2) improve; (3) regulate; (4) insult; (5) leave out.	4. ————	————
5. *wreak*	(1) crash; (2) search; (3) wrinkle; (4) estimate; (5) eliminate.	5. ————	————

(10 off for each mistake)   *Word Comprehension* without *contextual help* (I) ————

Word Comprehension with *contextual help*   (II) ————

TOTAL WORD COMPREHENSION SCORE ————

EXERCISES

With such matters as style, usage, punctuation, diction, spelling, and sentence structure in mind, make the best possible choices in the groupings that follow, circling your preference.

(a) Now, that   (a) done,   (a) Londoners   (a) beauty,
          much of the cleaning has been   delight in new
(b) Now that   (b) done   (b) Londoner's   (b) beauty

(a) beginning   (a) there   (a) had
but   with   was some uneasiness. We   become so accustomed to
(b) to begin   (b) their   (b) have

               (a) buildings, that   (a) people, felt   (a) their   (a) State.
the blackness of our great   many   that this was   proper
               (b) buildings that   (b) people felt   (b) its   (b) state.

         (a) Dean and Chapter   (a) St. Pauls'   (a) decided that   (a) london
When the   of   the new purity of the   air
         (b) dean and chapter   (b) St. Paul's   (b) decided, that   (b) London

         (a) huge   (a) Cathedral   (a) they   (a) prescribe
justified the   expense of cleaning the   stone,   asked the public to
         (b) corpulent   (b) cathedral   (b) it   (b) subscribe

         (a) money, for   (a) epistles   (a) Times
the necessary   many weeks afterwards   appeared in the   protesting the
         (b) money. For   (b) letters   (b) *Times*

(a) sacrifice.   (a) wreak   (a) familiar
         How dare anyone   such a change on the dear   blackness of St. Paul's!
(b) sacrilege.   (b) wreck   (b) familar

When you have finished, check your version with the original in Selection 69. Consult your dictionary or an English handbook to clear up any problems.

NAME_____ DATE_____ READING RATE_____ W.P.M.

COMPREHENSION CHECK QUESTIONS

1. In the last ten years the total annual number of divorces was said to have (1) leveled off; (2) dropped slightly; (3) risen steeply; (4) doubled.

  1. _____

2. Second marriages tend to have (1) a longer life span that the first; (2) the same life span; (3) an unpredictable life span; (4) a shorter life span.

  2. _____

3. Today what percent of the low-birth-weight babies are born to mothers in their teens? (1) 25; (2) 20; (3) 15; (4) not given.

  3. _____

4. It is said that divorce hangs over a young wife (1) when she first becomes pregnant; (2) as soon as she's married; (3) even before the ceremony; (4) the minute she stops working.

  4. _____

5. It is said that a good marriage takes (1) money; (2) similar backgrounds; (3) hard work; (4) parental help.

  5. _____

Receptive Comprehension _____

6. The main idea is to (1) indicate the problem; (2) suggest ways of dealing with the problem; (3) encourage more parental guidance; (4) persuade people to postpone getting married.

  6. _____

7. What best describes the attitude taken here toward new-style alternates to marriage? (1) noncritical; (2) critical; (3) evasive; (4) encouraging.

  7. _____

8. What factor appears most likely to lead to divorce? (1) lack of education; (2) early marriage; (3) health; (4) children.

  8. _____

9. In tone this selection is (1) sarcastic; (2) straightforward; (3) somewhat flowery; (4) colloquial.

  9. _____

10. By implication, it would seem most important for young couples to (1) read for new insights and ideas; (2) spend more time apart; (3) watch TV together more; (4) plan things to do with each other.

  10. _____

(10 off for each mistake)   *Reflective Comprehension* _____

TOTAL READING COMPREHENSION SCORE _____

VOCABULARY CHECK QUESTIONS

		without context I	*with context* II
1. *peers*	(1) superiors; (2) inferiors; (3) parents; (4) equals; (5) strangers.	1. _____	_____
2. *fending*	(1) using; (2) complaining; (3) concluding; (4) destroying; (5) managing.	2. _____	_____
3. *interloper*	(1) runner; (2) eloquent plea; (3) foreigner; (4) intruder; (5) foreman.	3. _____	_____
4. *ambivalence*	(1) conflicting feeling; (2) dexterity; (3) pleasantness; (4) slow gait; (5) slumber.	4. _____	_____
5. *limbo*	(1) leg; (2) indeterminate state; (3) distress signal; (4) dialect; (5) distaste.	5. _____	_____

(10 off for each mistake)   Word Comprehension without *contextual help* (I) _____

Word Comprehension with *contextual help* (II) _____

TOTAL WORD COMPREHENSION SCORE _____

EXERCISES

With such matters as style, usage, punctuation, diction, spelling, and sentence structure in mind, make the best possible choices in the groupings that follow, circling your preference.

Marriage and early pregnancy   (a) are   the main   (a) reason   today why girls drop out of   (a) school.   (b) is   (b) reasons   (b) school,

Perhaps   (a) returning.   In most   (a) communities there   (a) no place   in the   (a) high school   never   perhaps   (b) to return.   (b) communities, there   (b) noplace   is   (b) high-school

system for a   (a) young, married   (a) woman; let   alone for a young mother.   (a) Often, too,   (b) young married   (b) woman, let   (b) Often too

young husbands fail to go on with   (a) there   (a) schooling.   The freedom   (a) gained,   by leaving   (b) their   (b) education.   (b) gained

home and school   (a) becomes   the obligation to   (a) work —   to be   (a) self-supporting   and,   (b) becoming   (b) work;   (b) self supporting

for a young   (a) father,   to support a family. Lack of education in turn   (a) means,   that a   (a) very   large   (b) Father,   (b) means   (b) very,

(a) porportion   of the very young   (a) married, live   at the poverty   (a) level   without any   (b) proportion   (b) married live   (b) level;

reserves to fall back   (a) on (a) nor   any hope of getting out of   (a) poverty and debt.   (b) to (b) or   (b) poverty, and debt.

When you have finished, check your version with the original in Selection 70. Consult your dictionary or an English hand-book to clear up any problems.

NAME_____ DATE_____ READING RATE_____ W.P.M.

COMPREHENSION CHECK QUESTIONS

1. One allusion was to a Presidential (1) Screening Board; (2) Brain Trust; (3) In-Service Apprenticeship; (4) Academy.   1. _____

2. According to one authority, a President must be both preacher and (1) common man; (2) politician; (3) arm twister; (4) teacher.   2. _____

3. The selection refers to the (1) Civil War; (2) Viet Nam War; (3) Panama Canal; (4) Suez Canal.   3. _____

4. It was specifically said that the President must cope with the (1) Chinese; (2) Arabs; (3) Israelis; (4) Russians.   4. _____

5. What specific words were quoted? (1) with malice towards none . . . ; (2) . . . one nation, under God; (3) . . . a new deal for the American people; (4) . . . the great arsenal of democracy.   5. _____

Receptive Comprehension _____

6. This is mainly about (1) finding a Presidential candidate; (2) the problems facing a President; (3) the qualities voters should look for in a President; (4) the ideal schooling for a President.   6. _____

7. Electoral machinery and campaigning are considered (1) hopelessly antiquated; (2) rather useful; (3) in need of major overhaul; (4) exactly right as is.   7. _____

8. The comparison to a morality play was primarily to show that we are (1) a God-fearing country; (2) playing a world-wide role; (3) fighting evil; (4) being directed by God.   8. _____

9. What quality appears to be given most importance for a President? (1) wisdom; (2) character; (3) oratorial skill; (4) self-confidence.   9. _____

10. In tone, you would call this (1) highly optimistic; (2) strongly pessimistic; (3) critical; (4) authoritative.   10. _____

(10 off for each mistake)   *Reflective Comprehension* _____

TOTAL READING COMPREHENSION SCORE _____

VOCABULARY CHECK QUESTIONS

		without context I	with context II
1. *virtuosos*	(1) good women; (2) morals; (3) lessons; (4) groups; (5) skilled performers. 1.	_____	_____
2. *exultant*	(1) additional; (2) solid; (3) weak; (4) soothed; (5) triumphant. 2.	_____	_____
3. *militant*	(1) hopeless; (2) fearful; (3) strengthened; (4) matter-of-fact; (5) aggressive. 3.	_____	_____
4. *conciliator*	(1) attorney; (2) teacher; (3) guard; (4) appeaser; (5) foreman. 4.	_____	_____
5. *fiasco*	(1) exposition; (2) display; (3) complete failure; (4) wide fluctuation; (5) frivolity. 5.	_____	_____

(10 off for each mistake)   *Word Comprehension* without *contextual help* (I) _____

Word Comprehension with *contextual help* (II) _____

TOTAL WORD COMPREHENSION SCORE _____

EXERCISES

With such matters as style, usage, punctuation, diction, spelling, and sentence structure in mind, make the best possible choices in the groupings that follow, circling your preference.

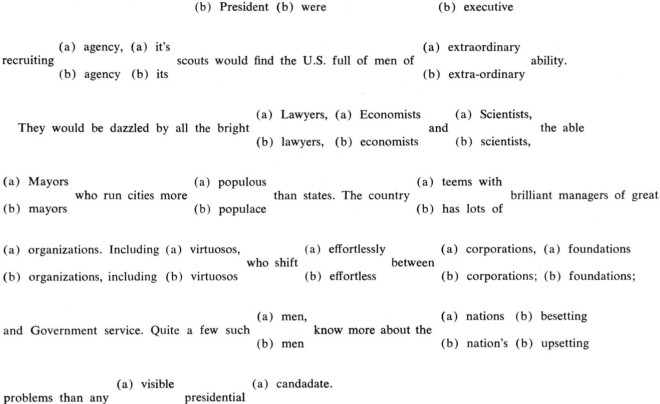

If the task of finding the ideal   (a) president (a) was   (a) Executive
                                             turned over to an
                             (b) President (b) were   (b) executive

         (a) agency, (a) it's   (a) extraordinary
recruiting   scouts would find the U.S. full of men of   ability.
         (b) agency (b) its   (b) extra-ordinary

                      (a) Lawyers, (a) Economists   (a) Scientists,
They would be dazzled by all the bright   and   the able
                      (b) lawyers, (b) economists   (b) scientists,

(a) Mayors   (a) populous   (a) teems with
       who run cities more   than states. The country   brilliant managers of great
(b) mayors   (b) populace   (b) has lots of

(a) organizations. Including (a) virtuosos,   (a) effortlessly   (a) corporations, (a) foundations
                      who shift   between
(b) organizations, including (b) virtuosos   (b) effortless   (b) corporations; (b) foundations;

                      (a) men,   (a) nations (b) besetting
and Government service. Quite a few such   know more about the
                      (b) men   (b) nation's (b) upsetting

          (a) visible   (a) candadate.
problems than any   presidential
          (b) visable   (b) candidate.

       (a) age   (a) out, for   (a) white house.
The   cries   greatness in the
       (b) Age   (b) out for   (b) White House.

When you have finished, check your version with the original in Selection 71. Consult your dictionary or an English handbook to clear up any problems.

NAME——————————————————— DATE——————— READING RATE——————— W.P.M.

COMPREHENSION CHECK QUESTIONS

1. For what percent was time and energy expenditure said to be out of step with life goals? (1) 45; (2) 60; (3) 75; (4) 90.   1. ————

2. One of the seven questions was specifically on (1) production of income; (2) environmental needs and life style; (3) sense of responsibility; (4) physical fitness as related to mental fitness.   2. ————

3. Who was quoted? (1) Kennedy; (2) Pogo; (3) Peanuts; (4) Hitler.   3. ————

4. At what age was parallel play said to be typical? (1) age 1; (2) age 2; (3) age 2 or 3; (4) age 3 or 4.   4. ————

5. Reference was made to (1) Hollywood; (2) Utopia; (3) Great Britain; (4) San Francisco.   5. ————

Receptive Comprehension ————

6. This selection is chiefly about how to (1) discover our problems; (2) solve our problems; (3) check up on our mental health; (4) strengthen our relationships with others.   6. ————

7. The aphorism "physician, heal thyself" was used to develop the idea that self-examination (1) is difficult; (2) is common; (3) should be done by physicians; (4) is actually impossible to do.   7. ————

8. The seven areas are ordered essentially on what basis? (1) from the global to the individual; (2) according to a developing time sequence; (3) from the particular to the general; (4) from most to least importance.   8. ————

9. By implication, an avocation is considered primarily as a way of (1) avoiding problems; (2) gaining emotional fulfillment; (3) finding needed relaxation; (4) developing stronger self-reliance.   9. ————

10. In style you would call this article (1) conversational; (2) lively; (3) dignified; (4) dreary.   10. ————

(10 off for each mistake)   *Reflective Comprehension* ————

TOTAL READING COMPREHENSION SCORE ————

VOCABULARY CHECK QUESTIONS

		without context I	*with context* II

1. *autonomy*   (1) technical perfection; (2) independence; (3) motor-driven; (4) composite; (5) welfare state.   1. ———— ————

2. *castigate*   (1) punish; (2) discard; (3) evolve; (4) tear down; (5) smooth over.   2. ———— ————

3. *pre-empt*   (1) suggest; (2) spare; (3) turn over; (4) get beforehand; (5) force into submission.   3. ———— ————

4. *germane*   (1) relevant; (2) cultivated; (3) original; (4) infected; (5) weakened.   4. ———— ————

5. *hallmark*   (1) shipping label; (2) entryway; (3) engraving tool; (4) symbol of excellence; (5) gift.   5. ———— ————

(10 off for each mistake)   *Word Comprehension* without *contextual help* (I) ————

Word Comprehension with *contextual help* (II) ————

TOTAL WORD COMPREHENSION SCORE ————

EXERCISES

With such matters as style, usage, punctuation, diction, spelling, and sentence structure in mind, make the best possible choices in the groupings that follow, circling your preference.

It is
(a) clear that
(b) clear, that
the
(a) capacaty
(b) capacity
to
(a) bring into existence
(b) establish
close,
(a) significant emotional
(b) significant, emotional

ties with others
(a) are
(b) is
characteristic of emotional maturity. It
(a) is
(b) being
(a) clear
(b) clear,
(a) moreover
(b) moreover,

that the work, the
(a) effort, and
(b) effort and
sometimes the
(a) pain of
(b) pain, of
doing
(a) so
(b) so,
is quite enough to discourage

(a) many. Especially
(b) many, especially
(a) when
(b) being that
the trends in our society
(a) is
(b) are
moving in the same direction. And

(a) yet, we
(b) yet we
are still
(a) disdainful
(b) disdainfull
of the empty
(a) superficiality
(b) superficially
of the
(a) "cocktail"
(b) cocktail
(a) party, even
(b) party. Even

when lessened by the
(a) illusion
(b) allusion
of
(a) intimacy, which
(b) intimacy which
alcohol
(a) can
(b) could
provide. . . .

Your relationships to
(a) others,
(b) others
do indeed
(a) image
(b) mirror
(a) your
(b) you're
relationship to yourself.

When you have finished, check your version with the original in Selection 72. Consult your dictionary or an English handbook to clear up any problems.

NAME——————————————— DATE———————— READING RATE————————— W.P.M.

COMPREHENSION CHECK QUESTIONS

1. Anthony Morley was for some time (1) a professor; (2) an office worker; (3) an engineer; (4) a clergyman.   1. ————

2. According to one source quoted, most of us face how many periods of crisis? (1) only one; (2) two; (3) three; (4) four.   2. ————

3. Howard Bede developed a special interest in (1) volcanoes; (2) bridges; (3) waterfalls; (4) windmills.   3. ————

4. The adults in this country were said to constitute a work force of what size? (1) eighty-one million; (2) seventy-three million; (3) sixty-seven million; (4) fifty-nine million.   4. ————

5. Of our young people, about what percent does the author estimate have no real goals? (1) 35; (2) 50; (3) 62; (4) 68.   5. ————

Receptive Comprehension ————

6. The main idea is to indicate (1) what the U.S. Office of Education is doing about career education; (2) the possibilities for volunteer work; (3) the specific kinds of training needed; (4) the changing role of education to meet the current situation.   6. ————

7. You would infer that the problem dealt with here is probably (1) a long-standing one; (2) of concern to retirees only; (3) a temporary one; (4) somewhat new.   7. ————

8. The author's chief concern is apparently to help in (1) dealing with changing technology; (2) solving present-day problems; (3) discovering a better life; (4) earning more money.   8. ————

9. As a tool in preparing for additional careers, which would you infer might be best? (1) a college degree program; (2) a graduate degree program; (3) a liberal education program; (4) a carefully laid out individual reading program.   9. ————

10. Judging from this article, you would infer that the ideal time to start thinking of additional careers would be (1) in your late forties; (2) in grade school; (3) during college; (4) after college.   10. ————

(10 off for each mistake)   *Reflective Comprehension* ————

TOTAL READING COMPREHENSION SCORE ————

VOCABULARY CHECK QUESTIONS

		without context I	*with context* II
1. *competencies*	(1) comparisons; (2) abilities; (3) collections; (4) groups; (5) plans.	1. ————	————
2. *integrity*	(1) number; (2) uprightness; (3) knowledge; (4) purpose; (5) curiosity.	2. ————	————
3. *envision*	(1) imagine; (2) change; (3) surround; (4) desire; (5) continue.	3. ————	————
4. *niche*	(1) cut; (2) element; (3) acid; (4) noise; (5) place.	4. ————	————
5. *shibboleths*	(1) twins; (2) stalls; (3) customs; (4) shields; (5) sand bars.	5. ————	————

(10 off for each mistake)   Word Comprehension without *contextual help* (I) ————

Word Comprehension with *contextual help* (II) ————

TOTAL WORD COMPREHENSION SCORE ————

EXERCISES

With such matters as style, usage, punctuation, diction, spelling, and sentence structure in mind, make the best possible choices in the groupings that follow, circling your preference.

Bede was one of those early
  (a) volunteers, and
  (b) volunteers and
is still at it, along with
  (a) two thousand
  (b) 2,000

other people of all
  (a) ages, most
  (b) ages. Most
of
  (a) who
  (b) whom
he inspired. The
  (a) program
  (b) programme
now reaches

  (a) twenty one
  (b) twenty-one
towns in the
  (a) Chicago
  (b) chicago
area. What does he talk to young people
  (a) about?
  (b) about.

Publishing,
  (a) of course. And
  (b) of course, and
writing and
  (a) volcanoes
  (b) volcanos
and how to set up a
  (a) darkroom to
  (b) darkroom; to

develop pictures in school or
  (a) "at home."
  (b) at home.
When the
  (a) children
  (b) kids
  (a) ask,
  (b) ask
he also

  (a) narrates
  (b) talks
about what
  (a) Life
  (b) life
was like in the
  (a) Depression;
  (b) depression;
many of
  (a) there
  (b) their
teachers

are themselves
  (a) too
  (b) to
young to
  (a) remember!
  (b) remember.
Most of
  (a) all
  (b) all,
he asks students what

they want to
  (a) do, with
  (b) do with
their lives and how they intend to get
  (a) there. He
  (b) there, he
asks them

to think ahead, to consider the options, and then
  (a) to chart
  (b) charting
a realistic career, intuitively,

without formal
  (a) cirriculums.
  (b) curriculums.

When you have finished, check your version with the original in Selection 73. Consult your dictionary or an English handbook to clear up any problems.

NAME————————————————— DATE——————— READING RATE——————— W.P.M.

COMPREHENSION CHECK QUESTIONS

1. One speaker specifically contrasted the work ethic with the (1) play ethic; (2) drink-and-drug ethic; (3) escape ethic; (4) welfare ethic.   1. ———

2. The unemployment percent mentioned was (1) 5.5; (2) 8.7; (3) 13; (4) 15.   2. ———

3. There is specific mention of (1) *The Greening of America;* (2) *Masks of Loneliness;* (3) *Beyond Freedom and Dignity;* (4) *Retreat from Sanity.*   3. ———

4. The selection quotes (1) Plato; (2) Demosthenes; (3) Aristotle; (4) Socrates.   4. ———

5. In a listing of aspects of work according to importance, what came first? (1) interesting work; (2) good pay; (3) pleasant surroundings; (4) fringe benefits.   5. ———

Receptive Comprehension ———

6. The main idea of this selection dealing with the work ethic was to (1) reveal its origin; (2) evaluate its present status; (3) determine the role of automation; (4) suggest providing varied work tasks.   6. ———

7. This article was apparently written for (1) union leaders; (2) the general public; (3) politicians; (4) job hunters.   7. ———

8. Christianity has apparently had what effect on the work ethic? (1) a weakening effect; (2) no effect; (3) a conflicting effect; (4) an establishing effect.   8. ———

9. Welfare figures were introduced as evidence to suggest (1) the loss of the work ethic; (2) changes in the work ethic; (3) the continued presence of the work ethic; (4) the growing need for a work ethic.   9. ———

10. The list of promising ideas tends to focus primarily on the (1) individual; (2) job; (3) surrounding; (4) fringe benefits.   10. ———

(10 off for each mistake)   *Reflective Comprehension* ———

TOTAL READING COMPREHENSION SCORE ———

VOCABULARY CHECK QUESTIONS

		without context I	*with context* II
1. *ethic*	(1) strength; (2) code of conduct; (3) reason; (4) length of time; (5) basic need.	1. ———	———
2. *pantheon*	(1) remedy; (2) disease; (3) temple; (4) formal speech; (5) investigation.	2. ———	———
3. *menial*	(1) servile; (2) virile; (3) helpless; (4) effective; (5) menacing.	3. ———	———
4. *hedonism*	(1) wickedness; (2) curved graph; (3) sadness; (4) pleasure-seeking; (5) heritage.	4. ———	———
5. *holistic*	(1) incomplete; (2) empty; (3) hopeful; (4) destructive; (5) organic.	5. ———	———

(10 off for each mistake)   *Word Comprehension* without *contextual help* (I) ———

Word Comprehension with *contextual help*   (II) ———

TOTAL WORD COMPREHENSION SCORE ———

EXERCISES

With such matters as style, usage, punctuation, diction, spelling, and sentence structure in mind, make the best possible choices in the groupings that follow, circling your preference.

The   (a) Puritans   were   (a) Calvinists,   and they brought the work ethic to   (a) America, they
      (b) puritans   (b) calvinists,   (b) America. They

punished idleness   (a) like   a serious misdemeanor. They filled   (a) there   (a) childrens'   ears
                  (b) as   (b) their   (b) children's

with copybook   (a) axioms   about the   (a) devil   finding work for idle   (a) hands,   and God   (a) helps
                (b) maxims   (b) Devil   (b) hands   (b) helping

those   (a) that   help themselves. Successive waves of   (a) immigrants   took those lessons
      (b) who   (b) emigrants

(a) "to heart,"   and they aimed   (a) for,   what they thought   (a) were   the ultimate
(b) to heart,   (b) for   (b) was

(a) success   (a) them — middle-class   status. They almost   (a) deified   Horatio   (a) Algers'
(b) Success   open to   (b) them. Middle-class   (b) defied   (b) Alger's

fictional   (a) heroes,   like Ragged   (a) Dick,   (a) whom   struggled   (a) up to   the   (a) Middle Class
         (b) heros,   (b) Dick   (b) who   (b) up, to   (b) middle class

by dint of   (a) hard work.
            (b) hard-work.

When you have finished, check your version with the original in Selection 74. Consult your dictionary or an English handbook to clear up any problems.

Name————————————————— Date——————— Reading Rate——————— w.p.m.

COMPREHENSION CHECK QUESTIONS

1. By 1985 we will be importing how much of our petroleum? (1) about one-fourth; (2) about one-third; (3) over half; (4) over two-thirds.   1. ————

2. Mention is made of (1) Lebanon; (2) Saudi Arabia; (3) Kuwait; (4) Tunisia.   2. ————

3. The world supply of high-quality protein is hampered in how many specified areas? (1) three; (2) two; (3) one; (4) an unspecified number.   3. ————

4. Since 1950 soybean yields in the U.S. have (1) leveled off; (2) almost doubled; (3) increased about 1 percent a year; (4) increased over 4 percent a year.   4. ————

5. One suggestion was to (1) reduce auto size; (2) limit auto production; (3) improve gas mileage; (4) double license fees on autos.   5. ————

Receptive Comprehension ————

6. This selection is mainly to get us to (1) reduce energy use; (2) recognize our environmental crisis; (3) reexamine our life style; (4) change our foreign-affairs budget.   6. ————

7. The discussion of the world energy market was intended primarily to point up the problem of (1) finding petroleum; (2) wasting our natural resources; (3) curbing our growing needs; (4) buying needed fuel.   7. ————

8. Most attention was given to supplies of (1) petroleum products; (2) a military nature; (3) needed minerals; (4) food.   8. ————

9. How would you summarize the fish production situation? (1) can be increased further; (2) is spotty; (3) is declining; (4) is at an upper level.   9. ————

10. The "crust of bread" illustration was used to reveal (1) the importance of food; (2) the effectiveness of our farm program; (3) our superaffluence; (4) our basic needs.   10. ————

(10 off for each mistake)   *Reflective Comprehension* ————

Total Reading Comprehension Score ————

VOCABULARY CHECK QUESTIONS

		without context I	*with context* II
1. *sector*	(1) center; (2) poison; (3) portion; (4) secret; (5) season.	1. ————	————
2. *rigorous*	(1) harsh; (2) religious; (3) bloody; (4) trusting; (5) resolute.	2. ————	————
3. *aspire*	(1) view; (2) feature; (3) exist; (4) explain; (5) desire.	3. ————	————
4. *presumed*	(1) claimed falsely; (2) divided; (3) taken for granted; (4) intended; (5) allocated.	4. ————	————
5. *enhanced*	(1) held; (2) stored away; (3) advised; (4) improved; (5) hindered.	5. ————	————

(10 off for each mistake)   *Word Comprehension* without *contextual help* (I) ————

Word Comprehension with *contextual help* (II) ————

Total Word Comprehension Score ————

EXERCISES

With such matters as style, usage, punctuation, diction, spelling, and sentence structure in mind, make the best possible choices in the groupings that follow, circling your preferences.

The ____ (a) 3rd (a) area ____ in which we have not been ____ (a) successful ____ is in ____ (a) raising ____ soybean
____ (b) third (b) area,   (b) successful,   (b) rising

(a) yeild ____ per acre. Soybeans are an ____ (a) extremely, ____ important ____ (a) global ____ source of ____ (a) high quality
(b) yield   (b) extremely   (b) Global   (b) high-quality

protein, but since 1950 soybean ____ (a) yields, ____ in the United ____ (a) States, (a) have ____ increased only about 1 percent a
                                  (b) yields   (b) States (b) has

(a) year (compared ____ with 4 percent a year for ____ (a) corn). ____ To my ____ (a) knowledge
(b) year. Compared   (b) corn.   (b) knowledge,

no experts expect any sort of breakthrough in the ____ (a) forseeable (a) future. The ____ crucial ____ (a) role
                                                    (b) foreseeable (b) future, the   (b) roll

of soybeans as a global protein ____ (a) source; and ____ the additional ____ (a) economic ____ importance of
                                   (b) source and   (b) Economic

(a) soybeans to ____ the United States ____ (a) is ____ underlined by the fact that soybeans ____ (a) constitute ____ our
(b) soybeans, to   (b) are   (b) constituted

(a) greatest single ____ export item ____ (a) (in dollar value) ____ in ____ (a) 1972.
(b) greatest, single   (b) in dollar value   (b) the year 1972.

When you have finished, check your version with the original in Selection 75. Consult your dictionary or an English handbook to clear up any problems.

APPENDIX

The general procedure for getting word-per-minute rate is to divide the number of words by the reading time in seconds and then multiplying that quotient by sixty. The conversion table provides, however, a convenient shortcut to that procedure for most reading times.

To use the table, find the figure in the left-hand column that is closest to your reading time. Then look along that line to the column headed by the number of the selection read to get your word-per-minute rate.

For reading times between one and two minutes (60 to 120 seconds), double your reading time before looking in the table. Then double the number in the table to get your rate.

For reading times over 400 seconds, divide your reading time by half before looking in the table. Then divide the number in the table by half to get your rate.

TIME IN SECONDS (AND MINUTES)	SELECTIONS BY NUMBER																						
	1	2	3	4	5	6	7	8	9	10	11	12	13	14	15	16	17	18	19	20	21	22	23
60(1)	1180	1620	1520	2250	3000	1740	1660	1320	910	2440	2245	2885	1930	1124	1734	1866	1275	1358	1050	2090	1056	732	1300
120(2)	590	810	760	1125	1500	870	830	660	455	1220	1123	1443	965	562	867	933	638	679	525	1045	528	366	650
130	545	746	702	1038	1384	803	766	609	420	1126	1036	1332	891	519	800	861	588	627	485	964	487	338	600
140	506	694	651	963	1284	746	711	566	390	1048	962	1236	827	482	743	799	546	583	450	896	453	314	555
150	472	648	608	900	1200	696	664	528	364	976	898	1154	772	450	694	746	510	543	420	836	422	293	520
160	443	606	570	843	1125	653	623	495	342	914	842	1082	724	422	650	699	478	507	394	783	396	275	486
170	417	572	536	794	1059	614	586	466	321	862	792	1018	681	397	612	659	450	480	371	737	373	258	459
180(3)	393	540	507	750	1000	580	553	440	303	814	748	962	643	375	578	622	425	453	350	697	352	244	433
190	373	511	480	710	947	549	524	417	287	770	709	911	609	355	548	589	403	429	332	660	333	231	410
200	354	485	456	675	900	522	498	396	273	732	674	866	579	337	520	560	383	408	315	627	317	220	390
210	338	463	434	642	856	498	474	377	260	698	641	824	551	321	495	533	364	388	300	597	302	209	372
220	322	441	415	612	818	475	453	360	248	666	612	787	526	307	472	509	347	370	286	570	288	200	354
230	308	422	397	587	782	454	433	344	237	636	586	753	503	293	452	485	332	354	274	545	275	191	339
240(4)	295	405	380	563	750	435	415	330	227	610	562	721	483	281	434	467	319	339	263	523	264	183	325
250	283	388	365	540	720	418	398	317	218	586	539	692	463	270	416	448	306	326	252	492	253	176	312
260	273	373	351	519	692	402	383	305	210	563	518	666	445	259	400	431	294	314	242	482	244	169	300
270	262	360	338	500	667	387	369	294	202	542	499	641	429	250	385	415	283	302	233	464	235	163	289
280	253	347	326	482	642	373	356	283	195	524	481	618	414	241	371	400	273	292	225	448	226	157	278
290	244	335	314	465	620	360	343	273	188	505	464	597	399	233	359	386	263	281	217	439	218	151	269
300(5)	236	324	304	450	600	348	332	264	182	488	449	577	386	225	347	373	255	272	210	418	211	146	260
310	228	313	294	435	580	337	322	256	176	472	435	558	374	218	336	359	247	263	203	404	204	142	251
320	221	303	285	422	563	326	312	248	171	458	421	541	362	211	325	350	239	253	197	392	198	137	243
330	215	294	276	409	545	316	302	240	165	444	408	525	351	204	315	339	232	247	191	380	192	133	236
340	209	286	268	397	530	307	293	233	161	432	396	509	341	198	306	329	225	240	185	369	186	129	230
350	202	278	261	386	514	298	284	226	156	418	385	495	331	193	297	319	219	233	180	358	181	125	223
360(6)	196	270	253	375	500	290	277	220	152	406	374	481	322	187	289	311	212	226	175	348	176	122	216
370	191	262	246	365	486	282	269	214	148	396	364	468	313	182	281	302	207	220	170	339	171	119	210
380	187	255	240	355	474	275	262	208	144	386	354	456	305	177	273	294	202	214	166	330	167	116	205
390	182	249	234	346	462	268	255	203	139	375	345	444	297	173	266	287	196	209	162	321	162	113	200
400	177	243	228	338	450	261	249	198	137	366	337	433	290	169	260	280	192	204	158	313	158	110	195
410	173	237	222	329	439	255	243	193	133	357	329	422	282	164	253	273	187	199	154	306	155	107	190
420(7)	169	231	217	321	429	249	237	186	129	348	321	412	276	161	248	267	182	194	150	299	151	105	186

SELECTIONS BY NUMBER

TIME IN SECONDS (AND MINUTES)	24	25	26	27	28	29	30	31	32	33	34	35	36	37	38	39	40	41	42	43	44	45	46	47	48	49
60(1)	1574	3364	1820	1220	2550	1390	1300	2090	1548	920	1870	1020	1320	1662	2352	2320	1050	1890	1704	2550	1590	1930	1910	2530	1220	820
120(2)	787	1682	910	610	1275	695	650	1035	774	460	935	510	660	831	1176	1160	525	945	852	1275	795	965	955	1265	610	410
130	726	1553	840	563	1176	642	600	964	714	425	884	471	609	767	1086	1070	484	872	786	1176	734	890	879	1168	563	379
140	675	1442	780	524	1092	596	555	896	663	394	802	437	566	712	1008	994	450	810	730	1092	682	828	819	1084	524	352
150	630	1346	728	488	1020	556	520	836	619	370	748	408	528	665	941	928	420	756	682	1020	636	772	764	1012	488	328
160	590	1262	683	457	954	521	486	783	580	345	702	383	495	623	882	870	394	709	639	954	596	724	716	948	457	308
170	556	1187	642	431	900	491	459	737	546	325	660	360	466	587	830	818	371	667	601	900	559	681	674	893	431	290
180(3)	525	1121	607	407	850	463	433	697	516	307	623	340	440	554	784	773	350	630	568	850	530	643	633	843	407	274
190	497	1062	575	385	804	439	410	660	488	291	590	322	417	525	743	733	332	597	538	804	502	609	602	798	385	260
200	472	1009	546	366	765	417	390	627	464	276	561	306	396	499	706	696	315	567	511	765	477	579	572	759	366	246
210	450	961	520	349	729	397	372	597	442	263	534	292	377	475	672	660	300	540	487	729	454	552	546	722	349	235
220	429	917	496	333	696	379	354	570	422	251	510	278	360	453	641	633	285	516	465	696	434	526	521	690	333	224
230	411	878	475	318	666	363	339	545	404	240	486	266	344	434	614	605	274	493	445	666	415	503	498	660	318	214
240(4)	394	841	455	305	638	348	325	518	387	230	468	255	330	416	588	580	263	473	426	638	398	483	478	633	305	205
250	378	807	437	293	612	334	312	492	371	221	449	245	317	399	564	557	252	454	409	612	382	463	458	607	293	197
260	363	776	420	282	588	321	300	482	357	212	442	236	305	384	543	535	242	436	393	588	367	445	439	584	282	189
270	350	748	404	271	566	309	289	464	344	204	416	227	294	369	523	516	233	420	379	566	353	429	424	562	271	182
280	337	721	390	262	546	298	278	448	331	197	401	218	283	356	504	497	225	405	365	546	341	414	409	542	262	176
290	326	696	377	252	527	288	269	439	320	190	387	211	273	344	487	480	217	391	353	527	329	399	394	523	252	170
300(5)	315	673	364	244	510	278	260	418	310	184	374	204	264	332	470	464	210	378	341	510	318	386	382	506	244	164
310	305	651	352	236	493	269	251	404	300	178	360	197	256	322	455	449	203	366	330	493	308	374	369	490	236	159
320	295	631	341	229	477	261	243	392	290	173	351	192	248	312	441	435	197	355	320	477	298	362	358	474	229	154
330	286	612	331	222	463	253	236	380	281	167	340	186	240	302	428	422	191	343	310	463	289	351	347	460	222	149
340	278	594	321	216	450	245	230	369	273	162	330	180	233	293	415	409	186	334	301	450	280	341	337	447	216	145
350	270	577	312	209	437	238	223	358	265	158	320	174	226	285	403	397	180	324	292	437	272	331	327	434	209	141
360(6)	262	561	303	203	425	232	216	348	258	153	312	170	220	277	392	387	175	315	284	425	265	322	317	422	203	137
370	255	546	295	198	413	225	210	339	251	149	303	164	214	270	381	377	170	306	276	413	258	314	310	410	198	133
380	249	531	287	193	402	219	205	330	244	145	295	161	207	262	371	367	166	299	269	402	251	305	301	399	193	130
390	242	518	280	188	392	214	200	321	238	142	288	157	203	256	362	357	161	291	262	392	245	297	294	389	188	126
400	236	505	273	183	383	209	195	313	232	138	281	153	198	249	353	348	158	284	256	383	239	289	286	379	183	123
410	230	492	266	179	373	203	190	306	226	135	274	149	193	243	344	340	154	277	249	373	233	282	280	370	179	120
420(7)	225	481	260	174	364	199	186	299	221	131	267	146	189	237	336	331	150	270	243	364	227	276	273	361	174	117

TIME IN SECONDS (AND MINUTES) — SELECTIONS BY NUMBER

TIME IN SECONDS (AND MINUTES)	50	51	52	53	54	55	56	57	58	59	60	61	62	63	64	65	66	67	68	69	70	71	72	73	74	75
60(1)	950	1320	1410	2490	2600	1400	2780	1380	800	1366	1600	1720	1090	2090	790	1532	2210	2654	5180	1898	2225	1280	3010	2108	2122	1812
120(2)	475	660	705	1245	1300	700	1390	690	400	683	800	860	545	1045	395	766	1105	1327	2590	949	1113	640	1505	1054	1061	906
130	438	609	650	1150	1200	646	1283	636	369	630	738	794	403	964	364	707	1020	1225	2388	876	1026	591	1389	973	979	836
140	407	566	604	1071	1110	600	1192	592	343	585	686	737	467	896	338	657	947	1137	2220	813	953	549	1290	903	909	777
150	380	528	564	996	1040	560	1112	552	320	546	640	688	436	836	316	613	884	1062	2072	759	890	512	1204	840	849	725
160	356	495	529	934	972	525	1043	518	300	512	600	645	409	783	296	575	829	995	1942	712	834	480	1129	790	796	680
170	335	466	498	879	918	494	981	486	283	482	566	607	385	737	279	541	780	937	1828	670	785	452	1062	744	749	640
180(3)	317	440	470	830	866	467	927	460	267	455	533	573	363	697	263	511	737	885	1727	633	742	427	1003	703	707	604
190	300	417	445	786	820	442	878	436	253	431	506	543	344	660	250	484	698	838	1636	599	703	404	951	665	670	572
200	285	396	423	747	780	420	834	414	240	410	480	516	327	627	237	460	663	796	1554	569	668	384	903	632	637	544
210	271	377	402	711	743	400	794	396	228	390	456	491	312	597	226	438	631	758	1480	542	636	366	860	602	606	518
220	259	360	385	680	708	382	760	376	218	373	436	469	297	570	215	418	603	724	1410	518	607	349	821	575	579	494
230	248	344	368	650	678	366	725	360	209	356	418	449	284	545	206	400	577	692	1351	495	580	334	785	550	554	473
240(4)	238	330	353	623	650	350	695	346	200	342	400	430	273	523	198	383	553	664	1295	475	556	320	753	527	531	453
250	228	317	338	598	624	335	667	332	192	328	384	413	262	492	189	368	531	637	1243	455	534	307	722	506	509	435
260	219	305	325	575	600	323	642	318	185	315	369	397	252	482	182	354	510	612	1194	438	513	295	695	486	490	418
270	211	294	313	553	578	311	618	306	178	304	356	382	242	464	176	340	491	590	1151	422	495	284	669	468	472	403
280	204	283	302	536	556	300	596	296	172	293	343	368	234	448	169	328	473	569	1110	407	477	274	645	451	455	388
290	197	273	292	515	538	289	575	286	166	283	331	356	226	439	163	317	457	549	1072	393	460	265	623	436	439	375
300(5)	190	264	282	498	520	280	556	276	160	273	320	344	218	418	158	306	442	531	1036	380	445	256	602	422	424	362
310	184	256	273	480	502	271	538	266	155	264	310	333	211	404	153	297	428	514	1003	367	431	248	583	408	411	351
320	178	248	265	467	486	263	522	258	150	256	300	323	205	392	148	287	415	498	971	356	417	240	564	395	398	340
330	173	240	256	453	472	254	505	250	146	248	291	313	198	380	144	279	402	483	942	345	405	233	547	383	386	329
340	168	233	249	440	460	247	491	244	142	241	283	303	193	369	139	270	390	468	914	335	393	226	531	372	374	320
350	163	226	242	427	446	240	476	236	137	234	274	295	187	358	135	263	379	455	888	325	381	219	516	361	364	311
360(6)	158	220	235	415	432	233	463	230	134	228	267	287	182	348	132	255	368	442	864	316	371	213	502	351	354	302
370	154	214	229	404	423	227	451	224	130	222	260	279	177	339	128	248	356	430	840	308	361	208	488	341	344	294
380	150	208	223	393	410	221	439	218	127	216	253	272	172	330	125	242	349	419	818	300	351	202	475	332	335	286
390	146	203	217	383	400	215	428	212	123	210	246	264	168	321	122	236	340	408	797	291	342	197	463	324	326	279
400	143	198	212	374	390	210	417	207	120	205	240	258	164	313	119	230	332	398	777	285	334	192	452	316	318	272
410	139	193	206	364	380	205	407	202	117	200	234	252	160	306	116	224	323	388	758	278	326	187	440	308	306	265
420(7)	136	186	201	356	371	200	397	197	114	195	229	246	156	299	113	219	316	379	740	271	318	183	430	301	303	259

INDEX ACCORDING TO ORDER OF DIFFICULTY

*With item-analyzed comprehension tests. Of the 330 items item-analyzed, only 6 percent needed to be revised because of low validity. Average validity of the remaining items was .477.

Tests closely equated in difficulty:
Easiest: Selections 25 and 52.
Easy: Selections 30, 45, and 62.
Difficult: Selections 5 and 55.
Most Difficult: Selections 56 and 60.

PROGRESS RECORD

Students and teachers alike will find a Progress Record invaluable. Such a record helps spot specific reading strengths and weaknesses, points up growth and improvement, and heightens the personal satisfaction found in achievement.

Some students may wish to use only the columns for word-per-minute rate and Total Comprehension. Others may wish to keep a much more complete record. Space is provided for the following kinds of information:

1. DATE

2. SELECTION NUMBER

3. DIFFICULTY. As a measure of difficulty, enter the *Reading Ease Score* and *Classification* from the Index on page 327.

4. INTEREST RATING. Enter your personal Interest Rating for the selection. Enter a *1* if you think it is "very interesting," a *2* if "somewhat interesting," a *3* if "of average interest," a *4* if "somewhat uninteresting," and a *5* if "very uninteresting." The effect of interest on rate and comprehension is often a necessary aid to interpreting and understanding results.

5. RATE W.P.M. Enter your word-per-minute reading rate for the selection.

6. TOTAL COMP. Enter the Total Comprehension Score here — ten off for each of the questions missed.

7. R. E. INDEX. It is often desirable to have a single figure to indicate Reading Efficiency, an index that reflects both rate and comprehension factors. A Reading Efficiency Index may be obtained by multiplying word-per-minute rate by comprehension and dividing by one hundred. For example, if you read a selection at 320 words a minute with 60 percent comprehension, your Reading Efficiency Index would be 192. $\left(\dfrac{320 \times 60}{100} = 192 \right)$

8. PERCENT OF IMPROVEMENT. Improvement is sometimes best understood in terms of percentage gain. To determine the percent of improvement, subtract your initial Reading Efficiency Index from the last Reading Efficiency Index. The difference will be the number of points gained. Add two zeros to the number of points gained and divide that amount by the initial Reading Efficiency Index. The result will be your percent of improvement.

9. VOCABULARY. If you do the vocabulary check questions, both without and with the help of context, score them by taking ten off for each of the ten missed. If you just check vocabulary without context, take twenty off for each one missed and enter your scores.

The grouping of ten entry lines for ten selections is done to facilitate the averaging of any of the scores.

PROGRESS RECORD

	DATE	SELECTION NUMBER	DIFFI-CULTY	INTEREST RATING	RATE W.P.M.	TOTAL COMP.	R.E. INDEX	PERCENT OF IMPROVEMENT	VOCAB-ULARY
1.									
2.									
3.									
4.									
5.									
6.									
7.									
8.									
9.									
10.									
Average									

1.									
2.									
3.									
4.									
5.									
6.									
7.									
8.									
9.									
10.									
Average									

1.									
2.									
3.									
4.									
5.									
6.									
7.									
8.									
9.									
10.									
Average									

329

PROGRESS RECORD

	Date	Selection Number	Diffi- culty	Interest Rating	Rate W.P.M.	Total Comp.	R.E. Index	Percent of Improvement	Vocab- ulary
1.									
2.									
3.									
4.									
5.									
6.									
7.									
8.									
9.									
10.									
Average									

1.									
2.									
3.									
4.									
5.									
6.									
7.									
8.									
9.									
10.									
Average									

1.									
2.									
3.									
4.									
5.									
6.									
7.									
8.									
9.									
10.									
Average									

330

PROGRESS RECORD

	Date	Selection Number	Diffi-culty	Interest Rating	Rate W.P.M.	Total Comp.	R.E. Index	Percent of Improvement	Vocab-ulary
1.									
2.									
3.									
4.									
5.									
6.									
7.									
8.									
9.									
10.									

Average

1.									
2.									
3.									
4.									
5.									

Average

PACING AID SHEETS

(For pacing at 500, 750, 1,000, 1,500, or 2,000 W.P.M.)

The figures below will serve as a substitute for individual reading accelerator machines. Through use of these figures an individual or entire class can be paced through any selection in this text at speeds of 500, 750, 1,000, 1,500, or 2,000 words a minute, thus expediting the development of superior reading, scanning, and skimming skills.

At the signal "Begin," the individuals or class are to begin reading at what they feel is the indicated rate. When they should be finishing the first column, reading at that rate, say, "Next." If they have not quite finished, they are to skip the remaining portion of the column and start reading the next column somewhat faster. In that way as they are paced through a selection, they are able to adjust their rate as closely as possible to the paced rate.

Following the selection numbers and pages in the left-hand column, you will notice two (or three) sets of figures, one for each column of print for the selection. They indicate the time in minutes and seconds for reading the column at the speed given in the heading (e.g., @ 500, @ 750, etc.). For Selection #1, for example, the figures 0/44 and, for the second column, 1/31, mean that the first column should be finished in exactly zero minutes and 44 seconds and the second column in one minute and 31 seconds, or 47 seconds of additional time, since the time figures are cumulative. These figures would apply for pacing at 500 wpm. For pacing at 750 wpm, the signal "Next" would come after 30 seconds and, for the next column, after 1 minute.

For pacing at 2,000 wpm, divide each reading-time figure in the column headed @ 1,000 by two. (Similarly, for 3,000 wpm, divide the figure in the column headed @ 1,500 by two.)

SELECTION AND PAGE	1ST COLUMN				2ND COLUMN			
	@ 500	@ 750	@ 1000	@ 1500	@ 500	@ 750	@ 1000	@ 1500
#1	0/44	0/30	0/22	0/15	1/31	1/0	0/45	0/30
p. 4	1/57	1/18	0/58	0/39	2/22	1/35	1/11	0/47
#2	0/15	0/10	0/7	0/5	0/35	0/23	0/17	0/12
p. 5	1/36	1/4	0/48	0/32	2/41	1/47	1/20	0/54
p. 6	2/57	1/58	1/29	59	3/14	2/10	1/37	1/5
#3	0/23	0/16	0/12	0/8	0/52	0/35	0/26	0/17
p. 7	1/55	1/17	0/58	0/38	2/57	1/58	1/28	0/59
p. 8	2/58	2/0	1/30	1/0	3/3	2/2	1/31	1/1
#4	0/37	0/25	0/19	0/12	1/16	0/51	0/38	0/25
p. 9	2/16	1/30	1/8	0/45	3/16	2/11	1/38	1/5
p. 10	3/54	2/36	1/57	1/19	4/29	3/0	2/15	1/30
#5	0/2	0/2	0/1	0/1	0/9	0/6	0/5	0/3
p. 11	1/6	0/44	0/33	0/22	2/4	1/23	1/2	0/41
p. 12	3/10	2/6	1/35	1/3	4/9	2/46	2/4	1/23
p. 13	5/3	3/23	2/32	1/42	6/1	4/1	3/1	2/0
#6	0/51	0/34	0/25	0/17	1/44	1/9	0/52	0/35
p. 15	2/36	1/44	1/18	0/52	3/29	2/19	1/44	1/10
#7	0/45	0/30	0/23	0/15	1/35	1/3	0/48	0/32
p. 17	2/28	1/39	1/14	0/49	3/20	2/13	1/40	1/7
#8	0/45	0/30	0/22	0/15	1/36	1/4	0/48	0/32
p. 19	2/7	1/25	1/4	0/42	2/38	1/45	1/19	0/53
#9	0/5	0/4	0/3	0/2	0/15	0/10	0/7	0/5
p. 20	1/2	0/41	0/31	0/21	1/49	1/13	0/55	0/36
#10	0/39	0/26	0/20	0/13	1/28	0/59	0/44	0/29
p. 22	2/31	1/40	1/15	0/50	3/31	2/21	1/46	1/10
p. 23	4/15	2/50	2/7	1/25	4/53	3/15	2/26	1/38
#11	0/48	0/32	0/29	0/16	1/40	1/7	0/50	0/33
p. 25	2/43	1/49	1/22	0/54	3/50	2/33	1/55	1/17
p. 26	4/10	2/46	2/5	1/23	4/29	2/59	2/15	1/30
#12	0/21	0/14	0/10	0/7	0/45	0/30	0/22	0/15
p. 27	1/43	1/9	0/52	0/34	2/37	1/45	1/19	0/52
p. 28	3/33	2/22	1/47	1/11	4/31	3/0	2/15	1/30
p. 29	5/10	3/26	3/35	1/43	5/46	3/51	2/53	1/55
#13	0/42	0/28	0/21	0/14	1/29	1/0	0/45	0/30
p. 31	2/27	1/38	1/14	0/49	3/27	2/18	1/43	1/9
p. 32	3/40	2/27	1/50	1/13	3/52	2/34	1/56	1/17
#14	0/24	0/16	0/12	0/8	0/52	0/34	0/26	0/17
p. 33	1/32	1/2	0/47	0/31	2/15	1/30	1/7	0/45
#15	0/48	0/32	0/24	0/16	1/37	1/4	0/48	0/32
p. 35	2/31	1/41	1/16	0/50	3/28	2/18	1/44	1/9

SELECTION AND PAGE	1ST COLUMN				2ND COLUMN			
	@500	@750	@1000	@1500	@500	@750	@1000	@1500
#16	0/48	0/32	0/24	0/16	1/39	1/6	0/50	0/33
p. 37	2/43	1/48	1/21	0/54	3/43	2/29	1/52	1/14
#17	0/49	0/33	0/25	0/16	1/40	1/7	0/50	0/33
p. 39	2/6	1/24	1/3	0/42	2/31	1/41	1/16	0/50
#18	0/13	0/9	0/6	0/4	0/30	0/20	0/15	0/10
p. 40	1/34	1/3	0/47	0/31	2/36	1/44	1/18	0/52
p. 41	2/39	1/46	1/20	0/53	2/42	1/48	1/21	0/54
#19	0/36	0/24	0/18	0/12	1/16	0/50	0/38	0/25
p. 42	1/40	1/6	0/50	0/33	2/5	1/24	1/3	0/42
#20	0/12	0/8	0/6	0/4	0/29	0/19	0/14	0/10
p. 43	1/36	1/4	0/48	0/32	2/40	1/46	1/20	0/53
p. 44	3/25	2/16	1/42	1/8	4/11	2/47	2/6	1/24
#21	0/52	0/35	0/26	0/17	1/46	1/10	0/53	0/35
p. 46	1/56	1/17	0/58	0/39	2/6	1/24	1/3	0/42
#22	0/28	0/19	0/14	0/9	1/5	0/43	0/32	0/22
p. 47	1/17	0/51	0/38	0/26	1/28	0/59	0/44	0/29
#23	0/29	0/19	0/15	0/10	1/3	0/42	0/32	0/21
p. 48	1/48	1/12	0/54	0/36	2/36	1/44	1/18	0/52
#24	0/41	0/28	0/21	0/14	1/30	1/0	0/45	0/30
p. 50	2/18	1/32	1/9	0/46	3/10	2/6	1/35	1/3
#25	0/47	0/31	0/23	0/16	1/37	1/5	0/49	0/32
p. 52	2/39	1/46	1/20	0/53	3/42	2/28	1/51	1/14
p. 53	4/43	3/9	2/22	1/34	5/44	3/49	2/52	1/55
p. 54	6/15	4/10	3/8	2/5	6/45	4/30	3/23	2/15
#26	0/9	0/6	0/5	0/3	0/23	0/16	0/12	0/8
p. 55	1/22	0/54	0/41	0/27	2/18	1/32	1/9	0/46
p. 56	2/59	1/59	1/29	0/59	3/39	2/26	1/49	1/13
#27	0/47	0/31	0/24	0/16	1/33	1/2	0/46	0/31
p. 58	2/0	1/20	1/0	0/40	2/36	1/38	1/13	0/49
#28	0/10	0/6	0/5	0/3	0/24	0/16	0/12	0/8
p. 59	1/20	0/53	0/40	0/27	2/11	1/27	1/5	0/44
p. 60	3/13	2/9	1/37	1/4	4/14	2/49	2/7	1/25
p. 61	4/41	3/7	2/20	1/33	5/5	3/23	2/33	1/42
#29	0/45	0/30	0/22	0/15	1/32	1/1	0/46	0/31
p. 63	2/8	1/25	1/4	0/43	2/46	1/50	1/23	0/55
#30	0/3	0/2	0/1	0/1	0/7	0/5	0/4	0/2
p. 64	1/6	0/44	0/33	0/22	2/12	1/28	1/6	0/44
p. 65	2/24	1/36	1/12	0/48	2/36	1/44	1/18	0/52
#31	0/27	0/18	0/13	0/9	0/59	0/40	0/29	0/20
p. 66	2/2	1/21	1/1	0/41	3/0	2/6	1/35	1/3
p. 67	3/39	2/26	1/49	1/13	4/10	2/47	2/5	1/23
#32	0/9	0/6	0/5	0/3	0/21	0/14	0/11	0/7
p. 68	1/22	0/54	0/41	0/27	2/23	1/35	1/11	0/48
p. 69	2/44	1/49	1/22	0/54	3/6	2/4	1/33	1/2
#33	0/19	0/13	0/10	0/7	0/41	0/27	0/20	0/14
p. 70	1/15	0/50	0/38	0/25	1/50	1/14	0/55	0/37
#34	0/5	0/4	0/3	0/2	0/10	0/7	0/5	0/3
p. 71	1/10	0/46	0/35	0/23	2/8	1/25	1/4	0/43
p. 72	2/57	1/58	1/29	0/59	3/44	2/29	1/52	1/15
#35	0/41	0/27	0/20	0/14	1/26	0/57	0/43	0/29
p. 74	1/45	1/10	0/52	0/35	2/3	1/22	1/1	0/41
#36	0/19	0/13	0/10	0/6	0/38	0/26	0/19	0/13
p. 75	1/36	1/4	0/48	0/32	2/32	1/41	1/16	0/51
p. 76	2/35	1/44	1/18	0/52	2/39	1/46	1/19	0/53
#37	0/35	0/23	0/17	0/12	1/12	0/48	0/36	0/24
p. 77	2/12	1/28	1/6	0/44	3/8	2/5	1/34	1/3
p. 78	3/14	2/9	1/37	1/5	3/20	2/13	1/40	1/7
#38	0/34	0/23	0/17	0/11	1/4	0/42	0/32	0/21
p. 79	2/0	1/20	1/0	0/40	2/54	1/56	1/27	0/58
p. 80	3/46	2/30	1/53	1/15	4/42	3/8	2/21	1/34
#39	0/45	0/30	0/23	0/15	1/34	1/3	0/47	0/31
p. 82	2/35	1/43	1/17	0/51	3/35	2/23	1/48	1/12
p. 83	4/7	2/45	2/4	1/22	4/38	3/5	2/19	1/33

333

SELECTION AND PAGE	1ST COLUMN				2ND COLUMN			
	@ 500	@ 750	@ 1000	@ 1500	@ 500	@ 750	@ 1000	@ 1500
#40	0/8	0/5	0/4	0/3	0/19	0/13	0/9	0/6
p. 84	1/12	0/48	0/36	0/24	2/3	1/22	1/1	0/41
#41	0/47	0/31	0/24	0/16	1/36	1/4	0/48	0/32
p. 86	2/38	1/45	1/19	0/53	3/35	2/24	1/48	1/12
p. 87	3/41	2/27	1/51	1/14	3/46	2/31	1/53	1/15
#42	0/34	0/23	0/17	0/11	1/11	0/47	0/36	0/24
p. 88	2/12	1/28	1/6	0/44	3/10	2/7	1/35	1/3
p. 89	3/19	2/12	1/39	1/6	3/46	2/17	1/43	1/9
#43	0/31	0/21	0/16	0/10	1/7	0/44	0/33	0/22
p. 90	2/3	1/22	1/1	0/41	3/1	2/1	1/30	1/0
p. 91	3/57	2/38	1/59	1/19	4/59	3/19	2/29	1/40
p. 92	5/5	3/23	2/32	1/42	5/11	3/27	2/35	1/43
#44	0/31	0/21	0/16	0/10	1/5	0/43	0/32	0/22
p. 93	2/4	1/23	1/2	0/41	2/59	1/59	1/29	0/59
p. 94	3/5	2/3	1/33	1/2	3/11	2/8	1/36	1/4
#45	0/31	0/21	0/16	0/10	1/7	0/44	0/33	0/22
p. 95	2/10	1/27	1/5	0/43	3/9	2/6	1/35	1/3
p. 96	3/31	2/21	1/46	1/10	3/53	2/35	1/56	1/18
#46	0/17	0/11	0/8	0/6	0/36	0/24	0/18	0/12
p. 97	1/40	1/7	0/50	0/33	2/46	1/51	1/23	0/55
p. 98	3/20	2/13	1/40	1/7	3/50	2/33	1/55	1/17
#47	0/9	0/6	0/4	0/3	0/21	0/14	0/11	0/7
p. 99	1/26	0/57	0/43	0/29	2/28	1/39	1/14	0/49
p. 100	3/27	2/18	1/44	1/9	4/28	2/58	2/14	1/29
p. 101	4/46	3/10	2/23	1/35	5/4	3/22	2/32	1/41
#48	0/19	0/13	0/10	0/6	0/40	0/27	0/20	0/13
p. 102	1/34	1/2	0/47	0/31	2/24	1/36	1/12	0/48
#49	0/36	0/24	0/18	0/12	1/20	0/54	0/40	0/27
p. 104	1/31	1/0	0/45	0/30	1/39	1/6	0/49	0/33
#50	0/27	0/18	0/14	0/9	1/3	0/42	0/31	0/21
p. 105	1/30	1/0	0/45	0/30	1/54	1/16	0/57	0/38
#51	0/13	0/9	0/7	0/4	0/30	0/20	0/15	0/10
p. 106	1/32	1/2	0/46	0/31	2/33	1/42	1/16	0/51
p. 107	2/35	1/43	1/17	0/52	2/37	1/45	1/19	0/52
#52	0/39	0/26	0/20	0/13	1/18	0/52	0/39	0/26
p. 108	2/1	1/21	1/1	0/40	2/49	1/52	1/24	0/56
#53	0/40	0/27	0/20	0/13	1/26	0/57	0/43	0/29
p. 110	2/20	1/34	1/10	0/47	3/18	2/11	1/39	1/6
p. 111	4/5	1/43	2/3	1/22	5/0	3/20	2/30	1/40
#54	0/43	0/28	0/21	0/14	1/30	1/0	0/45	0/30
p. 113	2/25	1/37	1/12	0/48	3/25	2/16	1/42	1/8
p. 114	4/18	2/52	2/9	1/26	5/11	3/27	2/36	1/44
#55	0/45	0/30	0/23	0/15	1/40	1/6	0/50	0/33
p. 116	2/16	1/30	1/8	0/45	2/49	1/52	1/24	0/56
#56	0/8	0/5	0/4	0/3	0/20	0/13	0/10	0/7
p. 117	1/21	0/54	0/40	0/27	2/20	1/34	1/10	0/47
p. 118	3/20	2/14	1/40	1/7	4/22	2/54	2/11	1/27
p. 119	4/58	3/19	2/29	1/39	5/34	3/43	2/47	1/51
#57	0/41	0/28	0/21	0/14	1/30	1/0	0/45	0/30
p. 121	2/6	1/24	1/3	0/42	2/46	1/51	1/23	0/55
#58	0/46	0/31	0/23	0/15	1/35	1/3	0/47	0/32
#59	0/50	0/33	0/25	0/17	1/43	1/9	0/52	0/34
p. 124	2/12	1/28	1/6	0/44	2/44	1/49	1/22	0/55
#60	0/11	0/7	0/5	0/4	0/23	0/15	0/12	0/8
p. 125	1/17	0/52	0/39	0/26	2/13	1/29	1/7	0/44
p. 126	2/44	1/49	1/22	0/55	3/12	2/8	1/36	1/4
#61	0/10	0/7	0/5	0/3	0/24	0/16	0/12	0/8
p. 127	1/26	0/57	0/43	0/29	2/28	1/38	1/14	0/49
p. 128	2/57	1/58	1/29	0/59	3/27	2/18	1/43	1/9
#62	0/12	0/8	0/6	0/4	0/27	0/18	0/14	0/9
p. 129	0/58	0/38	0/29	0/19	1/27	0/58	0/44	0/29
p. 130	1/48	1/12	0/54	0/36	2/11	1/28	1/6	0/44

SELECTION AND PAGE	1ST COLUMN				2ND COLUMN			
	@ 500	@ 750	@ 1000	@ 1500	@ 500	@ 750	@ 1000	@ 1500
#63	0/18	0/12	0/9	0/6	0/38	0/26	0/19	0/13
p. 131	1/36	1/4	0/48	0/32	2/33	1/42	1/17	0/51
p. 132	3/21	2/14	1/41	1/7	4/9	2/46	2/5	1/23
#64	0/40	0/26	0/20	0/13	1/25	0/56	0/42	0/28
p. 134	1/30	1/0	0/45	0/30	1/35	1/3	0/47	0/32
#65	0/41	0/27	0/20	0/14	1/25	0/57	0/43	0/28
p. 136	2/12	1/28	1/6	0/44	3/3	2/2	1/32	1/1
#66	0/49	0/33	0/25	0/16	1/37	1/5	0/49	0/32
p. 138	2/41	1/47	1/21	0/54	3/44	2/29	1/52	1/15
p. 139	4/6	2/44	2/3	1/22	4/27	2/58	2/14	1/29
#67	0/18	0/12	0/9	0/6	0/41	0/27	0/20	0/14
p. 140	1/39	1/6	0/50	0/33	2/40	1/46	1/20	0/53
p. 141	3/42	2/28	1/51	1/14	4/45	3/10	2/23	1/35
p. 142	5/3	3/22	2/32	1/41	5/18	3/38	2/39	1/46
#68	0/20	0/13	0/10	0/7	0/44	0/30	0/22	0/15
p. 143	1/46	1/10	0/53	0/35	2/46	1/40	1/23	0/55
p. 144	3/46	2/30	1/53	1/15	4/43	3/8	2/21	1/34
p. 145	5/44	3/50	2/52	1/55	6/33	4/28	3/21	2/14
p. 146	7/43	5/9	3/52	2/34	8/43	5/48	4/21	2/54
p. 147	9/31	6/20	4/46	3/10	10/23	6/55	5/11	3/28
#69	0/44	0/29	0/22	0/15	1/30	1/0	0/45	0/30
p. 149	2/16	1/31	1/8	0/45	3/14	2/10	1/37	1/5
p. 150	3/26	2/17	1/43	1/7	3/48	2/32	1/54	1/16
#70	0/26	0/17	0/13	0/9	0/56	0/37	0/28	0/19
p. 151	1/55	1/17	0/58	0/38	2/52	1/59	1/26	1/0
p. 152	3/42	2/28	1/51	1/14	4/27	2/58	2/13	1/29
#71	0/43	0/29	0/22	0/14	1/32	1/1	0/46	0/31
p. 154	2/1	1/21	1/1	0/40	2/34	1/42	1/17	0/51
#72	0/8	0/5	0/4	0/3	0/20	0/14	0/10	0/7
p. 155	1/18	0/52	0/39	0/26	2/16	1/31	1/8	0/45
p. 156	3/1	2/7	1/36	1/4	4/9	2/46	2/5	1/23
p. 157	5/5	3/23	2/32	1/41	5/49	3/53	2/55	1/56
#73	0/43	0/29	0/21	0/14	1/29	0/59	0/45	0/30
p. 159	2/31	1/40	1/15	0/50	3/26	2/17	1/43	1/9
p. 160	3/41	2/27	1/50	1/14	3/56	2/38	1/58	1/19
#74	0/24	0/16	0/12	0/8	0/51	0/34	0/25	0/17
p. 161	1/46	1/11	0/53	0/35	2/44	1/49	1/22	0/55
p. 162	3/28	2/18	1/44	1/9	4/15	2/50	2/7	1/25
#75	0/44	0/29	0/22	0/15	1/32	1/1	0/46	0/31
p. 164	2/32	1/42	1/16	0/51	3/30	2/20	1/45	1/10
p. 165	3/34	2/23	1/47	1/11	3/38	2/25	1/49	1/12

ANSWERS

COMPREHENSION CHECK QUESTIONS

	1	2	3	4	5	6	7	8	9	10	11	12	13	14	15	16	17	18	19	20	21	22	23	24	25	26	27	28	29	30	31	32	33	34	35	36	37	38
1.	2	4	1	2	3	4	1	1	1	2	2	2	4	4	4	4	4	3	2	1	2	1	3	2	2	4	3	3	3	3	3	3	3	4	3	1	3	1
2.	1	1	2	1	1	2	1	4	2	1	1	3	1	3	1	3	1	2	4	2	2	2	1	1	3	3	3	1	1	1	3	3	1	1	4	3	4	2
3.	1	2	1	1	4	1	3	2	2	3	3	1	1	3	3	2	1	2	2	4	4	2	3	3	1	3	4	4	4	4	4	4	4	4	1	1	1	1
4.	3	3	2	4	4	4	4	2	3	1	4	4	3	4	3	3	4	1	4	4	2	2	4	4	3	3	2	3	4	3	2	4	4	1	1	2	2	3
5.	2	3	3	2	2	4	3	2	1	4	2	3	4	4	2	2	2	4	3	4	2	4	1	4	4	3	2	2	1	2	4	2	3	3	3	2	2	4
6.	1	3	2	1	3	3	4	3	2	3	3	3	3	2	3	1	1	3	4	4	4	2	1	3	3	4	4	2	2	4	2	4	4	2	4	4	4	4
7.	4	4	4	2	4	2	3	4	4	4	4	4	1	2	2	3	3	4	2	2	2	2	4	3	3	2	2	1	3	3	3	3	3	1	2	1	3	4
8.	1	2	1	2	2	3	4	1	4	4	4	4	2	2	3	4	4	2	1	2	3	2	3	4	4	4	1	2	1	1	2	1	1	1	1	2	1	4
9.	2	3	4	2	1	1	1	2	4	4	2	4	4	4	4	1	2	4	1	3	1	3	1	2	4	4	2	2	4	3	2	2	2	4	2	3	3	4
10.	4	1	2	4	3	1	2	4	2	3	2	1	1	1	2	2	3	3	3	3	3	1	2	1	4	2	2	2	2	1	1	2	2	2	1	4	1	3

VOCABULARY CHECK QUESTIONS

	1	2	3	4	5	6	7	8	9	10	11	12	13	14	15	16	17	18	19	20	21	22	23	24	25	26	27	28	29	30	31	32	33	34	35	36	37	38
1.	4	5	1	3	3	5	2	5	4	3	5	4	5	3	3	3	4	2	4	4	5	4	1	5	4	1	2	4	5	4	5	5	5	1	1	4	5	4
2.	5	3	4	2	4	4	3	5	3	4	3	2	4	4	4	3	1	1	5	1	1	4	2	2	1	4	1	2	2	1	5	5	2	2	4	2	4	1
3.	4	1	3	1	2	3	1	1	3	2	1	4	4	2	2	1	2	4	5	2	3	5	3	5	1	2	5	4	5	5	5	1	1	3	3	3	3	4
4.	1	2	2	5	4	1	4	4	1	4	2	2	1	3	3	3	2	5	2	5	2	1	1	1	1	4	1	1	1	1	1	4	4	2	4	4	1	2
5.	2	4	2	2	4	5	5	3	2	3	4	1	4	2	4	4	3	3	1	4	4	2	2	4	2	5	4	2	3	2	3	3	3	4	3	2	1	2

COMPREHENSION CHECK QUESTIONS

	39	40	41	42	43	44	45	46	47	48	49	50	51	52	53	54	55	56	57	58	59	60	61	62	63	64	65	66	67	68	69	70	71	72	73	74	75
1.	4	1	1	3	2	4	1	1	2	4	4	4	4	2	3	3	4	2	4	3	2	3	1	4	4	1	2	3	4	2	3	4	4	4	4	4	3
2.	1	2	2	2	1	1	3	3	1	3	3	1	2	2	3	1	3	1	4	1	4	4	4	1	3	4	3	1	1	4	4	2	4	3	2	1	2
3.	3	4	2	3	1	3	1	4	3	1	3	4	4	4	4	1	1	4	2	3	3	2	2	3	1	3	4	3	4	3	3	1	2	1	1	1	1
4.	2	2	2	1	2	4	3	3	2	2	3	3	3	4	3	3	3	3	3	1	4	2	2	3	3	3	2	4	2	2	2	2	1	3	1	3	3
5.	1	4	3	2	2	4	1	4	4	2	4	2	3	2	1	2	1	2	1	2	1	1	2	4	4	2	4	3	3	4	2	3	1	3	1	3	1
6.	1	1	4	3	3	1	2	1	3	3	2	3	1	1	1	2	2	1	2	1	2	1	3	1	1	4	2	4	2	2	3	2	2	2	4	2	3
7.	3	2	3	2	4	2	4	2	2	2	2	2	1	3	3	2	2	2	4	3	2	1	2	3	1	2	2	4	2	2	2	1	3	4	4	4	3
8.	2	2	1	4	2	2	2	4	1	3	1	3	3	3	4	4	4	4	3	2	3	4	2	2	2	3	4	3	1	3	4	2	2	3	3	3	1
9.	3	3	4	4	2	2	2	4	3	4	3	4	2	3	3	3	2	3	1	3	4	2	3	4	3	2	2	3	3	4	3	4	2	4	4	2	3
10.	4	4	1	1	3	3	3	1	3	1	3	3	1	3	2	1	3	2	4	3	3	3	4	2	1	2	1	2	3	2	1	3	4	2	1	1	3

VOCABULARY CHECK QUESTIONS

	39	40	41	42	43	44	45	46	47	48	49	50	51	52	53	54	55	56	57	58	59	60	61	62	63	64	65	66	67	68	69	70	71	72	73	74	75
1.	4	3	5	2	4	5	2	1	4	4	2	5	4	5	4	4	4	2	5	2	5	3	4	1	2	3	5	2	5	3	5	3	5	2	2	2	3
2.	1	4	2	1	2	4	3	3	1	1	3	5	3	4	3	5	5	4	2	4	3	1	5	3	3	5	4	3	3	4	4	5	5	1	2	3	1
3.	5	2	1	2	5	4	5	2	2	3	5	2	4	3	2	1	1	3	1	3	1	3	1	1	4	1	1	1	4	3	5	4	5	2	4	1	5
4.	3	2	3	1	3	2	1	4	5	3	3	3	1	4	3	3	3	1	3	4	5	4	3	5	3	5	4	3	3	5	3	1	1	5	4	4	3
5.	2	2	2	2	4	4	4	5	1	1	1	1	4	2	2	1	2	5	2	1	5	2	1	4	2	4	1	5	4	4	5	5	2	3	3	5	4